THE WAITE GROUP®

LAFORE'S WINDOWS PROGRAMMING MADE EASY

Only What You Need to Know

ROBERT LAFORE

WAITE
GROUP
PRESS™

Corte Madera CA

Publisher: *Mitchell Waite*
Editorial Director: *Scott Calamar*
Managing Editor: *John Crudo*
Content Editor: *Harry Henderson*
Technical Reviewers: *John Botke and David Calhoun*
Production Director: *Julianne Ososke*
Design and Production: *Cecile Kaufman, Michele Cuneo*
Illustrations: *Carl Yoshihara*
Cover Design: *Michael Rogondino*

Printed in the United States of America
93 94 95 96 • 10 9 8 7 6 5 4 3 2 1

Part and Chapter Opening Illustrations: Part One Credit: Isabella Stewart Gardner Museum/Art Resource, NY. Carlo Crivelli, St. George and the Dragon. Boston, Isabella Stewart Gardner Museum. Parts Two through Eight Credit: Scala/Art Resource, NY. Part Two: Fogolino, Tournament scene. Malpaga, Castle. Part Three: Vittore Carpaccio, St. George slaying the dragon. Venice, S. Giorgio degli Schiavoni. Part Four: Cassoni Masters, Tournament. Tours, Museum. Parts Five and Eight: Vittore Carpaccio, St. George bringing the slain dragon into the city. Venice, S. Giorgio degli Schiavoni. Part Six: Paolo Ucello, Battle of San Romano. Florence, Uffizi. Part Seven: Andrea Mantegna, St. George, Venice, Gallerie dell'Accademia.

Library of Congress Cataloging-in-Publication Data
Lafore, Robert (Robert W.)
    [Windows programming made easy]
    Lafore's Windows programming made easy / Robert Lafore ; The Waite Group.
      p. cm.
    Includes index.
    ISBN: 1-878739-23-9 : $29.95
    1. Windows (Computer programs) 2. Microsoft Windows (Computer file) I. Waite Group. II. Title. III. Title: Windows programming made easy.
QA76.76.W56L34 1993
005.4'3--dc20
                         93-273
                         CIP

DEDICATION

This book is dedicated to William: who would have thought we could use a rain-fly as a spinnaker on the freezing waters of the Yukon?

ACKNOWLEDGMENTS

John Botke deserves the lion's share of thanks for his patient, painstaking and very expert critique of my Windows programming. His suggestions pulled the fat out of the fire on more occasions than I care to remember. David Calhoun and Harry Henderson also offered valuable help with technical details and broader issues. Mitch Waite of course is always after me to go the extra mile: is it funny yet? John Crudo somehow kept track of whether it was the third edit of the second draft or the third draft of the second edit.

Scott Calamar kept a firm hand on the whole process; his moral support was invaluable. In the production department Julianne Ososke, Michele Cuneo, and Cecile Kaufman did a bang-up job, as you can see, and threw themselves into the medieval theme with a vengeance. Kathy Carlyle, the copy editor, is one of the true gems of that demanding art, saving me from myself only when it was absolutely necessary.

Finally, Nan Borreson of Borland provided an essential liaison with the guys who make it all possible: the compiler developers.

ABOUT THE AUTHOR

*R*obert Lafore has been writing books about computer programming since 1982. His best-selling titles include *Assembly Language Programming for the IBM PC and XT, C Programming Using Turbo C++, Microsoft C Programming for the PC, Object-Oriented Programming in Turbo C++,* and *Object-Oriented Programming in Microsoft C++.* Mr. Lafore holds degrees in mathematics and electrical engineering, and has been active in programming since the days of the PDP-5, when 4K of main memory was considered luxurious. His interests include hiking, windsurfing, and recreational mathematics.

ABOUT THE DISK

The included disk makes it even easier to build the applications discussed in this book. The disk provides both source code and executable programs. The files have been organized into subdirectories corresponding to the eight parts of the book.

Requirements

In order to compile and run the programs you must be running Windows 3.1.

Since the executables (.EXE files) are provided, you can run the programs even if you don't have a C/C++ compiler; however, you cannot compile the programs without Borland C++ for Windows or Turbo C++ for Windows.

Copying the Files to the Hard Disk

We recommend that you copy the files from the diskette to your hard disk using Windows File Manager. Follow these steps to copy them:

1. With Windows running, click on the File Manager icon.
2. Switch to the hard disk drive's root directory.

To do this, click on the icon for the desired hard disk drive, then click on the folder icon at the top of the list of directories. This icon represents the root directory. If your hard disk is the C: drive, the icon is labeled c:\.

3. Create a subdirectory for the files you intend to copy.

To do this, click on "File" at the top menu bar. Select "Create Directory" from the menu, type a name for your new directory (for example, WINPROGS), then click on "OK."

4. Copy the contents of the diskette to the newly created subdirectory.

To do this, insert the diskette in the appropriate drive and double-click on the diskette drive icon. A second window opens. Move the mouse cursor over the folder labeled a:\ or b:\ (depending on your disk drive's designation) and hold down the left mouse button. Drag the icon to the new subdirectory, located in the original window. Release the mouse button and click on "OK" or "Yes" to begin copying.

After the files have copied to the hard disk, store the original diskette as a backup.

INTRODUCTION

$\mathcal{M}$any people think of Windows as an army of fire-breathing dragons: formidable obstacles that you must slay before you can pass on to the "holy grail" of writing Windows programs. Windows is said to be so difficult that only the most experienced knights (super-hackers who stay up all night drinking Jolt™) can overcome it. You've probably heard the weeping and wailing: Windows has hundreds of function calls, it's event-driven, it's object-oriented, it's message-based, and so on.

The goal of this book is to give you the confidence to attack these fire-breathing dragons. The fact is that Windows programming does not need to be difficult. The secret is that you don't need to know every detail about Windows to write useful and functional programs. To extend our dragon analogy (perhaps too far), to slay the dragon you don't need to know exactly what combustion process it uses to produce smoke and fire, or the name of every bone in its scaly tail.

Previous books on Windows programming devoted considerable space to discussing the dragon's combustion processes. They perpetuated the myth of Windows' difficulty by their minute coverage of every aspect of Windows programming. It seemed the only way to program Windows was to read and understand the entire book. Unfortunately, not everyone had six months or a year to devote to such a project.

Lafore's Windows Programming Made Easy takes a different approach. It concentrates on just what you need to know to slay the Windows dragons with a minimum of fuss and inconvenience. Its aim is not to make you into a Windows super-expert, but into a normal programmer who can write useful Windows programs. This approach means a simpler and shorter book, and a simpler and shorter road to becoming a productive Windows programmer.

WHO SHOULD READ THIS BOOK

This book is for anyone who wants a fast way to learn Windows programming. You might have a specific project in mind: a nifty Windows utility, or a DOS program you want to convert to Windows. Or perhaps you need to learn Windows professionally, but are intimidated by existing Windows books and their long learning curve. Or you may simply be curious about Windows programming, and want to experiment without making a major time commitment.

REAL WINDOWS PROGRAMMING

This book teaches you real Windows programming, using the C programming language and the functions of the Windows API (applications programming interface). This approach has many advantages:

- It produces the fastest, smallest applications.
- It gives you access to every Windows feature.
- Windows is designed to use this approach.
- Most examples in books and magazines follow this approach, so it's easier to learn more about Windows.
- Your program can be as sophisticated as you want; it isn't limited by artificial constraints.

There are other ways to program Windows, including Visual Basic, C++ class libraries (such as Borland's Object Windows Library) and Asymetrix ToolBox. Some of these systems offer a quick way to create prototypes and demonstration programs, but none offers the faster performance and the direct, efficient connection to all Windows features that C programming does.

BORLAND C COMPILERS

This book is based on the *Turbo C++ for Windows* and *Borland C++ for Windows* development systems, both from Borland International. (We'll abbreviate them TCW and BCW.) For Windows programmers using C, these products operate in essentially the same way. However, BCW can generate more optimized (faster or smaller) programs than TCW. Both products are complete Windows development systems; you don't need anything else.

TCW is a stand-alone product. BCW is sold as part of several other products, including *Borland C++ for Windows and DOS* and *Borland C++ & Application Frameworks*. Both packages include a DOS development system as well as the

BCW. *Borland C++ & Application Frameworks* includes various other products and utilities. For the C-language Windows developer, the most notable addition is a three-volume Windows reference. However, this reference is not worth the extra cost of the Application Frameworks package unless you want some of its other features. TCW is much less expensive than Borland C++ for Windows and DOS, which is in turn less expensive than Borland C++ and Application Frameworks.

The bottom line is that TCW is all you need to develop Windows programs. If you're wondering what to buy, it's all you need. If you already have BCW, that's fine too. By the way, don't be confused by the "C++" in the names: these products contain both C and C++ compilers, but we'll be using only the C compiler in this book.

TCW and BCW are among the easiest-to-use development systems for Windows. They are Windows-hosted, meaning that they run under Windows rather than DOS. This makes the development process easier, since you don't need to switch back and forth repeatedly between Windows and DOS during the development process. In fact, these products allow you to edit, compile, and run your program all from the same program. This convenience is a major contributor to ease of learning.

TCW and BCW are more popular than competing products, such as Microsoft's QuickC for Windows. TCW is also amazingly inexpensive. And yet these Borland compilers are powerful systems that will not limit your Windows programming as you become more proficient.

An alternative approach to C-language Windows development is to buy the Microsoft C/C++ compiler, which includes the Windows Software Development Kit (SDK). This approach has been around for many years, but it is considerably more complicated to use than the Borland products, and it is not currently Windows hosted.

WHAT YOU NEED TO KNOW

There are only two prerequisites for using this book. First, you should know something about C programming. You don't need to be a Grand Wizard in C, but you should feel reasonably comfortable with pointers, structures, and the other major aspects of the language. If you're hazy on C, consider *The Waite Group's C Programming Using Turbo C++*, described in the Bibliography at the end of this book.

Second, you should have spent some time exploring Windows from the user's viewpoint. You should be familiar with menus, dialog boxes, scroll bars, and the other aspects of the Windows GUI (graphic user interface). You should have some experience running Windows applications, and know how to use the Program Manager and File Manager. A background as a Windows user gives you an understanding of what Windows programs are supposed to do. You need to know what a user expects, so your program won't offer any unpleasant surprises.

You don't need any previous experience with Borland compilers; we explain how to use TCW and BCW as we go along.

HARDWARE AND SOFTWARE

What hardware and software do you need to use this book? First, you need a computer that can run Windows and TCW (or BCW). TCW and BCW each require about 20 megabytes of hard disk space if you install only what is necessary for Windows programming. (Installation is described in Chapter 1, *Installing Your System.*) The minimum system is a probably a 386SX processor, 4 megabytes of RAM, a hard disk with 80 megabytes, and a VGA monitor. A more comfortable system would be a 486 processor with 8 megabytes of RAM and a 200-megabyte hard disk. You might be able to use an 80286-based machine, but they are really too slow for frustration-free Windows program development.

You'll need Windows version 3.1 or later. This book discusses some features that were not available on earlier versions of Windows. You should run Windows on top of DOS version 5.0 or later.

This book is designed to be self-contained, but if you want to branch out and write your own Windows programs you'll need some additional documentation, such as the multivolume *Microsoft Windows 3.1 Programmer's Reference* or *The Waite Group's Windows API Bible* (described in the bibliography) that contains descriptions of each of the functions, structures, and other elements used in Windows programming.

WHAT THIS BOOK DOES

How does this book differ from other Windows programming books? Here are its unique features.

Focus on Essentials

As we've noted, we focus on the essentials. If you don't need to know some obscure fact, this book doesn't spend pages discussing it. Ah, but we can hear the Windows gurus now: "It's an outrage! This book tells about whiffle-snaffles, but it doesn't cover all six ways to create them, and it doesn't describe all 24 members of the WHIFFLE_SNAFFLE structure!" Well, that's just the point. It is this excess of detail that makes Windows so difficult to learn. So, if one way of creating whiffle-snaffles works for most programs, we describe that and ignore the other five.

This is the lean and mean approach. A knight in heavy armor with a supply train of horses carrying spare swords, helmets, hewberks, lances, and whatnot, cannot move as fast as one who travels alone with light armor and a few good weapons. In the same way you can learn Windows faster if you aren't burdened with unnecessary functions, structures, and other details.

Simple Example Programs

We've tried to simplify the example programs wherever possible. For instance, you don't really need to know exactly how big the characters are in order to display text with reasonable line spacing, so our initial example of text display leaves out the code that deals with this (although we get to it eventually). Reducing everything to its essentials in this way makes our example programs shorter and easier to understand.

We also make extensive use of predefined or "common" dialog boxes, which save an incredible amount of programming and, almost single-handedly, make it possible to write useful programs in a finite time.

Easy-to-Use Development Platform

Most Windows books are either generic—that is, they aren't based on a particular development system—or they are based on the venerable Microsoft Software Development Kit (SDK). Basing *Lafore's Windows Programming Made Easy* on Borland's TCW and BCW has two advantages. First, because we're talking about a specific system, we can give very detailed directions for its operation. We can tell you exactly what menu item to select to perform a certain activity. Second, the TCW and BCW systems are so much easier to use than the SDK that a substantial stumbling block is removed from the path of first-time Windows programmers.

One-Topic Chapters

We use many short chapters, each of which covers a single clearly defined topic, such as adding a scroll bar to a window, or creating a custom icon. This makes the book easier to understand and use. If you want to add a menu to your program, turn to the chapter devoted to this topic and follow the steps described.

Disk Included

The programs discussed in this book are available, as both source code and executables, on the disk that is included with every copy. You can run the executables to see what they do while you are reading about them. This makes it easier to see the relationship between a program's source code and its operation. It can also spare you a lot of typing. Later, when you're ready to develop your own Windows programs, you can use the source code on the disk to provide a template program you can modify to do what you want.

CHARGE!

The approach we take in this book (using the C language and the easy-to-use Borland compilers, along with our lean and mean approach) should have you writing real Windows programs more quickly than you thought possible. So buckle on your sword and armor, mount your trusty white charger, and—with a steely eye—gallop straight at the fierce Windows programming dragons. We think the dragons will grow nervous as you approach. You may even find, halfway through this book, that they have transformed themselves into harmless pussycats.

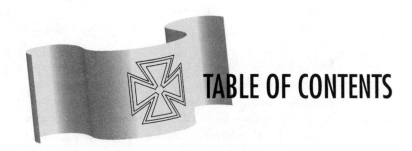

TABLE OF CONTENTS

CONTENTS

Part Eight: Larger Programs

Chapter 39: Fractal Flower Generator

Chapter 40: Roman Numeral Converter

PART ONE
GETTING STARTED

In the days of King Arthur, becoming a knight wasn't something that happened all at once. You started off as a *page*, taking lessons in horsemanship, chivalry, and jousting; and doing odd jobs around the castle, like polishing armor and waiting on tables. Then you became a *squire*, which was a sort of copilot for a knight. You helped him on with his armor, boosted him onto his horse, fought by his side in battle, rescued him if he was captured, and—if the occasion arose—buried him. Only after you had spent the requisite number of years as a page, and more years as a squire, could you aspire to the ultimate accolade of being knighted.

We're going to accelerate the process considerably. Part One of this book corresponds (in a highly tenuous way) with being a page. You'll learn some terminology and some important fundamentals of Windows programming. Then, toward the end of Part One, you'll undergo your first Trial (a test of your courage and valor). This trial appears in the form of a dragon called *event-driven programming*. Many would-be knights have been frightened by this dragon, but never fear. We supply a magic elixir that gives you the strength to overcome it with surprising ease.

CHAPTER 1

INSTALLING YOUR SYSTEM

To extend our knights-and-dragons metaphor a little further, you might think of the compiler as a horse: your trusty white charger. It should carry you bravely and uncomplainingly into the Windows battles. It is the foundation for all your programming efforts; without it, you would never get anywhere. It should respond to your commands quickly and naturally, without excessive use of the spurs, and it should not shy or bolt when one of the Windows dragons suddenly rears up, breathing fire and smoke.

Fortunately, Turbo C++ for Windows and Borland C++ for Windows meet these requirements. They are fast, flexible, and fun to use; worthy steeds in every way. In this chapter we'll show how to install these compilers. (Again, don't be confused by the "C++" in the names. Both products contain straight C compilers, which we'll be using in our examples.) These compilers work in essentially the same way, so most of our description covers them both. We'll point out places where they differ.

THE INSTALLATION PROGRAM

Installing TCW or BCW is not difficult. The installation program takes care of almost everything. In this section we'll explain the process.

Turbo C++ for Windows

In TCW you start the installation process from Windows. Insert the Install disk in the appropriate drive, go to the Program Manager, and select Run from the File menu. Then type

```
a:install
```

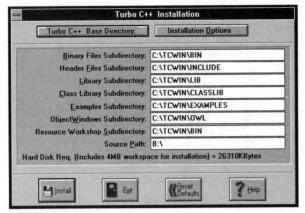

Figure 1-1
TCW Installation Window

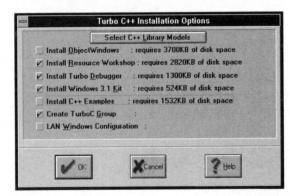

Figure 1-2
TCW Options Window

(or a different drive letter if that's where your disk is) and click on OK. You'll see a window listing various paths for different parts of the system. You probably won't need to change these. Figure 1-1 shows how this window looks.

Options

At the top of the Installation window there's a button called Installation Options. For this book you don't need all the optional applications provided in TCW, so click on this button. You'll see another window with a group of check boxes, as shown in Figure 1-2.

You don't need ObjectWindows and you don't need the C++ examples, so uncheck these boxes. This will save about 5 megabytes of hard disk space. Also, make sure the LAN Windows Configuration box remains unchecked (unless you're running with a local area network). You *do* need the Resource Workshop, Turbo Debugger, and the Windows 3.1 Kit; and you probably want to create the Turbo C++ group box for applications icons, so make sure these boxes are checked.

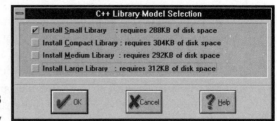

Figure 1-3
TCW Model Selection Window

Library Models

You don't need all the library models, so click the Library Models button at the top of the Installation Options window. This will bring up a Model Selection window, as shown in Figure 1-3.

You're probably familiar with library routines and memory models. The C compiler built into TCW, like most C compilers, comes with a library of routines for manipulating strings, handling math operations, and performing many other common operations. You use a different version of these routines depending on what memory model you're using.

The need for different memory models arises from the way Windows handles RAM (Random Access Memory). Windows thinks of memory as a group of *segments*. A segment cannot exceed 64 kilobytes in size. There are segments for code and segments for data. How many segments your program uses depends on how much code and how much data it requires. In TCW there are four possible arrangements, with a different function library for each arrangement, as shown in Table 1-1.

All the programs in this book are small enough to use the Small model for the function libraries, so you can uncheck the other boxes in the Model Selection window. Click on OK to return to the Installation Options window, and on OK again to return to the Installation window.

Table 1-1 TCW Library Models

Library Model	Code Segments	Data Segments
Small	One	One
Compact	Many	One
Medium	One	Many
Large	Many	Many

Installation

Click on Install. The installation program will now ask you to insert all the installation disks in order. This will take a little while, but an attractive speedometer will display your progress, and show you the number of kilobytes installed, while you wait. Even with the nonessential options and library models removed, you'll still need almost 20 megabytes of disk space.

After installation a message box tells you how to install additional icons for tools and help references. You don't need these, so click on OK to get rid of the box.

Follow the instructions for updating your CONFIG.SYS file and your AUTOEXEC.BAT file. Then exit to DOS, restart your system, and start Windows again.

Deleting Files

You can save a few megabytes of additional disk space by deleting several directories after TCW is installed. These directories are called CLASSLIB and OWL. The first is used for class libraries for the C++ language, and the second is used for Object Windows classes for Windows development in C++. If you're sure you won't be using object-oriented programming (we don't use it at all in this book), you can delete these directories and their contents. This is conveniently done with the File Manager, by clicking on the directory to be deleted and selecting Delete from the File menu.

Borland C++ for Windows

In BCW you start the installation from DOS. Simply put the Install diskette in the appropriate drive and enter

```
a:install
```

at the DOS prompt (or a different drive letter if your diskette isn't in the a: drive).

Options

If you're installing Borland C++ & Application Frameworks, you may not want all the options included with it. Installing all these options uses almost 50 megabytes on your hard disk. If your goal is simply developing Windows programs, as described in this book, you can reduce this considerably. The installation program will ask you what options you want, and you can eliminate the nonessentials. You'll be shown a screen that looks something like this:

```
Directories...        [ C:\BORLANDC ]
Windows Dir...        [ C:\WINDOWS ]
Install Options       [ CMD IDE TD TASM TPROF TV CLASS BGI DOC ]
Examples Options...   [ C/C++ TD TASM TPROF WIN RW OWL TV ]
Windows Options...    [ WIN DEV31 RW OWL DEBUG GRPS ]
Dos Library Models... [ S M C L H SRC ]
```

The Install program shows you how to use the arrow keys to select which of these options you want to install. All the options start out being marked Yes. Keep the options you do need set to Yes, and change everything else to No.

Directories

The directories shown in the first two lines tell you where Borland C++ will be installed, and where Windows is located. You don't usually need to change them unless you want to put Borland C++ somewhere else, or Windows is installed in a different directory.

Install Options

Under Install Options you only need one item. This is TD, which stands for Turbo Debugger.

▣ TD—enables Turbo Debugger

The debugger will prove useful in Windows development. The other items on this line are for DOS development, the C++ language, and other things we don't need to worry about, so you can eliminate them.

Under Examples you should select

▣ WIN—includes Windows examples

You don't need these examples to use this book, but you may want to look at them later. If you're really tight on disk space, you can forget this one. Eliminate everything else on this line.

Under Windows Options, you should select

▣ WIN—provides Windows capability
▣ DEV31—gives you the new capabilities of Windows 3.1
▣ RW—installs the Resource Workshop for creating dialog boxes and other items
▣ DEBUG—installs the 386 debugger
▣ GRPS—installs a group for program icons in the Windows Program Manager

If you're running on a 286 machine you can eliminate DEBUG. All the other options listed here are essential for Windows development, except OWL.

DOS Library Models

As we noted in the TCW installation section, all the examples in this book use the Small model. You can eliminate all the others unless you know you'll need them. Thus the only DOS Library Model you need is

▣ S—or the Small memory model

Minimum Options

When you're done making the changes noted above, the resulting screen should look like this:

```
Directories...         [ C:\BORLANDC ]
Windows Dir...         [ C:\WINDOWS ]
Install Options        [ TD ]
Examples Options...    [ WIN ]
Windows Options...     [ WIN DEV31 RW DEBUG GRPS ]
DOS Library Models...  [ S ]
```

When the screen is set up to your satisfaction, select Start Installation. The necessary files will be decompressed and loaded automatically. You'll need to feed in all the disks in order.

When installation is complete, the INSTALL program makes some suggestions before terminating. Follow the instructions about the FILES statement in your CONFIG.SYS file, and the PATH statement in your AUTOEXEC.BAT file. Restart your system, and run Windows. Borland C++ will ask if you want to install a group box in the Program Manager that contains the icons for the programs you've just installed. Answer Yes, and the group box with icons will appear in the Program Manager. One of these icons is named BCW; this is the one that launches Borland C++ for Windows. There are others, some of which we'll meet as we go along.

BUILDING A PROGRAM

$\mathcal{N}$ ow that you're safely mounted on your trusty steed, you're ready to canter around the practice field and make sure that everything works as it should. You don't want your helmet falling off or the cinch strap coming undone at a critical moment.

In this chapter we're going to go through the steps of building a simple Windows program. To *build* a program means to start with a source (text) file and turn it into an executable program. We aren't going to deal in this chapter with the *contents* of the program, only the build process. This way, you and your horse can learn to know and trust each other before encountering anything too scary, like a griffon or a dragon.

If you are already familiar with Turbo C++ for Windows or Borland C++ for Windows, you can probably skim parts of this chapter. Actually, TCW and BCW are remarkably similar to other Borland products, such as Turbo C++ for DOS, so familiarity with those systems may also give you a head start. TCW and BCW function almost identically, so we'll often refer to TCW when we mean both TCW and BCW. If their behavior differs, we'll tell you how.

STARTING YOUR SYSTEM

Start Windows in Standard or 386-Enhanced mode (use 386-Enhanced mode, the default for Windows 3.1, if possible). From the Program Manager, open the Turbo C++ (or Borland C++) group icon. You'll see icons for the applications you installed in the last chapter. Now double-click on the Turbo C++ or BCW icon to start the compiler. You'll see the screen shown in Figure 2-1. (If you're using BCW it will say Borland C++ at the top, instead of Turbo C++.)

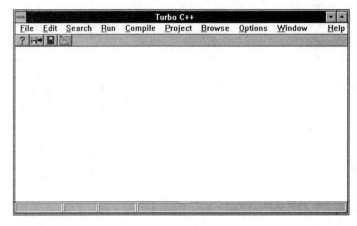

Figure 2-1

Startup Turbo
C++ Screen

A SHORT WINDOWS PROGRAM

Your first task is to enter a source file into the compiler. Here's the listing for a short
Windows program, SOLOMEM.C, that's suitable for such experimentation:

```
// solomem.c
// puts a message box on the desktop
// does not use main window

#define STRICT                  // strict type-checking
#include <windows.h>            // include file for all Windows programs

//////////////////////////////////////////////////////////////////////
// WinMain() -- program entry point                                   //
//////////////////////////////////////////////////////////////////////
#pragma argsused                // ignore unused arguments

int PASCAL WinMain(HINSTANCE hInstance,  // which program are we?
                   HINSTANCE hPrevInst,  // is there another one?
                   LPSTR lpszCmdLine,    // command line arguments
                   int nCmdShow)         // window size (icon, etc)
   {
   DWORD dwMemAvail;            // free memory (unsigned long)
   char szBuffer[80];          // buffer for string

   dwMemAvail = GetFreeSpace(0);  // get free memory

                               // make a string
   wsprintf(szBuffer, "Memory available: %lu", dwMemAvail);

                               // display message box
   MessageBox(NULL, szBuffer, "SOLOMEM", MB_OK);
   return NULL;                 // return to Windows
   } // end WinMain
```

The purpose of this program is to display a message box that tells you how much global memory is available in your system. Global memory is the total amount of RAM available for your program's use. Actually, if you're using Windows' 386-Enhanced mode, global memory includes *virtual memory*. This is an area of the disk set up to act like RAM. It offers what you might think of as emergency memory, if regular RAM is used up. (The disadvantage is that it's slower.) Thus you may find to your surprise that the SOLOMEM program reports more memory than there is RAM installed in your system.

As a Windows user you have other ways to check the global memory available. Select the About Program Manager item from the Program Manager's Help menu, and examine the number listed under Memory. It won't be quite the same as the number returned by SOLOMEM, since SOLOMEM itself uses up some space. Applications (as opposed to users) may need to employ the method shown in SOLOMEM to find out how much memory is available. They can use this information to arrange their storage space, or sometimes to inform the user that there isn't enough memory to run at all.

Don't worry if the contents of the SOLOMEM.C listing are Greek to you at this point. We'll explain how it works in the next chapter. For now, we'll concentrate on the process of turning it into an executable Windows program.

ENTERING THE PROGRAM

There are two ways to put the SOLOMEM.C source file into the compiler. You can type it in, or you can load it from the disk that accompanies this book. We recommend you type it in. Typing forces you to concentrate on the details of the listing. Even if you don't know what the listing means at this point, the more familiar you are with it, the better. Also, as you know, typing builds character, and what is a knight without character? We'll show you how to enter the file from the keyboard, and then (bowing to the pressures of the real world) we'll also explain how to load the file from the disk.

Typing in the Source File

To type in the source file, select New from the File menu. An empty Edit window will appear on the screen. Figure 2-2 shows the empty edit window.

You can type the SOLOMEM.C listing directly into this window. As a C programmer, you know you must be very careful of typos. Everything must be spelled correctly, and proper care must be paid to braces, semicolons, and other punctuation.

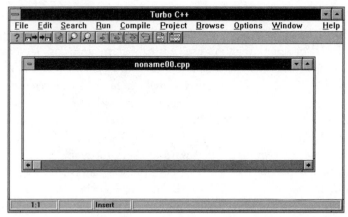

Figure 2-2

The Empty Edit Window

You'll find that operating the editor built into TCW or BCW is quite intuitive. What you type appears on the screen, at the *insertion point* (the blinking vertical line). You can move the insertion point with the mouse by repositioning the *cursor* (the I-shaped mouse pointer) and clicking the left button. You can also use the arrow keys to move the insertion point. Pressing the (ENTER) key inserts a new line, and drops the insertion point to the start of the line. The (BACKSPACE) key deletes the character to the left of the insertion point.

Table 2-1 shows some of the more important cursor commands.

You can scroll up and down and left and right with the scroll bars; and cut, copy and paste using the mouse and menu commands, as with many other Windows applications. The edit window can be resized, moved, or maximized. For more information about the editor, select Contents from the Help menu and then select Editor Tables. You'll see a list of cursor commands, among other things. You can use the Help window to learn more about all features of the editor's operation.

Arranging Your Hard Disk

Once you've typed in the source file you can save it to your hard disk. This is a good time to think about how to organize your hard disk for Windows program development.

When compiled and linked, each program you write will generate several files. At the least there will be (besides the .C file you typed in) an object file with the .OBJ extension, and an executable file with the .EXE extension. The compiler automatically generates backups, so when you modify the source file there will be a file with the .BAK extension. As our programs get more complicated we'll add other files as well, such as a resource script file with the .RC extension, a project file with the .PRJ extension, and so on.

Table 2-1 Editing Keys

Keyboard Key	Action
(↑)	Up one line
(↓)	Down one line
(←)	Left one character
(→)	Right one character
(CTRL)-(←)	Left one word
(CTRL)-(→)	Right one word
(HOME)	Start of line
(END)	End of line
(PGUP)	Scroll one screen up
(PGDN)	Scroll one screen down
(ENTER)	Insert line, go to next line
(BACKSPACE)	Delete character to left of insertion point
(DEL)	Delete character to right of insertion point
(INS)	Toggle insert/write-over

It's not very efficient to jumble all your programs, each with so many files, together in one large directory. A better approach is to allocate one directory for each program, or for each closely related group of programs. We recommend creating a directory off your root directory, called (for example) \WINPROGS. Then create subdirectories under this subdirectory for each section of the book, calling them PART_1, PART_2, and so on. You can switch to the Windows File Manager (press (CTRL)+(ESC) to bring up the Task List) and create a new directory at any time. Figure 2-3 shows our recommended directory arrangement.

You should definitely avoid mixing up your source files with the Borland executables, which are in the \TCWIN\BIN (or \BORLANDC\BIN) directory. This is easy to do, because that's the default directory that appears when you select Save As from the File menu. Don't forget to change this directory to the one you want when you save the source file.

Saving Your Source File

If you typed in your file, it's been given the default name of NONAME00.CPP. This isn't the name you want, so select Save As from the File menu to change the name and save the file. In the Save As dialog, change to the appropriate drive and directory. Then in the File Name field type the new file name and extension: SOLOMEM.C. Or you can type the drive, path, file name, and file extension directly into the File Name field. For instance, to save SOLOMEM.C to the PART_1 subdirectory in the WINPROGS directory, you would enter

```
c:\winprogs\part_1\solomem.c
```

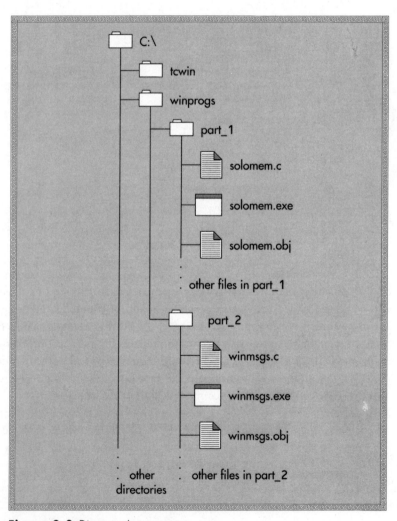

Figure 2-3 Directory Arrangement

Figure 2-4

The

SOLOMEM.C

File in the Edit

Window

```
Turbo C++ - [c:\winprogs\part_1\solomem.c]
  File   Edit   Search   Run   Compile   Project   Browse   Options   Window   Help

// solomem.c
// puts a message box on the desktop
// does not use main window

#define STRICT                   // strict type-checking
#include <windows.h>             // include file for all Windows programs

////////////////////////////////////////////////////////////////////////
// WinMain() -- program entry point                                    //
////////////////////////////////////////////////////////////////////////
#pragma argsused                 // ignore unused arguments

int PASCAL WinMain(HINSTANCE hInstance,   // which program are we?
                   HINSTANCE hPrevInst,   // is there another one?
                   LPSTR lpszCmdLine,     // command line arguments

 1:1            Insert
```

The file will be saved, and the new file name will appear at the top of the edit window. Figure 2-4 shows how this looks.

Copying Files to Your Hard Disk

As you know, a diskette, containing the source code and executables for the example programs, is included with this book. Unless you prefer to type in the programs, you will probably want to copy all the files from this diskette onto your hard disk. To do this, first use the Windows File Manager utility to create a WINPROGS directory off the root directory of your c: drive. Then (of course) make sure the diskette is in the a: drive (or whatever the appropriate drive letter is). Click on the icon for this drive to produce the file-folder icon for the root directory for the diskette. Now drag this folder to the WINPROGS folder on the c: drive. This will automatically copy all the folder icons (PART_1, PART_2, and so on) and their contents from the diskette into the WINPROGS directory on the hard disk. See "About the Disk" in the beginning of this book for more information.

Reading the Source File from Disk

Once the examples are installed on your hard disk, you can load the SOLOMEM.C source file from the disk into TCW (or BCW). Simply select Open from the File menu. The Open a File dialog box appears. An annoyance the first time you open this dialog is that it lists only those files with the .CPP extension. This extension is used only for programs written in the C++ language. We don't use that language for the programs in this book; we use C, and programs in C use the .C extension. So the first thing you should do is change the *.CPP in the File Name field to *.C. Now you can see lists of .C files, as shown in Figure 2-5.

Change the directory to \WINPROGS\PART_1, and double-click on SOLOMEM.C. Alternatively you could enter

`c:\part_1\solomem.c`

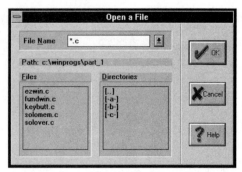

Figure 2-5
The Open a File Dialog

directly into the File Name field. Either way the SOLOMEM.C file should appear in the edit window.

Specifying the Output Directory

Various files, such as object files and executable files, are generated in the program development process. Unfortunately, TCW and BCW don't automatically put these files in the same directory as the source file. Before building your program, you should specify where such output files go. If you don't specify anything, they will go in the \TCWIN\BIN (or \BORLANDC\BIN) directory, where they will be hard to find among the dozens of application programs.

Select Directories from the Options menu. You'll see fields called Include Directories, Library Directories, and Output Directories. In the Output Directories field, type in the path name of the directory where you're putting your files. If you created a WINPROGS directory for the programs in this book and used a subdirectory called PART_1 for the programs of Part One, then you should enter

```
c:\winprogs\part_1
```

If you want, you can also delete references to the OWL directory, since we won't be using it. The result is shown in Figure 2-6. Click on the OK button to make the box go away. Then select Save from the Options menu to save these path-name changes to disk. That way the compiler will know about them when you start it up again.

Don't forget to change the Output Directory field when you change to a different directory, otherwise TCW or BCW will go right on putting your object and executable files in the old directory. Unfortunately, it's easy to forget to do this; this feature of TCW is judged a minor annoyance, since the compilers could have automatically put all output files in the same directory as the source file.

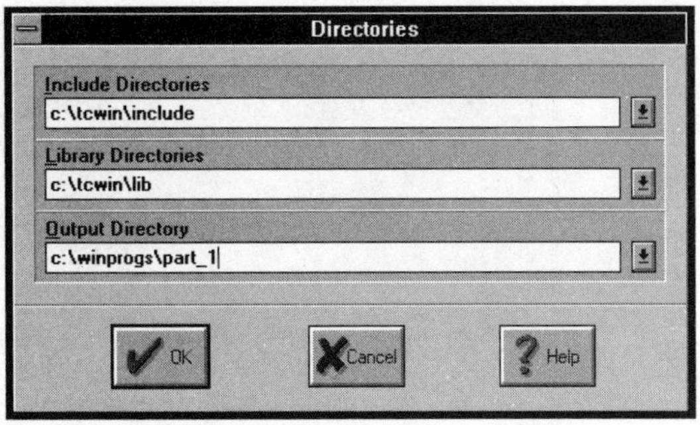

Figure 2-6
The Directories Dialog

COMPILING, LINKING, AND RUNNING YOUR PROGRAM

Now we're ready to convert our program from a text source file to an executable file that Windows can run. This involves compiling your .C file into an .OBJ object file, linking the .OBJ file to create an .EXE executable file, and executing the .EXE file.

First, make sure that the source file you're starting with has a .C extension and not the .CPP extension. That's the only way the compiler knows what language, C or C++, to use to compile the file.

One-Stop Shopping

You could build your program one step at a time, this way:

1. Select Compile from the Compile menu.
2. Select Link from the Compile menu.
3. Select Run from the Run menu.

However, you don't need to perform the separate steps listed above. It's usually more efficient to simply select Run from the Run menu, or press (CTRL)+(F9). This compiles, links, and runs your program. If your program has not been modified since the last time it was compiled or linked, the compile and link steps are skipped automatically.

Output of SOLOMEM

Assuming you didn't make any mistakes typing in your program, and that everything is set up correctly, you should see a message box appear on your screen, as shown in Figure 2-7.

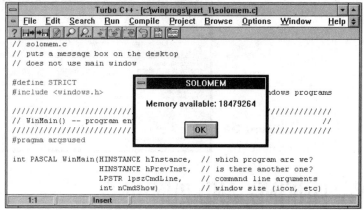

Figure 2-7
Output of
the SOLOMEM
Program

The message box appears directly over whatever else is on the screen, in this case TCW itself. Click on the OK button in the box to make it go way. This terminates the SOLOMEM program.

As we mentioned, this message box shows the global memory available in your system. This value varies considerably, depending on whether you're running Windows in Standard mode or in 386-Enhanced mode, and on how much RAM and disk space you have. The more memory, the higher the number; and (in 386-Enhanced mode) the more disk space the higher the number (up to a point), because the disk is used for virtual memory. For example, a system with 8 megabytes of memory and a 200-megabyte hard disk might report a number like 19,414,400 bytes of free memory. More than half of this is virtual memory on the disk. Another computer with only 4 megabytes of memory and a 40-megabyte hard disk might report 3,970,080 bytes free, mostly in RAM.

Linker Warning

The linker generates a warning when you develop this program. You can see this warning by selecting Message from the Window menu after running your program. The message window stores all the messages created during the compiling and linking process. If you have typed in the program correctly, there will be only one warning, which looks like this:

```
Linker Warning: No module definition file specified: using defaults
```

Some Windows compiler systems require a special file, called the *module definition* file (with file extension .DEF) to provide the linker with additional information. TCW and BCW don't need this .DEF file for the programs in this book, so we don't worry about it. The linker, however, feels a responsibility to remind us that we haven't supplied the file. You can ignore this message.

Other Errors

If you have made mistakes typing in the program, the compiler or the linker may signal other kinds of errors or warnings. You should correct your source code, as you would with any C program, until you can compile and link your program with only one warning—the module definition file warning mentioned above.

Running from Windows

Once your program has been compiled and linked, thus generating an executable file, you can run it directly from Windows; you don't need to run it from the compiler. It is now a complete stand-alone program. To run it under Windows, switch to the Program Manager by pressing (CTRL)+(ESC) and double-clicking on the "Program Manager" entry in the task list. Then select Run from the Program Manager's File menu, and type the complete path name of the program into the Command Line field of the resulting Run dialog box (or use the Browse button to see a list of files). For SOLOMEM, assuming the executable file is in \WINPROGS\PART_1, you would enter

```
\winprogs\part_1\solomem
```

You don't need the .EXE extension; it's the default. When you click on OK in the Run dialog, SOLOMEM will execute and you'll see the SOLOMEM message box, displaying the available memory as before. (You can also run a program by double-clicking on the icon for its .EXE file in the File Manager.) Figure 2-8 shows SOLOMEM running when the only other running application is the Program Manager.

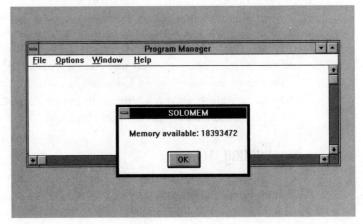

Figure 2-8
SOLOMEM Running Without the Compiler

OPTIONS

A menu is available in TCW and BCW that lists various options. We'll mention a few here; some are useful, but others are indispensible.

Warning Level

Most compilers issue both errors and warnings. An error means that the compiler has given up on your source code; it cannot create an object file. A warning, on the other hand, indicates that the compiler thinks you might have made a mistake, but it can still make a reasonable guess about what you mean, so it goes ahead and creates the object file. Most compilers allow you to specify what sorts of things generate warnings. We recommend that you tell the compiler to generate a warning for *everything*. It can be hard to track down errors in Windows programs, so the more suspicious situations the compiler tells you about, the better. Don't try to run your program until it compiles warning-free with all the warnings turned on.

Here's how to turn on all the warnings. Select Compiler from the Options menu, and then select Messages from the resulting submenu. Select Display from the sub-submenu. In the resulting Message Display dialog box, click on the All radio button. Then click on OK. (If you select other items besides Display in the sub-submenu, you can see the sorts of things that trigger warnings.)

Now you should select Save from the Options menu to record this option to disk. You should do this after changing any option that you want to apply to future programs. Saving the options ensures that the compiler will remember your selections when you load it the next time.

Precompiled Headers

You can speed up compilation significantly by precompiling the header files. This means that a file like WINDOWS.H (which we'll learn about later) is compiled only once, when you first build your program. For each build after that, the compiled version of the file is used, which saves a lot of time. The compiled header takes some disk space, but unless that poses a problem this is a really good idea.

To activate this option select Compiler from the Options menu, and then select Code Generation from the submenu. In the resulting Code Generation Options dialog, check the Precompiled Headers check box.

Highlighting

You may have noticed in the TCW or BCW editor that different parts of the program listing are automatically given different colors. If you select Environment from the Options menu, and then select Highlight from the resulting submenu, you can change the colors used for highlighting different parts of the code. For instance, you might want to make reserved words red, so they stand out better. Just click on Reserved Word in the Element list, click on the red block in the Color list, and click on OK.

Highlighting can help to prevent errors by making it clearer what's going on in the listing. You're less likely to make a mistake if program elements like strings and comments are in different colors. The colors you choose are largely a matter of choice (so long as they're legible).

Fonts

You may not like the default font that TCW uses for program listings. If you don't, it's easy to change. Select Environment from the Options menu, and then select Preferences from the submenu. You'll see a list of fonts. Select the one that appeals to you. Generally it's easier to program with a fixed-width font (where all characters are the same width, as on a typewriter). Courier 12 point is a good bet. Select the font, click on OK, and then select Save from the Options menu so this selection will be loaded the next time you start TCW.

NOT SO HARD AFTER ALL

Now you've cantered around the practice field. Hopefully, you stayed on your horse, and the horse (TCW or BCW) is behaving in a civilized way. Are you surprised how easy it is to develop a real working Windows program? So far it's really no more difficult than a DOS program. You may also be surprised to find how easy it to understand how the program works. That's the topic of the next chapter.

CHAPTER 3

TYPES AND NAMES

The page who wants to become a knight must learn a new vocabulary. For example, he must learn that a *hewberk* is a tunic made of chain mail, that *jesses* are straps fastened around the leg of a hawk or other bird used in falconry, and that to *foin* is to thrust with the point of a sword. The Windows programmer must also learn some new terminology.

In this chapter we're going to examine the SOLOMEM program, introduced in the last chapter, in considerable detail. Although it is short (for a Windows program), this program demonstrates many important features of Windows programming. We'll focus on two topics that deal with terminology: derived types and Hungarian notation. But we will also introduce the WinMain() function (which works like main() in non-Windows C programs) and its arguments, and show how to use the library functions built into Windows.

For your convenience, we'll reproduce here the listing for the SOLOMEM.C source file from the last chapter:

```
// solomem.c
// puts a message box on the desktop
// does not use main window

#define STRICT                  // strict type-checking
#include <windows.h>            // include file for all Windows programs


///////////////////////////////////////////////////////////////////////
// WinMain() -- program entry point                                    //
///////////////////////////////////////////////////////////////////////
#pragma argsused                // ignore unused arguments

int PASCAL WinMain(HINSTANCE hInstance,    // which program are we?
                   HINSTANCE hPrevInst,    // is there another one?
                   LPSTR lpszCmdLine,      // command line arguments
```

```
                    int nCmdShow)              // window size (icon, etc)
{
DWORD dwMemAvail;         // free memory (unsigned long)
char szBuffer[80];        // buffer for string

dwMemAvail = GetFreeSpace(0);  // get free memory

                          // make a string
wsprintf(szBuffer, "Memory available: %lu", dwMemAvail);

                          // display message box
MessageBox(NULL, szBuffer, "SOLOMEM", MB_OK);
return NULL;              // return to Windows
}  // end WinMain
```

DERIVED DATA TYPES

One of the first hurdles faced by a beginning Windows programmer is that, even though it is written in C, a Windows program doesn't *look* like a C program. Perhaps the biggest difference in appearance is that, in addition to normal C data types like **int** and **char**, you see unfamiliar type names written in capital letters. In SOLOMEM there are three such derived types: HINSTANCE, LPSTR, and DWORD. Other programs will use other such types, such as UINT, WORD, HWND, HGLOBAL, and so on.

These new type names are equivalent to, or derived from (hence the name), existing types. Let's see how Windows defines these types, and why you would want to use them.

What Are They Really?

A derived type is simply a normal C data type called by another name. You can find out the "real" meanings of derived data types by searching for them in the WINDOWS.H header file (which we'll discuss soon). In that file you'll find the statements

```
typedef unsigned long  DWORD;
```

and

```
typedef char FAR*  LPSTR;
```

Such typedef declarations create new names for existing data types. Thus DWORD is made equivalent to **unsigned long**. LPSTR, which stands for a Long (meaning **_far**) Pointer to a STRing, is made equivalent to **char** FAR*, where FAR is itself typedefed to be equivalent to **_far** (which designates a 32-bit pointer instead of a 16-bit **_near** pointer).

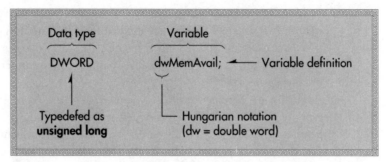

Figure 3-1 Defining a Variable

Finding the definition of HINSTANCE in WINDOWS.H is somewhat more obscure, but what it comes down to is that HINSTANCE is type **const void _near***
(a constant near pointer to void). Similarly you can figure out any derived type by looking it up in WINDOWS.H. Figure 3-1 annotates the definition of the dwMemAvail variable, which is the first statement in WinMain().

The surprising thing about these derived types is that, in most cases, you can use them without knowing or caring what the "real" underlying type is. This will become clearer as we go along. However, if you feel hazy on **_near** and **_far** pointers, what **const** means, or any other aspects of the C language, you can consult *Turbo C Programming for the PC* (listed in the Bibliography at the end of this book) or a similar tutorial.

Handles

A variable of type HINSTANCE is a kind of *handle*; specifically a handle to an *instance*. (We'll discuss instances soon.) A handle is simply an arbitrary number assigned by the system to a particular entity. It serves to identify the entity, whether it's an instance, a window, a control, or a block of memory. There are a dozen or so related data types for describing different kinds of handles. They all begin with the letter H. Thus HWND is the type for a window handle, HGLOBAL for a global memory handle, and so on. We'll see other examples of handles as we go along.

Advantages of Derived Types

Why use derived types instead of the basic types like **int** and **char**? One reason is that the derived type names convey more information to someone reading the listing. It's easy to recognize HINSTANCE as a handle to an instance, but **const void _near*** conveys very little about the purpose of the data type. Thus the derived types make the listing easier to understand. Also, they're often shorter, thus reducing clutter.

More importantly, the compiler will be able to check your code much more rigorously if different type names are used for different kinds of variables. It can tell if you are using the wrong kind of handle as a function argument, for example, and signal an error, even if both handles have the same underlying type. This will become clearer later.

Finally, as Windows evolves, Microsoft may choose to change the underlying types of certain entities. In previous versions of Windows, for example, instance handles (type HINSTANCE) were of type **unsigned int**, while now, as we've seen, they're a pointer to **void**. (This change was made to make Windows programs more portable to different processors.) If you had written your program using the underlying types, you would need to modify all your handle variables every time Microsoft revised Windows. By using the derived types you avoid having to change your source code.

Just Do It

The beginning Windows programmer may find the use of derived types disconcerting. If I can't even recognize the data types, you may be asking yourself, how far am I going to get? However, this does not turn out to be a major problem. After you've looked over a few Windows listings, you begin to accept the derived types, and even take them for granted. You may begin by feeling frustrated that you don't know immediately what basic type they represent, but, as we noted, you don't usually need to know about the underlying type. If a function returns an argument of type DWORD, and you want to assign this value to a variable, just declare a variable of type DWORD. You don't need to know that DWORD is defined as **unsigned long**. You can even get into trouble if you make use of the fact; as we noted, Microsoft may change the underlying type in a future version of Windows. In a nutshell: forget that derived types are derived from anything, and treat them simply as types.

Appendix A includes a list of the derived data types used in this book.

HUNGARIAN NOTATION

As if new data types weren't enough, there's a second terminology-related issue in Windows programs. Look at the variable names in SOLOMEM. They probably seem odd to you: hInstance, lpszCmdLine, dwMemAvail, and so on. These variable names are written using a system called *Hungarian notation*. This system is named after the birthplace of its inventor, Charles Simonyi, a programmer at Microsoft. (The name also seems to reflect the fact that to many people the notation is as obscure as the Hungarian language.)

Table 3-1 Hungarian Notation in SOLOMEM

Variable	Prefix	Meaning
hInstance, hPrevInst	h	Handle
szBuffer	sz	String
lpszCmdLine	lpsz	Long pointer to string
nCmdShow	n	Number (often type **int**)
dwMemAvail	dw	Double word (type DWORD)

The idea in Hungarian notation is to preface a variable name with several lowercase letters that describe its purpose or data type. Thus **h** stands for handle, **dw** means double word, **lp** is a long (**far**) pointer, **sz** is a zero-terminated string (a normal C string), **lpsz** is a long pointer to a zero-terminated string, and **n** means a number of something. Table 3-1 shows the Hungarian notation for the variables in SOLOMEM.

The name that these prefixes precede (Instance, Buffer, and so on) is also important. It should describe something about the variable's purpose, and should start with an uppercase letter. Thus adding h to Instance gives you hInstance, a handle to an instance, and adding dw to MemAvail gives you dwMemAvail, a double-word variable whose value is the memory available.

Why use Hungarian notation? The idea is to make it easier for the programmer to spot errors. If you find yourself using a variable called dwWhatsis (where the 'dw' indicates it's a variable of type DWORD) as an argument to a function that requires type HINSTANCE, you can see you've made a mistake just by looking at the variable name.

Of course you don't really need to use Hungarian notation when naming your variables; the compiler won't care if you're using it or not. It is simply a mnemonic device to help the programmer. However, Microsoft uses it in the Windows documentation, and it's a helpful approach to preventing errors. We'll use it in the examples in this book. However, bear in mind that Hungarian notation is an evolving discipline, with stylistic variations from one programmer to another. Appendix B shows some definitions of Hungarian notation used in this book.

Now that we've mentioned the two major notational features of Windows programs, derived types and Hungarian notation, we're ready to look at the SOLOMEM program line by line.

PRELIMINARIES

The SOLOMEM program starts with a #define, an #include, and a #pragma. Let's see what these directives do.

The STRICT Variable

Windows programs can be more difficult to debug than traditional MS-DOS programs, for reasons that will become clearer soon. Thus it's important to catch as many errors as possible at compile time, rather than waiting until run time. Windows versions starting with 3.1 allow the programmer to define a variable called STRICT, which switches on a more rigorous level of variable type checking. For instance, when STRICT is defined, the arguments to all Windows functions must be of the correct derived type. You can't use a variable of type HWND (handle to a window) when you're supposed to use type HINSTANCE (handle to an instance). Even though both these derived types have the same underlying type, STRICT allows the compiler to signal an error. Here's how STRICT is invoked:

```
#define STRICT
```

This directive must be placed *before* the #include for the WINDOWS.H file (described next). You don't need to use STRICT, but we recommend it highly, and will use it in all our program examples.

The WINDOWS.H Header File

The WINDOWS.H header file is one of the keys to Windows programming. It contains a multitude of definitions needed by all Windows programs, including prototypes (declarations) for the hundreds of Windows functions; and definitions of structures, constants, and (as we've seen) derived data types. All Windows programs must #include the WINDOWS.H header file. Don't leave home without this directive:

```
#include <windows.h>
```

You can use the WINDOWS.H file as a quick reference. For instance, if you want to know the data types of arguments used in a Windows function, just use your TCW (or BCW) editor to open WINDOWS.H as you would any other text file. It's in the \TCWIN\INCLUDE (or \BORLANDC\INCLUDE) directory. Then select Find from the Search menu and enter the name of the function you want to examine. You'll see the function prototype, which includes the data types of the arguments. Similarly you can look up the meaning of constants, structures, derived data types, and almost anything else you're curious about. (Of course you

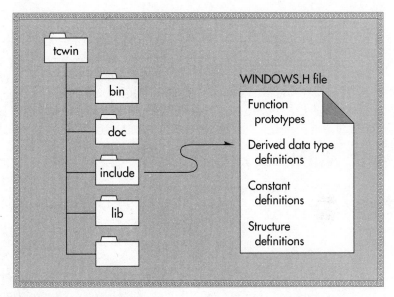

Figure 3-2 WINDOWS.H File

should make sure you don't inadvertently alter WINDOWS.H.) Figure 3-2 shows the WINDOWS.H file.

The argsused Pragma

As you'll see, none of the arguments to WinMain() is used in SOLOMEM. Most compilers will find this suspicious, and will generate warning messages like "Parameter hInstance is never used." Such messages can be annoying, because you're trying to create a warning-free compilation every time. The argsused pragma solves this problem by telling the compiler not to worry about function arguments that are not used. A pragma is a directive that works with specific compilers; it is not defined in the C language. It usually gives a specific instruction to the compiler about how to compile a program.

```
#pragma argsused
```

This pragma applies only to one function. You insert it before the function, and it disables the "unused argument" error messages for that function, but not for subsequent functions.

Comments

If you're an old-time C programmer, used to a comment syntax like

```
/* comment */
```

you may not be familiar with the new // (double-slash) style of comment. Everything following the // symbol is considered to be a comment until the end of the line. There is no symbol to terminate the comment; the end of the line is the terminator. This new style, originally introduced in C++, is perfectly acceptable in TCW and BCW, as well as most other C compilers. You can use the old style as well if you want; it's still useful for multiple-line comments.

THE WinMain() FUNCTION

Every journey starts with a single step, and every Windows program—no matter how many functions it has—starts with the WinMain() function. As you can see, WinMain() is the only function in SOLOMEM. This function plays the same role in Windows programs that main() does in normal C programs in MS-DOS. It is to this function that control is passed when an application is first executed by the operating system. When this function terminates, it returns control to Windows. Figure 3-3 shows what this looks like. Every Windows program must have a WinMain() function, although of course it may have many other functions as well.

In source file listings, the first line of a function, where the return type and arguments are specified, is called the *declarator*. Figure 3-4 annotates the declarator of WinMain().

We don't really need to worry at this point about any of the arguments to WinMain(), or its return value, but we'll discuss these details briefly so you won't go on wondering about them.

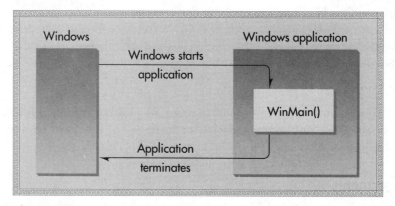

Figure 3-3 WinMain() and Windows

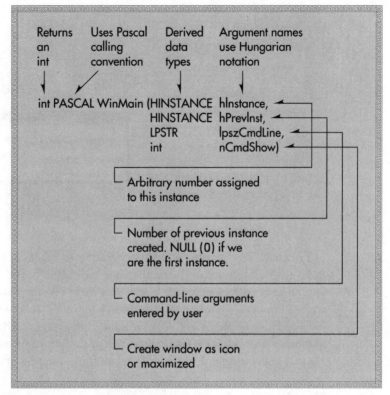

Figure 3-4 The WinMain() Declarator

Instances

The first two arguments to WinMain(), hInstance and hPrevInst, are concerned with *instances*. To see what an instance is, you can perform a simple experiment. Run SOLOMEM, and, without clicking on its OK button to terminate it, run it again. Run it a third time (or more, if you want). Now, by minimizing any full-size windows on your screen, and rearranging your desktop, you'll see three different versions of the SOLOMEM message box, as shown in Figure 3-5.

Because Windows is a multitasking operating system, many programs can run at the same time. Also, different *instances* of the same program can run at the same time. That's what's happening here. Each of the message boxes in Figure 3-5 represents one operating instance of SOLOMEM. As far as the user is concerned, each is an independent program. Notice that each instance reports a slightly different amount of memory. This is because each instance occupies some memory space, which is not available when the next one executes.

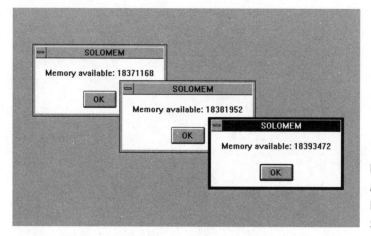

Figure 3-5
Multiple
Instances of
SOLOMEM

Internally (and for the Windows programmer), these instances are not entirely independent. They actually share the same code! That is, the executable instructions that make up the program are loaded into memory only once. This saves memory space. However, each instance does have its own data, so it can operate independently of the others. Also, Windows imposes considerable overhead on each instance, which accounts for the rather large amount of memory used by each one. Figure 3-6 shows how Windows handles multiple instances of the same program.

The hInstance Argument

Suppose that there are multiple instances of a program running, and that an application needs to know which instance it is (like asking yourself, "What's my name?"). It can find this out by checking the hInstance argument to WinMain(). This value is a number unique to a particular instance.

The hPrevInst Argument

An application can also tell if it is the *first* instance launched by the user. This will be true if the hPrevInst argument is NULL.

We won't worry about these instance-related arguments for the moment. Most simple applications don't need to know which instance they are, or (with one exception, which we'll explore later) whether they're the first one.

The lpszCmdLine Argument

The lpszCmdLine argument is a pointer to a string containing the text typed by the user to invoke the program. For example, you might use the Program Manager to start a program, and enter one or more words after the name of the program, like this:

```
\winprogs\progname one two three
```

Here "one," "two," and "three" are command-line arguments. This entire string is passed on to the application being executed. The command-line arguments may be file names that the application should open, or other information. This is similar to the way command-line arguments are used in the DOS environment. However, command-line arguments are somewhat less popular in Windows and other GUI environments than in DOS, because programs are more commonly launched by double-clicking an icon rather than by typing a file name.

The nCmdShow Argument

Finally, the nCmdShow argument tells the application whether it has been created as a full-size window or as an icon. Our program doesn't even have a main window, so we don't need to worry about this.

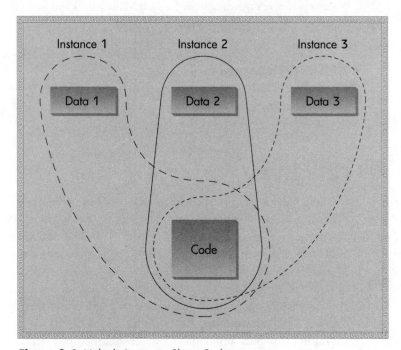

Figure 3-6 Multiple Instances Share Code

Return Value

As you can see from the declarator for WinMain(), the data type of the return value is **int**. The PASCAL keyword tells the compiler to generate WinMain() using the Pascal calling convention. This has to do with how function arguments are passed from a calling program to a function. Arguments are passed by being stored in a special area of memory called the *stack*, before control is transferred to the function. With the C calling convention, the last argument goes onto the stack first, which allows for functions with an undefined number of arguments (like printf() in traditional C programs). With the Pascal convention, the first argument goes first, which is slightly more efficient. Windows uses the Pascal convention for most functions because of this increased efficiency.

For this short kind of Windows program, the return value from WinMain() should be NULL (a constant defined as 0 in WINDOWS.H). Later we'll see that in more complicated programs WinMain() returns other values.

Older Versions of Windows

Programs written to run with older versions of Windows used different derived types for some arguments to WinMain() and for many other functions as well. For example, here's the declarator for WinMain() in Windows 3.0:

```
int PASCAL WinMain(HANDLE, HANDLE, LPSTR, int);
```

Here HANDLE is used for the first two arguments. The newer approach, using HINSTANCE, makes it possible for the compiler to do better type-checking (provided STRICT is defined). However, you may run across the old approach in books and magazines. We suggest you stick with the new approach in all your programs.

API FUNCTIONS

Three functions are called from SOLOMEM: GetFreeSpace(), wsprintf(), and MessageBox(). These functions are part of the Windows Applications Program Interface or, as it's usually called, the API. The API is simply a collection of functions built into Windows, which applications can call to perform Windows-related activities.

There are hundreds of API functions. They are used mostly for creating and manipulating elements of the Windows graphic user interface, such as windows, menus, and dialog boxes. They are also used for I/O activities such as text and graphics output, and mouse and keyboard input. In addition there are API functions that handle other activities like memory management and disk files. Figure 3-7 shows the relationship of Windows applications to the Windows API.

You can still use many of the traditional C library functions as well, but some of them, including traditional I/O functions like printf() and scanf(), are not relevant to the Windows environment. We'll learn more about this as we go along.

As we noted earlier, the prototypes (declarations) for the API functions are in the WINDOWS.H file, which you can examine with your editor. This is useful if you're not clear about the data types of a function's arguments or its return value. The code for the functions themselves is in one of several dynamic link libraries (DLLs) that come with Windows. You don't need to worry about linking these libraries to use the API functions; it's all handled automatically by TCW or BCW and Windows itself.

You'll be introduced to many new API functions in this book. If you want more details on the functions described, consult *The Waite Group's Windows API Bible* or a similar reference (several are described in the Bibliography). In addition to the functions themselves, these references describe constants, structures, and any other program elements you need to use the API.

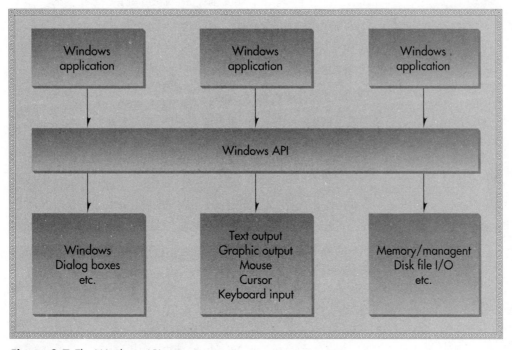

Figure 3-7 The Windows API

The GetFreeSpace() Function

The heart of the SOLOMEM program is the GetFreeSpace() API function, which returns the number of bytes of global memory available.

```
dwMemAvail = GetFreeSpace(O);  // get free memory
```

This function takes only one argument, of type UINT (which is **unsigned int**). This argument is ignored in the current version of Windows, so we set it to 0. GetFreeSpace() returns a value of type DWORD (**unsigned long**), representing the number of bytes of global memory, as discussed in the last chapter. (We'll discuss memory usage more thoroughly in Chapter 36, *Managing Memory*.)

The wsprintf() Function

You're probably familiar with the C function printf(), which is the most-used output function for C programs in DOS. It formats numerical and other values so they are displayed as part of a string. A related C function, sprintf(), uses the same approach as printf() to generate a formatted string, but instead of displaying the string, it inserts it into a buffer for later use. Windows includes the function wsprintf(), which is similar to sprintf(), but uses far instead of near pointers.

```
wsprintf(szBuffer, "Memory available: %lu", dwMemAvail);
```

In the SOLOMEM program, we use wsprintf() to combine the string "Memory available:" with the numerical value returned from GetFreeSpace(). The result (such as "Memory available: 4,243,746") is inserted into szBuffer. (The %lu type specification is used for variables that are type **long** and **unsigned**.) The contents of szBuffer will be used as an argument to the MessageBox() function.

The wsprintf() function has some peculiarities. One is that you can't use the floating-point format specifiers with it (%f, %g, and so on). It doesn't know anything about floating point. You *can* use the usual %c for characters, %d for signed integers, %s for strings, and so on. However, another peculiarity is that if you use a string variable as an argument to plug into the format string, as in

```
wsprintf(szBuffer, "Program name is %s", (LPSTR)szProgName);
```

then the string variable *must* be cast to type LPSTR (a far pointer to a string). Without this cast, the function compiles correctly, but doesn't display the string.

The MessageBox() Function

MessageBox() is the most Windows-oriented API function in SOLOMEM. It is a very useful function; there are few Windows applications that don't use it. MessageBox() creates a (what else?) message box and places it on the screen. A message box is a simple, fixed-size window that displays text and has one or more buttons that terminate the box.

```
MessageBox(NULL, szBuffer, "SOLOMEM", MB_OK);
```

The first argument to MessageBox() is the handle of a window that is the *parent* of the message box. We won't worry at this point what a parent window is. In any case, in SOLOMEM the message box has no parent, so this argument is set to NULL.

The second argument is the memory address of the text to be displayed in the box. We've already stored this text in szBuffer. The third argument is the text that will appear as the title of the message box. This is often the name of the application, "SOLOMEM" in this case. The message box is automatically sized to fit neatly around the text and title.

You can use various options with MessageBox(). These fall into two categories: the icon you want displayed alongside the text (an exclamation point, question mark, stop sign, and so on) and the buttons to be included in the box (such as OK, OK-and-Cancel, or Yes-and-No). SOLOMEM does not use an icon. (We'll see an example of a message box that uses an icon in the next chapter.)

However, our message box does contain a button. Table 3-2 shows the constants used to create various combinations of buttons. These constants (like most things in Windows programming) are defined in the WINDOWS.H file. You could look up the numerical values of these constants, but there's no need to. The symbolic names are all you need to know. The constants used with particular functions are usually listed in the description of the function in your reference book.

In SOLOMEM we use the MB_OK constant in the last argument to MessageBox() to cause a single OK button to appear in the box. When the user clicks on the OK

Table 3-2 Button Constants for MessageBox()

Constant	Buttons To Be Installed
MB_OK	OK button
MB_YESNO	Yes and No buttons
MB_OKCANCEL	OK and Cancel buttons
MB_RETRYCANCEL	Retry and Cancel buttons
MB_YESNOCANCEL	Yes, No, and Cancel buttons
MB_ABORTRETRYIGNORE	Abort, Retry, and Ignore buttons

button, the box vanishes, the MessageBox() function returns, and the program terminates. Pressing (ENTER) also causes the program to terminate, since this has the same effect as pushing the button.

SUMMARY

In this chapter we described almost everything you need to know about the SOLOMEM program. You've been introduced to derived data types, Hungarian notation, the WinMain() function, and several Windows API functions. You've also created a real live, running Windows program.

Notice how much bang for the buck we've gotten out of this program, which is just a few lines long. Imagine trying to write a DOS program that created a moveable message box, with a title, system menu, text, and an OK button that made the box go away when the user clicked on it. You'd be over 100 lines in no time. But Windows (once you get used to the nomenclature) makes it easy.

In the next chapter we'll look at a somewhat more complex variation of this program.

4

MACROS, ETCETERA

Let's look at another Windows program. This one is similar to the SOLOMEM program in the last chapter, but adds a few new wrinkles. You'll learn about Windows macros, and we'll introduce a few more derived types and their corresponding Hungarian notation. We'll also demonstrate some additional aspects of the MessageBox() function.

You won't learn about any major Windows features in this chapter. Its main purpose is simply to expose you again to the peculiar way Windows programs look, in an attempt to make it seem less peculiar. You will need to be at least slightly comfortable with derived types, Hungarian notation, and the other details of Windows nomenclature before we go on to the more challenging examples in the following chapters.

THE SOLOVER PROGRAM

This program reports which version of Windows you're running (such as 3.1 or whatever). Also, it allows you to choose whether to report the version of DOS (such as 5.0) as well. All this is done with message boxes. Here's the listing for SOLOVER:

```
// solover.c
// displays Windows version number
// uses standalone message box

#define STRICT                  // strict type-checking
#include <windows.h>            // include file for all Windows programs

/////////////////////////////////////////////////////////////////////
// WinMain() -- program entry point                                //
/////////////////////////////////////////////////////////////////////
```

```
#pragma argsused                    // ignore unused arguments

int PASCAL WinMain(HINSTANCE hInstance, HINSTANCE hPrevInst,
                LPSTR lpszCmdLine, int nCmdShow)
   {
   DWORD dwVersion;                 // packed version info
   WORD wMsdos;                     // MS-DOS;  high=major, low=minor
   WORD wWindows;                   // Windows; low=major, high=minor
   char szBuffer[80];               // buffer for string

   dwVersion = GetVersion();        // get version number
   wMsdos = HIWORD(dwVersion);      // MS-DOS info in high half
   wWindows = LOWORD(dwVersion);    // Windows info in low half

   if( MessageBox(NULL, "Do you want DOS version as well?",
               "SOLOVER", MB_YESNO | MB_ICONQUESTION) == IDNO )

                                    // do Windows but not DOS
      wsprintf( szBuffer, "Windows %u.%u",
               LOBYTE(wWindows), HIBYTE(wWindows) );

   else
                                    // do Windows and also DOS
      wsprintf( szBuffer, "Windows %u.%u\nMS-DOS %u.%u",
               LOBYTE(wWindows), HIBYTE(wWindows),
               HIBYTE(wMsdos), LOBYTE(wMsdos) );

                                    // display message box
   MessageBox(NULL, szBuffer, "SOLOVER", MB_OK | MB_ICONINFORMATION);
   return NULL;                     // return to Windows
   }  // end WinMain
```

When it's first executed, this program puts a message box on the screen that asks if you want to know the DOS version number as well as the Windows version. This box has Yes and No buttons, as shown in Figure 4-1.

If the user selects Yes, you'll see another message box, with two lines of text that give the Windows and DOS version numbers. This is shown in Figure 4-2. If the user selects No, a similar message box appears, but with only the Windows version number.

The GetVersion() API function shown in this program may be useful in serious programs. Many applications check to see which version number of Windows or DOS they are running under, so that they know what capabilities are available. Sometimes they might need to bail out entirely with a "Can't run under this version of Windows" message.

THE GetVersion() FUNCTION

The GetVersion() function retrieves the version numbers for both Windows and DOS. It requires no argument. All the version information is returned in a single

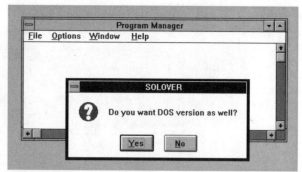

Figure 4-1

First Message Box
in SOLOVER

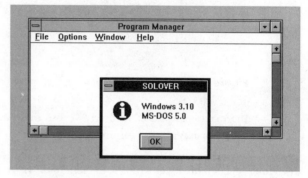

Figure 4-2

Second Message
Box in SOLOVER

variable of type DWORD (**unsigned long**), which contains four bytes. Figure 4-3 shows how this packing looks.

MACROS

As you no doubt remember, a macro is a #define directive that takes arguments. Macros operate much like small functions, except that they can be faster to execute. The WINDOWS.H file contains several macros that are convenient for manipulating data. Because these macros are defined in the WINDOWS.H file, they are available to all Windows programs without the need to #include any other header files, as there is in DOS programs. We use four such macros in SOLOVER to extract the version numbers, and major and minor parts of the version numbers, from the value returned by GetVersion(). Appendix A, *Derived Data Types*, lists the macros used in this book.

The HIWORD and LOWORD macros take a double word (4 bytes) as an argument, and return the high-order word (2 bytes) and the low-order word, respectively. (You could do the same thing with the bit manipulation operators, but

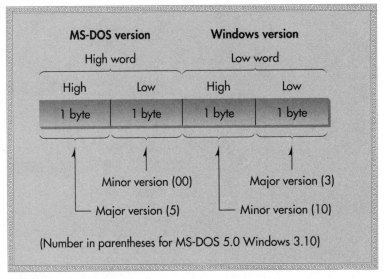

Figure 4-3 GetVersion() Return Value

the macros are easier to use.) We use these macros to separate the Windows and DOS version numbers from the dwVersion variable, in the lines

```
wMsdos = HIWORD(dwVersion);   // MS-DOS info in high half
wWindows = LOWORD(dwVersion); // Windows info in low half
```

The wMsdos and wWindows variables are of derived type WORD, which is defined in WINDOWS.H to be **unsigned short**. Variables declared to be of this type can use a lowercase 'w' as the Hungarian notation to indicate the type.

Once we've separated the double word into two words containing the MS-DOS version number and the Windows version number, we use the HIBYTE and LOBYTE macros to separate the major and minor version numbers from each word. These macros return the high-order byte and low-order byte of the word given them as an argument. Figure 4-4 shows how these macros work.

Instead of creating four additional variables, we use the HIBYTE and LOBYTE macros directly in calls to the wsprintf() function. To display only the Windows version, the call looks like this:

```
wsprintf( szBuffer, "Windows %u.%u",
        LOBYTE(wWindows), HIBYTE(wWindows) );  // values 3, 1
```

As you can see, the values returned from LOBYTE and HIBYTE are plugged directly into the formatting string, where the %u type specifiers appear. The resulting string is then stored in szBuffer.

There is an inconsistency between the DOS and Windows version numbers: in the DOS number the high-order byte contains the major version number, while in Windows it's the low-order byte. (How *does* this sort of thing happen?)

When both Windows and DOS versions are displayed, a similar call to wsprintf() inserts all four numbers into the formatting string:

```
wsprintf( szBuffer, "Windows %u.%u\nMS-DOS %u.%u",
    LOBYTE(wWindows), HIBYTE(wWindows),    // values 3, 1
    HIBYTE(wMsdos), LOBYTE(wMsdos) );      // values 5, 0
```

Notice how the Hungarian notation makes it easier to check whether you've used the correct arguments. For example, you know that the LOBYTE macro must take a word as an argument, so if you saw an expression like

```
LOBYTE(dwWhatsis)
```

you would know something was wrong.

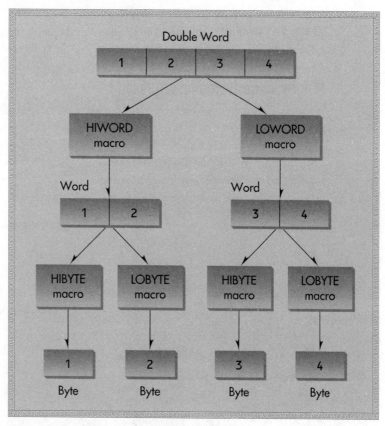

Figure 4-4 Macros Used with Bytes, Words, and Double Words

MessageBox() REPRISE

We've gotten a little fancier with the MessageBox() function in this example. The first call to it sports a decorative new icon in addition to the text, and we use the return value to direct the flow of control. We embed the MessageBox() function in an **if** statement so we can conveniently check its return value.

Here's the call:

```
if( MessageBox(NULL, "Do you want DOS version as well?",
          "SOLOVER", MB_YESNO | MB_ICONQUESTION) == IDNO )
```

Icons in MessageBox()

You can place an icon in a message box to accentuate your text message. Table 4-1 shows the possibilities. (MB in the constants stands, as you might guess, for Message Box.)

Because the purpose of our message box is to ask a question, we use the MB_ICONQUESTION constant to generate a question-mark icon. The logical OR operator, |, combines this with the MB_YESNO constant.

Return Value from MessageBox()

If a message box has two or more buttons, we need to determine which one the user pressed to terminate the box. We do this by checking the return value from MessageBox(). Table 4-2 shows the possible return values from this function.

In SOLOVER, if the user presses the Yes button, we set up a string (in the szBuffer array) that contains both MS-DOS and Windows version numbers. If the user presses No, we make a string with only the Windows version number. In either

Table 4-1 Icon Constants for MessageBox()

Constant	Icon
MB_ICONQUESTION	A green question mark (asks a question of the user)
MB_ICONINFORMATION	A blue letter 'i' (for 'info,' tells the user something)
MB_ICONEXCLAMATION	A yellow exclamation point (for more urgent messages)
MB_ICONSTOP	A red stop sign (for very urgent messages)

case we call MessageBox() a second time to display the string, this time with an information icon.

OTHER SYSTEM INFORMATION

If you want to experiment with the simple message-box type of program demonstrated in this and the previous chapter, you can use other API functions that return useful and interesting information about the system.

The GetNumTasks() function takes no arguments and returns the number of tasks, or program instances, that are currently running. It returns this number as an **int** (not a derived type, for a change). If you are running the File Manager, a word processor, a compiler, and your own program that uses GetNumTasks(), this function should return 5, because it always counts the Program Manager.

The GetWinFlags() function tells you what CPU and what mode (Standard or Enhanced) your program is running under.

You can also try the GetFreeSystemResources() function. However, this function is undocumented. That means that it may not exist in future versions of Windows, and should be used with caution. This function takes one argument, 0, and returns an **int** value which is the percentage of system resources in use. This is the same value you can obtain by Selecting About Program Manager from the Program Manager Help menu. When this percentage gets too low, say below 20 or 30 percent, strange things may start to happen in your system, and you may need to close some applications.

Table 4-2 Return Values from MessageBox()

Constant	Meaning
IDOK	The OK button was pushed
IDYES	The Yes button was pushed
IDNO	The No button was pushed
IDCANCEL	The Cancel button was pushed
IDIGNORE	The Ignore button was pushed
IDABORT	The Abort button was pushed
IDRETRY	The Retry button was pushed

CHAPTER 5

CREATING A MAIN WINDOW

You may feel that, in your role as a page, you've spent entirely too many hours in the classroom, learning terminolgy and syntax in simple Windows programs that didn't really accomplish much. These programs could display a few items of information, and they could distinguish between yes and no, but that's about all. What about windows, menus, dialog boxes, and all the other features of a real GUI (graphic user interface)?

Well, classroom time is over. We're about to head out into the the world of real fire-breathing Windows programs. In this chapter we'll meet something a little less fierce than a dragon: a hungry lion. So make sure your lance is sharp, and listen for heavy breathing in the tall grass. The lion we're stalking is the fierce *main window*, which we're going to display on the screen. This is a real window, as opposed to the message boxes we have generated before. You can move it, resize it, maximize it (make it fill the screen), and minimize it (turn it into an icon). It has a system menu that lets you do these things from the keyboard, and—more importantly—that lets you close the window and thereby terminate the program.

THE FUNDWIN PROGRAM

Our example could be called the fundamental Windows program. You'll see the elements of this program reproduced, often with very little change, in almost all Windows programs. The listing is not so short as that of the previous SOLOMEM and SOLOVER programs, but don't panic. It's not all *that* big, and we'll take time to explain what's going on, in this and the next chapter.

Before we examine the listing, it might be helpful to preview the overall organization of the program. There are two functions in the FUNDWIN.C listing: WinMain(), which we've seen before in SOLOMEM and SOLOVER, and WndProc().

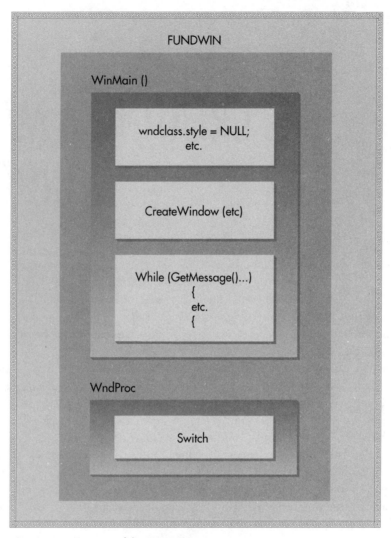

Figure 5-1 Contents of the FUNDWIN program

WinMain() contains three major new sections of code. First we assign values to various members of a structure called wndclass. Then we execute a function called CreateWindow(), which has many arguments. And finally we enter a short **while** loop.

WndProc(), the second function in the program, is considerably shorter than WinMain(), and consists mostly of a **switch** statement. Figure 5-1 shows this arrangement. We'll describe in detail what the code does in this and the next chapter. Here's the listing for FUNDWIN.C:

```
// fundwin.c
// puts a window on the screen

#define STRICT           // strict type checking (put before #include)
#include <windows.h>      // include file for all Windows programs
                          // prototype for WndProc()
LRESULT CALLBACK _export WndProc(HWND, UINT, WPARAM, LPARAM);

///////////////////////////////////////////////////////////////////
// WinMain() -- program entry point                              //
///////////////////////////////////////////////////////////////////
#pragma argsused                              // ignore unused arguments

int PASCAL WinMain(HINSTANCE hInstance,       // which program are we?
                   HINSTANCE hPrevInst,       // is there another one?
                   LPSTR lpCmdLine,           // command line arguments
                   int nCmdShow)              // window size (icon, etc)
   {
   HWND hWnd;                        // window handle from CreateWindow
   MSG msg;                          // message from GetMessage
   WNDCLASS wndclass;                // window class structure

   if(!hPrevInst)                    // if this is first such window
      {
      wndclass.style          = NULL;        // default style
                                             // WndProc address
      wndclass.lpfnWndProc    = (WNDPROC)WndProc;
      wndclass.cbClsExtra     = 0;           // no extra class data
      wndclass.cbWndExtra     = 0;           // no extra window data
      wndclass.hInstance      = hInstance;   // which program?
                                             // stock arrow cursor
      wndclass.hCursor        = LoadCursor(NULL, IDC_ARROW);
                                             // stock blank icon
      wndclass.hIcon          = LoadIcon(NULL, IDI_APPLICATION);
      wndclass.lpszMenuName   = NULL;        // no menu
                                             // white background
      wndclass.hbrBackground  = GetStockObject(WHITE_BRUSH);
      wndclass.lpszClassName  = "fundwinClass"; // window class name

      RegisterClass(&wndclass); // register the class
      } // end if

   hWnd = CreateWindow("fundwinClass",       // window class name
                       "FundWin",            // caption
                       WS_OVERLAPPEDWINDOW,  // style
                       CW_USEDEFAULT,        // default x position
                       CW_USEDEFAULT,        // default y position
                       CW_USEDEFAULT,        // default width
                       CW_USEDEFAULT,        // default height
                       NULL,                 // parent's handle
                       NULL,                 // menu handle
                       hInstance,            // which program?
                       NULL);                // no init data
```

```
    ShowWindow(hWnd, nCmdShow);          // make window visible

    // message loop
    while( GetMessage(&msg,0,0,0) )      // get message from Windows
        {
        TranslateMessage(&msg);          // convert keystrokes
        DispatchMessage(&msg);           // call window procedure
        }
    return msg.wParam;                   // return value from
    }  // end WinMain                           PostQuitMessage()

///////////////////////////////////////////////////////////////////
// main window procedure -- receives messages                     //
///////////////////////////////////////////////////////////////////
LRESULT CALLBACK _export WndProc(HWND hWnd,   // our window's handle
                                 UINT msg,      // message number
                                 WPARAM wParam, // word parameter
                                 LPARAM lParam) // long parameter
    {
    switch(msg)                         // which message?
        {
        case WM_DESTROY:                // we handle this message
            PostQuitMessage(0);         // send WM_QUIT
            break;
                                        // all other messages are
        default:                        // handled by DefWindowProc
            return( DefWindowProc(hWnd, msg, wParam, lParam) );
        }   // end switch(msg)

    return 0L;                          // return if we handled msg
    }  // end WndProc
```

Build the program and run it. It displays a window titled FundWin, as shown in Figure 5-2. This window is called a *main window*. It is similar to the windows placed on the screen by most Windows programs. Try changing the window's size and moving it around. Use the maximize and minimize buttons to expand the window and shrink it to an icon. Use the system menu to switch to the Task List window. You'll see FUNDWIN on the task list. Switch back to it. Finally, select Close from the system menu to close the window. This terminates the program.

ORGANIZATION OF A WINDOWS PROGRAM

As we noted, there are two functions in the FUNDWIN program: WinMain() and WndProc(). We've seen WinMain() in previous examples. The WndProc() function is an example of a *window procedure* (as the name indicates). Almost every Windows program includes these two functions—WinMain() and a window procedure—as essential parts of its architecture.

Figure 5-2
Output of the
FUNDWIN
program

Yin and Yang

In the FUNDWIN example, the major role of WinMain() is to create the main window—that is, the lion—that is the subject of this chapter. But this lion never goes anyplace without its consort, the event-driven dragon. This dragon lives in the WndProc() function. The lion and the dragon are so closely intertwined that it's hard to talk about one without the other. However, we have to begin someplace, so we're going to start with the easier one: creating the main window in WinMain(). We'll defer a discussion of WndProc() until the next chapter. However, WndProc() and what it does will creep into the discussion in this chapter from time to time. So what does WndProc() do? It handles mysterious entities known as *messages*. Be patient; we'll get to WndProc(), messages, and event-driven programming soon enough.

We should note that, while WinMain() must always be named WinMain(), the window procedure, which we call WndProc(), can be named anything you like, although it's nice if the name reflects the function's purpose. Some programmers favor WinMainProc(), for example.

More Detail

Actually, WinMain() does more than simply create a main window. Looking at it in more detail, we can say that it registers a window class, creates a main window of that class, and supplies a message loop (there come messages, creeping in). Figure 5-3 is a functional interpretation of the FUNDWIN program. The message loop, since it involves messages, will be discussed in the next chapter. But what are classes? And how do they relate to creating a main window?

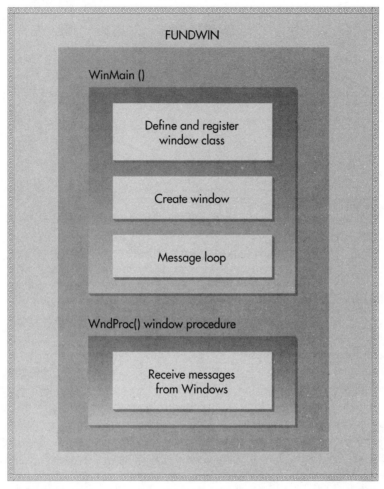

Figure 5-3 Functionality of the FUNDWIN Program

There are two parts to specifying a window. First you specify a class, then you specify an individual window of that class. We'll look at these two aspects of describing a window in turn.

WINDOW CLASSES

A window _class_ is a template, or plan, for creating a number of windows with similar characteristics. It's like a blueprint for an item you want to manufacture, say a toaster. You create blueprints for the toaster, then you send them down to the factory, where they're used to create many actual toasters. Each toaster has the characteristics specified in the blueprints.

When we create a window class we specify certain attributes the window will have, such as what mouse cursor will appear in the window, what icon will appear when the window is minimized, and the menu structure it will use. Then we use this class as a blueprint to create actual windows that have these attributes. (We'll learn more about specific features such as icons and menus later.) Figure 5-4 shows several windows created from a single class.

If you're familiar with object-oriented programming, you'll recognize a similarity to classes in that context. However, although the concept of window classes is derived from OOP concepts, Windows does not use any other object-oriented features, and cannot really be said to be object oriented.

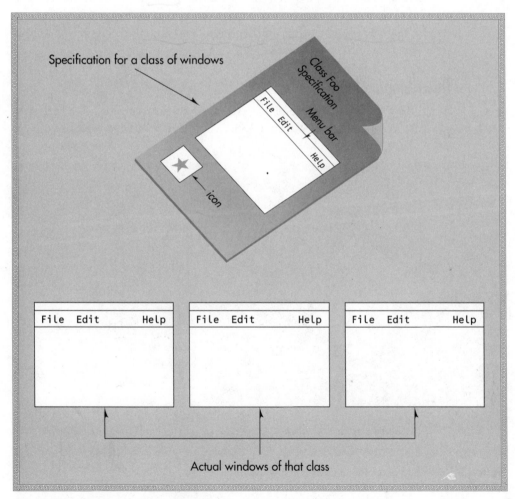

Figure 5-4 Windows and Classes

Why bother with classes at all? Why not simply specify attributes, such as cursors and icons, for each individual window? Windows was first designed to run on 286 computers in an era when memory was scarce. Conserving memory was therefore a high priority. One way to minimize memory usage was to lump together those window attributes that used a lot of memory. This collection of attributes was called a "class." Then if you had several windows that all used these same attributes, it wasn't necessary to store the attributes repeatedly for each window; you simply defined the window to be of that class, and it acquired the attributes automatically.

Actually, most simple Windows programs don't realize the advantages of classes, because they use only one main window. However, the class approach must be followed anyway.

There are two parts to specifying the class. First you *describe* the class by assigning values to the members of a structure of type WNDCLASS. Then you *register* the class by executing the RegisterClass() function. Figure 5-5 shows, somewhat fancifully, how this looks.

Describing a Class

A window class is described by assigning values to the members of a structure variable of type WNDCLASS. We declare a variable wndclass of type

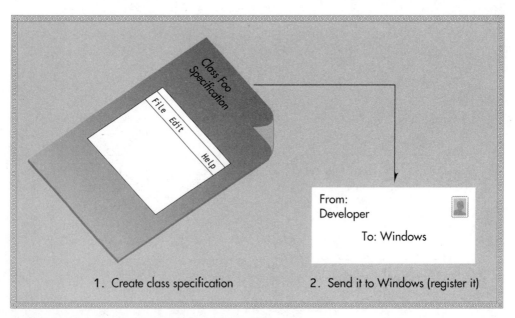

Figure 5-5 Creating and Registering a Window Class

WNDCLASS, and then assign values to the various members of the structure, as reproduced here:

```
WNDCLASS wndclass;       // create structure variable wndclass
...
                         // assign values to structure members
wndclass.style         = NULL;                     // default style
wndclass.lpfnWndProc   = (WNDPROC)WndProc;         // WndProc address
wndclass.cbClsExtra    = 0;                         // no extra class data
wndclass.cbWndExtra    = 0;                         // no extra window data
wndclass.hInstance     = hInstance;                // which program?
wndclass.hCursor       = LoadCursor(NULL, IDC_ARROW); // stock cursor
wndclass.hIcon         = LoadIcon(NULL, IDI_APPLICATION); // stock icon
wndclass.lpszMenuName  = NULL;                      // no menu
wndclass.hbrBackground = GetStockObject(WHITE_BRUSH); // white background
wndclass.lpszClassName = "fundwinClass";           // class name
```

important .

To avoid MEGO (the My Eyes Glaze Over phenomena) we won't discuss every member of this structure. However, you might like to note a few items.

The class defined by the wndclass variable uses a stock arrow cursor, specified in the statement

```
wndclass.hCursor = LoadCursor(NULL, IDC_ARROW);
```

Here we set the hCursor member of the wndclass variable to the return value of the API function LoadCursor(). This function loads a cursor, which can be either a stock cursor built into the system or one we create ourselves, and connects it to the wndclass class. The IDC_ARROW constant specifies the stock cursor that consists of an arrow pointing up and left; it's the same cursor used by the Program Manager and other systems programs. By changing this constant we could specify other cursors, including ones we create ourselves, but we'll use the stock cursor for the time being.

Similarly, the statement

```
wndclass.hIcon = LoadIcon(NULL, IDI_APPLICATION);
```

uses the LoadIcon() API function to specify the icon that will be used to represent the window when it's minimized. The IDI_APPLICATION constant produces a stock application icon, which resembles a little multicolored flag. Again, by changing this statement, we could specify an icon we create ourselves.

The wndclass class in this program doesn't include a menu, but if we want one we can add it by changing the line

```
wndclass.lpszMenuName = NULL;
```

We'll see how to add custom icons and cursors, and how to create menus, later. All these items—cursors, icons, and menus—can potentially require a good deal of memory. That's why they're specified as part of a class: so they won't need to be duplicated if more than one window uses them.

You should also note the statement

```
wndclass.lpfnWndProc = (WNDPROC)WndProc;
```

This tells the class where to find the window procedure: it's the address of the WndProc() function that appears later in FUNDWIN. This is one of the ways the lion and the dragon are intertwined.

Other members of the WNDCLASS structure are seldom altered in simple Windows programs. You can ignore them until you need to do something unusual. (Note, however, that they must all be set to a value; don't try to save space by eliminating the statements that do this.)

ix class: a collection of Attributes

Registering the Class

Once a window class has been specified by assigning values to the various values of the wndclass variable, we must tell Windows to store this information in memory (along with any custom icons, cursors, and menus). The RegisterClass() function does this:

```
RegisterClass(&wndclass); // register the class
```

This function takes as its only argument the address of the structure defining the class; here the address of wndclass.

Note: the lower case Wndclass

Now that Windows knows about the specification of the wndclass variable, we can create an individual window of this class.

CREATING A WINDOW

As we've seen, some of a window's characteristics, such as its icon, cursor, and menu, are specified by the class from which it is derived. Additional characteristics, including its caption, its dimensions, and whether it has a system menu, minimize and maximize icons, and so on, are specified for each individual window. The API function CreateWindow() creates an individual window and gives it these additional characteristics. Here's how that looks in the FUNDWIN example:

```
hWnd = CreateWindow("fundwinClass",    // window class name
                    "FundWin",         // caption
                    WS_OVERLAPPEDWINDOW,  // style
                    CW_USEDEFAULT,     // default x position
                    CW_USEDEFAULT,     // default y position
                    CW_USEDEFAULT,     // default width
                    CW_USEDEFAULT,     // default height
```

```
NULL,              // parent's handle
NULL,              // menu handle
hInstance,         // which program?
NULL);             // no init data
```

Class and Caption

The first argument to CreateWindow() is the name of the class from which the window is to be created. Here it's the string "fundwinClass". This must be the same as the string assigned to lpszClassName member of the wndclass structure. If these names don't agree, your program will compile without error, but no window will appear when you run it. This sort of bug is hard to track down, so be careful that the names match (including case).

The second argument is the caption that will appear in the window's title bar. Here it's "FundWin". In a main window this caption is generally the name of the program.

Style

The most complex characteristic set by CreateWindow() is the window *style*. The style specifies a certain set of window features. Choosing which of these features you want is like ordering the options for your car. You want power steering and a sunroof, but you don't want power windows or an automatic transmission.

For the window in FUNDWIN, we want a title bar (in which the caption is displayed), a system menu, maximize and minimize buttons, and a "thick" border that can be used to resize the window. This creates a "standard" window. We could specify these options separately, using constants like WS_CAPTION, WS_SYSMENU, WS_THICKFRAME, and so on (where WS means Window Style). However, there is another constant that allows us to specify all these options at once: WS_OVERLAPPEDWINDOW. The main window in a program often uses this standard style. We'll use it on most of the main windows in this book.

Size and Position

Arguments 4 through 7 of CreateWindow() specify the window's size and position. The constant used for all these arguments in FUNDWIN is CW_USEDEFAULT. This constant tells Windows to use its own judgment in locating and sizing the window when it first appears. (After it's on the screen, of course, the user can move it and resize it as desired.) If you want a window to first appear at a particular position on the screen, or be a particular size, you can fill in specific numbers for these arguments. The coordinates are measured in pixels from the top left corner of the screen.

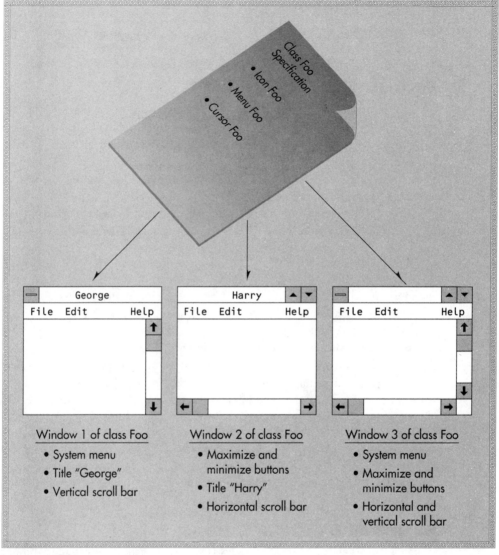

Figure 5-6 Window Features

Other Arguments

We don't need to dwell on the last four arguments to CreateWindow(). Our window has no parent, so argument 8 is NULL. Argument 9 is an alternative way to specify a menu, which we won't use, so it's also NULL. Argument 10 is the hInstance value we obtained as a parameter of WinMain(), and argument 11 is used only in specialized situations, so it's NULL.

The CreateWindow() function returns a handle to the window. This handle can then be used by other functions that do things to, or get information from, the window.

To summarize, some of a window's features, such as its icon and cursor, are specified as part of the class description, while others, such as the style and dimensions, are specified for each individual window. Figure 5-6 shows how some features of a window are specified in the class, while others are specified for each individual window of that class.

Making the Window Visible

When you first create the window it's not visible. To make it visible we use the ShowWindow() function:

```
ShowWindow(hWnd, nCmdShow);        // make window visible
```

which takes as its arguments the window handle returned by CreateWindow() and the value of nCmdShow retrieved as a parameter to WinMain(). Windows uses this parameter to tell the program, when it first starts, whether the window should be created as an icon or a full-size window.

Figure 5-7 summarizes the process of creating a window class, creating a window of that class, and making the window visible.

As we mentioned, in simple programs you will probably create only one window from the class you specified. That's what happens in FUNDWIN, where we use the CreateWindow() API function to create a single main window.

OTHER DETAILS

We've left a few loose ends about the window creation process, so let's go back and tidy them up.

Don't Do It More than Once

You may wonder why the statements that define and register the class are all part of an **if** statement. Here's how this conditional looks, with the details removed:

```
if(!hPrevInst)                 // if this is first such window
   {
   // statements to define the wndclass structure
   // function call to register the window
   }
```

To understand the need for this conditional, imagine that two or more instances of the same program are running. (Refer to Chapter 3, *Types and Names*, if you've

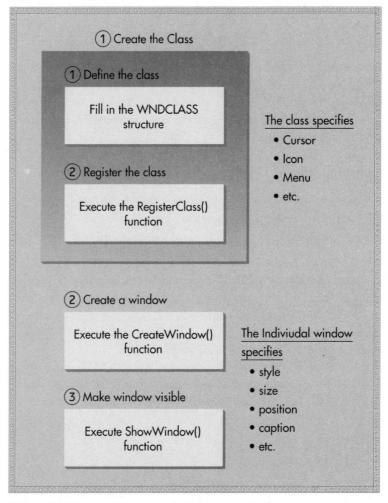

Figure 5-7 Steps in Creating and Displaying a Window

forgotten what an instance is.) Each instance needs to create a window based on the wndclass class. Now, the first instance must create the class (specify and register it), but all subsequent instances should not do this; they just create windows based on the already-defined class. So how does an instance know whether it should create a class?

The hPrevInst parameter to WinMain() is NULL if there was no previous instance of the program; that is, if our instance is the first instance. In the **if** statement we check for this value. If we are the first instance, we go ahead and define the class. If not, we skip defining the class and go right on to create a specific window of the class using CreateWindow(). Figure 5-8 shows a flowchart of the WinMain() function.

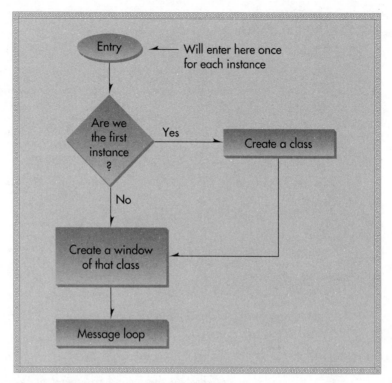

Figure 5-8 Flowchart of WinMain() Function

Prototype

The first few lines of FUNDWIN.C are similar to those of SOLOMEM.C, except for the prototype for the WndProc() function:

```
LRESULT CALLBACK _export WndProc(HWND, UINT, WPARAM, LPARAM);
```

As you know if you program in ANSI C, you must declare every function before using it. We'll discuss the argument types and return value of this function when we discuss the WndProc() function in the next chapter.

Return Value

You may have noticed that the return value of WinMain() is no longer NULL as it was in SOLOMEM and SOLOVER:

```
return msg.wParam;
```

This return value is connected with messages, which we'll discuss in the next chapter.

The Big Switch

Although we won't discuss the WndProc() function in detail here, you should note its overall structure as a preview of coming attractions. We've reproduced it here:

```
LRESULT CALLBACK _export WndProc(HWND hWnd,   // our window's handle
                                 UINT msg,    // message number
                                 WPARAM wParam,  // word parameter
                                 LPARAM lParam)  // long parameter
   {
   switch(msg)                        // which message?
      {
      case WM_DESTROY:                // we handle this message
         PostQuitMessage(0);          // send WM_QUIT
         break;
                                      // all other messages are
      default:                        // handled by DefWindowProc
         return( DefWindowProc(hWnd, msg, wParam, lParam) );
      }    // end switch(msg)
   return NULL;
   }  // end WndProc
```

As you can see, the entire function body consists of a single **switch** statement. There is only one **case** in this statement:

```
case WM_DESTROY:
```

This **case** is executed when the second parameter to WndProc(), msg, has the value WM_DESTROY. As we'll see in the next chapter, WM_DESTROY is a *message*. More complex programs will have more **case** statements because they handle more messages.

Perhaps the strangest thing about the WndProc() function is that it is *never called from WinMain()*. How can this be? If our program doesn't call it, who does? And why? Again, have patience.

Error Returns

In a serious, full-scale Windows program it's important to program very conservatively. This means checking for errors that don't usually occur, but could under some conditions. One way to do this is to check the return value of any API function that might produce an error value. If an error return is found, it is reported to the user and the program can be terminated or other appropriate action taken.

In the listings in this book we don't generally check for such error returns, except for certain high-risk functions. Doing so would make the listings longer and much harder to understand. Also, most Windows programs work perfectly well in most circumstances without such checking. However, you should be aware that you might want to add such code to your programs at some point. We'll discuss this issue further in Chapter 38, *Debugging*.

SUMMARY

You have successfully met and mastered the main-window lion. You've learned that there are two major parts to creating a main window: creating a window class, and creating a window of that class. Creating the class also has two parts: defining the class by filling in the members of a WNDCLASS structure; and registering it (telling Windows about it) by executing the RegisterClass() function. Certain details about the window are specified in the class definition (such as its icon, cursor, and menu), and other details are specified in the CreateWindow() function (such as its style, size, and caption). Finally the window is made visible with the ShowWindow() function.

However, these activities are only part of what you need to do to make a fully functional Windows program. You also need to make the window—or the window procedure, which is in some ways the same thing—respond to messages. To do these things, you'll need to meet and master the event-driven dragon, the subject of the next chapter.

CHAPTER 6

EVENT-DRIVEN PROGRAMMING

rom miles away you can hear it, deep in its forest lair, stomping and roaring and breathing fire. It's the most fierce and terrible beast in all of Windows programming: it's the event-driven programming dragon. In a way it's unfair that you must encounter such a fierce beast so early in your Windows programming career. Scarcely out of the classroom and the practice paddock, you must ride out to face an adversary that has proven a challenge to many a battle-hardened knight.

But fear not. The elixir we promised, the secret to mastering event-driven programming, is contained in a single magic phrase. Repeat this phrase whenever the dragon's breath grows too hot: *A program never does anything until Windows sends it a message*. We'll spend the rest of this chapter explaining what this means.

In the last chapter we referred to *messages* several times in passing. We mentioned that the WinMain() function contains a section of code called a message loop, and that the purpose of the WndProc() function is to receive messages. But what exactly are messages?

In King Arthur's time a message was what happened when you saw a knight approaching the castle, galloping as fast as he could. He clattered over the drawbridge, jumped from his horse with a great clashing of armor, and handed a scroll to the astonished king, saying "Sire, it's from Sir Lancelot!"

Messages in Windows are slightly more complicated, although perhaps quieter. To understand what Windows messages are, we need to learn a new approach to writing programs—a new program architecture. This is what is called *event-driven programming*.

You don't need to vanquish the event-driven dragon all at once. If you don't follow everything in this chapter, that's all right. You can come back and read it again later, when you've seen some more Windows programs at work. Eventually, everything will begin to make sense.

THE KEYBUTT PROGRAM

The best way to understand how event-driven programming works, and what messages are, is to experiment with a program that handles messages that can be generated directly by the user. We therefore present a program example that does just this. Here's the listing for KEYBUTT.C:

```c
// keybutt.c
// responds to keyboard and mouse messages

#define STRICT                  // strict type checking
#include <windows.h>            // include file for all Windows apps
                                // prototype
LRESULT CALLBACK _export WndProc(HWND, UINT, WPARAM, LPARAM);

PSTR szProgName = "keybutt";    // application name

//////////////////////////////////////////////////////////////////
// WinMain() -- program entry point                               //
//////////////////////////////////////////////////////////////////
#pragma argsused                // ignore unused arguments

int PASCAL WinMain(HINSTANCE hInstance, HINSTANCE hPrevInst,
                LPSTR lpCmdLine, int nCmdShow)
   {
   HWND hWnd;                   // window handle from CreateWindow
   MSG msg;                     // message from GetMessage
   WNDCLASS wndclass;           // window class structure

   if(!hPrevInst)              // if this is first such window
      {
      wndclass.style        = NULL;
      wndclass.lpfnWndProc  = (WNDPROC)WndProc;
      wndclass.cbClsExtra   =  wndclass.cbWndExtra  = 0;
      wndclass.hInstance    = hInstance;
      wndclass.hCursor      = LoadCursor (NULL, IDC_ARROW);
      wndclass.hIcon        = LoadIcon(NULL, IDI_APPLICATION);
      wndclass.lpszMenuName = NULL;
      wndclass.hbrBackground = GetStockObject(WHITE_BRUSH);
      wndclass.lpszClassName = "keybuttClass";
      RegisterClass(&wndclass);    // register the class
      } // end if
                                   // create the window
   hWnd = CreateWindow("keybuttClass", szProgName,
                WS_OVERLAPPEDWINDOW, CW_USEDEFAULT, CW_USEDEFAULT,
                CW_USEDEFAULT, CW_USEDEFAULT, NULL, NULL,
                hInstance, NULL);
   ShowWindow(hWnd, nCmdShow);     // make window visible
   while( GetMessage(&msg,0,0,0) ) // get message from Windows
      {
      TranslateMessage(&msg);      // convert keystrokes
      DispatchMessage(&msg);       // call window procedure
```

```
      }
   return msg.wParam;                    // return to Windows
   }  // end WinMain

///////////////////////////////////////////////////////////////
// main window procedure -- receives messages                 //
///////////////////////////////////////////////////////////////
LRESULT CALLBACK _export WndProc(HWND hWnd,      // window handle
                          UINT msg,        // message number
                          WPARAM wParam,   // word parameter
                          LPARAM lParam)   // long parameter
   {
   char szString[100];                    // for wsprintf()

   switch(msg)                            // which message?
      {
      case WM_CHAR:                       // user presses a keyboard key
         MessageBox(hWnd, "Keyboard key pressed", szProgName,
                  MB_OK | MB_ICONINFORMATION );
         break;

      case WM_LBUTTONDOWN:                // user presses left mouse button
         wsprintf( szString, "Left button pressed at x=%d, y=%d",
                  LOWORD(lParam), HIWORD(lParam) );
         MessageBox(hWnd, szString, szProgName,
                  MB_OK | MB_ICONINFORMATION );
         break;

      case WM_DESTROY:                    // we handle this message
         PostQuitMessage(0);              // send WM_QUIT
         break;
                                          // all other messages are
      default:                            // handled by DefWindowProc
         return( DefWindowProc(hWnd, msg, wParam, lParam) );
      }   // end switch(msg)

   return 0L;                             // return if we handled msg
   }  // end WndProc
```

The listing for this program is almost identical to that of FUNDWIN, except that it includes two additional **case** statements (shown in bold) in the WndProc() function. When you run the program, the main window appears on the screen as it did in FUNDWIN. However, when you press the left button, a message box pops up in the main window, as shown in Figure 6-1. (You can run this program directly from the Program Manager, or from TCW.)

The coordinates in the message box indicate the position of the mouse pointer, relative to the window, when the button was pressed. You can see the coordinates change as you move the pointer and press the button. A similar message box appears (with no coordinates displayed) when you press a keyboard key. Clicking the OK button in either box makes it go away.

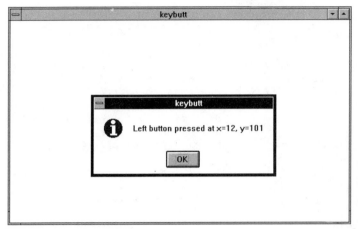

Figure 6-1

Output of the

KEYBUTT Program

Experiment with this program. Size the main window so it only occupies part of the screen. Notice that mouse clicks don't have any effect on KEYBUTT unless the mouse pointer is positioned on KEYBUTT's main window. Also notice that keystrokes don't affect it unless this window's title bar is colored (rather than plain white). The colored title bar means the window has the *keyboard focus* and is listening for keystrokes. If a window doesn't have the focus, some other window does and keystrokes go to it instead. Normally, you give a window the keyboard focus by clicking with the mouse anywhere in the window.

Examine the listing. What do the two new **case** statements do? What do WM_CHAR and WM_LBUTTONDOWN mean? Is it just a coincidence that there are two new **case** statements and that the program now handles two new events, left-button presses and key presses? This chapter will answer these (and several other) questions.

TRADITIONAL ARCHITECTURE

We've said that Windows uses an event-driven architecture. To see why we need a new kind of program architecture, let's first review how a traditional MS-DOS program works. In an MS-DOS program, the user and the program may type at each other on the screen, something like this:

```
Program: Enter your name
User:     Wannabea Knight
Program: Press F to load a file, or X to exit
User:     F
Program: Enter file name
User:     DATA22.JUN
Program: Press A to analyze the file, or P to print it
```

And so on. Of course some applications may use a more elaborate approach, with screens that display lists of options and other refinements; but the effect is the same. The application waits for the user to respond. Then it takes a particular action, prompts the user again, and waits again for the user's input. Internally, as it waits for the user, the program is busy in a wait loop, querying the keyboard to see if the user has typed anything, using (in C) a function like scanf() or getche(). Even when the program is waiting for user input, it's still executing CPU instructions. Usually the program monopolizes all the CPU time and memory, and most other resources (such as disk drives) in the system.

In this traditional scenario, the role of the operating system is simply to find and load the correct application file and transfer control to it. Once it has launched the program, the operating system bows out of the picture until the application terminates. The application may call functions in the operating system to access files and perform other tasks, but it's the application that has control. When an I/O event occurs, such as the user pressing a keyboard key, this information goes directly to the application, as shown in Figure 6-2.

WINDOWS ARCHITECTURE

Now the traditional architecture is all very well in a single-tasking system, where we assume that only one program at a time will be loaded into memory and running. But in Windows there can be many different programs in memory at the same time, sharing CPU time, each one represented by a window on the screen. This requires a bit more complexity.

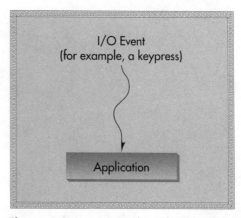

Figure 6-2 Events in Traditional Programs

Where Do Mouse Clicks Go?

In Windows, if an application is running and the user pushes a system-key combination like (CTRL)+(ESC), who handles it? If several applications are running and the user presses *any* keyboard key, who decides which program it is intended for? If the user clicks a mouse button, who decides which program is affected? If two programs both want to use the printer, who decides which one should go first?

If you think about these questions, you'll see that the traditional MS-DOS programming model won't work in Windows. One application can't seize control of all the I/O and other system resources, because other applications also need to receive user input, and need to access other I/O devices. Some sort of super program must keep control of I/O, figure out which of the running applications should be notified about a particular I/O event such as a keypress, and pass data about the event to that application (or act on the event itself). That's the role played by Windows.

It turns out that Windows must be responsible for *all* mouse clicks and moves, all keystrokes, all disk and printer accesses, and indeed all I/O-related events. No single program can take direct control of an I/O device. If it could, other programs would not get the input intended for them.

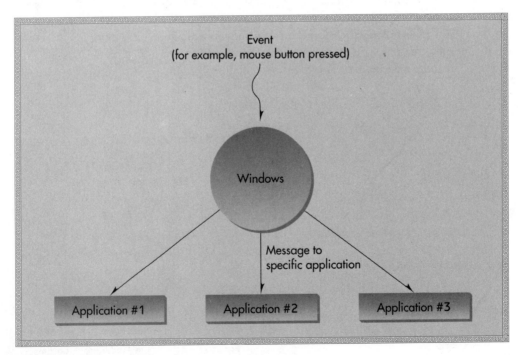

Figure 6-3 Events in Windows Programs

When the user clicks the mouse button, Windows figures out where the mouse cursor is, and transmits the mouse click information to the application whose window lies directly below the cursor. Other programs, which may also have windows on the screen, are unaffected. When the user presses a keyboard key, Windows figures out which window has the keyboard focus and sends the keystroke information to that window and no other. Figure 6-3 shows how events are handled in Windows.

CPU Time

A traditional operating system gives up control to an application for as long as the application runs. Windows, however, gives control to an application only when an event occurs that affects the application. If the user presses a key when an application's window has the focus, Windows transmits this information to the application, and the application takes appropriate action, such as displaying the character. When the application has processed the keystroke, it returns control to Windows so Windows can check for the next keystroke or mouse click, which may or may not be intended for the same application. When an application is not executing, Windows or another application is. Figure 6-4 shows the distribution of processor time in traditional and in Windows programs.

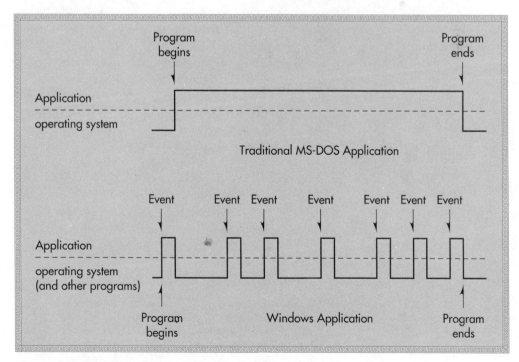

Figure 6-4 Distribution of Processor Time

It's important to get used to the idea that your application only takes control of the processor for brief periods, as the result of some external event.

Messages

How does Windows tell an application about an event like a keystroke or mouse click? It sends it a *message*. A message is a small unit of information, like a Post-it™ note. A message is sent by Windows to an application's window any time an event takes place that affects the application. A message consists of information like "the user clicked the left mouse button with the pointer at coordinates (56,175)" or "the user pressed the Ⓖ key" or "the user selected the Edit menu item" or "the user clicked the OK button."

What is the mechanism for transmitting messages? Windows transmits a message to an application by *calling a function in that application.* Think about that. It is one of the key concepts in Windows programming: *Transmitting a message* (which is another way of saying "sending information") *means calling a function.*

What function in the application does Windows call? You can imagine all sorts of possible arrangements. There might be one message-receiving function for all messages directed to an application. Or there might be different functions for different kinds of messages. However, it turns out that in many ways a *window* is the key unit of program organization in Windows. So *there is one message-receiving function associated with each window class.* (This is another space-saver, because several windows, provided they are of the same class, can share the same message-receiving function.)

In the KEYBUTT program (and in FUNDWIN too) there is one window class, one window, and one message-receiving function, called WndProc(). Such a message-receiving function is called a *window procedure* or sometimes a *window function.* Figure 6-5 shows how messages are sent to window procedures.

Kinds of Messages

So Windows calls a window procedure to transmit a message. The call by itself says "Here's a message!" But how does the window procedure learn the *meaning* of the message? How can it tell whether it's a notification of a mouse button press, or a keyboard key press, or a menu selection, or something else? As you might have guessed, Windows passes the information that constitutes the message as *parameters to the window procedure.*

Here's the declarator (the first line) of the WndProc() function:

```
LRESULT CALLBACK _export WndProc(HWND hWnd,      // window handle
                                 UINT msg,       // message number
                                 WPARAM wParam,  // word parameter
                                 LPARAM lParam)  // long parameter
```

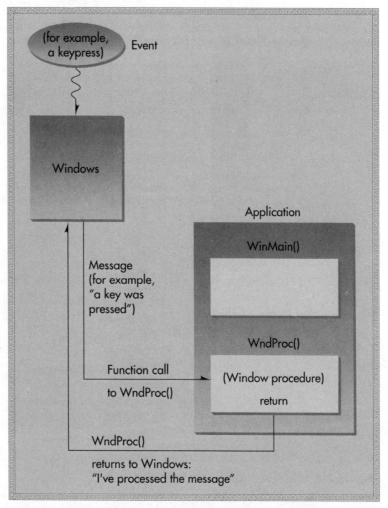

Figure 6-5 Messages and Window Procedures

As you can see, there are four parameters to this window procedure. The first is the handle of the particular window receiving the message, hWnd. This is the same window handle, of type HWND, returned from the CreateWindow() function in WinMain(). This window handle is used as an argument to other functions, as we'll see later, so it's a convenience to have it passed to the window procedure.

The second parameter to WndProc() is central to our discussion: it's the *message number*, represented in KEYBUTT by the variable msg. The message number is an important variable in a Windows program, since the entire window procedure is organized around it. In WndProc(), a **switch** statement causes different actions to be taken depending on the value of the message number. Figure 6-6 shows how this looks.

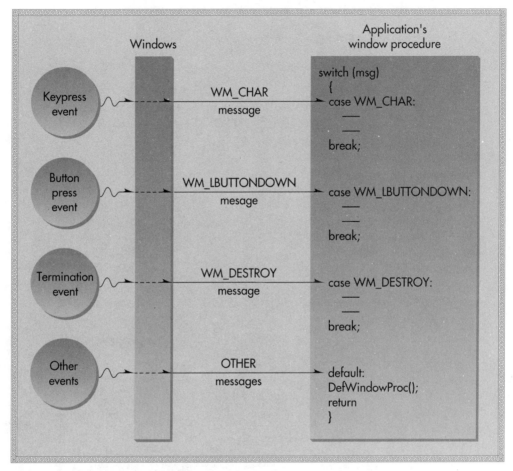

Figure 6-6 Messages and the switch Statement

Of course, since we're talking about Windows, constants defined in WINDOWS.H are used for message number values, rather than actual numbers. Table 6-1 shows some typical message constants.

These are just a few of the window-oriented messages; there are more than 100. Fortunately, only a handful are critical: those shown here and a few more. We'll introduce them individually as we go along.

Many messages include information other than just the message number. The last two parameters to the window procedure, wParam and lParam, are used to convey this additional information. The derived type WPARAM is currently type **unsigned int** (two bytes), and LPARAM is type **long** (four bytes).

The specific information in wParam and lParam depends on the message. In KEYBUTT we use the information returned in lParam, when we receive a

Table 6-1 Some Typical Messages Sent to a Window

Constant	Meaning
WM_CHAR	User pressed a keyboard key
WM_CLOSE	Window will be closed
WM_COMMAND	User selected menu item
WM_CREATE	Window is being created
WM_DESTROY	Window is being destroyed
WM_LBUTTONDOWN	User pressed the left mouse button
WM_RBUTTONDOWN	User pressed the right mouse button
WM_MOVE	Window was moved
WM_PAINT	Window needs to be redrawn
WM_SIZE	Size of window was changed

WM_LBUTTONDOWN message, to figure out the coordinates of the mouse pointer. The X-coordinate is in the low word of this parameter, and the Y-coordinate in the high word. We use the LOWORD and HIWORD macros (introduced in Chapter 4, *Macros, Etcetera*) to extract these values for wsprintf(), so we can display them in the message box.

The WM_DESTROY Message

In the FUNDWIN program, the WndProc() procedure handled only one message: WM_DESTROY. KEYBUTT also handles this message. In fact, all Windows applications must handle WM_DESTROY; it's the only message that's not optional. It is sent by Windows when the window has been removed from the screen. It means "You've lost your window, you better terminate." One common reason for this message is that the user selected Close from the system menu. When a window procedure receives this message, it must execute the PostQuitMessage() function, with a single argument of 0. This function (in a sequence worthy of a Rube Goldberg machine) then causes a WM_QUIT message to be transmitted to the application. This causes the program to terminate, as we'll see when we examine the message loop. (If you forget to include PostQuitMessage(), your program's window will disappear, but the program itself will run forever, being unable to break out of the message loop.)

Returning from the Window Procedure

When an application executes the **return** statement in a window procedure like WndProc() in KEYBUTT, control is given back to Windows. Windows can then give control to another application if it needs to, or it can wait for another event to occur. This is one of the two usual ways in which an application gives up control of the CPU. Because Windows is a *nonpreemptive* operating system, an application must actively pass control back to Windows every so often (preferably after a short length of time), otherwise other applications won't get a chance to run. Figure 6-5, shown earlier, demonstrates the return from WndProc() to Windows. (By contrast, a *preemptive* operating system, like Windows NT or OS/2, can interrupt an application at any time; the application doesn't need to worry about being quick to pass control back to the system.)

THE MESSAGE LOOP

The last part of WinMain() in KEYBUTT (and FUNDWIN) is a section of code called the *message loop*. Here it is again:

```
while( GetMessage(&msg,0,0,0) )    // get message from Windows
   {
   TranslateMessage(&msg);         // convert keystrokes
   DispatchMessage(&msg);          // call windows procedure
   }
```

What does this code do, and why is it necessary? The answer is rather involved, and it is not something you need to understand perfectly (or indeed hardly at all) in order to write Windows programs. All you really need to do is insert the code for the message loop into your program and let it run. For the curious, however, here is a rough explanation.

Sending Versus Posting

There are actually two ways to transmit a message to a window procedure: it can be *sent* or it can be *posted*. Either way the result is that the window procedure is called with the message number and other data as arguments, as we've described. However, the route taken by the message on its way to the window procedure is more circuitous if the message is posted than if it is sent.

Sending a message is like making a phone call. A message is sent when it is important that it arrive immediately at the window procedure. The WM_DESTROY message is an example. No matter what else is happening, the window procedure needs to deal with this message quickly. To send a message, Windows uses the straightforward approach: it makes a direct call to the application's window procedure.

The majority of messages are sent, rather than posted. Figure 6-7 shows the route taken by a message that is sent.

Posting a message is like mailing a letter. A message is posted when it may be part of a series of messages that needs to be dealt with in order. The WM_CHAR message, posted when a keystroke generates a character, is an example of this. To keep the keystrokes from getting out of order and scrambling the words typed by the user, Windows places WM_CHAR messages in a *queue*. A queue is simply a storage buffer that works on a first-in-first-out basis, like the line of people at a bank teller's window. The application removes these messages from the queue when it has time, just as you take letters out of your mailbox when it's convenient. Figure 6-8 (on the next page) shows the route taken by a message that is posted.

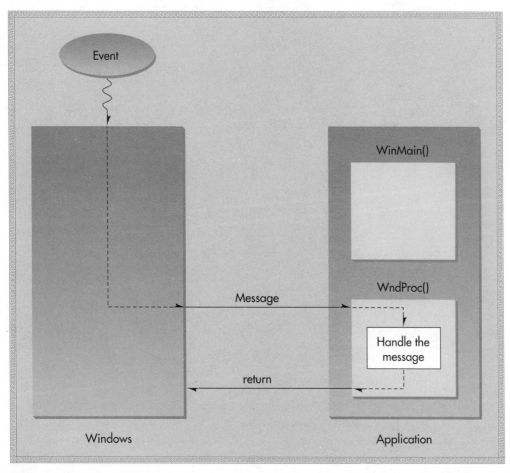

Figure 6-7 Sending a Message

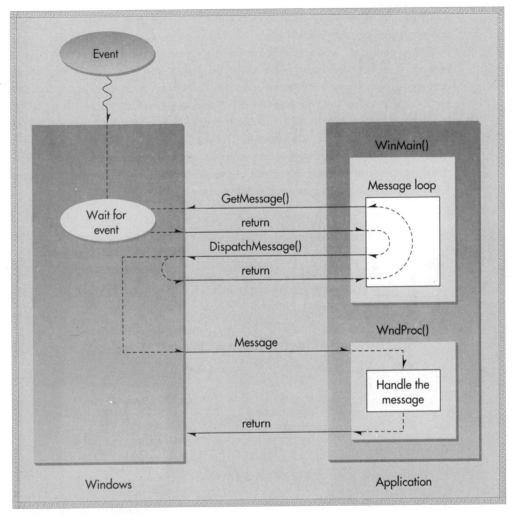

Figure 6-8 Posting a Message

Messages that are posted are sometimes called *queued* messages, while those that are sent are *non-queued*.

Getting Messages from the Queue

When a message is sent, your application doesn't need to take any action to receive the message; its window procedure just sits back and waits to be called with the message. But when a message is posted, the application must work a little harder. It must actively remove the message from the queue and *relay it to its own window procedure*. (Is that weird or what?)

Removing the Message from the Queue

How does the application get the message out of the queue and transmit it to its window procedure? That's where the message loop comes in. The message loop is a **while** loop with two important API functions: GetMessage() and DispatchMessage(). The application executes GetMessage() to tell Windows that it isn't processing any messages at the moment, and that it's ready to get the next posted message out of its queue. If the queue is empty, this function does not return; Windows just keeps control. This is the second way that an application can turn control over to Windows, so that other applications have a chance to run.

Windows allows GetMessage() to return to the application when an event occurs that causes a message to be posted, such as a key being pressed. The information returned from GetMessage() about this event is stored in a structure of type MSG, which in our program is the variable msg.

Passing the Message to the Window Procedure

As soon as GetMessage() returns, your application immediately executes DispatchMessage(). This function causes Windows to call the application's window procedure with the contents of the message, taken from the msg structure.

This process continues over and over, with GetMessage() getting a message from Windows, and DispatchMessage() passing it on to the window procedure.

Translating Keystrokes

As you can see from the listing, there is a third function in the message loop in FUNDWIN: TranslateMessage(). The inclusion of this function in the loop is a bit of a kludge. It is needed because a keypress does not actually generate a WM_CHAR message (which reports a character code), but a lower-level message indicating a particular keyboard key. TranslateMessage() translates these lower-level messages into a WM_CHAR message, which is more convenient for most programs to handle.

Not a Central Issue

You don't ordinarily need to worry too much about the message loop. You don't need to remember which messages are sent and which are posted, because Windows takes care of the details of transmitting messages. You also don't need to access the MSG structure, or even know what it looks like. The bottom line is that a message that is posted eventually ends up at the window procedure just as a message that is sent does. (You *do* need to worry about how messages are handled in the window procedure.)

Exiting from the Message Loop

The message loop cycles as long as the application is running. But how do you exit from this loop? As you can see from the listing, the loop will terminate if GetMessage() returns a value of 0. There is only one way that it returns this value, and that is when the message it receives from Windows is WM_QUIT. What causes WM_QUIT? The application does this itself by executing the PostQuitMessage() function. It does this when it receives a WM_DESTROY message. WM_DESTROY is sent when, for example, the user clicks on Close in the System menu. When the application executes the PostQuitMessage() function, Windows posts the WM_QUIT message. Figure 6-9 shows the process.

The WM_DESTROY message says "You should get ready to terminate yourself," and WM_QUIT says "You're being terminated." Once it has exited from

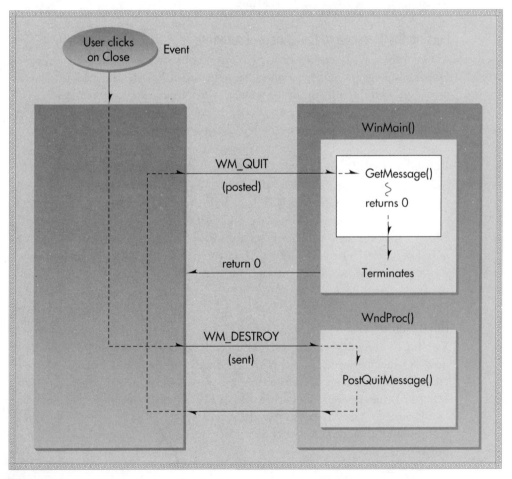

Figure 6-9 Messages at Program Termination

the message loop, the application returns to Windows, using part of the data obtained by GetMessage() from the WM_QUIT message as a return value. (Windows uses this value for internal processing.)

Why Put the Message Loop in the Application?

Why didn't the designers of Windows embed the message loop inside Windows, instead of making every application contain its own message loop? In most situations that approach would be fine, but a few programs need to examine posted messages before they are forwarded to the window procedure. Putting the message loop in the application allows this.

The operation of the message loop and the way Windows programs terminate may seem rather baroque, but as we've noted you don't need to worry about it. The message loop operates automatically. Just type it into WinMain() at the appropriate place, and let it do its work.

PASSING THE BUCK

There's one function in the KEYBUTT and FUNDWIN programs we haven't mentioned yet. It's called DefWindowProc(), and it plays a unique and important role in Windows programs. To see why we need it, ask yourself this question: what happens to messages that we do *not* handle in our application's window procedure? In FUNDWIN, the only message we actually handle is WM_DESTROY, and in KEYBUTT we handle only three messages. Supposing Windows calls WndProc() with some other message, say WM_PAINT; do we just throw it away?

As it turns out, a window procedure like WndProc() must take some action on every single message sent to it. Because there are more than 100 messages, it would make even a simple program very long and complicated if we had to write a **case** statement to handle every possible message. To keep the listing manageably small, Windows provides a way to avoid the responsibility for handling those messages that the application doesn't take action on itself. The application does this by calling DefWindowProc(). This function takes a default action (hence the name) for any message given it as a parameter. Figure 6-6, shown earlier, indicates how DefWindowProc() works.

In KEYBUTT, as in most programs, DefWindowProc() is installed in the window procedure following the **default** keyword in the **switch** statement. Here it will be called for any message not specifically coded into the **switch** statement. We don't need to know what the default processing that DefWindowProc() performs for each message actually is. We just need to remember to install it appropriately in our window procedure.

THE WndProc() RETURN VALUE

We haven't yet mentioned the return value for the window procedure. Here's the declarator for WndProc():

```
LRESULT CALLBACK _export WndProc(HWND, hWnd, UINT msg,
                             WPARAM wParam, LPARAM lParam)
```

LRESULT is defined in WINDOWS.H as type **long**, and CALLBACK is **_far _pascal**, so WndProc() has a **_far** address, is called with the Pascal calling convention, and returns type **long**. Functions that are called by Windows are often called *callback functions*. The CALLBACK type reflects this nomenclature.

The **_export** keyword is intended for the linker. It indicates that this function must be visible to other applications, not just other functions in the same application. As we've seen, WndProc() is called by Windows. For Windows to be able to find it, the function must be tagged as exportable.

LET IT SINK IN

An encounter with the event-driven dragon is never easy. We hope that you are only slightly singed, and that the fang marks on your shield are not too deep.

You may need to stop for a while and think about event-driven programming. It represents such a major change from traditional MS-DOS programs that some mental gymnastics are necessary to feel comfortable about it. Remember the magic incantation: *A program never does anything until Windows sends it a message.* Much of the time your application sits around doing absolutely nothing. It may be "running" in the sense that it's in memory and listed in Windows' Task List, but none of its instructions are being executed; it's not using the CPU at all. Instead, Windows itself is executing, or has turned over control temporarily to some other application.

Your program gets a chance to run only when an event occurs that causes a message to be transmitted (sent or posted) to it. An event is the user clicking a mouse button while the pointer is in your program's window, or the user pressing a keyboard key when your application has the keyboard focus, or the user selecting Close from the System menu, or any one of dozens of other causes. To transmit a message to your program, Windows calls a window procedure in your program. The parameters to this procedure indicate the type of message and other data. Your window procedure uses a **switch** statement to sort out the different messages, and takes action accordingly. When the action is completed, the window procedure returns, which returns control to Windows. When another event occurs, Windows calls your window procedure with another message.

In Part Two, *The User Interface—An Introduction*, we'll see how another group of messages is processed: those that occur when the user manipulates your application's window. But first we need to learn how to clone one program from another.

7
CLONING A PROGRAM

When you sit down to write a new MS-DOS program, you may very well begin by typing new lines of code into an empty file. That sounds like a reasonable thing to do, doesn't it? But if you are writing a Windows program, it is unlikely that you will follow this approach. There is just too much code that is common to all Windows programs. Instead, you will copy the source file of an existing program, rename the new file, and modify it to create the new program.

You can see why this approach makes sense by looking at the programs in the last two chapters: FUNDWIN and KEYBUTT. Most of the code in these programs is the same, or at least almost the same. This is true with most Windows programs. Usually they have a WinMain() function that creates a window class, registers it, creates a window of that class, and provides a message loop. They also have a window procedure that processes messages for the window created in WinMain(). Some of these messages, such as WM_DESTROY, are handled the same way in most programs. All this may amount to several pages of code that is more or less common to most Windows programs.

Thus it saves a lot of time for the programmer to start a program by copying a standard or "generic" file, and modifying the result as necessary. Actually, the FUNDWIN program in the last chapter comes close to being a generic program. However, we can improve on it in several ways. In this chapter we're going to create a generic Windows program by modifying FUNDWIN, and learn how to clone (that is, copy, rename, and modify) the result to create new programs.

TWO SOURCE FILES

For our generic Windows program we're going to break FUNDWIN into two source files: an .INC file and a .C file. The .INC (which stands for INClude) file will contain code that doesn't change from one program to another. The .C file will contain code that is different in each program. We'll simply #include the .INC file in the .C file for each new program. This way we need to show the .INC file only once.

Basically the .INC file will contain the WinMain() function, and the .C file will contain the WndProc() function, which usually varies substantially from one program to another.

We use this two-file approach to make the listings in this book easier to read. A long listing is harder to understand, and if a good part of the listing is material that does not vary from program to program, and therefore doesn't teach you anything new, it makes sense not to reproduce it over and over. By standardizing WinMain() and putting it in the .INC file, we can focus on the new material for each new

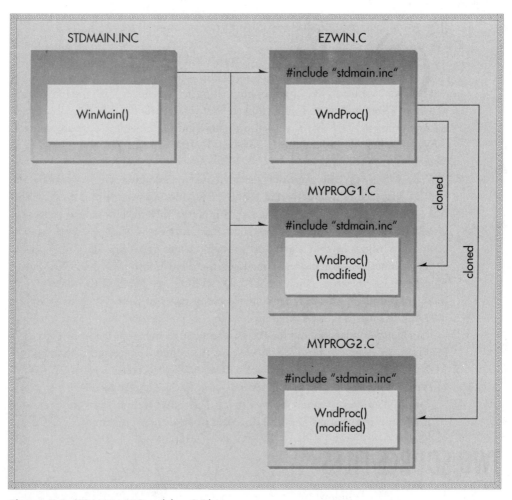

Figure 7-1 STDMAIN.INC and the .C Files

program. (We also could have split FUNDWIN into two .C files and combined them using the linker, but this would have required a Project file, which complicates the build process.)

We'll call our generic program EZWIN.C, and the include file STDMAIN.INC. When we make a new program, we can copy EZWIN.C, change its name (to MYPROG.C or whatever), and modify it. We don't need to modify STDWIN.INC; we simply #include it in each program. Figure 7-1 shows the relationship of these files.

The STDMAIN.INC File

As we noted, the The STDMAIN.INC file contains nothing more than the code for WinMain() and the argsused pragma that disables the "unused argument" warnings for WinMain(). Here's the listing for the STDMAIN.INC include file:

```
// stdmain.inc -- standard WinMain() function

#pragma argsused                       // ignore unused arguments

int PASCAL WinMain(HINSTANCE hInstance,      // which program are we?
                   HINSTANCE hPrevInst,      // is there another one?
                   LPSTR lpCmdLine,          // command line arguments
                   int nCmdShow)             // window size (icon, etc)
    {
    HWND hWnd;                         // window handle from CreateWindow
    MSG msg;                           // message from GetMessage
    WNDCLASS wndclass;                 // window class structure

    if(!hPrevInst)                     // if this is first such window
        {
        wndclass.style        = CS_HREDRAW | CS_VREDRAW; // style
        wndclass.lpfnWndProc  = (WNDPROC)WndProc; // WndProc address
        wndclass.cbClsExtra   = 0;            // no extra class data
        wndclass.cbWndExtra   = 0;            // no extra window data
        wndclass.hInstance    = hInstance;    // which program?
                                              // stock arrow cursor
        wndclass.hCursor      = LoadCursor (NULL, IDC_ARROW);
                                              // stock blank icon
        wndclass.hIcon        = LoadIcon(NULL, IDI_APPLICATION);
        wndclass.lpszMenuName = szProgName;   // menu name
                                              // white background
        wndclass.hbrBackground = GetStockObject(WHITE_BRUSH);
        wndclass.lpszClassName = szProgName;  // window class name

        RegisterClass(&wndclass); // register the class
        }  // end if

    hWnd = CreateWindow(szProgName,          // window class name
                        szProgName,          // caption
```

```
                    WS_OVERLAPPEDWINDOW,    // style
                    CW_USEDEFAULT,          // default x position
                    CW_USEDEFAULT,          // default y position
                    CW_USEDEFAULT,          // default width
                    CW_USEDEFAULT,          // default height
                    NULL,                   // parent's handle
                    NULL,                   // menu handle
                    hInstance,              // which program?
                    NULL);                  // no init data

    ShowWindow(hWnd, nCmdShow);        // make window visible

    // message loop
    while( GetMessage(&msg,0,0,0) )    // get message from Windows
       {
       TranslateMessage(&msg);         // convert keystrokes
       DispatchMessage(&msg);          // call windows procedure
       }
    return msg.wParam;                 // return to Windows
    }  // end WinMain
```

This file is almost identical to the WinMain() part of FUNDWIN. However, we have made several small additions so that STDMAIN.INC will work in a wider variety of situations.

Application Name

The most significant change is the way we handle the application name. The lines concerned with names are shown in bold. Instead of strings, we use the szProgName variable, which is defined in the .C file. We'll return to this when we discuss the .C file.

Style

Another change is in the style member of the wndclass structure, in the statement

```
wndclass.style = CS_HREDRAW | CS_VREDRAW;
```

Before we set the style member to NULL. The reason for this addition won't be clear until later, when we discuss how to display images in our window. Briefly, the CS_HREDRAW and CS_VREDRAW constants specify that an image in our window will be redrawn whenever the window changes size. This provides additional flexibility for some programs.

Menu Name

Finally, we added a menu name, using the statement

```
wndclass.lpszMenuName = szProgName
```

This will make it easier to add a menu to future programs. Note that the menu name is the same as the application name.

The EZWIN.C File

The EZWIN.C source file is a generic Windows program that #includes
STDMAIN.INC. It is a file we can clone to create other programs. Here's the
listing for EZWIN.C:

```
// ezwin.c
// puts a window on the screen
// WinMain() is #included in the stdwin.inc file

#define STRICT                   // strict type checking
#include <windows.h>             // include file for all Windows apps
                                 // prototype
LRESULT CALLBACK _export WndProc(HWND, UINT, WPARAM, LPARAM);

PSTR szProgName = "EzWin";       // application name

#include "stdmain.inc"           // standard WinMain() function
///////////////////////////////////////////////////////////////////
// main window procedure -- receives messages                     //
///////////////////////////////////////////////////////////////////
LRESULT CALLBACK _export WndProc(HWND hWnd,     // our window's handle
                                 UINT msg,       // message number
                                 WPARAM wParam,  // word parameter
                                 LPARAM lParam)  // long parameter
   {
   switch(msg)                           // which message?
      {
      case WM_DESTROY:                    // we handle this message
         PostQuitMessage(0);              // send WM_QUIT
         break;

                                          // all other messages are
      default:                            // handled by DefWindowProc
         return( DefWindowProc(hWnd, msg, wParam, lParam) );
      }   // end switch(msg)

   return 0L;                             // return if we handled msg
   }   // end WndProc
```

CHANGING THE PROGRAM NAME

We can simplify the process of cloning new programs from old if we standardize
various names used in the listing. In FUNDWIN.C we used string constants (such
as "fundwinClass") for names in three locations. (Refer to the listing of FUNDWIN
in the last chapter.) Our plan is to change all these string constants to string
variables, and then set this variable to a single name at the beginning of the
EZWIN.C file, before #including STDMAIN.INC. This will be a sort of universal
name, used wherever an application-specific name is needed.

Let's examine all the lines in FUNDWIN.C where string-constant names appear.

The Class Name

The class name shows up in two places in WinMain(). The first is in the definition of wndclass:

```
wndclass.lpszClassName = "fundwinClass";
```

and the second is in the CreateWindow() function:

```
hWnd = CreateWindow("fundwinClass", .., .., .., .., .., .., .., .., ..
```

(where two dots represent an omitted argument). The names in these two statements must agree: having defined a class, it is this class name we use when creating a window of that class. In STDMAIN.INC we change both these occurrences to the variable szProgName.

Caption Name

The third place we use a string constant in FUNDWIN is the caption name, "FundWin", which is the second argument to CreateWindow():

```
hWnd = CreateWindow(.., "FundWin", .., .., .., .., .., .., .., .., ..);
```

In STDWIN.INC we'll change this string as well to szProgName.

Menu Name

The fourth place we need a name doesn't use one in FUNDWIN. This is in the lpszMenuName member of the WNDCLASS structure, where the menu handle name is set to NULL to indicate there is no menu bar:

```
wndclass.lpszMenuName = NULL;
```

We're going to use menus in programs in the future, so—although there will be no menu in EZWIN—we'll insert szProgName to make things easier later. Doing this doesn't add the menu bar to the program, but it makes it easier to do so when we're ready.

Defining the Universal Name

Now all we need to do in EZWIN.C is define szProgName to be a particular string constant. In the EZWIN example we chose "EzWin", although we could have chosen anything we wanted to appear in the caption. Some programmers like all lowercase, some like all uppercase, but the majority prefer a combination, often using initial caps so the caption is easier to read.

Here's the line that defines and initializes the string variable szProgName:

```
PSTR szProgName = "EzWin";    // application name
```

We use the PSTR derived type for this, which is typedefed to be **char** *, a pointer to **char**.

Defining all the names in one place, as we show here, avoids the common error of forgetting to change a name somewhere when you clone your program. It also simplifies the listing. (However, see the discussion of names in Chapter 38, *Debugging*.)

Including WinMain( )

Once we've defined the application name, we can include the STDMAIN.INC file, with the directive

```
#include "stdmain.inc"
```

FINDING #include FILES

You will encounter a problem compiling EZWIN if your compiler doesn't know where to look for the STDMAIN.INC include file. You will probably want to put STDMAIN.INC in the same directory as your EZWIN.C source file. However, no matter where you put the .INC file, the compiler needs to be told where it is.

To do this, select Directories from the Options menu, and add the path name for the appropriate directory to the string in the Include Directories field. This field already tells where normal include files like WINDOWS.H are: in \TCWIN\INCLUDE (or BORLANDC\INCLUDE for Borland C++ for Windows). You need to add the path where STDMAIN.INC is, separating the path names with a semicolon. The resulting Include Directories field is shown in Figure 7-2. You should have already modified the Output Directory field, as mentioned in Chapter 2, *Building a Program*. (In BCW the path is \BORLANDC\INCLUDE instead of \TCWIN\INCLUDE.)

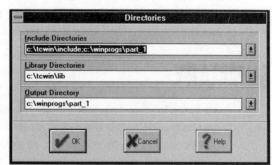

Figure 7-2

Changing the Include
Directories Field

The failure to look automatically for include files in the same directory as the source file is one of TCW's (and BCW's) little peculiarities.

CLONING EZWIN

Now that we've created a two-file version of our generic program, let's see how to clone it to create new programs.

Copy and Rename the Files

First, make sure STDMAIN.INC is in the subdirectory where you want to create your program. (Actually it can be anywhere, as long as the compiler knows where to find it.) Then copy EZWIN.C to this same subdirectory. Third, rename EZWIN.C to the new program name, say MYPROG.C.

Change the Listing

Now you're ready to modify the listing. First, change the comments that specify the file name and its description at the top of the listing. Then change the definition of szProgName to the new name. Here's how the first part of the modified .C file looks, with the changes in bold:

```
// myprog.c
// new program description
// WinMain() is #included in the stdwin.inc file

#define STRICT                  // strict type checking
#include <windows.h>            // include file for all windows apps
                                // prototype
LRESULT CALLBACK _export WndProc(HWND, UINT, WPARAM, LPARAM);

PSTR szProgName = "MyProg";     // application name

#include "stdmain.inc"          // standard WinMain() function
```

You can then modify the balance of the program to add new functionality, as we'll see in Part Two, *The User Interface—An Introduction.*

SUMMARY

In Part One you have learned all you need to know to create a generic Windows program. You've been exposed to derived data types and Hungarian notation. You've successfully faced the lion of window creation, and you have met the event-driven dragon and lived to tell the tale.

Having reached this point, you have completed your training as a mere page. We will now, with high hopes and glad heart, confer upon you the title of Squire, with all the rights and privileges pertaining thereto. You can feel confident of your ability to handle the various giants, wyverns, and lesser dragons you'll encounter in the balance of this book. We could almost say that from now on it's mostly a matter of filling in the blanks: adding a message here and an API function there, but that's not completely true. There will be some major new ideas, and quite a few surprises. However, you will never again encounter anything quite as hair-raising as the event-driven dragon.

PART TWO
THE USER INTERFACE— AN INTRODUCTION

*I*n medieval times the tapestry was a major art form. Tapestries were rug-like wall-hangings with scenes woven into the design. Some tapestries chronicled historical events like battles and coronations, others showed scenes from daily life, including knights hunting in the forest and jousting at tournaments. Unicorns and other fabulous beasts also appeared. The tapestry was the TV set of the Middle Ages, providing a visual record of the events of the time.

In Windows our tapestry is the Graphical User Interface (GUI). It's a visual representation of events in the computer. However, the Windows GUI has a feature the tapestry did not have (and indeed which no visual medium ever had before): it is interactive. The user not only receives information from the GUI, but can cause the GUI to reveal more information or to affect the action of the computer. It is as if a medieval sorcerer could, by touching a scene in a tapestry, cause the scene to change or events to occur in distant places.

In Part Two we introduce three topics connected with the Windows GUI. We show how to display text on the screen, how to create menus, and how to use "common" dialog boxes. There is, of course, a great deal more to programming the Windows' GUI, and we'll continue to explore aspects of it in future sections. The material in this section provides an introduction to the topic, and enough specifics so that you can begin to write real Windows programs.

We also introduce a subject not typically associated with the user interface: disk files, which are essential for most programs. This lets us put the common dialog boxes to work opening and saving files. At the end of the section we put together what we've learned so far into a mini-application that allows you to analyze text files and display the results.

*I*n the next chapter, we're going to show how to display text on the screen. However, to understand how text is displayed in Windows, you need to be familiar with how Windows handles certain messages. It's like learning horsemanship before learning how to handle the lance at full gallop. In this chapter, we present a program that demonstrates the messages that are involved with changes to a program's main window.

THE WINMSGS PROGRAM

As we saw in Part One, *Getting Started*, Windows sends messages to tell our application about events that may affect it. One kind of event that affects our program occurs when the user manipulates our main window, (for example, by uncovering it, resizing it, or moving it). Our example program reacts to these user activities by reacting to the three messages WM_PAINT, WM_SIZE, and WM_MOVE. It also responds to WM_CREATE, WM_CLOSE, and the ubiquitous WM_DESTROY. (You've guessed by now that WM stands for Window Message, right?)

As the program receives each of these messages, it displays a message box that names the message. By running this program, you can become familiar with the circumstances that trigger these messages. The primary message involved with displaying text on the screen is WM_PAINT, but the other messages are important too. Here's the listing for WINMSGS.C:

```
// winmsgs.c
// notifies user of several messages

#define STRICT
#include <windows.h>
```

```
LRESULT CALLBACK _export WndProc(HWND, UINT, WPARAM, LPARAM);

PSTR szProgName = "WinMsgs";     // program name
#include "stdmain.inc"           // standard WinMain() function

//////////////////////////////////////////////////////////////////
// main window procedure -- receives messages                    //
//////////////////////////////////////////////////////////////////
LRESULT CALLBACK _export WndProc(HWND hWnd, UINT msg,
                                 WPARAM wParam, LPARAM lParam)
   {
   PAINTSTRUCT ps;               // structure for paint info

   switch(msg)
      {
      case WM_CREATE:
         MessageBox(hWnd, "WM_CREATE received", szProgName, MB_OK);
         break;

      case WM_MOVE:
         MessageBox(hWnd, "WM_MOVE received", szProgName, MB_OK);
         break;

      case WM_SIZE:
         MessageBox(hWnd, "WM_SIZE received", szProgName, MB_OK);
         break;

      case WM_PAINT:
         BeginPaint(hWnd, &ps);            // prepare for painting
         MessageBox(hWnd, "WM_PAINT received", szProgName, MB_OK);
         EndPaint(hWnd, &ps);              // end painting
         break;

      case WM_CLOSE:
         MessageBox(hWnd, "WM_CLOSE received", szProgName, MB_OK);
         DestroyWindow(hWnd);
         break;

      case WM_DESTROY:
         // don't put a message box here
         PostQuitMessage(0);
         break;

      default:
         return( DefWindowProc(hWnd, msg, wParam, lParam) );
      }   // end switch(msg)

   return 0L;
   } // end WndProc
```

Cloning WINMSGS

You can clone this program from EZWIN as described in the last chapter. Make a copy of the EZWIN.C file, and rename it WINMSGS.C. Change the comments at the top of the listing to reflect the new name, and change the value of the szProgName variable in the listing to "WinMsgs". Then you can add the additional code, as shown in the listing for WINMSGS.C, and recompile. Of course if you're ambitious, you can type the entire file from scratch. Or if you're pressed for time, you can load the file from the disk.

In any case, remember that WINMSGS.C (as do all the programs in this section) requires the STDMAIN.INC file to be located where the compiler can find it. Copy it into your PART_2 directory if it's not there already. Don't forget to change the path names the compiler is using for include and output files. Select Directories from the Options menu as described in the last chapter, and insert the path \WINPROGS\PART_2 in the Include Directories and the Output Directory fields.

THE WM_CREATE MESSAGE

As we describe the messages handled by the WINMSGS program, keep in mind that a message is nothing more than a call by Windows to your WndProc() window procedure. The second parameter to this function, msg, is a message number with a value like WM_CREATE, WM_PAINT, and so on. Our WndProc() function uses a **switch** statement to take different actions, depending on the value of this parameter.

The WM_CREATE message is sent by Windows to signal that a window has been created. Typically, window creation is the result of a CreateWindow() function executed by the application. (Thus the program indirectly causes messages to be sent to itself!) We execute CreateWindow(), as you may recall, in WINMSGS in WinMain(), which is in the include file STDMAIN.INC. The WM_CREATE message appears before the window is made visible, so when you run WINMSGS you'll see the message box, which announces that this message has been received, displayed on the screen all by itself as shown in Figure 8-1.

Because this message arrives only once, when the main window is first created, we can use its **case** statement as a place to perform any initialization necessary in the program. (As we'll see later, a typical use is to find the size of the characters in the current font.)

When the message box appears, announcing that WM_CREATE has arrived, click on the OK button to make the message box go away. This will cause the application's main window to appear. However, this main window doesn't appear alone. It is accompanied by more message boxes. Following WM_CREATE, there

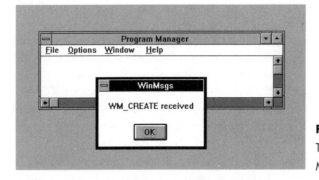

Figure 8-1
The WM_CREATE
Message Box

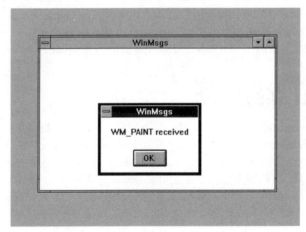

Figure 8-2
The WM_PAINT
Message Box

is WM_PAINT, then WM_SIZE, and finally WM_MOVE. Figure 8-2 shows the first of these: WM_PAINT.

When you click on the OK button in each box, the box disappears, to be replaced by the next one. These four messages always arrive in the same order when you start your application and create a window.

THE WM_PAINT MESSAGE

The WM_PAINT message is central to displaying text—or anything else, for that matter—on the screen. Here is a key concept in Windows programming: *WM_PAINT is sent to an application whenever the screen needs to be redrawn.* This statement goes to the heart of event-driven programming. What does it mean? Why does the screen need to be redrawn? When did it get drawn in the first place?

Play with the Program

To see what WM_PAINT does, play with the main window in WINMSGS. Make it bigger: you get a WM_PAINT message and a WM_SIZE message. Make it smaller. The same thing happens (although if you had not used the window styles CS_HREDRAW and CS_VREDRAW when defining the window class, you would not get a WM_SIZE message when making the window smaller). Try covering up the WINMSGS window with another program's window. Now click on the WINMSGS window to bring it to the top, or move the other window off it. You'll get a WM_PAINT message all by itself. Moving the window doesn't generate a WM_PAINT message, but a WM_MOVE message instead. Figure 8-3 shows these results.

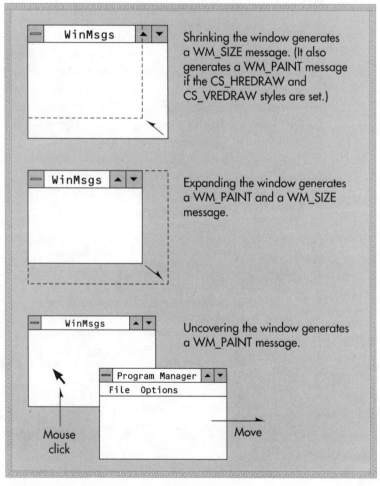

Figure 8-3 Actions Eliciting a WM_PAINT Message

What can we infer about the WM_PAINT message from these experiments? It appears in three circumstances: when a window is first created, when the window's size changes, and when any part of the window is uncovered by another window. To see why this is so, think about what a window does.

They Never Rest

As you have just demonstrated—by resizing, moving, covering, and uncovering the WINMSGS window—a window is not a static object (as the screen is in a simple DOS program, for example). At any moment a window can change its size and shape. Yet this window is where we want to display text or other information. Because our window is a dynamic object, we must send output to it in a dynamic way.

Suppose our application needs to display some text—say 30 lines—in a window, and the window (at the moment, anyway) is big enough to hold only 10 lines of text. We'll display 10 lines. But then the user makes the window twice as high; big enough to hold 20 lines of text. What happens? If you experiment with Windows programs that handle text (like the accessories Notepad and Write), you'll see that when you make a window larger, or uncover it, the newly displayed area is filled in immediately with the appropriate text. In our case, because our window will now hold 20 lines, we want to display all 20 lines. Figure 8-4 shows how additional text is drawn in the expanded part of a text window.

How do we cause our program to draw the added text? How does the program even know when the window has become larger?

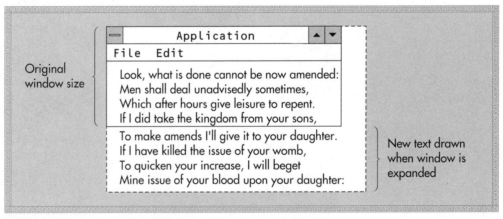

Figure 8-4 Text in Expanded Window

<u>Not</u> How It's Done

One possible scenario is that Windows itself takes care of filling in text when a window is enlarged. Windows might maintain a sort of subwindow underlying the window that we see on the screen. This subwindow is very large—it can hold many screenfulls—and our application writes all the text in the file to this subwindow. The window we see on the screen is just a frame that looks into the subwindow, so when the user makes the frame larger, Windows simply reveals more of the text that was already there. This may sound plausible, but it is *not* how Windows works. Why not? In this scenario, Windows would need to store all the text somewhere, and be ready to display any part of it as the user moved the window around on top of it.

But Windows does not want this responsibility. Keeping track of multipage documents or complicated graphics images would be too much of a strain on Windows' time and memory. Besides, the application may need to reformat the image to suit a larger window. A word processor, for example, may need to change where the line breaks occur if a window is made narrower. So Windows turns over the responsibility for all screen displays to the application.

The Application Does It

Your application is responsible for displaying whatever should appear in its window, and for *redisplaying* this information if necessary. If the user makes the window larger, or if part of it is uncovered, then the part that was uncovered needs to be filled with data. How does the application know when to do this? The WM_PAINT message is the signal that the window needs to be redisplayed. Often only part of a window needs to be redrawn. An application can find out exactly how much of its new area needs to be redrawn, but in most cases it's simpler to redraw everything in the window whenever a WM_PAINT message is received. (The exception might be a complex drawing that would take too long to redraw completely.)

When the Window is Created

You might get the impression that WM_PAINT is sent only when the window needs to be *re*painted. But what about the first time, when the program first starts to run? No problem. Remember that Windows sends a WM_PAINT message when the window is first made visible. The application can do the initial display then. So WM_PAINT covers all the bases. The application never needs to display data when it *doesn't* receive a WM_PAINT message, but it *always* needs to when it does.

Other Functions

There are two APIs in the WM_PAINT **case** statement besides the MessageBox() function, BeginPaint() and EndPaint(). In the next chapter we'll see why they're necessary. For now we'll continue our exploration of messages.

We should note that, although this program works fine when compiled with TCW or BCW, some compilers require you to insert a function called ValidateRect() following the call to MessageBox() in the WM_PAINT section:

```
ValidateRect(hWnd, NULL);
```

This avoids an infinite loop if a WM_PAINT message is generated when the message box terminates. Don't worry about this unless you're using a different compiler.

THE WM_SIZE MESSAGE

Whenever the window is made smaller or larger, a WM_SIZE message is sent. The application can use this message if it needs to recalculate something that is based on the window size. Usually, however, a size change also triggers a WM_PAINT message, and the program waits for this message to discover the new size and recalculate the display.

THE WM_MOVE MESSAGE

Windows, in a sudden burst of generosity, actually helps out when a window is moved. It could leave it to the application to redraw the screen when the window is moved, but instead it transfers all the pixels to the new location. The application doesn't usually even need to know that a move has taken place. But if it does need to know this, it can intercept the WM_MOVE message.

THE WM_CLOSE MESSAGE

Windows sends a WM_CLOSE message when a window is about to be destroyed (caused by the user selecting Close from the System menu, for example). This message precedes the WM_DESTROY message described in the last chapter. However, unlike WM_DESTROY, which tells the application it's being shut down whether it wants to be or not, WM_CLOSE is simply a suggestion that the application terminate. There is still time to cancel the termination if the application (or the user) decides it's not a good idea after all. WM_CLOSE gives the application a chance to see if all the appropriate housekeeping has been done prior to termination. For example, it can check to see if there are open files, and if so close them. Or it can ask the user "Do you really want to exit?" and forget the whole thing if the answer is no.

MESSAGE INTUITION

Make sure you can predict which message will be received when you do something to the program's window. What messages are received when you minimize it? When you maximize it? Does WM_PAINT always appear when it should? Do the other messages make sense? This sort of experimentation will give you an intuitive feeling for these messages.

This chapter has focused on messages that are sent to an application concerning changes to its window. In the next chapter we'll see how to put one of these, the WM_PAINT message, to work displaying text.

CHAPTER 9

DISPLAYING TEXT

Your next job as a squire is to learn how to weave your own tapestry: that is, how to create pictures. In our case the pictures will be displayed in our program's window, and they will consist of text, rather than some complicated scene of knights and ladies. However, in Windows, text is just another kind of graphics: it is handled in many ways like a picture. Medieval weavers often included text (usually in Latin) in their tapestries in the same way.

THE EZTEXT PROGRAM

As we learned in the last chapter, we display information when our application receives a WM_PAINT message. Our example program, EZTEXT, demonstrates this with a short prose selection. The text is stored as an array of pointers to strings, with each string holding one line of text. The Windows TextOut() API function is used to display each string on a different line in the window. Here's the listing for EZTEXT.C.

```
// eztext.c
// displays text on the screen

#define STRICT
#include <windows.h>

#define LINES   12        // number of lines to display
#define TMARGIN  3        // top margin, in pixels
#define LMARGIN 10        // left margin, in pixels
#define CYCHAR  18        // height of characters, in pixels

PSTR ashley[LINES] = {    // array of pointers to strings
"Then Sir Ashley, arriving at the River Shattuck at evensong, found the",
```

```
"ford guarded by a knight-errant on horseback, armed at all points,",
"his shield in black with bend sinister.",
"    \"Let me pass,\" Sir Archbald said, \"for I am sore pressed to",
"succor the damosel Milvia, kept prisoner in yon dark castle.\"",
"    \"Ye shall not pass,\" quoth the knight, \"for wit ye well I am",
"master of yon castle, and shall take the damosel to wife before",
"Saint Swithn's day.\"",
"    Therewith they hurtled together with great raundon, and the spears",
" of both were shattered and twirled skyward in the waining light.",
"",
"From \"Sir Ashley and the Blue Pavillion,\" by Robert Malgre Louis" };


                           // prototype
LRESULT CALLBACK _export WndProc(HWND, UINT, WPARAM, LPARAM);


PSTR szProgName = "ezText";    // program name
#include "stdmain.inc"         // standard WinMain() function
///////////////////////////////////////////////////////////////////
// main window procedure -- receives messages                     //
///////////////////////////////////////////////////////////////////
LRESULT CALLBACK _export WndProc(HWND hWnd, UINT msg,
                                 WPARAM wParam, LPARAM lParam)
    {
    HDC hDC;                    // handle for the device context
    PAINTSTRUCT ps;             // holds PAINT information
    int iIndex;                 // loop index

    switch(msg)
        {
        case WM_PAINT:                      // repaint the screen
            hDC = BeginPaint(hWnd, &ps);    // get device context

            // display the text from buffer
            for(iIndex = 0; iIndex < LINES; iIndex++ )  // for each line
                TextOut( hDC,                       // device context
                        LMARGIN,                    // horiz position
                        TMARGIN + CYCHAR*iIndex,     // vert position
                        ashley[iIndex],             // address of line
                        lstrlen( ashley[iIndex]) ); // length of line

            EndPaint(hWnd, &ps);                // painting complete
            break;  //  End of WM_PAINT

        case WM_DESTROY:
            PostQuitMessage(0);
            break;

        default:
            return( DefWindowProc(hWnd, msg, wParam, lParam) );
        }   // end switch(msg)

    return 0L;
    } // end WndProc
```

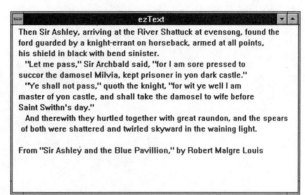

Figure 9-1

Output of EZTEXT

This program displays the text in its main window, as shown in Figure 9-1.

Run this program and try resizing the window. Make it very small and then enlarge it. When you enlarge it, text appears to fill in the newly created part of the window. It's as if the text were already there, waiting to be revealed, but of course it's not. When you enlarge the window, Windows sends a WM_PAINT message to the program, which causes the program to redisplay all the text lines.

You'll notice that (aside from the text itself) most of the new material in this program occurs in the WM_PAINT section.

THE BeginPaint() AND EndPaint() FUNCTIONS

The TextOut() function, which actually displays the text, is surrounded by a pair of functions, BeginPaint() and EndPaint(). It is absolutely essential to use this pair of functions whenever you process the WM_PAINT message. If you don't, your application—and even Windows itself—will probably die a horrible death. Also, don't try to use BeginPaint() and EndPaint() when you have *not* received a WM_PAINT message. Here's the drill: you need to wait for the WM_PAINT message, you need both BeginPaint() and EndPaint(), and any functions that display anything on the screen must be placed between them. Figure 9-2 shows the way display functions are organized.

It may sound odd to have messages and functions with the word "paint" in them when we're displaying text. Remember that Windows treats text as just another form of graphics: characters are drawn pixel by pixel, rather than being sent as ASCII code to the display as in DOS programs.

The BeginPaint() function tells Windows that we're about to begin displaying something. It takes two arguments. The first is the handle of the main window, which we obtain from the first argument to WndProc(). This tells Windows what

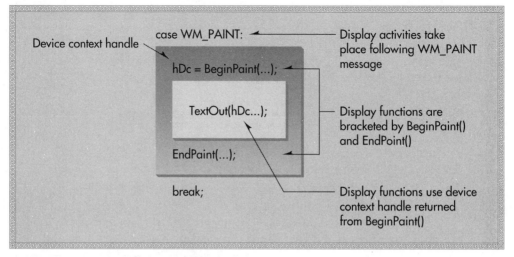

Figure 9-2 Display Functions and WM_PAINT

window we want to use for the display (although in this case there's only one window, there could be more).

The second argument to BeginPaint() is the address of a structure of type PAINTSTRUCT; this is the variable we call ps in our program. BeginPaint() fills this structure with such information as the coordinates of the area to be repainted and whether the background needs to be redrawn. For now we don't need to worry about what's in this structure. Just remember to provide a copy of it for use by BeginPaint() and EndPaint(). The EndPaint() function tells Windows that we're through painting.

THE DEVICE CONTEXT

BeginPaint() returns a handle (remember that a handle is just an ID number) to something called a *device context*. This forbidding name describes a rather abstract entity. There are two important aspects to a device context.

First, as its name implies, it is associated with a particular device. In this case the device is the screen display. The other common device is the printer, but any piece of hardware that generates graphics output can be associated with a device context.

Second, the device context serves as a place to store various graphics attributes such as color palettes, pen sizes, fill patterns (called brushes), and so on. We'll see examples of these attributes in Part Five, *Graphics*.

You might want to think of the device context as an artist (the kind with a beret). Perhaps your knightly skills don't extend as far as creating good-looking scenes of knights and horses and legendary beasts and fair ladies. But, for a few gold pieces, you can hire an expert to create whatever scene you want. "Put a knight here," you might say, "and a fierce giant there, with a castle in the background." In the same way, you don't give instructions to the screen display hardware directly, but to the device context, which translates your instructions into an appropriate form for the particular device. Figure 9-3 shows the relationship of a device context and a device.

Figure 9-3 A Device Context

In EZTEXT, the BeginPaint() function obtains a device context handle from Windows. The TextOut() function then uses this handle to actually display the text. Finally the EndPaint() function returns the device context to Windows.

A device context is a system resource that takes up memory space. Windows maintains only a limited number of device contexts, so you shouldn't keep them in use for long or use too many at once. Ordinarily you probably won't be tempted to commit either of these *faux pas*, since you execute the BeginPaint() and EndPaint() only when you're processing a WM_PAINT message. As long as you give the device context back before you finish processing WM_PAINT, you're probably all right.

THE TextOut() FUNCTION

The TextOut() function displays a text string. Its parameters are the device context handle, the horizontal position of the text to be displayed, the vertical position of the text, the address of the buffer containing the text string, and the length of the string.

```
TextOut( hDC,                        // device context
         LMARGIN,                    // horiz position
         TMARGIN + CYCHAR*index,     // vert position
         ashley[index],             // address of line
         lstrlen(ashley[index]) );  // length of line
```

Remember that TextOut() is a *graphics* function. It thinks of the display as being composed of pixels, and positions text using pixel coordinates, just like functions that draw lines and rectangles. By contrast, traditional C-library functions like printf() are *text* functions. They can place text only in fixed rows and columns determined by the display hardware.

The coordinates for TextOut() are normally measured in pixels from the upper left corner of the window (not of the screen). The X-coordinate increases rightward, and the Y-coordinate increases downward. In EZTEXT, the TextOut() function is embedded in a **for** loop. Each time through the loop, one string, representing a line of text, is displayed. All the lines start LMARGIN pixels from the left of the screen. The vertical position is TMARGIN plus the height of the characters CYCHAR (which we assume is 18 pixels) multiplied by the line number. This causes each line to be displayed lower than the last. The last two arguments are the address of the line, ashley[iIndex] and its length; we'll examine the lstrlen() function in a moment.

You should know that the TextOut() function is a member of the *Graphics Device Interface* (GDI). This is a frequently used term in Windows. The GDI is the collection of functions that provide output to all graphics devices, such as the display screen, the printer, plotters, and so forth. The term "GDI" is also used to refer to the whole approach Windows takes to graphics.

The Lstrlen() Function

The Windows API includes several string-handling functions that duplicate the actions of C-library functions. These Windows functions have the same name as their C-library counterparts, but preceded by a lowercase letter l. They are lstrcat(), lstrcmp(), lstrcmpi(), lstrcpy(), and lstrlen(). The Windows versions require **far** pointers to strings, while the C-library versions take **near** pointers. Otherwise they operate in the same way.

There are two advantages to using the Windows string-handling functions. First, there's no need to include the STRING.H header file in your source code. Second, the string-handling routines from the C library don't need to be linked to your program. Thus you can decrease compilation time and make your program smaller by using the Windows string functions. We recommend doing this whenever possible (although not all string functions have Windows counterparts).

In EZTEXT we use lstrlen() to find the length of each string, as required by the final argument to TextOut().

CONSTANTS FOR DIMENSIONS

In EZTEXT we use the constants TMARGIN, LMARGIN, and CYCHAR to specify the left and top margins for the text, and the height of the characters. We could figure out the actual character dimensions, and use them to calculate the margins and line spacing. However, we don't need to deal with this detail now. If you think the text lines in EZTEXT are too close together or too far apart, you can change the CYCHAR constant until you like the spacing. In Part Three, *Text*, we'll see how your program can determine the dimensions of the characters, but for now we'll avoid the added complexity this would entail.

SUMMARY

Here are the basics of displaying text:

1. Do display processing when (and only when) you receive a WM_PAINT message.
2. Start with BeginPaint().
3. Use the device context handle from BeginPaint() in display functions like TextOut().

4.   Finish with EndPaint().

There is much more to be said about displaying text, such as changing fonts, scrolling the screen display, and (as we noted) accounting for the exact size of the text. We'll look into these topics in Part Three, *Text.* In the next chapter we'll look at a more abstract concept: resources, which will prove valuable for creating menus, dialog boxes, and many other Windows entities.

CHAPTER

10
RESOURCES AND PROJECTS

*I*n ancient mythology, there were various beasts that were part something and part something else. For example, centaurs (which first appeared in ancient Greece) had the head and arms of a man but the body and legs of a horse. A griffon had the head and wings of an eagle and the body of a lion. The dreaded manticore had the head of a man, the body of a lion, and the tail of a dragon. Many a knight made his reputation fighting these sorts of monsters.

In this chapter we're going to introduce an entity called the *resource*, which is also partly one thing and partly another. In some ways a resource is part of your program, but in some ways it's more like a data file; it occupies a sort of twilight zone between the two.

Resources include menus, dialog boxes, icons, cursors, bitmaps, fonts, and strings. In this chapter we're going to discuss resources in general. In the next chapter we'll show how to use resources to create a menu system. We'll cover some of the other kinds of resources later in this book.

A resource may not be quite as scary as a manticore, but it still takes some getting used to. We'll try to explain what resources are all about. The discussion may seem rather abstract, but it will come into focus in the next chapter when we discuss the specific details of the menu resource.

To create resources you must know how to use the TCW (or BCW) Project feature. This is the capability, built into your compiler, to combine several different source files to produce a single executable file. In the second part of the chapter we'll see how to use the project feature to combine resources with your program.

A NEW WAY TO STORE DATA

Traditional MS-DOS programs divide the world into two categories. There is the program itself, and there is everything outside the program. Suppose the program uses a certain kind of data. You can put that data inside the program, in the form of constants (like 27 or "escape velocity". Or, you can put the data outside the program, in a separate disk file, or as something the user must type in.

This division between program data and nonprogram data can be rather inflexible. There may be certain information needed for your program that is inconvenient to compile along with the program, but that is also inconvenient to keep around as a separate file. Resources are a new way to store data, occupying the twilight zone between program and data file. Figure 10-1 shows how this looks.

WHY USE RESOURCES?

There are three primary reasons for using resources. First, you may want to change certain kinds of data in your program without recompiling it. Second, it may be difficult to create some kinds of information using the normal edit-compile process. And third, it may not be efficient to load certain information into memory every time you load your program. Let's examine these three points.

Avoid Recompiling

Most programs use text for various purposes in the user interface: for window titles, menu items, control names in dialog boxes, and so on. This text is probably all in a particular language, say English. Now suppose you want to create a French version of your program. You could go into the source code and insert French text. However, by doing this you run the risk that you will inadvertently change something in the code that will introduce a bug. It's always dangerous to fiddle with the source code.

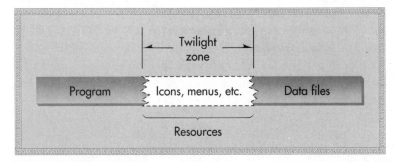

Figure 10-1 The Twilight Zone

Another disadvantage of recompiling is that you may not want to distribute your source code. Your company may have a software distributor in France, which must come up with the French text. But you may not want to let the source code for your application out of your main office in the United States. You would rather send the already-compiled object code to the French office, and let them combine it with a language-specific part of the program that's appropriate for their particular country.

One answer to this problem is to remove all language-specific material from the .EXE executable file, and distribute both the executable file and a language-specific data file. However, this means the user must keep two files loaded on the hard disk. It's cleaner and easier if the user has only one file to worry about. What we really need is something that is part of the .EXE file, and yet not part of the source file that generates the .EXE file.

Non-Text Editors

Some information is difficult to create in a form that can be placed in an ordinary .C source file. As we'll see in Part Four, *Dialog Boxes*, there are two ways to create a dialog box. You can use your normal program editor to create a text file that describes the dialog box. For example, if there's an OK button in the dialog box, you can type the coordinates where this OK button should go. However, there's an easier way to create a dialog box. You can use a graphics editor that allows you to position the OK button and other controls visually. You slide the OK button around until it's just where you want it. A graphics editor uses your visual input to create a text file that describes the dialog. (In TCW and BCW this graphics editor is called the Resource Workshop.)

Now suppose dialog box text files were part of the source file. You create several dialog boxes and paste the resulting text files into your source file; then compile the source file. That's fine, but suppose you decide later to change the dialog box; perhaps the OK button isn't in quite the right place after all. Now you have to go into your source file, cut out the old dialog box, and paste in the new one. This brings up the disadvantages, noted earlier, involved in changing your source code. It would be better if the descriptions of dialog boxes could be kept separate from the source code for the program. But again, they should be part of the .EXE file to simplify distribution of your program.

Managing Memory

Resources can take a lot of memory space. This is especially true of graphics resources like icons, cursors, and bitmaps. If all of a program's resources were loaded into memory when the program itself was loaded, the program would occupy substantially more space. To conserve memory, Windows waits until a resource is

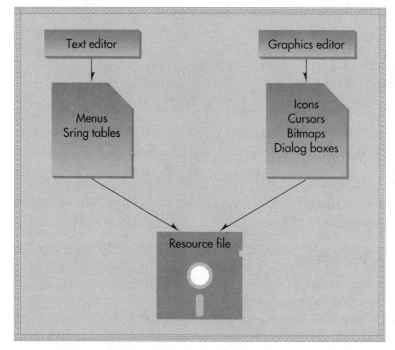

Figure 10-2 Combining Resources into a Single File

actually needed in the course of program execution before loading it. This would not be possible if the resources were part of the source file.

Resources: .EXE But Not .EXE

The solution to the problems posed above requires several steps. First, resources are created by various editors and combined into a single file, as shown in Figure 10-2.

This resource file is then (after various steps which we'll discuss next) combined with a program's .EXE file to create a new, improved .EXE file. This is shown in Figure 10-3.

This final executable file includes a program's resources in a format that Windows can read separately from the executable part of the file. Thus Windows can wait and load the resources when they are needed, not when the program's executable code is loaded. On the other hand, the user only has one file to load and store.

Let's look more closely at how resources are created, compiled, and combined with the executable file.

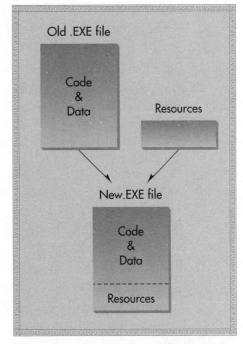

Figure 10-3 Resource and Executable Files

CREATING RESOURCES

Some resources begin life as text files. This is true of the resource we'll describe first, menus. You can create a complete menu system using nothing but the text editor built into TCW (or BCW). You can in theory use a text editor to create dialog boxes, but it's easier to use a graphics editor that in turn creates a text file. (Actually, you can use a special editor to create menus as well, but it is just as easy to type a text description of the menu structure.)

Other resources, like bitmaps, cursors, and icons, must be created pixel by pixel using a graphics editor.

Resource Script File

When you create a resource, you place it in a special file called the *resource script file*, which has the .RC extension. All of a program's resources go in this one .RC file. It is a text file, like the .C source file, so you can examine and modify it with a text editor. However, the .RC file can #include files that are not text files, so that it can handle graphic resources like icons and bitmaps. The resource script file is usually given the same name as your application's .EXE file: if your executable is MYAPP.EXE, the script file would be MYAPP.RC.

The Resource Compiler

A special compiler called the Resource Compiler (file name RC.EXE), is used to compile the .RC resource script file into object (binary) form. The RC compiler is included with TCW and BCW. The compilation process results in a file with the .RES file extension: MYAPP.RES. This file contains the results of resources that started off as text files, as well as resources that started as graphic files, such as icons. This compilation process is somewhat like compiling a normal .C source file into an .OBJ object file, except that it deals with data, not code.

The Resource Compiler Again

Now we have a .RES file. You might think we would use the linker to combine it with the .OBJ file produced by the normal compiler, but this isn't how it's done. Instead, the .RES file is combined with the .EXE file produced by the linker.

How do we do this? Surprisingly, to combine the .RES file with the .EXE file, we invoke the RC compiler a second time, but this time it plays the role of a file-combiner rather than that of a compiler.

The Header File

Usually a program's .C source file and .RC resource script file must both have access to the values of certain constants. These constants identify menu items and control items (such as pushbuttons) in dialogs, among other things. An easy way for two files to share such information is to place it in a header file, and then #include the header file in both files.

Figure 10-4 shows the various steps and files involved in creating a resource script file, compiling it, and combining it with an application's .EXE file.

Now that we know in a general way what files are used for resources, let's look at the mechanism TCW provides for handling operations on these files.

THE PROJECT FEATURE

As you've proven to yourself already, TCW (or BCW) has no problem compiling and linking a single source file to create an executable Windows file. You select Run from the Run menu, and off she goes. However, things get a little more complicated when we introduce resources. As we've seen, we need to generate a .RES resource object file from a .RC resource script file, and we need to combine the .RES file with our .EXE file. TCW and BCW can't handle this without some additional instructions about what to do. These additional instructions take the form of something called a *project*.

Actually, the Project feature in TCW is rather clever. If you tell it the names of the source files you plan to use (the .C and .RC files), it will know that the .C file

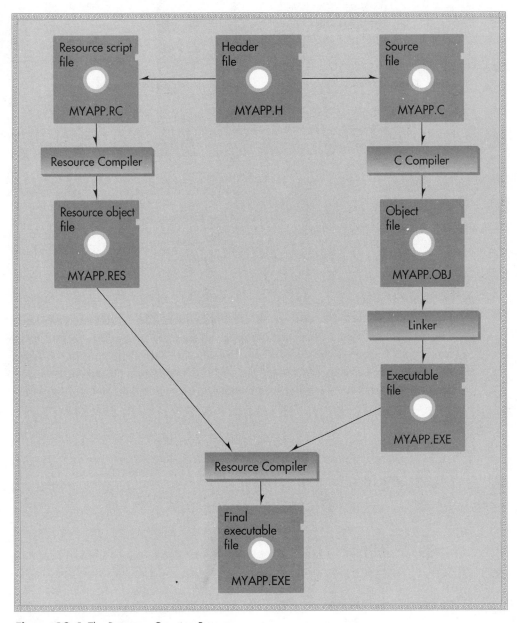

Figure 10-4 The Resource Creation Process

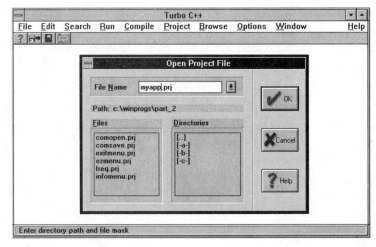

Figure 10-5

The Open

Project

File Dialog

should be compiled with the normal C compiler and linked into an .EXE file, and it will also know that the .RC file should be compiled with the Resource Compiler, and that the resulting .RES file should be combined with the .EXE file again using Resource Compiler. The project feature uses the file extensions to figure all this out. All you have to do is tell the Project feature the names of the source files.

Open a Project

In TCW (or BCW), start with all source files closed. Then select Open Project from the Project menu. You'll see the usual file-opening dialog box, called Open Project File. Change to the directory where you want to develop your project. Now type the project file name into the File Name field, as shown in Figure 10-5.

The project file name should be the name of your program (that is, the name you want to use for the final executable file), plus the .PRJ extension. Thus if you want to generate MYAPP.EXE, type MYAPP.PRJ. Click on OK. The dialog box will go away, and you'll see a Project window open on the bottom of your screen.

Put the Source Files in the Project

Now that you've opened a project file, you need to insert the names of your source files into it. Select Add Item from the Project menu. A dialog box called Add To Project List will open, as shown in Figure 10-6.

All the files in your directory should be shown in this dialog. You want to add your source files to the project: in this example the two files MYAPP.C and MYAPP.RC. Double-click on the first one in the Files list, or type its name into the File Name field. Then click on the Add button. The file name will appear in the

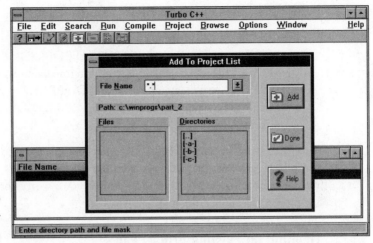

Figure 10-6

The Add To Project
List Dialog

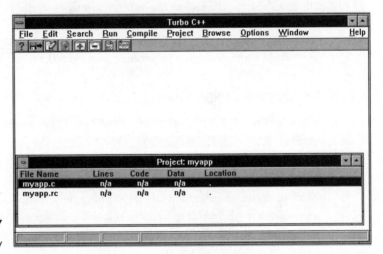

Figure 10-7

The Project Window

Project window at the bottom of the screen. Do the same with the second file. Now click on the Done button in the dialog box. The resulting Project window is shown in Figure 10-7.

If you look in your directory with the Windows File Manager, you'll see that the file MYAPP.PRJ has been created.

Building the Project

Now that you've created the project, you can use it to build your program. That's the easy part. As you did with previous programs, simply select Run from the Run menu. When you do this, the project feature will cause the following steps to take place:

1. MYAPP.C will be compiled into MYAPP.OBJ.
2. MYAPP.OBJ will be linked into an intermediate version of MYAPP.EXE.
3. MYAPP.RC will be compiled into MYAPP.RES.
4. MYAPP.RES will be combined with MYAPP.EXE to produce the final version of MYAPP.EXE.

Notice how smart the project feature is. It knows to use the RC resource compiler to generate the .RES file from the .RC file, and to use it again to combine the .RES file with the .EXE file. You don't need to worry about any of this, because the project feature handles it all.

Opening an Existing Project File

Once you've created a project file, you can simply open this file each time you want to work on your application. Select Open Project from the Project menu and then double-click on the .PRJ file you want to open. You can then edit your source files and rebuild your application by selecting Run from the Run menu as described above.

Modifying a Project File

You can delete files from the project file by selecting Delete Item from the Project menu. You can also add additional files by selecting Add Item.

More Source Files

We've discussed the situation where you have only one .C source file. Many larger applications are divided into multiple source files, such as MYAPP1.C, MYAPP2.C, and so on. When this is the case you must add all these .C files to your project. The linker will combine them into a single .OBJ file, which will, as before, create a single .EXE file, which can be combined with the .RES file. The final .EXE file always has the same name as the project file, regardless of the names of the source files.

SUMMARY

This chapter has described resources and shown you how to use the project tool to combine resources with your program. But until you come face to face with a real live resource, it's hard to picture what all this means. In the next chapter we'll show how to use the project feature to create menus, which are key resources in Windows programs.

CHAPTER 11
MENUS

Suppose that Merlin, King Arthur's favorite sorcerer, suddenly appears in a puff of orange smoke next to your computer. He tells you that you can have one wish. You name it, and Merlin will carry it out. Sounds too good to be true, doesn't it? But menus in a Windows program operate in a similar almost magical way. You choose one action to be performed, and the program carries it out. In fact, menus are even better because you can see at a glance (or with a few mouse clicks) what all your options are. This keeps you from making choices that can't be carried out. (Merlin denies you anything on his long list of forbidden wishes: things that are illegal, immoral, or unchivalrous).

Menus are the most common way users interact with Windows programs; almost every program uses them. They provide a quick and intuitive way to access a program's major features. Also, for users who are unfamiliar with a program, the menu names at the top of the window give the first clues about what the application does; they provide a starting point for exploration. In this chapter we're going to demonstrate several programs with simple menu systems.

There are three new concepts in this chapter, all of which are part of the process of adding a menu to a program. First is the process of combining a resource script file with your program. We covered that in a general way in the last chapter. Second, you need to know how to actually write the resource script file: how do you use it to specify the menu structure? And third, you need to know how to modify your program so that it can respond appropriately when the user selects a menu item.

MENU NOMENCLATURE

To help in our discussion of menus, we should be clear about various terms.

The *menu bar* is the narrow horizontal area of window, just below the title bar, where pop-up menu names appear.

Pop-up menus appear on the menu bar. For example, the pop-up menu names on the menu bar in the Windows Program Manager are File, Options, Window, and Help. Confusingly, pop-up menus are sometimes called pull-down menus, or simply menus. We'll call them pop-up menus because that's the term used in the menu definition in the .RC file. However, the term is misleading, because pop-up menus normally drop *down* from the menu bar.

Menu items appear in a list on a pop-up menu when it is activated by the user. (For example, the menu items in the File pop-up in the Program Manager are New, Open, Move, and so on.) When the user selects one of these items by clicking on it, the program takes the appropriate action. A menu item can also appear directly on the menu bar, instead of on a pop-up menu, although this arrangement is less common.

Technically, the word *menu* by itself refers to the whole organization of the menu bar, the pop-up menus on the menu bar, and menu items in each pop-up menu. A menu in this sense is associated with a particular window (actually with a window class, in most cases). The menu is usually defined in the .RC file, and given a name that can be referred to by other functions.

The *system menu* is triggered by clicking on the box whose icon is a horizontal line, located at the left end of the title bar. (The horizontal line is supposed to represent the (SPACEBAR) on the keyboard. You can bring up the system menu by pressing the (ALT)+(SPACEBAR) key combination.) The system menu pop-up normally contains the menu items Restore, Move, Size, Minimize, Maximize, Close, and Switch To. One important reason for the system menu is to provide users who don't have mice (if there are still any holdouts) with a way to move and resize the window from the keyboard. Also, the Close item gives you a convenient way to terminate a program when the program itself lacks such a menu item.

THE EZMENU PROGRAM

Our first example program is called EZMENU. When you run this program, a menu bar appears with the names File and Edit on it. If you click on File, a pop-up menu will appear with the items Open and Save, as shown in Figure 11-1.

If you select Edit, the resulting pop-up contains the items Cut and Copy. When you select any menu item, a message box appears that reports the selection made.

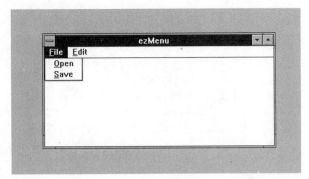

Figure 11-1

File Pop-Up in EZMENU

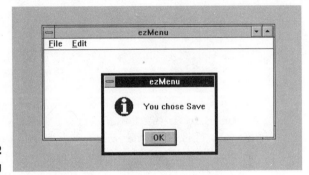

Figure 11-2

Result of Save Item in EZMENU

Figure 11-2 shows the output of the program when the user selects Save from the File menu.

You can also select the pop-up menus and the menu items from the keyboard using the (ALT) key and the key representing the letter that is underlined in each selection. (This feature is built into Windows; you get it for free, with no additional programming on your part.)

THE THREE FILES

When an application uses resources, we must use three different files to describe it. Besides the usual .C source file, there is the .RC resource script file and the .H header file. You create these files with your editor, just as you've been creating .C source files all along.

The Resource Script File

Since we've been describing resources, we'll show how the resource script file looks first. Here's the listing for EZMENU.RC:

```
// ezmenu.rc
// resource script file for ezmenu

#include "ezmenu.h"

ezMenu MENU  // name must agree with szProgName (no quotes)
   BEGIN
      POPUP "&File"
         BEGIN
            MENUITEM "&Open", IDM_OPEN
            MENUITEM "&Save", IDM_SAVE
         END
      POPUP "&Edit"
         BEGIN
            MENUITEM "Cu&t", IDM_CUT
            MENUITEM "&Copy", IDM_COPY
         END
   END
```

Let's look at this file in detail. First there is an #include for the header file EZMENU.H. This file, which we'll examine next, contains #defines for the four menu ID numbers used in the program: IDM_OPEN and so on. As we noted in the last chapter, both the .C source file and the .RC resource script file use these constants, so they must both know what they are. Thus it's convenient to put the constants in a header file and #include this file in both the source and the resource script files.

Next the menu definition is created. It looks a little like a Pascal program, with its BEGIN and END blocks. (You can use braces, as in C programs, if you want; but most programmers prefer the Pascal style.) The menu definition for EZMENU is shown in Figure 11-3.

The basic structure of the menu definition in the resource script file looks like this:

```
ezMenu MENU
   BEGIN
   // popups and menu items
   END
```

The MENU keyword in the first line specifies that we're going to define a menu, rather than some other resource. The name of this menu is ezMenu. Note that it's not enclosed in quotes here.

This menu name in the resource script file must agree with the name referred to in the line

```
wndclass.lpszMenuName = szProgName;
```

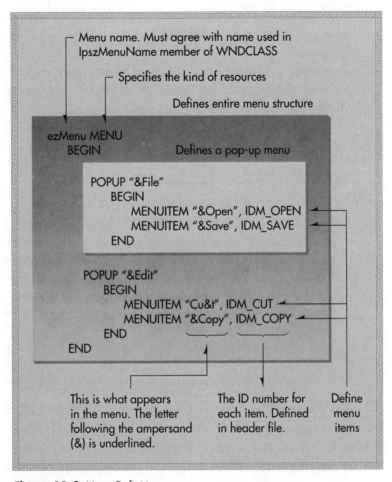

Figure 11-3 Menu Definition

which appears in the STDMAIN.INC file. This name is specified in our .C file in the line

```
PSTR szProgName = "ezMenu";    // quotes
```

Here (of course) you use quotes because you're defining a string constant. Remember, no quotes in the menu definition, but quotes in the .C file.

If the menu name in the resource script file doesn't agree exactly (including case) with the name in the .C file, the menu bar will not appear. And don't expect the compiler (or anything else) to warn you about this. It's another situation where it's better to get it right the first time.

By the way, don't worry about the ninth argument to the CreateWindow() function in the STDMAIN.INC file, which is set to NULL but includes the comment "menu handle". This argument is used only if we have more than one window of the same class, and we want to give each one a different menu. Otherwise the same menu is used for all windows of a class. Usually, as we've noted, there's only one such window per class.

To specify a pop-up menu with a group of menu items, we use an arrangement like

```
POPUP "&Edit"
    BEGIN
        MENUITEM "Cu&t", IDM_CUT
        MENUITEM "&Copy", IDM_COPY
    END
```

The first line specifies, in quotation marks, the name of a pop-up menu. This is the text that will actually appear on the menu bar. We put an ampersand before the letter that the keyboard-oriented user will type (with the (ALT) key) to select the item. In this example, to select the Edit pop-up menu, you would press (ALT)+(E) and to select Cut you would press (ALT)+(T). The ampersand causes the appropriate letter to be underlined when the menu is displayed. If you don't use the ampersand, the first letter of the item will respond to the (ALT) key selection by default. (Don't confuse this way of selecting pop-ups and items with another menu feature, *accelerators*, which allow you to select a menu item with a shortcut or hot-key combination. We cover accelerators in Chapter 33, *Menu Accelerators*.)

BEGIN and END statements surround all the specific menu items. Again, the name that will appear on the pop-up menu, like "&Open", is in quotes. The constants, like IDM_CUT, connect a menu item with a number that can be recognized by the window procedure in our program, as we'll see soon.

Of course you can have many more pop-up menus than we show in this example, and many more menu items in each pop-up.

The Header File

A header file defines the constants used in both the EZMENU.RC and EZMENU.C files. Here's the listing for EZMENU.H:

```
// ezmenu.h
// header file for ezmenu

#define IDM_OPEN    101
#define IDM_SAVE    102
#define IDM_CUT     201
#define IDM_COPY    202
```

The numbers used for the constants can be almost anything you want, but one scheme is to use 101, 102, 103, and so on for the items on the first pop-up, 201,

202, 203, and so on for the items on the second pop-up, and similarly for any other pop-ups.

Needless to say, you should make sure the constants, like IDM_OPEN, are exactly the same in all the files. If you use a constant in the .RC file that doesn't match a definition in the .H file, you'll get strange error messages from the resource compiler, like "END expected." This can be rather mystifying. If you see a message like this, check the spelling of these constants.

The Source File

Here's the key to menu programming: *When the user selects any menu item, Windows sends a WM_COMMAND message to the application's window procedure.* The wParam argument that accompanies this message carries the ID number of the particular menu item selected. This is the basic mechanism a program uses to act on menu item selections. The following program excerpt shows how this looks:

```
switch(msg)
   {
   case WM_COMMAND:        // user selected a menu item
      switch(wParam)
         {
         case IDM_Open:   // user selected Open
         // take appropriate action for Open
         break;

         case IDM_SAVE:   // user selected Save
         // take appropriate action for Save
         break;

         // cases for other menu items
         }
   break;
   // cases for other messages
   }
```

This is a **switch** within a **switch** arrangement. The outer **switch** depends on the message. If the message is WM_COMMAND, the inner **switch** is activated. The inner switch depends on the wParam argument sent with WM_COMMAND.

There are four menu items in the EZMENU program: Open, Save, Cut, and Copy. Each has its own **case** statement within the WM_COMMAND section. Here's the EZMENU.C file:

```
// ezmenu.c
// puts a menu bar in main window

#define STRICT
#include <windows.h>
#include "ezmenu.h"            // header file for IDM_OPEN, etc.
```

```
LRESULT CALLBACK _export WndProc(HWND, UINT, WPARAM, LPARAM);

PSTR szProgName = "ezMenu";          // application name
#include "stdmain.inc"               // standard WinMain function
//////////////////////////////////////////////////////////////////
// main window procedure -- receives messages                    //
//////////////////////////////////////////////////////////////////
LRESULT CALLBACK _export WndProc(HWND hWnd, UINT msg,
                                 WPARAM wParam, LPARAM lParam)
  {
  switch(msg)
    {
    case WM_COMMAND:                 // user selects a menu item
       switch(wParam)                // wParam holds item ID
          {
          case IDM_OPEN:             // user selects Open
             MessageBox(hWnd,"You chose Open",
                 szProgName, MB_OK | MB_ICONINFORMATION);
             break;

          case IDM_SAVE:             // user selects Save
             MessageBox(hWnd,"You chose Save",
                 szProgName, MB_OK | MB_ICONINFORMATION);
             break;

          case IDM_CUT:              // user selects Cut
             MessageBox(hWnd,"You chose Cut",
                 szProgName, MB_OK | MB_ICONINFORMATION);
             break;

          case IDM_COPY:             // user selects Copy
             MessageBox(hWnd,"You chose Copy",
                 szProgName, MB_OK | MB_ICONINFORMATION);
             break;
          }   // end switch wParam
       break;  // end case WM_COMMAND

    case WM_DESTROY:
       PostQuitMessage(0);
       break;

    default:
       return( DefWindowProc(hWnd, msg, wParam, lParam) );
    }   // end switch(msg)

  return 0L;
  } // end WndProc
```

THE INFOMENU PROGRAM

Let's make a slightly more functional menu program. We'll start with the capabilities of the SOLOMEM and SOLOVER programs from Chapters 3, *Types and Names*, and Chapter 4, *Macros Etcetera*, which found respectively the total memory available and the DOS and Windows version numbers. To this we'll add the ability to find out how many programs, or *tasks*, are running in Windows. We'll let the user select one of these three options using a pop-up menu. Figure 11-4 shows what happens when the the user clicks on the Info pop-up.

As you can see, there are three menu items on this pop-up: Memory, Version, and Tasks. Selecting any one of these items causes a message box to appear. The Memory item shows the global memory available, Version shows the Windows and DOS version numbers, and Tasks shows the number of currently executing programs.

The resource script file defines this menu structure: one pop-up with three items. Here's the listing for INFOMENU.RC:

```
// infomenu.rc
// resource script file for infomenu

#include "infomenu.h"

infoMenu MENU  // name must agree with szProgName
   BEGIN
      POPUP "&Info"
         BEGIN
            MENUITEM "&Memory", IDM_MEMORY
            MENUITEM "&Version", IDM_VERSION
            MENUITEM "&Tasks", IDM_TASKS
         END
   END
```

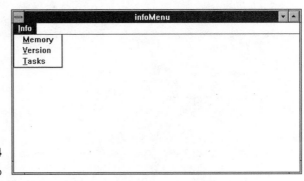

Figure 11-4
Selecting the Info Pop-Up

The header file reflects the ID numbers for the three menu items. Here's the listing for INFOMENU.H:

```
// infomenu.h
// header file for infomenu

#define IDM_MEMORY    101
#define IDM_VERSION   102
#define IDM_TASKS     103
```

The source file installs three **case** statements, within the WM_COMMAND **case** statement, to handle the three menu items. The code in these **case** statements is a bit longer than in EZMENU, but the principle is the same: the code following the **case** for a particular menu item will be executed when the item is selected. Here's the listing for INFOMENU.C:

```
// infomenu.c
// uses menu to select which kind of system info to display

#define STRICT
#include <windows.h>
#include "infomenu.h"

LRESULT CALLBACK _export WndProc(HWND, UINT, WPARAM, LPARAM);

PSTR szProgName = "infoMenu";      // application name
#include "stdmain.inc"             // standard WinMain function
///////////////////////////////////////////////////////////////
// main window procedure -- receives messages                  //
///////////////////////////////////////////////////////////////
LRESULT CALLBACK _export WndProc(HWND hWnd, UINT msg,
                              WPARAM wParam, LPARAM lParam)
   {
   char szBuffer[80];        // buffer for string
   DWORD dwMemAvail;         // free memory
   DWORD dwVersion;          // packed version info
   WORD wMsdos;              // MS-DOS; high=major, low=minor
   WORD wWindows;            // Windows; low=major, high=minor
   UINT nTasks;              // number of tasks running in Windows

   switch(msg)
      {
      case WM_COMMAND:                // user selects a menu item
         switch(wParam)              // wParam holds item ID
            {
            case IDM_MEMORY:          // user selects Memory
               dwMemAvail = GetFreeSpace(0);  // get free memory
               wsprintf(szBuffer, "Mem available: %lu", dwMemAvail);
               MessageBox(hWnd, szBuffer, szProgName, MB_OK);
               break;
```

```
    case IDM_VERSION:            // user selects Version

        dwVersion = GetVersion();        // get version number
        wMsdos = HIWORD(dwVersion);    // MS-DOS in high half
        wWindows = LOWORD(dwVersion); // Windows in low half
        if( MessageBox(NULL, "Find DOS version as well?",
                    szProgName, MB_YESNO | MB_ICONQUESTION)
                    == IDYES )
                                       // do Windows and DOS
            wsprintf( szBuffer, "Windows %u.%u\nMS-DOS %u.%u",
                LOBYTE(wWindows), HIBYTE(wWindows),
                HIBYTE(wMsdos), LOBYTE(wMsdos) );
        else                           // do only Windows
            wsprintf( szBuffer, "Windows %u.%u",
                LOBYTE(wWindows), HIBYTE(wWindows) );
        MessageBox(hWnd, szBuffer, szProgName, MB_OK);
        break;

    case IDM_TASKS:              // user selects Tasks
        nTasks = GetNumTasks();
        wsprintf(szBuffer, "Number of tasks: %u", nTasks);
        MessageBox(hWnd, szBuffer, szProgName, MB_OK);
        break;

    }   // end switch wParam
    break;  // end case WM_COMMAND

case WM_DESTROY:
    PostQuitMessage(0);
    break;

default:
    return( DefWindowProc(hWnd, msg, wParam, lParam) );
}   // end switch(msg)

return 0L;
}  // end WndProc
```

The code to handle the first two menu items in this program should be familiar from the SOLOMEM and SOLOVER program in Part One, *Getting Started.* For the third item, we find the number of tasks running in Windows by calling GetNumTasks(). This API function returns the number of tasks as an integer of type UINT, which we display in a message box in the usual way.

THE EXITMENU PROGRAM

Our last example introduces three new wrinkles in menu usage: menu separators, the use of menu items directly on the menu bar, and programming an Exit menu item. Here's the listing for EXITMENU.RC:

```
// exitmenu.rc
// resource file for exitmenu

#include "exitmenu.h"

ExitMenu MENU   // name must agree with szProgName
    BEGIN
        POPUP "&File"
            BEGIN
                MENUITEM "&Open", IDM_OPEN
                MENUITEM "&Save", IDM_SAVE
                MENUITEM SEPARATOR
                MENUITEM "E&xit", IDM_EXIT
            END
        MENUITEM "&About", IDM_ABOUT
        MENUITEM "&Help", IDM_HELP
    END
```

Menu Separators

A menu separator is a line that separates two menu items on a pop-up menu. It is often used to divide the menu items into two categories. In EXITMENU we use a separator in the File menu. This is accomplished with the keyword SEPARATOR, used with MENUITEM, as shown in this fragment from EXITMENU.RC:

```
MENUITEM "&Open", IDM_OPEN
MENUITEM "&Save", IDM_SAVE
MENUITEM SEPARATOR
MENUITEM "E&xit", IDM_EXIT
```

The Open and Save items are above the separator, and Exit is below. The separator implies that the items above it and the items below have different purposes: file-related actions above and exit actions below. Figure 11-5 shows the File pop-up.

Menu Items on the Menu Bar

When you click on About and Help, which appear on the menu bar, you don't get a pop-up, but instead a message box, as if you had selected a menu item. In fact, About and Help are actual menu items, even though they appear on the menu bar. Figure 11-6 shows what happens when you select About.

Selecting Help evinces another message box, that says "This function not implemented." The Open and Save items on the File menu produce this same message box.

We put the About and Help menu items directly on the menu bar by not enclosing them in a POPUP/BEGIN/END arrangement in the menu definition. When you select one of these items, an action happens immediately.

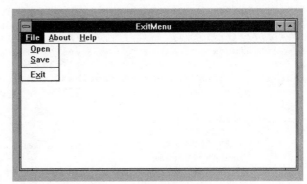

Figure 11-5

File Pop-Up in EXITMENU

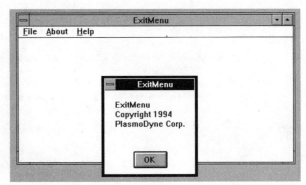

Figure 11-6

Result of Selecting About

Here's the listing for EXITMENU.H:

```
// exitmenu.h
// header file for exitmenu

#define IDM_OPEN    101
#define IDM_SAVE    102
#define IDM_EXIT    103
#define IDM_HELP    200
#define IDM_ABOUT   300
```

And finally, here's the listing for EXITMENU.C:

```
// exitmenu.c
// shows Exit as a menu item

#define STRICT
#include <windows.h>
#include "exitmenu.h"    // header file for IDM_ABOUT, etc.

LRESULT CALLBACK _export WndProc(HWND, UINT, WPARAM, LPARAM);
```

```
PSTR szProgName = "ExitMenu";        // application name
#include "stdmain.inc"               // standard WinMain function
///////////////////////////////////////////////////////////////////
// main window procedure -- receives messages                     //
///////////////////////////////////////////////////////////////////
LRESULT CALLBACK _export WndProc(HWND hWnd, UINT msg,
                                 WPARAM wParam, LPARAM lParam)
   {
   switch(msg)
      {
      case WM_COMMAND:                 // menu processing
         switch(wParam)
            {
            case IDM_ABOUT:          // user selects About
               MessageBox(hWnd,
               "ExitMenu\nCopyright 1994\nPlasmoDyne Corp.\n",
                        szProgName, MB_OK);
               break;

            case IDM_OPEN:           // user selects Open
            case IDM_SAVE:           // user selects Save
            case IDM_HELP:           // if user selects Help
               MessageBox(hWnd,"This function not implemented",
                   "No Cause For Alarm", MB_OK | MB_ICONINFORMATION);
               break;

            case IDM_EXIT:           // user selects Exit
               if( MessageBox(hWnd, "Terminate the program?",
                   szProgName, MB_YESNO | MB_ICONQUESTION) == IDYES )
                  DestroyWindow(hWnd);
               break;
            }    // end switch wParam
         break;  // end case WM_COMMAND

      case WM_CLOSE:                   // Close selected on system menu
         if( MessageBox(hWnd, "Terminate the program?",
            szProgName, MB_YESNO | MB_ICONQUESTION) == IDYES )
            DestroyWindow(hWnd);
         break;

      case WM_DESTROY:
         PostQuitMessage(0);
         break;

      default:
         return( DefWindowProc(hWnd, msg, wParam, lParam) );
      }    // end switch(msg)

   return 0L;
   } // end WndProc
```

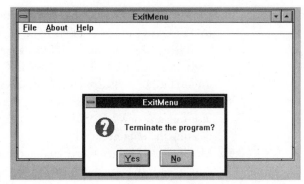

Figure 11-7

Result of Selecting Exit

Handling an Exit Menu Item

What does our program do with the Exit menu item? As you can see in the EXITMENU.C file, the program's response to this message is a message box that asks "Terminate the program?" and provides Yes and No buttons, as shown in Figure 11-7.

If the user selects No, no further action is taken. If the user selects Yes, the program executes the DestroyWindow() function, which sends the WM_DESTROY message to the window, causing the program to terminate (as we discussed earlier). This mechanism provides a way to ensure that the user really means to terminate, and didn't select Exit by accident. We could also insert code here to carry out shutdown activities like closing files.

But what happens if the user selects Close from the system menu? This generates a WM_CLOSE message, which causes the same result as the IDM_EXIT selection: a dialog box that asks "Terminate the program?" We've ensured that the user can't terminate without getting a message box.

SUMMARY

How do you create a new program that uses menus? If you're not trying to add menus to an already-existing program, you can clone the EZMENU program from this chapter and modify it with pop-ups and menu items of your choice. (Of course there are other ways to begin, such as writing all your files from scratch or cloning some other program.) To clone EZMENU, follow these steps:

1. Copy the files EZMENU.RC, EZMENU.H, and EZMENU.C, renaming them at the same time (to MYPROG.RC, and so on, or whatever your program name is).

2. Create a new project file that contains the new source file names (MYPROG.C and MYPROG.RC).

3. Modify the .RC resource script file, changing the comment at the beginning, the name of the include file, the name of the menu (this is important!), and the contents of the menu structure.

4. Modify the .H header file, changing the comment at the beginning, inserting any new constants used in the resource script file and, of course, deleting the ones not used.

5. Modify the .C source file, changing the comment at the beginning, the #include for the header file, and the szProgName variable (which must agree with the menu name in the .RC file). Change the arrangement of the WM_COMMAND section so there is a **case** for each menu item, and incorporate the new functionality triggered by selecting these items.

6. Build your program by selecting Run from the Run menu.

Sometimes you start with an existing program and want to add menus to it. Here are the steps necessary to add menu capability to an application that consists of a .C source file.

1. Create an .RC file (MYPROG.RC) with the menu definition in it. Make sure the menu name in the definition agrees with the lpszMenuName member of the WNDCLASS structure in WinMain().

2. Create an .H (MYPROG.H) header file that #defines the constants used for menu items in the .RC file.

3. Add code to your .C source file (MYPROG.C) to process the WM_COMMAND message. This should consist of a switch statement in which there is a **case** statement for each of the menu-item constants defined in the .H file. The code in the **case** section will be executed when the menu item is selected.

4. Create a project file, and add the .C and .RC source files to it.

5. Build your program by selecting Run from the Run menu.

Although we've covered the most basic aspects of using menus, there is a great deal more to know. For instance, while a program is running you can *check* a menu item (place a check mark next to it) to indicate it is already selected, *gray* an item when an option is not available in certain circumstances, and add and delete items. We'll demonstrate such advanced menu features in Part Six, *Getting Fancy with the GUI*.

CHAPTER 12

DISK FILES

*I*n the days of King Arthur, permanent storage of data was handled by monks in monasteries, who kept entire rooms full of parchment scrolls. Parchment was made from sheep or goat skin, and could be written upon with ink and then rolled up. When a particular scroll became too old and crumbly, after a hundred years or so, a monk (working in a room called the scriptorium) was assigned to copy it onto a new piece of parchment. In this way monks managed to keep the records of Greek and Roman civilization alive for more than a thousand years.

Disk files are no doubt faster and more convenient than sheepskin scrolls, but they serve the same purpose: keeping data safe for a period of time. Most programs need to use disk files. Although they are not part of the user interface, we introduce them in this section because they are an indispensable element in most Windows programs, and because interacting with them gives us an excuse to introduce common dialog boxes, a topic which definitely is part of the user interface and which we cover in the next chapter.

WINDOWS FILE FUNCTIONS

Beginning with version 3.0, Windows supplies its own set of file-management functions. (Actually Microsoft merely decided to acknowledge functions that existed before but had been undocumented.) We'll introduce these functions in this chapter. They are sophisticated functions designed specifically for Windows. Table 12-1 lists these functions and their roles in file handling.

Be careful writing these function names. Note the underscore before the names. This is left over from older versions of Windows when these functions were

Table 12-1 Windows File Functions

Function	Purpose
_lcreat()	Creates or opens a file (truncates existing file to zero length)
_lopen()	Opens a file (it must already exist)
_lread()	Reads data from a file into a buffer
_lwrite()	Writes data from a buffer to a file
_llseek()	Moves the file pointer
_lclose()	Closes a file

undocumented. The "l" indicates that the functions take long pointers to the data buffer. Note the lack of the second "e" in _lcreat(), and the double "l" in _llseek().

We should note that there are other approaches to reading and writing files in Windows. One common one is to use the Windows API function OpenFile() to open a file, and then operate on the file with the normal C-library low-level file functions read(), write(), seek(), close(), and so on. One disadvantage with this approach is that these C functions take near pointers to the data buffer (unless you're using a Large or Compact memory model). Thus these functions won't work with data in segments outside your program's data segment, such as memory allocated with GlobalAlloc(), which would present a problem for large files. (We'll discuss memory management in Part Seven, *Other Topics*). Also, the C functions may not work in future versions of Windows. We'll stick with the native Windows file functions for their clarity and simplicity.

We use two example programs in this chapter. The first, OUTFILE, writes text data to a file; and the second, INFILE, reads the data back from the file and displays it. Neither of these programs uses menus or other resources (as the programs in the last chapter did), so you can compile them without a project file.

THE OUTFILE PROGRAM

This program does only one thing: it writes text to a file. The text is one stanza of the poem "Kubla Khan" (for variety, not all our text examples are concerned with knights). The file it is written to is called FILETEST.DAT. We assume this file will be placed in a directory called C:\DATA which has already been created—that is, you need to create it before running the program. Since the program does not involve any interaction with the user, we dispense with the main window and the WndProc() function, as we did in the SOLOMEM and SOLOVER programs in Part One, *Getting Started*. Here's the listing for OUTFILE.C:

```c
// outfile.c
// writes text to file

#define STRICT              // strict type-checking
#include <windows.h>        // include file for all Windows programs

#define LINES 7             // number of text strings
#define MAXLENGTH 80        // maximum length of each string

char khan[LINES][MAXLENGTH] = {  // array of fixed-length buffers
"In Xanadu did Kubla Khan",      // initialized with strings
"   A stately pleasure-dome decree",
"Where Alph, the sacred river, ran",
"Through caverns measureless to man",
"   Down to a sunless sea.",
"",
"from \"Kubla Khan\" by Samuel Taylor Coleridge" };

PSTR szProgName = "OutFile";     // application name
//////////////////////////////////////////////////////////////////
// WinMain() -- program entry point                              //
//////////////////////////////////////////////////////////////////
#pragma argsused                 // ignore unused arguments

int PASCAL WinMain(HINSTANCE hInstance, HINSTANCE hPrevInst,
                LPSTR lpszCmdLine, int nCmdShow)
   {
   HFILE hFile;                   // file handle
   UINT cbLength;                 // characters written

                                  // create the file
   hFile = _lcreat("c:\\data\\filetest.dat", 0);
   if(hFile == HFILE_ERROR)
      {
      MessageBox(NULL,"Error: Cannot create file",
            szProgName, MB_OK | MB_ICONINFORMATION);
      return NULL;
      }
                                  // write entire array to file
   cbLength = _lwrite(hFile, khan, LINES*MAXLENGTH);
   if(cbLength == (UINT)HFILE_ERROR)
      {
      MessageBox(NULL,"Error: Cannot write to file",
            szProgName, MB_OK | MB_ICONINFORMATION);
      return NULL;
      }
   _lclose(hFile);                // close file
```

```
    return NULL;     // return NULL if no message loop
}   // end WinMain
```

We could have used an array of pointers to strings for the text, this is more efficient in terms of memory usage. Using a two-dimensional array, however, simplifies the programming.

The _lcreat() Function

The _lcreat() function creates a new file, or opens an existing file and truncates it to zero length. (Be careful not to use this function on an existing file whose contents you want to keep.) Here's the statement in OUTFILE that invokes this function:

```
hFile = _lcreat("c:\\data\\filetest.dat", 0);
```

The _lcreat() function takes two parameters. The first is the file name or the path-plus-file name, in the form of a pointer to a null-terminated character string (type LPCSTR, a far pointer to a constant string). The double backslashes in the path name are necessary because C interprets a single backslash as an escape character (used for such characters as '\t' and '\n'). Doubling it makes it read as a single backslash.

In OUTFILE we use a string constant. The second parameter is an integer specifying the file attributes. Table 12-2 shows these attributes. In most situations you use a value of 0 for the Normal attribute.

The _lcreat() function returns a file handle of type HFILE if the function is successful, and the constant HFILE_ERROR otherwise. We use a message box in OUTFILE to inform the user if the file could not be created. This error commonly happens because the specified path does not exist.

If you specify only a file name instead of a path-plus-file name as the first argument to _lcreat(), the file will be written to the current directory. In OUTFILE we use a

Table 12-2 Attributes for _lcreat()

Value	Attribute
0	Normal—no restriction on reading and writing
1	Read-only—cannot be opened for writing
2	Hidden—does not appear in directory
3	System—does not appear in directory

complete path name. If you used only the file name, then when you ran OUTFILE from within your compiler, the file would be written to the directory where the compiler itself was located, rather than the directory where your application is. That is, it would be placed in \TCWIN\BIN (or BORLANDC\BIN). Whereas, if you ran the application directly from the Program Manager, the file would be written to the same directory as the application. Using the full path name ensures the file will be created in the same directory every time.

The _lwrite() Function

The _lwrite function, which writes data from a buffer to a file, takes three parameters. The first is the file handle, of type HFILE, obtained from _lcreat() or _lopen(). The second is a pointer, of type **const void _huge***, to the data buffer. The third is the size of the buffer, which is type UINT. In our example, this length is found by multiplying the number of text lines (the constant LINES) by the length of each line (MAXLENGTH). Here's our invocation of this function in OUTFILE:

```
cbLength = _lwrite(hFile, khan, LINES*MAXLENGTH);
```

This function returns the number of bytes actually written, or the constant HFILE_ERROR if the operation was unsuccessful. The return value is type UINT. We again use a message box to inform the user if the data could not be written to the file.

Notice that we write the entire array, consisting of LINES times MAXLENGTH characters, to the file. This is not a very efficient way to store text, since many of the lines are shorter than MAXLENGTH. However, it simplifies the program.

The _lclose() Function

When we've finished writing to the file, we close it with the _lclose() function, which takes the file handle as its only argument.

THE INFILE PROGRAM

The INFILE program reads the FILETEST.DAT file created by OUTFILE, and displays the data. This requires a full-scale Windows program with a WndProc() function. We read the data when the program is first started, which is signaled by a WM_CREATE message, and store the data in a buffer. We display the buffer contents every time we get a WM_PAINT message. Figure 12-1 shows the output of INFILE.

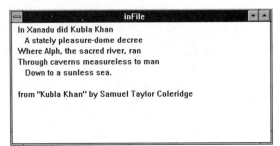

Figure 12-1

Output of INFILE Program

Here's the listing for INFILE.C:

```
// infile.c
// reads and displays text from file

#define STRICT
#include <windows.h>

#define LINES      11     // number of text lines
#define MAXLENGTH  80     // maximum length of line
#define TMARGIN    3      // top margin, in pixels
#define LMARGIN    10     // left margin, in pixels
#define CYCHAR     18     // height of characters, in pixels

                          // prototype
LRESULT CALLBACK _export WndProc(HWND, UINT, WPARAM, LPARAM);

char aText[LINES][MAXLENGTH]; // array of characters

PSTR szProgName = "inFile";   // program name
#include "stdmain.inc"        // standard WinMain() function
//////////////////////////////////////////////////////////////
// main window procedure -- receives messages               //
//////////////////////////////////////////////////////////////
LRESULT CALLBACK _export WndProc(HWND hWnd, UINT msg,
                            WPARAM wParam, LPARAM lParam)
   {
   HDC hDC;                 // handle for the device context
   PAINTSTRUCT ps;          // holds PAINT information
   HFILE hFile;             // file handle
   UINT cbLength;           // characters read
   int index;               // loop counter

   switch(msg)
      {
      case WM_CREATE:        // when program first runs
                             // open file
         hFile = _lopen("c:\\data\\filetest.dat", READ);
         if(hFile == HFILE_ERROR)
            {
```

```
        MessageBox(NULL,"Error: Cannot open file",
                "OutFile", MB_OK | MB_ICONINFORMATION);
        return NULL;
        }
                            // read entire array from file
    cbLength = _lread(hFile, aText, LINES*MAXLENGTH);
    if(cbLength == (UINT)HFILE_ERROR)
        {
        MessageBox(NULL, "Error: Cannot read from file",
                "OutFile", MB_OK | MB_ICONINFORMATION);
        return NULL;
        }
    _lclose(hFile);    // close file

    break;

case WM_PAINT:                      // repaint the screen
    hDC = BeginPaint(hWnd, &ps);    // get device context

    for(index = 0; index < LINES; index++ )    // for each line
        TextOut( hDC, LMARGIN, TMARGIN + CYCHAR*index, // display
                aText[index], lstrlen(aText[index]) ); // text

    EndPaint(hWnd, &ps);            // painting complete
    break;  //  End of WM_PAINT

case WM_DESTROY:
    PostQuitMessage(0);
    break;

default:
    return( DefWindowProc(hWnd, msg, wParam, lParam) );
}   // end switch(msg)

return 0L;
} // end WndProc
```

In OUTFILE, to simplify the programming, we use the constants LINES and MAXLENGTH for the number of text lines in the file and their length. However, in most programs you wouldn't know in advance how large the file to be read was. We'll see how to handle more complex situations in future chapters.

How Long Should Files Be Open?

You need to think about the issue of how long a file should be kept open. There are two philosophies about this. The first holds that files should be opened and closed again during the processing of a single message; that is, before returning from WndProc(). The second view is that there's no harm in keeping files open as long as necessary.

Close Them Quick

According to the first school of thought, files should be open just long enough to read data into memory, or to write it to disk. The user selects Open, the file is opened, the data is read into memory, and the file is closed immediately with _lclose(). The user then works with the data in memory. When the user selects Save, the file is opened again, the data is written to it, and the file is closed again. This approach avoids potential problems, such as one application trying to write to a file that has been opened by another.

A corollary of this doctrine is that the file should be opened, read or written to, and then closed, all during the processing of a single message. If this weren't done, another application might take over the system before the file could be closed. Further, if it's necessary to close the file before returning from the message, it follows that you should read or write to the file as quickly as possible, using one or just a few _lread() or _lwrite() statements. You shouldn't nibble away at it byte by byte. This is because every message should be processed quickly to avoid denying other applications access to the system.

Don't Worry About It

The second school of thought points out that Windows has built-in protections against one application trashing the files of another. Programs that subscribe to this second approach can keep a file open for the entire time that the user wants to work with it. The user selects Open, the file is opened, the user works with the file (adding new data to it, searching it, or whatever) and later, when the user selects Save, the file is closed.

Which approach is right? The bottom line is that it's probably somewhat safer to close files before returning from WndProc(), but if there's a good reason for keeping a file open longer, go ahead and do it.

But Always Close Floppies

The above discussion applies only to the hard disk. Files on floppies should always be closed immediately, since the user can remove a floppy from the drive at any time. If this happens while a file is open, disaster results.

The _lopen() Function

The _lopen() function opens an existing file. Here's how it looks in INFILE:

```
hFile = _lopen("c:\\data\\filetest.dat", READ);
```

This function takes two parameters. The first is the file name, or path-plus-name, in the form of a far pointer to a null-terminated string, just as with _lcreat(). The

Table 12-3 Access Modes for _lopen()

Constant	Access Mode
READ	File open for reading only
WRITE	File open for writing only
READ_WRITE	File open for both reading and writing

second parameter is a file-access code (type **int**). There are two parts to this code: an access mode and a share mode. The share mode specifies whether other applications can read or write to the file while our application has it open. We'll ignore this option. The access mode specifies whether we want to open the file for reading, writing, or both, as shown in Table 12-3.

The _lopen() function returns the handle to the file if successful, and otherwise the HFILE_ERROR value.

The _lread() Function

Like _lwrite(), the _lread() function takes as its three arguments the handle of the file to be read, the address of the buffer to write the data into, and the size of the buffer. Here's how it looks in INFILE:

```
cbLength = _lread(hFIle, aText, LINES*MAXLENGTH);
```

The return value (type UINT) is the number of bytes actually read. If this is less than the size of the buffer, then we can assume the EOF was reached. If the return value is HFILE_ERROR, the read was unsuccessful.

The _llseek() Function

Although we don't use it in our example programs, we'll mention the _llseek() function for completeness. This function sets the *file pointer*—the byte number where the next read or write will begin. It allows you to read or write data in the middle of a file, or to determine a file's size. It takes three arguments, of which the first is the file handle (type HFILE). The second is the *offset* (type LONG). This is the number of bytes between the origin and the place where the file pointer should be moved. The third argument is an *origin code* (type **int**) that specifies where the origin is located. The possibilities are shown in Table 12-4.

Table 12-4 Origin Code for _llseek()

Code	Origin Location
0	Beginning of file
1	Current position
2	End of file

For example, if the offset is 10 and the origin code is 0, the file pointer will be moved to a position 10 bytes from the beginning of the file. Figure 12-2 shows these offsets.

The return value (type LONG) of _llseek() is the new file position, measured in bytes from the beginning of the file. If the function is unsuccessful, the return value is HFILE_ERROR. You can use _llseek() to find a file's size by using an offset of 0 and an origin code of 2. The return value is then the file size.

FUNCTIONS FOR HUGE DATA

If you are using huge data objects (single data items like arrays that are larger than one 64K segment), you'll need to use different Windows file functions for reading and writing: _hread() and _hwrite(). The normal functions can't handle the

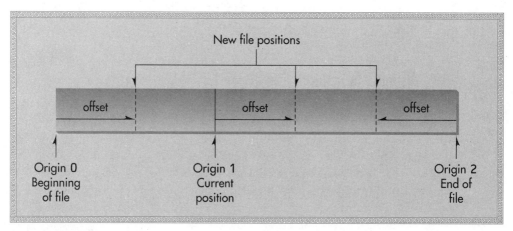

Figure 12-2 Origins, Offsets, and the _llseek() Function

situation where a single object crosses a segment boundary, but _hread() and _hwrite() can. These functions have arguments and return values similar to _lread() and _lwrite(), except that the data argument for the length of the buffer to be read or written is type **long** instead of type UINT.

SUMMARY

To write to a file:

1. Use _lcreat() to create and open the file.
2. Use _lwrite() to write data from a buffer to the file.
3. Use _lclose() to close the file.

To read from a file:

1. Use _lopen() to open the file.
2. Use _lread() to read data from the file to a buffer.
3. Use _lclose() to close the file.

Be sure to check the return values from _lcreat(), _lopen(), _lread(), and _lwrite(), because these operations may cause errors even if your program is perfect.

Now that you know how to work with disk files, let's see how the user-interface part of file handling works.

CHAPTER 13

THE FILE COMMON DIALOGS

Legend has it that young Arthur proved he was the rightful king of Britain by pulling a sword from a stone. He used this sword throughout his life in many battles and adventures; it was called *Excalibur*, or the singing sword. It had magic powers, and gave the person using it an almost insurmountable advantage on the battlefield, with the power to fight like ten ordinary knights.

In this chapter we're going to introduce a Windows feature that gives the programmer a similar kind of power. It enables you to cut some of the most-dreaded Windows problems down to size. In Windows this magic sword is called a *common dialog box*. Dialog boxes are special windows that appear on the screen and invite the user to enter data. They contain various kinds of *controls*, such as pushbuttons, static text, radio buttons, check boxes, list boxes, edit fields, and combo boxes. Figure 13-1 shows these typical controls.

Each kind of control is appropriate for a certain kind of information. An edit field lets the user type in a text string, radio buttons let the user make a choice among several mutually exclusive options, and so forth.

When you mention dialog boxes, a Windows programmer will probably think of *custom* dialog boxes: those that are designed and implemented by the programmer. In custom dialogs, the programmer specifies exactly what controls will appear in the dialog, where they will be placed, and what they will do. Programming custom dialog boxes, even simple ones, requires some work. Programming more complex custom dialogs, such as those typically used to open files, can be a major challenge, even for experienced Windows programmers. They are like powerful and evil knights, impossible to defeat without a lengthy and bloody battle.

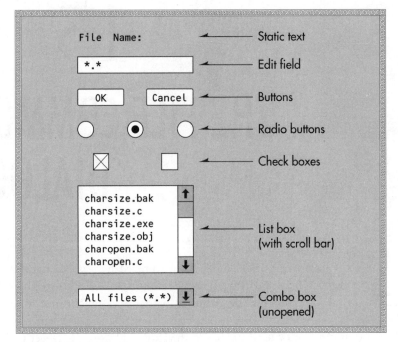

Figure 13-1 Dialog Box Controls

However, beginning in version 3.1, there are also dialog boxes built into Windows. They are called *common* dialogs, because they can be used by any Windows application. Common dialogs are much easier to program than custom dialogs, because the placement and functionality of the controls has already been defined. They can multiply your programming efforts manyfold, and are truly the "singing swords" of Windows programming.

COMMON DIALOGS

Common dialogs perform a variety of tasks in Windows programming. They are used in situations where it would be complicated and time consuming for a programmer to achieve the same effect. Table 13-1 shows the common dialog boxes available.

In this chapter we'll examine two of the most useful common dialogs: those that allow the user to open and save files. As we noted, creating full-featured custom Open and Save dialog boxes is quite complicated. Fortunately, common dialogs make the process easy.

The file-oriented programs in the last chapter always worked on the same file, FILETEST.DAT. Of course this is rather limiting. Most applications allow the user to

Table 13-1 Common Dialogs

Dialog Name	Function	Purpose
Open	GetOpenFileName()	Open a file
Save As	GetSaveFileName()	Name and save a file
Color	ChooseColor()	Define a custom color
Font	ChooseFont()	Choose a text font, style, size, and color
Print	PrintDlg()	Print a file
Find	FindText()	Enter a search string
Replace	ReplaceText()	Enter search and replacement strings

specify the name of the file to be read or written. In Windows programs, file selection is usually handled with a dialog box, into which the user enters the file name.

There are two example programs in this chapter, COMOPEN and COMSAVE. The first imitates the action of INFILE in the last chapter, which opened a text file and displayed its contents, except that COMOPEN supplies an Open dialog box so the user can open any file. The COMSAVE example works like OUTFILE, writing text to a file, except that it uses the Save As dialog to permit the user to save the text under any file name.

In the next chapter we'll show a more sophisticated application that uses the Open common dialog, file functions, and text display. We'll see some other kinds of common dialogs later in this book.

THE OPEN COMMON DIALOG

The COMOPEN example has a single pop-up menu called File, which in turn contains a single menu item called Open. When the user selects Open, the Open common dialog appears. Figure 13-2 shows what it looks like.

This dialog box provides amazing functionality. You can open a file by double-clicking on a name in the list of files, or by typing the name into the edit field. You can change directories by double-clicking on the folders in the Directories list box; this will display the files in the new directory. You can selectively display files with different file extensions, using the combo box called List Files of Type; and you can

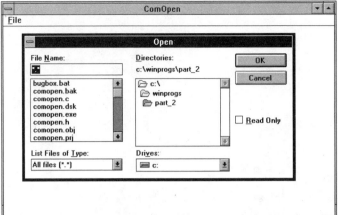

Figure 13-2

The Open Common

Dialog Box

change the drive letter using the Drives combo box. You can even request that files be opened as read-only files by clicking on the Read Only check box.

COMOPEN uses the Open dialog to get a file name. It then opens and displays a text file of this name, using the file functions discussed in Chapter 12, *Disk Files*. The user can open any file; but to display correctly, this file must be in the same format as the file used in the last chapter, which was named FILETEST.DAT and was placed in the \DATA directory. So (unless you want to change its name) this is the only file you'll be able to display.

To use the Open dialog in COMOPEN, select a file, changing directories if necessary, and click on OK. The Open dialog vanishes and the text is displayed. (See Figure 12-1 in the last chapter.)

Because COMOPEN uses a menu, it requires a resource script file and a header file. The resource script file is very simple, since there's only one pop-up and one menu item. Here's the listing for COMOPEN.RC:

```
// comopen.rc
// resource file for comopen

#include "comopen.h"

ComOpen MENU     // must agree with szProgName
    BEGIN
        POPUP "&File"
            BEGIN
                MENUITEM "&Open", IDM_OPEN
            END

    END
```

There's only one item on the header file: the ID of the Open menu item. Here's the listing for COMOPEN.H:

```
// comopen.h
// ID for comopen

#define IDM_OPEN        100
```

The COMOPEN program responds to only one message: WM_COMMAND, with a wParam value of IDM_OPEN. When it receives this message, it displays the Open common dialog. The bulk of the program is involved with handling the Open dialog. Here's the listing for COMOPEN.C:

```
// comopen.c
// uses "Open" common dialog box to open file for display

#define STRICT
#include <windows.h>
#include <commdlg.h>              // for GetOpenFileName()
#include <memory.h>               // for memset()
#include "comopen.h"              // for menu #defines

#define LINES      11             // number of text lines
#define MAXLENGTH 80              // maximum length of line
#define TMARGIN    3              // top margin, in pixels
#define LMARGIN   10              // left margin, in pixels
#define CYCHAR    18              // height of characters, in pixels
#define BUFFSIZE 256              // buffer size
char szPath[BUFFSIZE];            // buffer for file path+name
char szTitle[BUFFSIZE];           // buffer for file name (no path)
char szString[BUFFSIZE];          // buffer for various strings

char aText[LINES][MAXLENGTH];     // array of characters

                                  // prototype
LRESULT CALLBACK _export WndProc(HWND, UINT, WPARAM, LPARAM);

PSTR szProgName = "ComOpen";      // application name
#include "stdmain.inc"            // standard WinMain() function
////////////////////////////////////////////////////////////////
// main window procedure -- receives messages                  //
////////////////////////////////////////////////////////////////
LRESULT CALLBACK _export WndProc(HWND hWnd, UINT msg,
                            WPARAM wParam, LPARAM lParam)
   {
   HDC hDC;                       // handle for the device context
   PAINTSTRUCT ps;                // holds PAINT information
   HFILE hFile;                   // file handle
   UINT cbLength;                 // characters read
   int index;                     // loop counter
```

```
OPENFILENAME ofn;               // for GetOpenFileName()
LPCSTR szFilter[] = { "All files (*.*)", "*.*",     // extension
                   "Data files (*.dat)", "*.dat",  // filters
                   "" };
switch(msg)
   {
   case WM_COMMAND:            // menu command
      switch(wParam)
         {
         case IDM_OPEN:        // user chose Open
            {
            szPath[0] = '\0';                  // empty the name field
                                               // zero the structure
            memset( &ofn, 0, sizeof(OPENFILENAME) );
                                               // size of structure
            ofn.lStructSize = sizeof(OPENFILENAME);
            ofn.hwndOwner = hWnd;              // owner is main window
            ofn.lpstrFilter = szFilter[0]; // filter string array
            ofn.lpstrFile = szPath;           // path+name buffer
            ofn.nMaxFile = BUFFSIZE;          // size of above
            ofn.lpstrFileTitle = szTitle;  // file name buffer
            ofn.nMaxFileTitle = BUFFSIZE;  // size of above
                                               // require valid names
            ofn.Flags = OFN_PATHMUSTEXIST | OFN_FILEMUSTEXIST;

            if( !GetOpenFileName(&ofn) )   // get the path+name
               break;                         // user pressed Cancel
                              // open file
            hFile = _lopen(szPath, READ);
            if(hFile == HFILE_ERROR)
               {
               MessageBox(NULL,"Error: Cannot open file",
                      szProgName, MB_OK | MB_ICONINFORMATION);
               return NULL;
               }
                              // read entire array from file
            cbLength = _lread(hFile, aText, LINES*MAXLENGTH);
            if(cbLength == (UINT)HFILE_ERROR)
               {
               MessageBox(NULL, "Error: Cannot read from file",
                      szProgName, MB_OK | MB_ICONINFORMATION);
               return NULL;
               }
            _lclose(hFile);    // close file
            InvalidateRect(hWnd, NULL, TRUE); // paint window
            }  // end IDM_OPEN block
         }  // end switch wParam
      break;  // end case WM_COMMAND

   case WM_PAINT:                        // repaint the screen
      hDC = BeginPaint(hWnd, &ps);     // get device context
      for(index = 0; index < LINES; index++ )    // for each line
```

```
        TextOut( hDC, LMARGIN, TMARGIN + CYCHAR*index, // display
                  aText[index], lstrlen( aText[index]) ); // text
      EndPaint(hWnd, &ps);              // painting complete
      break;  //  End of WM_PAINT

   case WM_DESTROY:
      PostQuitMessage(0);
      break;

   default:
      return( DefWindowProc(hWnd, msg, wParam, lParam) );
   }   // end switch(msg)

 return 0L;
}  // end WndProc
```

PROGRAMMING THE OPEN DIALOG

As we'll see when we get to custom dialogs, common dialogs do a lot of the programmer's work. The Open common dialog not only displays the dialog box on the screen, it also takes care of handling the messages sent to the dialog's controls, so you don't have to worry about what to display in the list boxes, how to handle button pushes, and most of the other interactions between the program and the dialog box. It also makes sure that the file you're trying to open actually exists. (You probably won't appreciate how hard the Open common dialog works until you've seen how to program custom dialogs.)

There are only two steps to creating a common dialog box. You fill in the members of a structure, and you call a function. For the Open common dialog, the structure is OPENFILENAME and the function is GetOpenFileName(). When you call this function, the dialog box is displayed and the user can interact with it. When the user selects the desired file from the dialog and clicks on the OK button, GetOpenFileName() places the name of the selected file in a buffer pointed to by a member of the OPENFILENAME structure. When GetOpenFileName() returns, your program can use the names to open a file, using _lopen() or another appropriate function. Figure 13-3 shows the process.

Let's look at the OPENFILENAME structure and the GetOpenFileName() function in detail.

The OPENFILENAME Structure

We create a structure called ofn, of type OPENFILENAME in the line

```
OPENFILENAME ofn;
```

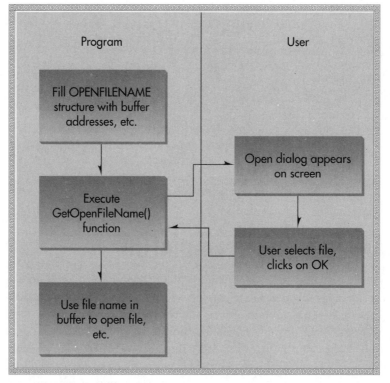

Figure 13-3 Flowchart of Open Dialog

Once the structure is created, we need to provide values for its various members. The most important information is the address of the buffer where the path-plus-file name string for the selected file will be placed by GetOpenFileName(). This is the string that will be used to open a file. However, some other data must be placed in the OPENFILENAME structure as well. This data includes addresses where additional information will be returned, and instructions to GetOpenFileName(). Here are the key members of the OPENFILENAME structure.

The Path-Plus-File Name

The GetOpenFileName() function places the path-plus-file name string in a buffer before it returns. In COMOPEN we set up a buffer 256 characters long called szPath, and tell the function where it is by setting the lpstrFile member of ofn to the buffer's address, with the statement

```
ofn.lpstrFile = szPath;
```

We also tell ofn the size of the buffer, using the nMaxFile member, in the line

```
ofn.nMaxFile = BUFFSIZE;
```

After the GetOpenFileName() function returns, we'll pass the path-plus-file name on to the _lopen() function to open the file. Using the entire path-plus-file name (sometimes called a "fully qualified" file name) ensures that _lopen() can find the file no matter what directory it's in. Although the file name by itself is returned in another buffer, you don't ordinarily use it to open a file, because it applies only to files in the current directory.

Before calling GetOpenFileName(), we must also empty the buffer used to hold the path-plus-file name:

```
szPath[0] = '\0';
```

This puts a null character (a zero) in the first element, thus making a zero-length string.

The File Name

One place where the file name alone is helpful is in the title of your main window. Many programs show not only the application name, but also the name of the file currently being processed. We don't use the file name field in COMOPEN, but we can still provide a buffer to hold it. We set up the szTitle buffer, and assign its address to the lpstrFileTitle member. We also assign the size of the buffer to the nMaxFileTitle member. Here are the statements that do that:

```
ofn.lpstrFileTitle = szTitle;
ofn.nMaxFileTitle = BUFFSIZE;
```

The Filter

When you run COMOPEN and bring up the Open dialog box, you'll see a combo box called List Files of Type:. Clicking on the arrow in this box will cause a short list to drop down, like this:

```
All files (*.*)
Data files (*.dat)
```

Clicking on the first line will cause all files to be displayed in the File Name list box. Clicking on the second line will display only those files with the .DAT extension. Designations like *.dat are called filters, because they filter out files you don't want to look at. As another example, a program editor might use the following filters to display only one type of program file at a time:

```
All files (*.*)
Source files (*.c)
Header files (*.h)
Resource files (*.rc)
```

You can see how to program these filters by comparing the display in the dialog box in COMOPEN with the code that generated it in COMOPEN.C. An array of

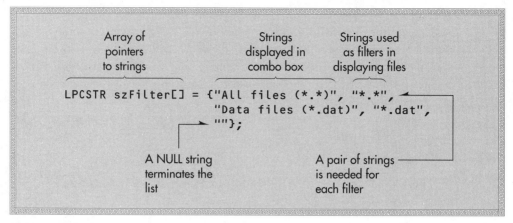

Figure 13-4 Filters

pointers to strings is filled in with the appropriate values. Figure 13-4 shows how this array is arranged.

We set up szFilter, an array of type LPCSTR (far pointers to constant strings), before we assign values to the ofn structure. Each filter requres two strings: the first holds the text displayed in the combo box, and the second is the actual wildcard expression used to select which files to display. The entire array of strings in szFilter must be terminated with a null string (specified by two quote marks with no space between). The address of the first string in the array, szFilter[0], is placed in the lpstrFilter member of OPENFILENAME:

```
ofn.lpstrFilter = szFilter[0];
```

The filter that will be displayed initially in the combo box is selected from the list using the nFilterIndex member of ofn. This is often the first filter, which has an index of 0 in the array of strings, so we use a value of 0 for this member.

The Flags

A member of OPENFILENAME called Flags specifies various aspects of the Open dialog's behavior. In the COMOPEN program we specify two flags: OFN_PATHMUSTEXIST and OFN_FILEMUSTEXIST, which we OR together, in the line

```
ofn.Flags = OFN_PATHMUSTEXIST | OFN_FILEMUSTEXIST;
```

These flags specify that the Open dialog will complain to the user if an incorrect path name, or file name, is entered. Another useful flag is OFN_HIDEREADONLY, which can be used to eliminate the Read Only check box. This check box is not completely appropriate in COMOPEN, because we're only reading from the files anyway. We've left it so you can see what it looks like.

If you were creating a new file, rather than opening an existing file, you would eliminate the OFN_FILEMUSTEXIST flag.

Other Structure Members

We set the lStructSize member to the size of the structure itself, in the line

```
ofn.lStructSize = sizeof(OPENFILENAME);
```

Why do this? Well, if GetOpenFileName() finds the wrong size, it knows something is seriously wrong; perhaps the structure has never been initialized. It can then bail out immediately, returning a FALSE value to your program.

The hwndOwner member is set to the handle of the window that will own the dialog box. In this example, that's the main window:

```
ofn.hwndOwner = hWnd;
```

There are various other members of the OPENFILENAME structure that we don't discuss here. You don't need to worry about them unless you want to do something fancy. (As with other Windows functions, you can consult Microsoft's documentation or the equivalent to learn the details.)

Fortunately, the default value for these other structure members is 0. We can set everything in the structure to 0 with the C library function memset(). This handy function sets every byte in a block of memory to a constant character value. The first argument is the address of the memory block, the second is the character to insert, and the third is the size of the block, in bytes. We use the statement

```
memset(&ofn, 0, sizeof(OPENFILENAME));
```

to zero the entire structure before filling in those members of the structure that *do* have nonzero values.

The GetOpenFileName() Function

Once the OPENFILENAME structure is filled in, you execute the GetOpenFileName() function to display the Open dialog box. This function takes as its only argument the address of the OPENFILENAME structure.

```
if( !GetOpenFileName(&ofn) )
    break;
```

The function returns TRUE if a file was successfully located, and FALSE otherwise. The most common reason for returning FALSE is that the user pressed the Cancel button. Assuming you've specified the OFN_FILEMUSTEXIST flag, as we have in the example, you won't get a FALSE if the user asks for a nonexistent file because GetOpenFileName() won't let you specify a nonexistent file. Instead it pops up a message box of its own inviting the user to try again, and doesn't return until the user has selected an existing file or pushed the Cancel button.

In COMOPEN we use the return value of the function to decide whether to open a file. If the function returns FALSE, then we break out of the **case** statement and wait for another message. Otherwise, we go ahead and open the file.

SENDING MESSAGES TO YOURSELF

You may have noticed an unfamiliar API function, located just after the _lclose() statement that finishes our file processing:

```
InvalidateRect(hWnd, NULL, TRUE);
```

What does this function do? Try deleting it from the listing (or commenting it out), and running COMOPEN again. You'll find that you can open the file all right with the Open dialog, but when the dialog goes away, the window is blank! What happened to the text? Change the window's size, or cover it with another window and then uncover it. Suddenly the text appears! What's going on?

Recall your interaction with the program. First you selected Open from the File menu. This caused a WM_COMMAND message with a wParam value of IDM_OPEN to be sent to WndProc(). In the corresponding **case** statement the Open common dialog was called up. As a user you then selected a file. This caused the file to be opened and read into the buffer. All this took place in the WM_COMMAND section of code. But where does text display take place? That's right, in the WM_PAINT section. Making a menu selection and manipulating the Open dialog doesn't generate a WM_PAINT message, so there's no display. However, changing the size of the window does generate WM_PAINT (because of the CS_HREDRAW and CS_VREDRAW constants in the style member or the wndclass structure in STDMAIN.INC), so the text appears when you resize the window.

Intra-Program Communication

It seems the two parts of our program, the WM_COMMAND part where we read the file, and the WM_PAINT part where we display it, are disconnected. The WM_PAINT part doesn't know we've read the file, so the file is never displayed. We need a way for the WM_COMMAND part of the program to tell the WM_PAINT part, "Hey, I've read a file, so display the buffer, darn it."

It would be nice if the WM_COMMAND part of the program generated a WM_PAINT message. This would activate the display. How could we cause that to happen? Windows generates a WM_PAINT message when it thinks some part of the window is invalid (that is, needs to be redrawn). So, if we tell it the entire window is invalid, it will send a WM_PAINT message and redraw the entire window. And, you guessed it, we tell Windows the window is invalid by executing the InvalidateRect() function. The scheme is shown in Figure 13-5.

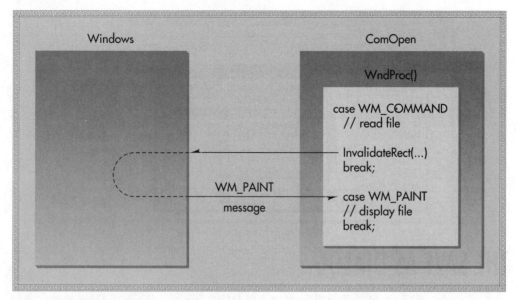

Figure 13-5 InvalidateRect() and WM_PAINT

The first argument to InvalidateRect() is the handle to the window. The NULL value in the second argument tells Windows to make the entire area of the window invalid. A TRUE value in the third parameter tells Windows to erase the background in the window before redrawing:

```
InvalidateRect(hWnd, NULL, TRUE);
```

With the InvalidateRect() statement installed, we get a WM_PAINT message and display the text every time we read a file. Without this function we don't get a WM_PAINT message until we generate it some other way, by expanding or uncovering the window.

Thus InvalidateRect() serves as a useful way for one part of the program to communicate with another. It may seem rather odd, but using InvalidateRect() this way is the correct approach in Windows programming.

Don't Call Yourself

By the way, don't be tempted to do something like calling your own window procedure directly with a message, like this:

```
WndProc(hWnd, WM_PAINT, 0, 0L);  // don't even think of it
```

Windows must keep track of all the messages being transmitted in the sytem. If you call your own window procedure directly, you short-circuit this process, and fierce knights in black armor slay you immediately.

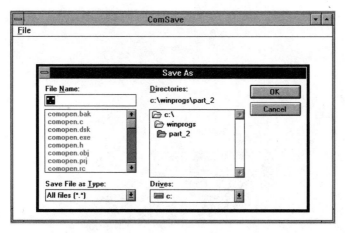

Figure 13-6

The Save As Dialog

THE SAVE AS DIALOG

The Save As common dialog is similar to the Open common dialog. The COMSAVE example program displays the Save As dialog when the user selects Save As (the only selection) from the File menu. Figure 13-6 shows what the resulting Save As dialog looks like.

You can do the same sorts of things with this dialog that you could do with Open: select files from the list or type them into the edit field, change directories, and so on. The main difference in the way the dialog looks is that the file names in the list box are grayed. This indicates that they are existing files, and that you might not want to delete their contents by overwriting them with your file. However, you can do this if you want, simply by double-clicking on a name. Normally you type a new file name into the edit field.

Once the user has selected a file name, COMSAVE writes a stanza of a poem to the file. The user can write the poem to as many different files as seems desirable.

Programming the Save As dialog is similar to programming the Open dialog. It uses the same OPENFILENAME structure. However, the function used to create Save As is called GetSaveFileName(). Like GetOpenFileName(), the GetSaveFileName() function takes as its only argument the address of a structure of type OPENFILENAME.

Here is the listing for COMSAVE.RC:

```
// comsave.rc
// resource file for comsave.c

#include "comsave.h"

ComSave MENU    // must agree with szProgName
   BEGIN
      POPUP "&File"
```

```
        BEGIN
            MENUITEM "Save &as...", IDM_SAVEAS
        END

    END
```

This is the listing for COMSAVE.H:

```
// comsave.h
// ID for comsave.c

#define IDM_SAVEAS      100
```

And here is the listing for COMSAVE.C:

```
// comsave.c
// uses "Save As" common dialog box to open file for writing

#define STRICT
#include <windows.h>
#include <commdlg.h>            // for "Open" and "Save as..." dialogs
#include <memory.h>            // for memset()
#include "comsave.h"           // for menu #define

#define BUFFSIZE 256           // buffer size
char szPath[BUFFSIZE];         // buffer for file path+name
char szTitle[BUFFSIZE];        // buffer for file name (no path)

#define LINES        7         // number of text lines
#define MAXLENGTH 80           // maximum length of line
char khan[LINES][MAXLENGTH] = {  // array of strings
"In Xanadu did Kubla Khan",
"   A stately pleasure-dome decree",
"Where Alph, the sacred river, ran",
"Through caverns measureless to man",
"   Down to a sunless sea.",
"",
"from \"Kubla Khan\" by Samuel Taylor Coleridge" };

                               // prototype
LRESULT CALLBACK _export WndProc(HWND, UINT, WPARAM, LPARAM);

PSTR szProgName = "ComSave";   // application name
#include "stdmain.inc"         // standard WinMain() function
////////////////////////////////////////////////////////////////
// main window procedure -- receives messages                  //
////////////////////////////////////////////////////////////////
LRESULT CALLBACK _export WndProc(HWND hWnd, UINT msg,
                         WPARAM wParam, LPARAM lParam)
    {
    HFILE hFile;              // file handle
    UINT cbLength;            // characters read
    OPENFILENAME ofn;         // for GetSaveFileName()
```

```
        LPCSTR szFilter[] = { "All files (*.*)", "*.*",      // extension
                        "Data files (*.dat)", "*.dat",  // filters
                        "" };
    switch(msg)
       {
       case WM_COMMAND:              // menu command
          switch(wParam)
             {
             case IDM_SAVEAS:    // user chose Save as...
                {
                szPath[0] = '\0';                      // empty the name field
                                                       // zero the structure
                memset( &ofn, 0, sizeof(OPENFILENAME) );
                                                       // size of structure
                ofn.lStructSize = sizeof(OPENFILENAME);
                ofn.hwndOwner = hWnd;          // owner is main window
                ofn.lpstrFilter = szFilter[0]; // filter string array
                ofn.lpstrFile = szPath;        // path+name buffer
                ofn.nMaxFile = BUFFSIZE;       // size of above
                ofn.lpstrFileTitle = szTitle;  // file name buffer
                ofn.nMaxFileTitle = BUFFSIZE;  // size of above
                                               // require valid paths
                ofn.Flags = OFN_PATHMUSTEXIST | OFN_HIDEREADONLY |
                            OFN_OVERWRITEPROMPT; // notify on overwrite

                if( !GetSaveFileName(&ofn) )   // get the path+name
                   break;                      // user pressed Cancel
                                 // open file
                hFile = _lcreat(szPath, READ);
                if(hFile == HFILE_ERROR)
                   {
                   MessageBox(NULL,"Error: Cannot create file",
                           szProgName, MB_OK | MB_ICONINFORMATION);
                   return NULL;
                   }
                                 // write entire array to file
                cbLength = _lwrite(hFile, khan, LINES*MAXLENGTH);
                if(cbLength == (UINT)HFILE_ERROR)
                   {
                   MessageBox(NULL, "Error: Cannot write to file",
                           szProgName, MB_OK | MB_ICONINFORMATION);
                   return NULL;
                   }
                _lclose(hFile);      // close file
                } // end case IDM_SAVEAS
             }    // end switch wParam
          break;  // end case WM_COMMAND

       case WM_DESTROY:
          PostQuitMessage(0);
          break;
```

```
    default:
        return( DefWindowProc(hWnd, msg, wParam, lParam) );
    }    // end switch(msg)

  return 0L;
  }  // end WndProc
```

We set up the structure just as we did for the Open dialog. When GetSaveFileName() returns, we use the path-plus-file name to create a file, using the _lcreat() function. Then we write the poem, in the same format as in OUTFILE, to the file name selected.

The only difference in setting up the OPENFILENAME structure for Save As instead of Open is in the Flags member. We don't care if the file exists, so there's no OFN_FILEMUSTEXIST constant. In fact, if the file does exist, we want to alert the user, since the exisiting file will be overwritten by the new file, with possible loss of data. Therefore we use the OFN_OVERWRITEPROMPT constant, which causes a message box to appear if a file with the same name already exists. The user can choose to either overwrite the file or not. Here's the code for setting the Flags member:

```
ofn.Flags = OFN_PATHMUSTEXIST | OFN_HIDEREADONLY | OFN_OVERWRITEPROMPT;
```

We saw the OFN_PATHMUSTEXIST flag before. The OFN_HIDEREADONLY constant removes the Read Only check box from the dialog.

SUMMARY

The Open and Save As common dialog boxes are created the same way. Here are the steps:

1. Fill in the members of the OPENFILENAME structure. The most important data in this structure is the address of a buffer in which to put the path-plus-file name of the file selected.
2. Call GetOpenFileName() for the Open dialog, or GetSaveFileName() for the Save As dialog, using the address of the structure as its argument.
3. When the function returns, the path-plus-file name selected by the user will be installed in the buffer.
4. Use this name to open or create a file, or to save it.

14

THE FREQ PROGRAM

major occupation of the knights in King Arthur's time was the quest. This was a long journey, usually involving hardship and danger. It's purpose was to perform good works, like rescuing damsels in distress or seeking the Holy Grail. A quest increased a knight's self-knowledge and helped form his character.

In your role as aspiring knight, you've learned a great deal about such things as the event-driven dragon and the sword *Excalibur.* Now it's time to embark on a quest to see if what you've learned is actually useful in the real world. The quest in this chapter consists of creating a small application. This application, FREQ, reads a text file and performs a letter-frequency analysis on it. That is, it determines how many letter A's are in the file, how many B's, how many C's, and so on. It then displays the results. Letter-frequency analysis is useful in cryptanalysis (code breaking) and many other fields that deal in information content and data transmission. You might even find it helpful in solving crosswords and similar puzzles. Even if you're not a cryptanalyst, this program will demonstrate that, using what you've learned so far, you can write programs that perform at least somewhat useful tasks. You could adapt this program to analyze any sort of data stored in a disk file.

WHAT IT DOES

FREQ uses the Open common dialog to get the name of a text file from the user, and then reads in the file. It then goes through the file character by character, incrementing a count specific to each character. If the character is a K, for example, the count of K's is incremented; if it's an X, the count of X's is incremented. When it's done analyzing the file, the program displays a table of the resulting letter

```
┌───────────────────────────────────────────────┐
│  ─              Freq                    ▼ ▲ │
├───────────────────────────────────────────────┤
│ File                                           │
├───────────────────────────────────────────────┤
│ File FREQ.C contains 6560 characters           │
│ A –  211                                       │
│ B –   70                                       │
│ C –  135                                       │
│ D –  125                                       │
│ E –  404                                       │
│ F –  174                                       │
│ G –   46                                       │
│ H –  106                                       │
│ I –  235                                       │
│ J –    5                                       │
│ K –   11                                       │
│ L –  183                                       │
│ M –   93                                       │
│ N –  252                                       │
│ O –  149                                       │
│ P –   86                                       │
│ Q –    9                                       │
│ R –  205                                       │
│ S –  182                                       │
│ T –  256                                       │
│ U –   97                                       │
│ V –   12                                       │
│ W –   56                                       │
│ X –   37                                       │
│ Y –   25                                       │
│ Z –   49                                       │
│ Nonletters – 3347                              │
└───────────────────────────────────────────────┘
```

Figure 14-1

Output of the FREQ Program

frequencies. Figure 14-1 shows what this table looks like when FREQ analyzes its own .C file.

This display will be similar no matter what file you analyze; only the numbers will be different. It shows the total number of characters in the file, the number of times each letter occurs, and the number of nonletters. The sum of all the letters, plus the nonletters, should add up to the total number of characters. In a program listing there will be many more nonletters than in a pure text file, since there are so many braces, parentheses, and so on. The carriage-return and linefeed at the end of each line also count as two nonletters.

Unlike our previous example programs, FREQ works on files of arbitrary length. It does this by repeatedly reading data from the file into a small fixed-size buffer and analyzing it.

We use a simple menu structure with one pop-up and two menu items, Open and Quit, with a separator between them. Here's the listing for FREQ.RC:

```
// freq.rc
// resource file for freq

#include "freq.h"

Freq MENU    // must agree with szProgName
   BEGIN
      POPUP "&File"
         BEGIN
            MENUITEM "&Open", IDM_OPEN
            MENUITEM SEPARATOR
            MENUITEM "&Quit", IDM_QUIT
         END
   END
```

This simple menu structure is reflected in the header file, which has only two constants to define. Here's the listing for FREQ.H:

```
// freq.h
// header file for freq

#define IDM_OPEN        101
#define IDM_QUIT        102
```

The source file is somewhat longer than those you've seen before. Except for the function called analyze(), at the end of the listing, it should be relatively familiar. Here's the listing for FREQ.C:

```
// freq.c
// analyzes a text file's letter-frequency distribution

#define STRICT
#include <windows.h>
#include <commdlg.h>          // for GetOpenFileName()
#include <memory.h>           // for memset()
#include "freq.h"             // for menu #defines

#define LMARGIN      10      // left margin, in pixels
#define CYCHAR       13      // height of characters, in pixels
#define NUMLETS      26      // number of letters in the alphabet
#define UBUFFSIZE    256     // utility text buffer size
#define TBUFFSIZE    2048    // input text-file buffer size

char InBuffer[TBUFFSIZE];    // buffer for text-file input
DWORD Table[NUMLETS];        // table of frequencies
BOOL bIsFile = FALSE;        // true if file opened

char szPath[UBUFFSIZE];      // buffer for file path+name
char szTitle[UBUFFSIZE];     // buffer for file name (no path)
char szString[UBUFFSIZE];    // buffer for various strings

DWORD cbTotal;               // total characters in file
DWORD nonLetters;            // nonletters (punctuation, etc.)
HWND hWnd;                    // main window handle
                             // prototypes
LRESULT CALLBACK _export WndProc(HWND, UINT, WPARAM, LPARAM);
void analyze(void);

PSTR szProgName = "Freq";    // application name
#include "stdmain.inc"        // standard WinMain() file
////////////////////////////////////////////////////////////////////
// main window procedure -- receives messages                      //
////////////////////////////////////////////////////////////////////
LRESULT CALLBACK _export WndProc(HWND hWnd, UINT msg,
                                 WPARAM wParam, LPARAM lParam)
   {
   HDC hDC;                   // handle for the display device
   PAINTSTRUCT ps;            // holds PAINT information
```

```
int index;              // loop index
char ch;                // character
OPENFILENAME ofn;       // for GetOpenFileName()
LPCSTR szFilter[] = { "All files (*.*)", "*.*",      // extension
                      "Source files (*.c)", "*.c",   // filters
                      "Header files (*.h)", "*.h",
                      "Resource files (*.rc)", "*.rc",
                      "" };
switch(msg)
   {
   case WM_COMMAND:      // some menu item selected
      switch(wParam)
         {
         case IDM_OPEN: // menu item Open selected
            {
            szPath[0] = '\0';                // empty the name field
            memset( &ofn, 0, sizeof(OPENFILENAME) ); // clear struct
            ofn.lStructSize = sizeof(OPENFILENAME);  // strct size
            ofn.hwndOwner = hWnd;            // owner is main window
            ofn.lpstrFilter = szFilter[0]; // filter
            ofn.lpstrFile = szPath;         // path+name buffer
            ofn.nMaxFile = UBUFFSIZE;       // size of above
            ofn.lpstrFileTitle = szTitle;   // file name buffer
            ofn.nMaxFileTitle = UBUFFSIZE; // size of above
                                            // require valid names
            ofn.Flags = OFN_PATHMUSTEXIST | OFN_FILEMUSTEXIST;

            if( !GetOpenFileName(&ofn) )    // get the path+name
               break;                       // if no name, forget it
            analyze();                      // read file and analyze
            InvalidateRect(hWnd, NULL, TRUE);  // repaint window
            bIsFile = TRUE;                 // file data exists
            }  // end case IDM_OPEN
            break;

         case IDM_QUIT:
            DestroyWindow(hWnd);
            break;

         }   // end switch wParam
      break; // end case WM_COMMAND

   case WM_PAINT:                       // repaint the screen
      hDC = BeginPaint(hWnd, &ps);      // get device context
      if(bIsFile)                       // if file has been read
         {
         // display file size
         wsprintf(szString, "File %s contains %lu characters",
                  (LPSTR)szTitle, cbTotal);
         TextOut( hDC, LMARGIN, 0, szString, lstrlen(szString) );
```

```
            // display the table of letter frequencies
            for(index = 0; index < NUMLETS; index++ )   // 26 times
                {
                ch = index + 'A';                   // make the character
                wsprintf( szString,                 // create a string
                        "%c -- %5ld\n",             // "A -- 277" etc.
                        ch, Table[index] );         // character, count
                TextOut(hDC, LMARGIN,               // display string
                        CYCHAR*(index+1), szString, 10);
                // display number of non-letters
                wsprintf(szString, "Non-letters -- %lu", nonLetters);
                TextOut( hDC, LMARGIN, CYCHAR*27,
                        szString, lstrlen(szString) );
                }  // end for
            }  // end if
        EndPaint(hWnd, &ps);
        break;  //  End of WM_PAINT

    case WM_DESTROY:
        PostQuitMessage(0);
        break;

    default:
        return( DefWindowProc(hWnd, msg, wParam, lParam) );
    }    // end switch(msg)

    return 0L;
    }  // end WndProc

//////////////////////////////////////////////////////////////////
// analyze() function -- reads and analyzes text file             //
//////////////////////////////////////////////////////////////////
void analyze(void)
    {
    HFILE hFile;                        // file handle
    UINT index;                         // index to table
    UINT j;                             // index to input buffer
    UINT cbLength;                      // characters read
    char ch;

    cbTotal = 0;                        // no characters read yet
    hFile = _lopen(szPath, READ);       // open the file
    if(hFile == HFILE_ERROR)
        {
        MessageBox(hWnd, "Can't Open File", szProgName,
                MB_ICONSTOP | MB_OK);
        return;
        }
    memset(Table, 0x00, NUMLETS*4);     // clear the table
    nonLetters = 0;                     // clear nonletters
```

```
do                                   // for each buffer-full,
    {                                // read bytes into buffer
    cbLength = _lread(hFile, InBuffer, (UINT)TBUFFSIZE);
    if(cbLength == (UINT)HFILE_ERROR)
        {
        MessageBox(NULL,"Can't read file", szProgName,
                MB_ICONSTOP | MB_OK);
        return;
        }
    cbTotal += cbLength;                 // update total length
    for(j=0; j<cbLength; j++)            // for each char,
        {
        ch = (char)*(InBuffer + j);      // get char from buffer
        if( ch >= 'A' && ch <= 'Z' )     // uppercase
            {
            index = ch - 'A';
            Table[index]++;                  // count it
            }
        else if( ch >='a' && ch <= 'z' )  // lowercase
            {
            index = ch - 'a';
            Table[index]++;                  // count it
            }
        else                             // nonletters
            nonLetters++;
        }  // end for
    } while(cbLength != 0);
_lclose(hFile);            // close the file
}  // end analyze
```

READING AND ANALYZING

The Open common dialog box is used to obtain the path-plus-file name when the
user selects Open from the File menu. This is how previous examples worked.
However, we handle the file reading differently. To be able to read and analyze a file
of arbitrary length, rather than being restricted to fixed-length files, we make
multiple reads into a small (2,048 bytes) buffer, alternately reading and analyzing
each buffer-full of data, in a **do while** loop. We perform the read using the _lread()
function. If the number of bytes returned from this function (the bytes actually
read) is less than the buffer size, the end-of-file has been reached, and the **do while**
loop terminates.

We've placed the reading and analysis in a separate function called analyze().
Figure 14-2 shows the overall structure of this function.

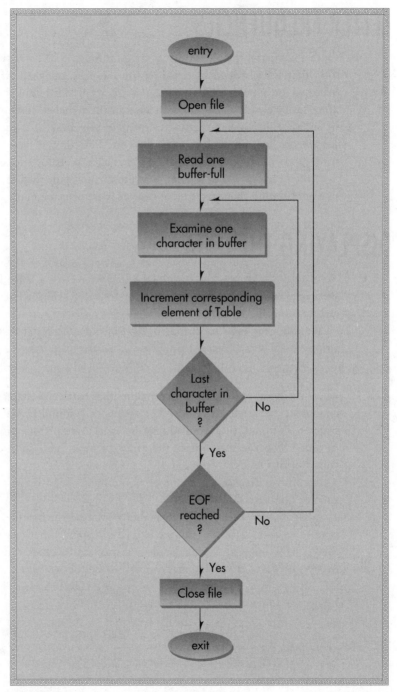

Figure 14-2 Flowchart of the analyze() Function

LETTER FREQUENCIES

Once a section of the file is read in, we go through it character by character in a **for** loop that is embedded in the **do while** loop in analyze(). If the character is a lowercase or uppercase letter, a value in an array called Table is incremented. This array has 26 elements, one for each letter of the alphabet. If the program finds an 'A' or an 'a,' it increments the first element in this array; if it finds a 'B' or a 'b,' it increments the second element, and so on. This array is type DWORD, so it can count up to 4 billion instances of each character, probably enough for most files.

If the character is not a letter, it is presumably punctuation, a graphics symbol, or a nonprinting character. In that case we increment the nonLetters variable.

DISPLAYING THE DATA

We display the data using TextOut() when we receive a WM_PAINT message, as we've seen before. First we display the total file size, which we've accumulated in the cbTotal variable.

We use a **for** loop to display one string for each letter of the alphabet. Each string, which is constructed by wsprintf(), has the form

```
A -- 277
```

where the number shows how many times that particular character (or its lowercase equivalent) occurred in the file. The character is found by taking the loop index, which runs from 0 to 25 and adding the value 'A' to it. This produces all the letters in order. The count is simply the array element Table[index], the accumulated count for that letter.

Finally we display the count of nonletters, which we've accumulated in the variable nonLetters.

A flag, bIsFile, keeps track of whether we've read the first file. If we haven't, there is no data in OutBuffer, and we skip the display functions when we receive a WM_PAINT message. This avoids a display of 0 values. The BOOL data type means "Boolean," a variable that can have either of two values, TRUE (nonzero) or FALSE (zero). It is typedefed as **int** in WINDOWS.H. A lowercase 'b' is the Hungarian notation for a Boolean value.

SUMMARY

In Part Two you've learned how to display text on the screen using TextOut(), how to create menus, how to use disk files, and how to create the Open and Save As common dialogs. As you have seen in this chapter, these are all the skills you need for simple programs that read disk files, analyze them, and display results.

However, there are some limitations in what we've learned. We can't display more text than will fit in our window, since we can't use scroll bars; and we can't handle text of different sizes. We also don't know how to input text. In the next section we'll deal with these deficiencies, and examine various other text-related Windows features as well.

PART THREE

TEXT

*I*magine all those medieval monks, sequestered away in cold and dismal monasteries, laboring over their parchment manuscripts by the light of flickering candles. The results were beautiful; hand-drawn script was an artform. But creating it was incredibly time consuming. Every line, every letter, every gargoyle and angel in the margin was drawn by hand; and if they made a mistake, they started over with a new page. As a consequence, books and literacy were rare in King Arthur's time (although junk mail was less of a problem).

There have been two revolutions in text since then: the printing press in the 15th century and computers in the 20th. The text capability of early computer systems was crude: only one typeface (usually Courier) was supported and only in one size. Now Windows brings the ability to display and print thousands of typefaces in any reasonable size.

There may be a third revolution at some point in the future: text will disappear entirely and be replaced by thought waves. In the meantime we need to know how to handle text, both input and output, in our Windows programs. That's the subject of Part Three.

The first few chapters of Part Three focus on text output. We've shown the rudiments of text output already, but here we'll extend what we've learned to give you far more power and flexibility. You'll learn how to display text in any size, font, and style; and position it anywhere on the screen. You'll also find out how to use scroll bars to view documents that are larger than a window. Because Windows text is displayed using a graphics-based approach, much of what you learn in these chapters is relevant for displaying graphics images (pictures) as well as text.

In the last few chapters of Part Three, we'll discuss text input from the keyboard. There are two approaches to text input: the easy way, using edit control windows and the hard way, where messages are intercepted for each keypress. We'll cover them both. At the end of Part Three we'll put together what we've learned to create a mini-editor that lets the user type text into a window, save the resulting document file to disk, and read document files back into the editor. The monks of King Arthur's time would have envied us (if envy had not been a mortal sin).

CHAPTER 15

STOCK FONTS

*I*t's easy for a monk with a pen to change from one typeface to another; all he has to do is draw the letters differently. He can use any typeface, and any size characters, anyplace on the page. This is a lot more versatility than existed in the days of character-based computer displays. Then you had an undemocratic choice of one: the font built into the PC hardware.

Things have changed with the advent of Windows. Now most applications let you access any font that's loaded into Windows, of which there can be dozens. This gives you amazing versatility in creating documents; it is one of the most exciting things about Windows, and has lead to the whole desktop publishing industry.

So far in this book we have not used different fonts; we've used only the System font; which is also the normal font for titles and menu items. In the next two chapters we'll remedy this omission by showing you how to use different fonts to display text. This chapter examines stock fonts, which are included with Windows and are relatively easy for your program to access. The next chapter demonstrates installable fonts, which offer considerably more flexibility but are not quite so easy to program.

CHARACTERISTICS OF STOCK FONTS

Every copy of Windows comes with several standard fonts, called *stock fonts*, built into the GDI. (As you may recall from Part Two, *The User Interface—An Introduction*, GDI stands for Graphics Device Interface, and refers to the approach Windows takes to displaying graphics.) Because stock fonts are standard in all Windows installations, your application can assume they exist and use them at any time. This is not true of installable fonts, which may be loaded or removed by the user. Knowing a font is always available is a considerable convenience for the programmer, so stock fonts are a useful part of the programmer's arsenal.

Table 15-1 Stock Fonts

Font Designation	Purpose
SYSTEM_FONT	Proportional; used for titles, menus, etc.
SYSTEM_FIXED_FONT	Fixed system font for older versions of Windows
ANSI_FIXED_FONT	Fixed pitch "typewriter" font (Courier)
ANSI_VAR_FONT	Proportional sans serif font (MS Sans Serif)
DEVICE_DEFAULT_FONT	Font preferred by a specific device
OEM_FIXED_FONT	Fixed pitch, with IBM character set

There are six stock fonts in Windows 3.1, as shown in Table 15-1.

The System font is the one we've been using all along. It is normally used by Windows for titles, menus, dialog box information, and so on. It's also the default font for displaying text if you don't specify something else. Our EZTEXT and other programs used it for text output. The System font is a *proportional* font, meaning the letters are different sizes: the 'i' is narrower than the 'm', for example.

Serifs are the little lines at the end of the straight lines that make up some letters. The text you're reading is a serif font; the short lines on the top and bottom of this uppercase 'I' are serifs. The System font is a *sans serif* font, so it doesn't have these little lines (the word *sans* is French for "without").

The System Fixed font is *not* proportional; that is, all the characters are the same width. A nonproportional font is said to have "fixed pitch". Text drawn with fixed-pitch fonts looks like it came from a typewriter. The System Fixed font is also a serif font. It is included only for compatibility with older versions of Windows, which used this font as the default font.

The ANSI Fixed font is useful when you're arranging text and figures in columns. To make the columns line up nicely, it's common to use a fixed-pitch font, as we'll see later in this chapter. The ANSI fixed font is a serif font. (ANSI is an acronym for American National Standards Institute, which developed the character set used by this font.)

The ANSI Variable font is a proportional sans serif font like the System font, but with a smaller, finer character design.

The Device Default font is tailored to work effectively on specific devices. Each device has its own Device Default font. On the screen display it's a fixed-pitch serif font.

The OEM Fixed font is a fixed serif font somewhat like the ANSI Fixed font, although it's a bit bolder. The major difference is that it uses a different character set.

Character Sets

As you know, characters are stored in most computer systems as 8-bit numbers. This accommodates 256 possible characters, one for each number from 0 to 255. A *character set* is the list of characters that correspond to these numerical codes. The normal characters 'a' to 'z' and 'A' to 'Z', and the normal punctuation marks and numerals, usually correspond to the same numbers in all character sets. However, other numbers may represent different characters in different sets. For years MS-DOS computers used the IBM character set. Besides the standard letters and punctuation, this set includes many characters for drawing lines and boxes. This was a useful capability on machines that had no graphics capability. Microsoft calls this the OEM character set. It's shown in Figure 15-1.

In Windows it's easy to draw boxes and lines with graphics API functions (as we'll see in Part Five, *Graphics*), so the OEM character set is not as useful. Windows therefore usually uses fonts based on the ANSI character set instead. This character set doesn't have characters for drawing lines and boxes, but instead contains a large selection of accented letters, which are useful in languages other than English, such as French and German; and business-oriented characters such as ® and ©. The ANSI character set is shown in Figure 15-2.

Occasionally you may require compatibility with a DOS program, or need to use the line- and box-characters from the IBM character set, so the OEM Fixed

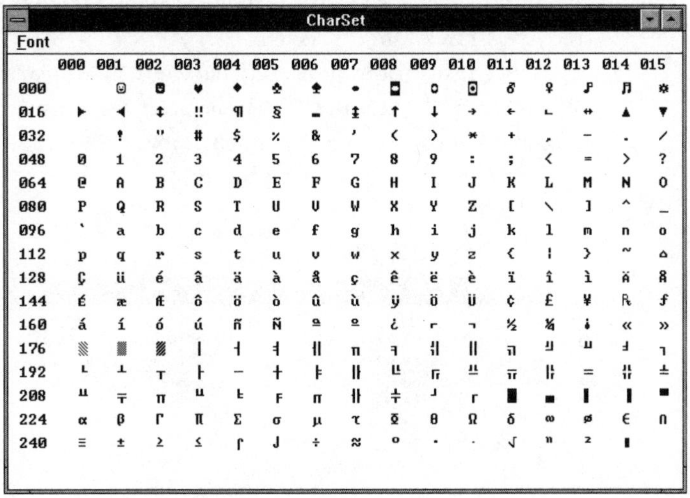

Figure 15-1

The OEM Character Set

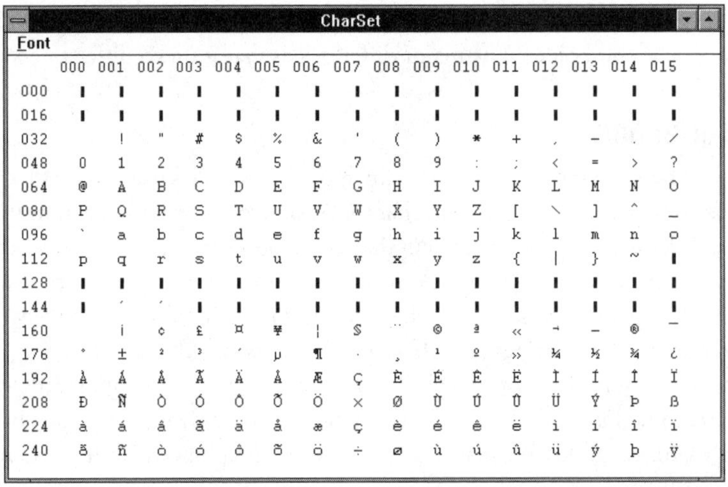

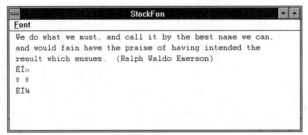

Figure 15-2

The ANSI

Character Set

font is included as a stock font. Generally you can ignore it. For most purposes, the System font, ANSI Fixed font, and ANSI Variable font are the most useful of the stock fonts.

THE STOCKFON PROGRAM

Our example program allows you to select any one of the stock fonts and use it to display several lines of text and some graphics characters. Selecting Fonts on the menu bar brings up a menu with the items System, System Fixed, Ansi Fixed, Ansi Proportional, Device Default, and OEM Fixed. Figure 15-3 shows the output when the ANSI Fixed font is selected.

Notice that various nonletter characters are displayed following the lines of text. When fonts that use the ANSI character set are used, these characters appear as accented letters and other symbols. However, if you select the OEM Fixed font, they appear as the corners and sides of a small box. Figure 15-4 shows how this looks.

Figure 15-3

STOCKFON Displays the ANSI Fixed Font

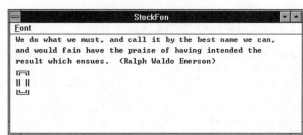

Figure 15-4

STOCKFON Displays the
OEM Fixed Font

The graphics characters don't quite join together to make a contiguous box because the line spacing doesn't take into account the size of the different fonts. We'll see how to fix that problem in Chapter 17, *Text Size*.

We use a pop-up to find what font the user wants, so we must use a three-file program. Here's the STOCKFON.RC file:

```
// stockfon.rc
// resource script file for stockfon

#include "stockfon.h"

StockFon MENU  // name must agree with szProgName
   BEGIN
      POPUP "&Font"
         BEGIN
            MENUITEM "System", IDM_SYSTEM
            MENUITEM "System Fixed", IDM_SYSFIX
            MENUITEM "Ansi Fixed", IDM_ANSIFIX
            MENUITEM "Ansi Proportional", IDM_ANSIPRO
            MENUITEM "Device Default", IDM_DEVICE
            MENUITEM "OEM Fixed", IDM_OEMFIX
         END
   END
```

This is the corresponding STOCKFON.H file:

```
// stockfon.h
// header file for stockfon

#define IDM_SYSTEM    101
#define IDM_SYSFIX    102
#define IDM_ANSIFIX   103
#define IDM_ANSIPRO   104
#define IDM_DEVICE    105
#define IDM_OEMFIX    106
```

The program handles three messages: WM_CREATE, WM_COMMAND, and WM_PAINT. Here's the listing for STOCKFON.C:

```
// stockfon.c
// displays text using stock font selected by user

#define STRICT
#include <windows.h>
#include "stockfon.h"      // header file for menu IDs

#define TMARGIN  3         // top margin, in pixels
#define LMARGIN 10         // left margin, in pixels
#define CYCHAR  18         // height of characters, in pixels
#define LINES    6         // number of lines to display

PSTR Emerson[LINES] = {    // array of pointers to strings
"We do what we must, and call it by the best name we can,",
"and would fain have the praise of having intended the",
"result which ensues.  (Ralph Waldo Emerson)",
"\xC9\xCD\xBB",            // box made with graphics characters
"\xBA \xBA",
"\xC8\xCD\xBC" };
                                        // prototype
LRESULT CALLBACK _export WndProc(HWND, UINT, WPARAM, LPARAM);

PSTR szProgName = "StockFon";          // application name
#include "stdmain.inc"                 // standard WinMain() function
////////////////////////////////////////////////////////////////////
// main window procedure -- receives messages                      //
////////////////////////////////////////////////////////////////////
LRESULT CALLBACK _export WndProc(HWND hWnd, UINT msg,
                              WPARAM wParam, LPARAM lParam)
   {
   HDC hDC;                   // handle for the device context
   PAINTSTRUCT ps;            // holds PAINT information
   int index;                 // loop index
   static int iFontType;      // SYSTEM_FONT, etc. (note: static)
   HFONT hFont, hOldFont;     // font handles

   switch(msg)
      {
      case WM_CREATE:
         iFontType = SYSTEM_FONT;
         break;

      case WM_COMMAND:                  // user selects a menu item
         switch(wParam)                 // wParam holds item ID
            {
            case IDM_SYSTEM:
               iFontType = SYSTEM_FONT; break;
            case IDM_SYSFIX:
               iFontType = SYSTEM_FIXED_FONT; break;
            case IDM_ANSIFIX:
               iFontType = ANSI_FIXED_FONT; break;
            case IDM_ANSIPRO:
               iFontType = ANSI_VAR_FONT; break;
```

```
        case IDM_DEVICE:
          iFontType = DEVICE_DEFAULT_FONT; break;
        case IDM_OEMFIX:
          iFontType = OEM_FIXED_FONT; break;
      }    // end switch wParam
    InvalidateRect(hWnd, NULL, TRUE);   // redraw after selection
    break;  // end case WM_COMMAND

  case WM_PAINT:                          // repaint the screen
    hDC = BeginPaint(hWnd, &ps);         // get device context
    hFont = GetStockObject(iFontType); // get stock font object
    hOldFont = SelectObject(hDC, hFont);  // select font object
    // display text from buffer
    for(index = 0; index < LINES; index++ ) // for each line
      TextOut( hDC,                       // device context
               LMARGIN,                   // horiz position
               TMARGIN + CYCHAR*index,    // vert position
               Emerson[index],            // address of line
               lstrlen( Emerson[index]) ); // length of line
    SelectObject(hDC, hOldFont);         // restore original font
    EndPaint(hWnd, &ps);                 // painting complete
    break;  //  End of WM_PAINT

  case WM_DESTROY:
    PostQuitMessage(0);
    break;

  default:
    return( DefWindowProc(hWnd, msg, wParam, lParam) );
  }   // end switch(msg)

return 0L;
}  // end WndProc
```

When we receive a WM_COMMAND message with a wParam value corresponding to one of the menu selections, we use a **switch** statement to set the iFontType variable to one of the font designations in Table 15-1.

The SYSTEM_FONT designation is also set when the WM_CREATE message is received. This ensures that the display will use the System font when the program first runs. When a WM_PAINT message arrives we display the text in the usual way, but not before executing two new functions: GetStockObject() and SelectObject(). To see what these functions do, we need to know about GDI objects.

GDI OBJECTS

In Windows, a stock font is considered to be a kind of GDI *object*. What is an "object" in this context? In Part Two, *The User Interface—An Introduction*, we discussed the idea of a device context. The device context is a rather amorphous entity with several characteristics. We saw that it acts as a conduit between our program and the hardware device: we don't write text directly to the screen, for example, but to the device context for the display, which relays the text to the screen. You might think of the device context as a professional artist: rather than painting on a canvas ourselves, we give instructions to the artist, who then carries out our request, using special skills and knowledge about the paint and canvas (the graphics display system).

Another role played by the device context (the artist in this analogy) is to supply a paintbox containing such items as a drawing pen, which determines line width and color when drawing graphics figures, and a brush, which determines the pattern when filling an area. The pen and the brush are called *objects*. (There isn't much connection here with "objects" as used in object-oriented programming.) We'll discuss pens and brushes in Part Five, *Graphics*. Of more interest to us in this chapter is that the device context also supplies a *font object* for use in displaying text. (There are actually six kinds of GDI objects in all. Besides fonts, pens, and brushes; there are bitmaps, regions, and palettes.)

Our artist's paintbox is unusual in that it can contain only one of each kind of object at a time: one pen, one brush, and one font. If we want our artist to use a different pen or a different font, we must obtain the new object and put it in the paintbox, where it replaces the old object. Figure 15-5 shows a version of the artist with the paintbox.

We get an object and put it in the paintbox with two API functions. GetStockObject() obtains a stock font object, and SelectObject() puts it into the paintbox, where it will replace whatever font was there before. Let's see how these functions are used.

The GetStockObject() Function

The font designation, such as SYSTEM_FONT, is used as an argument to the GetStockObject() function, which returns a handle to the font. This handle is of type HFONT and, like other handles, uses the 'h' character as Hungarian notation. In the STOCKFON program, we set a variable called iFontType to one of the five font designations, depending on which menu selection the user made. Then we use iFontType as the argument to GetStockObject() to retrieve a handle to that font, as shown in this code fragment:

```
iFontType = ANSI_FIXED_FONT;
  .
  .
  .
hFont = GetStockObject(iFontType);
```

Selecting Objects

Getting a handle to a font (or any other kind of object) doesn't mean that it automatically becomes part of a device context's paintbox. We must pass the object's handle to the device context, as we would pass a pen or a brush to an artist. This is called *selecting an object into* the device context. The SelectObject() function carries out this task. Because there is only one of each kind of object in the device context,

Figure 15-5 The Artist and the Paintbox

SelectObject() in effect substitutes a new object for the old one. Here it gets rid of whatever font was in use before, and substitutes the font whose handle we obtained with GetStockObject():

```
hOldFont = SelectObject(hDC, hFont);
```

Like other functions that use the device-context handle as an argument, the SelectObject() function must be used only when a device context has been obtained; that is, between BeginPaint() and EndPaint().

When we obtain the device context, we must save the original font object, which we do in the statement above in the hOldFont variable. This is necessry because this original object must be restored to the device context before we give back the device context with EndPaint(). We do this after displaying the text, in the statement

```
SelectObject(hDC, hOldFont);    // restore original font
```

(Actually it's not a catastrophe if you don't do this with stock fonts, but it's good programming style and for installable fonts it's essential.)

As we'll see in the next chapter, installable fonts must be deleted with the DeleteObject() function. However, stock fonts should not be deleted. In fact, it's bad form to try to delete a stock font.

STATIC VARIABLES

You may have noticed in the WndProc() function in STOCKFON that the iFontType variable is declared with the storage class **static**. As you no doubt remember, in C a static variable, unlike a normal automatic variable, retains its value between calls to the function in which it's declared. If a function sets a static variable to 3, for example, then the next time the function is called the variable will still be 3 (while a normal automatic variable would have some random garbage value).

Why does iFontType need to retain its value between calls to WndProc()? Remember that every message from Windows is conveyed by a function call to WndProc(). If a variable must retain its value between messages, it must retain it between calls to its WndProc() function, since that's what a message is. Declaring a variable static is one way to do this.

The iFontType variable is given a value in two places. The first is when a WM_CREATE message is received, which happens when the program first starts and iFontType is initialized to SYSTEM_FONT. The second is when a WM_COMMAND message is received, as a result of the user selecting an item from the Font menu.

Later, the value of iFontType is accessed when a WM_PAINT message is received. This value is used in GetStockObject() to set the font selected by the user.

Thus iFontType is given a value when we receive WM_CREATE and WM_COMMAND, but this value is not used until we receive WM_PAINT. To make sure that its value is not destroyed between messages, iFontType is declared static.

Variables that must retain their values between messages can also be made external, defined outside any function. This is appropriate for variables referred to by several different functions, but in STOCKFON, iFontType is referenced only in the WndProc() function, so it's more appropriate to make it **static**.

Failure to declare variables **static** (or external) when they are referenced by more than one message is a frequent and insidious source of errors in Windows programs. Your program won't work, but the reason won't be obvious. The moral is to look very carefully at every variable *as you type its declaration*. Ask yourself, does this variable need to retain its value between messages? If so, make it **static** (or external).

We should also note that static variables can cause trouble if you create more than one window of the same class. Why is that? Because all windows of the same class share the same window procedure. Thus all the variables declared in the window procedure will be shared between windows, which could lead to one window trashing another window's variables. We don't create multiple windows of the same class in the examples in this book, so we don't worry about this problem.

DISPLAYING TEXT IN COLUMNS

Now that we know how to obtain different fonts, we can introduce another wrinkle in displaying text: setting text in columns. A fixed-pitch font makes columnized text look better, because the characters line up directly over each other. This is especially nice with columns of numbers. Our example program, COLUMNS, displays some geological information. Besides a fixed-pitch font, it uses a useful new API function called TabbedTextOut(), which allows us to set tab stops at arbitrary locations on the screen. Figure 15-6 shows the output of this program.

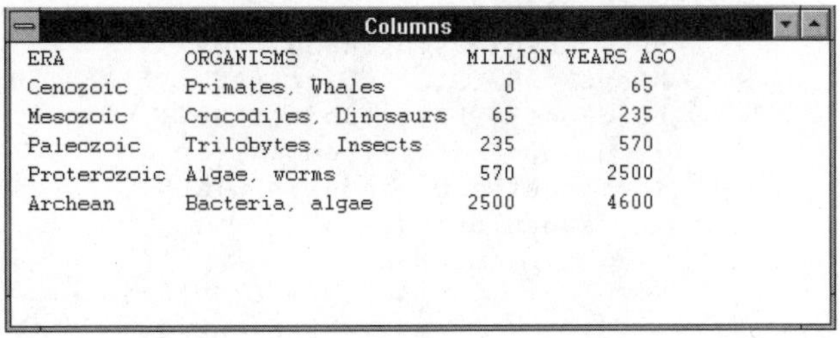

ERA	ORGANISMS	MILLION	YEARS AGO
Cenozoic	Primates, Whales	0	65
Mesozoic	Crocodiles, Dinosaurs	65	235
Paleozoic	Trilobytes, Insects	235	570
Proterozoic	Algae, worms	570	2500
Archean	Bacteria, algae	2500	4600

Figure 15-6
Output of
COLUMNS Program

We don't use any menus with COLUMNS, so there's no need for .H or .RC files. Here's the listing for COLUMNS.C:

```c
// columns.c
// uses fixed-pitch font to display output in columns

#define STRICT
#include <windows.h>

#define TMARGIN  3          // top margin, in pixels
#define LMARGIN 10          // left margin, in pixels
#define CYCHAR  18          // height of characters, in pixels
#define LINES    6          // number of lines to display
#define NTABS    3          // number of tabs

PSTR apszTable[LINES] = { // array of pointers to strings
"ERA\tORGANISMS\tMILLION YEARS AGO",
"Cenozoic\tPrimates, Whales\t  0\t  65",
"Mesozoic\tCrocodiles, Dinosaurs\t  65\t 235",
"Paleozoic\tTrilobytes, Insects\t 235\t 570",
"Proterozoic\tAlgae, worms\t 570\t2500",
"Archean\tBacteria, algae\t2500\t4600" };
                            // array of tabstops
int anTabs[NTABS] = {100,280,370};

                                      // prototype
LRESULT CALLBACK _export WndProc(HWND, UINT, WPARAM, LPARAM);
PSTR szProgName = "Columns";          // application name
#include "stdmain.inc"                // standard WinMain() function
//////////////////////////////////////////////////////////////////
// main window procedure -- receives messages                    //
//////////////////////////////////////////////////////////////////
LRESULT CALLBACK _export WndProc(HWND hWnd, UINT msg,
                         WPARAM wParam, LPARAM lParam)
   {
   HDC hDC;                 // handle for the device context
   PAINTSTRUCT ps;          // holds PAINT information
   int index;               // loop index
   HFONT hFont, hOldFont;   // font handles

   switch(msg)
      {
      case WM_PAINT:                          // repaint the screen
         hDC = BeginPaint(hWnd, &ps);         // get device context
         hFont = GetStockObject(ANSI_FIXED_FONT); // get stock font
         hOldFont = SelectObject(hDC, hFont);     // select font object
         // display text from buffer
         for(index = 0; index < LINES; index++ ) // for each line
            TabbedTextOut( hDC,               // device context
                    LMARGIN,                  // horiz position
                    TMARGIN + CYCHAR*index,   // vert position
                    apszTable[index],         // address of line
                    lstrlen( apszTable[index] ),  // length of line
```

```
                 NTABS,                         // number of tabs
                 anTabs,                        // array of tab stops
                 LMARGIN);                      // start of tabs
      SelectObject(hDC, hOldFont);       // restore original font
      EndPaint(hWnd, &ps);               // painting complete
      break;  //  End of WM_PAINT

   case WM_DESTROY:
      PostQuitMessage(0);
      break;

   default:
      return( DefWindowProc(hWnd, msg, wParam, lParam) );
   }   // end switch(msg)

return 0L;
}  // end WndProc
```

In this program we use GetStockObject() and SelectObject() to install the ANSI Fixed font into the device context whenever we get a WM_PAINT message. Everything we draw will be drawn with this font.

The TabbedTextOut() Function

The TabbedTextOut() function is similar to TextOut(), except that it includes several extra arguments that allow it to specify tab stops. Each time a tab character '\t' is encountered in a line of text, the text display skips to the next tab stop. This makes it easy to line up the text in columns.

Here's how the tab-stop mechanism works. The locations of all the tab stops are placed in an array of type **int**, which we call anTabs. This is sort of like installing tabs on the ruler bar of your word processor: each tab goes to a location measured from the left margin of the paper. These measurements are made in pixels, not character widths.

The array of tabs is the major new argument to TabbedTextOut(). Here's how it looks in COLUMNS.C:

```
int anTabs[NTABS] = { 100, 280, 370 };
```

Each number represents the X-coordinate of a tab stop. Figure 15-7 shows the relation of the tab stops and the array.

The origin for these measurements is specified by the last argument to TabbedTextOut(). We use a value of LMARGIN so the tab-stop origin is the same as the text origin (which is the second argument to the TabbedTextOut() function). This is 10 pixels from the left of the window, the same as in previous programs that used TextOut(). The second column starts 100 pixels to the right of LMARGIN, the third column is 280 pixels from LMARGIN, and the last column is 370 pixels from LMARGIN.

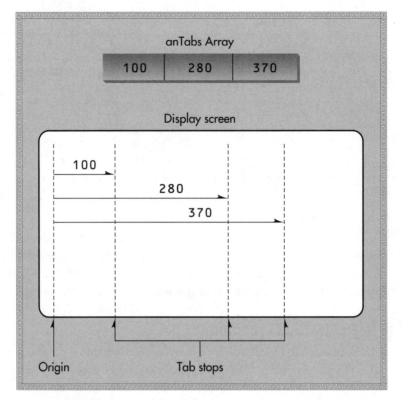

Figure 15-7 Tab Stops and the aTabs Array

Here's how the call to TabbedTextOur() looks:

```
TabbedTextOut( hDC,                        // device context handle
         LMARGIN,                          // X-coordinate of text
         TMARGIN + CYCHAR*index,           // Y-coordinate of text
         apszTable[index],                 // text address
         lstrlen(apszTable[index]),        // length of text string
         NTABS,                            // number of tab stops in array
         anTabs,                           // address of tab-stop array
         LMARGIN );                        // tab origin
```

The last three arguments are the new ones, not shared by TextOut(). The first two of these are the number of elements in the tab-stop array and the address of the array. The third (the last argument) specifies the X-coordinate where the tab-stop measurements should begin.

As you may have guessed, the Hungarian notation in apszTable means an array of pointers to zero-terminated strings, and anTabs means an array of numbers.

SUMMARY

In this chapter we've learned how to use stock fonts. The following code fragment summarizes the use of GetStockObject() and SelectObject() to install a stock font:

```
case WM_PAINT:
    hDC = BeginPaint(hWNd, &ps);
    hFont = GetStockObject(ANSI_VAR_FONT);   // get new stock font
    hOldFont = SelectObject(hDC, hFont);     // select new font
    TextOut(...                              // draw with new font
    SelectObject(hOldFont);                  // restore original font
    EndPaint(hWnd, &ps);
    break;
```

Stock fonts are convenient because you know they're always in Windows; you can use them whenever you want. But the selection of fonts is woefully limited. In the next chapter we'll see how to access an almost unlimited number of fonts.

Remember that any variable that should retain its value between messages must be made **static** or external. An evil sorcerer is waiting to cast a particularly ugly spell on anyone who fails to heed this warning. (Ominous music.)

CHAPTER 16

INSTALLABLE FONTS

There are only a few stock fonts, but Windows gives you access to literally thousands of *installable* fonts, which can be purchased from a variety of manufacturers and loaded into your system. Besides the usual character fonts in a wide assortment of type faces, sizes, and styles, you can also use fonts for foreign languages like Greek and Hebrew, and for mathematical and other symbols.

How does an application find out what fonts are installed in the Windows system? And how does it access these fonts? We'll answer these questions in this chapter. To make things easy, we'll use another one of the famous Excalibur-like magic swords, that give you a great deal of power without much effort on your part. This magic sword is the Font common dialog.

THE COMFONT EXAMPLE

Our example program, COMFONT, is similar to programs we've seen before, such as the EZTEXT program of Chapter 9, *Displaying Text*, in that it displays text on the screen. (Here it's a stanza from "The Song of Hiawatha," by Henry Wadsworth Longfellow.) However, COMFONT goes beyond a simple text display. It contains a single menu item, Fonts. Selecting this item brings up a Font common dialog box that allows you to change the font, the font style (italic, bold, etc.), and the size of the text. Figure 16-1 shows the Font common dialog.

As you can see, this dialog box contains combo boxes that let you select the font name, style, and size. In addition, a text field provides a sample of the resulting selection so you can see what you're getting before clicking on the OK button. (We'll see how to add some bells and whistles to this dialog in the next chapter.)

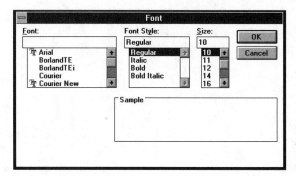

Figure 16-1

The Font Common Dialog in
the COMFONT Program

Once you've made your selection, the poem is displayed in the newly selected font. Figure 16-2 shows the display when a 12-point Lucida Blackletter font (a TrueType font from Microsoft) is selected.

Of course, individual Windows installations may have different fonts installed, so your system may not include the font we show here. Fonts are available from a variety of manufacturers, including Microsoft. Your Windows documentation will guide you through the installation process, which is usually done using the Fonts item in the Control Panel utility.

You can use COMFONT to experiment with the different fonts available in your system. All the available fonts will appear in the Font dialog. Select different fonts. Try using italic, bold, and bold italic. Not all fonts have all these styles. Try out different sizes. Many fonts come only in specific sizes. You can type an unlisted size in the Size combo box, and Windows will try to create the specified size, but the results aren't always all you might hope for. Using the font in the sizes provided gives the cleanest look.

In experimenting with sizes, you may discover that if you use too large a size, the lines of text overlap each other, as shown in Figure 16-3. In the next chapter we'll see how to avoid this unsightly situation.

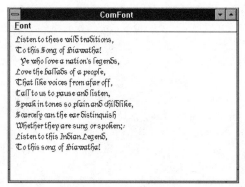

Figure 16-2

Output of the COMFONT Program

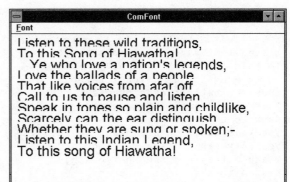

Figure 16-3

The Dreaded Line Overlap

Because we use a menu item in the program, we require an .RC file to specify the menu arrangement, although this file structure is as simple as it can be. Here's the listing for COMFONT.RC:

```
// comfont.rc
// resource script file for comfont

#include "comfont.h"

ComFont MENU   // name must agree with szProgName
   BEGIN
      MENUITEM "&Font", IDM_FONT
   END
```

The header file is correspondingly short. Here's the listing for COMFONT.H:

```
// comfont.h
// header file for comfont

#define IDM_FONT    101
```

This program is an embellished version of EZTEXT. The statements that display the text are the same, but additional code has been added to allow the user to change the font. Here's the listing for COMFONT.C:

```
// comfont.c
// chooses font with common dialog

#define STRICT
#include <windows.h>
#include <commdlg.h>        // for common dialogs
#include <memory.h>         // for memset()
#include "comfont.h"        // header file for IDM_FONT

#define TMARGIN  3          // top margin, in pixels
#define LMARGIN 10          // left margin, in pixels
#define CYCHAR  18          // height of characters, in pixels
```

```
#define LINES    11           // number of lines to display

PSTR Hiawatha[LINES] = {  // array of pointers to strings
"Listen to these wild traditions,",
"To this Song of Hiawatha!",
"   Ye who love a nation's legends,",
"Love the ballads of a people,",
"That like voices from afar off,",
"Call to us to pause and listen,",
"Speak in tones so plain and childlike,",
"Scarcely can the ear distinguish",
"Whether they are sung or spoken;-",
"Listen to this Indian Legend,",
"To this song of Hiawatha!"  };
                                         // prototype
LRESULT CALLBACK _export WndProc(HWND, UINT, WPARAM, LPARAM);


PSTR szProgName = "ComFont";         // application name
#include "stdmain.inc"               // standard WinMain() function
//////////////////////////////////////////////////////////////////
// main window procedure -- receives messages                    //
//////////////////////////////////////////////////////////////////
LRESULT CALLBACK _export WndProc(HWND hWnd, UINT msg,
                          WPARAM wParam, LPARAM lParam)
   {
   HDC hDC;                   // handle for the device context
   PAINTSTRUCT ps;            // holds PAINT information
   int index;                 // loop index
   CHOOSEFONT chf;            // structure for ChooseFont()
   HFONT hFont, hOldFont;     // font handle
   static LOGFONT lf;         // logical font info (note: static)
   static BOOL bFontChosen = FALSE;  // not chosen yet (note: static)

   switch(msg)
      {
      case WM_COMMAND:              // user selects a menu item
         switch(wParam)            // wParam holds item ID
            {
            case IDM_FONT:         // user selects Font
               memset(&chf, 0, sizeof(CHOOSEFONT)); // zero struct
               chf.lStructSize = sizeof(CHOOSEFONT); // struct size
               chf.hwndOwner = hWnd;                 // owner
               chf.lpLogFont = &lf;                  // struct addr
               chf.Flags = CF_SCREENFONTS;           // screen fonts

               if( ChooseFont(&chf) )      // get new font from user
                  {                        // (results in lf)
                  bFontChosen = TRUE;              // font was chosen
                  InvalidateRect(hWnd, NULL, TRUE); // redraw display
                  }
               break;  // end case IDM_FONT

            }   // end switch wParam
```

```
            break;  // end case WM_COMMAND

      case WM_PAINT:                        // repaint the screen
         hDC = BeginPaint(hWnd, &ps);       // get device context
         if(bFontChosen)                    // if font chosen
            {
            hFont = CreateFontIndirect(&lf);    // create logical font
            hOldFont = SelectObject(hDC, hFont);    // select it

            // display text from buffer
            for(index = 0; index < LINES; index++ ) // for each line
               TextOut( hDC,                    // device context
                        LMARGIN,                // horiz position
                        TMARGIN + CYCHAR*index, // vert position
                        Hiawatha[index],        // address of line
                        lstrlen( Hiawatha[index]) ); // length of line
            }
         SelectObject(hDC, hOldFont);       // restore original font
         DeleteObject(hFont);               // delete installable font
         EndPaint(hWnd, &ps);               // painting complete
         break;  // End of WM_PAINT

      case WM_DESTROY:
         PostQuitMessage(0);
         break;
      default:
         return( DefWindowProc(hWnd, msg, wParam, lParam) );
      }  // end switch(msg)
   return 0L;
}  // end WndProc
```

There are two main areas of activity in this program. First, when we receive a WM_COMMAND message with a wParam value of IDM_FONT (as a result of the user's selecting the Font menu item), we set up a structure of type CHOOSEFONT and call the ChooseFont() function. This invokes the Font common dialog, which allows the user to select a font. Second, when a WM_PAINT message arrives, we create a font based on the user's selection, and display the text using that font. The following code fragment shows the essentials of the COMFONT program in condensed form:

```
case WM_COMMAND:
   ...
   ChooseFont(&chf);                  // fill in LOGFONT structure lf
   ...
   break;

case WM_PAINT:
   hDC = BeginPaint(...
   hFont = CreateFontIndirect(&lf); // create new font object using lf
   hOldFont = SelectObject(hDC, hFont); // select new font
   TextOut(...                       // display text
```

```
SelectObject(hDC, hOldFont);        // restore old font
DeleteObject(hFont);                // delete new font
EndPaint(...
break;
```

There are several new API functions involved in displaying text using an installable font. ChooseFont() allows the user to select the font using the Font common dialog, CreateFontIndirect() uses the specifications of the font to create a font object, and DeleteObject() tells Windows we're done with the font. We'll explain each of these functions in turn. We already made the acquaintance of the SelectObject() function in Chapter 15, *Stock Fonts*.

Storing Font Data

Before getting to the API functions, however, let's ask a leading question: how is the information about the font (its name, size, and so on) communicated from the first part of the program, where we receive a WM_COMMAND message and use ChooseFont() to discover what font the user wants; to the second part, where we receive a WM_PAINT message and actually display text based on that font? The answer is that a variable of type LOGFONT, called lf, holds the information about the font. This structure is filled in by ChooseFont(), and the information it contains is used to create the font used to display the text.

What does this tell you about how the lf variable should be declared? That's right: since lf must retain its value between being set in WM_COMMAND and used in WM_PAINT, it must be declared static.

Has a Font Been Chosen?

We don't want to display any text before the user chooses a font. To keep this from happening, we set a flag, bFontChosen, to FALSE when the program is first started. If the ChooseFont() function returns successfully in the WM_COMMAND section, we set bFontChosen to TRUE. In the WM_PAINT section we check its value and only display text if it's TRUE. Again, bFontChosen must be declared static, since it's assigned a value when we receive one message, and this value is used when we receive another.

THE LOGFONT STRUCTURE

When you work with fonts in Windows, you'll find that a central item is usually a structure of type LOGFONT. This structure describes a font in considerable detail. Here's how it's defined in WINDOWS.H:

```
typedef struct tagLOGFONT
   {
   int    lfHeight;                       // height of text
   int    lfWidth;                        // average width of characters
   int    lfEscapement;                   // angle (for italics, etc.)
   int    lfOrientation;                  // not currently used
   int    lfWeight;                       // light, normal, bold, etc.
   BYTE   lfItalic;                       // italic text
   BYTE   lfUnderline;                    // underline text
   BYTE   lfStrikeOut;                    // strikeout (line through text)
   BYTE   lfCharSet;                      // ANSI, OEM, etc.
   BYTE   lfOutPrecision;                 // font selection rules
   BYTE   lfClipPrecision;                // clipping rules
   BYTE   lfQuality;                      // quality rules
   BYTE   lfPitchAndFamily;               // pitch, font family (script, etc.)
   char   lfFaceName[LF_FACESIZE];        // font name (Times New Roman, tc.)
   } LOGFONT;
```

The most important member of this structure is lfFaceName (the last member). This specifies the name of the font; it's this name that the user selects from the menu in the Font common dialog. Also important is lfHeight (the first member), which gives the size of the font. This is related to the list of sizes displayed in the Font common dialog.

The lfItalic and lfUnderline members are set to TRUE or FALSE to specify if the font will be in italic or underlined, and the lfWeight member contains a number that specifies if the font will be in normal or boldface. (It can actually specify a degree of boldness from 100, which is very light, to 900, which is very bold.)

You don't really need to be concerned with the details of the LOGFONT structure, but you do need to be aware of its existence and how it's used.

Logical and Physical Fonts

Note that LOGFONT stands for *logical font*. This structure specifies a logical font, as opposed to a *physical* font. What's the difference? A logical font is merely a *specification* for a font. A physical font, on the other hand, is the detailed information necessary to actually construct characters in the font. The description of a logical font is stored in the LOGFONT structure. The description of a physical font is contained in a .FON file, which is stored in the \WINDOWS\SYSTEM directory. You install this file when you buy a font from the manufacturer. Think of a logical font as representing a wish or desire, and a physical font as representing what you actually get. Sometimes these are not the same. You might desire a handsome white stallion, but end up with a spavined mule. Similarly you may specify a font with certain characteristics, but end up with something a little different.

To understand why we need logical and physical fonts—why we need to deal with the difference between desire and reality—consider the following situation. Suppose you use a word processor to create a document on your computer. You specify a certain font (say Courier) and font size for the document. Then you copy the document to a floppy, and give the floppy to a coworker to edit on another computer. Unfortunately, the Window system on this coworker's computer does not include the same font that you used to create the document. How can the document be displayed?

Here's another situation: suppose you are using a font that comes only in certain sizes, and you request a different size. How does Windows manage to display the document?

The Closest Match

Windows is very clever. If it can't find a physical font that exactly matches the logical font requested, it will try to find a physical font that is *as close a match as possible*. If the font name you requested does not exist in the system, Windows will try to match the general characteristics of the font (serif or not, fixed pitch or not, and so on) and the size. Or, if the specified size is not available, Windows will try to scale the font to the new size, or use another font that does have that size.

Of course, if there is a physical font in the system that does match the logical font, there's no problem. This is the case if your application always runs on the same system, or if (as in the COMFONT program) we let the user choose from the available fonts in the system. Font matching is necessary only when a document (a letter created on a word processor, for example) codes the logical font information into the data file, and this file is then used on a different system.

THE FONT COMMON DIALOG

The COMFONT program uses the Font common dialog box to allow the user to select a font. Before the introduction of this common dialog in Windows 3.1, choosing a font was a surprisingly complex process. A Windows application first found out what fonts were available in the system by reading the WIN.INI file, where all the fonts and the files that contain them, are listed. The application was then responsible for creating a menu (or dialog) to list the font names. It had to create other menus as well to allow the user to select the style and size. Because the font names were not known by the application before it executed, this involved creating menus on the fly, among other complexities. This approach made you feel you were entering the font battles with a rusty teaspoon instead of a sword. Fortunately, the Font common dialog does almost everything for you, with a minimum of fuss.

As with the File common dialogs we saw in Chapter 13, there are two parts to setting up the Font common dialog. First you create a structure and assign values to its members; then you call a function that takes the address of this structure as an argument. There are only four members that need to be filled into the CHOOSEFONT structure. Here's how to fill in these members and call the ChooseFont() function:

```
chf.lStructSize = sizeof(CHOOSEFONT);   // size of CHOOSEFONT structure
chf.hwndOwner = hWnd;                    // our window's handle
chf.lpLogFont = &lf;                     // address of LOGFONT structure
chf.Flags = CF_SCREENFONTS;             // flag: show screen fonts

ChooseFont(&chf);                        // display Font common dialog
```

The first two lines are familiar from the File common dialogs, which also required the size of the structure and our window's handle. In the third member we specify the address of the structure of type LOGFONT. This is where the font information will be stored when the user has chosen the font and ChooseFont() returns. The CF_SCREENFONTS flag specifies that we want to list screen fonts in the Font dialog, as opposed to CF_PRINTERFONTS which would specify only fonts available for printing. (Many times these are the same, but not always.) There are other flags for this member as well, but we'll ignore them for the moment. There are also other members in CHOOSEFONT; they too can be ignored.

The ChooseFont() function invokes the Font common dialog. It returns TRUE if a valid font was chosen, otherwise it returns FALSE (if the user pressed Cancel, for example). If the function is successful, we set a flag called bFontChosen. This flag is used to prevent any display of text until a font is chosen. We then call InvalidateRect() so Windows will send a WM_PAINT message back to our WndProc() function (as discussed in Chapter 13, *The File Common Dialogs*) so we can display the text in the new font.

Creating Objects

When we used stock font objects in the last chapter, we simply obtained a handle to the font and selected it into the device context. However, an installable font object must be *created* before it can be used. Creating an object means that we give Windows a description of the object. Windows then stores this description for later use.

In the case of fonts, creating an object doesn't mean that we design the font in the sense of designing each character (specifying the radius of the curve in the C, how the bottom of the Q curves around, and so on). It simply means that we give Windows the specifications of a logical font: a font name, a size, whether it's italic, and so on. The usual way to do this is to put the description of the font in a LOGFONT structure, and call the CreateFontIndirect() function. That's what we do to create the font in COMFONT. (Another function, CreateFont(), does a similar job but uses arguments to specify the font characteristics, rather than a structure.)

A GDI object created this way has a surprising characteristic: once it has been created, it belongs, not to the program that created it, but to the system as a whole. It can be used by any program running under Windows. This is another potential memory-saving device, because the object doesn't need to be loaded into memory for each program.

Deleting Objects

Because an installable font is a system-wide resource, it is not removed from memory automatically when your program terminates. It can't be, since other programs may be using it. However, if no other programs are using the object, we do want it removed so it doesn't become an orphan, taking up memory space forever (or at least until we reboot the system). To make sure objects are eventually removed, Windows requires your application to execute a DeleteObject() function when it's done with an object. When you do this, Windows deletes the object if no other application is using it. If other applications are using it, Windows keeps track of how many such applications there are, and deletes the object from memory only when *all* the applications are through with it.

You must call DeleteObject() for each graphics object you create. However, don't do this until after you've selected the *original* object back into the device context. After you've done this you can delete the new object whenever you want, either before or after EndPaint(). This is true of any graphics object (such as pens and brushes), not just fonts. The sequence is always

```
hObj = Create...                     // create new object
hOldObj = SelectObject(hDC, hFont);  // select new object into DC
                                     // draw text or graphics
SelectObject(hDC, hOldObj);          // restore old object
DeleteObject(hObj);                  // delete new object
```

If you don't delete graphics objects, you will cause a phenomenon called *memory leakage*. The object will remain in the system, taking up memory space, even though no application is using it. If enough of these objects accumulate in the system, system memory will become too full and Windows will crash. You can check how much space is available for GDI objects by selecting About Program Manager from the Help menu in the Program Manager. The System Resources field tells you the percentage of memory available for graphics objects. When this percentage gets too low, say below 30%, your system may start to behave strangely. Eventually, as the percentage gets lower and lower, Windows will die.

To check if a program has a memory leak, you can run it over and over. If the percentage shown in the System Resources field decreases each time, your program may not be deleting a graphics object. The moral is to be careful to install a DeleteObject() function to match each function that creates an object, such as CreateFontIndirect().

SUMMARY

Here's how to use different installable fonts to display text. Step 1 in the following list takes place when the user requests the Font common dialog box, probably in the WM_COMMAND part of the program when the user makes a menu selection. The remaining steps take place when a WM_PAINT message is received.

1. Display a Font common dialog box by calling the ChooseFont() function. This function gets a font selection from the user, and fills in a LOGFONT structure with the font characteristics.
2. Create a logical font, based on the information in the LOGFONT structure, using the CreateFontIndirect() function.
3. Execute BeginPaint() to obtain a device context handle.
4. Select the new font into the device context using the SelectObject() function.
5. Draw the text in the new font, using TextOut() or a similar function.
6. Reselect the old font object back into the device context with SelectObject().
7. Delete the new font object using the DeleteObject() function (this can also be done after EndPaint().
8. Execute EndPaint() to release the device context.

Remember that if a variable must retain its value between messages (calls to the window procedure), then it must be static or external.

There is much more to learn about the subject of fonts. However, you now know how to use stock fonts, and how to use the Font common dialog to obtain an installable-font selection from the user and display text with it. In the next chapter we'll look at issues connected with the size of the font.

17

TEXT SIZE

*I*n the last chapter we saw that the approach we took to display text was deficient. Using larger fonts resulted in the lines of text being written on top of each other. In this chapter we'll see how to fix this situation by determining the actual size of the font being used, and adjusting our display accordingly. We'll also add some additional features to the Font common dialog that allow us to display text in different colors and use underlining and strikeouts (lines through the middle of the text).

THE TEXTSIZE PROGRAM

Our example program, TEXTSIZE, displays the poem "Jenny Kissed Me," by Leigh Hunt (1784-1859). Also, like the COMFONT program in the last chapter, TEXTSIZE allows you to use any installable font and vary its size by bringing up the Font common dialog box. However, TEXTSIZE (at last!) spaces the lines of text correctly no matter what font you use or what size you specify. Figure 17-1 shows the output when the Script font is used with 26-point type. TEXTSIZE uses a single menu item, Font, to call up the Font dialog box. Thus it needs a resource and header files. Here's the listing for TEXTSIZE.RC:

```
// textsize.rc
// resource script file for textsize

#include "textsize.h"

TextSize MENU   // name must agree with szProgName
   BEGIN
      MENUITEM "&Font", IDM_FONT
   END
```

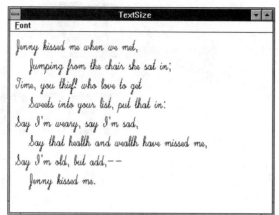

Figure 17-1

Output of the TEXTSIZE Program

Here's the corresponding header file, TEXTSIZE.H:

```
// textsize.h
// header file for textsize

#define IDM_FONT    101
```

There are quite a few new API functions in this program. Here's the listing for TEXTSIZE.C:

```
// textsize.c
// adapts line-spacing to different-size text
// also colors fonts, provides stock fonts

#define STRICT
#include <windows.h>
#include <commdlg.h>            // for common dialogs
#include "textsize.h"           // header file for IDM_FONT

#define LINES   8               // number of lines to display
PSTR Jenny[LINES] = {           // array of pointers to strings
"Jenny kissed me when we met,",
"   Jumping from the chair she sat in;",
"Time, you thief! who love to get",
"   Sweets into your list, put that in:",
"Say I'm weary, say I'm sad,",
"   Say that health and wealth have missed me,",
"Say I'm old, but add,--",
"   Jenny kissed me." };
                                        // prototype
LRESULT CALLBACK _export WndProc(HWND, UINT, WPARAM, LPARAM);
PSTR szProgName = "TextSize";   // application name
#include "stdmain.inc"          // standard WinMain function
////////////////////////////////////////////////////////////////
// main window procedure -- receives messages                  //
////////////////////////////////////////////////////////////////
```

```
LRESULT CALLBACK _export WndProc(HWND hWnd, UINT msg,
                            WPARAM wParam, LPARAM lParam)
   {
   HDC hDC;                   // handle for the device context
   PAINTSTRUCT ps;            // holds PAINT information
   int index;                 // loop index
   static CHOOSEFONT chf;     // struct for ChooseFont() (note: static)
   static LOGFONT lf;         // logical font info (note: static)
   static HFONT hFont;        // font handle (note: static)
   HFONT hOldFont;            // handle for original font
   int cxChar, cyChar;        // character width and height
   TEXTMETRIC tm;             // structure for current font info

   switch(msg)
      {
      case WM_CREATE:                 // start with system font
         hFont = GetStockObject(SYSTEM_FONT);  // get font handle
         GetObject(hFont, sizeof(LOGFONT), &lf);  // put font in lf
         break;

      case WM_COMMAND:                // user selects a menu item
         switch(wParam)              // wParam holds item ID
            {
            case IDM_FONT:           // user selects Font
               chf.lStructSize = sizeof(CHOOSEFONT);  // struct size
               chf.hwndOwner = hWnd;                  // owner
               chf.lpLogFont = &lf;                   // structure
                                      // do screen fonts and color
               chf.Flags = CF_SCREENFONTS | CF_EFFECTS;
               chf.rgbColors = RGB(0,0,0);            // color value
                                                      // (black)
               if( ChooseFont(&chf) )     // get new font from user
                   InvalidateRect(hWnd, NULL, TRUE); // if OK, redraw
               break;  // end case IDM_FONT

            }   // end switch wParam
         break;  // end case WM_COMMAND

      case WM_PAINT:                          // repaint the screen
         hDC = BeginPaint(hWnd, &ps);         // get device context
         hFont = CreateFontIndirect(&lf);     // get logical font
         hOldFont = SelectObject(hDC, hFont); // select it

         SetTextColor(hDC, chf.rgbColors); // set color

         GetTextMetrics(hDC, &tm);           // get text metrics
                                             // find line height
         cyChar = tm.tmHeight + tm.tmExternalLeading;
         cxChar = tm.tmAveCharWidth;         // find char width

         // display text from buffer
         for(index = 0; index < LINES; index++ )  // for each line
            TextOut( hDC,                    // device context
```

```
                    cxChar,                   // horiz position
                    cyChar/3 + cyChar*index,  // vert position
                    Jenny[index],             // address of line
                    lstrlen( Jenny[index]) ); // length of line

        SelectObject(hDC, hOldFont);      // select original font
        DeleteObject(hFont);              // delete new font
        EndPaint(hWnd, &ps);              // painting complete
        break;  // End of WM_PAINT

    case WM_DESTROY:
        PostQuitMessage(0);
        break;

    default:
        return( DefWindowProc(hWnd, msg, wParam, lParam) );
    }   // end switch(msg)

    return 0L;
}   // end WndProc
```

DETERMINING TEXT SIZE

In terms of describing a text font, the LOGFONT structure is only the tip of the iceberg. It specifies the most obvious features of a font: its size, its name, whether it's underlined or not, and several other characteristics. But as we noted, it describes only a logical font; a wish list of what we'd like a font to be. A different structure must be used to describe the details of an actual, existing, physical font: It's called TEXTMETRIC.

The TEXTMETRIC Structure

The TEXTMETRIC structure includes various technical details about an existing physical font. The difference between the LOGFONT and TEXTMETRIC structures is a little like the difference between wishing vaguely for a shiny new helmet for your suit of armor, and being given detailed specifications of a real helmet, including the visor dimensions, eye-hole spacing, rivet lengths, and so on. (Although even TEXTMETRIC doesn't tell you everything about the font, and should certainly not be confused with the actual font itself.) Here's how this structure is defined in WINDOWS.H:

```
typedef struct tagTEXTMETRIC
    {
    int    tmHeight;          // height of cell (ascent+descent)
    int    tmAscent;          // height of cell above baseline
    int    tmDescent;         // depth of cell below baseline
    int    tmInternalLeading;  // top of cell to top of line
```

```
    int    tmExternalLeading;      // vertical space between cells
    int    tmAveCharWidth;         // average character width
    int    tmMaxCharWidth;         // width of widest character
    int    tmWeight;               // line weight (normal, bold, etc.)
    BYTE   tmItalic;               // TRUE if italic
    BYTE   tmUnderlined;           // TRUE if underlined
    BYTE   tmStruckOut;            // TRUE if strikeout
    BYTE   tmFirstChar;            // value of first char defined in font
    BYTE   tmLastChar;             // value of last char defined in font
    BYTE   tmDefaultChar;          // used to represent nonprinting chars
    BYTE   tmBreakChar;            // used for word breaks
    BYTE   tmPitchAndFamily;       // pitch and family
    BYTE   tmCharSet;              // character set
    int    tmOverhang;             // extra width for bold and italic
    int    tmDigitizedAspectX;     // aspect ratio of device for which
    int    tmDigitizedAspectY;     //     font was designed
} TEXTMETRIC;
```

Many members of this structure refer to the dimensions of the font. Figure 17-2 shows some of these dimensions.

Let's examine these dimensions for a moment. Characters are assumed to sit on a *baseline*. Most of the characters extend only upward from the baseline, into the area known as the *ascent*; but those with descenders, such as g, q, and p, extend below the baseline as well, into the *descent*. The highest characters extend to the top of the ascent. Above the ascent is *internal leading*, used for accents as well as line separation. (The term "leading" arose because old-time printers used strips of lead to separate the lines of text.) Some font designers also specify *external leading* as well, which further separates the lines. *Line spacing* is the ascent plus the descent, which together make up the *cell height*, plus any external leading.

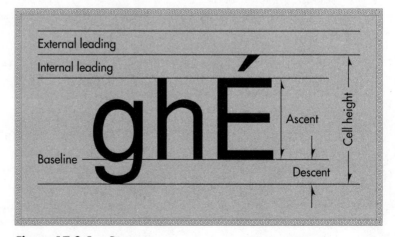

Figure 17-2 Font Dimensions

You'll notice that some of the information in TEXTMETRIC duplicates what's in the LOGFONT function. However, remember the conceptual difference between these two structures. The LOGFONT structure describes the specification for an idealized, logical font. It's typically specified by a document that wants to be printed in a font with those characteristics. The TEXTMETRIC structure provides details of an actual, already-designed physical font. The specifications returned in TEXTMETRIC are determined by the designer of the font; they're the real thing, not a vague desire.

The GetTextMetrics() Function

To obtain the information necessary to fill in a structure of type TEXTMETRIC, we call the GetTextMetrics() function. This function fills the TEXTMETRIC structure with the characteristics of the currently selected physical font. We can make use of any of these dimensions or other attributes in our program. In TEXTSIZE we want to know how far apart to space lines of text, so we're interested in the overall height of the characters and the external leading. We also want to know the width of the letters in the font. We'll use this dimension to set the left margin. In TEXTSIZE we obtain this information directly from the TEXTMETRIC structure, with the lines

```
GetTextMetrics(hDC, &tm);                          // fill in tm structure
cyChar = tm.tmHeight + tm.tmExternalLeading;       // line spacing
cxChar = tm.tmAveCharWidth;                         // character width
```

The line spacing is the cell height (ascent and descent), which is represented by the tmHeight member of TEXTMETRIC, plus the external leading, represented by the tmExternalLeading member. The average character width, represented by tmAveCharWidth, makes a nice separation between the left border of the window and the beginning of the lines of text.

We use these dimensions when drawing the lines of text with TextOut():

```
TextOut( hDC,
         cxChar,                        // left margin
         cyChar/3 + cyChar*index,       // top margin plus line spacing
         Jenny(index),
         lstrlen(Jenny[index]) );
```

The left margin is the average character width, cxChar; the top margin is 1/3 of the line spacing, cyChar/3; and the lines are spaced cyChar apart.

It is common practice to use GetTextMetrics() to find the line spacing even when an application will use only the System stock font. This ensures that text lines will be correctly spaced even on systems with quite different display dimensions. You should definitely use this approach unless you know in advance that your program will be used only on specific display systems.

TEXT COLOR AND EFFECTS

We've added two embellishments to the Font common dialog box in TEXTSIZE. One permits the selection of the color used for text display, using a combo box that allows the user to select one of a number of colored squares. The other provides check boxes called Strikeout and Underline, which allow the text to be displayed with a strikeout line running across it (used in legal documents to show the text of a previous version) or underlined. Figure 17-3 shows what the Font common dialog looks like with these additions. Figure 17-4 shows the result when underline is selected. Unfortunately, we can't show you what color looks like, but trust us, you really can display text in color (if you have a color display, of course).

The color and the strikeout/underline capabilities are achieved by modifying one program statement and adding another in the section where we set up the CHOOSEFONT structure. These statements are

```
chf.Flags = CF_SCREENFONTS | CF_EFFECTS;   // color and effects
chf.rgbColors = RGB(0,0,0);                // set color to black
```

A new flag, CF_EFFECTS, activates both the color combo box and the effects check boxes. We also set the rgbColors member to a value obtained with a macro

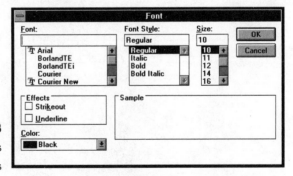

Figure 17-3

Font Dialog with Color and Effects Selections

·Figure 17-4

Underlining Selected in TEXTSIZE

called RGB. We're not going to discuss colors at this point, so we'll defer a discussion of RGB until Part Five, *Graphics*. However, the effect of this statement is to set the initial color selection to black (0 red, 0 green, and 0 blue makes black). The user can select a different color by making a selection from the Color combo box in the Font dialog. This modifies the rgbColors member accordingly.

During WM_PAINT processing we set the color to the one chosen by the user. For this we use the SetTextColor() function:

```
SetTextColor(hDC, chf.rgbColors);
```

SUMMARY

Here's how to space lines of text correctly. All these steps are executed after a device context has been obtained.

1. Select the desired logical font into the device context.
2. Execute the GetTextMetrics() function to write the dimensions of the resulting physical font into a TEXTMETRIC structure.
3. Add the tmHeight and tmExternalLeading members of the TEXTMETRIC structure together to obtain the line spacing.
4. Display the text with TextOut() or a similar function, moving the Y-coordinate for each line the distance determined in Step 3.

Similarly, the average character width is useful for positioning the text horizontally. It's returned in the tmAveCharWidth member of TEXTMETRIC. You may also find uses for the other members of this structure.

CHAPTER

18

TEXT POSITION

*I*n this chapter we're going to focus on positioning text within a window. In the old days of character-mode displays, when the user and the application typed text at each other, the programmer didn't need to worry too much about where text would be displayed. Text was sent to the display with printf() or a similar function, and each line of text appeared under the preceding line, often at the bottom of the screen, where its arrival caused the the screen contents to scroll upward. In Windows, programmers have much more freedom. You can place text anywhere on the screen. It's as if you were a graphics designer laying out articles for a magazine, moving the titles, text, pictures, and other visual elements around to achieve the most pleasing result.

To position text accurately, we need to know the size of the window the text will appear in and the dimensions of an entire line of text (as opposed to a single character). This chapter discusses these topics. We'll also see how to fit text into a rectangular area. Besides being useful in themselves, the techniques we learn in this chapter will be valuable when we encounter scroll bars in the following chapter.

THE WINSIZE PROGRAM

Our first example program, WINSIZE, draws a short line of text at the exact center of the window. Figure 18-1 shows what this looks like. There are no menus associated with this program, so it confines itself to a single file. Here's the listing for WINSIZE.C:

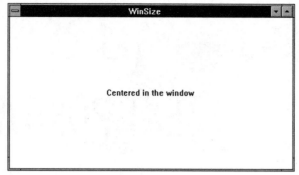

Figure 18-1

Output of WINSIZE

```
// winsize.c
// centers text in window

#define STRICT
#include <windows.h>
                                 // string
PSTR strCenter = "Centered in the window";
                                 // prototype
LRESULT CALLBACK _export WndProc(HWND, UINT, WPARAM, LPARAM);

PSTR szProgName = "WinSize";   // program name
#include "stdmain.inc"          // standard WinMain() function
/////////////////////////////////////////////////////////////////////
// main window procedure -- receives messages                       //
/////////////////////////////////////////////////////////////////////
LRESULT CALLBACK _export WndProc(HWND hWnd, UINT msg,
                                 WPARAM wParam, LPARAM lParam)
   {
   HDC hDC;                       // handle for the device context
   PAINTSTRUCT ps;                // holds PAINT information
   DWORD dwExtent;                // got GetTextExtent
   WORD cxText, cyText;           // length and height of text
   WORD cxPos, cyPos;             // string start location
   RECT rcClient;                 // rectangle structure for window size
   int cxClient, cyClient;        // width and height of window

   switch(msg)
      {
      case WM_PAINT:                       // repaint the screen
         hDC = BeginPaint(hWnd, &ps);      // get device context
                                           // get text dimensions
         dwExtent = GetTextExtent(hDC, strCenter, lstrlen(strCenter));
         cxText = LOWORD(dwExtent);        // extract width and height
         cyText = HIWORD(dwExtent);        //    of entire string

         GetClientRect(hWnd, &rcClient); // get window width and height
         cxClient = rcClient.right;        // (rcClient.left always 0)
```

```
            cyClient = rcClient.bottom;      // (rcClient.top always 0)
                                             // calculate drawing position
            cxPos = (cxText < cxClient) ? (cxClient-cxText)/2 : 0;
            cyPos = (cyClient-cyText)/2;

            // display text string in center of window
            TextOut( hDC,                     // device context
                     cxPos,                   // horiz position
                     cyPos,                   // vert position
                     strCenter,               // address of line
                     lstrlen(strCenter) );    // length of line

            EndPaint(hWnd, &ps);             // painting complete
            break;  //  End of WM_PAINT

       case WM_DESTROY:
          PostQuitMessage(0);
          break;
       default:
          return( DefWindowProc(hWnd, msg, wParam, lParam) );
       }    // end switch(msg)
   return 0L;
}   // end WndProc
```

When we receive a WM_PAINT message, we calculate the size of the text and the size of the window, and then use these dimensions to draw the text in the center of the window.

Text Size

To position the text correctly we must know how big it is. This means not just how big the individual characters are, which we could discover with the GetTextMetrics() function, but how long the entire string of characters is. Since we are using a proportional font, this is not a trivial calculation: the width of each character must be obtained, and the results added together to determine the length of the entire string.

Fortunately a function exists that performs this calculation for us: GetTextExtent(). It returns the height and length of the entire text string. These two word values are compressed into a single, double-word (DWORD) return value. We use the LOWORD macro to extract the width, and HIWORD to extract the height.

GetTextExtent() works with the currently selected font, so it must be executed in a particular device context. The arguments to GetTextExtent() are the device context handle (as usual), the address of the text string, and the number of characters in the string. Here's how that looks:

```
case WM_PAINT:
   hDC = BeginPaint(...
   dwExtent = GetTextExtent(hDC, strCenter, lstrlen(strCenter));
```

```
cxText = LOWORD(dwExtent);        // length of text
cyText = HIWORD(dwExtent);        // height of text
...
EndPaint(...
break;
```

The result is cxText, the length of the entire line of text; and cyText, its height.

Window Size

The rectangular area of a window that is available for drawing is called the *client area* (since an application is thought of as a client of the operating system). This is the blank white (or other color, if you changed it with the control panel) area of a standard window. We can find the dimensions of this client area with the API function GetClientRect(). This function takes two arguments: the handle of the window, and the address of a structure in which GetClientRect() will place the coordinates of the client area.

The structure, of type RECT, is commonly used in Windows for storing the coordinates of rectangles. It's a rather simple structure, compared with those we've been grappling with to describe fonts. Here's how it's defined in WINDOWS.H:

```
typedef struct tagRECT
    {
    int left;
    int top;
    int right;
    int bottom;
    } RECT;
```

The members of this structure are the coordinates of the four sides of a rectangle, measured from the upper left corner of the window's client area. We call our RECT structure variable rcClient (rc is the Hungarian for rectangle). Since we're discussing the entire client area of the window, the left and top members are always 0, and the right and bottom members represent the client area's width and height.

For convenience we set our own variables, cxClient and cyClient, to the client area's width and height (the Hungarian cx and cy mean a count in the X or Y direction.) Thus finding the dimensions of our window's client area looks like this:

```
RECT rcClient;
...
GetClientRect(hWnd, &rcClient);   // fill RECT structure with dimensions
cxClient = rcClient.right;        // width of window's client area
cyClient = rcClient.bottom;       // height of window's client area
```

We should note that the width and height of the client area can also be found by extracting the low word and high word of the lParam value that accompanies the WM_SIZE message. Some programmers use this approach, but it is not as straightforward as calling GetClientRect() when WM_PAINT arrives.

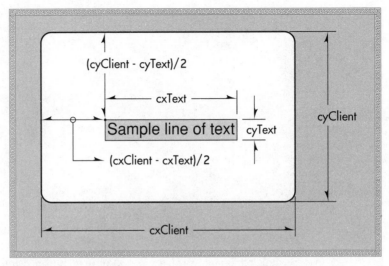

Figure 18-2 Positioning Text in WINSIZE

Calculating the Text Position

As we've seen, the TextOut() function must be told the coordinates of the upper left corner of the text line to be displayed. These are the coordinates we need to position the text. They depend on the text dimensions and client area dimensions previously found. The simple solution is

```
cxPos = (cxClient - cxText)/2;
cyPos = (cyClient - cyText)/2;
```

This is shown in Figure 18-2. This looks good if the window is big enough to hold the entire text string. However, what happens if the string is wider than the window? There are several ways to handle this, but what looks best is to chop off the string on the right side but not the left, so the beginning of the string is always visible. Thus when the text is wider than the window, we want cxPos to be 0. That's what this statement accomplishes:

```
cxPos = (cxText < cxClient) ? (cxClient-cxText)/2 : 0;
```

using C's conditional operator. Figure 18-3 shows the result.

THE DRAWTEXT PROGRAM

So far the text output functions we've used, like TextOut() and TabbedTextOut(), draw only one line of text at a time. This is fine if our text is neatly stored in the program so that each string contains one line of text. But what happens if we're

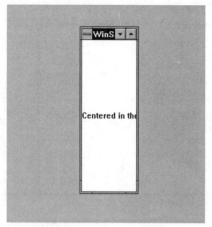

Figure 18-3

WINSIZE Text Wider
than the Window

given a whole paragraph (or many pages) of text crammed into a single string? If we used TextOut(), most of a long string would extend invisibly beyond the right edge of the window; this would not be very satisfactory for the viewer. However, an amazing Windows function called DrawText() solves this problem. It takes a text string of arbitrary length and displays it in a rectangular area, automatically breaking lines at word boundaries when necessary. (This is called "word wrap" in word processing programs.)

Our example program, DRAWTEXT, uses DrawText() to display a short prose selection. Figure 18-4 shows what this looks like when two instances of the program use different-sized windows.

There's no need for a resource or a header file in the DRAWTEXT example. Here's the listing for DRAWTEXT.C:

```c
// drawtext.c
// writes text in rectangle using DrawText()

#define STRICT
#include <windows.h>
#define BORDER 5              // size of border around text
                             // string
PSTR strLong = "When Hortense found that Rodney had absconded \
with the gems, leaving naught but empty sacks as evidence that \
they had ever existed, she immediately thought of Colonel \
Farlough. He would know what to do. Wasn't he the man who had \
tracked the vile Mr. Blathly to his lair in Rangoon? She dashed \
off a note and rang for the footman.\n \
\n \
from \"A Duchess in the Offing\" by Violet Trundle-Hyde";

                             // prototype
LRESULT CALLBACK _export WndProc(HWND, UINT, WPARAM, LPARAM);
```

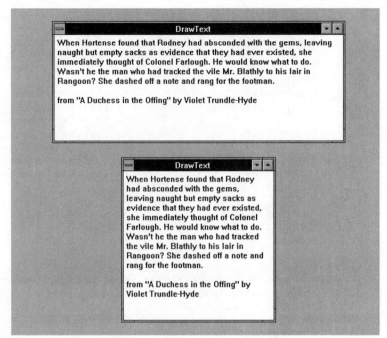

Figure 18-4

Output of the
DRAWTEXT Program

```
PSTR szProgName = "DrawText";   // program name
#include "stdmain.inc"          // standard WinMain() function
///////////////////////////////////////////////////////////////////
// main window procedure -- receives messages                    //
///////////////////////////////////////////////////////////////////
LRESULT CALLBACK _export WndProc(HWND hWnd, UINT msg,
                                 WPARAM wParam, LPARAM lParam)
    {
    HDC hDC;                    // handle for the device context
    PAINTSTRUCT ps;             // holds PAINT information
    int cxClient, cyClient;     // size of window
    RECT rcText;                // rectangle for text dimensions
    RECT rcClient;              // rectangle for window dimensions

    switch(msg)
        {
        case WM_PAINT:                          // repaint the screen
            hDC = BeginPaint(hWnd, &ps);        // get device context

            // get window width and height
            GetClientRect(hWnd, &rcClient);
            cxClient = rcClient.right;          // (rcClient.left always 0)
            cyClient = rcClient.bottom;         // (rcClient.top always 0)

            // set rectangle to window coordinates, less border
            SetRect(&rcText,                    // address of rectangle
```

```
                      BORDER,              // left
                      BORDER,              // top
                      cxClient-BORDER*2,   // right
                      cyClient-BORDER*2);  // bottom

          // display text string in rectangle
          DrawText(hDC,                    // device context
                   strLong,                // string
                   -1,                     // if it's null-terminated
                   &rcText,                // address of rectangle
                   DT_LEFT | DT_WORDBREAK);  // left justified,
                                             // break on words
          EndPaint(hWnd, &ps);             // painting complete
          break;  //  End of WM_PAINT

       case WM_DESTROY:
          PostQuitMessage(0);
          break;

       default:
          return( DefWindowProc(hWnd, msg, wParam, lParam) );
       }   // end switch(msg)

    return 0L;
}  // end WndProc
```

The SetRect() Function

As we'll see, the DrawText() function requires a structure of type RECT as one of its arguments. It is within this rectangle that it will draw the text. What are the coordinates of this rectangle? Generally we want the rectangle to coincide with our window, so that when we display text it will fill the window.

In DRAWTEXT we get the coordinates of the window as we did in the last program, by calling GetClientRect() and assigning the values returned in a structure of type RECT to the variables cxClient and cyClient. These represent the width and height of the window. Actually, it's more pleasing visually if we provide a small margin around the edges of the rectangle, so the text doesn't butt right up to the window edges. We'll #define the size of this margin as the constant BORDER (equal to 5 pixels).

The origin of the window coordinate system is the upper left corner of the window, so the coordinates of the rectangle in which we want to display our text are

```
BORDER                     // left
BORDER                     // top
cxClient - BORDER*2        // right
cyClient - BORDER*2        // bottom
```

The RECT structure to be used as an argument to DrawText() is called rcText. We could simply assign the coordinates shown above to the members of this structure, as in

```
rcText.left = BORDER;
rcText.top = BORDER;
rcText.right = cxClient - BORDER*2;
rcText.bottom = cyClient - BORDER*2;
```

but it's somewhat more elegant to use a function, SetRect() to do this for us. Here's how that looks:

```
SetRect(&rcText,                    // address of RECT structure
        BORDER,                     // left
        BORDER,                     // top
        cxClient-BORDER*2,          // right
        cyClient - BORDER*2 );      // bottom
```

Once the rcText structure is filled in with the appropriate coordinates, we're ready to call DrawText().

The DrawText() Function

The DrawText() function displays a string within a rectangle. Here's how the call to it looks in the DRAWTEXT program:

```
DrawText(hDC,                       // device context handle
         strLong,                   // address of string
         -1,                        // length, or -1 if null-terminated
         &rcText,                   // address of rectangle structure
         DT_LEFT | DT_WORDBREAK);   // flags
```

Besides the device context handle, we have the address of the string as the second argument, and its length as the third. If the length is set to –1, Windows knows that the string is null-terminated (the way strings are supposed to be in C). The address of the RECT structure is the fourth argument. In the fifth argument, the DT_LEFT flag tells DrawText() to left-justify the text. You could also use DT_CENTER or DT_RIGHT. The DT_WORDBREAK flag means that the text should break at the spaces between words. Various other flags can also be used to achieve more specialized results.

SUMMARY

This chapter has introduced several useful API functions that relate to text dimensions. You can find the dimensions of a text string with GetTextExtent(). GetClientRect() will return the dimensions of the rectangle in which you must fit the text in your window. It takes as an argument a structure of type RECT, whose four members represent the coordinates of a rectangle. The SetRect() function fills in a structure of type RECT with a rectangle's coordinates. The DrawText() function uses a RECT structure as an argument, and displays a long text string in the rectangle, breaking the lines at the rectangle boundaries.

In the next chapter we'll put our knowledge of text size and position to work in adding scroll bars to a text display.

CHAPTER 19

SCROLL BARS IN THE WINDOW

Some medieval tapestries stretched the entire length of rather large castle rooms. Sometimes they even turned corners, covering more than one wall (as does the famous Bayeux tapestry, which depicts the Norman conquest of England and is 231 feet long). You can't see all the scenes in such a large tapestry at once; you must walk slowly along it, focusing on one part at a time.

In a similar way a Windows text document may be too large to view all at once. However, rather than walking to a different part of the document, you use the mouse to scroll the document in the window. As all Windows users know, this is handled with controls called *scroll bars*, which are the sliders at the right edge, and often the bottom, of a window. When a display is too large to fit in a window, scroll bars allow the user to move the image vertically or horizontally so any part of it can be seen. You can imagine other ways to view a document too large to fit in a window (selecting Up and Down items from a menu, for example), but scroll bars offer a simple, fast, and intuitive solution.

In this chapter we'll show how to add scroll bars to a main window. There are three example programs. The first demonstrates a vertical scroll bar; the second, which is similar, demonstrates a horizontal scroll bar; and the third uses both vertical and horizontal scroll bars and in addition includes the ability to select different fonts and type sizes to show how scrolling can be made to work with any size text.

SCROLLING TERMINOLOGY

We should agree, before we begin our discussion of scroll bars, what the various parts of the scroll bar are called and what they're supposed to do. Figure 19-1 shows a vertical scroll bar.

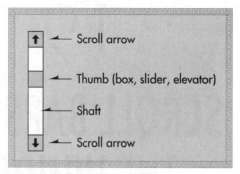

Figure 19-1 Vertical Scroll Bar

The scroll bar consists mostly of a *shaft*, by analogy with an elevator shaft in a building. At the top and bottom of the shaft are *scroll arrows*. In the shaft, and able to slide up and down it, is a square shape variously called the *thumb, box, slider*, or *elevator*. We'll call it the thumb.

When displaying text, manipulating the various parts of a vertical scroll bar should have the effects shown in Table 19-1.

Notice that the text moves in the opposite direction to the thumb and the arrows. When you click on the up arrow or move the thumb upward, the concept is that you're moving the window *upward* over the text; thus the text moves *downward*.

Dragging the thumb should scroll the text to a position proportional to the scroll bar's position in the shaft. That is, if the thumb is at the top of the shaft, the top screen of text should be displayed. If the thumb is in the middle, the middle screen of text should be displayed, and so on. The position of the thumb thus provides an indication to the user of which part of the document is being displayed.

Table 19-1 Vertical Scroll Bar Actions

Action	Moves Text	wParam Value
Click on up scroll arrow	Down one line	SB_LINEUP
Click on shaft above thumb	Down one screen	SB_PAGEUP
Drag the thumb	To instantaneous position	SB_THUMBTRACK
Release the thumb	To position at release	SB_THUMBPOSITION
Click on shaft below thumb	Up one screen	SB_PAGEDOWN
Click on down scroll arrow	Up one line	SB_LINEDOWN

Dragging the thumb can have one of two different effects, depending on how the program is written. Ideally, the text should move at the same time the thumb is dragged. However, on slower machines this may slow down the scrolling process too much, so some programs are written to move the text only when the thumb is released.

Whenever the user interacts with a vertical scroll bar, Windows sends a WM_VSCROLL message to the window procedure of the window containing the scroll bar. The wParam parameter of this message uses one of the constants shown in Table 19-1 to tell the application what the user did.

VERTICAL SCROLLING

Our example program, EZVSCROL, displays a poem with quite a few lines, and adds a vertical scroll bar so all the lines can be viewed by the user, even when the window is sized much smaller than the vertical extent of the text. Figure 19-2 shows the window when viewing the last few lines of the poem in a small window.

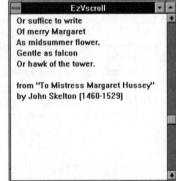

Figure 19-2

Output of EZVSCROL Program

There's no need for a resource file with EZVSCROL, so all we need is the EZVSCROL.C file:

```
// ezvscrol.c
// scrolls the screen vertically

#define STRICT
#include <windows.h>

#define TMARGIN   3        // top margin, in pixels
#define LMARGIN  10        // left margin, in pixels
#define CYCHAR   18        // height of characters
#define LINES    22        // number of lines to be displayed

PSTR margaretCLINES] = {   // array of strings
```

```
         "Merry Margaret,",
         "As midsummer flower,",
         "Gentle as falcon",
         "Or hawk of the tower;",
         "With solace and gladness,",
         "Much mirth and no madness,",
         "All good and no badness;",
         "So joyously,",
         "So maidenly,",
         "So womanly,",
         "Her demeaning;",
         "In every thing",
         "Far far passing",
         "That I can indite",
         "Or suffice to write",
         "Of merry Margaret",
         "As midsummer flower,",
         "Gentle as falcon",
         "Or hawk of the tower.",
         "",
         "from \"To Mistress Margaret Hussey\"",
         "by John Skelton (1460-1529)" };
                                           // prototype
LRESULT CALLBACK _export WndProc(HWND, UINT, WPARAM, LPARAM);

PSTR szProgName = "EzVscroll";       // application name
#include "stdmain.inc"               // standard WinMain function
///////////////////////////////////////////////////////////////////
// main window procedure -- receives messages                     //
///////////////////////////////////////////////////////////////////
LRESULT CALLBACK _export WndProc(HWND hWnd, UINT msg,
                                 WPARAM wParam, LPARAM lParam)
   {
   HDC hDC;                       // handle for the device context
   PAINTSTRUCT ps;                // holds PAINT information
   RECT rcClient;                 // dimensions of client window
   int cyClient;                  // height of client window
   static int nPos;               // vertical scroll-bar position (static)
   int index;                     // loop index

   switch(msg)
      {
      case WM_CREATE:
         nPos = 0;                 // start at first line
         SetScrollRange(hWnd,      // window handle
                        SB_VERT,   // vertical scroll bar
                        0,         // minimum position
                        LINES-1,   // maximum position
                        FALSE);    // don't redraw thumb
         break;  // end WM_CREATE

      case WM_VSCROLL:       // handle scroll bar messages
```

```
        GetClientRect(hWnd, &rcClient);  // get height of
        cyClient = rcClient.bottom;       // client window
        switch(wParam)                    // type of vert scroll message
            {                             // one line up or down
            case SB_LINEUP:   nPos--; break;
            case SB_LINEDOWN: nPos++; break;
                                          // one screen up or down
            case SB_PAGEUP:   nPos -= cyClient/CYCHAR - 1; break;
            case SB_PAGEDOWN: nPos += cyClient/CYCHAR - 1; break;
                                          // set to thumb position
            case SB_THUMBTRACK:      // before release (if too slow,)
        //  case SB_THUMBPOSITION:   // after release  (use this one)
                            nPos = LOWORD(lParam); break;
            default: break;
            }                             // keep in range
        nPos = max( 0, min(nPos, LINES-1) );
                                          // has thumb moved at all?
        if( nPos != GetScrollPos(hWnd, SB_VERT) )
            {                             // if so, reposition it
            SetScrollPos(hWnd,            // window handle
                      SB_VERT,    // vertical scroll bar
                      nPos, // position of thumb
                      TRUE);      // redraw the thumb

            InvalidateRect(hWnd, NULL, TRUE);  // redraw window
            }
        break;  // end WM_VSCROLL

    case WM_PAINT:                        // repaint the screen
        hDC = BeginPaint(hWnd, &ps);  // get device context

        // display the output buffer
        for(index = 0; index < LINES; index++ )  // for each line
            TextOut( hDC,                         // DC
                     LMARGIN,                     // horiz pos
                     TMARGIN + CYCHAR*(index-nPos), // vert pos
                     margaret[index],             // string
                     lstrlen( margaret[index]) ); // str length

        EndPaint(hWnd, &ps);  // tell Windows painting complete
        break;  //  end WM_PAINT

    case WM_DESTROY:
        PostQuitMessage(0);
        break;
    default:
        return( DefWindowProc(hWnd, msg, wParam, lParam) );
    }   // end switch(msg)
return 0L;
}  // end WndProc
```

Adding a scroll bar to a program requires several new sections of code, which are summarized in the following list:

1. Set the scroll range with SetScrollRange().
2. Find the client window size with GetClientRect().
3. React to different kinds of WM_VSCROLL messages.
4. Set the thumb position with SetScrollPos().
5. Display the appropriate lines of text.

The variable nPos ties all this together. This variable represents two things. First, it's the position of the thumb on the shaft, from 0 at the top to some maximum value at the bottom. Second, it's the number of the line of text that should appear at the top of the screen. That is, if line number 5 of the poem is at the top of the screen, nPos should be 5.

The implication here is that the position of the thumb is tied to the line numbers of text to be displayed. The range of thumb positions should equal the number of lines of text. If there are 10 lines of text, the scroll positions should run from 0 to 9. For each scroll position (each value of nPos), a different line of text appears at the top of the display. Most of the sections of code listed above interact with nPos. Let's examine these sections in more detail.

Setting the Scroll Range

Before we do anything with the scroll bars, we need to tell Windows the possible range of positions the thumb can assume. This allows Windows to position the thumb correctly when we send it a new thumb position. For example, suppose we tell Windows that the scroll range will be from 0 to 9. Then if we tell it to position the thumb at 5, it knows to position it in the middle of the scroll bar. Or if we tell it to position the thumb at 1, it positions it one-tenth of the way down.

The function used to set the scroll range is the aptly named SetScrollRange(). Here's how it looks in EZVSCROL:

```
SetScrollRange(hWnd,    // handle of window containing scroll bar
            SB_VERT,    // for vertical bar (SB_HORZ for horizontal)
            0,          // lower end of range
            LINES-1,    // upper end of range
            FALSE);     // don't redraw thumb now
```

The third and fourth parameters specify the range. For text, the lower end of the range is usually set to 0, and the upper end to the number of lines of text to be displayed (less 1, since we start at 0).

The last parameter specifies whether the scroll bar should be redrawn to reflect a new thumb position that might result from executing this function. The thumb starts out at the top of the scroll bar, which is where we want it, so we set this argument to FALSE.

When the number of lines of text to be displayed is fixed, as in EZVSCROL, then SetScrollRange() can be executed when a WM_CREATE message is received.

However, if you were displaying a text file you had just read from disk, whose length you didn't know in advance, you would probably want to execute SetScrollRange() each time you read in a file.

Besides setting the scroll range, this function plays another significant role in EZVSCROL: it causes the scroll bar to be displayed. Without this function, the scroll bar does not appear. Many programmers add a WS_VSCROLL constant to the dwStyle argument to the CreateWindow() function to create the scroll bar. (This function, as you may remember, is located in our STDMAIN.INC file and creates our program's main window.) However, this isn't necessary. Simply executing SetScrollPos() causes Windows to add the scroll bar to the window at the same time the range is set.

Finding the Client Window Size

When the user clicks on the shaft, we scroll the text up or down one screen, depending on whether the mouse pointer was above or below the thumb. (The word "screen," while commonly used in this context, actually means the client area of the window.) To scroll the text one screen, we need to know how large the client area is, so we will know how many lines of text to scroll. As in the last chapter, we find these dimensions with the GetClientRect() function:

```
GetClientRect(hWnd, &rcClient);
cyClient = rcClient.bottom;        // height of client area
```

We'll use this value later when we process messages from the scroll bar.

We should note a nuance in screen-by-screen scrolling. Microsoft recommends that when you scroll one screen upward, the text line that was at the bottom of the old screen should appear at the top of the new one. For example, if five lines of text, say lines 1 to 5, are displayed in the window, scrolling one screen upward should display lines 5 to 9, not lines 6 to 10. Similarly, when you scroll one screen downward, the text line that was at the top of the old screen should appear at the bottom of the new one. Repeating one line this way provides a sense of continuity to the user; a reassurance that the program has not lost any of the text.

Reacting to WM_SCROLL Messages

The most complex part of installing a scroll bar in your program is reacting to the messages that arrive from the scroll bar. Actually there is only one message for a vertical scroll bar: WM_VSCROLL. (The corresponding message for a horizontal scroll bar is WM_HSCROLL.) However, this message conveys different meanings depending on the value of its wParam argument. We listed these values earlier in Table 19-1.

Here's how we handle these wParam values in EZVSCROL:

```
switch(wParam)
   {
   case SB_LINEUP:      nPos--;                              break; // line up
   case SB_LINEDOWN:    nPos++;                              break; // line down
   case SB_PAGEUP:      nPos -= cyClient/CYCHAR - 1; break; // screen up
   case SB_PAGEDOWN:    nPos += cyClient/CYCHAR - 1; break; // screen dn
   case SB_THUMBTRACK:  nPos = LOWORD(lParam);       break; // thumb pos
   default: break;
   }
```

As we noted, the nPos variable specifies which text line will appear at the top of the screen. The SB_LINEUP and SB_LINEDOWN constants increase or decrease this variable by one line. The SB_PAGEUP and SB_PAGEDOWN constants increase or decrease it by the number of lines on the screen (minus one line). The number of lines on the screen is cyClient/CYCHAR, the height of the window divided by the height of one line of text. We subtract 1 from this quantity to scroll one fewer lines than are on the screen, as we discussed earlier.

In the last line of code we handle SB_THUMBTRACK. This wParam value is received whenever the thumb moves. It is accompanied by an lParam value whose low-order word is the new thumb position. We simply set nPos to this value.

If you have an older computer, you may find that your text scrolls too slowly when you use SB_THUMBTRACK as we show here. This is because the text is redisplayed for each individual thumb position. When you slide along 20 positions, the text is redrawn 20 times. On slower machines this causes scrolling to be reduced to an unacceptable rate for many users. To fix this, you can respond to a different wParam value: SB_THUMBPOSITION. This value is received only when the thumb is released, not whenever it moves. You handle this message the same way, by setting nPos to the low-order word of lParam, which represents the position of the thumb:

```
case SB_THUMBPOSITION: nPos = LOWORD(lParam); break; // thumb position
```

Now when the user slides the thumb, the text doesn't move; but when the thumb is released, the text snaps into the new position. This isn't as nice as a continuous scroll, but on slow computers it may be the only acceptable approach.

Once we've found the new nPos value, we need to make sure it's within the permissible range of values, which in our program is between 0 and LINES−1. We do this by calling on two macros, max() and min(), which are defined in WINDOWS.H. These macros return the maximum and the minimum values, respectively, of their two arguments. Thus the statement

```
nPos = max( 0, min(nPos, LINES-1) );
```

sets nPos to 0 if it's less than 0, and to LINES−1 if it's greater than LINES−1. Otherwise it's unchanged.

There is a question of what should be displayed in the lowest screen; that is, what will be visible when the thumb is at the bottom of the shaft. Different applications handle this in different ways. Some show a completely blank screen, some show the last few lines of text at the top of the screen, and some show the entire last screenful of text.

In EZVSCROL we elect to show the single last line of text at the top of the screen, with everything else blank. This assures the user that the text is still there, but also indicates that the end of the text has been reached, saying in effect, "See, there's nothing after the last line."

If you want to keep more lines on the screen when the thumb is at the bottom, the −1 in the line shown above can be altered. For example, if you want to keep 7 lines on screen, use the line

```
nPos = max( 0, min(nPos, LINES-7) );
```

A similar substitution of LINES–7 for LINES–1 must be made in the SetScrollRange() function.

Setting the Thumb Position

Once we receive the WM_VSCROLL message telling us what the user is doing to the scroll bar, we need to set the thumb to the new position. You might think that Windows would take care of this for us, but leaving it to the application presumably provides increased flexibility. Positioning the thumb is done with the SetScrollPos() function. We also need to send ourselves a WM_PAINT message to cause the window to be redrawn, which we do with the usual InvalidateRect() function.

However, we don't want to reset the thumb position or redraw the window if the thumb position hasn't actually changed when we receive a WM_VSCROLL message. For example, the thumb may already be at the top of the scroll bar when the user clicks on the up arrow. Now nPos can't change, since it's already at its minimum value. If we redraw the screen when this happens, we make the display jiggle (as a result of the redraw) without accomplishing anything. To eliminate this behavior, we get the current thumb position with a function called GetScrollPos(), and compare it with our current value of nPos. If they're the same, we don't need to do anything. Here's how this section of code looks:

```
if( nPos != GetScrollPos(hWnd, SB_VERT) )
   {
   SetScrollPos(hWnd,        // our window handle
             SB_VERT,    // vertical scroll bar (horiz is SB_HORZ)
             nPos,       // new position
             TRUE);      // redraw the thumb
   InvalidateRect(hWnd, NULL, TRUE);  // redraw window with new text
   }
```

The arguments to SetScrollPos() are similar to those for SetScrollRange() except that we use a single position value instead of two range values. Also, we set the last argument to TRUE so the thumb will be redrawn whenever its position changes.

Displaying the Text

We draw the text when we receive a WM_PAINT message, as we've seen in many previous programs. The difference is in where we position the line in the window. Here's how the TextOut() function looks:

```
TextOut( hDC,                            // device context handle
         LMARGIN,                        // horizontal position
         TMARGIN + CYCHAR*(index-nPos),  // vertical position
         margaret(index),                // address of string
         lstrlen(margaret[index]) );     // length of string
```

The unusual argument here is the third, which specifies the vertical position of the text line being drawn. Instead of CYCHAR*index, as in previous examples, it's CYCHAR*(index–nPos). This has the effect of displaying the line with the value of nPos at the top of the window.

Improvements

There are several embellishments you could make to our scroll bar routine that we don't show here. For one thing, we have assumed a constant line spacing, CYCHAR, instead of calculating it using GetTextMetrics() as we showed in Chapter 17, *Text Size*. In a serious program, you would want to use this more accurate approach to line spacing.

Also, we always display all the lines of text, running our **for** loop from 0 to LINES–1. We leave it to Windows to clip off the lines that don't fit in the window. This approach works fine if the total number of lines is fairly small. However, if you have 1,000 lines of text, displaying them all can be rather time consuming, even if most of them don't actually appear in the window. This is easily fixed by changing the limits in the **for** loop to start at the first line to be displayed, nPos, and to end at either the total number of lines or the number of lines that will fit in the window, whichever is smaller. That looks like this:

```
for(index = nPos; index < min(LINES, nPos+cyClient/CYCHAR+1); index++)
    {
    TextOut(...
    }
```

This is the preferred approach if the total number of lines is large. We'll incorporate these improvements in the SCROLFON example later in this chapter.

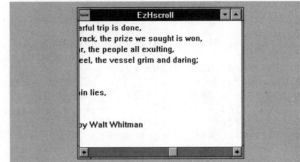

Figure 19-3

Output of the

EZHSCROL Program

HORIZONTAL SCROLLING

So far we've concentrated on vertical scrolling, but horizontal scrolling is accomplished in a similar way. Our next example program, EZHSCROL, shows how it's done. It displays another stanza of a poem, this one with fewer but longer lines (it's about the assassination of President Lincoln). Figure 19-3 shows the output when the window is too narrow for the line lengths, and the poem is scrolled toward the right ends of the lines.

The code to accomplish horizontal scrolling is almost identical to that for vertical scrolling. Here's the listing for EZHSCROL.C:

```
// ezhscrol.c
// scrolls the screen horizontally

#define STRICT
#include <windows.h>

#define TMARGIN  3        // top margin, in pixels
#define LMARGIN 10        // left margin, in pixels
#define CYCHAR  18        // height of characters
#define CXCHAR   7        // width of characters
#define LINES   10        // number of lines to display
#define COLS    52        // number of columns

PSTR captain[LINES] = {
"Oh Captain! my Captain! our fearful trip is done,",
"The ship has weathered every rack, the prize we sought is won,",
"The port is near, the bells I hear, the people all exulting,",
"While follow eyes the steady keel, the vessel grim and daring;",
"But O heart! heart! heart!",
"   O the bleeding drops of red,",
"     Where on the deck my Captain lies,",
"       Fallen cold and dead.",
```

```
"",
"from \"O Captain! My Captain!\" by Walt Whitman" };
                                    // prototype
LRESULT CALLBACK _export WndProc(HWND, UINT, WPARAM, LPARAM);

PSTR szProgName = "EzHscroll";      // application name
#include "stdmain.inc"              // standard WinMain function
////////////////////////////////////////////////////////////////////
// main window procedure -- receives messages                      //
////////////////////////////////////////////////////////////////////
LRESULT CALLBACK _export WndProc(HWND hWnd, UINT msg,
                                 WPARAM wParam, LPARAM lParam)
  {
  HDC hDC;                          // handle for the device context
  PAINTSTRUCT ps;                   // holds PAINT information
  RECT rcClient;                    // client window dimensions
  int cxClient;                     // client window width
  static int nPos;                  // horiz scroll-bar position (static)
  int index;                        // loop index

  switch(msg)
    {
    case WM_CREATE:
      SetScrollRange(hWnd,          // window handle
                     SB_HORZ,       // horizontal scroll bar
                     0,             // minimum position
                     COLS-1,        // maximum position
                     FALSE);        // don't redraw thumb
      break;  // end WM_CREATE

    case WM_HSCROLL:       // handle scroll bar messages
      GetClientRect(hWnd, &rcClient);  // get width of
      cxClient = rcClient.right;       // client window
      switch(wParam)
        {                              // one line left or right
        case SB_LINELEFT: nPos--; break;
        case SB_LINERIGHT: nPos++; break;
                                       // one screen left or right
        case SB_PAGELEFT:  nPos -= cxClient/CXCHAR; break;
        case SB_PAGERIGHT: nPos += cxClient/CXCHAR; break;
                                       // set to thumb position
        case SB_THUMBTRACK:            // before release (if too slow,)
      // case SB_THUMBPOSITION:        // after release  (use this one)
                     nPos = LOWORD(lParam); break;
        default: break;
        }                              // keep in range
      nPos = max( 0, min(nPos, COLS) );
                                       // has thumb moved at all?
      if( nPos != GetScrollPos(hWnd, SB_HORZ) )
        {                              // if so, reposition it
        SetScrollPos(hWnd,            // window handle
                     SB_HORZ,         // horizontal scroll bar
                     nPos, // position of thumb
```

```
                        TRUE);          // redraw the thumb

           InvalidateRect(hWnd, NULL, TRUE);  // redraw window
           }
       break;  // end of WM_HSCROLL

   case WM_PAINT:                    // repaint the screen
       hDC = BeginPaint(hWnd, &ps);  // get device context

       // display the output buffer
       for(index = 0; index < LINES; index++ )      // for each line
           TextOut( hDC,                            // DC
                    LMARGIN - CXCHAR*nPos,           // horiz position
                    TMARGIN + CYCHAR*index,          // vert position
                    captain[index],                  // string
                    lstrlen( captain[index]) );      // string length

       EndPaint(hWnd, &ps);  // tell Windows painting complete
       break;         //  End of WM_PAINT

   case WM_DESTROY:
       PostQuitMessage(0);
       break;

   default:
       return( DefWindowProc(hWnd, msg, wParam, lParam) );
   }   // end switch(msg)
return 0L;
}  // end WndProc
```

Windows sends a WM_HSCROLL message when the user interacts with a horizontal scroll bar. The wParam constants for this message are shown in Table 19-2.

Table 19-2 Horizontal Scroll Bar Actions

Action	Move Text	wParam Values
Click on left scroll arrow	Right one column	SB_LINELEFT
Click on shaft to left of thumb	Right one screen	SB_PAGELEFT
Drag the thumb	To instantaneous position	SB_THUMBTRACK
Release the thumb	To position at release	SB_THUMBPOSITION
Click on shaft to right of thumb	Left one screen	SB_PAGERIGHT
Click on right scroll arrow	Left one column	SB_LINERIGHT

The new constants here are SB_LINELEFT, SB_LINERIGHT, SB_PAGELEFT, and SB_PAGERIGHT. Actually "line" is the wrong word; it should be "column" or maybe "character," since you usually want to scroll horizontally by one average character width when you click on the left and right scroll buttons. Our example program shows how these wParam values are processed.

There is much less standardization among applications when dealing with horizontal scroll bars than with vertical ones. For instance, when the shaft is clicked, some applications scroll a fixed distance left or right, while others scroll a fixed percentage of the line length or one screen-width of text. Some leave a little text on the left side when the thumb is at the far right, some don't leave any, and some only scroll until the right edge of the longest line is at the right edge of the window. We scroll one screen-width, and leave a little bit of text on the left.

As in the previous program, you could make various improvements to EZHSCROL. For example, we use an arbitrary value of 7 pixels for the character width CXCHAR, but you might want to obtain a more accurate value by checking the tmWidth member of TEXTMETRICS. We also guess at the number of characters in the longest line, giving a value of 52 to the COLS variable. A serious program could do something like measuring the length of the longest line and dividing by the average character width to determine this value. In practice it's not important to do this accurately, since the user is usually not aware of exactly how much the display shifts when the text is scrolled horizontally.

SCROLLING DIFFERENT TEXT SIZES

In our final program for this chapter, we've put together what we've learned about scroll bars. This example shows both vertical and horizontal scroll bars, and uses the Font common dialog to allow the user to select different fonts and sizes. This is a more realistic situation.

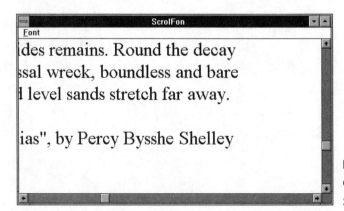

Figure 19-4
Output of the
SCROLFON Program

The program gets the line spacing and average character width of the text by calling GetTextMetrics(), as discussed in Chapter 17, *Text Size.* The resulting variables cxChar and cyChar are then used instead of the constants CXCHAR and CYCHAR as in previous examples. Figure 19-4 shows the situation when the text has been scrolled to view the lower right corner of large text. This program uses a resource file to create a one-item menu. Here's the listing for SCROLFON.RC:

```
// scrolfon.rc
// resource script file for scrolfon

#include "scrolfon.h"

ScrolFon MENU  // name must agree with szProgName
   BEGIN
      MENUITEM "&Font", IDM_FONT
   END
```

The header file handles the constant for this one menu item. Here's the listing for SCROLFON.H:

```
// scrolfon.h
// header file for scrolfon

#define IDM_FONT    101
```

The listing for the source file is rather lengthy, but we've seen all the parts of it in previous examples. It's a combination of the COMFONT, EZHSCROL, and EZVSCROL programs, with a hint of TEXTSIZE thrown in. Here's the listing for SCROLFON.C:

```
// scrolfon.c
// uses scroll bar with different fonts

#define STRICT
#include <windows.h>
#include <commdlg.h>        // for common dialogs
#include <memory.h>         // for memset()
#include "scrolfon.h"       // header file for IDM_FONT

#define COLS  50            // number of columns
#define LINES 16            // number of lines to display
PSTR ozyman[LINES] = {      // array of pointers to strings
"I met a traveler from an antique land",
"Who said: Two vast and trunkless legs of stone",
"Stand in the desert. Near them, on the sand,",
"Half sunk, a shattered visage lies, whose frown,",
"And wrinkled lip, and sneer of cold command,",
"Tell that its sculptor well those passions read",
"Which yet survive, stamped on these lifeless things,",
"The hand that mocked them and the heart that fed;",
"And on the pedestal these words appear:",
```

```
         "\"My name is Ozymandias, king of kings:",
         "Look on my works, ye Mighty, and despair!\"",
         "Nothing besides remains. Round the decay",
         "Of that colossal wreck, boundless and bare",
         "The lone and level sands stretch far away.",
         "",
         "     \"Ozymandias\", by Percy Bysshe Shelley" };
                                       // prototype
LRESULT CALLBACK _export WndProc(HWND, UINT, WPARAM, LPARAM);

PSTR szProgName = "ScrolFon";        // application name
#include "stdmain.inc"               // standard WinMain function
//////////////////////////////////////////////////////////////////////
// main window procedure -- receives messages                       //
//////////////////////////////////////////////////////////////////////
LRESULT CALLBACK _export WndProc(HWND hWnd, UINT msg,
                               WPARAM wParam, LPARAM lParam)
    {
    HDC hDC;                  // handle for the device context
    PAINTSTRUCT ps;           // holds PAINT information
    TEXTMETRIC tm;            // structure for current font info
    int index;               // loop index
    static CHOOSEFONT chf;    // struct for ChooseFont()
    static LOGFONT lf;        // logical font info
    static HFONT hFont;       // font handle
    HFONT hOldFont;          // handle for original font
    RECT rcClient;           // client window dimensions
    int cxClient, cyClient;  // client window width and height
    static int nVPos, nHPos;      // scroll-bar positions
    static int cxChar, cyChar;    // character dimensions

    switch(msg)
       {
       case WM_CREATE:              // set scroll ranges
          SetScrollRange(hWnd, SB_VERT, O, LINES-1, FALSE);
          SetScrollRange(hWnd, SB_HORZ, O, COLS-1, FALSE);
                                    // start with system font
          hFont = GetStockObject(SYSTEM_FONT);    // get font handle
          GetObject(hFont, sizeof(LOGFONT), &lf); // put font in lf
          break;

       case WM_HSCROLL:     // handle horiz scroll bar messages
          GetClientRect(hWnd, &rcClient);  // get width of
          cxClient = rcClient.right;       // client window
          switch(wParam)
             {                              // one line left or right
             case SB_LINELEFT:   nHPos--; break;
             case SB_LINERIGHT:  nHPos++; break;
                                           // one screen left or right
             case SB_PAGELEFT:   nHPos -= cxClient/cxChar; break;
             case SB_PAGERIGHT:  nHPos += cxClient/cxChar; break;
```

```
                                 // set to thumb position
      case SB_THUMBTRACK: nHPos = LOWORD(lParam); break;
      default: break;
      }                          // keep in range
   nHPos = max( 0, min(nHPos, COLS) );
                                 // has thumb moved at all?
   if( nHPos != GetScrollPos(hWnd, SB_HORZ) )
      {                          // if so, reposition it
      SetScrollPos(hWnd, SB_HORZ, nHPos, TRUE);
      InvalidateRect(hWnd, NULL, TRUE);  // redraw window
      }
   break;  // end of WM_HSCROLL

case WM_VSCROLL:       // handle vertical scroll bar messages
   GetClientRect(hWnd, &rcClient);  // get height of
   cyClient = rcClient.bottom;      // client window
   switch(wParam)
      {                          // one line up or down
      case SB_LINEUP:      nVPos -= 1; break;
      case SB_LINEDOWN:    nVPos += 1; break;
                                 // one screen up or down
      case SB_PAGEUP:      nVPos -= cyClient/cyChar - 1; break;
      case SB_PAGEDOWN:    nVPos += cyClient/cyChar - 1; break;
                                 // set to thumb position
      case SB_THUMBTRACK: nVPos = LOWORD(lParam); break;
      default: break;
      }                          // keep in range
   nVPos = max( 0, min(nVPos, LINES-1) );
                                 // has thumb moved at all?
   if( nVPos != GetScrollPos(hWnd, SB_VERT) )
      {                          // if so, reposition it
      SetScrollPos(hWnd, SB_VERT, nVPos, TRUE);
      InvalidateRect(hWnd, NULL, TRUE);  // redraw window
      }
   break;      // end of WM_VSCROLL

case WM_COMMAND:                 // user selects a menu item
   switch(wParam)                // wParam holds item ID
      {
      case IDM_FONT:             // user selects Font
         memset( &chf, 0, sizeof(CHOOSEFONT) ); // zero struct
         chf.lStructSize = sizeof(CHOOSEFONT);  // struct size
         chf.hwndOwner = hWnd;                  // owner
         chf.lpLogFont = &lf;                   // structure
                                 // do screen fonts and color
         chf.Flags = CF_SCREENFONTS | CF_EFFECTS;
         chf.rgbColors = RGB(0,0,0);            // color value

         if( !ChooseFont(&chf) )       // get new font from user
            break;                     // if no font, forget it
         InvalidateRect(hWnd, NULL, TRUE); // if OK, redraw
         break;  // end case IDM_FONT
```

```
            }   // end switch wParam
        break;  // end case WM_COMMAND

    case WM_PAINT:                          // repaint the screen
        hDC = BeginPaint(hWnd, &ps);        // get device context
        GetClientRect(hWnd, &rcClient);     // get height of
        cyClient = rcClient.bottom;         // client window

        hFont = CreateFontIndirect(&lf);    // create font
        hOldFont = SelectObject(hDC, hFont);  // put font in DC
        SetTextColor(hDC, chf.rgbColors);   // set color

        GetTextMetrics(hDC, &tm);           // get text metrics
                                            // find line height
        cyChar = tm.tmHeight + tm.tmExternalLeading;
        cxChar = tm.tmAveCharWidth;         // find char width

        // display text from buffer
        for(index = nVPos;
            index < min(LINES, nVPos+cyClient/cyChar); index++ )
            TextOut( hDC,                        // DC
                    cxChar - cxChar*nHPos,      // horiz position
                    cyChar*(index-nVPos),       // vert position
                    ozyman[index],              // string
                    lstrlen( ozyman[index]) );  // string length

        SelectObject(hDC, hOldFont);        // restore original font
        DeleteObject(hFont);                // delete new font
        EndPaint(hWnd, &ps);                // painting complete
        break;  // end WM_PAINT

    case WM_DESTROY:
        PostQuitMessage(0);
        break;
    default:
        return( DefWindowProc(hWnd, msg, wParam, lParam) );
    }   // end switch(msg)
    return 0L;
}  // end WndProc
```

SUMMARY

Here's how to add a vertical scroll bar to your program. Adding a horizontal scroll bar is similar.

1. Create a variable, nPos, that represents the thumb position as well as the number of the text line that will appear at the top of the window.

2. When you get a WM_CREATE message, or whenever you know how many lines to display, set the scroll range with SetScrollRange(). This also turns on the scroll bar display. The nPos variable must stay within this range.

3. React to different kinds of WM_VSCROLL messages. Depending on the wParam argument, the nPos variable should be adjusted as shown in Table 19-3.

4. Set the thumb position with SetScrollPos().

5. Display the appropriate lines of text, positioning them so the line numbered nPos is at the top of the window. For short documents, you can display text above and below the window, and let Windows clip it to the window's borders. For faster operation with documents with many lines, display only the lines that actually appear in the window.

With this chapter we conclude our discussion of text output. You now know how to use different stock and installable fonts, how to position text and account for its size and the size of the window, and how to add scroll bars to your program. In the next chapter we'll turn our attention to text *input*: reading what the user has typed at the keyboard.

Table 19-3 Modifications to nPos for Different Message Parameters

wParam Value	Modification to nPos Variable
SB_LINEUP	−1
SB_LINEDOWN	+1
SB_PAGEUP	− (number of lines on screen − 1)
SB_PAGEDOWN	+ (number of lines on screen − 1)
SB_THUMBTRACK (continuous adjustment)	LOWORD(lParam)
SB_THUMBPOSITION (adjust on release)	LOWORD(lParam)

20

TEXT INPUT: THE EASY WAY

Battles between knights traditionally began with a joust. Two knights on horseback faced each other from opposite ends of a field. Protected by armor (with padding inside), and armed with long spears called lances, they galloped toward each other at full speed. As they met, each knight tried to knock the other off his horse with the point of the lance. There was much crashing and bashing as the unseated knight fell to earth. Although jousting was dangerous, the lance was favored in the initial stages of a conflict because it prevented the knights from approaching close enough to use their swords, which were far more deadly. Jousting was practiced as a sport as well as a means of battle, and formed the heart of the knightly tournament.

This chapter deals with text input; that is, text typed into the keyboard by the user. One approach to text input (which we'll explore in the next chapter) is complicated and involves attention to numerous troublesome details. In this chapter, to simplify the programming, we're going to use a Windows tool we can liken to a knight's lance. It's a powerful weapon that enables the programmer to keep this host of details out of reach. It's called the *edit control*.

The edit control automatically handles reading and interpreting keyboard characters, as well as displaying the resulting text, including breaking the text at word boundaries, installing scroll bars if necessary, and responding to editing commands. In its way, the edit control is as powerful a tool for program simplification as the Excalibur-like common dialogs we've seen before.

THE EZEDIT PROGRAM

Our example program creates a standard window with another window inside it. This is our first exposure to the possibility of creating more than just the standard window. The window we create is rather special. It is called an *edit control* window, and its purpose in life is to accept text typed by the user and display it.

We should note that there are many kinds of control windows besides the edit control. There are buttons, combo boxes, list boxes, and so on. Controls are most often used as parts of a dialog box, but the edit control is so versatile that it's useful as a stand-alone window, as we show here. (Paradoxically, it's easier to create a program that obtains a whole window-full of text from the user, than to create a dialog box with an edit control that reads a single word.)

When you first run EZEDIT, the standard window appears on the screen, with a black border just inside it. This black border marks the boundary of the edit control window. Any text you type will appear inside this black border. Figure 20-1 shows what this looks like when the user has typed some sample paragraphs.

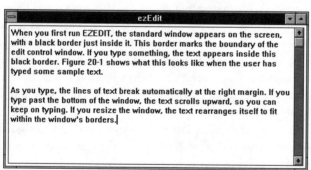

Figure 20-1

Output of the
EZEDIT Program

As you type, the lines of text automatically break at the right border. If you type past the bottom of the window, the text scrolls upward, so you can keep typing. You can scroll upward to view what you typed before. If you resize the window, the text rearranges itself to fit within the window's borders.

You can use the arrow keys or the mouse to position the cursor, and the (BACKSPACE) and (DEL) keys to delete text. Text will be inserted wherever the cursor is.

This example program needs only a .C source file. Here's the listing for EZEDIT.C:

```
// ezedit.c
// uses multiline edit box for text input

#define STRICT
#include <windows.h>
#define IDC_EDIT   100        // ID of edit window
```

```
#define BORDER      4           // border around edit window
                                // prototype
LRESULT CALLBACK _export WndProc(HWND, UINT, WPARAM, LPARAM);

PSTR szProgName = "ezEdit";   // application name
#include "stdmain.inc"        // standard WinMain()
////////////////////////////////////////////////////////////////
// main window procedure -- receives messages                  //
////////////////////////////////////////////////////////////////
LRESULT CALLBACK _export WndProc(HWND hWnd, UINT msg,
                              WPARAM wParam, LPARAM lParam)
   {
   static HWND hWndEdit;                // edit window handle
   HINSTANCE hInst;                     // handle of this instance

   switch(msg)
      {
      case WM_CREATE:          // get instance handle
         hInst = (HINSTANCE)GetWindowWord(hWnd, GWW_HINSTANCE);
                              // create edit control window
         hWndEdit = CreateWindow(
                    "EDIT",          // class is "EDIT"
                    NULL,            // no caption
                    WS_CHILD | WS_VISIBLE | ES_MULTILINE |
                    WS_BORDER | WS_VSCROLL | ES_AUTOVSCROLL,
                    0, 0, 0, 0,      // will be sized later
                    hWnd,            // parent window
                    (HMENU)IDC_EDIT, // ID for WM_COMMAND
                    hInst,           // this instance
                    NULL);           // no data passed in struct
         break;  // end WM_CREATE

      case WM_COMMAND:
         switch(wParam)          // if edit runs out of memory
            {
            case IDC_EDIT:
               if(HIWORD(lParam)==EN_ERRSPACE)
                  MessageBox(hWnd, "Edit control is out of Memory",
                           szProgName, MB_OK | MB_ICONEXCLAMATION);
               break;
            // (other menu commands can go here)
            }
         break;  // end WM_COMMAND


      case WM_SIZE:            // if main window resized
         // size edit window to fit main window, inside border
         MoveWindow(hWndEdit,                  // edit-window handle
                 BORDER,                       // left edge of window
                 BORDER,                       // top of edit window
                 LOWORD(lParam)-BORDER*2,  // width of edit window
                 HIWORD(lParam)-BORDER*2,  // height of edit window
```

```
                            TRUE);
            break;  // end WM_SIZE

        case WM_SETFOCUS:        // whenever main window gets focus
            SetFocus(hWndEdit);  // give it to the edit window
            break;

        case WM_DESTROY:
            PostQuitMessage(0);
            break;

        default:
            return( DefWindowProc(hWnd, msg, wParam, lParam) );
        }   // end switch(msg)

    return 0L;
}   // end WndProc
```

This listing has several new features. The central function is CreateWindow(), which creates the edit control; but we must also learn how to get an instance handle, how to handle messages sent by Windows to the edit control window, how to move and size the edit control window, and how to change the keyboard focus.

The CreateWindow() Function Revisited

We last saw the CreateWindow() function many pages ago when we discussed the creation of our main window in Chapter 5, *Creating a Main Window*. This function has been included in our example programs ever since, even though it's been hidden in the STDMAIN.INC file we #include with each program.

As we learned in Chapter 5, when we create a main window we must first create a class of windows by assigning values to the members of a WNDCLASS structure. We then create a window of that class, using CreateWindow(). However, it's easier to create an edit control window, because this class of window is predefined. That is, the characteristics of the class are built into Windows. Therefore there's no need to fill in a WNDCLASS structure. We need only set the first argument of CreateWindow() to the string "EDIT", the name of the predefined edit control window class. Here's how the call to CreateWindow() looks in the program:

```
hWndEdit = CreateWindow(
        "EDIT",              // class is "EDIT"
        NULL,                // no caption
        WS_CHILD | WS_VISIBLE | ES_MULTILINE |     // style
        WS_BORDER | WS_VSCROLL | ES_AUTOVSCROLL,
        0, 0, 0, 0,          // will be sized later
        hWnd,                // parent window
        (HMENU)IDC_EDIT,     // ID for WM_COMMAND (note cast)
        hInst,               // this instance
        NULL);               // no data passed in structure
```

We don't use a caption in an edit window, so we set the second argument to NULL. The third argument is the style. We've ORed together several constants here to create exactly the kind of edit window we want. The constants that start with WS (for Window Style) apply to all windows, while the ES (Edit Style) constants apply only to edit control windows. Here's what these constants specify about our edit window:

- WS_CHILD means the edit window is a child of the main window. Its coordinates will be based on the main window's coordinates.
- WS_VISIBLE—the edit window is visible.
- ES_MULTILINE—allows multiple lines of text input in the edit window (without this constant, only a single line is allowed).
- WS_BORDER—gives the edit window a visible border.
- WS_VSCROLL—gives the edit window a vertical scroll bar. (The WS_HSCROLL constant could be used to install a horizontal scroll bar.)
- ES_AUTOVSCROLL—scrolls the text automatically. (The constant ES_AUTOHSCROLL scrolls text horizontally.)

Parameters 4, 5, 6, and 7 of CreateWindow() set the left and top coordinates of the window and its width and height. We're going to base these on the main window, so we'll wait until later to give them values; for now they're set to 0.

The parent of the edit control window is the main window. The main window's handle is hWnd, which we use as the 8th argument. The 9th argument is a constant, in this case IDC_EDIT, that will be used by Windows to identify the edit window when it sends WM_COMMAND messages. To avoid compiler warning messages, this constant must be cast to HMENU. The 10th argument is our instance handle. The 11th and final argument could be a pointer to a data structure that conveys additional information to CreateWindow(), but we don't use it, so we set it to NULL.

The CreateWindow() function does most of the work of creating an edit window control, but it needs some supporting functions to help it out. Let's see what they do.

The GetWindowWord() Function

We discussed instances in Chapter 5, *Creating a Main Window*. As you may recall, there can be more than one instance of the same program running at the same time. Instances share code, but each has its own data. Some API functions, such as CreateWindow(), need to know which instance they're being called from, because they're going to alter some data and they need to know which instance's data to alter. Therefore to call such a function, we must know our instance handle. We saw in Chapter 5 that the instance handle is one of the arguments to WinMain().

However, because WinMain() is hidden in the STDMAIN.INC header file, it's not convenient to access this argument. Fortunately, there are several other ways to get the instance handle. One is to execute the GetWindowWord() function.

GetWindowWord() is a portmanteau function that can tell you several different things, depending on the constant you supply as its second argument. Here we want the instance handle, so we use the GWW_HINSTANCE constant. Other possibilities are GWW_HWNDPARENT, which retrieves the handle of the parent window, and GWW_ID, which retrieves a child window's control ID. Because this function can return values with different data types, we must cast the return value to HINSTANCE.

We call GetWindowWord() when we get a WM_CREATE message. It returns the instance handle, which we then use as the 10th argument to CreateWindow().

The WM_SIZE Message

We can tell Windows to reposition or resize any window at any time. The user usually resizes main windows, so there's ordinarily no reason for the application to do it. However, our edit control window is supposed to fit inside the main window. When the user resizes the main window, we want the edit window to resize itself so it will continue to fit exactly within the main window.

In Chapter 18, *Text Position,* we learned how to find the dimensions of the client area of a main window using GetClientRect(). We executed this function when we received a WM_PAINT message, so we could arrange text output to fit the window. In EZEDIT we also need to know the size of the client area, but here we want to apply this information whenever the size of the main window changes. Thus it's more appropriate to resize the edit window whenever our main window receives a WM_SIZE message.

The lParam value that accompanies WM_SIZE contains the width and height of the main window's client area, with the width in the low-order word and the height in the high-order word. We can extract them with the LOWORD and HIWORD macros, as we've seen before.

The MoveWindow() Function

Using the dimensions of the main window's client area, obtained from the lParam argument to WM_SIZE, we can then resize the edit window. The MoveWindow() function does this:

```
case WM_SIZE:                // if main window resized,
   // size edit window to fit main window, inside border
   MoveWindow(hWndEdit,                // edit window handle
         BORDER,                       // left edge of edit window
```

```
            BORDER,                    // top edge of edit window
            LOWORD(lParam)-BORDER*2,   // width of edit window
            HIWORD(lParam)-BORDER*2,   // height of edit window
            TRUE);
break;
```

The upper left corner of the main window has the coordinates (0,0), so the edit window installs itself BORDER units down and to the right from there. The LOWORD(lParam) and HIWORD(lParam) values are the width and height of the main window (when we get a WM_SIZE message), so the edit window sizes itself to be BORDER*2 narrower and shorter than the main window. That gives it a border of BORDER pixels all the way around.

If you don't want the border, you can #define BORDER as 0, or you can eliminate it altogether. Then the black line around the edit window will coincide with the line around the main window. This is the more usual approach to using edit windows, but a visible edit window border makes it easier to understand what's going on.

The SetFocus() Function

When a main window is created, it is usually given the keyboard focus; that is, any keystrokes typed by the user will be directed to that window. However, we want the keystrokes to go to the edit window rather than the main window. To cause this to happen, we must change the focus. This is easily accomplished with the SetFocus() function, which is given as its only argument the handle of the window that will get the focus.

The focus can change as the user clicks on different Windows applications. When the user clicks on the EZEDIT main window, this application is always sent a WM_SETFOCUS message. We want to restore the focus to the edit window every time this happens, so we execute the SetFocus() function when we receive the WM_SETFOCUS message.

Messages to the Edit Control Window

In the current version of Windows, edit controls normally hold up to 30,000 characters. If the user types more characters than this, or if there isn't enough system memory available, the edit control will send a WM_COMMAND message to the window procedure. The wParam value of this message is the IDC_EDIT value that we specified as the 9th argument to CreateWindow(). If there's no more memory, the lParam value will be set to the constant EN_ERRSPACE. Should this message arrive, our application will display a message box telling the user that there's no more memory.

Cut, Copy, Paste, and Clear

If you experiment with the EZEDIT program, you'll notice that you can use the mouse or the keyboard to select text. Drag across the text to select it with the mouse, or hold down the (SHIFT) key and press the cursor keys to select it from the keyboard. Once text is selected, you can use control-key combinations to cut, copy, paste, and clear it. Here are the key combinations that carry out these actions:

- (CTRL)+(X) or (SHIFT)+(DEL) cuts the selected text to the clipboard (deleting it from edit window).
- (CTRL)+(C) or (CTRL)+(INS) copies the selected text to the clipboard (leaving it in edit window).
- (CTRL)+(V) or (SHIFT)+(INS) pastes the text from clipboard to edit window.
- (DEL)+(CTRL) or (DEL) clears the selected text without saving it to the clipboard.

This editing capability is built into the edit control. You get it gratis, with no further programming effort on your part. Truly the edit control is the long lance of programming. However, even such a powerful tool can be improved.

THE EDITMENU PROGRAM

It's nice to be able to cut, copy, and paste text using the keyboard keys, as we could with the edit window in the last example. However, it's often even nicer to be able to do these things from a menu, especially if you have trouble remembering the key combinations. After all, a major advantage of a GUI is making it obvious how to do things. Our next example, EDITMENU, shows how to add menu-driven editing functions to an edit control window.

This example also shows how the text you typed into an edit control can be saved to memory, and loaded from memory back into the window. We've created menu items to carry out these functions. This is one step toward learning how to save the contents of an edit control to a file, which we'll explore in Chapter 22, *The MINIEDIT Program*.

Figure 20-2 shows how this looks when the Edit menu is activated.

We've taken the liberty of removing the border between the edit window and the main window in this program, by removing the BORDER variable. Now the edit window is exactly the same size as the client area of the main window, so it looks as if you're typing directly into the main window.

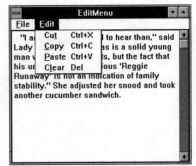

Figure 20-2

Edit Menu in EDITMENU Program

Because the EDITMENU program uses menus, it has a resource script file and a header file. Here's the listing for EDITMENU.RC:

```
// editmenu.rc
// resource script file for editmenu

#include "editmenu.h"

EditMenu MENU  // name must agree with szProgName
   BEGIN
      POPUP "&File"
         BEGIN
            MENUITEM "&Save to memory" IDM_SAVEMEM
            MENUITEM "&Load from memory", IDM_LOADMEM
         END
      POPUP "&Edit"
         BEGIN
            MENUITEM "Cu&t\tCtrl+X" IDM_CUT
            MENUITEM "&Copy\tCtrl+C", IDM_COPY
            MENUITEM "&Paste\tCtrl+V", IDM_PASTE
            MENUITEM "C&lear\tDel", IDM_CLEAR
         END

   END
```

And here's the corresponding header file, EDITMENU.H:

```
// editmenu.h
// header file for editmenu

#define ID_EDIT      1000    // edit control window ID
#define IDM_SAVEMEM 101      // menu item IDs
#define IDM_LOADMEM 102
#define IDM_CUT      201
#define IDM_COPY     202
#define IDM_PASTE    203
#define IDM_CLEAR    204
```

The souurce file contains all the elements we examined in the EZMENU
program, and in addition handles a variety of menu items when it receives a
WM_COMMAND message. Here's the listing for EDITMENU.C:

```
// editmenu.c
// uses multiline edit box for text input
// includes edit menu, and loading and saving text to buffer

#define STRICT
#include <windows.h>
#include "editmenu.h"
#define NMAX   20000            // size of text buffer (not too big!)
char szTextBuff[NMAX];          // text buffer
                                // prototype
LRESULT CALLBACK _export WndProc(HWND, UINT, WPARAM, LPARAM);

PSTR szProgName = "EditMenu";   // application name
#include "stdmain.inc"          // standard WinMain()
/////////////////////////////////////////////////////////////////////
// main window procedure -- receives messages                       //
/////////////////////////////////////////////////////////////////////
LRESULT CALLBACK _export WndProc(HWND hWnd, UINT msg,
                                 WPARAM wParam, LPARAM lParam)
   {
   static HWND hWndEdit;                    // edit window handle
   HINSTANCE hInst;

   switch(msg)
      {
      case WM_CREATE:          // get instance handle
         hInst = (HINSTANCE)GetWindowWord(hWnd, GWW_HINSTANCE);
                               // create edit control window
         hWndEdit = CreateWindow(
                     "EDIT",            // class is "EDIT"
                     NULL,              // no caption
                     WS_CHILD | WS_VISIBLE | ES_MULTILINE |
                     WS_BORDER | WS_VSCROLL | ES_AUTOVSCROLL,
                     0, 0, 0, 0,        // will be sized later
                     hWnd,              // parent is main window
                     (HMENU)ID_EDIT,    // ID for WM_COMMAND
                     hInst,             // this instance
                     NULL);             // no data structure
         break;

      case WM_COMMAND:
         switch(wParam)
            {
            case IDM_SAVEMEM:  // contents of edit window into buffer
               GetWindowText(hWndEdit, (LPSTR)szTextBuff, NMAX);
               break;
```

```
     case IDM_LOADMEM:   // contents of buffer into edit window
        SetWindowText(hWndEdit, (LPSTR)szTextBuff);
        break;

     case IDM_CUT:       // user selects cut
        SendMessage(hWndEdit, WM_CUT, 0, 0L);
        break;

     case IDM_COPY:      // user selects copy
        SendMessage(hWndEdit, WM_COPY, 0, 0L);
        break;

     case IDM_PASTE:     // user selects paste
        SendMessage(hWndEdit, WM_PASTE, 0, 0L);
        break;

     case IDM_CLEAR:     // user selects clear
        SendMessage(hWndEdit, WM_CLEAR, 0, 0L);
        break;

     case ID_EDIT:       // if edit runs out of memory
        if(HIWORD(lParam)==EN_ERRSPACE)
           MessageBox(hWnd, "Edit Control is out of Memory",
                      szProgName, MB_OK | MB_ICONEXCLAMATION);
        break;
     }
   break;  // end switch

case WM_SIZE:              // give edit window a 4 pixel border
   MoveWindow(hWndEdit,    // edit window handle
              0,           // left edge
              0,           // top edge
              LOWORD(lParam),  // width
              HIWORD(lParam),  // height
              TRUE);
   break;

case WM_SETFOCUS:          // give edit window the focus
   SetFocus(hWndEdit);     // whenever main window gets focus
   break;

case WM_DESTROY:
   PostQuitMessage(0);
   break;
default:
   return( DefWindowProc(hWnd, msg, wParam, lParam) );
}   // end switch(msg)
return 0L;
} // end WndProc
```

Sending Messages to Windows

It would be nice if simply adding an Edit menu to our program automatically connected the menu commands with the edit window. However, this isn't the case. Our application has to make the connection by telling the edit window what to do in response to the user selecting an Edit menu item. We tell the edit window that we want to cut, copy, paste, or clear text by sending it messages. These messages have surprisingly logical names: WM_CUT, WM_COPY, WM_PASTE, and WM_CLEAR. But how do we send messages? We've seen in almost every program how Windows sends messages *to* our window procedure. How do we turn this around and send messages *from* our window procedure?

It turns out this isn't very complicated. We need only execute the SendMessage() function to send a message to a window procedure, provided we know the window's handle. For example, here's the code that's activated if the user selects the Cut item from the Edit menu:

```
case IDM_CUT:
    SendMessage(hWndEdit, WM_CUT, 0, 0L);
    break;
```

This sends the WM_CUT message to the window procedure of the hWndEdit window. Since the edit window belongs to the predefined EDIT class, this procedure is built into Windows; we can't see it, but we know it's there.

The arguments to SendMessage() are the handle of the window to which the message is being sent (hWndEdit), the message number (WM_CUT), and two parameters that depend on the message being sent. If you look up any window message in the appropriate reference (see the Bibliography), you'll find values listed for these parameters. For WM_CUT and the other edit messages used in EDITMENU, these values are always set to 0 and 0L respectively (L meaning type **long**).

It may be of academic interest that SendMessage(), as the name implies, *sends* its message as opposed to posting it. That means that Windows calls the window's procedure directly with this message. To *post* a message we could use the PostMessage() function, which causes Windows to insert the message into the application's message queue. See Chapter 6, *Event-Driven Programming*, for a discussion of sending versus posting.

Transferring Text Between the Edit Window and Memory

Usually, when a user types text into an edit window, we need to process this text in some way; by writing it to disk, analyzing it, or whatever. Conversely, we often want to take existing text and load it into an edit window. This happens, for instance, if we read a file from disk and want to edit it.

The EDITMENU program allows us to save the contents of the edit window to memory, and load it back again from memory into the edit window. To see the effect of saving text to memory, type something in the edit window, and then choose the Save To Memory item from the File menu. Now select the entire text selection and delete it. The edit window is now blank, but you can restore the deleted text by selecting the Load From Memory item from the File menu. The text will be written from memory back into the window.

Here's the code that responds to these menu selections:

```
case IDM_SAVEMEM:
   GetWindowText(hWndEdit, (LPSTR)TextBuff, NMAX);
   break;

case IDM_LOADMEM:
   SetWindowText(hWndEdit, (LPSTR)TextBuff);
   break;
```

The GetWindowText() function copies the text from the edit window into a buffer. The first argument is the handle of the edit window, the second is the address of the buffer (which must be cast to LPSTR, a long pointer to a string), and the third is the size of the buffer. In general the text to be copied will be shorter than the buffer, but if it's not, this argument ensures the buffer isn't overfilled.

The companion function SetWindowText() transfers text from a buffer into the edit window. It takes the same arguments as GetWindowText() except that it doesn't need a length argument, since it will go on copying until the edit window is full.

In Chapter 22, *The MINIEDIT Program,* we'll see how GetWindowText() and SetWindowText() can be used to transfer text between disk files and the edit window, thus creating a real text editor.

Limitations

We should note some limitations to the edit-control approach to text input. First, as we mentioned, the number of characters you can input is limited to about 30,000, or about 30 pages of text. This is fine for notes, diary entries, and the like, but it's not enough for major reports or book chapters. Second, you can't conveniently vary the font, font size, or font style in an edit control; you get the plain vanilla system font, take it or leave it. Third, you can't format the text except in paragraphs. You can't use columns, set margins, and so on. Thus while this approach is fine in some situations, you won't be able to use it to write a full-featured word processing program.

SUMMARY

Here are the steps necessary to create an edit window inside your main window:

1. Get the instance handle by executing the GetWindowWord() function. This will be needed for CreateWindow().
2. When you get a WM_CREATE message, execute CreateWindow() with the class name "EDIT". Set the style parameter to the desired combination of style constants. Use a constant for the 9th argument; this constant will be used by Windows when messages are sent to the edit window. (Cast this constant to HMENU.)
3. Respond to any WM_COMMAND messages that have a wParam value that is the ID of the edit window and an lParam value of EN_ERRSPACE by telling the user that the edit window is out of memory.
4. Whenever a WM_SIZE message is received, resize the edit window to fit just inside the main window (leaving a border if desired).
5. Whenever a WM_SETFOCUS message is received, use SetFocus() to set the focus to the edit window.

In this chapter we've demonstrated an approach to text input that gives you considerable power for not much effort. In the next chapter, we'll see how considerably more effort buys you a more flexible approach.

CHAPTER 21

TEXT INPUT: THE HARD WAY

*I*n the last chapter we used an edit control as a long lance to keep our adversary—complexity—at bay while performing text input. All we had to do was create the edit control. It took care of the details of responding to keystrokes and displaying appropriate characters in the window, as well as luxuries like handling word wrap, scroll bars, and editing.

In this chapter we're going to plunge into the murky forest of direct character manipulation. Here amongst the trees and vines there's no room to use our lance; we must proceed on foot, and deal hand-to-hand with each typed character as it appears suddenly out of the gloom.

Why do we need this close-up approach, if we already have available a powerful way to read text using edit windows? There are many potential reasons. You might want to display text in different sizes or styles as it's typed in, as commercial Windows-based word processors do. You might want to handle larger files than are possible in an edit window. Or you might want to handle certain keystrokes in unusual ways, such as executing a certain task when a function key is pressed.

This new way of reading and displaying text has many new aspects. Accordingly we're going to present four sample programs, each of which demonstrates a different feature. The first focuses on normal character keyboard keys, the second on noncharacter keys like the function keys, and the third on keys that influence the text input process, like the cursor-control keys and the (DELETE) key. Finally, in the fourth example, we show how to add what Microsoft calls a "caret" (the blinking vertical line where new text is inserted) so you can see where your next keystroke will appear in the display.

CHARACTER KEYSTROKES

Our first program, CHARSIN, is rather basic. The user types at the keyboard, and the characters appear on the first line of the window. Only this top line can be used. The noncharacter keys don't work. For example the (BACKSPACE) key causes a little box to be displayed, and the cursor keys have no effect at all. There's no caret, so you can't see where your next keystroke will go; you're flying blind. But for all its limitations, this program does demonstrate the basics of reading keystrokes. Figure 21-1 shows the window after the user has typed some text.

Figure 21-1

Interaction with the CHARSIN Program

When the buffer is full, you can't type any more and the program beeps at you for each additional keystroke. Here's the listing for CHARSIN.C:

```c
// charsin.c
// displays keyboard characters on screen
// no caret, no backspace, no cursor keys, etc.

#define STRICT
#include <windows.h>
#define MAXLENGTH 80            // size of buffer
                               // prototype
LRESULT CALLBACK _export WndProc(HWND, UINT, WPARAM, LPARAM);

PSTR szProgName = "CharsIn";    // application name
#include "stdmain.inc"          // standard WinMain() function
/////////////////////////////////////////////////////////////
// main window procedure -- receives messages              //
/////////////////////////////////////////////////////////////

LRESULT CALLBACK _export WndProc(HWND hWnd, UINT msg,
                                 WPARAM wParam, LPARAM lParam)
   {
   PAINTSTRUCT ps;                     // info for painting
   HDC hDC;                            // device context handle
   static char achString[MAXLENGTH];   // text buffer
   static UINT cLength = 0;            // number of chars

   switch(msg)
      {
      case WM_CHAR:                    // user typed a char
         if(cLength > MAXLENGTH)       // check if buffer full
            {
```

```
            MessageBeep(0);                // beep and exit if full
            break;
            }                              // put character in buffer
         achString[cLength] = LOBYTE(wParam);
         cLength++;                        // count it
         InvalidateRect(hWnd, NULL, TRUE); // repaint window
         break;

      case WM_PAINT:                       // window needs repainting
         hDC = BeginPaint(hWnd, &ps);      // prepare window for paint
         TextOut(hDC, 10, 10, achString, cLength ); // draw text
         EndPaint(hWnd, &ps);              // painting is over
         break;

      case WM_DESTROY:
         PostQuitMessage(0);
         break;

      default:
         return( DefWindowProc(hWnd, msg, wParam, lParam) );
      }    // end switch(msg)

   return OL;
   }  // end WndProc
```

The WM_CHAR Message

The basic feature of this program is that it responds to the WM_CHAR message. This message is posted whenever an ASCII character is typed at the keyboard and our application has the input focus. It is *not* posted for noncharacter keys like the function keys, the cursor control keys, and keys like (INS), (DEL), (HOME), and (END). Nondisplaying character keys, like (ESC), (TAB), (BACKSPACE), and (ENTER), show up as little vertical boxes; this is the character used for nondisplayable characters in the ANSI character set.

Here's how the WM_CHAR message is processed:

```
case WM_CHAR:
   if(cLength > MAXLENGTH)
      {
      MessageBeep(0);
      break;
      }
   achString[cLength] = LOBYTE(wParam);
   cLength++;
   InvalidateRect(hWnd, NULL, TRUE);
   break;
```

When this message arrives, signalling that a character has been typed, the wParam argument carries the ASCII code of the character. We set up a text buffer,

achString (the Hungarian notation means array of characters), to store the
characters as they arrive, and we keep track of how many characters are in this
buffer with the cLength variable.

Table 21-1 Common Virtual Key Codes

Virtual Key Code	Keyboard Key
VK_BACK	BACKSPACE
VK_TAB	TAB
VK_RETURN	ENTER
VK_ESCAPE	ESC
VK_PRIOR	PGUP
VK_NEXT	PGDN
VK_END	END
VK_HOME	HOME
VK_LEFT	Left Arrow ←
VK_UP	Up Arrow ↑
VK_RIGHT	Right Arrow →
VK_DOWN	Down Arrow ↓
VK_SNAPSHOT	PRINT SCREEN
VK_INSERT	INSERT
VK_DELETE	DELETE
VK_NUMPAD0 to VK_NUMPAD9	Numeric Keypad 0 to 9 (NumLock off)
VK_MULTIPLY	Numeric Keypad *
VK_ADD	Numeric Keypad +
VK_SUBTRACT	Numeric Keypad -
VK_DIVIDE	Numeric Keypad /
VK_DECIMAL	Numeric Keypad .
VK_F1 to VK_F12	Function keys F1 to F12
VK_NUMLOCK	NUM LOCK

If cLength becomes larger than the size of the buffer, we beep and ignore the keystroke. The function used to sound the beep is MessageBeep(). The argument to this function is not used, and should be set to 0. MessageBeep() causes a short, rather anemic beep, suitable for indicating that the user has made a minor typing mistake.

Every time a WM_CHAR message is processed, we execute an InvalidateRect() function so we'll get a WM_PAINT message and be able to redraw the text string with the new character. This makes for a slightly jumpy display, but it's the simplest approach to displaying each keystroke as it arrives.

NONCHARACTER KEYSTROKES

When any keyboard key is pressed, whether it's a character key like 'A' or a noncharacter key like F1, it generates a WM_KEYDOWN message. (When it's released it generates a WM_KEYUP message, but we won't worry about that.) Applications typically use WM_KEYDOWN to find out when a noncharacter key has been pressed.

When a WM_KEYDOWN message arrives, the wParam argument contains a constant indicating which key was pressed. This constant is called a *virtual key code*. Table 21-1 lists the most common virtual key codes.

Our next example program shows how virtual key codes are processed. Here's the listing for KEYSIN.C:

```
// keysin.c
// handles noncharacter keys using virtual key codes

#define STRICT
#include <windows.h>
LRESULT CALLBACK _export WndProc(HWND, UINT, WPARAM, LPARAM);

PSTR szProgName = "KeysIn";        // application name
#include "stdmain.inc"             // standard WinMain() function
/////////////////////////////////////////////////////////////////////
// main window procedure -- receives messages                       //
/////////////////////////////////////////////////////////////////////
LRESULT CALLBACK _export WndProc(HWND hWnd, UINT msg,
                                 WPARAM wParam, LPARAM lParam)
   {
   switch(msg)
      {
      case WM_KEYDOWN:                   // user presses any key
         switch(wParam)
            {
            case VK_LEFT:                // left cursor key
               MessageBox(hWnd, "Left arrow key",
                         szProgName, MB_OK | MB_ICONINFORMATION);
               break;
```

```
        case VK_RIGHT:          // right arrow key
           MessageBox(hWnd, "Right arrow key",
                       szProgName, MB_OK | MB_ICONINFORMATION);
           break;

        case VK_F1:             // F1 function key
           MessageBeep(0);      // beep
           break;

        case VK_ESCAPE:         // Escape key
           if(MessageBox(hWnd, "Terminate the program?",
                        szProgName, MB_YESNO | MB_ICONQUESTION)
              == IDYES)
              DestroyWindow(hWnd);
           break;
        } // end switch wParam
     break;  // end case WM_KEYDOWN

  case WM_DESTROY:
     PostQuitMessage(0);
     break;

  default:
     return( DefWindowProc(hWnd, msg, wParam, lParam) );
  }  // end switch(msg)

return 0L;
} // end WndProc
```

The program monitors four keys: the left ⊖ and right ⊙ arrow keys, the F1 function key, and the ESC key. Notice that because ESC is an ASCII character, it generates a WM_CHAR message as well as a WM_KEYDOWN message; we could check for either one to determine if it had been pressed. We display message boxes for the arrow keys, beep for the F1 key, and ask the user "Terminate the program?" if the ESC key is pressed. If the answer is yes, we terminate the program with DestroyWindow().

THE ARROW KEYS

Now that we know how to handle virtual key codes, we'll put them to use in a program called ARROWS. This example uses the left ⊖ and right ⊙ arrow keys to change the insertion point of a line of text we type in. Any characters to the right of the insertion point will be shifted right to make room for new characters, as shown in Figure 21-2.

We'll also use the DEL key to delete the character at the insertion point, and the BACKSPACE key to delete the character to the left of the insertion point. In these cases

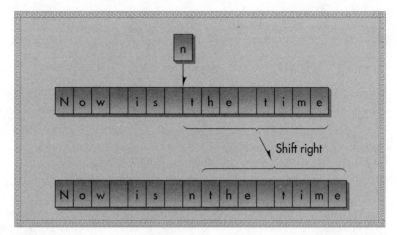

Figure 21-2 Inserting a Character

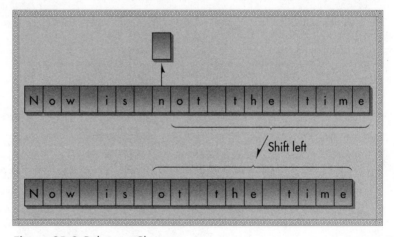

Figure 21-3 Deleting a Character

if there is any text to the right of the insertion point, we shift it left to fill in the empty space, as shown in Figure 21-3. We don't have a caret yet, so you're still flying blind: you can move the insertion point, but you can't see where it is.

Here's the listing for ARROWS.C:

```
// arrows.c
// displays keyboard characters on screen
// handles cursor keys and delete key, but not caret

#define STRICT
#include <windows.h>

#define XSTART      10          // text starting position
```

```
#define YSTART    30
#define MAXLENGTH 80 ·             // size of buffer
char achString[MAXLENGTH];         // text buffer
                                   // prototype
LRESULT CALLBACK _export WndProc(HWND, UINT, WPARAM, LPARAM);

PSTR szProgName = "KeysIn";        // application name
#include "stdmain.inc"             // standard WinMain() function
//////////////////////////////////////////////////////////////////
// main window procedure -- receives messages                    //
//////////////////////////////////////////////////////////////////
LRESULT CALLBACK _export WndProc(HWND hWnd, UINT msg,
                                 WPARAM wParam, LPARAM lParam)
    {
    PAINTSTRUCT ps;                // info for painting
    HDC hDC;                       // device context handle
    static int cCaretPos = 0;      // number of chars to left of caret
    static int cLength = 0;        // total chars in string
    int j;                         // loop index

    switch(msg)
        {
        case WM_CHAR:              // user typed a char
            if(wParam=='\b')       // if it's backspace,
                {
                if(cCaretPos>0)    // if any chars to the left of us
                    {
                    for(j=cCaretPos-1; j<cLength; j++) // shift text
                        achString[j] = achString[j+1]; //    to left
                    achString[--cLength] = '\0';       // shorten string
                    cCaretPos--;                       // move caret
                    InvalidateRect(hWnd, NULL, TRUE);  // repaint window
                    }
                else
                    MessageBeep(0);
                break;
                }

            if(cLength > MAXLENGTH)                // ignore if buffer full
                {
                MessageBeep(0);
                break;
                }
                                                  // it's a displayable char
            for(j=cLength; j>=cCaretPos; j--)     // shift right side of
                achString[j+1] = achString[j];    //    text to the right
            achString[cCaretPos++] = wParam;      // insert character
            cLength++;                            // lengthen string
            InvalidateRect(hWnd, NULL, TRUE);     // repaint window
            break;

        case WM_KEYDOWN:
```

```
    switch(wParam)
      {
      case VK_RIGHT:                 // right keyboard arrow
         if(cCaretPos < cLength)     // if caret not at right end
            cCaretPos++;             // move caret right
         else
            MessageBeep(0);
         break;

      case VK_LEFT:                  // left keyboard arrow
         if(cCaretPos > 0)           // if caret not at left end
            cCaretPos--;             // move caret left
         else
            MessageBeep(0);
         break;

      case VK_DELETE:                // the Del key
         if(cCaretPos < cLength)     // if caret not at right end
            {
            for(j=cCaretPos; j<cLength; j++)    // shift text
               achString[j] = achString[j+1];   // to left
            achString[--cLength] = '\0';        // shorten string
            InvalidateRect(hWnd, NULL, TRUE);   // paint window
            }
         else
            MessageBeep(0);
         break;
      }  // end switch wParam
   break;

   case WM_PAINT:                    // window needs repainting
      hDC = BeginPaint(hWnd, &ps);   // prepare window for paint
      TextOut(hDC, XSTART, YSTART,   // draw text from buffer
            achString, cLength );
      EndPaint(hWnd, &ps);           // ok, painting is over
      break;

   case WM_DESTROY:
      PostQuitMessage(0);
      break;

   default:
      return( DefWindowProc(hWnd, msg, wParam, lParam) );
   }   // end switch(msg)

return 0L;
}  // end WndProc
```

You can see that things are starting to get more complicated. When we delete or insert a character, we must check to see if we're at the right end of the text line. If we are, we simply delete the character. If not, we must shift the characters to the right of the insertion point either left (if we're deleting a character) or right (if we're inserting one).

Although in ARROWS we don't display a caret, we maintain a variable, cCaretPos, to indicate the insertion point in the line of text. This variable is incremented as we insert characters or move right with the arrow key, and decremented as we delete characters or move left with the arrow key. Let's see how to connect this variable to a real, displayable caret.

THE CARET

The caret (which is also called the insertion point, and often confused with the mouse cursor) is the blinking vertical line that indicates where characters that you type will be inserted into the text. In the previous three examples there was no caret, so there was no visual indication where the characters that we typed would appear. In the next example program, CARET, we'll correct this problem.

There are three major aspects to using a caret:

1. On receipt of a WM_SETFOCUS message, create the caret with CreateCaret() and display it with ShowCaret().
2. Whenever the insertion point moves, move the caret to the new location with SetCaretPos().
3. On receipt of a WM_KILLFOCUS message, destroy the caret with DestroyCaret().

Our example program is similar to the ARROWS program, except for the addition of these caret-support features. Note that moving the caret is sufficiently complex, and required in so many places in the program, that we handle it in a separate function called MoveCaret(). Here's the listing for CARET.C:

```
// caret.c
// text input, uses caret

#define STRICT
#include <windows.h>

#define XSTART 10                        // text starting position
#define YSTART 30
#define XCARETWIDTH 2                     // caret size
#define YCARETHEIGHT 15
#define MAXLENGTH 80                      // size of buffer
char achString[MAXLENGTH];               // text buffer
                                         // prototypes
LRESULT CALLBACK _export WndProc(HWND, UINT, WPARAM, LPARAM);
void MoveCaret(HWND, int);
```

```
PSTR szProgName = "Caret";            // application name
#include "stdmain.inc"                // standard WinMain() function
//////////////////////////////////////////////////////////////////
// main window procedure -- receives messages                    //
//////////////////////////////////////////////////////////////////
LRESULT CALLBACK _export WndProc(HWND hWnd, UINT msg,
                                 WPARAM wParam, LPARAM lParam)
    {
    PAINTSTRUCT ps;                   // info for painting
    HDC hDC;                          // device context handle
    static int cCaretPos = 0;         // numb chars to left of caret
    static int cLength = 0;           // total chars in string
    int j;                            // loop index

    switch(msg)
        {
        case WM_SETFOCUS:             // can type in our window
            CreateCaret(hWnd, NULL, XCARETWIDTH, YCARETHEIGHT);
            MoveCaret(hWnd, cCaretPos);  // position caret
            ShowCaret(hWnd);          // display caret
            break;

        case WM_KILLFOCUS:            // no typing in our window,
            DestroyCaret();           //    so no caret
            break;

        case WM_CHAR:                 // user typed a char
            if(wParam=='\b')          // if it's backspace,
                {
                if(cCaretPos>0)       // if chars to the left of us
                    {
                    for(j=cCaretPos-1; j<cLength; j++) // shift text
                        achString[j] = achString[j+1];  //    to left
                    achString[--cLength] = '\0';    // shorten string
                    cCaretPos--;                    // move caret
                    MoveCaret(hWnd, cCaretPos);     // position caret
                    InvalidateRect(hWnd, NULL, TRUE); // repaint window
                    }
                else
                    MessageBeep(0);
                break;
                }

            if(wParam < ' ' || cLength > MAXLENGTH) // if Tab,
                {                                   // Enter, etc.,
                MessageBeep(0);                     // or if buffer full,
                break;                              // ignore it
                }
                                            // it's a displayable char
            for(j=cLength; j>=cCaretPos; j--) // shift right side of
                achString[j+1] = achString[j]; // text to right
            achString[cCaretPos++] = wParam;   // insert character
```

```
        MoveCaret(hWnd, cCaretPos);        // position caret
        cLength++;                         // lengthen string
        InvalidateRect(hWnd, NULL, TRUE);  // repaint window
        break;

    case WM_KEYDOWN:
        switch(wParam)
            {
            case VK_HOME:              // Home key
                cCaretPos = 0;         // caret to beginning of line
                MoveCaret(hWnd, cCaretPos);
                break;
            case VK_END:               // End key
                cCaretPos = cLength;   // caret to end of line
                MoveCaret(hWnd, cCaretPos);
                break;
            case VK_RIGHT:             // right keyboard arrow
                if(cCaretPos < cLength) // if caret not at right end
                    MoveCaret(hWnd, ++cCaretPos);  // move caret right
                else
                    MessageBeep(0);
                break;
            case VK_LEFT:              // left keyboard arrow
                if(cCaretPos > 0)      // if caret not at left end
                    MoveCaret(hWnd, --cCaretPos);  // move caret left
                else
                    MessageBeep(0);
                break;
            case VK_DELETE:            // the Del key
                if(cCaretPos < cLength) // if caret not at right end
                    {
                    for(j=cCaretPos; j<cLength; j++)   // shift text
                        achString[j] = achString[j+1]; // to left
                    achString[--cLength] = '\0';       // shorten string
                    InvalidateRect(hWnd, NULL, TRUE);  // paint window
                    }
                else
                    MessageBeep(0);
                break;
            }  // end switch wParam
        break;

    case WM_PAINT:                      // window needs repainting
        hDC = BeginPaint(hWnd, &ps);    // prepare window for paint
        TextOut(hDC, XSTART, YSTART,
                achString, cLength );   // draw text from buffer
        EndPaint(hWnd, &ps);            // ok, painting is over
        break;

    case WM_DESTROY:
        PostQuitMessage(0);
        break;
```

```
      default:
         return( DefWindowProc(hWnd, msg, wParam, lParam) );
      }   // end switch(msg)

   return OL;
   }  // end WndProc

/////////////////////////////////////////////////////////////////////
// MoveCaret function                                                //
/////////////////////////////////////////////////////////////////////
void MoveCaret(HWND hWnd, int cCaretPosition)
   {
   HDC hDC;                       // device context handle
   DWORD dwExtent;                // text dimensions
   WORD xExtent;                  // text length

   hDC = GetDC(hWnd);             // get device context
                                  // get text info
   dwExtent = GetTextExtent(hDC, achString, cCaretPosition);
   xExtent = LOWORD(dwExtent);    // get text line length
   ReleaseDC(hWnd, hDC);          // release device context
   SetCaretPos(xExtent+XSTART, YSTART);  // position caret
   }
```

Creating and Showing the Caret

There can be only one caret on the screen at any time, and it should appear in the window that has the keyboard focus, since that's where typed characters will be directed. Thus we arrange to create and display the caret when we get the WM_SETFOCUS message, indicating that we now have the focus. We destroy it when we get the WM_KILLFOCUS message, indicating that we've lost the focus.

Here's how this is handled in the CARET program:

```
case WM_SETFOCUS:
   CreateCaret(hWnd, NULL, XCARETWIDTH, YCARETHEIGHT);
   MoveCaret(hWnd, cCaretPos);
   ShowCaret(hWnd);
   break;
...
case WM_KILLFOCUS:
   DestroyCaret();
   break;
```

The CreateCaret() function installs a caret in the window whose handle is the first argument. The second argument can be a handle to a bitmap, which you can use for specialized caret shapes. Because we're using only the normal vertical-line caret, we set this to NULL. The third and fourth arguments are the horizontal and vertical dimensions of the caret, in pixels. Usually you want a caret that can be accurately positioned between letters, so it should be fairly narrow. We make it 2 pixels wide and 15 pixels high. (In more complex programs you would probably want to size it to the text being displayed.)

You must not only create the caret, you must also tell Windows to make it visible. You do this with ShowCaret(). This function takes as its only argument the handle to the caret's window. (You can temporarily hide the caret with the HideCaret() function, although we don't use it in this program.)

When a window loses the keyboard focus it should remove the caret with the DestroyCaret() function, which takes no arguments.

Moving the Caret

The caret is moved to any position on the screen with the SetCaretPos() function, which takes two arguments: the X- and Y-coordinates of the new position.

Moving the caret is easy; but figuring out where to put it requires some thought. Remember that we are using a proportional font, in which the characters have different widths. Even if we know that the caret should go after, say, the 7th character, we can't calculate this position by simply multiplying the character width by 7. Instead we must use the GetTextExtent() function (discussed in Chapter 18, *Text Position*) to calculate the length of the first 7 characters. Here's how that looks in our MoveText() function in the CARET program:

```
dwExtent = GetTextExtent(hDC, achString, cCaretPosition);
xExtent = LOWORD(dwExtent);
...
SetCaretPos(xExtent+XSTART, YSTART);
```

These instructions are executed whenever we need to move the caret. This happens whenever we move the caret with the arrow keys, as well as whenever we type or delete a displayable character.

Device Context Without WM_PAINT

Using GetTextExtent() poses an interesting problem. To call it, we need a device context handle, which is used as its first argument. This is because only the device context knows what font we're using, and GetTextExtent() needs to know this to calculate the length of a string. So far in this book, the only way we've obtained a device context is as the return value of a BeginPaint() function, when a WM_PAINT message is received. But we don't want to repaint the window every time we move the caret; pressing the arrow keys should move the caret but leave the text unchanged.

It turns out that Windows provides a way to obtain a device context handle without waiting for WM_PAINT and executing BeginPain(). This is the function GetDC(). You can execute this function at any time; you don't need to wait for

WM_PAINT. As you can see, we use it in our MoveCaret() function to obtain a device context handle that we can use as the first argument to GetTextExtent().

When the device context is no longer needed, it is released with the ReleaseDC() function. These two functions always form a pair. Here's how this looks:

```
hDC = GetDC(hWnd);
// functions that require a device context
ReleaseDC(hWnd, hDC);
```

This arrangement is typically used to find out something about the device context, such as what font, pen, or brush objects are being used, or the dimensions of a particular graphics element, which in this case is a line of text.

SUMMARY

We have emerged from the forest with some new skills, but perhaps a bit scratched by thorns and briars. As you can see, processing text input using WM_CHAR and WM_KEYDOWN messages is not a trivial undertaking. Our CARET program is already fairly complex, and we haven't even considered what happens with multiple lines of text. For text input in simple Windows programs, you may be better off sticking with the edit control approach, as shown in Chapter 20, *Text Input: The Easy Way*. Of course, if you're writing a real word processor, you'll need to push further into the dark forest of character manipulation, whose outskirts we've briefly toured here.

In traditional character-based DOS programs, the function keys and some of the other noncharacter keys were an important part of the user interface. You probably memorized many key-combinations for your old pre-Windows word processor, for example. However, in Windows applications, keyboard keys are less important, because menu selections, dialog boxes, and other GUI devices are the preferred methods for the user to input information to the application. Thus you can go a long way in Windows programming without worrying about the approach to text input we've explored in this chapter. However, when you need to know exactly what key the user has pressed, this is how to do it.

22

THE MINIEDIT PROGRAM

*I*t's time to embark on another quest. This time our quarry is an actual, working text-editor program. The user can type text into a window, save the results to disk, and read files back from the disk for display or further editing. This program, called MINIEDIT, operates in much the same way as the NOTEPAD accessory program that comes with Windows, except that it does automatic word wrap at the right margin, rather than allowing very long lines. MINIEDIT is useful any time you want to create small ASCII text files, without the bother of pressing (ENTER) at the end of each line.

On our quest, we carry both a magic sword and a long lance: that is, the File common dialog and the edit control window. MINIEDIT is a combination of the COMOPEN and COMSAVE programs from Chapter 13, *The File Common Dialogs*, which demonstrated common File dialogs, and the EDITMENU program of Chapter 20, *Text Input: The Easy Way*, which demonstrated edit control windows. The sword and lance do so much for us in this program that it's surprising there's any code left to write, but there are a few odds and ends, as you'll see.

OPERATION OF MINIEDIT

There aren't many surprises in the operation of MINIEDIT. You can type text into the window; select parts of it with the mouse or keyboard; and cut, copy, paste, and clear the resulting selections, using menu or keyboard commands. If you resize the window, the text automatically rearranges itself to fit the new margins. The big change from the EDITMENU program is that you can save the resulting text file to disk, and read it back in. Figure 22-1 shows the MINIEDIT program with the Edit menu selected.

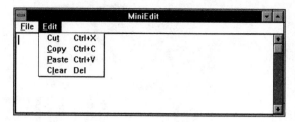

Figure 22-1
The MINIEDIT Program
and the Edit Menu

Because this program uses a menu system, it requires an .RC file. Here's the listing for MINIEDIT.RC:

```
// miniedit.rc
// resource script file for miniedit

#include "miniedit.h"

MiniEdit MENU  // name must agree with szProgName
   BEGIN
      POPUP "&File"
         BEGIN
            MENUITEM "&Open...", IDM_OPEN
            MENUITEM "&Save", IDM_SAVE
            MENUITEM "Save &As...", IDM_SAVEAS
         END
      POPUP "&Edit"
         BEGIN
            MENUITEM "Cu&t\tCtrl+X", IDM_CUT
            MENUITEM "&Copy\tCtrl+C", IDM_COPY
            MENUITEM "&Paste\tCtrl+V", IDM_PASTE
            MENUITEM "C&lear\tDel", IDM_CLEAR
         END

   END
```

Here's the corresponding MINIEDIT.H header file:

```
// miniedit.h
// header file for miniedit

#define ID_EDIT     1000      // ID of edit control window
#define IDM_OPEN    101       // menu IDs
#define IDM_SAVE    102
#define IDM_SAVEAS  103
#define IDM_CUT     201
#define IDM_COPY    202
#define IDM_PASTE   203
#define IDM_CLEAR   204
```

The source file is fairly large, but you've already seen the major sections of code in previous programs. Here's the listing for MINIEDIT.C:

```
// miniedit.c
// uses multiline edit box for text input
// includes edit menu, and loading and saving text to file

#define STRICT
#include <windows.h>
#include <memory.h>          // for memset()
#include <commdlg.h>         // for common dialogs
#include "miniedit.h"        // for menu item IDs
#define NMAX    20000        // size of text buffer (not too big!)
#define SBSIZE    256        // buffer size for file names, etc.


char szText[NMAX];           // text buffer
char szFile[SBSIZE];         // file name for OPENFILENAME
char szPath[SBSIZE];         // path+file name for OPENFILENAME
char szString[SBSIZE];       // general string
HFILE hFile;                 // file handle
BOOL bValidFile;             // TRUE if valid file is in memory
                             // filters for Open and Save as
LPCSTR szFilter[] = { "Text files (*.txt)", "*.txt",
                      "All files (*.*)",     "*.*",
                      "" };
                             // prototypes
LRESULT CALLBACK _export WndProc(HWND, UINT, WPARAM, LPARAM);
void DoOpen(HWND, HWND);
void DoSave(HWND, HWND);
void DoSaveAs(HWND, HWND);


PSTR szProgName = "MiniEdit";       // application name
#include "stdmain.inc"              // standard WinMain()
//////////////////////////////////////////////////////////////////
// main window procedure -- receives messages                    //
//////////////////////////////////////////////////////////////////
LRESULT CALLBACK _export WndProc(HWND hWnd, UINT msg,
                          WPARAM wParam, LPARAM lParam)
    {
    static HWND hWndEdit;            // edit window handle
    HINSTANCE hInst;                 // instance handle

    switch(msg)
        {
        case WM_CREATE:
            bValidFile = FALSE;      // no file opened yet
                                     // get instance handle
            hInst = (HINSTANCE)GetWindowWord(hWnd, GWW_HINSTANCE);
            hWndEdit = CreateWindow(      // create edit control window
                        "EDIT",           // class is "EDIT"
                        NULL,             // no caption
                        WS_CHILD | WS_VISIBLE | ES_MULTILINE |
                        WS_BORDER | WS_VSCROLL | ES_AUTOVSCROLL,
                        0, 0, 0, 0,       // will be sized later
                        hWnd,             // parent is main window
```

279

```
                    (HMENU)ID_EDIT,  // ID for WM_COMMAND
                    hInst,           // this instance
                    NULL);           // no data structure
      break;

   case WM_COMMAND:              // menu item selected
      switch(wParam)
         {
         case IDM_OPEN:
            // if text modified since last save, and
            if( SendMessage(hWndEdit, EM_GETMODIFY, 0, 0L) )
               if( MessageBox(hWnd,          // if user says save it
                  "There is unsaved data. Save it?",
                  szProgName, MB_YESNO | MB_ICONQUESTION) == IDYES )
                  if(bValidFile)                 // if file "open"
                     DoSave(hWnd, hWndEdit);     // save it
                  else                           // otherwise,
                     DoSaveAs(hWnd, hWndEdit);   // get name, save
            DoOpen(hWnd, hWndEdit);  // open new file
            break;

         case IDM_SAVE:
            // if valid file, save text to old name
            if(bValidFile)
               DoSave(hWnd, hWndEdit);
            else                               // otherwise, to new name
               DoSaveAs(hWnd, hWndEdit);
            break;

         case IDM_SAVEAS:
            DoSaveAs(hWnd, hWndEdit);   // save text to old name
            break;

         case IDM_CUT:        // user selects cut
            SendMessage(hWndEdit, WM_CUT, 0, 0L);
            break;

         case IDM_COPY:       // user selects copy
            SendMessage(hWndEdit, WM_COPY, 0, 0L);
            break;

         case IDM_PASTE:      // user selects paste
            SendMessage(hWndEdit, WM_PASTE, 0, 0L);
            break;

         case IDM_CLEAR:      // user selects clear
            SendMessage(hWndEdit, WM_CLEAR, 0, 0L);
            break;

         case ID_EDIT:        // if edit control runs out of memory
            if(HIWORD(lParam)==EN_ERRSPACE)
               MessageBox(hWnd, "Edit Control is out of Memory",
```

```
                              szProgName, MB_OK | MB_ICONEXCLAMATION);
               break;
           }
         break;  // end case WM_COMMAND

      case WM_SIZE:               // edit window same as main window
         MoveWindow(hWndEdit, 0, 0, LOWORD(lParam),
                                    HIWORD(lParam), TRUE);
         break;  // end case WM_SIZE

      case WM_SETFOCUS:           // give edit window the focus
         SetFocus(hWndEdit);      // whenever main window gets focus
         break;

      case WM_CLOSE:
         // if text modified since last save, and
         if( SendMessage(hWndEdit, EM_GETMODIFY, 0, 0L) )
            if( MessageBox(hWnd,                 // if user says save it
               "There is unsaved data. Save it?",
               szProgName, MB_YESNO | MB_ICONQUESTION) == IDYES )
               if(bValidFile)                    // if file "open"
                  DoSave(hWnd, hWndEdit);    // save it
               else                              // otherwise
                  DoSaveAs(hWnd, hWndEdit);  // open file, save it
         DestroyWindow(hWnd);
         break;  // end case WM_CLOSE

      case WM_DESTROY:
         PostQuitMessage(0);
         break;
      default:
         return( DefWindowProc(hWnd, msg, wParam, lParam) );
      }    // end switch(msg)
   return 0L;
   }  // end WndProc

///////////////////////////////////////////////////////////////////////
// DoOpen -- "Open" dialog box, opens a file                           //
///////////////////////////////////////////////////////////////////////
void DoOpen(HWND hWnd, HWND hEdit)
   {
   OPENFILENAME ofn;                    // structure for GetOpenFileName()
   UINT cbRead;                         // bytes read by _lread()

   szPath[0] = '\0';                    // empty name field
   memset(&ofn, 0, sizeof(OPENFILENAME) );  // zero the structure
   ofn.lStructSize = sizeof(OPENFILENAME);  // size of structure
   ofn.hwndOwner = hWnd;                // owner is main window
   ofn.lpstrFilter = szFilter[0]; // filter
   ofn.lpstrFile = szPath;         // path+file name buffer
   ofn.nMaxFile = SBSIZE;          // size of above
   ofn.lpstrFileTitle = szFile;    // file name buffer
```

```
      ofn.nMaxFileTitle = SBSIZE;     // size of above
      ofn.Flags = OFN_PATHMUSTEXIST   // require valid path and file
                | OFN_FILEMUSTEXIST;

      if( !GetOpenFileName(&ofn) )    // get the path+name
         return;                      // user pressed Cancel
      hFile = _lopen(szPath, READ);   // open file
      if( !hFile )
         goto file_error;
      memset(szText, 0, NMAX );                 // zero the buffer
      cbRead = _lread(hFile, szText, NMAX);     // read file
      _lclose(hFile);                           // close file
      if(cbRead == (UINT)HFILE_ERROR)           // check for error
         goto file_error;
      SetWindowText(hEdit, (LPSTR)szText);      // put text in edit window
      wsprintf(szString, "%s -- %s",            // put program name
               (LPSTR)szProgName, (LPSTR)szFile); // and file name
      SetWindowText(hWnd, (LPSTR)szString);     // in main title
      bValidFile = TRUE;                        // valid file in memory
      return;                                   // successful return
   file_error:
      MessageBox(hWnd, "Can't open file or can't read file",
               szProgName, MB_OK | MB_ICONEXCLAMATION);
      return;                                   // error return
      }  // end DoOpen()


   ////////////////////////////////////////////////////////////////////
   // DoSave function  -- saves memory to file                        //
   ////////////////////////////////////////////////////////////////////
   void DoSave(HWND hWnd, HWND hEdit)
      {
      int cbLength;                   // return from GetWindowTextLength()
      UINT cbWrite;                   // bytes written by _lwrite()

      hFile = _lcreat(szPath, 0);     // open file, truncate to 0 length
      if( hFile == HFILE_ERROR )
         goto file_error;
      GetWindowText(hEdit, (LPSTR)szText, NMAX);
      cbLength = GetWindowTextLength(hEdit);
                                      // write buffer to file
      cbWrite = _lwrite(hFile, szText, cbLength);
      _lclose(hFile);                 // close file
      if(cbWrite==(UINT)HFILE_ERROR)
         goto file_error;
      // reset edit control to "not modified"
      SendMessage(hEdit, EM_SETMODIFY, FALSE, OL);
      return;                         // successful return
   file_error:
      MessageBox(hWnd, "Can't open or can't write to file",
               szProgName, MB_OK | MB_ICONEXCLAMATION);
      return;                         // error return
```

```
    }  // end DoSave()

///////////////////////////////////////////////////////////////////
// DoSaveAs   -- "Save as..." common dialog box                  //
///////////////////////////////////////////////////////////////////
void DoSaveAs(HWND hWnd, HWND hEdit)
    {
    OPENFILENAME ofn;              // create structure
    int cbLength;                  // return from GetWindowTextLength()
    UINT cbWrite;                  // bytes written by _lwrite()

    szPath[0] = '\0';             // empty the name field
    memset( &ofn, 0, sizeof(OPENFILENAME) );  // zero structure
    ofn.lStructSize = sizeof(OPENFILENAME);   // size of structure
    ofn.hwndOwner = hWnd;         // owner is main window
    ofn.lpstrFilter = szFilter[0]; // filter
    ofn.lpstrFile = szPath;       // path+name buffer
    ofn.nMaxFile = SBSIZE;        // size of above
    ofn.lpstrFileTitle = szFile;  // file name buffer
    ofn.nMaxFileTitle = SBSIZE;   // size of above
                                  // require valid path
    ofn.Flags = OFN_PATHMUSTEXIST | OFN_HIDEREADONLY |
            OFN_OVERWRITEPROMPT;  // warn on file overwrite
    if( !GetSaveFileName(&ofn) )  // get the path+name
       return;                    // user pressed Cancel
    hFile = _lcreat(szPath, 0);   // create new file
    if( hFile == HFILE_ERROR )
       goto file_error;
    GetWindowText(hEdit, (LPSTR)szText, NMAX);
    cbLength = GetWindowTextLength(hEdit);      // get length
    cbWrite = _lwrite(hFile, szText, cbLength); // write text to file
    _lclose(hFile);               // close file
    if(cbWrite==(UINT)HFILE_ERROR)
       goto file_error;
    wsprintf(szString, "%s -- %s",              // put program name
            (LPSTR)szProgName, (LPSTR)szFile);  // and file name
    SetWindowText(hWnd, (LPSTR)szString);       // in main title
    bValidFile = TRUE;                          // valid file in memory
    // reset edit control to "not modified"
    SendMessage(hEdit, EM_SETMODIFY, FALSE, 0L);
    return;                       // successful return
file_error:
    MessageBox(hWnd, "Can't open or can't write to file",
            szProgName, MB_OK | MB_ICONEXCLAMATION);
    return;                       // error return
    }  // end DoSaveAs()
```

As you can see, the code for responding to the Open, Save, and Save As menu selections has been placed in functions called DoOpen(), DoSave(), and DoSaveAs(), which appear at the end of the listing.

Figure 22-2

The MINIEDIT Program
and the File Menu

FILE STRATEGY

When an application begins to interact with disk files in a serious way, the programmer must make some decisions. One is how many and what items to put on the file menu. Another is how to protect the user from making mistakes that would lead to loss of data.

File Menu Selections

At a minimum you'll see Open, Save, and Save As items on a File menu. Some programs also include New and Close. Other items may be used in more specialized situations, and of course the File menu may also include items that are not directly related to loading and saving files, such as Print, Exit, Change directory, and so on. In MINIEDIT we use the simplest arrangement. Figure 22-2 shows the MINIEDIT program with the File menu selected.

Probably the user starts using MINIEDIT by typing some text—a grocery list, a note to be sent to Jennifer on E-mail, or whatever—into the edit control window. Once there's text in the edit control, the user wants the capability to give it a file name and save it to disk. This is done with the Save As menu item, which calls up the Save As common file dialog. After the user specifies a directory path and a file name using this dialog, the text is written to disk using the specified name.

The user may later make changes to the text, and then want to save the revised text under the same name. This is done by selecting Save, which simply writes the text directly to the same file (erasing the previous contents).

The user may also want to view and edit a previously written text file. The Open menu item accomplishes this by calling up the Open common dialog, which allows the user to specify a file name and path. It then reads the contents of this file into the edit window.

We could have added a New menu item. This would delete the text in the edit window, and forget the name of a previously specified file, so the user could start with a clean slate. However, this isn't strictly necessary, since the programmer can achieve the same effect by restarting the program or by erasing the contents of the screen and saving new material to a new file.

Another possibility is a Close item. However, this isn't necessary either, because files are closed automatically when necessary.

"Open" Is Not Open

In Chapter 12, *Disk Files*, we mentioned that files could either be left open while the user worked on them, or closed immediately after each read or write. In MINIEDIT we elect to take the second approach. The result is that the user's idea of what "open" means, and the program's idea, may be different.

Suppose the user selects Open from the File menu, edits the resulting text in the edit window, and then saves the result to disk. The user probably thinks the file is open the whole time the text is being edited. But in fact, when Open is selected, the program opens the file, reads the contents into the edit window, and then *closes* the file. When the user selects Save or Save As, the program opens the file, writes the contents of the edit window to the file, and then closes the file.

What the user thinks of as being "open" is really just the program becoming aware of a valid file name. When the user successfully executes Open or Save As, the program remembers the file name (actually a complete path-plus-file name). If the user selects Save, it is to this file name that the text in the edit window is saved. Before the first Open or Save As selection, the program is not aware of any such name.

The program keeps track of whether it has stored a valid file name with the bValidFile flag. This variable is set to TRUE whenever a file has been read into the edit window with Open, or whenever the text in the window has been saved to a file with Save As. The program uses this flag to remember whether a file is "open" in the user's sense of the term. We may fall into using "open" this way ourselves, although we'll try to remember to put quotation marks around it to indicate that we're not really "opening" a file.

Saving Users from Themselves

Programmers' lives would be much simpler if they could assume that all users were perfectly rational. Unfortunately, it's easy for a user to make a mistake that results in irretrievable data loss. In programs like MINIEDIT, a common mistake is for a user to create or modify one file, and then try to "open" a second file, without saving the edited version of the first file. Doing this overwrites the contents of the edit window with the second file, losing any changes made to the first file since the last save. Another user mistake is exiting from the program without saving the edited text.

Our application looks for these situations. If the user is about to open a file, the application checks to see if the contents of the edit window have been modified. If they have been, the program puts up a message box asking if the user wants to save the data. If the answer is yes, the program saves the data if a valid file is "open," and otherwise calls the Save As dialog box so the user can supply a file name for saving the file. Figure 22-3 uses flowcharts to show how the program behaves in these situations.

A similar check is made when the user attempts to exit from the program (by selecting Close from the System menu). This happens when the WM_CLOSE message is received.

Also, if the user selects the Save item when no file is "open," then the application calls up the Save As common dialog so the user can supply a file name.

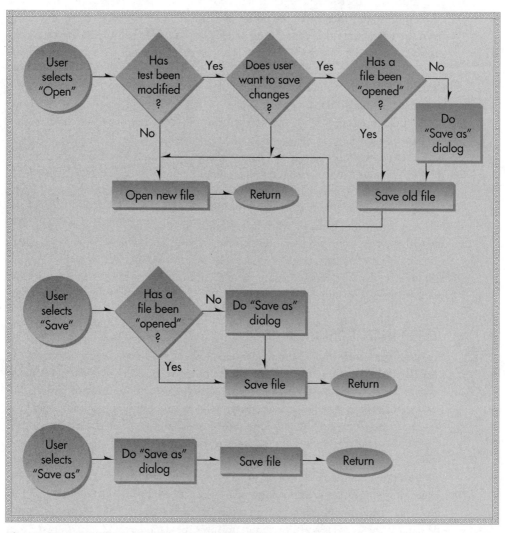

Figure 22-3 MINIEDIT Response to File Menu Selections

There are other potential user errors we don't respond to in MINIEDIT. For example, the user may use the Save or Save As menu items to save an empty file. The program doesn't check to see if the user has actually typed any text, before writing to the file. This usually doesn't do any harm besides creating a 0-length file. We also don't check to see if the user is attempting to save a file that has not been modified since the last save. This usually doesn't do any harm either, except for taking a few seconds to perform the unnecessary save.

MONITORING EDIT CONTROL CHANGES

To know whether to complain to the user that there is unsaved data, we need to know if the user has modified the text in the edit control window. Fortunately Windows makes this easy. We send a message to the edit control with SendMessage(), and the return value of this function tells us if the text was modified. Here's how that looks:

```
answer = SendMessage(hWndEdit, EM_GETMODIFY, 0, 0L);
```

The message EM_GETMODIFY causes a return of TRUE if the edit window was modified, and FALSE otherwise. In MINIEDIT we place this function in an **if** statement.

When we ask whether the edit window has been modified, the question arises, modified since when? The answer is, since the last time the contents of the edit window were saved to disk. We need a way to tell the edit window, "OK, forget you were modified before, since the user saved the text to disk. Just tell me if you're modified starting now." This is accomplished by sending an EM_SETMODIFY message to the edit window, like this:

```
SendMessage(hWndEdit, EM_SETMODIFY, FALSE, 0L);
```

When the third parameter is FALSE, the edit window resets itself to "unmodified;" if it's TRUE, it sets itself to "modified." We execute this statement at the end of the DoSave() and DoSaveAs() functions, when we've successfully saved the contents of the window to disk.

FILE NAMES IN THE WINDOW TITLE

When a program works with files, it's nice if the name of the file that is currently "open" can appear, along with the program name, in the title bar of the main window. This reminds the user what file is currently being processed. For example, if our MINIEDIT program were working on a file named DATA8.TXT, we would like the window title to read "MINIEDIT - DATA8.TXT".

We implement this in MINIEDIT using SetWindowText(). As we've seen, this function can be used to install the entire contents of an edit window. However, when applied to a window with a title bar, it inserts text into the title. We use wsprintf() to combine the program name and the file name into one string. Here's the code:

```
wsprintf(szString, "%s -- %s", (LPSTR)szProgName, (LPSTR)szFile);
SetWindowText(hWnd, (LPSTR)szString);
```

This happens in both the DoOpen() and DoSaveAs() functions, after the user has successfully read a file with Open or saved it with Save As.

Note the casts of string variables to LPSTR in wsprintf(). It is essential to cast string variables this way (although casts are unnecessary on other kinds of variables). Without the casts, the function won't work (and sometimes the program dies as well).

SUMMARY

The MINIEDIT program gives you a chance to see some of the elements of a real Windows application in action. It can serve as the basis for any simple program that reads and writes disk files. For different applications you can keep the file-handling logic of this program, and substitute your own data handling code. The DATAB program in Part Eight, *Larger Programs,* of this book uses this approach.

In Part Three you've learned the basics of text input and output. You now know how to use different fonts for text display, and how to account for the text size and the dimensions of the client window. You can add scroll bars to a window so you can see all parts of a large document. You also know how to input text typed by the user, either using an edit control window, which makes the job easy; or by responding to the the WM_CHAR and WM_KEYDOWN messages, which makes the job complicated but provides a more flexible approach. Finally we investigated a semi-serious application that shows one approach to handling disk access in a realistic way.

PART FOUR
DIALOG BOXES

*a*s legend has it, King Arthur invented the round table so all the knights would be equal; no one could claim superiority by virtue of sitting at the head of the table. This promoted a free exchange of views; if everyone was equal, no one was afraid to speak out. Knights who had been on quests in distant lands brought back new ideas, which were considered and discussed by all. In this way, Camelot became a center of culture, commerce, and innovation.

In Windows, the dialog box plays (by a fairly long leap of the imagination) a role similar to the round table. It promotes the exchange of ideas between the user and the program. The program makes suggestions and encourages the user to express preferences and desires.

The dialog box provides a rich selection of tools to facilitate this exchange of ideas. Text and numbers can be displayed by the application or entered by the user. The user can select an entry from various kinds of lists. The application can also present yes-or-no options and lists of mutually exclusive options for the user to choose from. Using scroll bars, the user has a visually intuitive way to select from a range of values.

These information-exchange tools, provided by the dialog box, are called *controls*. The dialog box itself is a fixed-size window that (usually) appears on top of an application's main window. It groups together related controls, and is displayed in specific circumstances, often as the result of the user making a menu selection.

We've already seen examples of common dialog boxes, such as Open and Save As. However, common dialogs are predesigned; you don't need to create them yourself or even write the code for what they do. Here in Part Four we're going to discuss how to create your own "custom" dialog boxes, which look and work the way you want.

In Turbo (and Borland) C++ for Windows, creating custom dialogs and installing controls in them is most conveniently carried out using a utility called the Resource Workshop (RW). We'll discuss the RW and dialog boxes in general in the first chapter, show how to write the corresponding source file in the next chapter, and focus on individual controls in later chapters.

CHAPTER 23

THE RESOURCE WORKSHOP

a dialog box, like some mythological beast, has two faces. The first is what the user sees on the screen: a certain visual arrangement of controls within a dialog window. The second is a description of the dialog box created by the programmer. In the same way a source file for a program generates an executable file, so the text description of a dialog box generates the visual dialog box on the screen. Figure 23-1 shows a dialog box with several controls: an edit control, a line of static text, and two pushbuttons. This is the user's view of a dialog box.

The text description of the dialog is what you, the programmer, create. Because a dialog box is a resource, this text description forms part of a program's resource script (.RC) file. We discussed .RC files in Chapter 11, *Menus*. As you learned then, the .RC compiler translates the text description of a menu resource into binary code that creates the visual menu on the screen. The text descriptions of dialog resources are similar, but more complicated. This added complexity results from the need to specify where the various controls will be positioned in the dialog, and from the larger number of options available for each control.

Here's the text description of the dialog box shown in Figure 23-1:

```
NameDlg DIALOG 18, 18, 179, 49
STYLE DS_MODALFRAME | WS_POPUP | WS_CAPTION | WS_SYSMENU
CAPTION "Name entry"
BEGIN
        LTEXT "Enter your name:", -1, 12, 18, 83, 8
        EDITTEXT IDD_EDIT, 12, 29, 104, 12,
            ES_LEFT | WS_CHILD | WS_VISIBLE | WS_BORDER | WS_TABSTOP
        PUSHBUTTON "OK", IDOK, 129, 6, 38, 14,
            WS_CHILD | WS_VISIBLE | WS_TABSTOP
        PUSHBUTTON "Cancel", IDCANCEL, 129, 27, 38, 14,
            WS_CHILD | WS_VISIBLE | WS_TABSTOP
END
```

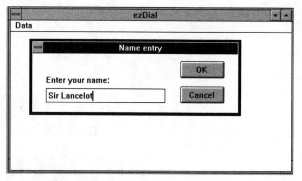

Figure 23-1

A Simple
Dialog Box

This description is sometimes called a *dialog script*. Figure 23-2 shows the relationship of the visual appearance of a dialog box, the dialog script, and the compiled binary code for the resource.

We won't worry about the details of the dialog script now. However, you should note a few major aspects. The keyword DIALOG specifies a dialog resource. LTEXT, EDITTEXT, and PUSHBUTTON are types of controls. The four numbers associated with each control specify the location and size of the control within the dialog box. A major part of designing a dialog is positioning the controls in a way that's logical, easy-to-use, and visually pleasing.

In the earliest days of Windows programming this dialog script was created "by hand," using a text editor. This meant guessing at the values of each control's coordinates, and then compiling and running the program to see how it looked when displayed on the screen. Usually the coordinates needed adjusting, so the programmer would edit the .RC file again, and then recompile. This process would be repeated over and over until the dialog looked right. Of course this was time consuming and not much fun.

Fortunately more powerful tools have been developed that make the creation of dialog boxes much easier. Here we'll be concerned with Borland's Resource Workshop tool, which provides a simple visual approach to creating the dialog script. Most of this chapter will be devoted to explaining how to use the RW. But before we get to the specifics, let's summarize the types of controls that are normally used in dialog boxes.

CONTROLS

A dialog box doesn't do anything by itself. It exists only as a frame to hold a group of related controls. Let's look at the common controls and see what they're supposed to do. Figure 23-3 shows these controls in a dialog box.

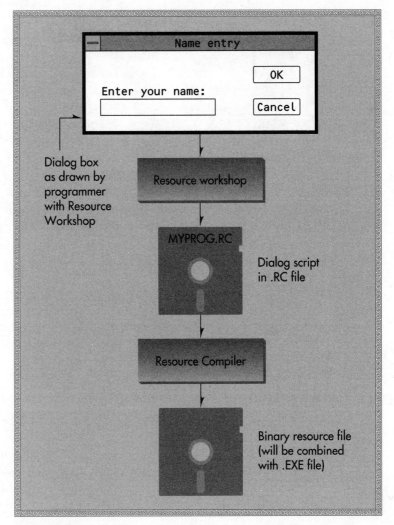

Figure 23-2 Visual, Script, and Binary Representations of a Dialog Box

Pushbuttons

A pushbutton is a rounded rectangle with a text caption inside. The caption is most often a single word, such as OK, Cancel, Yes, or No. Pressing a pushbutton usually causes some action related to the dialog box, such as exiting from it. Buttons are sometimes used to bring up a second dialog as an adjunct to the first. Such buttons have captions like Options... or Setup... .

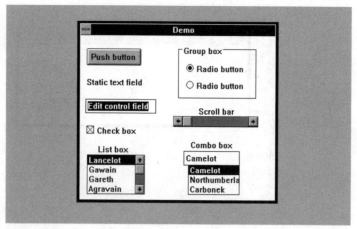

Figure 23-3
The Major
Dialog Controls

Static Text

Static text is simply a text string that appears in the dialog. Technically, static text is a kind of control, but the designation doesn't fit very well, because static text doesn't control anything, and the user can't interact with it. Static text is normally used to label other controls, such as edit controls. Although static text is usually permanently installed in the dialog, it can also be changed by the program.

Edit Controls

An edit control is a rectangular area into which the user can type text from the keyboard. We already saw an edit control in Chapter 20, *Text Input: The Easy Way*, where it occupied an entire main window and could accept multiple lines of text. However, in dialog boxes, edit controls usually accept only a single line of text, such as a name or number. Edit controls are the equivalent of the one-line text input allowed at the old-fashioned DOS prompt.

Radio Buttons

A radio button appears as a small circle. If the user clicks on a radio button, it acquires a smaller black circle in the middle to show that it has been selected. Radio buttons usually appear in a group. Only one button in a group can be selected at a time. Radio buttons allow the user to choose one from a mutually exclusive list of choices, thus imitating the behavior of the buttons on a car radio.

Group Boxes

A group box is a border with a title. Like static text, group boxes don't control anything. They are most often used to form a border around a number of radio buttons, thus providing a visual indication to the user that the radio buttons form a group from which only one can be selected.

Check Boxes

Check boxes are small square boxes that either have an X in them or not. They are used as On/Off switches to decide between two possible states. A check box is either checked (with a cross) or it isn't. Clicking on it changes it from one state to another. Each check box handles one decision. Unlike radio buttons, they aren't grouped together logically (although they may be grouped visually). The Italic and Bold check boxes in the Font common dialog are examples. Either one may be checked independently of the other.

List Boxes

A list box contains a list of text strings. These strings are typically names, such as file names, font names, or lists of data from the application, like employee names. The user selects one of these text strings by clicking on it. If there are too many strings to fit in the list box, they may be scrolled to bring all the entries into view.

Combo Boxes

A combo box is a combination of a list box and either an edit field or a static text field. The user can make a selection from the list, or type a name into the edit field. The list box part of the control may be visible all the time, or it may appear only when the user selects the control. Combo boxes are typically used for file name input.

Scroll Bars

We've already discussed how scroll bars can be added to a main window so you can see all parts of a large document. You can also use scroll bars as dialog box controls. They allow the user to select a value from a continuously varying range, like the volume control on a radio or the accelerator on a car. You might use a scroll bar to select a shade of gray on a scale that varies smoothly from white to black.

Common Usage

Every dialog box needs some way for the user to make it go away. On a few dialogs it is possible to invoke the System menu by clicking on the icon in the upper left corner of the dialog, and then selecting Close. However, most dialogs rely on pushbuttons. We've seen that in message boxes a single OK button suffices if the message box is simply reporting information. Message boxes can also provide Yes or No buttons, among other options.

Dialog boxes are different because they can accept input from the user. If all goes well, the user enters data into edit controls, clicks on radio buttons, chooses an option from a list, and so on. When all the information has been entered into the dialog, the user presses an OK button to tell the dialog to return the information to the application and disappear from the screen.

However, sometimes the user makes a mistake, and decides not to enter the information after all. Or maybe the user just wants to look at the dialog, without influencing the program at all. In such cases it's nice to be able to make the dialog vanish without having its data transferred to the application. The usual mechanism for this is the Cancel button. Thus most dialogs have OK and Cancel buttons.

By convention, pressing (ENTER) on the keyboard has the same effect as clicking the OK button, and pressing (ESC) is the same as clicking the Cancel button.

RESOURCES AND THE RW

Using the Resource Workshop to create resources means learning how to operate a fairly sophisticated application. The RW is perhaps a shade less complicated than the Turbo C++ or Borland C++ compilers. However, because of its visual nature, it's a lot more fun; it's like working with a paint program. Once you get the hang of it, you'll find it intuitive and easy. Using Windows, it's also easy to switch back and forth between the compiler and the RW, which makes program development fast and convenient.

In this chapter we'll explain in detail how to use the RW to create the resource script file shown earlier, which generates the dialog box of Figure 23-1. In the Summary section at the end of the chapter we'll condense these steps into several easy-to-follow lists, which you can use for reference when you design your own dialog boxes. We don't explain everything there is to know about the RW; just enough to get you started. To learn more, consult Borland's *Resource Workshop User's Guide*, which accompanies your compiler.

It Does Menus Too

We've said we're going to use the Resource Workshop to create dialog scripts. However, the RW can be used to create almost any kind of resource; it's not limited to dialogs. A menu is a resource, and the RW can be used to generate menu scripts as well. In the past we've generated menu scripts "by hand" with the regular Turbo C++ editor. We could continue to make menu scripts this way, but if we're going to be using the RW anyway, it's easier to use it to create our menu resource at the same time we create dialog resources. In this chapter we'll explain how to use the RW for both menus and dialog boxes. (In Part Six, *Getting Fancy with the GUI,* we'll show how to use the RW to create icons, another kind of resource.)

Resources Contained in the .RC File

The primary role of the RW is to create an .RC file and place resources in it. Creating different resources requires different kinds of editors. These editors are built into the RW and are started automatically when you want to create a new resource (or edit an old one). Here's how the overall process looks:

1. Open the Resource Workshop.
2. Create a resource script (.RC) file.
3. Use special editors to create resources (such as menus and dialog boxes) to go in the .RC file.
4. Save the .RC file.
5. Switch to the Turbo C++ compiler and use it to compile the .RC file and combine it with your program's .EXE file.

There are variations to this approach, such as using separate files for each resource and simply referencing them from the .RC file. However, for small programs the approach we show here is the simplest.

Strategies

At this point we might stop to consider overall approaches to designing Windows programs. One important question is, do you start with the internals of the program, or do you start with the user interface? For example, if you're writing a statistics program, do you write the mathematics functions first, or the code that handles getting data from the user and outputting the results? In a traditional MS-DOS program, a developer might reasonably start by coding the internals first, and leave the user interface for last. After all, it's just a few printf() and scanf() statements.

However, in Windows this strategy might not work so well. The user interface is more complex and powerful in Windows, and the event-driven architecture that it requires has a greater influence on the way the internals are written. For these reasons it's probably better to start by designing the user interface. When all the menus, dialog boxes, and so forth are just the way you (or your clients) like them, you can go on to write the "guts" of the program around them. If you write the internals first, you'll probably need to change a lot of code when you begin to experiment with the user interface.

In creating small Windows programs, the strategy question simplifies itself into a choice between which file to create first: the .C source file or the .RC resource script file. Usually it works better to start with the .RC file: design your menu and dialog resources first. We'll follow this approach in creating the EZDIAL program. We'll create the EZDIAL.RC file in this chapter, and then show how to write the EZDIAL.C source code in Chapter 24, *Invoking Dialog Boxes*.

CREATING EZDIAL.RC

Let's suppose we want to write a program that allows the user to call up a dialog box like that shown in Figure 23-1. The dialog box should appear when the user selects an item called Name from a pop-up menu called Data. When the dialog appears, the user can type a name into the edit field, and when the user clicks the OK button on the dialog, the dialog disappears, and the name is displayed in a message box (to prove that the program can read information from the edit control).

We'll call this program EZDIAL. This program does not aspire to be a megabucks commercial application, but it does demonstrate the basics of how dialog boxes are created, and how their controls interact with a program's code. As we discussed, we'll create the resources first, then we'll write the C code for the program.

Starting the Resource Workshop

To start the RW, double-click on the Workshop icon in the Turbo C++ (or Borland C++) group in the Program Manager. You'll see an attractive graphic, followed by the Resource Workshop window with File and Help menus. Select New Project from the File menu. In the resulting dialog, make sure the .RC radio button is selected, and press OK. A window will appear titled UNTITLED.RC, and additional menus will appear on the menu bar. The result is shown in Figure 23-4.

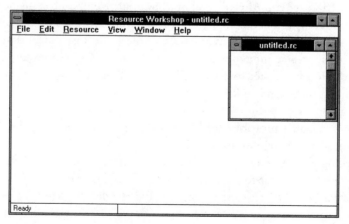

Figure 23-4

The Resource Workshop with the .RC Window

We should note a possible source of confusion. The RW refers to something called a *project* (as in the New Project, Open Project, and similar menu items in the File menu). What the RW means by "project" is, in this context, simply the .RC resource script file. To open a project means to open an .RC file. The various resources we will place in this file are parts of the project.

The Turbo C++ compiler, on the other hand, uses the term "project" in quite a different way: as a facility for keeping track of the files that need to be compiled, linked, and combined to create an .EXE executable file. The project file that results from this process has the .PRJ extension.

In both cases a *project* is the combination of several things into a single result. The RW project combines resources into an .RC file, and Turbo C++ combines source files into an executable file. Don't confuse the two uses of the term.

Creating Files

For our example, we want to name the .RC file EZDIAL.RC, so select Save File As from the RW File menu. In the resulting dialog, change to the directory where you're developing your program, and type in EZDIAL.RC. Click on OK. The .RC window will reflect the new name.

When we worked with menus we created a header file to hold the definitions used to identify the menu items, such as

```
#define IDM_OPEN  101
#define IDM_CLOSE 102
```

The RW can create the .H file for you and place the appropriate #defines in it automatically. This is a real convenience, as we'll see. To tell it to create the .H file, select Add To Project from the File menu. Enter your program's name with the .H extension, EZDIAL.H, in the File Name field. Click on OK. Answer Yes to the "All right to create new file?" query that pops up in a message box.

You've created an .RC resource script file and an .H header file. Now all you need to do is use the menu editor in the RW to create a menu, and the dialog editor to create a dialog. The results will be placed automatically in the .RC file, and the appropriate definitions will be placed in the .H file.

Creating a Menu

To create a menu, select New from the Resource menu. A dialog box will appear, with a list of resource types: ACCELERATOR, BITMAP, DIALOG, and so on. Select MENU and Click on OK. This brings up the Menu editor, as shown in Figure 23-5.

There are three parts to the menu editor window. Borland calls them *panes*. The important one is the Outline pane, on the lower right. It presents the menu

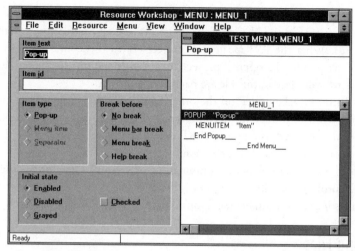

Figure 23-5
The Menu Editor

structure in outline form. You'll modify and extend this outline to create your menu. Each line in the outline represents a pop-up or a menu item (or the end of a pop-up). You'll see that the contents of this pane are somewhat like the menu scripts we've worked with before, but without the details such as the identifier (IDM_OPEN) for each item. The outline comes with one pop-up and one menu item already installed.

The Test Menu pane on the upper right shows what the menu bar will look like, and lets you interact with the pop-ups by dropping down the list of items. The idea is to let you test the menu structure you created in the Outline pane.

The Dialog pane on the left displays additional information about the item that's highlighted in the Outline pane. ("Item" as used here means a pop-up or menu item.) You can change the characteristics of the item by interacting with this dialog box.

Setting the Text

We'll want to change the text in the pop-up and the menu item. This is the text that will be displayed when the program runs. Click on the pop-up (it's labelled "pop-up"), and type the text "Data" into the Item Text field in the dialog pane (type over the text "pop-up").

Now click on the menu item (labelled "Item"), and type the text "Name" into the Item Text field (type over "Item"). You've created a menu with one pop-up, Data, which has one menu item on it, Name.

Setting the Item ID

You also need to assign an identifier, IDM_NAME, to the menu item. As you saw in Chapter 11, *Menus*, this identifier will be used in the .C file when the WM_COMMAND message is received, to tell what menu item was selected.

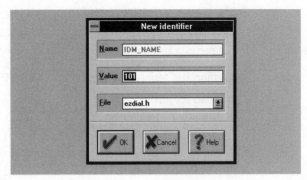

Figure 23-6

The New Identifier Dialog

When you select a menu item in the Outline pane, the Item ID field in the Dialog pane will display a value, like 101. Type over this value with the identifier IDM_NAME. The number will reappear in the adjacent text field, but the identifier will remain in the edit field.

Press (ENTER) and a message box will ask if you mean to create the new identifier. Answer Yes. The New Identifier box will appear, as shown in Figure 23-6.

This dialog displays the identifier name IDM_NAME and the corresponding value, 101. If it's not the value you want, you can change it. The File field should contain your EZDIAL.H file. (If it doesn't, you didn't create this file as described above in the "Creating Files" section. Better go back and do that now.) When you're ready, click on Yes. If you have multiple menu items, you'll need to do this for each one.

Modifying the Outline Pane

We don't need to modify the structure of the Outline pane for the EZDIAL example, since it uses one pop-up and one item, which is, fortuitously, just what the program needs. In general, however, you will want to add and rearrange the items in the Outline pane.

To insert a new pop-up or item, click on the line in the template *above* where you want the new item to go. (You can insert an item at the top of the menu by clicking on the MENU_1 line at the top of the Outline pane.) Then select the item to be inserted, using a selection from the Menu menu (that's *not* a typo), such as New Pop-up, New Item, or New Separator. The pop-up or menu item will be installed in the outline. Don't forget to add an identifier to each new menu item. To delete an item, select it, and then select Delete from the Edit menu.

Exiting from the Menu Editor

When you're finished organizing the menu and applying the appropriate text to each pop-up and menu item (and an identifier to each menu item), you can exit from the menu editor. Do this by selecting Close from the document control menu. (The document control menu is invoked by clicking on the document control icon, which is the box with the short rectangle in it at the upper corner of the menu bar). This returns you to the RW screen. The menu editor has transformed your menu into a menu script and placed it in the .RC file.

Renaming the Menu Resource

The menu resource is initially given a name like MENU_1. You need to give it the same name you will use in the szProgName string in your .C file, so it will agree with the lpszMenuName member of the WNDCLASS structure. We'll call it "ezDial" in this case. To set the menu to this name, you should be in the RW window (not the menu editor). Click on MENU_1 in the .RC window, select Rename from the Resource menu, type ezDial into the New Name field, and click on OK. Answer No to the query "Create a new identifier?" You don't need an identifier for the menu name.

Saving the Menu Resource

You should save your work after creating each resource by saving the entire .RC file (which you've already named EZDIAL.RC in this example). To do this, select Save Project from the File menu.

Incidentally, if you mistakenly create an entire resource you don't want, such as a menu, click on its name in the .RC window, and select Delete from the Edit menu.

Creating a Dialog

Creating a dialog resource is different from creating a menu resource, because they use different editors. However, as with menus, you should start off in the RW with an already-opened .RC file; in this case EZDIAL.RC. Then select New from the

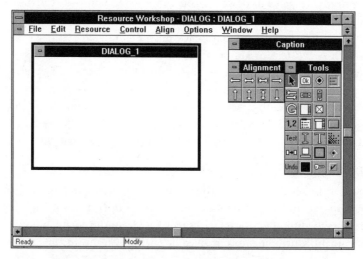

Figure 23-7

The Dialog

Editor

Resource menu. In the resulting New Resource dialog, select DIALOG from the Resource Type list, and click on OK. This brings up the Dialog editor, as shown in Figure 23-7. The frame on the left is an empty dialog box that serves as a starting point for your custom dialog.

Adding Controls to the Dialog

To add a control, simply drag it from the Tools palette and position it in the dialog frame. (A *palette* in this context is a group of square buttons with icons on them representing the controls). Figure 23-8 shows the tools we'll discuss in this Part Four, *Dialog Boxes*. (See Borland's documentation for a more complete description of the tools palette).

To create the dialog for our EZDIAL example, drag a static text field, an edit control, and two pushbuttons from the Tools palette into the dialog frame. Your

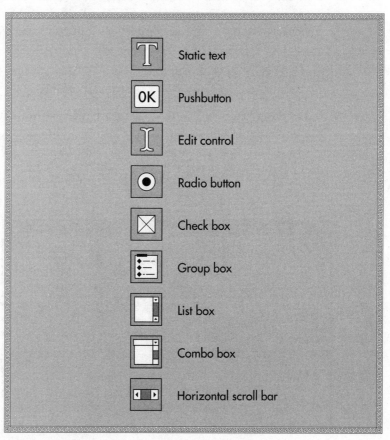

Figure 23-8 Control Icons on the Tools Palette

goal is to make this dialog look like Figure 23-1. To do this you'll need to position the controls, resize them, and change their captions.

Positioning and Naming Controls

To resize a control (or the dialog itself, which may also be necessary) click once on it. A sizing border will appear around it. You can use this border to resize it or drag it to a new location. The editor adds sizing borders to the controls so you can resize them; the borders don't appear in the final dialog. The user (as opposed to the programmer) can't ordinarily change the size of a dialog box or its controls.

To change the text in a control (which starts out as the text "Text"), select the control by clicking on it, and type the new text into the Caption window, which is located just above the Tools palette. Resize the control if the text doesn't fit. You can change the text in the dialog caption the same way.

In our EZDIAL example you need to change the text in the dialog caption to "Name entry". The static text control should be changed to "Enter your name", and the pushbuttons to "OK" and "Cancel". The edit field doesn't require a caption.

Once the text appears in the controls, you'll probably need to reposition them to achieve a pleasing effect. This is where your skill as a graphics designer comes into play.

Giving a Control an Identifier

We saw that you must give menu items identifiers like IDM_NAME. You must also give identifiers to any dialog controls that will be referred to in your .C source file. Naming conventions vary for these identifiers. They commonly start with ID, followed by a letter or word that identifies the dialog box (since many programs have more than one dialog box). There follows an underscore and then a word referring to the specific control. For instance, IDOPEN_EDIT might refer to an

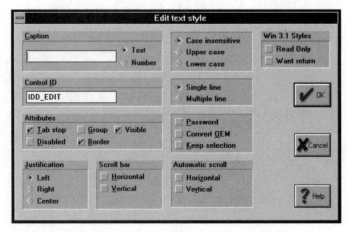

Figure 23-9

Edit Style Dialog

edit control in the Open dialog, and IDC_BLUE might be a Blue radio button in the Color dialog. Of course you're free to use any convention you want, however misguided it may be.

To apply an identifier, double-click on the control. For example, double-click on the edit control. A Style dialog appears called Edit Style (it will be Button Style for buttons, and so on). Figure 23-9 shows the Style dialog for the edit control.

The Control ID field in this box contains the ID number of the control, like 101. (The number depends on the order in which you installed the controls.) Type over this number with the identifier you want to use. In the case of the edit control for EZDIAL, we'll call this IDD_EDIT. Click on OK. A message box appears, asking, "Create a new identifier, IDD_EDIT?" Click on Yes.

As with menu resources, the New Identifer dialog appears, with the identifier and the corresponding number. This dialog should list EZDIAL.H in the File field. If it doesn't, you forgot to create this file as described earlier.

You can, and probably should, change the number in the Value field of this dialog. A common convention for dialog controls is to number them 1001, 1002, 1003, and so on for the first dialog box, 2001, 2002, 2003 for the second, and so on for subsequent dialogs. You'll probably want to change the dialog editor's choice of 101 (or whatever it is) to 1001. When you're done, click on OK to make the New Identifier go away.

Table 23-1 shows the constants and values for each control.

If you have a dialog box with more controls, you'll need to continue this process for each control that will be referenced in the .C file. Here the only remaining controls that need identifiers are the pushbuttons, which require special treatment.

Don't assign identifiers to controls that won't be referenced, such as the static text field in this example. It gets a value of −1 by default.

Table 23-1 Control Identifiers in EZDIAL

Constant	Identifier	Value
Static text	None	−1 (default)
Edit control	IDD_EDIT	1001
OK pushbutton	IDOK	Defined in WINDOWS.H
Cancel pushbutton	IDCANCEL	Defined in WINDOWS.H

Special Identifiers for OK and Cancel Buttons

As we mentioned, it's usual for your dialog box to respond to the keyboard keys (ENTER) and (ESC) as if the OK and Cancel buttons had been pushed. It's easy to arrange for this to happen by giving special identifier names to these buttons. Simply type the names IDOK and IDCANCEL into the Control ID field in the Button Style window for these buttons, and click on OK. These identifiers are already defined in WINDOWS.H, so you don't need to assign them values yourself. Using these values automatically arranges for keyboard support for these buttons. (Incidentally, the values for IDOK and IDCANCEL are 1 and 2, so don't use these values for other identifiers. To be on the safe side, don't use any values less than 100.)

Naming the Dialog

You'll need to give the dialog box itself a name so it can be referred to inside your program's .C file. The name should distinguish the dialog from others in your program, and, to avoid confusion, it's nice if the name includes "dlg" or "Dialog". The convention is to use upper- and lowercase letters, as in DataEntryDlg or ChooseColorDialog.

To rename the dialog, first close the dialog editor by clicking on the document control icon at the left of the title bar and selecting Close. You'll be back in the RW window. The dialog will initially have a name like DIALOG_1. To change this name, click on the name in the .RC window. Then select Rename Resource from the Resource menu, and enter the new name—which we'll call "NameDlg" in the EZDIAL program—into the New Name field in the resulting dialog. Click on OK. Answer No (*not* Yes) when it asks if you want to create a new identifier. The new name will show up under DIALOG in the .RC window.

Other Items in the Style Dialog

There are all sorts of other items in the Style dialogs for the different controls. For instance, in the Edit Text Style dialog, you can select justification, specify single or multiline, add scroll bars, and so on. For the time being, don't worry about any of these options. The default values will work just fine. Later on we'll use a few of these other style items.

When you're done creating the dialog resource, save the entire .RC file by choosing Save Project from the File menu.

THE .RC AND .H FILES

You've used the RW to create two files for our EZDIAL application. The first is an .RC resource script file, and the second is an .H header file. You can verify the creation of these files by looking for them with the File Manager, and you can examine them with the Turbo C++ editor or the Notepad accessory.

Actually, there's a more convenient option. You can examine the script for individual resources in the .RC file while you're in the RW. Select a resource in the .RC window, and select Edit As Text from the Resource menu. The resource script will appear in a text window, where you can examine it or edit it.

It's not really necessary for you to understand everything about the contents of the .RC file. The RW goes to a lot of trouble to generate this file for you, so why agonize over the details? However, it's always interesting to know something about the internal workings of things, so let's briefly examine the completed .RC and .H files. The RW creates some very long lines, so we've altered the listing somewhat so all the lines fit on the page. We also added some introductory comments. Here's the complete listing for EZDIAL.RC:

```
// ezdial.rc
// resource file for ezdial

#include "ezdial.h"

ezDial MENU
BEGIN
        POPUP "Data"
        BEGIN
                MENUITEM "Name", IDM_NAME
        END
END

NameDlg DIALOG 18, 18, 179, 49
STYLE DS_MODALFRAME | WS_POPUP | WS_CAPTION | WS_SYSMENU
CAPTION "Name entry"
BEGIN
   LTEXT "Enter your name:", -1, 12, 18, 83, 8
   EDITTEXT IDD_EDIT, 12, 29, 104, 12,
      ES_LEFT | WS_CHILD | WS_VISIBLE | WS_BORDER | WS_TABSTOP
   PUSHBUTTON "OK", IDOK, 129, 6, 38, 14,
      WS_CHILD | WS_VISIBLE | WS_TABSTOP
   PUSHBUTTON "Cancel", IDCANCEL, 129, 27, 38, 14,
      WS_CHILD | WS_VISIBLE | WS_TABSTOP
END
```

The RW also generated an .H file. We've added a title comment to this file. Here's the listing for EZDIAL.H:

```
// ezdial.h
// header file for ezdial

#define IDD_EDIT        1001
#define IDM_NAME         101
```

The menu script in the .RC file should present no surprises, since you've written such scripts yourself in previous programs. However, we haven't yet explored the dialog script. Let's look at it in detail.

Dialog Definitions

The first three lines of the dialog script define the dialog box itself.

```
NameDlg DIALOG 18, 18, 179, 49
STYLE DS_MODALFRAME | WS_POPUP | WS_CAPTION | WS_SYSMENU
CAPTION "Name entry"
```

NameDlg is the name of the dialog. The DIALOG keyword specifies the type of resource. The four numbers that follow are the upper left corner (18,18), and the length and height (179,49) of the dialog.

The next line specifies the dialog's style. DS_MODALFRAME indicates a modal frame, which has thick lines and is the usual choice. This style dialog can optionally include a title bar and System menu. WS_CAPTION and WS_SYSMENU provide them. WS_POPUP makes this a pop-up window, as opposed to a child window. A pop-up window is not confined within the borders of its parent. Dialogs need this option so they will appear full size, even if their parent (the main window) is too small to contain them.

The CAPTION keyword is followed by the dialog's caption, "Name entry".

The BEGIN and END keywords then delimit the list of controls that will go in the dialog.

Control Definitions

Each control gets one line in the original .RC file (although we've folded the longer ones to make them fit).

Static Text

This statement creates the static text control:

```
LTEXT "Enter your name:", -1, 12, 18, 83, 8
```

The LTEXT keyword creates a left-justified text string. It's followed by the string itself. As we noted, the −1 is the default ID value given to controls when we don't need to specify a value or an identifier. Because we don't reference this static control in the .C file, we don't need an identifier for it. The next four numbers specify the coordinates of the upper right corner of the control, relative to the dialog box; and the size of the control.

Edit Control

This statement creates the edit control into which the user will type text:

```
EDITTEXT IDC_EDIT, 12, 29, 104, 12,
ES_LEFT | WS_CHILD | WS_VISIBLE | WS_BORDER | WS_TABSTOP
```

EDITTEXT specifies an edit control. We gave this control the identifier IDC_EDIT. As usual, the four numbers are the coordinates of the upper left corner of the control, and its width and height.

There follow various constants specifying the style of the edit control. ES_LEFT means that the text is left-justified. WS_CHILD specifies that the control is a child of the dialog window; that is, it will move when the dialog moves. WS_VISIBLE makes the control visible, and WS_BORDER gives it a border. The WS_CHILD and WS_VISIBLE styles are common to most controls.

When the user presses the ⓉⒶⒷ key, the focus moves from one control to another, provided the control was created with the WS_TABSTOP style. This allows the dialog box to be controlled from the keyboard. Controls that don't accept user input, such as static text, don't normally have the WS_TABSTOP style.

Pushbuttons

The two pushbuttons are created with similar statements:

```
PUSHBUTTON "OK", IDOK, 129, 6, 38, 14,
WS_CHILD | WS_VISIBLE | WS_TABSTOP
PUSHBUTTON "Cancel", IDCANCEL, 129, 27, 38, 14,
WS_CHILD | WS_VISIBLE | WS_TABSTOP
```

Following the keyword PUSHBUTTON are the captions we specified in the RW, the identifiers IDOK and IDCANCEL, the coordinates and dimensions of the buttons, and the usual styles.

MODIFYING EXISTING RESOURCES

One of the major payoffs for using the RW as we've described here is that, as well as creating new resources, you can modify existing ones. This is quite easy. Start the RW, and open your program's .RC ("project") file. The resources will be listed in the .RC window. Double-click on the name of the resource you want to modify. The editor for that resource will appear, with the resource ready for editing.

For a menu resource, you can delete pop-ups and items, insert other ones, copy and paste to create a new arrangement, and change the text and identifier of any item. For a dialog, you can drag controls to new locations, delete controls, insert new ones, change their size, and change their text and identifiers.

When you're done with the modification, save the .RC file. Now you can use the revised dialog in your program.

SUMMARY

It's often hard to remember all the steps necessary to use the Resource Workshop, especially if you haven't used it for a while. Accordingly, in the following lists we summarize the steps for creating resource files, menu resources, and dialog resources.

Creating a Resource Script (.RC) File

1. Double-click on the Workshop icon in the Turbo C++ (or Borland C++ group) to bring up the Resource Workshop window with File and Help menus.
2. Select New Project from the File menu.
3. In the resulting dialog, make sure the .RC radio button is selected, and press OK. A window appears titled UNTITLED.RC. You've opened a resource script (.RC) file.
4. To name the new .RC file, select Save File As from the File menu. In the resulting dialog, change to the appropriate directory, and type in the file name with the .RC extension (MYPROG.RC). Click on OK. The .RC window will reflect this new name.
5. To create the header file to hold the #defines needed for menu items and dialog controls, select Add To Project from the File menu. Enter the file name with the .H extension in the File Name field (MYPROG.H). Click on OK. Answer Yes to the "All right to create new file?" query.
6. At this point you can create resources, like menus and dialogs, as outlined below.
7. To save the resource script file, select Save Project from the File menu. You should do this every time you create a new resource (or more frequently).
8. If you create a resource you don't want, click on its name in the .RC window and select Delete from the Edit menu.
9. To close the resource script file, close any editors that are open, so you're in the RW window. Click on the .RC window's document control icon, and select Close.

Creating a Menu Resource

Here are the steps for creating a menu. You should be in Resource Workshop with an already-opened .RC file.

1. Select New from the Resource menu to bring up the New Resource dialog.
2. Select MENU from the Resource Types list, and Click on OK. This launches the Menu editor. A window with three sections or "panes" appears. The Outline pane is on the lower right. You'll modify and extend this outline to create your menu.
3. To modify an item in the Outline pane, click on it. Details of the item appear in the Dialog pane on the left. Change the Item Text, Item ID, and Item Type to be what you want.
4. To insert a new pop-up or item, click on the line in the template above where you want the new item to go. Then select the appropriate item from the Menu menu, such as New Pop-up, New Item, and New Separator. It will be installed in the template. To delete an item, select it, and then select Delete from the Edit menu.
5. Add an identifier to menu items like Open and Save (but not to pop-up names, like File and Edit), as detailed in the list below.
6. When the menu structure is the way you like it, exit from the menu editor by selecting Close from the document menu (the one you get by clicking on the box with the short rectangle at the upper corner of the menu bar).
7. The menu resource is initially given a name like MENU_1. Rename it to match the szProgName variable in your .C file by clicking on the menu name in the .RC window, selecting Rename from the Resource menu, typing the desired name into the New Name field (MyProg), and clicking on OK. Answer No to the query "Create a new identifier?"
8. Don't forget to select Save Project from the File menu to save the entire .RC file.

Applying Identifiers to Menu Items

1. When you select a menu item in the Outline pane, the Item ID field in the Dialog pane will display a value, like 101.
2. Type over the Item ID value with an identifier, like IDM_NAME. The number will reappear in the adjacent text field, but the identifier will remain in the edit field.
3. Press any key and a message box will ask if you mean to create the new identifier. Answer Yes.
4. The New Identifier box will appear, with the identifier name and the corresponding value, like 101. You can change this value if you like. The File field should contain your .H file (entered in Step 5 of Creating a Resource File).

5. Type the identifier you want to use, like IDM_OPEN, over the number in the Value field. Click on Yes. This will create a statement #defining IDM_OPEN as 101, and place it in the .H file.

6. Repeat this process for each menu item.

Creating a Dialog Resource

To create a dialog resource, you should be in Resource Workshop with an already-opened .RC file.

1. Select New from the Resource menu.
2. In the resulting New Resource dialog, select DIALOG from the Resource Type list and click on OK. This brings up the dialog editor.
3. The rectangle on the left is an empty dialog box. You add controls to it to create the dialog box you want.
4. To place a control in the dialog, use the mouse to drag it from the Tools palette.
5. Arrange the controls in the template, resizing the template if necessary by dragging its sizing border.
6. To change the text in a control (or in the dialog), click on the control and type the text into the Caption window. Most controls can be resized by dragging their sizing borders. You'll need to do this if a control's text doesn't fit.
7. Follow the instructions below for applying identifiers to the controls.
8. To close the dialog editor, click on the document control icon at the left of the menu bar, and select Close.
9. The dialog will initially have a name like DIALOG_1. To change this name to something more descriptive, click on it in the .RC window. Then select Rename Resource from the Resource menu, and enter the name (for example, OpenFileDlg) in the New Name field in the resulting dialog. Click on OK. Answer No when asked if you want to create a new identifier.
10. Don't forget to select Save Project from the File to save the entire .RC file.

Applying Identifiers to Controls

1. Make sure you're in the Dialog editor with the dialog box displayed in it.
2. Double-click on a control (edit field, pushbutton, or whatever) that you want to give an identifier to. A Style dialog appears (such as Button Style for buttons, or Edit Text Style for edit fields).
3. The Control ID field in this box contains the ID number of the control, like 101. Change this to the #define constant you want to use, such as ID_OPEN. Click on OK.

4. A message box appears, asking, "Create a new identifier?" Click on Yes.
5. The New Identifer dialog appears, with the identifier and the number. It should also have the name of the header file (MYFILE.H) in the File field. You can change the number in the Value field if you want (from 101 to 1021, for example). Click on OK.
6. Repeat steps 2 to 5 for all the controls that will be referenced in the program. (Controls that won't be referenced, such as static text and group boxes, don't need identifiers.)
7. Use the special identifiers IDOK and IDCANCEL for OK and Cancel buttons, to enable keyboard control of these buttons. Steps 4 and 5 are automatically eliminated for these IDs, because they have already been defined.

Now you know how to create menu and dialog resources and install them in an .RC file. In the next chapter we'll show how to write a .C source file that uses these resources to display the menu and dialog box on the screen, and allow the user to interact with them.

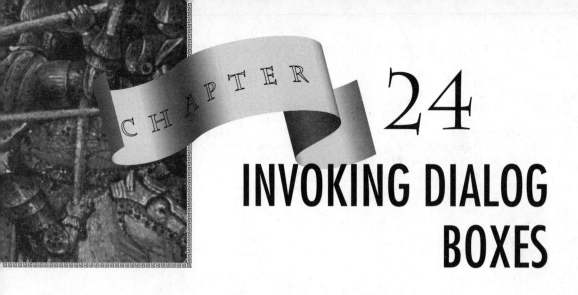

CHAPTER 24

INVOKING DIALOG BOXES

*I*n the last chapter we created the EZDIAL.RC resource script file that described the menu and dialog box resources for the EZDIAL program. In this chapter we'll examine the EZDIAL.C source file that invokes these resources. You've already seen how this is done for menus, so we'll concentrate on how you cause the dialog box to appear on the screen, and how to handle the user's interactions with the dialog.

THE EZDIAL.C SOURCE FILE

There are two major new parts in the source file. The first results from the user selecting the Name menu item; it follows the **case** IDM_NAME line in WndProc(). It is here that we cause the dialog to appear on the screen, using the DialogBox() API function. However, various supporting functions are executed as well.

The second major addition to the program is the *dialog procedure*, which is called NameDlgProc(). This is a separate function. It is similar but not identical to the WndProc() window procedure we've been using all along. We'll look at these two parts of the program in turn. Here's the listing for EZDIAL.C:

```
// ezdial.c
// adds a dialog box to a program

#define STRICT
#include <windows.h>
#include "ezdial.h"          // for menu and control #defines

                             // prototypes
LRESULT CALLBACK _export WndProc(HWND, UINT, WPARAM, LPARAM);
BOOL CALLBACK _export NameDlgProc(HWND, UINT, WPARAM, LPARAM);
```

```
#define BUFFSIZE    256             // buffer size
char szName[BUFFSIZE];              // space for file name
char szString[BUFFSIZE];            // space for general string

PSTR szProgName = "ezDial";         // application name
#include "stdmain.inc"              // standard WinMain() function
//////////////////////////////////////////////////////////////////
// main window procedure -- receives messages                   //
//////////////////////////////////////////////////////////////////
LRESULT CALLBACK _export WndProc(HWND hWnd, UINT msg,
                                 WPARAM wParam, LPARAM lParam)
   {
   HINSTANCE hInst;                 // instance handle
   DLGPROC lpNameDlgProc;           // pointer to dialog proc

   switch(msg)
      {
      case WM_COMMAND:
         switch(wParam)
            {
            case IDM_NAME:          // user selected Name
               // get instance handle
               hInst = (HINSTANCE)GetWindowWord(hWnd, GWW_HINSTANCE);

               // get pointer to this instance of procedure
               lpNameDlgProc = (DLGPROC)MakeProcInstance(
                                  (FARPROC)NameDlgProc, hInst );
               // execute dialog box
               DialogBox(hInst, "NameDlg", hWnd, lpNameDlgProc);

               // free this instance of procedure
               FreeProcInstance( (FARPROC)lpNameDlgProc );
               break;
            }    // end switch wParam
         break;  // end case WM_COMMAND

      case WM_DESTROY:
         PostQuitMessage(0);
         break;

      default:
         return( DefWindowProc(hWnd, msg, wParam, lParam) );
      }    // end switch(msg)

   return 0L;
   }  // end WndProc


//////////////////////////////////////////////////////////////////
// dialog window procedure -- receives messages for dialog box   //
//////////////////////////////////////////////////////////////////
#pragma argsused
```

```
BOOL CALLBACK _export NameDlgProc(HWND hDlg, UINT msg,
                                  WPARAM wParam, LPARAM lParam)
   {
   switch(msg)
      {
      case WM_COMMAND:                    // msg from dlg box control
         switch(wParam)
            {
            case IDOK:                     // user pushes OK button
                                           // read text from edit field
               GetDlgItemText(hDlg, IDD_EDIT, szName, BUFFSIZE);
               EndDialog(hDlg, NULL);  // terminate dialog box

                                           // display text in msg box
               wsprintf(szString, "You entered %s", (LPSTR)szName);
               MessageBox(NULL, szString, "Just checking", MB_OK);
               break;  // end case IDOK

            case IDCANCEL:                 // user pushes Cancel button
               EndDialog(hDlg, NULL);  // terminate dialog box
               break;
            } // end switch wParam
         break;  // end case WM_COMMAND

      default:
         return FALSE;                     // if we don't handle msg
      } // end switch msg
   return TRUE;                            // if we handled message
   } // end NameDlgProc
```

INVOKING THE DIALOG

The code that calls up the dialog box is repeated here. It is executed when the user selects Name from the Data menu.

```
case IDM_NAME:               // user selected Name
   // get instance handle
   hInst = (HINSTANCE)GetWindowWord(hWnd, GWW_HINSTANCE);

   // get pointer to this instance of procedure
   lpNameDlgProc = (DLGPROC)MakeProcInstance(
                        (FARPROC)NameDlgProc, hInst);

   // execute dialog box
   DialogBox(hInst, "NameDlg", hWnd, lpNameDlgProc);

   // free this instance of the procedure
   FreeProcInstance( (FARPROC)lpNameDlgProc );
   break;
```

The key function here is DialogBox(). It displays the dialog box, and doesn't return until the user exits from the dialog. That much is relatively straightforward. However, there are various other support functions—GetWindowWord(), MakeProcInstance(), and FreeProcInstance()—whose roles are more difficult to unravel. Like many things in Windows you don't really need to know what these functions do to write perfectly good programs. The code is the same (except for variable names) for every dialog. You can treat it like a mantra: don't ask what it means, just plug it in when you need to invoke a dialog box. However, it's interesting and possibly even useful to know something about what all these support functions do, so we'll discuss them briefly.

Data and Instances

We've already mentioned that several copies, or *instances,* of a program can be running at the same time. These instances all share the same code, but each has its own separate data area (actually a data segment). A dialog box uses this data area for various purposes, such as storing user input. When a particular instance of the EZDIAL program creates a dialog box, the dialog must store its data in the same data area that is being used by that specific instance of the program. If it uses the data area of any other instance, then massive confusion, probably followed by an unpleasant error message, will result. The purpose of the various support functions used with DialogBox() is to ensure that the correct data area is used for each dialog box's data.

The Instance Handle

First we need to find out which instance we are. We saw in Chapter 20, *Text Input: The Easy Way,* how to do this using the GetWindowWord() function. It returns an instance handle, which is what other functions need to identify a particular instance.

GetWindowWord() doesn't need to be executed just before the dialog box is invoked, as we show here. You can use it at any point in the program, as long as the instance handle is available when you invoke the dialog box. Many programmers get the instance handle at WM_CREATE time, and store it as a global (external) variable. Global variables are stored in the data segment, so each instance has its own version.

The MakeProcInstance() Function

To access the data area for its particular instance, the dialog box requires the creation of a small piece of code called a *thunk* (a great name). There's one thunk for each instance, so the complete term is *instance thunk* (there are other kinds of

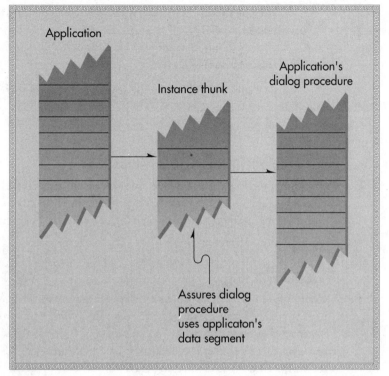

Figure 24-1 The Instance Thunk

thunks, which we won't get into here). The thunk simply ensures that the correct data area will be used by the dialog box as shown in Figure 24-1.

The dialog box needs to know where this thunk is. The MakeProcInstance() function creates the thunk and returns its address. It takes as its arguments the address of the dialog procedure (which we'll discuss soon) and the instance handle.

The DialogBox() Function

The DialogBox() function creates and displays the dialog box. The description of the dialog box to be created comes from the dialog resource. This function takes four arguments:

1. The instance handle, hInst. This tells DialogBox() which instance of our program is calling it.
2. The name of the dialog box, which is "NameDlg" in the EZDIAL.RC file. As you may recall from the last chapter, this is the name we gave the dialog resource with the RW, by selecting Rename from the Resource menu.

3. Our main window handle, hWnd, which will be the owner of the dialog window.

4. A pointer to our instance's thunk, lpNameDlgProc, which we obtained from MakeProcInstance().

DialogBox() displays the dialog on the screen, and keeps it there until the user frees it, usually by pressing the OK or Cancel button. Until the user does this, DialogBox() does not return.

The FreeProcInstance() Function

This function frees the instance thunk created with MakeProcInstance(). Don't forget this function. Note that the three functions MakeProcInstance(), DialogBox(), and FreeProcInstance() must appear for every dialog box, and must appear in the same order.

Special Warning

Controls are members of window classes. These classes are predefined, so you don't need to worry about creating them, as you did with your program's main window. The names of these classes have not appeared so far, since the statements that the RW generates to create static text, edit fields, and pushbuttons (LTEXT, EDITTEXT, and PUSHBUTTON) don't include class names. However, these statements are later expanded into information that does include class names. The class names for all the control windows are STATIC, EDIT, BUTTON, LISTBOX, COMBOBOX, and SCROLLBAR.

Ordinarily you don't need to worry about these names, since the RW and Windows take care of the details for you. However, if you are unfortunate enough to use one of these predefined class names as the class name of your program's main window, your program won't work. Windows will confuse the main window with the control and send messages to one that are intended for the other. This will lead to fatal bugs that are exceedingly difficult to track down. The moral is *Don't use a predefined class name for your window's class name.* In the approach we use, with the STDMAIN.INC include file, we give the program name to the main window's class. So in this case, be careful not to use one of the predefined names shown above as your szProgName value.

THE DIALOG PROCEDURE

In almost every program in this book we've seen an example of a window procedure, which we usually called WndProc(). The purpose of this procedure is to receive and process messages sent from Windows to our main window. Now, a dialog box is also a window. We create it differently than we do a main window, using the DialogBox() function and a dialog resource in the .RC file rather than the CreateWindow() function. However, it has a great deal in common with a main window. One common element is that they both need a procedure to receive messages from Windows. For a dialog box, this procedure is called a *dialog procedure.* It's similar to a window procedure, but there are some differences.

Dialog Procedures Versus Window Procedures

The dialog procedure in EZDIAL is called NameDlgProc(). You can compare it with WndProc(), which it follows in the listing. In fact, you might want to review Chapter 6, *Event-Driven Programming*, to refresh your understanding of window procedures.

Here's the declarator for the dialog procedure:

```
BOOL CALLBACK _export NameDlgProc(HWND hDlg, UINT msg,
                         WPARAM wParam, LPARAM lParam)
```

The return type is BOOL CALLBACK, instead of LRESULT CALLBACK as it is in WndProc(). So the dialog procedure returns a Boolean value rather than a long value. This is reflected in the values we return from the dialog function: TRUE if we handle the mesassage, FALSE if we don't. CALLBACK means **far pascal**. The dialog procedure must be exported, just as WndProc() must, so that Windows can call it. We don't need the DefWindowProc() function to handle messages that we don't handle ourselves, as we do in WndProc(). In fact, using it would cause problems.

The arguments to a dialog procedure are the same as those for a window procedure. The first argument is the handle to the dialog, the second is the message number, and the third and fourth parameters, wParam and lParam, have meanings that depend on the message.

Don't forget to provide a prototype for the dialog procedure, just as you did for the window procedure.

Responding to Dialog Messages

Most of the code in simple dialog procedures involves responding to messages from the controls that are located in the dialog. Like menu selections in the main window, all dialog controls generate WM_COMMAND messages. The wParam value of this message is the ID of the control; it tells what control sent the message. In EZDIAL there are three controls that can generate messages: the OK button, the Cancel button, and the edit field. The wParam values corresponding to these controls are IDOK, IDCANCEL, and IDD_EDIT. These are the identifiers we gave to these controls with the RW. Here's the code, copied from EZEDIT.C, that responds to these wParam values of WM_COMMAND:

```
case WM_COMMAND:                    // msg from dlg box control
    switch(wParam)
        {
        case IDOK:                  // user pushes OK button
                                    // read text from edit field
            GetDlgItemText(hDlg, IDD_EDIT, szName, BUFFSIZE);
            EndDialog(hDlg, NULL);  // terminate dialog box

                                    // display text in msg box
            wsprintf(szString, "You entered %s", (LPSTR)szName);
            MessageBox(hDlg, szString, "Just checking", MB_OK);
            break;  // end case IDOK

        case IDCANCEL:              // user pushes Cancel button
            EndDialog(hDlg, NULL);  // terminate dialog box
            break;
        }  // end switch wparam
    break;  // end case WM_COMMAND
```

The IDOK Value

This is the bread-and-butter value of wParam. It arrives when the user presses the OK button. When we receive it we know that whatever changes the user made in the dialog box are to be accepted by our program. In EZDIAL, that means that the user is finished entering a new name into the edit control. It's at this time that we want to read the name from the edit control. To do this, we execute the GetDlgItemText() function. Here's how that looks:

```
GetDlgItemText(hDlg, IDD_EDIT, szName, BUFFSIZE);
```

This function takes whatever text is in a specified control and copies it into a buffer. The first argument is the handle to the dialog window, which we received as an argument to NameDlgProc(). The second is the identifier for the particular control in the dialog; here it's IDD_EDIT for the edit window. The third is the buffer for the text, and the fourth is the size of the buffer, which is provided so the function won't overflow the buffer.

Once we have the text in the szName buffer, we display it in a message box to demonstrate that we can indeed read the text from an edit field.

When the user presses an OK button, interaction with the dialog is over. Therefore, after the dialog procedure has obtained all the information it wants from the controls in the dialog, it executes the EndDialog() function.

```
EndDialog(hDlg, NULL);
```

This function removes the dialog box from the screen and causes the DialogBox() function in WndProc(), which we executed to create the dialog, to return. The first argument is the handle of the dialog window. The second can be used to provide a return value to DialogBox(), but we don't bother with that here, so we set it to NULL.

The IDCANCEL Value

If the user pushes the Cancel button, it means we should not try to read any data from the dialog; we just want to make the dialog go away. Accordingly we execute EndDialog() without taking any other action.

The IDD_EDIT Value

You may be surprised that we don't respond to messages generated by the edit control itself. After all, it's the data in this control that is the purpose of the dialog in the first place. The user types it in, and our program siphons it out of the dialog and takes whatever action is desirable with it.

However, we don't know that the user has finished entering data in the edit control until the OK button is pushed. The edit control does generate messages, it sends one every time the user changes something. But we don't normally need to know when something changes; we just want to know when the user has finished with the changes. So we ignore messages from the edit control, and concentrate on the OK button.

Figure 24-2 shows the general approach to invoking dialogs and handling messages from them.

Building EZDIAL

Now that we have all the building blocks of our program, the .RC, .H, and .C files, how do we turn them into a complete, executable file? The process is just the same as for any program with an .RC file. Using Turbo (or Borland) C++ for Windows, we open a project and put EZDIAL.C and EZDIAL.RC in the project. Then we select Run from the Run menu. You should end up with the executable file EZDIAL.EXE. When you run this program you'll find that selecting the Name menu item from the Data menu invokes the dialog box we constructed with the RW in the last chapter.

Remember that you must rebuild your program every time you change the .RC or .H files. This doesn't happen automatically, and it's easy to forget.

It's Unfocused

The dialog box as it's written has an annoying peculiarity. When it is first displayed, the edit window doesn't have the keyboard focus. No keyboard caret (cursor) is

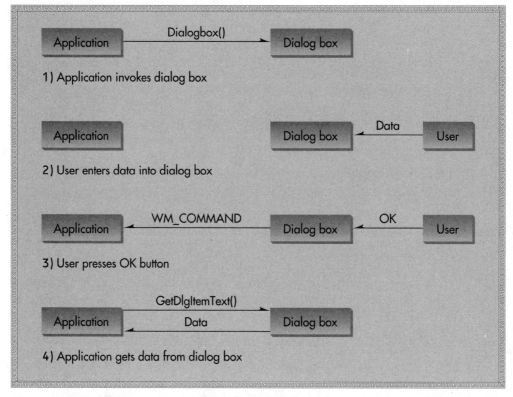

Figure 24-2 Dialog Box Operation

displayed. If the user starts typing, nothing happens, except an annoying beep. The user must click on the edit field with the mouse to give it the focus. Then the caret appears, and the user can type text into the edit field.

It would be nice if the edit field was given the focus as soon as the dialog appeared. We'll see how to do this in the next example, and improve the dialog in other ways as well.

THE KEYBOARD FOCUS

Besides dealing with the keyboard focus problem mentioned above, our example program, BUTEDIT, also introduces a related topic: default pushbuttons. It also shows how to copy text from the application into the edit control. BUTEDIT is similar to EZDIAL, but has some subtle changes. It invokes the dialog box shown in Figure 24-3.

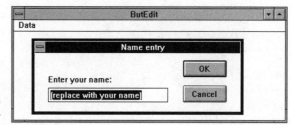

Figure 24-3

Dialog Box in BUTEDIT

There are two differences in appearance between this dialog and the one in EZDIAL (see Figure 23-1). First, there's text in the edit control when the dialog first appears, and this text is selected (shown as white-on-black). The second difference is more subtle. Look at the OK button. In BUTEDIT it has a darker border than in EZDIAL. That's because it's a *default* pushbutton. We'll see what this means soon.

The code for our example program is similar to EZDIAL, but with modifications to the .C file and the .RC file.

Here's the listing for BUTEDIT.RC:

```
// butedit.rc
// resource file for butedit

#include "butedit.h"

ButEdit MENU
BEGIN
    POPUP "Data"
    BEGIN
            MENUITEM "Name", IDM_NAME
    END
END

NameDlg DIALOG 18, 18, 179, 49
STYLE DS_MODALFRAME | WS_POPUP | WS_CAPTION | WS_SYSMENU
CAPTION "Name entry"
BEGIN
    LTEXT "Enter your name:", -1, 12, 18, 83, 8
    EDITTEXT IDD_EDIT, 12, 29, 104, 12,
        ES_LEFT | WS_CHILD | WS_VISIBLE | WS_BORDER | WS_TABSTOP
    DEFPUSHBUTTON "OK", IDOK, 129, 6, 38, 14,
        WS_CHILD | WS_VISIBLE | WS_TABSTOP
    PUSHBUTTON "Cancel", IDCANCEL, 129, 27, 38, 14,
        WS_CHILD | WS_VISIBLE | WS_TABSTOP
END
```

There's only one change in this file: the OK button control type is listed as a DEFPUSHBUTTON control rather than PUSHBUTTON.

The .H file is the same as that in EZDIAL. Here's the listing for BUTEDIT.H:

```
// butedit.h
// header file for butedit

#define IDD_EDIT        1001
#define IDM_NAME        101
```

The major change in the .C file is in the dialog procedure, where we handle a new message: WM_INITDIALOG. Here's the listing for BUTEDIT.C:

```
// butedit.c
// demonstrates buttons and edit controls

#define STRICT
#include <windows.h>
#include "butedit.h"        // for menu and control #defines

                            // prototypes
LRESULT CALLBACK _export WndProc(HWND, UINT, WPARAM, LPARAM);
BOOL CALLBACK _export NameDlgProc(HWND, UINT, WPARAM, LPARAM);

#define BUFFSIZE    256                 // buffer size
char szName[BUFFSIZE];                  // space for file name
char szString[BUFFSIZE];                // space for general string

PSTR szProgName = "ButEdit";            // application name
#include "stdmain.inc"                  // standard WinMain() function
//////////////////////////////////////////////////////////////////////
// main window procedure -- receives messages                        //
//////////////////////////////////////////////////////////////////////
LRESULT CALLBACK _export WndProc(HWND hWnd, UINT msg,
                                 WPARAM wParam, LPARAM lParam)
    {
    HINSTANCE hInst;                    // instance handle
    DLGPROC lpNameDlgProc;              // pointer to dialog proc

    switch(msg)
        {
        case WM_COMMAND:
            switch(wParam)
                {
                case IDM_NAME:              // user selected Name
                    // get instance handle
                    hInst = (HINSTANCE)GetWindowWord(hWnd, GWW_HINSTANCE);
                    // do dialog box
                    lpNameDlgProc = (DLGPROC)MakeProcInstance(
                                        (FARPROC)NameDlgProc, hInst );
                    DialogBox(hInst, "NameDlg", hWnd, lpNameDlgProc);
                    FreeProcInstance( (FARPROC)lpNameDlgProc );
                    break;
                }   // end switch wParam
            break;  // end case WM_COMMAND
```

```
          case WM_DESTROY:
             PostQuitMessage(0);
             break;

          default:
             return( DefWindowProc(hWnd, msg, wParam, lParam) );
          }    // end switch(msg)

      return 0L;
      } // end WndProc

//////////////////////////////////////////////////////////////////
// dialog window procedure -- receives messages for dialog box    //
//////////////////////////////////////////////////////////////////
#pragma argsused

BOOL CALLBACK _export NameDlgProc(HWND hDlg, UINT msg,
                                    WPARAM wParam, LPARAM lParam)
    {
    HWND hControl;                        // control window handle
    char* szInit = "(replace with your name)";

    switch(msg)
        {
        case WM_INITDIALOG:               // dialog box created
           hControl = GetDlgItem(hDlg, IDD_EDIT);
           SetFocus(hControl);            // set focus to edit control
           SetDlgItemText(hDlg, IDD_EDIT, szInit); // set text in edit
           SendMessage( hControl, EM_SETSEL, 0,    // select it
                     MAKELONG(0, -1) );
           return FALSE;                  // note the return value

        case WM_COMMAND:                  // msg from dlg box control
           switch(wParam)
              {
              case IDOK:                  // user pushes OK button
                                          // read text from edit field
                 GetDlgItemText(hDlg, IDD_EDIT, szName, BUFFSIZE);
                 EndDialog(hDlg, NULL);   // terminate dialog box

                                          // display text in msg box
                 wsprintf(szString, "You entered %s", (LPSTR)szName);
                 MessageBox(NULL, szString, "Just checking", MB_OK);
                 break;  // end case IDOK

              case IDCANCEL:              // user pushes Cancel button
                 EndDialog(hDlg, NULL);   // terminate dialog box
                 break;
              }  // end switch wparam
           break;  // end case WM_COMMAND

        default:
           return FALSE;                  // if we don't handle msg
```

```
      }  // end switch msg
   return TRUE;                              // if we handled message
   }  // end NameDlgProc
```

Setting the Focus with SetFocus()

It is often the case that, when a dialog box is first placed on the screen, one particular control should have the input focus. In the EZDIAL and BUTEDIT programs it's most convenient for the user to start typing as soon as the edit box appears, rather than having to first click on the edit field with the mouse pointer. Thus we want to give the edit field the focus when the dialog first appears. In other dialogs you may want to give a pushbutton or some other control the focus. Knowing what control should get the focus requires some experience with Windows applications. You can experiment with various applications to get a feeling for how the keyboard focus is handled in different kinds of dialogs.

In EZDIAL no control got the focus when the dialog box appeared. BUTEDIT solves this problem. Here's the procedure used in the program:

1. In the dialog procedure, install a **case** for the WM_INITDIALOG message.
2. When this message is received, use the SetFocus() function to give the focus to a particular control.
3. Return a value of FALSE after handling WM_INITDIALOG.

The SetFocus() function sets the focus to whichever window's handle is used as an argument. How do we find the handle of the edit control? We know its identifier, because we assigned it using the RW; but we don't know its handle. However, we can find the handle using the GetDlgItem() function. Given the handle of the dialog box, and the identifier of a control, it returns the handle to the control. It's this value we use in SetFocus().

```
case WM_INITDIALOG:
   hControl = GetDlgItem(hDlg, IDD_EDIT);
   SetFocus(hControl);
   return FALSE;
```

The normal approach in our dialog procedure is to return TRUE if we handle the message, but the WM_INITDIALOG message must be handled differently. The description of this message in the documentation specifies that in this particular situation we must return FALSE.

Setting the Focus with .RC File Arrangement

We should note that there's another way to set the focus to a particular control. Here's how it works:

1. Put the control first in the dialog script in the .RC file.

2. In the dialog procedure install a **case** for the WM_INITDIALOG message.
3. Return a value of TRUE after handling WM_INITDIALOG.

You can use the Edit As Text item in the Resource menu in the RW to rearrange the lines in the dialog script. (There's also a special tool to do the same thing.) When WM_INITDIALOG returns TRUE, whatever control is listed first will get the focus.

This method has the advantage of not requiring the use of the SetFocus() function, but there's a potential danger in requiring a certain arrangement of lines in the .RC file: you may change this arrangement inadvertently, forgetting that the focus depends on the precise arrangement.

The OK and Cancel Buttons

Setting the focus when the dialog first appears has another advantage. It allows you to use the (ENTER) key to activate the OK button, and the (ESC) key to activate the Cancel button, as soon as the dialog appears. You can't use these keyboard equivalents until the focus has been set. Users commonly press (ENTER) when they've finished typing a selection into the edit control; it's more convenient than reaching for the mouse to click on OK. They may also press (ESC) to make the dialog go away if they decide they don't need it at all.

Remember that the (ENTER) and (ESC) keys won't have this effect unless the OK and Cancel buttons have been given the identifiers IDOK and IDCANCEL, which are predefined in WINDOWS.H.

Tab Stops

Once the focus is set, you can take advantage of another convenience provided by the dialog box. To see how this works, bring up the dialog box in BUTEDIT, and press (TAB). You'll see the focus move from one control to another. This allows the user to conveniently select a particular control using only the keyboard.

The focus moves in order to all the controls that have the WS_TABSTOP style set. As you can see in BUTEDIT.RC, this includes all the controls except the static text, which doesn't interact with the user and has no need of keyboard control. The order followed in moving tabbing from one control to another is the order in which the controls are listed in the .RC file.

Default Pushbuttons

When you first invoke the dialog box in BUTEDIT, you'll see that the OK button has a dark border around it. This border provides a visual clue to the user that the OK button will be activated when the user presses (ENTER).

In BUTEDIT the OK button has this role because it has been given the IDOK identifier. However, making a pushbutton into a default pushbutton can override the OK button identifier. If you made the Cancel button into a default pushbutton, it would be activated when the user pressed (ENTER), even if the OK button has the IDOK identifier.

You use the RW to make a pushbutton into a default pushbutton. Here's how to do it. You should have RW running, with your .RC file opened.

1. In the .RC window, double-click on the dialog resource, NameDlg in the BUTEDIT example.
2. In the dialog template, double-click on the button to be changed (the OK button).
3. In the Button Style dialog, click on the Default Push Button selection in the Button Type list. Then click on OK.
4. Select Save Project from the File menu.

This process replaces the PUSHBUTTON statement with DEFPUSHBUTTON in the description of the OK pushbutton in the .RC file.

Inserting Text into a Control

You can insert text into most controls using the SetDlgItemText() API function. This function takes three arguments: the handle of the dialog box, the identifier for the particular control, and the text string to be inserted. Here's how it looks in BUTEDIT:

```
SetDlgItemText(hDlg, IDD_EDIT, szInit);
```

The szInit string is "(replace with your name)", an added reminder to the user as to what should be typed into the edit control. You can use this same function to place text in buttons and other controls.

The SendMessage() Function

Users will probably want the "(replace with your name)" string to vanish automatically when they start typing into the edit field. This will happen if the string is selected (so it appears as white letters on a black background). To select the string, we use another API function: SendMessage(). This is a more general-purpose approach than the SetDlgItemText() function we just looked at. SendMessage(), which we saw before in Chapter 20, *Text Input: The Easy Way,* can send any message to any window, provided we know the window's handle. Here we use it because there is no API function designed specifically to select text in an edit control. Instead, we send it an EM_SETSEL message:

```
SendMessage( hControl, EM_SETSEL, 0, MAKELONG(0, -1) );
```

The key to this function is the message value, which is the second parameter. The return value of the function, and the values of the third and fourth parameters depend on the message value. The first parameter is always the control's handle.

The messages that are appropriate to send to specific kinds of controls are listed under Messages in your reference manual. (See the Bibliography.) Different message prefixes correspond to certain controls (although you can send other messages, like WM_ messages, to controls as well). Table 24-1 shows the most common prefixes and some typical messages.

Check boxes and radio buttons are considered to be buttons, so there's no special prefix for them. Scroll bar controls aren't listed, since they use WM_ messages. You can find out some interesting things about how to interact with controls by reading about the messages with the appropriate prefix.

Notice that, for the EM_GETSEL message, the fourth argument to SendMessage() is a type LONG whose low word is the character position at the beginning of the text to be selected, and whose high word is the character position at the end. However, to select the entire text, we need only put a –1 in the high-word part. The MAKELONG macro puts the two words together into a LONG. (The low word is the first argument to MAKELONG, the high word is the second.)

The SendMessage() function may look like the answer to all sorts of problems, and in fact it's a highly versatile function. However, you can't send just any message with it. The WM_SIZE message, for example, is sent by Windows to our window

Table 24-1 Control Message Prefixes

Type of Control	Message Prefix	Examples
Button	BM_	BM_GETSTATE, BM_SETCHECK
Combo box	CB_	CB_ADDSTRING, CB_GETCURSEL
Edit control	EM_	EM_GETSEL, EM_GETMODIFY
List box	LB_	LB_ADDSTRING, LB_SETCURSEL

procedure. If we try to send this message ourselves, we will be knocked off our horse in short order.

SUMMARY

To handle a dialog box, two additions must be made to the code in the .C file. First the dialog box must be invoked. Here's an outline of the process:

```
hInst = GetWindowWord(...                       // get instance handle
lpDlgProc = MakeProcInstance(DlgProc, hInst);   // make the thunk
DialogBox(hInst, "DlgName", hWnd, lpDlgProc);   // make the dialog
FreeProcInstance(lpDlgProc);                     // release the thunk
```

Second, every dialog box must have a dialog procedure, DlgProc(). The dialog procedure responds to messages from Windows that result from user interaction with the dialog box. It's quite similar to a window procedure, which responds to messages resulting from user interaction with a window. Here's the skeleton of a dialog procedure:

```
BOOL CALLBACK _export DlgProc(HWND hDlg, UINT msg,
                        WPARAM wParam, LPARAM lParam)
  {
  switch(msg)
    {
    case WM_INITDIALOG:
       // set the focus
       return FALSE;
    case WM_COMMAND:
       {
       case IDOK:
          // handle OK
          break;
       case IDCANCEL:
          // handle Cancel
          break;
       }
    default:
       return FALSE:
    }
  return TRUE;
  }
```

The description of the dialog box, including what controls it has and how they are placed, is stored in the .RC file, created with the Resource Workshop.

You need to be careful to match the names used in different places in your program. Failure to use the right names can lead to hard-to-diagnose bugs, such as your dialog box or menu not appearing at all, controls not working, and other problems. Table 24-2 shows the places the various variables and other names are used.

Table 24-2 Name and Variable Correspondences for Dialog Boxes

Name	Example	Places Used
Dialog procedure name	DlgProc	1. Prototype for dialog procedure in .C file
		2. First argument to MakeProcInstance() in .C file
		3. Dialog procedure declarator in .C file
Pointer to thunk	lpDlgProc	1. Declaration in WndProc in .C file
		2. Return value of MakeProcInstance() in .C file
		3. Second argument to DialogBox() in .C file
		4. Argument to FreeProcInstance() in .C file
Name of menu	"AppName"	1. Value of external variable szProgName in .C file
		2. Name of MENU resource in .RC file
Name of dialog box	"ChoicesDlg"	1. Second argument of DialogBox() in .C file
		2. Name of DIALOG resource in .RC file
IDs of controls	IDD_EDIT	1. #defined in .H file
		2. In **case** statements following WM_COMMAND in dialog procedure in .C file
		3. In control specifications in .RC file
Name of header file	appname.h	1. #included in .C file
		2. #included in .RC file

Besides learning to create dialog boxes, you've also seen how to set the keyboard focus to particular controls, how to insert text into an edit control, and how to select text.

In the last two chapters you've learned about dialog boxes in general. You've also learned something about pushbuttons, edit controls, and static text. In subsequent chapters you'll learn about other controls, such as radio buttons, check boxes, list and combo boxes, and scroll bars.

25

RADIO BUTTONS AND CHECK BOXES

*I*n this chapter we'll examine radio buttons and check boxes. These controls are alike in that they are both small controls that have two states: on or off. Also, the programming for them is similar. However, radio buttons are used in groups to select mutually exclusive options, while check boxes are used alone to indicate yes-or-no states. Radio buttons are round, with a dark circle inside when they're selected, while check boxes are square, with an X inside when they're checked.

RADIO BUTTONS

Radio buttons allow the user to choose one of a fixed group of options. The number of options is usually fairly small; between 2 and 10 or so. Also, the options don't often vary during the course of the program. If the list of options changes as the program runs, then a list box or combo box may be a more appropriate control.

Examples of situations that use radio buttons are choosing from the Small, Medium, Compact, or Large memory models in a compiler; from All, Current Page, or Page Range when printing a file; and from Forward or Backward in a text search dialog.

The AUTORAD Example

Our example program, AUTORAD, displays some text and allows the user to select from single-space, one-and-a-half-space, or double-space when formatting the display. The user clicks on the menu item Options, which invokes a dialog box whose caption is Output Options. This dialog contains three radio buttons, two pushbuttons—OK and Cancel—and a group-box control. The group box

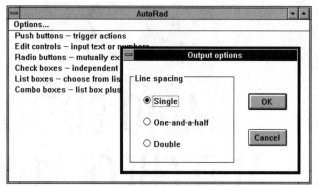

Figure 25-1

Dialog Box in
AUTORAD Program

surrounds the radio buttons and indicates to the user that the radio buttons are part of a group and that only one of them can be checked at a time. Figure 25-1 shows what this dialog box looks like.

When a particular line spacing has been selected using the radio buttons, and the OK button clicked, the dialog vanishes and the output is displayed using the indicated spacing. Figure 25-2 shows the output when double-space is selected.

Constructing the Resource File

We'll assume you're familiar with the contents of Chapter 23, *The Resource Workshop*. Use the RW to construct a menu with one item: Options. Add the dialog box resource shown in Figure 25-1. Drag the radio buttons from the Tools palette just as you do other controls. Be careful to install the radio buttons in order: the Single-space button first, One-and-a-half-space second, and Double-space third. Drag the group box and position it around the radio buttons.

Add identifiers to the controls. Make sure the values of identifiers for the radio buttons are arrannged in ascending order by ones, starting with the first button. That is, number them 1001, 1002, 1003, or 2005, 2006, 2007, or a similar sequence.

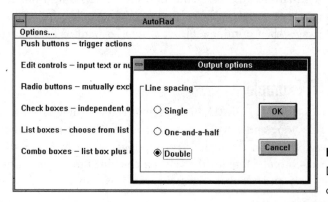

Figure 25-2

Double-Spaced Output
of AUTORAD Program

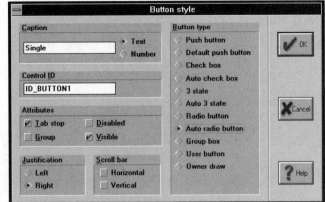

Figure 25-3

The Button

Style Dialog

Auto Radio Buttons

In this example we're going to use a variation of radio buttons called auto radio buttons. With an ordinary radio button, the application is responsible for selecting (putting a dot in the middle of) the button when the user clicks on it, and clearing (deselecting) the other buttons in the group. Auto radio buttons are more sophisticated: they automatically select themselves when the user clicks on them, and the other buttons automatically clear themselves.

Here's how to use the RW to change an ordinary radio button to an auto radio button. Double-click on the radio button in the dialog template. The Button style dialog appears, as shown in Figure 25-3.

The Radio button radio button will be checked in the Button type group. Click on the Auto radio button radio button. (Sorry about all those radio buttons.) Press OK. Change the other two radio buttons to the auto style in the same way.

The AUTORAD.RC File

When you're done with the RW, the resource script file, AUTORAD.RC, should look something like this:

```
// autorad.rc
// resource script file for autorad

#include "autorad.h"

AutoRad MENU
BEGIN
    MENUITEM "Options...", IDM_OPTIONS
END

OutputDlg DIALOG 18, 18, 150, 92
STYLE DS_MODALFRAME | WS_POPUP | WS_CAPTION | WS_SYSMENU
CAPTION "Output options"
```

```
BEGIN
   CONTROL "Single", ID_BUTTON1, "BUTTON",
      BS_AUTORADIOBUTTON | WS_CHILD | WS_VISIBLE | WS_TABSTOP,
      18, 27, 39, 12
   CONTROL "One-and-a-half", ID_BUTTON2, "BUTTON",
      BS_AUTORADIOBUTTON | WS_CHILD | WS_VISIBLE | WS_TABSTOP,
      18, 45, 60, 12
   CONTROL "Double", ID_BUTTON3, "BUTTON",
      BS_AUTORADIOBUTTON | WS_CHILD | WS_VISIBLE | WS_TABSTOP,
      18, 63, 39, 12
   CONTROL "Line spacing", 104, "BUTTON",
      BS_GROUPBOX | WS_CHILD | WS_VISIBLE, 6, 9, 90, 76
   DEFPUSHBUTTON "OK", IDOK, 108, 27, 33, 14,
      WS_CHILD | WS_VISIBLE | WS_TABSTOP
   PUSHBUTTON "Cancel", IDCANCEL, 108, 57, 33, 14,
      WS_CHILD | WS_VISIBLE | WS_TABSTOP
END
```

The CONTROL Statement

Let's examine how radio buttons are handled in the .RC file. Again, this isn't vital information, since presumably the RW does what you want automatically; but you may be curious about how it's done.

The three radio buttons and the group box all use the same statement name: CONTROL. This statement uses a somewhat different format than we saw for the LTEXT, EDITTEXT, PUSHBUTTON, and DEFPUSHBUTTON statements in previous .RC files. Those statements are actually abbreviated forms of the CONTROL statement, which can be adapted to produce any control. There is an analogous RADIOBUTTON statement, so it's not clear why the RW chooses to specify buttons using the CONTROL statement approach, but it does.

In a CONTROL statement, the string following the CONTROL keyword is the caption that will appear with the control (next to a radio button, for example). Next comes the control's ID value, and following that is a string representing the class name. In AUTORAD.RC, the class name in every line is BUTTON. (There are six classes in all: BUTTON, STATIC, EDIT, LISTBOX, COMBOBOX, and SCROLLBAR. We'll see how some of these are used later.)

Following the class name are various style flags, ORed together. These are the same flags we saw in PUSHBUTTON and similar statements. The flags starting with BS_ specify the style to be used for the BUTTON class. In the AUTORAD.RC example they are BS_AUTORADIOBUTTON and BS_GROUPBOX. (The group box is considered a kind of button, even though it's nothing like a button.) Ordinary radio buttons have the BS_RADIOBUTTON style. The other style flags should be familiar from Chapter 23.

The header file should have been automatically generated by the RW. It reflects the increased number of controls. Here's the listing for AUTORAD.H:

```
// autorad.h
// header file for autorad

#define IDM_OPTIONS        101

#define ID_BUTTON1         1002
#define ID_BUTTON2         1003
#define ID_BUTTON3         1004
```

Constructing the Source File

In the source file, the dialog box is invoked, just as in the programs in the last chapter, when the user selects a menu item. However, we also process the WM_PAINT message to draw the text on the screen, using a for loop and the TextOut() function as we've seen before. More importantly, we use several new functions in the dialog procedure. Here's the listing for AUTORAD.C:

```
// autorad.c
// demonstrates auto radio buttons

#define STRICT
#include <windows.h>
#include "autorad.h"           // for menu and control #defines
                               // prototypes
LRESULT CALLBACK _export WndProc(HWND, UINT, WPARAM, LPARAM);
BOOL CALLBACK _export ButtonDlgProc(HWND, UINT, WPARAM, LPARAM);

#define CYCHAR  18             // line spacing
#define LINES    6             // number of text lines
PSTR szCont[LINES] = {         // array of pointers to strings
"Push buttons -- trigger actions",
"Edit controls -- input text or numbers",
"Radio buttons -- mutually exclusive choices",
"Check boxes -- independent on/off switches",
"List boxes -- choose from list of names",
"Combo boxes -- list box plus edit field" };

int iSpacing = 2;                      // 2=single, 3=1.5, 4=double

PSTR szProgName = "AutoRad";           // application name
#include "stdmain.inc"                 // standard WinMain() function
/////////////////////////////////////////////////////////////////
// main window procedure ñ receives messages                    //
/////////////////////////////////////////////////////////////////
LRESULT CALLBACK _export WndProc(HWND hWnd, UINT msg,
                         WPARAM wParam, LPARAM lParam)
   {
   PAINTSTRUCT ps;                     // info for painting
   HDC hDC;                            // device context handle
   HINSTANCE hInst;                    // instance handle
   DLGPROC lpButtonDlgProc;            // pointer to dialog proc
   int index;                          // loop variable
```

```
     switch(msg)
        {
        case WM_COMMAND:
           switch(wParam)
               {
               case IDM_OPTIONS:                // user selected Options
                  // get instance handle
                  hInst = (HINSTANCE)GetWindowWord(hWnd, GWW_HINSTANCE);
                  // execute dialog box
                  lpButtonDlgProc = (DLGPROC)MakeProcInstance(
                                           (FARPROC)ButtonDlgProc, hInst );
                  DialogBox(hInst, "OutputDlg", hWnd, lpButtonDlgProc);
                  FreeProcInstance( (FARPROC)lpButtonDlgProc );

                  InvalidateRect(hWnd, NULL, TRUE);  // paint window
                  break;
               }    // end switch wParam
           break;  // end case WM_COMMAND

        case WM_PAINT:
           hDC = BeginPaint(hWnd, &ps);
           for(index=0; index < LINES; index++)
              TextOut(hDC, 10,
                      (index * iSpacing * CYCHAR)/2,
                      szCont[index], lstrlen( szCont[index]) );
           EndPaint(hWnd, &ps);
           break;

        case WM_DESTROY:
           PostQuitMessage(0);
           break;

        default:
           return( DefWindowProc(hWnd, msg, wParam, lParam) );
        }    // end switch(msg)

     return 0L;
     }  // end WndProc

//////////////////////////////////////////////////////////////////////
// dialog window procedure -- receives messages for dialog box      //
//////////////////////////////////////////////////////////////////////
#pragma argsused

BOOL CALLBACK _export ButtonDlgProc(HWND hDlg, UINT msg,
                                    WPARAM wParam, LPARAM lParam)
   {
   static int iTempSpacing;                 // temporary spacing value

   switch(msg)
      {
      case WM_INITDIALOG:                    // check appropriate button
         CheckRadioButton(hDlg, ID_BUTTON1, ID_BUTTON3, iSpacing+1000);
```

```
        break;

    case WM_COMMAND:                      // msg from dlg box control
        switch(wParam)
            {
            case ID_BUTTON1:
            case ID_BUTTON2:
            case ID_BUTTON3:
                iTempSpacing = wParam-1000;  // 2=single-space, etc
                break;

            case IDOK:                    // user pushes OK button
                iSpacing = iTempSpacing;  // save last spacing
                EndDialog(hDlg, NULL);    // terminate dialog box
                break;

            case IDCANCEL:                // user pushes Cancel button
                EndDialog(hDlg, NULL);    // terminate dialog box
                break;
            }  // end switch wparam
        break;  // end case WM_COMMAND

    default:
        return FALSE;
    }  // end switch msg
return TRUE;
}  // end ButtonDlgProc
```

A key variable in the program is iSpacing, which determines the line spacing. It can have one of three values: 2 for single-space, 3 for one-and-a-half space, and 4 for double-space. This variable is used in the TextOut() function, in the expression for the Y-coordinate of the text to be drawn. It's this variable that we want to change when the user selects a button in the Output Options dialog and presses OK. The possible values for iSpacing are twice the actual spacing because we want to avoid floating-point numbers, which cause an additional library to be linked to our program, making the .EXE file larger.

Initializing the Buttons

In the dialog procedure for the Output Options dialog, when we receive the WM_INITDIALOG message, we want to check (select) the radio button that corresponds to the current state of the program. That is, if iSpacing has the value 2, we should check the Single-space radio button, if it has a value of 3 we should check one-and-a-half space, and if it has a value of 4, we should check Double-space. This way, when the user first invokes the dialog, the radio buttons will give a visual indication of the current spacing.

There are several ways to check a radio button. The one we'll use is the CheckRadioButton() function. It takes four arguments: the handle to the dialog, the IDs of the first and last buttons in the group, and the ID of the button to be checked. This function simultaneously checks the designated button and unchecks all the others in the group. For this to work, the numerical values of the IDs of all the buttons in the group must be in order, as we described earlier.

We've arranged things so that the values of the button identifiers are exactly 1000 greater than the corresponding value of iSpacing. For example, the value of ID_BUTTON1, which is the button for single spacing, is 1002, which is 1000 greater than the value iSpacing uses to indicate single spacing. So by adding 1000 to iSpacing we obtain the ID of the appropriate button. This is then used as the third argument to CheckRadioButton(), which is the ID of the button to be checked:

```
CheckRadioButton(hDlg, ID_BUTTON1, ID_BUTTON3, iSpacing+1000);
```

This is a bit tricky, but it saves several if...else statements.

Responding to Button Presses

There are several ways to figure out what radio button is currently checked. One is to send messages to individual buttons with the SendDlgItemMessage() function, which returns TRUE if the button is checked. However, in this example it's simpler to respond to messages from the buttons themselves, and remember which one was pressed last. We monitor WM_COMMAND messages with wParam values of ID_BUTTON1, ID_BUTTON2, and ID_BUTTON3. When we receive one of these messages, we set a variable, iTempSpacing, to the value of wParam less 1000. Because we've given values of 1002, 1003, and 1004 to ID_BUTTON1, ID_BUTTON2, and ID_BUTTON3, the result is a value for iTempSpacing of 2, 3, or 4.

We can't assign this value directly to iSpacing because the user may decide not to change the spacing after all, and press the Cancel button instead. If we changed iSpacing every time a button was pressed, we would lose its original value.

Responding to OK

It's not until the user presses the OK button that we can be sure that the last button press should actually determine the line spacing. So when we get a WM_COMMAND message with an sParam value of IDOK, we set iSpacing equal to iTempSpacing. Then we end the dialog and return from the dialog procedure. This causes a return from DialogBox() in WndProc(), at which point we execute an InvalidateRect() function to cause the display to be redrawn with the new line spacing.

If we had not used auto (as opposed to normal) radio buttons, we would have had to worry about which button was checked whenever we received a button message, checked the selected button, and unchecked the other buttons. Using auto radio buttons relieves us of this responsibility.

CHECK BOXES

Our next example deals with check boxes, which allow the user to choose between one of two states. Examples of check boxes are the Read Only box in a File Open dialog, the Case Sensitive box in a Find Text dialog, and the Create Backup File box in a text editor. In each case the user can choose to do something or not. The button represents an on/off state; either something will be done, or it won't.

In some situations it's hard to decide whether to use two radio buttons or a check box. In the examples above, two radio buttons could have been used (Read Only and Read/Write, for example, instead of a Read Only check box). However, in these cases a check box seems more appropriate. On the other hand, selecting AM or PM in a clock program might be better handled with two radio buttons. The deciding factor is whether one thinks of the situation more as "do it" versus "don't do it," in which case a check box is more appropriate; or a choice between two equal things, ("hot" and "cold"), where two radio buttons should be used.

The AUTOCHK Example

The user of our next example program can use check boxes to determine how the program will handle the exit process. Selecting the Options menu item brings up a dialog with two check boxes in it, labelled Notify on exit and Exit on escape key. Figure 25-4 shows what this looks like.

Normally if the user selects the Exit menu item, or chooses Close from the System menu, the program exits immediately. However, if the Notify on exit box is checked when the user tries to exit, a message box appears asking "Terminate the program?" The user can then click on Yes or No.

Normally pressing (ESC) has no effect on the program, but if the Exit on escape key check box is checked, then pressing (ESC) will cause the program to terminate (or to display the "Terminate the program?" message box if the Notify on exit box is checked).

Notice that the two check boxes control unrelated states; either one can be on or off, independent of the other.

Figure 25-4

The Exit Options

Dialog in AUTOCHK

Constructing the Resource File

Call up the RW and create a menu and a dialog that looks something like Figure 25-4. Give identifiers to the controls. (Use the identifier names shown in the .RC file.) As you did with radio buttons, you should change the style of the check boxes to auto check boxes. To do this, double-click on a check box, and in the Button style dialog (which is used for all buttton styles), click on the Auto check box radio button and then press OK. Your check box will be given the BS_AUTOCHECKBOX style, as you can see by examining the .RC file. Here's the listing for AUTOCHK.RC:

```
// autochk.rc
// resource file for autochk

#include "autochk.h"
AutoChk MENU
BEGIN
        MENUITEM "Exit", IDM_EXIT
        MENUITEM "Options...", IDM_OPTIONS
END


ExitDlg DIALOG 18, 18, 129, 73
STYLE DS_MODALFRAME | WS_POPUP | WS_CAPTION | WS_SYSMENU
CAPTION "Exit options"
BEGIN
        CONTROL "Notify on exit", ID_CHECK1, "BUTTON",
          BS_AUTOCHECKBOX | WS_CHILD | WS_VISIBLE | WS_TABSTOP,
          30, 9, 75, 12
        CONTROL "Exit on escape key", ID_CHECK2, "BUTTON",
          BS_AUTOCHECKBOX | WS_CHILD | WS_VISIBLE | WS_TABSTOP,
          30, 27, 75, 12
        PUSHBUTTON "OK", IDOK, 21, 51, 33, 14,
          WS_CHILD | WS_VISIBLE | WS_TABSTOP
        PUSHBUTTON "Cancel", IDCANCEL, 66, 51, 33, 14,
          WS_CHILD | WS_VISIBLE | WS_TABSTOP
END
```

The header file should hold no surprises. Here's the listing for AUTOCHK.H:

```
// autochk.h
// header file for autochk

#define IDM_EXIT        101
#define IDM_OPTIONS     102
#define ID_CHECK1       1001
#define ID_CHECK2       1002
```

Constructing the Source File

In the source file we handle the Options menu item by invoking the dialog box in the usual way. If the Notify on exit box is checked, we handle the Exit menu item and the WM_CLOSE message (received when the user selects Close from the System menu) by invoking a "Terminate the program?" message box and executing DestroyWindow() if the response is Yes.

In addition we handle the WM_KEYDOWN message to see if the user has pressed the (ESC) key. If so, and if the Exit on escape check box is checked, we exit. Here's the listing for AUTOCHK.C:

```c
// autochk.c
// demonstrates auto check boxes

#define STRICT
#include <windows.h>
#include "autochk.h"          // for menu and control #defines
                              // prototypes
LRESULT CALLBACK _export WndProc(HWND, UINT, WPARAM, LPARAM);
BOOL CALLBACK _export CheckDlgProc(HWND, UINT, WPARAM, LPARAM);

BOOL bNotify = FALSE;         // state of check boxes (checked=TRUE)
BOOL bEscape = FALSE;

PSTR szProgName = "AutoChk";          // application name
#include "stdmain.inc"                // standard WinMain() function
//////////////////////////////////////////////////////////////////
// main window procedure -- receives messages                    //
//////////////////////////////////////////////////////////////////
LRESULT CALLBACK _export WndProc(HWND hWnd, UINT msg,
                                 WPARAM wParam, LPARAM lParam)
    {
    HINSTANCE hInst;                      // instance handle
    DLGPROC lpCheckDlgProc;               // pointer to dialog proc

    switch(msg)
        {
        case WM_COMMAND:
            switch(wParam)
                {
                case IDM_OPTIONS:             // user selected Options
                    hInst = (HINSTANCE)GetWindowWord(hWnd, GWW_HINSTANCE);
                    // execute dialog box
                    lpCheckDlgProc = (DLGPROC)MakeProcInstance(
                                        (FARPROC)CheckDlgProc, hInst);
                    DialogBox(hInst, "ExitDlg", hWnd, lpCheckDlgProc);
                    FreeProcInstance( (FARPROC)lpCheckDlgProc );
                    break;  // end case IDM_OPTIONS

                case IDM_EXIT:         // user selected Exit
                    SendMessage(hWnd, WM_CLOSE, 0, OL);  // tell ourselves
                    break;  // end case IDM_EXIT

                }   // end switch wParam
            break;  // end case WM_COMMAND
```

```
       case WM_KEYDOWN:            // user presses any key
          switch(wParam)
             {
             case VK_ESCAPE:       // if it's the escape key
                if(bEscape)        // if "Exit on escape key" box checked
                   SendMessage(hWnd, WM_CLOSE, 0, 0L);  // tell
ourselves
                break;
             }  // end switch wParam
          break;  // end case WM_KEYDOWN

       case WM_CLOSE:              // user chose Close from System menu
          if(bNotify)             // if "Notify before exit" box checked
             {
             if( MessageBox(hWnd, "Terminate the program?", szProgName,
                            MB_YESNO | MB_ICONQUESTION) == IDYES )
             DestroyWindow(hWnd);
             }
          else
             DestroyWindow(hWnd);
          break;  // end case WM_CLOSE

       case WM_DESTROY:
          PostQuitMessage(0);
          break;

       default:
          return( DefWindowProc(hWnd, msg, wParam, lParam) );
       }   // end switch(msg)

    return 0L;
    }  // end WndProc

////////////////////////////////////////////////////////////////////
// dialog window procedure -- receives messages for dialog box     //
////////////////////////////////////////////////////////////////////
#pragma argsused

BOOL CALLBACK _export CheckDlgProc(HWND hDlg, UINT msg,
                                   WPARAM wParam, LPARAM lParam)
    {
    HWND hCon;                          // check box handle

    switch(msg)
       {
       case WM_INITDIALOG:
          // set initial state of Notify box
          if(bNotify)
             CheckDlgButton(hDlg, ID_CHECK1, MF_CHECKED);
          else
             CheckDlgButton(hDlg, ID_CHECK1, MF_UNCHECKED);
          // set initial state of Escape box
          if(bEscape)
```

```
            CheckDlgButton(hDlg, ID_CHECK2, MF_CHECKED);
        else
            CheckDlgButton(hDlg, ID_CHECK2, MF_UNCHECKED);
        break;

    case WM_COMMAND:                    // msg from dlg box control
        switch(wParam)
            {
            case IDOK:                  // user pushes OK button
                // get state of Notify check box, set bNotify
                hCon = GetDlgItem(hDlg, ID_CHECK1);
                if( SendMessage(hCon, BM_GETSTATE, 0, 0L) )
                    bNotify = TRUE;
                else
                    bNotify = FALSE;
                // get state of Escape check box, set bEscape
                hCon = GetDlgItem(hDlg, ID_CHECK2);
                if( SendMessage(hCon, BM_GETSTATE, 0, 0L) )
                    bEscape = TRUE;
                else
                    bEscape = FALSE;
                EndDialog(hDlg, NULL);  // terminate dialog box
                break;

            case IDCANCEL:              // user pushes Cancel button
                EndDialog(hDlg, NULL);  // terminate dialog box
                break;
            } // end switch wparam
        break;  // end case WM_COMMAND

    default:
        return FALSE;
    } // end switch msg
return TRUE;
} // end CheckDlgProc
```

Two Boolean variables, bNotify and bEscape, record the state of the program's internal exit policy. If bNotify is true, a message box appears when the user attempts to exit. If bEscape is true, pressing the ⎋ESC key causes the program to exit. These variables should mirror the state of the Notify on exit and Exit on escape key check boxes.

Initializing the Check Boxes

In the dialog procedure we initialize the check boxes to reflect the current state of bNotify and bEscape when we receive a WM_INITDIALOG message. This is similar to what we did with radio buttons in the last example, but we use a different function: CheckDlgButton(). This function can be used for any kind of button, and is more appropriate for nonradio buttons.

```
CheckDlgButton(hDlg, ID_CHECK1, MF_CHECKED);
```

The first argument to this function is the dialog handle, and the second is the ID of the check box. The third can be either MF_CHECKED or MF_UNCHECKED, which cause the box to be checked or unchecked, respectively. Whether we check the boxes or not depends on the state of bNotify and bEscape variables.

(We could have written the if...else statements more succinctly as conditional expressions, but at the expense of clarity.)

Responding to OK

When we receive a WM_COMMAND message with a wParam of IDOK in the dialog procedure, we know the user is through using the dialog, so we want to set bNotify and bEscape in accordance with the current state of the check boxes. We discover these states using the SendMessage() function and the BM_GETSTATE message. (SendMessage() was discussed in Chapter 24, *Invoking Dialog Boxes*.) We then use if...else statements to set bNotify and bEscape to the appropriate values.

Acting on the Flag Values

Back in the main window procedure, we monitor three messages that indicate the program might be terminating. The first is the the WM_COMMAND message with a wParam value of IDM_EXIT, which is received when the user selects Exit. The second is the WM_KEYDOWN message with a wParam value of VK_ESCAPE, which is received when (ESC) is pressed; and the third is the WM_CLOSE message, which is received when the user selects Close from the System menu.

In the case of WM_CLOSE, we check if bNotify is TRUE; if so we put up a message box asking the user "Terminate the Program?" If the answer is Yes, we terminate with DestroyWindow(); if it's No, we don't do anything. If bNotify is FALSE, we destroy the window without asking.

We want to do exactly the same thing if the user selects the Exit menu item, or presses (ESC) when bEscape is TRUE. However, let's suppose that we don't want to duplicate the code in all three locations. In this situation, you might be tempted to use a **goto** to transfer control from the case IDM_EXIT section and the case VK_ESCAPE section to the case WM_CLOSE section. Resist this temptation! Using a **goto** to cross from one message case to another is bad form, making your program harder to read and maintain. Instead, use the SendMessage() function as we do for IDM_EXIT and VK_ESCAPE:

```
SendMessage(hWnd, WM_CLOSE, 0, 0L);
```

This function causes Windows to send the WM_CLOSE message to our window procedure. The window procedure processes this message in the usual way, so the effect is the same as if the user had selected Close from the System menu.

You can use SendMessage() in many similar situations to transfer control from one message case to another.

SUMMARY

To use auto radio buttons and auto check boxes, you first need to select the appropriate style by clicking the correct button in the Button style dialog in the RW. These are the Auto radio button and Auto check box buttons, respectively.

In the dialog procedure in your source file, you need to initialize the state of the buttons when you receive a WM_INITDIALOG message. Use the CheckRadioButton() function for radio buttons, and the CheckDlgButton() function for check boxes.

When you receive a WM_COMMAND message with a wParam of IDOK, you need to find out how the buttons are set. Use the SendMessage() function with the message BM_GETSTATE for both radio buttons and check boxes. This function requires the handle of the control that is being queried. You can discover this handle with the GetDlgItem() function.

SendMessage() is also handy for transferring control from the code that handles one message to the code that handles another.

26

LIST BOXES AND COMBO BOXES

List boxes allow the user to select an item from a list; typically a list of named items, such as files, fonts, patterns, or device drivers. Combo boxes are similar to list boxes in that they also display a list of names. However, a combo box adds an edit control or a static text field above the list box.

The programming of list boxes and combo boxes is similar in many ways. What you learn about one will probably be applicable to the other.

LIST BOXES

A list box appears to the user as a rectangle containing a list of names. Typically, the user selects a name by clicking on it, and then presses the OK button. This causes the desired action to take place, such as opening a file, displaying text in a font selected from the list, and so forth.

Our example program allows the user to select from a list of the largest islands in the world, such as Greenland and New Guinea. For simplicity, we use the selection only to display a message box. One selection is always "current." If the user presses OK after making a selection, the newly selected island becomes current, and is displayed in a message box. If the user presses Cancel, no change is made to the current selection.

The LISTBOX Program

In this example there is only one menu item: Islands. Making this selection brings up the dialog box containing the list box, as shown in Figure 26-1.

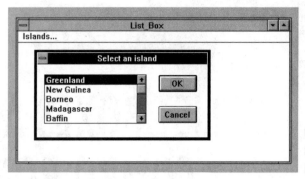

Figure 26-1
Dialog Box in
LISTBOX Program

If the list box has the keyboard focus, the currently selected item will be highlighted (white on black or whatever). The user can click on an island in the list box, and then click on OK. The message box then reports the changed selection.

Use the RW to create this dialog box. Call the dialog "IslandDlg". Install the OK and Cancel buttons in the usual way. Drag the list box icon from the Tools palette into the dialog template. You'll need to make one modification to the standard list box: the installation of a vertical scroll bar. We need the scroll bar because there are too many names to fit in a list box of the dimensions we show.

Here's how to add a scroll bar to a list box. In the dialog editor in the RW, double-click on the list box in the dialog template. The List Box Style dialog window will appear. Check the Vertical box in the group called Scroll Bar, then click on OK. This adds the WS_VSCROLL style to the dialog script. Here's the resulting LISTBOX.RC file:

```
// listbox.rc
// resource file for listbox

#include "listbox.h"

List_Box MENU
BEGIN
        MENUITEM "Islands...", IDM_ISLANDS
END


IslandDlg DIALOG 18, 18, 148, 61
STYLE DS_MODALFRAME | WS_POPUP | WS_CAPTION | WS_SYSMENU
CAPTION "Select an island"
BEGIN
        LISTBOX IDD_LISTBOX, 7, 9, 88, 39,
            LBS_NOTIFY | WS_CHILD | WS_VISIBLE | WS_BORDER | WS_VSCROLL
        PUSHBUTTON "OK", IDOK, 106, 9, 33, 14,
            WS_CHILD | WS_VISIBLE | WS_TABSTOP
        PUSHBUTTON "Cancel", IDCANCEL, 106, 35, 33, 14,
            WS_CHILD | WS_VISIBLE | WS_TABSTOP
END
```

The .H file has only two entries, the IDs of the single menu item and the list box itself. Here's the listing for LISTBOX.H:

```
// listbox.h
// header file for listbox

#define IDD_LISTBOX    1001
#define IDM_ISLANDS    101
```

The broad outline of the source file should be familiar to you. The dialog box is invoked in the usual way when the user selects the Islands menu item, thus generating a WM_COMMAND message with a wParam value of IDM_ISLANDS. The new material takes place in the dialog procedure.

Note that we give the szProgName variable the value "List_Box" rather than "ListBox" to avoid giving our main window class the same name as a control class. Here's the listing for LISTBOX.C:

```
// listbox.c
// demonstrates list box

#define STRICT
#include <windows.h>
#include "listbox.h"        // header file for menu IDs
                            // prototypes
LRESULT CALLBACK _export WndProc(HWND, UINT, WPARAM, LPARAM);
BOOL CALLBACK _export IslandDlgProc(HWND, UINT, WPARAM, LPARAM);

#define NUMISLANDS 9        // number of selections
PSTR aList[] = { "Greenland", "New Guinea", "Borneo",
                "Madagascar", "Baffin", "Sumatra",
                "Honshu", "Great Britain", "Victoria" };
char szString[80];          // utility buffer
int iSelect = 0;            // index of listbox selection (0 to n)

PSTR szProgName = "List_Box";       // application name
#include "stdmain.inc"              // standard WinMain() function
//////////////////////////////////////////////////////////////////
// main window procedure -- receives messages                    //
//////////////////////////////////////////////////////////////////
LRESULT CALLBACK _export WndProc(HWND hWnd, UINT msg,
                                 WPARAM wParam, LPARAM lParam)
    {
    HINSTANCE hInst;            // instance handle
    DLGPROC lpIslandDlgProc;   // pointer to dialog proc

    switch(msg)
        {
        case WM_COMMAND:                // user selects a menu item
            switch(wParam)              // wParam holds item ID
                {
                case IDM_ISLANDS:       // user selected Islands
```

```
                                    // get instance handle
                hInst = (HINSTANCE)GetWindowWord(hWnd, GWW_HINSTANCE);
                                    // execute dialog box
                lpIslandDlgProc = (DLGPROC)MakeProcInstance(
                                    (FARPROC)IslandDlgProc, hInst );
                DialogBox(hInst, "IslandDlg", hWnd, lpIslandDlgProc);
                FreeProcInstance( (FARPROC)lpIslandDlgProc );
                                    // display current selection
                wsprintf(szString, "Current island is %s",
                                    (LPSTR)aList[iSelect]);
                MessageBox(hWnd, szString, szProgName, MB_OK);
            }   // end switch wParam
        break;  // end case WM_COMMAND

    case WM_DESTROY:
        PostQuitMessage(0);
        break;

    default:
        return( DefWindowProc(hWnd, msg, wParam, lParam) );
    }   // end switch(msg)

    return 0L;
    } // end WndProc

///////////////////////////////////////////////////////////////////////
// dialog window procedure -- receives messages for dialog box         //
///////////////////////////////////////////////////////////////////////
#pragma argsused

BOOL CALLBACK _export IslandDlgProc(HWND hDlg, UINT msg,
                                    WPARAM wParam, LPARAM lParam)
    {
    int j;                              // loop variable

    switch(msg)
        {
        case WM_INITDIALOG:
            // put strings in list box
            for(j=0; j<NUMISLANDS; j++)
                SendDlgItemMessage(hDlg, IDD_LISTBOX, LB_ADDSTRING, 0,
                                    (LPARAM)((LPCSTR)aList[j]));
            // select the current string
            SendDlgItemMessage(hDlg, IDD_LISTBOX, LB_SETCURSEL,
                                                iSelect, 0L);

            break;

        case WM_COMMAND:                // msg from dlg box control
            switch(wParam)
                {
                case IDOK:              // user pushes OK button
                    // get index of currently selected string
```

```
            iSelect = (int)SendDlgItemMessage(hDlg, IDD_LISTBOX,
                                         LB_GETCURSEL, 0, 0L);
            EndDialog(hDlg, NULL);   // terminate dialog box
            break;

         case IDCANCEL:             // user pushes Cancel button
            EndDialog(hDlg, NULL);   // terminate dialog box
            break;

      }  // end switch wparam
     break;  // end case WM_COMMAND

   default:
      return FALSE;
   }  // end switch msg
 return TRUE;
}  // end IslandDlgProc
```

The strings representing island names are stored in an array. The variable iSelect is the index number of the string that is currently selected. We use this value to display the correct string in the "Current Island Is" dialog. The value of iSelect is set when the user selects a string from the dialog. We must also remember to initialize it when the program starts, so something will be selected initially.

Interacting with the List Box

In the LISTBOX example, when we receive the WM_INITDIALOG message, we use the SendDlgItemMessage() function twice. The first time we use it to put all the island names into the list box. We do this in a **for** loop, sending the LB_ADDSTRING message. For this message the fourth parameter is always 0, and the fifth is the address of the string to be added to the list box.

```
SendDlgItemMessage(hDlg, IDD_LISTBOX, LB_ADDSTRING, 0,
                              (LPARAM)((LPCSTR)aList[j]));
```

The address of the string must be cast, first to a long pointer to a constant string (LPCSTR), and then to the LPARAM type that the function expects.

The second use of SendDlgItemMessage() is to select an item in the list box. It's nice to show the user what the currently selected string is when the list box appears. We select an item with the LB_SETCURSEL message:

```
SendDlgItemMessage(hDlg, IDD_LISTBOX, LB_SETCURSEL, iSelect, 0L);
```

With this message, the string selected will be the one with the index given in the fourth argument, iSelect in this case. The fifth argument is always 0.

When we receive a WM_COMMAND message with a wParam value of IDOK, we use SendDlgItemMessage() again, this time to send a LB_GETCURSEL message to the list box. This message causes the function to return the index number of the current selection (where the index of the topmost string is 0). The fourth and fifth parameters are always set to 0 and 0L.

```
iSelect = SendDlgItemMessage(hDlg, IDD_LISTBOX, LB_GETCURSEL, 0, 0L);
```

Although it's not relevant in this example, you might someday need to know that if you don't select a string when WM_INITDIALOG is received using LB_SETCURSEL, as described above, and if the user presses OK without making any selection, the return value from LB_GETCURSEL will be LB_ERR. You should check for this value if there's a possibility of no selection being made in the list box.

Variations

You can cause the items in the list box to be automatically sorted into alphabetical order. To do this, you need to change the style of the list box using the Dialog editor in the RW. Double-click on the list box, and then check the Sort box in the List Box group in the List Box Style dialog. This gives the list box the LBS_SORT style. Then whenever you place an item in the box with LB_ADDSTRING, it will be inserted in the correct alphabetical position. (If you've given a list box the LBS_SORT style and want to insert some names that are *not* in alphabetical order, use the LB_INSERTSTRING message instead of LB_ADDSTRING.)

If you want to delete a string from a list box, use the LB_DELETESTRING message.

COMBO BOXES

A combo box is a list box combined with either an edit control or a static text field. The list box part of the combo box can either be displayed all the time, or it can appear only when the user wants. These variations result in three kinds of combo boxes: simple, drop-down, and drop-down-list.

In a *simple* combo box, the list box is always displayed along with an edit control. The user can select an item from the list, or type a different selection directly into the edit field. You've probably seen this type of combo box used to open files.

In the *drop-down* combo box only the edit field is initially visible. The list box does not appear until the user clicks on an arrow-shaped icon to the right of the edit field. The user can then either select from the list, or type a new selection directly into the edit field. This type of combo box is used to save space. To see some examples, activate the Ports utility in the Windows Control Panel utility, then click on Settings. You'll see a number of drop-down combo boxes, used to select the baud rate, number of data bits, parity, and so on.

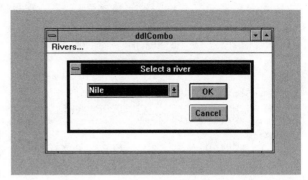

Figure 26-2

Drop-Down-List Combo
Box in DDLCOMBO Program

The *drop-down-list* combo box is similar to the drop-down combo box in that the list doesn't appear until the user clicks on the arrow icon. However, it has a static text control rather than an edit control. The user cannot type in a new selection; all selections must be made from the list. This is a useful arrangement when space is too restricted for a list box.

We show an example of the drop-down-list combo box first, since it's so similar to a list box. Then we'll show the simple combo box, which is actually more complicated to program. You can infer how to handle the drop-down combo box from these examples.

The Drop-Down-List Combo Box

Our example program, DDLCOMBO, is derived from the LISTBOX program of the last example. It operates in a similar way, but uses a drop-down-list combo box instead of a list box. When the combo box first appears, it looks like an edit field with an arrow icon on the right side, as shown in Figure 26-2.

However, you can't type anything into the "edit field" because it's really a static text control. If you click on the arrow icon, the list box part of the combo box appears. Whenever you make a selection from the list box, it's repeated in the static text field. If the combo box has the focus, the current selection will be highlighted. When you've selected what you want, click on OK to make the dialog box go away.

Use the RW to create the dialog. Install the OK and Cancel buttons as usual. Drag the combo box icon from the Tools palette to the dialog template. The default value for a combo box is Simple, so you'll need to change this to Drop-Down-List. To do this, double-click on the combo box to bring up the Combo Box Style dialog. Then push the Drop-Down-List radio button and click on OK.

Here's the listing for DDLCOMBO.RC:

```
// ddlcombo.rc
// resource file for ddlcombo

#include "ddlcombo.h"
```

```
ddlCombo MENU
BEGIN
        MENUITEM "Rivers...", IDM_RIVERS
END


RiverDlg DIALOG 18, 18, 156, 46
STYLE DS_MODALFRAME | WS_POPUP | WS_CAPTION | WS_SYSMENU
CAPTION "Select a river"
BEGIN
        CONTROL "", IDD_COMBO, "COMBOBOX", CBS_DROPDOWNLIST |
            WS_CHILD | WS_VISIBLE | WS_VSCROLL | WS_TABSTOP,
            15, 7, 79, 47
        PUSHBUTTON "OK", IDOK, 103, 7, 33, 14,
            WS_CHILD | WS_VISIBLE | WS_TABSTOP
        PUSHBUTTON "Cancel", IDCANCEL, 103, 25, 33, 14,
            WS_CHILD | WS_VISIBLE | WS_TABSTOP
END
```

And here's the listing for the associated header file, DDLCOMBO.H:

```
// ddlcombo.h
// header file for ddlcombo

#define IDD_COMBO       1001
#define IDM_RIVERS      101
```

In the source file, we handle the interaction with the combo box in the same way we did with the list box in the last example, using messages sent with SendDlgItemMessage(). The only difference is that the messages have the CB_ prefix instead of LB_. Here's the listing for DDLCOMBO.C:

```
// ddlcombo.c
// demonstrates drop-down-list combo box

#define STRICT
#include <windows.h>
#include "ddlcombo.h"       // header file for menu IDs
                            // prototypes
LRESULT CALLBACK _export WndProc(HWND, UINT, WPARAM, LPARAM);
BOOL CALLBACK _export RiverDlgProc(HWND, UINT, WPARAM, LPARAM);

#define NUMRIVS 9           // number of selections
PSTR aList[] = { "Nile", "Amazon", "Mississippi",
                "Yangtze", "Yenisei-Angara", "Amur-Argun",
                "Ob-Irtysh", "Plata-Parana", "Yellow" };
char szString[80];          // utility buffer
int iSelect = 0;            //. index of listbox selection (0 to n)

PSTR szProgName = "ddlCombo";    // application name
#include "stdmain.inc"           // standard WinMain() function
```

```
/////////////////////////////////////////////////////////////////
// main window procedure -- receives messages                    //
/////////////////////////////////////////////////////////////////
LRESULT CALLBACK _export WndProc(HWND hWnd, UINT msg,
                                 WPARAM wParam, LPARAM lParam)
    {
    HINSTANCE hInst;                   // instance handle
    DLGPROC lpRiverDlgProc;            // pointer to dialog proc

    switch(msg)
        {
        case WM_COMMAND:                // user selects a menu item
            switch(wParam)              // wParam holds item ID
                {
                case IDM_RIVERS:        // user selected Rivers
                                        // get instance handle
                    hInst = (HINSTANCE)GetWindowWord(hWnd, GWW_HINSTANCE);
                                        // execute dialog box
                    lpRiverDlgProc = (DLGPROC)MakeProcInstance(
                                       (FARPROC)RiverDlgProc, hInst );
                    DialogBox(hInst, "RiverDlg", hWnd, lpRiverDlgProc);
                    FreeProcInstance( (FARPROC)lpRiverDlgProc );
                                        // display current selection
                    wsprintf(szString, "Current river is %s",
                                       (LPSTR)aList[iSelect]);
                    MessageBox(hWnd, szString, szProgName, MB_OK);
                }    // end switch wParam
            break;  // end case WM_COMMAND

        case WM_DESTROY:
            PostQuitMessage(0);
            break;

        default:
            return( DefWindowProc(hWnd, msg, wParam, lParam) );
        }    // end switch(msg)

    return 0L;
    } // end WndProc

/////////////////////////////////////////////////////////////////
// dialog window procedure -- receives messages for dialog box   //
/////////////////////////////////////////////////////////////////
#pragma argsused

BOOL CALLBACK _export RiverDlgProc(HWND hDlg, UINT msg,
                                   WPARAM wParam, LPARAM lParam)
    {
    int j;                             // loop variable

    switch(msg)
```

```
      {
   case WM_INITDIALOG:                // when dialog starts
      // put names into listbox part of combobox
      for(j=0; j<NUMRIVS; j++)
         SendDlgItemMessage(hDlg, IDD_COMBO, CB_ADDSTRING, 0,
                              (LPARAM)((LPCSTR)aList[j]));
      // copy current string into static field
      SendDlgItemMessage(hDlg, IDD_COMBO, CB_SETCURSEL,
                                          iSelect, 0);
      break;

   case WM_COMMAND:                   // msg from dlg box control
      switch(wParam)
         {
         case IDOK:                   // user pushes OK button
            // get index of currently selected string
            iSelect = (int)SendDlgItemMessage(hDlg, IDD_COMBO,
                                     CB_GETCURSEL, 0, OL);
            EndDialog(hDlg, NULL);     // terminate dialog box
            break;

         case IDCANCEL:               // user pushes Cancel button
            EndDialog(hDlg, NULL);     // terminate dialog box
            break;

         }  // end switch wparam
      break;  // end case WM_COMMAND

   default:
      return FALSE;
   }  // end switch msg
return TRUE;
}  // end RiverDlgProc
```

The Simple Combo Box

The simple combo box features a list box and a real edit field. The user can type a string into the edit field, and it will be added to those already in the list box. The new string will also be stored in the program, so that it will appear in the list box whenever the dialog that contains it is activated.

The list-box part of a simple combo box is always visible, unlike the situation with drop-down and drop-down-list combo boxes. In our example program, SIMCOMBO, the user can select the single menu item Rivers. This invokes a dialog box with a simple combo box, as shown in Figure 26-3.

Use the RW to create the combo box as in the last example. Since the simple combo box is the default, you don't need to change this setting. However, if the number of items in the combo box is greater than can be displayed in the list-box

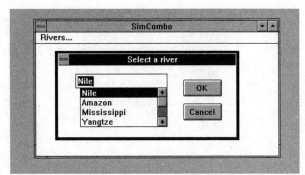

Figure 26-3

Single Combo Box
SIMCOMBO Program

part of the combo box, then you need to add a vertical scroll bar. That's the case in
SIMCOMBO. In the dialog editor in the RW, double-click on the combo box to
bring up the Combobox Style dialog. In this dialog, check the Vertical Scroll box,
and press OK. Here's the resulting SIMCOMBO.RC file:

```
// simcombo.rc
// resource file for simcombo

#include "simcombo.h"
#include "listbox.h"


SimCombo MENU
BEGIN
        MENUITEM "Rivers...", IDM_RIVERS
END



RiverDlg DIALOG 18, 18, 154, 60
STYLE DS_MODALFRAME | WS_POPUP | WS_CAPTION | WS_SYSMENU
CAPTION "Select a river"
BEGIN
        CONTROL "", IDD_COMBO, "COMBOBOX", CBS_SIMPLE |
            WS_CHILD | WS_VISIBLE | WS_VSCROLL | WS_TABSTOP,
            15, 7, 79, 47
        PUSHBUTTON "OK", IDOK, 108, 12, 33, 14,
            WS_CHILD | WS_VISIBLE | WS_TABSTOP
        PUSHBUTTON "Cancel", IDCANCEL, 108, 32, 33, 14,
            WS_CHILD | WS_VISIBLE | WS_TABSTOP
END
```

Here's the corresponding header file:

```
// simcomb.h
// header file for simcombo

#define IDD_COMBO       1001
#define IDM_RIVERS       101
```

The code in the simple combo box must be able to handle the new strings entered by the user. Instead of storing the strings as an array of pointers, we use a two-dimensional character array. This provides space for new strings to be stored. (This arrangement would be more efficient if we used dynamic memory allocation, but we'll defer our discussion of that topic until Chapter 36, *Managing Memory*.) Here's the listing for SIMCOMBO.C:

```c
// simcombo.c
// demonstrates simple combo box

#define STRICT
#include <windows.h>
#include "simcombo.h"        // header file for menu IDs
                             // prototypes
LRESULT CALLBACK _export WndProc(HWND, UINT, WPARAM, LPARAM);
BOOL CALLBACK _export RiverDlgProc(HWND, UINT, WPARAM, LPARAM);

#define INITRIVS  9          // initial number of selections
#define MAXNUM   30          // maximum number of selections
#define MAXLEN   30          // maximum length of selection
char aList[MAXNUM][MAXLEN] = { "Nile", "Amazon", "Mississippi",
                    "Yangtze", "Yenisei-Angara", "Amur-Argun",
                    "Ob-Irtysh", "Plata-Parana", "Yellow" };
char szString[80];           // utility buffer
int iSelect = 0;             // index of listbox selection (0 to n)
int nRivers = INITRIVS;      // number of rivers in array

PSTR szProgName = "SimCombo";    // application name
#include "stdmain.inc"           // standard WinMain() function
///////////////////////////////////////////////////////////////////
// main window procedure -- receives messages                     //
///////////////////////////////////////////////////////////////////
LRESULT CALLBACK _export WndProc(HWND hWnd, UINT msg,
                              WPARAM wParam, LPARAM lParam)
    {
    HINSTANCE hInst;                    // instance handle
    DLGPROC lpRiverDlgProc;             // pointer to dialog proc

    switch(msg)
        {
        case WM_COMMAND:                // user selects a menu item
            switch(wParam)              // wParam holds item ID
                {
                case IDM_RIVERS:        // user selected Rivers
                                        // get instance handle
                    hInst = (HINSTANCE)GetWindowWord(hWnd, GWW_HINSTANCE);
                                        // execute dialog box
                    lpRiverDlgProc = (DLGPROC)MakeProcInstance(
                                    (FARPROC)RiverDlgProc, hInst );
                    DialogBox(hInst, "RiverDlg", hWnd, lpRiverDlgProc);
                    FreeProcInstance( (FARPROC)lpRiverDlgProc );
                                        // display current selection
```

```
                wsprintf(szString, "Current river is %s",
                             (LPSTR)aList[iSelect]);
            MessageBox(hWnd, szString, szProgName, MB_OK);
         }    // end switch wParam
      break;  // end case WM_COMMAND

   case WM_DESTROY:
      PostQuitMessage(0);
      break;

   default:
      return( DefWindowProc(hWnd, msg, wParam, lParam) );
   }    // end switch(msg)

   return 0L;
   }  // end WndProc

//////////////////////////////////////////////////////////////////
// dialog window procedure -- receives messages for dialog box    //
//////////////////////////////////////////////////////////////////
#pragma argsused

BOOL CALLBACK _export RiverDlgProc(HWND hDlg, UINT msg,
                             WPARAM wParam, LPARAM lParam)
   {
   int j;                             // loop variable

   switch(msg)
      {
      case WM_INITDIALOG:               // when dialog starts
         // put names into listbox part of combobox
         for(j=0; j<nRivers; j++)
            SendDlgItemMessage(hDlg, IDD_COMBO, CB_ADDSTRING, 0,
                    (LPARAM)((LPCSTR)aList[j]));
         // copy current string into edit field
         SendDlgItemMessage(hDlg, IDD_COMBO, CB_SETCURSEL,
                          (WPARAM)iSelect, 0);
         break;

      case WM_COMMAND:                   // msg from dlg box control
         switch(wParam)
            {
            case IDOK:                    // user pushes OK button
               // get index of currently selected string
               iSelect = (int)SendDlgItemMessage(hDlg, IDD_COMBO,
                                      CB_GETCURSEL, 0, 0L);

               if( iSelect==(int)CB_ERR )  // if user typed new string
                  {
                  // copy text from edit part of combo box to array
                  GetDlgItemText(hDlg, IDD_COMBO, aList[nRivers++],
                                          MAXLEN);
                  iSelect = nRivers-1;
```

```
                }
            EndDialog(hDlg, NULL);      // terminate dialog box
            break;

        case IDCANCEL:                  // user pushes Cancel button
            EndDialog(hDlg, NULL);      // terminate dialog box
            break;

        }  // end switch wparam
      break;  // end case WM_COMMAND

    default:
        return FALSE;
    }  // end switch msg
  return TRUE;
}  // end RiverDlgProc
```

Our actions when we receive a WM_INITDIALOG message are the same as those in the last example: we copy the strings into the list-box part of the combo box, and then select one string to be displayed in the edit field. However, when we receive a WM_COMMAND message with a wParam of IDOK, we must be prepared to handle the case where the user has typed something into the edit field rather than selecting from the list. We can tell if this has happened by checking the return value from SendDlgItemMessage() when we send the CB_GETCURSEL message.

```
iSelect = (int)SendDlgItemMessage(hDlg, IDD_COMBO, CB_GETCURSEL, 0, OL);
if( iSelect==(int)CB_ERR)
    {
    GetDlgItemText(hDLg, IDD_COMBO, aList[nRivers++], MAXLEN);
    iSelect = nRivers - 1;
    }
```

If the return value is CB_ERR, we know the user has typed in a new string. In this case we get the text from the edit field just as we did in EZDIAL, with the GetDlgItemText() function, and copy it into the next available space in the text array. The nRivers variable records the number of strings in the array, so we increment it. Finally we change the iSelect variable to make the newly entered string the current selection. In a serious program we should also check that we have not overflowed the aList array; that is, that nRivers is less than MAXNUM.

The Drop-Down Combo Box

The drop-down combo box is handled similarly to the simple combo box. The main difference is that, in the RW, the Drop Down option must be selected from the Combo Box Style dialog when specifying the type of combo box. This gives you the capabilities of a simple combo box in the small space of a drop-down-list combo box.

SUMMARY

List boxes and different kinds of combo boxes all put strings into the list in the same way, when a WM_INITDIALOG message is received:

```
case WM_INITDIALOG:
   for(j=0; j<MAX; j++)
      SendDlgItemMessage(hDlg, IDD_LISTBOX, LB_ADDSTRING,
                                    0, (LPARAM)((LPCSTR)aList[j]));
   SendDlgItemMessage(hDlg, IDD_LISTBOX, LB_SETCURSEL, iSelect, 0);
   break;
```

Here the first SendDlgItemMessage() inserts the strings into the box, and the second selects the current item, as designated by the index iSelect. This code shows how to initialize a list box. For a combo box, simply change the LB_ message prefixes to CB_.

To get the input selection from a list or combo box when the user presses OK, we process the following code:

```
case IDOK:
   iSelect = (int)SendDlgItemMessage(hDlg, IDD_LISTBOX,
                                    LB_GETCURSEL, 0, OL);
   break;
```

Again, change the LB_ messages to CB_ messages if you're working with a combo box.

If you've created a simple or drop-down combo box, you'll need to handle the situation where the user types a new string into the edit field. If the return from the LB_GETCURSEL message is LB_ERR (or CB_ERR for combo boxes), then the user typed something new. Read it with GetDlgItemText() and add it to the array holding the other strings.

CHAPTER 27

27

SCROLL BARS AS CONTROLS

We've already seen scroll bars at work, scrolling text in main windows. Scroll bars can also be installed in a dialog box and used to select a number from a range of values, like the sliding volume controls on stereo equipment. Scroll bars are used in this way in the Windows Control Panel to specify mouse tracking speed, cursor blink rate, and keyboard repeat rate. Scroll bars are the only controls that give the user the feeling of selecting from a continuum of values.

You can't use a scroll bar for everything. They're appropriate when the number of possible values is large but not infinite, and known in advance. Also the values should be in a readily understandable series, such 1, 2, 3, 4; or 1, 10, 100, 1000. If the selection is to be made from a small number of integral values, such as selecting line spacing (see the AUTORAD example in Chapter 25, *Radio Buttons and Check Boxes*), then radio buttons should be used instead of scroll bars. If the range is infinite (such as asking the user to enter any positive integer) or not known, then an edit field is more appropriate. If the possible values aren't in a regular series, such as baud rates or the denominations of coins, then a list box or a group of radio buttons presents the choices more clearly.

THE SLIDER PROGRAM

Our example program, SLIDER, not only demonstrates scroll bars, but shows how static text controls and edit controls can be used to display numbers. The dialog box in our example functions as a special-purpose calculator. The purpose of the calculator is to find the volume and surface area of a box. You might use it to see if a parcel is too large to ship, or how much wrapping paper it needs. Scroll bars allow

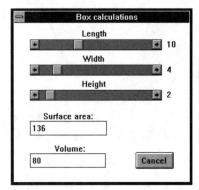

Figure 27-1

The Box Calculations Dialog Box in the SLIDER Program

the user to specify the length, width, and height of the box. The resulting volume and area are then displayed.

The dialog box appears when you run SLIDER and select the Calculate menu item. In Figure 27-1 the user has already dialed in some numbers.

Each scroll bar has a value of 0 when the thumb (slider, elevator) is on the left, and 30 when it's on the right. The position of each bar is reflected by the number to the right of the bar, which also ranges from 0 to 30.

Edit fields at the bottom of the dialog show the surface area and volume of a box with the dimensions indicated by the bars. The calculations are made and the answers displayed in real time, as the user slides the bars. In the example the length of the box is 10, the width is 4, and the height is 2. This gives a surface area of 136 and a volume of 80.

The surface area is found from the formula

```
2*(iLength*iWidth+iLength*iHeight+iWidth*iHeight)
```

and the volume is

```
iLength*iWidth*iHeight
```

When you're through with the dialog, press Cancel to make it vanish.

To create the dialog box and position the controls, use the RW, as we've seen before. Drag the horizontal scroll bar icons and edit field icons from the Tools palette to the dialog template. Drag static text icons not only to label the scroll bars and edit fields but to install numerals at the right ends of the scroll bars. These static text controls can be given captions of '0' for the moment; the program will change them later. Here's the listing for SLIDER.RC:

```
// slider.rc
// resource file for slider

#include "slider.h"

Slider MENU
```

```
BEGIN
        MENUITEM "Calculate...", IDM_CALC
END

BoxDlg DIALOG 18, 18, 153, 133
STYLE DS_MODALFRAME | WS_POPUP | WS_CAPTION | WS_SYSMENU
CAPTION "Box calculations"
BEGIN
        SCROLLBAR IDC_LENGTH, 14, 14, 115, 9,
            SBS_HORZ | WS_CHILD | WS_VISIBLE
        SCROLLBAR IDC_WIDTH, 14, 35, 115, 9,
            SBS_HORZ | WS_CHILD | WS_VISIBLE
        SCROLLBAR IDC_HEIGHT, 14, 56, 115, 9,
            SBS_HORZ | WS_CHILD | WS_VISIBLE
        LTEXT "Surface area:", -1, 26, 74, 50, 8
        LTEXT "Volume:", -1, 36, 101, 30, 8
        EDITTEXT IDC_AREA, 14, 82, 67, 12,
            ES_LEFT | WS_CHILD | WS_VISIBLE | WS_BORDER | WS_TABSTOP
        EDITTEXT IDC_VOLUME, 14, 109, 66, 12,
            ES_LEFT | WS_CHILD | WS_VISIBLE | WS_BORDER | WS_TABSTOP
        PUSHBUTTON "Cancel", IDCANCEL, 106, 108, 33, 14,
            WS_CHILD | WS_VISIBLE | WS_TABSTOP
        LTEXT "Length", -1, 59, 5, 26, 8
        LTEXT "Width", -1, 60, 26, 21, 8
        LTEXT "Height", -1, 59, 47, 27, 8
        LTEXT "0", IDC_EDITLENGTH, 133, 14, 16, 8,
            WS_CHILD | WS_VISIBLE | WS_GROUP
        LTEXT "0", IDC_EDITWIDTH, 133, 35, 16, 8,
            WS_CHILD | WS_VISIBLE | WS_GROUP
        LTEXT "0", IDC_EDITHEIGHT, 133, 56, 16, 8,
            WS_CHILD | WS_VISIBLE | WS_GROUP
END
```

This is a somewhat complex dialog, but, with the exception of the scroll bars, you've seen all the controls before. The scroll bars are represented in the .RC file by SCROLLBAR statements. Scroll bars have no captions. Otherwise they are similar to buttons or other controls.

The header file has quite a few identifiers. Here's the listing for SLIDER.H:

```
// slider.h
// header file for slider

#define IDM_CALC         101
#define IDC_LENGTH       1001
#define IDC_WIDTH        1002
#define IDC_HEIGHT       1003
#define IDC_AREA         1004
#define IDC_VOLUME       1005
#define IDC_EDITLENGTH   2001
#define IDC_EDITWIDTH    2002
#define IDC_EDITHEIGHT   2003
```

HANDLING SCROLL BARS

When we receive a WM_INITDIALOG message, we set the range of each scroll bar with the SetScrollRange() function, and the position of the thumb with SetScrollPos(). We examined these functions earlier, in Chapter 19, *Scroll Bars in the Window*. The three scroll bars are handled one after the other in a **for** loop, since they are all set to the same value. Here's the listing for SLIDER.C:

```c
// slider.c
// demonstrates scroll bars

#define STRICT
#include <windows.h>
#include "slider.h"        // for menu and control #defines
#define MAX  30            // maximum slider position
#define MIN   0            // minimum slider position

                          // prototypes
LRESULT CALLBACK _export WndProc(HWND, UINT, WPARAM, LPARAM);
BOOL CALLBACK _export SlideDlgProc(HWND, UINT, WPARAM, LPARAM);

PSTR szProgName = "Slider";        // application name
#include "stdmain.inc"             // standard WinMain() function
//////////////////////////////////////////////////////////////////
// main window procedure -- receives messages                    //
//////////////////////////////////////////////////////////////////
LRESULT CALLBACK _export WndProc(HWND hWnd, UINT msg,
                        WPARAM wParam, LPARAM lParam)
   {
   HINSTANCE hInst;                 // instance handle
   DLGPROC lpSlideDlgProc;          // pointer to dialog proc

   switch(msg)
      {
      case WM_COMMAND:
         switch(wParam)
            {
            case IDM_CALC:          // user selected Calculate
               // get the instance handle
               hInst = (HINSTANCE)GetWindowWord(hWnd, GWW_HINSTANCE);
               // execute dialog box
               lpSlideDlgProc = (DLGPROC)MakeProcInstance(
                                 (FARPROC)SlideDlgProc, hInst);
               DialogBox(hInst, "BoxDlg", hWnd, lpSlideDlgProc);
               FreeProcInstance( (FARPROC)lpSlideDlgProc );
               break;  // end case IDM_CALC
            }    // end switch wParam
         break;  // end case WM_COMMAND

      case WM_DESTROY:
         PostQuitMessage(0);
```

```
            break;

        default:
            return( DefWindowProc(hWnd, msg, wParam, lParam) );
        }   // end switch(msg)

    return 0L;
    }   // end WndProc

//////////////////////////////////////////////////////////////////
// dialog window procedure -- receives messages for dialog box    //
//////////////////////////////////////////////////////////////////
#pragma argsused

BOOL CALLBACK _export SlideDlgProc(HWND hDlg, UINT msg,
                                WPARAM wParam, LPARAM lParam)
    {
    int iWidth, iLength, iHeight, iArea, iVolume;
    int j;
    static int nPos[3];
    HWND hScroll;

    switch(msg)
        {
        case WM_INITDIALOG:
            for(j=0; j<3; j++)
                {
                hScroll = GetDlgItem(hDlg, IDC_LENGTH + j);  // get handle
                SetScrollRange(hScroll, SB_CTL,              // set range
                            MIN, MAX, FALSE);
                SetScrollPos(hScroll, SB_CTL, MIN,  TRUE);
                }
            break;

        case WM_HSCROLL:
            // get scroll bar handle
            hScroll = (HWND)HIWORD(lParam);
            // make index number from ID number of scroll bar
            j = GetDlgCtrlID(hScroll) - IDC_LENGTH;  // (0 to 2)
            switch(wParam)
                {
                case SB_LINERIGHT:  nPos[j]++;     break;
                case SB_LINELEFT:   nPos[j]--;     break;
                case SB_PAGERIGHT:  nPos[j]+=10;   break;
                case SB_PAGELEFT:   nPos[j]-=10;   break;
                case SB_THUMBTRACK: nPos[j]=LOWORD(lParam); break;
                }  // end switch wParam

            nPos[j] = max( MIN, min(nPos[j], MAX) ); // keep in range
                                        // has thumb moved at all?
            if( nPos[j] != GetScrollPos(hScroll, SB_CTL) )
                {                          // if so, reposition it
                SetScrollPos(hScroll,      // scroll bar handle
```

```
                    SB_CTL,        // bar is a control
                    nPos[j],       // position of thumb
                    TRUE);         // redraw the thumb
        iLength=nPos[0];
        iWidth= nPos[1];
        iHeight=nPos[2];
        iArea =
            2*(iWidth*iLength + iWidth*iHeight + iLength*iHeight);
        iVolume = iWidth * iLength * iHeight;
        SetDlgItemInt(hDlg, IDC_EDITLENGTH, iLength, TRUE);
        SetDlgItemInt(hDlg, IDC_EDITWIDTH, iWidth, TRUE);
        SetDlgItemInt(hDlg, IDC_EDITHEIGHT, iHeight, TRUE);
        SetDlgItemInt(hDlg, IDC_AREA, iArea, TRUE);
        SetDlgItemInt(hDlg, IDC_VOLUME, iVolume, TRUE);
        }
    break;

    case WM_COMMAND:                        // msg from dlg box control
        switch(wParam)
            {
            case IDCANCEL:                  // user pushes Cancel button
                EndDialog(hDlg, NULL);      // terminate dialog box
                break;
            } // end switch wparam
        break;  // end case WM_COMMAND

    default:
        return FALSE;
    } // end switch msg
return TRUE;
} // end SlideDlgProc
```

Most of the action in the program takes place when we receive a WM_HSCROLL message. The same message arrives no matter which scroll bar is being adjusted or what the adjustment is. To figure out which bar it is, we examine the high word of lParam, which is the scroll bar handle. To simplify the programming, we put the positions of the three scroll bars in an array with three elements: nPos[ ]. We convert the scroll bar handle to an index into this array by using the GetDlgCtrlID() function, which, given a control's handle, returns its ID. From this ID we subtract the ID of the first scroll bar, which gives us the index j, which can have the values 0, 1, or 2.

We handle the scroll bar messages, SB_LINERIGHT and so forth, in much the same way we did in Chapter 19, *Scroll Bars in the Window*, changing the nPos[ ] variable for the particular scroll bar appropriately and resetting the position of the scroll bar.

Each time the scroll bar moves, we set the variables' length, width, and height equal to the new scroll bar positions. The values of these variables are displayed in the three static text fields next to the scroll bars. Finally we recalculate the area and volume, and write these values into the two edit fields.

INSERTING NUMBERS IN CONTROLS

We saw in Chapter 24, *Invoking Dialog Boxes*, how we can put text into edit controls using the SetDlgItemText() function. It's also possible to insert integers directly into controls. This is done with the function SetDlgItemInt(). You could achieve the same effect by converting the integer to a string with wsprintf() or itoa() and then using SetDlgItemText(), but SetDlgItemInt() provides a one-step approach. (Unfortunately there is no corresponding function for floating-point numbers.)

```
SetDlgItemInt(hDlg, IDC_EDITLENGTH, length, TRUE);
```

The first argument is the dialog handle, the second is the control ID, the third is the integer whose value we want to display, and the fourth is TRUE if the integer in the third argument is a signed value (an int), and FALSE if it is unsigned (a UINT).

We use this function not only to put the area and volume into the edit controls, but also to set the static text. It seems that static text isn't so static after all; it can be changed, but only by the program, not by the user.

SUMMARY

Scroll bars are handled in much the same way in dialog boxes as they are in main windows. Their range and initial positions are set when the WM_INITDIALOG message is received.

When the user moves a scroll bar, the dialog receives a WM_HSCROLL message (or WM_VSCROLL if it's a vertical scroll bar). The lParam value to this message carries the handle to the scroll bar, which is useful if there's more than one. The wParam argument tells how the user has moved the scroll bar, with values like SB_LINERIGHT, and so on. Responding to these messages is the same as responding to them in a main window, except that the resulting nPos value is not used to position text in a window, but for numerical input to the program.

This concludes, at least for the time being, our discussion of dialog boxes. We'll return to dialogs later when we discuss stand-alone dialogs in Chapter 35, *Stand-Alone Dialogs*. In Part Five, *Graphics*, we'll examine graphics programming, and there we'll have a chance to put dialogs to work.

PART FIVE
GRAPHICS

*I*n medieval times, there was no art for art's sake. There were no stand-alone paintings to hang on the wall, or sculptures to sit in the alcove. Instead, art was applied to objects with a practical or religious value: engravings on sword hilts, scenes on tapestries which warmed the castle walls, pictures or "illuminations" in the margins of manuscripts, and religious scenes painted on altarpieces in the church. The concept of the "famous artist," so important in today's art scene, was unknown. Medieval artists were members of guilds, who created art anonymously, as part of a collaborative effort.

A picture on a computer screen also serves (usually) a practical purpose and requires a collaborative effort. A bar chart, a map, and the view from the cockpit of an F-18, all have a purpose beyond themselves, and all require collaboration among the software, the hardware, the programmer, the user, and maybe a designer or artist.

In this section we're going to discuss how to draw graphics (that is, pictures as opposed to text) on the screen. Graphics is becoming an increasingly important part of programming, as users grow accustomed to the advantages of, for example, charts instead of tables of figures. It's also a lot of fun for the programmer: you're rewarded in a very visible way for your code-writing efforts.

Windows has some remarkable advantages when it comes to writing graphics programs. Your application doesn't need to worry (usually) about what kind of graphics system it's running on. One of Windows' great strengths is that it takes care of translating graphics output to specific display devices. You no longer have to query the system to see what graphics adaptor—EGA, VGA, 8514a, or whatever—is in use, and modify your output accordingly. You can work in "generic" graphics and let Windows take care of the hardware-related details.

You also know that your application is not running on a character-based display (if anyone is still using such a thing). If the hardware is running Windows, it must have a graphics-based display.

Finally, because text in Windows is simply another form of graphics, there's no problem mixing text and graphics in the same display. This makes it easy to liven up otherwise dull text displays with pictures (like illuminations in medieval manuscripts), or add to the value of pictures with captions and explanations.

We're going to start off showing how to display simple graphics shapes like lines, rectangles, and ellipses. Then we'll discuss two new graphics entities: pens, which allow you to vary the color and thickness of lines; and brushes, which allow you choose the pattern and color used to fill shapes.

In Windows the mouse is an essential tool for graphics manipulation. We show how to use the mouse to create graphics shapes. This leads into some interesting topics such as raster operations (ROPs) and rubber banding.

We'll finish off with a mini-application: a paint-type program that lets you draw dots, lines, rectangles, and ellipses, vary the width and style of lines and the pattern used to fill shapes, and use different colors on each graphics element.

Clearly we're not going to cover all there is to know about Windows graphics; that would require several large books. We will show you a few of the most useful graphics functions and how to use them. This will get you started in the exciting world of Windows graphics.

28
DRAWING SHAPES

*I*n this chapter we show how to display rectangles, ellipses, polygons, and lines. If you've come this far, you'll find this is easy. Because text is displayed as a graphics element, and you learned how to display text, you've already mastered most of what you need to know to display graphics.

At the end of this chapter we'll discuss mapping modes, which allow you to specify the coordinates for graphics figures in inches or millimeters, instead of pixels.

FUNCTIONS FOR DRAWING SHAPES

As we noted in earlier chapters, the system Windows uses to display graphics, including the various API functions, is called the GDI, for Graphics Device Interface. Our first example program demonstrates several GDI functions. It doesn't use resources, so there's only one file. Here's the listing for SHAPES.C:

```
// shapes.c
// displays simple graphics shapes

#define STRICT
#include <windows.h>

LRESULT CALLBACK _export WndProc(HWND, UINT, WPARAM, LPARAM);

PSTR szProgName = "Shapes";              // application name
#include "stdmain.inc"                   // standard WinMain() function
/////////////////////////////////////////////////////////////////////
// main window procedure -- receives messages                       //
/////////////////////////////////////////////////////////////////////
LRESULT CALLBACK _export WndProc(HWND hWnd, UINT msg,
                         WPARAM wParam, LPARAM lParam)
    {
```

```
HDC hDC;
PAINTSTRUCT ps;
int xLeft=20, yTop=20, xRight=320, yBottom=220;
POINT apt[] = { {20, 120}, {170, 20}, {319, 120}, {170, 219} };

switch(msg)
    {
    case WM_PAINT:
        hDC = BeginPaint(hWnd, &ps);    // get device context

        // start drawing
        Rectangle(hDC, xLeft, yTop, xRight, yBottom); // rectangle
        Ellipse(hDC, xLeft, yTop, xRight, yBottom);   // ellipse
        MoveTo(hDC, xLeft, yTop);                     // line: begin
        LineTo(hDC, xRight, yBottom);                 //        end
        Polygon(hDC, apt, 4);                         // polygon
        // end drawing

        EndPaint(hWnd, &ps);                // release device context
        break;

    case WM_DESTROY:
        PostQuitMessage(0);
        break;
    default:
        return( DefWindowProc(hWnd, msg, wParam, lParam) );
    }   // end switch(msg)
return 0L;
}   // end WndProc
```

This program creates a design consisting of a rectangle, an ellipse, a line, and a polygon, as shown in Figure 28-1.

In Chapter 9, *Displaying Text,* we discussed the WM_PAINT message and the BeginPaint() and EndPaint() functions, and showed how they were used together to display text. As you can see in SHAPES, graphics figures are displayed in the same way. We wait for a WM_PAINT message, get a device context handle with

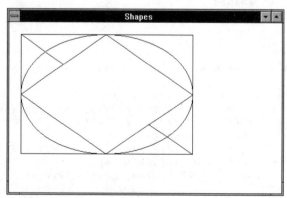

Figure 28-1
Output of SHAPES Program

BeginPaint(), display whatever graphics we want, and then return the device context to Windows with EndPaint().

Rectangles

The Rectangle() function takes five arguments. As is true with almost all graphics functions, the first argument is the device context handle. You may recall that the device context acts as an intermediary between our program and the display hardware: it's the professional artist that draws what we tell it. (The device context also provides various graphics objects—or tools—such as fonts, pens, and brushes. We'll discuss graphics objects in the next chapter.)

The final four arguments to Rectangle() are the coordinates of the rectangle to be drawn, in the order left, top, right, and bottom. You might want to memorize this order, since it's used in many graphics functions.

```
Rectangle(hDC, xLeft, yTop, xRight, yBottom);
```

Logical Coordinates

The coordinates used in GDI functions like Rectangle() are called *logical* coordinates, because they may be transformed in various ways before a drawing appears on an actual physical display device. By default, logical coordinates are expressed in pixels, as they are in this example (although in the next example we'll see how this can be changed). As you've seen, the origin of the coordinate system in the GDI is normally the upper left corner of the window (not the screen). Y-coordinates are measured downward, and X-coordinates to the right.

Colors

The default color scheme is a black line outlining an interior filled with white, and that's what you see in the output from SHAPES in Figure 28-1. We'll see how to change these colors in the next chapter.

Frames

We should note that the imaginary line outlining a rectangle (or similar shape) is called a *frame*. The frame is assumed to have no width, unlike the actual line that is usually (but not always) drawn on top of the frame. In this program the actual line has a default width of 1 pixel. The frame is important because when a figure is filled, it's filled out to the frame. Also, there are different ways to draw the outline relative to the frame, as we'll see when we look at pens.

Other Details

There's a minor lack of symmetry in the way the coordinates are used. The rectangle's frame starts at the given coordinates on the left and top, but falls one pixel short of the given coordinates on the right and bottom. In the Rectangle() statement above, the leftmost pixel that's part of the rectangle's frame is xLeft, and the rightmost one is xRight–1. The topmost pixel is yTop, and the bottommost one is yBottom–1. So the width of the rectangle is xRight–xLeft, and the height is yBottom –yTop.

There's a not-very onerous limitation on the size of rectangles: their width and height must be greater than 2 and less than 32,767.

Ellipses

The Ellipse() function is almost identical to Rectangle(). As you can see from the figure, it draws an ellipse that just fits inside a rectangle drawn with the same coordinates.

```
Ellipse(hDC, xLeft, yTop, xRight, yBottom);
```

Like rectangles, ellipses extend up to but do not include the right and bottom coordinates, and their width and height must be greater than 2 and less than 32,767.

Lines

Windows uses the concept of the *current position*. This is an imaginary point on the drawing surface where certain functions, like LineTo(), start drawing. In order to draw a line, we must first move the current position to the starting point of the line. The function that does this is MoveTo(). This function doesn't draw anything, it simply changes the current position. Once the current position is set, we use LineTo() to actually draw the line from the current position to an end point specified as an argument to LineTo().

```
MoveTo(hDC, xLeft, yTop);        // set the current position
LineTo(hDC, xRight, yBottom);    // draw line
```

In our example the line is drawn from the coordinates xLeft, yTop to xRight, yBottom. As you can see from the Figure 28-1, this is a diagonal line from the upper left corner of the previously drawn rectangle to the bottom right. (Actually, the very last pixel in the line, at xRight, yBottom, is not drawn. This makes it more efficient to draw a number of connected lines, but doesn't have any visible effect in this example.)

We don't see the line under the polygon because, although the line was drawn all the way across, the polygon drew over it.

Points

Many graphics functions use variables of type POINT. This is a structure defined this way in WINDOWS.H:

```
typedef struct tagPOINT
   {
   int x;
   int y;
   } POINT;
```

A variable of type POINT represents a location on a two-dimensional surface. If you have a structure of type POINT called ptStart, then its X-coordinate is ptStart.x, and its Y-coordinate is ptStart.y. We'll use this structure with the Polygon() function.

Polygons

Polygons are created with a simple function, but they require some preparation. A polygon is a figure consisting of a number of points connected by straight lines. To draw a polygon, you must create an array to hold these points. The Polygon() function requires these points to be of type POINT. In our example we've arranged four points to lie on the midpoints of the lines forming the rectangle, so the polygon creates a diamond shape.

```
POINT apt[ ] = { {20, 120}, {170, 20}, {319, 120}, {170, 219} };
...
Polygon(hDC, apt, 4);
```

The first point has an X-coordinate of 20 and a Y-coordinate of 120, and so on for the other three points. We don't need to specify the starting point twice. Polygon() is smart enough to complete the figure by drawing a final line from the last point specified (170,219), back to the starting point.

The polygon function takes three arguments: the device context handle (surprise!), the address of the array holding the points, and the number of points in the array.

MAPPING MODES

The default way to express coordinates for graphics functions is in pixels. This may not be advantageous in some situations, since a drawing will appear smaller on a device with smaller pixels. If you're using a laser printer, for example, graphics that are a reasonable size on the screen will appear tiny on the printer. So instead of pixels, you may want to use absolute units, such as inches or millimeters. This way a drawing will be the same size on all devices.

The Windows GDI provides several different *mapping modes* to solve this problem. A mapping mode is a transformation of logical coordinates (those specified in GDI functions) to device coordinates (those used on a physical device).

Our example program draws the same design as SHAPES, but uses a mapping mode where coordinates are specified in thousandths of an inch. Here's the listing for ENGLISH.C (so-named because inches are part of the English measurement system):

```
// english.c
// displays simple graphics shapes using coordinate in inches

#define STRICT
#include <windows.h>
                                        // prototype
LRESULT CALLBACK _export WndProc(HWND, UINT, WPARAM, LPARAM);

PSTR szProgName = "English";           // application name
#include "stdmain.inc"                 // standard WinMain() function
//////////////////////////////////////////////////////////////////////
// main window procedure -- receives messages                       //
//////////////////////////////////////////////////////////////////////
LRESULT CALLBACK _export WndProc(HWND hWnd, UINT msg,
                                 WPARAM wParam, LPARAM lParam)
   {
   HDC hDC;
   PAINTSTRUCT ps;
   int xLeft=200, yTop=200, xRight=3200, yBottom=2200;
   POINT apt[] = { {200, 1200}, {1700, 220},
                   {3190, 1200}, {1700, 2200} };
   RECT rcClient;
   int yClient;

   switch(msg)
      {
      case WM_PAINT:
         hDC = BeginPaint(hWnd, &ps);
         GetClientRect(hWnd, &rcClient);    // get client dimensions
         yClient = rcClient.bottom;         // get height of window

         SetMapMode(hDC, MM_HIENGLISH);     // use 1/1000ths of an inch
         SetViewportOrg(hDC, 0, yClient);   // origin at lower left

         // draw the usual design
         Rectangle(hDC, xLeft, yTop, xRight, yBottom);
         Ellipse(hDC, xLeft, yTop, xRight, yBottom);
         MoveTo(hDC, xLeft, yTop);
         LineTo(hDC, xRight, yBottom);
         Polygon(hDC, apt, 4);
         EndPaint(hWnd, &ps);
         break;

      case WM_DESTROY:
         PostQuitMessage(0);
         break;
```

```
    default:
        return( DefWindowProc(hWnd, msg, wParam, lParam) );
    }    // end switch(msg)
return 0L;
}   // end WndProc
```

The SetMapMode() Function

The SetMapMode() function specifies how the logical coordinates used in GDI functions will be interpreted. For instance, the statement

```
SetMapMode(hDC, MM_HIENGLISH);
```

uses the MM_HIENGLISH constant, which specifies thousandths of an inch. Table 28-1 shows the other possibilities.

Changing the Origin with SetViewportOrg()

The MM_TEXT mapping mode is the default; it's what we've been using all along. As you know, in this mode Y-coordinates are measured *downward* from a default origin assumed to be at the upper left corner of the window. However, in the other modes Y-coordinates are measured *upward*. This corresponds to standard practice on the coordinate plane in most noncomputer situations. Since we use MM_HIENGLISH, the Y-coordinate is measured upward in our example. However, the mapping mode doesn't change the origin. This means that our drawing will appear above the window and be invisible, as shown in Figure 28-2.

Table 28-1 Mapping Modes

Constant	One Logical Unit Is Interpreted As
MM_TEXT	One pixel (default)
MM_HIENGLISH	0.001 inch
MM_LOWENGLISH	0.01 inch
MM_HIMETRIC	0.01 millimeter
MM_LOWMETRIC	0.1 millimeter
MM_TWIPS	1/20 point (1/1440 inch)
MM_ISOTROPIC	Arbitrary (X-and Y-axes equal)
MM_ANISOTROPIC	Arbitrary (X-and Y-axes not equal)

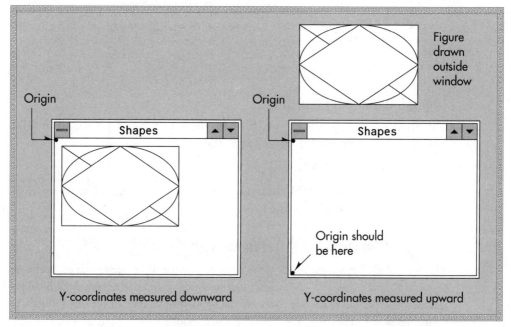

Figure 28-2 Y-Coordinates Measured Upward

If we want our drawing to be visible, we must move the origin to the bottom of the screen. The function that does this is SetViewPortOrg():

```
SetViewPortOrg(hDC, 0, yClient);
```

The arguments to this function are the device context and the X- and Y-coordinates of the new origin. These coordinates are always measured in device coordinates (pixels), rather than logical coordinates. Thus it isn't influenced by the mapping mode.

How do we know where to put the new origin? In our example we find the height of the client area of our window with GetClientRect(). We use the resulting value, yClient, as the Y-coordinate for SetViewPortOrg(), while leaving the X-coordinate at 0. This moves the origin to the lower left corner of the window. Figure 28-3 shows the output of the program.

The drawing now grows upward from the bottom of the window, rather than downward from the top. (This results in a mirror image, which explains why the diagonal line is reversed.)

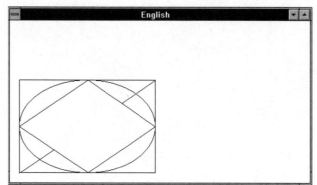

Figure 28-3
Output of
ENGLISH Program

SUMMARY

You draw graphics on the screen the same way as text: wait for a WM_PAINT message, execute BeginPaint(), use various GDI functions, and finish up with EndPaint(). (You can also use the GetDC() function, as we'll see soon.) Functions like Rectangle(), Ellipse(), and LineTo() do the actual drawing. The coordinates used by these functions are called logical coordinates. Normally they're specified in pixels, but you can change this so they're specified in physical units like inches and millimeters.

So far the figures we've drawn have all consisted of black lines on a white background. In the next chapter we'll see how to liven things up with colors and patterns.

PENS, BRUSHES, AND COLOR

*I*n this chapter we're going to look at two graphics objects: pens and brushes. These objects let us determine the color and other characteristics of lines and of closed figures like rectangles and ellipses. We'll show example programs that use both pens and brushes. But before we get into the details, let's stop for a minute to review the big picture.

GRAPHICS OBJECTS

Graphics objects are surprisingly abstract entities. What are they? And how are they used? How do they relate to another abstract entity, the device context? We touched on these issues in Chapter 15, *Stock Fonts*. Now let's examine the situation in a different way.

Why Are Graphics Objects Necessary?

You've seen that the functions used to draw graphics shapes are comparatively simple. The function to draw a rectangle, for example, takes only five arguments, four of which are the dimensions of the rectangle. It would be quite inconvenient if the function to draw a rectangle had to include all the additional data necessary to specify every aspect of the drawing process, such as the width and color of the rectangle's outline, the color and pattern of its interior, and other details. Graphics functions would become large and unwieldy.

For this reason the designers of Windows arranged to have many characteristics of the drawing process specified before any actual drawing takes place. These characteristics will then apply to *any* figure that's drawn. You specify that the line color is blue, for example, and following this all lines will be drawn in blue, until you specify a different color. This keeps graphics functions simple.

What Are Graphics Objects?

Groups of drawing characteristics (color, line width, and so on) are combined into entities called *graphics objects*. This makes them conceptually easier to understand, and easier for Windows to handle. The characteristics for drawing lines are combined into a graphics object called a *pen*, and the characteristics for filling the interiors of closed figures like rectangles are combined into an object called a *brush*. This imitates the real world of pen and paper, at least to some extent: a pen determines many things about how a line will be drawn, and a brush determines many things about how a surface will be painted.

In Windows you think about these groups of characteristics—these graphics objects—as being stored in a place called the *device context*. As we discussed in Chapter 15, you can imagine the device context as an artist (the kind that paints pictures). The artist has a paintbox that contains various graphics objects, but it can hold only one of each kind of object: one font, one pen, and one brush (so the analogy isn't perfect).

Telling Windows you want to use a certain set of characteristics is called *selecting an object into the device context*. Thus specifying how lines will be drawn is selecting a pen into the device context, and specifying how figures will be filled is selecting a brush into the device context. You can think of it as giving the painter a different pen or a different brush and taking away the old one. Really it's just substituting a new set of characteristics.

So much for abstract discussion. Let's see how objects work in actual programs.

PENS

Our first example program, PENS, draws the same design we saw in the SHAPES program, but it does it using four different pens for the four different graphics figures (rectangle, ellipse, line, and polygon). Figure 29-1 shows the output of PENS (unfortunately not in color).

As we saw with fonts, there are four aspects to using a graphics object. First you must create the new object. In the case of a pen, this is done with the CreatePen() function. Following this you must select the new object into the device context using SelectObject(). When you've finished using the new object, you must first restore the original one, using SelectObject() again, and then delete the new object with DeleteObject(). Here's the listing for PENS.C:

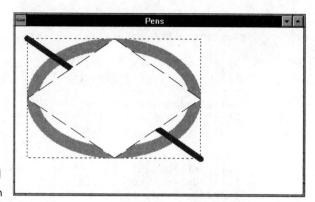

Figure 29-1

Output of PENS Program

```
// pens.c
// draws lines using different pens

#define STRICT
#include <windows.h>
                                 // prototype
LRESULT CALLBACK _export WndProc(HWND, UINT, WPARAM, LPARAM);

PSTR szProgName = "Pens";            // application name
#include "stdmain.inc"               // standard WinMain() function
///////////////////////////////////////////////////////////////////
// main window procedure -- receives messages                    //
///////////////////////////////////////////////////////////////////
LRESULT CALLBACK _export WndProc(HWND hWnd, UINT msg,
                            WPARAM wParam, LPARAM lParam)
   {
   HDC hDC;
   PAINTSTRUCT ps;
   HPEN hOldPen;

   int xLeft=20, yTop=20, xRight=320, yBottom=220;
   POINT apt[] = { {20, 120}, {170, 20}, {319, 120}, {170, 219} };

   static HPEN hBluePen, hInsidePen, hRedDotPen, hDashPen;

   switch(msg)
      {
      case WM_CREATE:                        // create pens
         hBluePen =   CreatePen(PS_DOT, 1, RGB(0,0,255) );   // blue
                                                             // cyan
         hInsidePen = CreatePen(PS_INSIDEFRAME, 20, RGB(0,255,255));
         hRedDotPen = CreatePen(PS_SOLID, 10, RGB(255,0,0)); // red
         hDashPen =   CreatePen(PS_DASH, 1, RGB(0,0,0) );   // black
         break;

      case WM_PAINT:
         hDC = BeginPaint(hWnd, &ps);
```

```
        hOldPen = SelectObject(hDC, hBluePen);  // select blue pen
        Rectangle(hDC, xLeft, yTop, xRight, yBottom);  // draw rect

        SelectObject(hDC, hInsidePen);              // select inside pen
        Ellipse(hDC, xLeft, yTop, xRight, yBottom);  // draw ellipse

        SelectObject(hDC, hRedDotPen);              // select red pen
        MoveTo(hDC, xLeft, yTop);                   // draw line
        LineTo(hDC, xRight, yBottom);

        SelectObject(hDC, hDashPen);                // select dash pen
        Polygon(hDC, apt, 4);                       // draw polygon
        SelectObject(hDC, hOldPen);                 // restore old pen
        EndPaint(hWnd, &ps);
        break;

    case WM_DESTROY:
        DeleteObject(hBluePen);                     // delete new pens
        DeleteObject(hInsidePen);
        DeleteObject(hRedDotPen);
        DeleteObject(hDashPen);

        PostQuitMessage(0);
        break;

    default:
        return( DefWindowProc(hWnd, msg, wParam, lParam) );
    }   // end switch(msg)
   return 0L;
}   // end WndProc
```

We use four pens in the program. They're created when we receive a WM_CREATE message, selected into the device context when we receive WM_PAINT, and deleted from the system when we receive WM_DESTROY.

You can create, select, and delete objects at other points in the program. For instance, you might create, select, use, and delete an object all while processing WM_PAINT, as we'll see in the next chapter. But no matter how you do it, remember to delete any graphics objects you create. Failure to do so means that the object remains in memory after your program terminates, taking up valuable space. If you create too many objects without deleting them, your system will begin to have problems, and eventually it will die. Here's the sequence, as demonstrated by the first pen we create in our example:

```
hBluePen = CreatePen(PS_DOT, 1, RGB(0,0,255));  // create new pen
...
hOldPen = SelectObject(hDC, hBluePen);              // select new pen into DC
...
SelectObject(hDC, hOldPen);                         // restore original pen
...
DeleteObject(hBluePen);                             // delete new pen
```

Real Windows gurus like to make things very efficient, so if they're selecting the old object and deleting the new one at the same time, they do it like this:

```
DeleteObject( SelectObject(hDC, hOldPen) );
```

This works because, besides selecting hOldPen, SelectObject() returns the handle of the existing object, which is then used as an argument to, and deleted by, DeleteObject().

The pen currently selected into the device context determines how lines will be drawn, so by selecting different pens we can change the characteristics of what we draw. We use a different pen for each graphics element in PENS.

Pens have three characteristics: style, width, and color. These are the three arguments to the CreatePen() function.

Style

Style determines whether the line drawn by a pen is solid, or has a pattern, like dots or dashes. Figure 29-2 shows the possibilities.

The styles that produce broken lines, PS_DASH, PS_DOT, and so on, can be used only when the width of the line is 1 unit. If you use a wider pen, the pattern reverts to a solid line.

When you draw a closed figure like a rectangle or ellipse, the frame or outline of the figure will be drawn using the current pen. If you're using a thick pen, there are several ways the line could be drawn. Normally it's drawn so the center of the line lies on top of the frame. However, sometimes you want the line, no matter how thick, to remain completely inside the frame. That's what the PS_INSIDEFRAME style is for. Figure 29-3 shows these possibilities.

In the PENS example the ellipse is drawn using the PS_INSIDEFRAME style. You can see that the outline lies just inside the ellipse's frame.

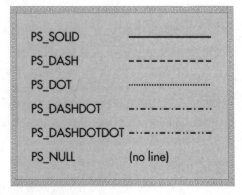

Figure 29-2 Pen Styles

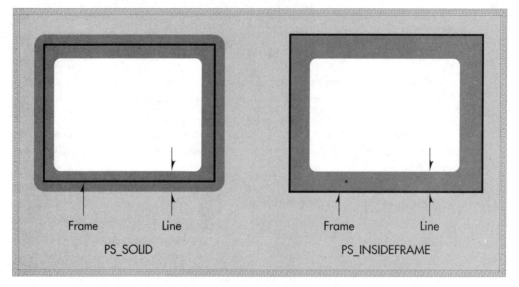

Figure 29-3 PS_SOLID and PS_INSIDEFRAME

Width and Color

The final two arguments to CreatePen() specify the width and color to be used for drawing lines. The width is given in logical units; pixels in this example. We draw the rectangle and polygon with a pen width of 1, and the ellipse and line with widths of 20 and 10, respectively. Remember that you can't use a width greater than 1 on dashed or dotted lines.

Color is a complex issue we'll discuss in the next section. Briefly, RGB is a macro used to create color values. Its three arguments specify the amount of red, green, and blue in the color. Thus RGB(0,0,255) specifies blue, RGB(0,255,255) is cyan, RGB(255,0,0) is red, and RGB(0,0,0) is black.

Stock Pens

In addition to creating your own custom pens as we described above, you can also choose from three *stock pens*. These are handled in much the same way as custom pens, except that instead of using the CreatePen() function to obtain a pen handle, you use the GetStockObject() function (discussed in Chapter 15, *Stock Fonts*). There are three stock pens: black, white, and invisible. Here's how you get the handle for the white pen:

```
hPen = GetStockObject(WHITE_PEN);
```

Stock pens are represented by the constants BLACK_PEN, WHITE_PEN, and NULL_PEN. Stock objects are built into Windows; you don't need to create them,

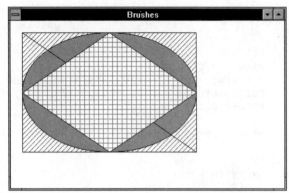

Figure 29-4

Output of BRUSHES Program

so they don't use up system resources. The black stock pen is the default; you've been using it all along. The white pen is useful for drawing on dark backgrounds. If you're going to draw in black or white, you should consider using them. The null pen doesn't draw any line at all. As with other stock objects, you should not attempt to delete stock pens.

BRUSHES

A brush is a graphics object whose characteristics determine the pattern and color to be used when filling a closed figure like a rectangle or ellipse. Our example program, BRUSHES, uses three different brushes to fill the same three closed figures we saw in SHAPES. The rectangle is filled with a red diagonally hatched pattern, the ellipse with a solid cyan, and the polygon with a green cross-hatched pattern. Note that the *outline* of a shape—as opposed to its interior—is determined by the pen, not the brush. In this example the default pen is used throughout, so all the shapes are outlined by a black line one pixel wide. Figure 29-4 shows how this looks.

Notice that each graphics element lies on top of the ones drawn earlier; they aren't transparent. Here's the listing for BRUSHES.C:

```
// brushes.c
// fills shapes with color and pattern

#define STRICT
#include <windows.h>
                                  // prototype
LRESULT CALLBACK _export WndProc(HWND, UINT, WPARAM, LPARAM);

PSTR szProgName = "Brushes";      // application name
#include "stdmain.inc"            // standard WinMain() function
//////////////////////////////////////////////////////////////
// main window procedure -- receives messages                //
//////////////////////////////////////////////////////////////
```

```
LRESULT CALLBACK _export WndProc(HWND hWnd, UINT msg,
                                 WPARAM wParam, LPARAM lParam)
   {
   HDC hDC;
   PAINTSTRUCT ps;
   int xLeft=20, yTop=20, xRight=320, yBottom=220;
   POINT apt[] = { {20, 120}, {170, 20}, {319, 120}, {170, 219} };
   HBRUSH hOldBrush;
                                               // declare brushes
   static HBRUSH hRedBrush, hCyanBrush, hGreenBrush;


   switch(msg)
      {
      case WM_CREATE:                          // create brushes
         hCyanBrush = CreateSolidBrush( RGB(0,255,255) ); // cyan
                                       // red diagonal pattern
         hRedBrush =   CreateHatchBrush( HS_BDIAGONAL, RGB(255,0,0) );
                                       // green cross pattern
         hGreenBrush = CreateHatchBrush( HS_CROSS, RGB(0,255,0) );
         break;

      case WM_PAINT:
         hDC = BeginPaint(hWnd, &ps);
                                          // select brush
         hOldBrush = SelectObject(hDC, hRedBrush);
         Rectangle(hDC, xLeft, yTop, xRight, yBottom);

         SelectObject(hDC, hCyanBrush);    // select brush
         Ellipse(hDC, xLeft, yTop, xRight, yBottom);

         MoveTo(hDC, xLeft, yTop);
         LineTo(hDC, xRight, yBottom);
         SelectObject(hDC, hGreenBrush);   // select brush
         Polygon(hDC, apt, 4);

         SelectObject(hDC, hOldBrush);     // restore old brush
         EndPaint(hWnd, &ps);
         break;

      case WM_DESTROY:
         DeleteObject(hRedBrush);          // delete brushes
         DeleteObject(hCyanBrush);
         DeleteObject(hGreenBrush);
         PostQuitMessage(0);
         break;

      default:
         return( DefWindowProc(hWnd, msg, wParam, lParam) );
      }  // end switch(msg)
   return 0L;
   }  // end WndProc
```

Brushes are used in much the same way as pens. Once they're created, the same functions, SelectObject() and DeleteObject(), are used to select them and delete them. However, creating the brushes requires different functions. There are two possibilities, depending on whether the brush will apply a solid color or a pattern: CreateSolidBrush() and CreateHatchBrush(). Here's how the three brushes are created in BRUSHES:

```
hCyanBrush = CreateSolidBrush( RGB(0,255,255) );
hRedBrush = CreateHatchBrush( HS_DIAGONAL, RGB(255,0,0) );
hGreeenBrush = CreateHatchBrush( HS_CROSS, RGB(0,255,0) );
```

CreateSolidBrush() takes only one argument, the color to be used for filling. CreateHatchBrush() takes two: a style and a color. Style in this context means pattern. The possible styles are shown in Figure 29-5.

Stock Brushes

Windows comes with several stock brushes. As with stock fonts and pens, stock brushes are built into Windows so you don't consume system resources by using them. Table 29-1 shows the available stock brushes.

Our next example program, STOCKBRU, uses three stock brushes to create the same figure as in BRUSHES, but filled with different patterns, as shown in Figure 29-6.

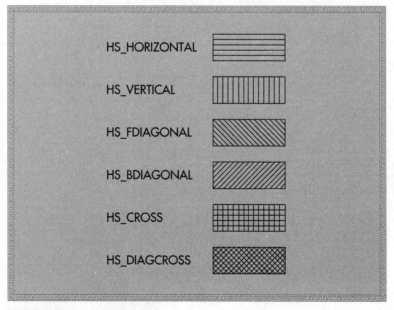

Figure 29-5 Hatch Brush Styles

Table 29-1 Stock Brushes

Constant	Resulting Solid Fill
WHITE_BRUSH	White
BLACK_BRUSH	Black
LTGRAY_BRUSH	Light gray
GRAY_BRUSH	Gray
DKGRAY_BRUSH	Dark gray
NULL_BRUSH	Transparent
HOLLOW_BRUSH	Same as NULL_BRUSH

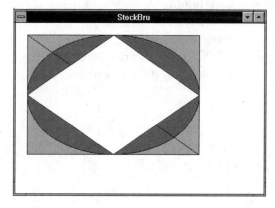

Figure 29-6
Output of STOCKBRU Program

Here's the listing for STOCKBRU.C:

```
// stockbru.c
// fills shapes using stock brushes

#define STRICT
#include <windows.h>
                                        // prototype
LRESULT CALLBACK _export WndProc(HWND, UINT, WPARAM, LPARAM);

PSTR szProgName = "StockBru";           // application name
#include "stdmain.inc"                  // standard WinMain() function
/////////////////////////////////////////////////////////////////////
// main window procedure -- receives messages                       //
/////////////////////////////////////////////////////////////////////
```

```
LRESULT CALLBACK _export WndProc(HWND hWnd, UINT msg,
                                 WPARAM wParam, LPARAM lParam)
   {
   HDC hDC;
   PAINTSTRUCT ps;
   int xLeft=20, yTop=20, xRight=320, yBottom=220;
   POINT apt[] = { {20, 120}, {170, 20}, {319, 120}, {170, 219} };
   HBRUSH hOldBrush;
                                          // declare brushes
   static HBRUSH hLtGrayBrush, hGrayBrush, hWhiteBrush;

   switch(msg)
      {
      case WM_CREATE:                     // create stock brushes
          hLtGrayBrush =  GetStockObject(LTGRAY_BRUSH);
          hGrayBrush =  GetStockObject(GRAY_BRUSH);
          hWhiteBrush = GetStockObject(WHITE_BRUSH);
          break;

      case WM_PAINT:
          hDC = BeginPaint(hWnd, &ps);
                                          // select brush
          hOldBrush = SelectObject(hDC, hLtGrayBrush);
          Rectangle(hDC, xLeft, yTop, xRight, yBottom);

          SelectObject(hDC, hGrayBrush);    // select brush
          Ellipse(hDC, xLeft, yTop, xRight, yBottom);

          MoveTo(hDC, xLeft, yTop);
          LineTo(hDC, xRight, yBottom);

          SelectObject(hDC, hWhiteBrush);   // select brush
          Polygon(hDC, apt, 4);

          SelectObject(hDC, hOldBrush);     // restore old brush
          EndPaint(hWnd, &ps);
          break;

      case WM_DESTROY:
          PostQuitMessage(0);
          break;
      default:
          return( DefWindowProc(hWnd, msg, wParam, lParam) );
      }    // end switch(msg)
    return 0L;
   }  // end WndProc
```

We use this statement to obtain the handle to the first stock brush:

```
hGrayBrush = GetStockObject(LTGRAY_BRUSH);
```

Remember: do not delete stock brushes.

COLOR

Color provides one of the most exciting differences between Windows and old-fashioned character-mode programs. Not only is an application that employs color more fun to use, it can actually make the application easier to operate. A good example is the color-coding of the different program elements (comments, constants, keywords, and so on) in Turbo C++ for Windows.

Enough Colors?

Most computers that have the graphics capability to run Windows also have color. (The exceptions these days are mostly laptop systems.) This is another plus for the Windows programmer, who can assume that a color display is available in most cases.

However, while you may be able to assume color capability, the number of available colors varies greatly from one system to another. You may have an EGA system with 16 colors, or a super VGA system with 256 colors. The minimum is 4 colors in some old CGA systems, and the maximum is 16.7 million, available with specialized adaptors.

This spectrum of color capabilities leads to a potential problem: what happens if a program specifies that something be drawn in a certain color, but the system it's running on can't reproduce that color?

Windows deals with this situation in somewhat the same way it deals with fonts. It does its best to match the specified color, and if it can't match it exactly, it tries to come as close as possible. It can do this in two ways. It can pick a solid color that's as close as possible to the specified color, or it can create a *dithered* color to imitate the original color.

Dithering is mixing pixels of several different colors to create another color. A similar process takes place in magazine illustrations, where dots of a few primary colors are combined to create a full spectrum. You can usually tell when a color has been created by dithering: there is a characteristic texture that results from the intermixing of different-colored pixels. Depending on your graphics system, you may have the opportunity to see dithered colors when you run the EZCOLOR example, coming up soon.

Specifying Colors

Images on a typical computer screen are created by turning on small phosphor dots. These dots come in three colors: red, green, and blue. You can verify this for yourself by using a strong (say 10-power) magnifying glass to examine the surface of your display screen. Figure 29-7 shows these dots.

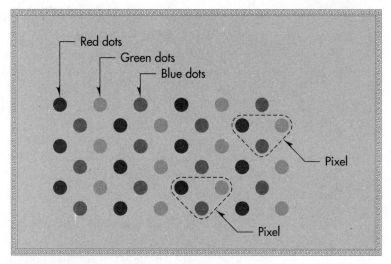

Figure 29-7 Phosphor Dots on the Display Screen

A pixel consists of three phosphor dots, one of each color. Each dot can appear in a range of intensities. The color of a pixel can be changed by varying the relative intensities of the three dots. To make pure red, the red dot is turned on, and the green and blue dots are turned off. To make magenta, the red and blue dots are turned on, and the green dot is turned off. Just as they told you in grade-school science class, white is made up of primary colors: the red, green, and blue dots are all turned on. Black results from turning off all three colors.

Many Windows functions take an argument that specifies a color value. CreatePen() and CreateSolidBrush() are examples. In these functions the color is specified using the derived type COLORREF, which is typedefed to be the same as DWORD, a 4-byte unsigned value. Of these four bytes, one is unused, one determines the amount of red in the color, one the amount of green, and the last one the amount of blue. Figure 29-8 shows how these bytes are arranged.

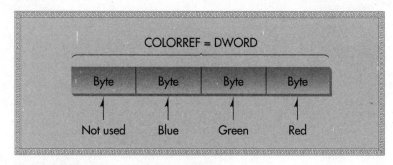

Figure 29-8 The COLORREF Data Type

The value of each byte can run from 0 to 255. A COLORREF specification thus includes 256 shades of red, 256 of green, and 256 of blue. The total number of colors you can specify with this arrangement is 256 times 256 times 256, or 16,777,216. This is enough colors for almost any situation. Even the most advanced display hardware does not exceed these limits.

Table 29-2 shows some typical colors and the values of red, green, and blue used to create them.

The RGB macro simplifies the creation of COLORREF values by putting together three bytes representing individual color values into one variable of type COLORREF. For example, the statement

```
rgbColor = RGB(255,0,0);
```

would give the rgbColor variable a value corresponding to red. In previous programs we used this macro to specify the colors for pens and brushes.

As we noted, even though your program specifies a certain color out of the 16.7 million possibilities, the graphics system in your computer may not be able to reproduce it. A color specified as RGB(175,37,76), for example, may be translated to something simpler, like RGB(255,0,128), or it may be dithered.

Table 29-2 Typical RGB Values

Color	Red	Green	Blue
Black	0	0	0
Red	255	0	0
Green	0	255	0
Blue	0	0	255
Yellow	255	255	0
Magenta	255	0	255
Cyan	0	255	255
White	255	255	255
Dark gray	128	128	128
Light gray	192	192	192
Olive	128	128	0
Orange	255	128	0
Dark brown	128	64	0

The Color Common Dialog

The best way to see how Windows handles colors is to experiment with a program that allows you to select different colors using color swatches, or squares of color. This is much more natural than choosing color names from a list. Fortunately, Windows provides a powerful common dialog box for this purpose. The Color common dialog is definitely another "Excalibur" Windows feature; it provides a great deal of almost magical power. It not only allows you to choose colors from color swatches, it shows you the RGB values of the color you've chosen, and lets you create new custom colors and display them.

Our example program invokes the Color common dialog and, when the user has selected a color, displays a rectangle in this color. Figure 29-9 shows the Color common dialog.

This dialog displays 48 "basic" colors on the upper left. (You may not actually see 48 different colors, since your system may not be capable of reproducing them all.) You can also choose from among 16 "custom" colors, displayed on the lower left.

Notice in the Color common dialog that the proportions of red, green, and blue for the selected color are displayed on the right, as numerical values. You can choose a color and examine the resulting values, or type in values and see the resulting colors. Comparing the values with the colors they produce will soon give you a feeling for how the RGB values relate to actual colors.

You can also use the Color common dialog to create your own custom colors. Use the mouse to move the pointer around in the large colored square. You can adjust the hue (color) by going left and right, and the saturation (grayness) by going up and down. You can adjust the luminosity (blackness or whiteness) with the slide on the far right. Once you've selected a color, you can click on the Add To Custom Colors button to insert the new color into one of the 16 Custom Color blocks.

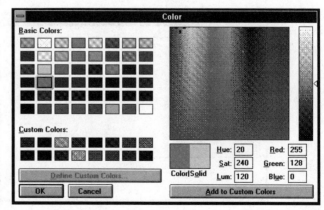

Figure 29-9

Color Common Dialog

If your system doesn't support a particular color in pure form, the color may be displayed as a dithered color. The color swatch will show a pattern made of several different colors, which approximates, with varying degrees of success, the color you want.

The EZCOLOR Example

We use a menu selection to bring up the Color common dialog, so our program, EZCOLOR, requires a resource file with one menu item. Here's the listing for EZCOLOR.RC:

```
// ezcolor.rc
// resource script file for ezcolor

#include "ezcolor.h"

ezColor MENU  // name must agree with szProgName
   BEGIN
      MENUITEM "&Color", IDM_COLOR
   END
```

The header file is correspondingly short. Here's the listing for EZCOLOR.H:

```
// ezcolor.h
// header file for ezcolor

#define IDM_COLOR    100
```

It's easy to program the Color common dialog. We do that when we receive a WM_COMMAND message with a wParam value of IDM_COLOR, as a result of the user selecting the Color menu item. Then we display a rectangle using the color value selected. Figure 29-10 shows the resulting output (unfortunately in black and white).

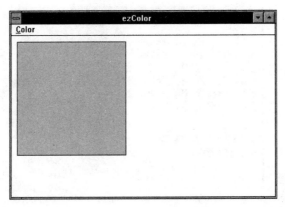

Figure 29-10

Output of EZCOLOR Program

Here's the listing for EZCOLOR.C:

```
// ezcolor.c
// demonstrates Color common dialog

#define STRICT
#include <windows.h>
#include <commdlg.h>            // for ChooseColor()
#include "ezcolor.h"            // header file for IDM_OPEN, etc.

LRESULT CALLBACK _export WndProc(HWND, UINT, WPARAM, LPARAM);

PSTR szProgName = "ezColor";           // application name
#include "stdmain.inc"                 // standard WinMain function
///////////////////////////////////////////////////////////////
// main window procedure -- receives messages                 //
///////////////////////////////////////////////////////////////
LRESULT CALLBACK _export WndProc(HWND hWnd, UINT msg,
                                 WPARAM wParam, LPARAM lParam)
   {
   HDC hDC;
   PAINTSTRUCT ps;
   int xLeft=10, yTop=10, xRight=200, yBottom=200;

   CHOOSECOLOR chc;                       // color info structure
   COLORREF rgbCustColors[16];            // custom colors
   static COLORREF rgbColor = RGB(0,0,0); // current color
   static HBRUSH hBrush;                  // brush handles
   HBRUSH hOldBrush;

   switch(msg)
      {
      case WM_COMMAND:                    // user selects a menu item
         switch(wParam)                   // wParam holds item ID
            {
            case IDM_COLOR:               // user selects Color
               chc.lStructSize = sizeof(CHOOSECOLOR);
               chc.hwndOwner = hWnd;
               chc.rgbResult = rgbColor;
               chc.lpCustColors = rgbCustColors;
               chc.Flags = CC_FULLOPEN | CC_RGBINIT;

               if( ChooseColor(&chc) )
                  {
                  rgbColor = chc.rgbResult;
                  InvalidateRect(hWnd, NULL, TRUE);
                  }
               break;
            }    // end switch wParam
         break;  // end case WM_COMMAND

      case WM_PAINT:
         hDC = BeginPaint(hWnd, &ps);
```

```
        hBrush = CreateSolidBrush(rgbColor);    // brush in new color
        hOldBrush = SelectObject(hDC, hBrush); // select brush
                                                // draw rectangle
        Rectangle(hDC, xLeft, yTop, xRight, yBottom);
        SelectObject(hDC, hOldBrush);           // restore old brush
        DeleteObject(hBrush);                   // delete new brush
        EndPaint(hWnd, &ps);
        break;

    case WM_DESTROY:
        PostQuitMessage(0);
        break;
    default:
        return( DefWindowProc(hWnd, msg, wParam, lParam) );
    }    // end switch(msg)
 return OL;
}   // end WndProc
```

The programming for the Color common dialog is similar to that of the other common dialogs. You first set up a structure of type CHOOSECOLOR, then you call the ChooseColor() function. This function returns a Boolean value indicating whether the operation was successful.

A key variable in this program is rgbColor. The user chooses a color from the Color common dialog, and the ChooseColor() function causes this color value to be assigned to rgbColor. In EZCOLOR we use this value in the CreateSolidBrush() function to specify the color of the rectangle. Every time the color changes, we execute InvalidateRect() so the rectangle will be redrawn in the new color.

DRAWING MODES

When you draw a line, you probably expect it to appear on the screen in the color of the current pen. If you draw a blue line on a red background, for example, you expect the resulting line to be blue. However, in the world of graphics things aren't necessarily so simple.

Suppose you want to draw a line across a background that consists of areas of many different colors, but you want the line to stand out against whatever color it's on. If the color of the line is limited to the pen color, it will disappear when it crosses a background area of that same color. A blue line on a blue background is invisible. What to do?

It turns out that Windows includes a sophisticated way of handling the interaction of a line drawn on a background color. This is called the *drawing mode* or *raster operation* (ROP). There are 16 drawing modes. Some of them are rather obscure; it's hard to imagine when they would be used. Table 29-3 shows a few of the most useful—or at least the most comprehensible—drawing modes.

Table 29-3 Some Drawing Mode Values

Constant	Line Drawn on Background Is Colored
R2_BLACK	Black
R2_WHITE	White
R2_NOP	Same as background color (so it's invisible)
R2_NOT	Inverse of background color (always visible)
R2_COPYPEN	Same as pen color (default)
R2_NOTCOPYPEN	Inverse of pen color

These modes are set using the SetROP2() function, which takes as its two arguments the device context handle and a mode constant:

```
SetROP2(hDC, R2_COPYPEN);
```

The R2_COPYPEN mode is the default. It draws a line using the current pen color, no matter what color the background is. This is usually what you want. Another useful mode is R2_NOT. It draws a line that is the *inverse of the background* (so it's not related to the pen color at all). Such a line is always visible, no matter what colors it crosses. Not only that, but if you use this mode to draw a line, and then draw another line in the same place, the line will disappear, restoring the background to its original state. This is because the inverse of the inverse is the original color. We're going to make use of this drawing mode in the next chapter.

SUMMARY

Pens and brushes are graphics objects that are selected into the device context. The currently selected pen determines how all subsequent lines will be drawn, whether they are stand-alone lines, or the outlines of closed figures like rectangles and ellipses. The currently selected brush determines how closed figures will be filled: what color will be used, and whether there will be a pattern.

Like other graphics objects, pens and brushes are first created using specialized functions. This can be done at any time before they are selected. The SelectObject() function is used to select a pen or brush into the device context. After this function is executed, the pen or brush will determine how all subsequent line-drawing or figure-fills are carried out. Before exiting, and sooner if possible, pens and brushes must be removed from the system with the DeleteObject() function.

Remember not to delete a graphics object while it is still selected into the device context. Use SelectObject() to reselect the original object back into the DC first. Then delete the new object. (Also, don't delete stock objects, which are a permanent part of the system.)

30

THE MOUSE AND GRAPHICS

So far we've talked about graphics output: how to draw different figures on the screen. What about graphics input? In Windows the mouse is the indispensible input device. You can use it to indicate points on the screen, to drag objects to different locations, and even to create freehand drawings. If you had to type in the coordinates to perform these activities you might go mad, but the mouse makes it easy.

In this chapter we're going to show how the mouse can allow the user to draw simple graphics shapes. In the next chapter we'll put this capability together with what we've learned in previous chapters to create a mini paint program.

DRAWING PIXELS WITH THE MOUSE

Windows provides functions for drawing many geometrical elements: lines, ellipses, rectangles, and so on. But sometimes none of these elements are just what you want, and you must fall back on placing individual pixels on the screen. Our next example shows how to do this using the mouse. It permits you to draw almost any figure, if you have enough patience. All you need to do is hold down the left mouse button and move the mouse. A trail of pixels will appear on the screen. If you move the pointer slowly you'll see a solid line, as shown in Figure 30-1.

If you move more rapidly the pixels will appear as a series of dots; the faster you go, the farther apart they'll be separated.

Figure 30-1

Output of MOUPIXEL Program

The only file necessary for this program is the source file. Here's the listing for MOUPIXEL.C:

```c
// moupixel.c
// draws pixels on screen using mouse

#define STRICT
#include <windows.h>
                                           // prototype
LRESULT CALLBACK _export WndProc(HWND, UINT, WPARAM, LPARAM);

PSTR szProgName = "MouPixel";         // application name
#include "stdmain.inc"                // standard WinMain() function
///////////////////////////////////////////////////////////////////
// main window procedure -- receives messages                     //
///////////////////////////////////////////////////////////////////
LRESULT CALLBACK _export WndProc(HWND hWnd, UINT msg,
                                 WPARAM wParam, LPARAM lParam)
   {
   HDC hDC;

   switch(msg)
      {
      case WM_MOUSEMOVE:                        // mouse moved
         if(wParam & MK_LBUTTON)                // left button was down
            {
            hDC = GetDC(hWnd);                  // open DC

            SetPixel( hDC, LOWORD(lParam),      // draw the point
                           HIWORD(lParam), RGB(0,0,0) );
            ReleaseDC(hWnd, hDC);               // close DC
            }
         break;

      case WM_DESTROY:
         PostQuitMessage(0);
         break;
      default:
```

```
        return( DefWindowProc(hWnd, msg, wParam, lParam) );
    }   // end switch(msg)
 return OL;
 }  // end WndProc
```

This program is short, but it introduces a new message, WM_MOUSEMOVE, and a new function, SetPixel().

The WM_MOUSEMOVE Message

Your window procedure receives a WM_MOUSEMOVE message every time the mouse moves. It doesn't matter whether the mouse buttons are pressed or what else is happening, as long as the mouse is moving you'll get a series of these messages.

The wParam value that accompanies this message indicates whether a mouse button or various keyboard keys were pressed when the mouse moved. Table 30-1 shows the possible values.

These values take the form of bits set in wParam. Any of these states can be set or not set, independently of the others. We use MK_LBUTTON to see if the left button is pressed when the mouse moves by ANDing it with wParam:

```
if(wParam & MK_LBUTTON)
```

If the left button is pressed, we draw the pixel at the mouse cursor location. The lParam value carries the coordinates of the mouse cursor. The low-order word is the X-coordinate, and the high-order word is the Y-coordinate. We extract these values with the LOWORD and HIWORD macros, as we've seen before, and use them as arguments to the SetPixel() function.

Table 30-1 wParam Values for WM_MOUSEMOVE

Constant	When Mouse Moved
MK_LBUTTON	Left mouse button was down
MK_MBUTTON	Middle mouse button was down
MK_RBUTTON	Right mouse button was down
MK_CONTROL	CTRL key was down
MK_SHIFT	SHIFT key was down

The SetPixel() Function

We place an individual pixel on the screen with SetPixel(). This function takes four arguments: the device context handle, the X- and Y-coordinates of the pixel, and the pixel's color, which is a variable of type COLORREF.

In the majority of cases we display information on the screen when, and only when, we receive a WM_PAINT message. In MOUPIXEL, however, we want to display a new pixel whenever the mouse is moved (if the left button is pressed). We saw how to deal with a similar situation in Chapter 21, *Text Input: The Hard Way*, where we introduced the GetDC() function. This function obtains a device context, and allows display functions to be executed, when no WM_PAINT message has been received. We'll make extensive use of GetDC() in this chapter. Remember that GetDC() is always matched with the ReleaseDC() function, which frees the device context.

DRAWING LINES WITH THE MOUSE

We've seen how to draw freehand lines created from individual pixels. We can also use the mouse to create straight lines. In our next example, the user presses the left mouse button at the point where the line should begin, and moves the mouse, keeping the button depressed. As the mouse moves, a line "rubber-bands" or appears to stretch from the starting point to the mouse cursor. A whole series of lines is drawn as the mouse moves, but each one is erased when a new one is drawn, so there is only one line at any given moment. At the point where the user wants the line to end, the button is released. This "disconnects" the line from the mouse; and makes the line permanent. Figure 30-2 shows some lines drawn using our example program, MOULINE1.

The programming for line-drawing is a bit more complicated than it is for a series of pixels. We must examine a new message, and apply one of the drawing modes or ROPs (raster operations) discussed in the last chapter. We'll also introduce a new macro for dealing with points. Here's the listing for MOULINE1.C:

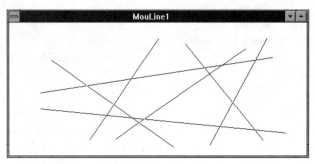

Figure 30-2
Output of the
MOULINE1 Program

```
// mouline1.c
// draws lines on screen using mouse

#define STRICT
#include <windows.h>
                                // prototype
LRESULT CALLBACK _export WndProc(HWND, UINT, WPARAM, LPARAM);

PSTR szProgName = "MouLine1";  // application name
#include "stdmain.inc"         // standard WinMain()
/////////////////////////////////////////////////////////////////
// main window procedure -- receives messages                  //
/////////////////////////////////////////////////////////////////
LRESULT CALLBACK _export WndProc(HWND hWnd, UINT msg,
                              WPARAM wParam, LPARAM lParam)
    {
    static POINT ptBegin, ptNew, ptOld;
    HDC hDC;

    switch(msg)
        {
        case WM_LBUTTONDOWN:
            ptBegin = MAKEPOINT(lParam);           // save start point
            ptOld = ptBegin;
            break;

        case WM_MOUSEMOVE:
            if(wParam & MK_LBUTTON)
                {
                ptNew = MAKEPOINT(lParam);         // latest point
                hDC = GetDC(hWnd);                  // open DC

                SetROP2(hDC, R2_NOT);              // opposite of bkgrnd
                MoveTo(hDC, ptBegin.x, ptBegin.y); // erase old line
                LineTo(hDC, ptOld.x, ptOld.y);
                MoveTo(hDC, ptBegin.x, ptBegin.y); // draw new line
                LineTo(hDC, ptNew.x, ptNew.y);

                ReleaseDC(hWnd, hDC);              // close DC
                ptOld = ptNew;                     // old becomes new
                }
            break;

        case WM_DESTROY:
            PostQuitMessage(0);
            break;
        default:
            return( DefWindowProc(hWnd, msg, wParam, lParam) );
        }   // end switch(msg)
    return 0L;
    }   // end WndProc
```

The WM_LBUTTONDOWN Message

In order to know where the user wants to start drawing the line, we want to record where the mouse cursor is at the moment when the left button is first pressed. To do this, we intercept the WM_LBUTTONDOWN message. Just as WM_MOUSEMOVE did, this message returns a constant in wParam indicating if another mouse button or the (SHIFT) or (CTRL) key is pressed. We don't use this information. We do use the coordinates of the mouse pointer, which are returned in lParam. However, we use a new macro to extract the coordinates, instead of LOWORD and HIWORD as in the last example.

The MAKEPOINT Macro

When we start talking about several different points in the same program, it becomes conceptually easier to use a single variable that represents a point, rather than two variables that represent the two coordinates of a point. We've already discussed the POINT structure in Chapter 28, *Drawing Shapes,* where it was required by the Polygon() function. Here we use POINT variables to hold three points. The ptBegin variable records where the left button was pressed, ptNew holds the current location of the mouse cursor, and ptOld is the last location of the mouse cursor.

A macro, MAKEPOINT, defined in WINDOWS.H, is convenient for converting the two coordinates of a point from their packed format in lParam, into members of the POINT structure.

Erasing the Old Line

The tricky part of MOULINE1 is erasing each old line before drawing the new one. This is what creates the rubber-band effect, where a line appears to move without leaving any trace of its former position.

To carry out this operation we use the SetROP2() function to draw the lines. As we noted earlier, this function, when used with the R2_NOT drawing mode, draws a line that is always the inverse color of the background. This makes the line visible against any background. Also, when the same line is drawn twice using this mode, the original background is restored. This makes it easy to erase a line: we just draw another line on top of the previous one.

When we get a WM_LBUTTONDOWN message, we record the point as ptBegin. That's where we'll start drawing our new line. We give ptOld the same value; we'll see how this variable is used next.

When we get a WM_MOUSEMOVE message, we record the current point as ptNew. Then we draw over the old line, which runs from ptBegin, where the mouse button was pressed, to ptOld, which is the previous ptNew. We draw the new line

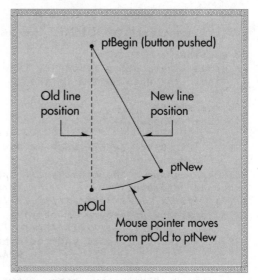

Figure 30-3 Rubber-Banding

from ptBegin to ptNew, and finally set ptOld to ptNew so the process can start again. Figure 30-3 shows how this looks.

Fixing the Intersection Problem

There's a subtle defect in MOULINE1, which you can see if you draw two lines that lie almost on top of each other, as shown in Figure 30-4.

The problem occurs where the lines intersect: if both lines occupy the same space, the result is white instead of black. Normally we want an entire line to be black (or another color); we don't want it to be white just because some other line crosses it. This problem is a consequence of the drawing mode we used to simplify erasing the old lines.

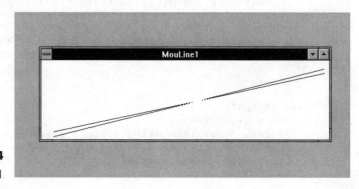

Figure 30-4
Defect in MOULINE1

The solution is to redraw the line when the user lifts the left mouse button. Our next example, MOULINE2, does just that. Here's the listing for MOULINE2.C:

```
// mouline2.c
// draws lines, using temporary lines while dragging,
// final line when button lifted

#define STRICT
#include <windows.h>
                                // prototype
LRESULT CALLBACK _export WndProc(HWND, UINT, WPARAM, LPARAM);

PSTR szProgName = "MouLine2";   // application name
#include "stdmain.inc"          // standard WinMain()
///////////////////////////////////////////////////////////////////
// main window procedure -- receives messages                     //
///////////////////////////////////////////////////////////////////
LRESULT CALLBACK _export WndProc(HWND hWnd, UINT msg,
                                 WPARAM wParam, LPARAM lParam)
    {
    static POINT ptBegin, ptNew, ptOld;
    HDC hDC;

    switch(msg)
        {
        case WM_LBUTTONDOWN:
            ptBegin = MAKEPOINT(lParam);        // get starting point
            ptOld = ptBegin;                    // it's first old point
            break;

        case WM_MOUSEMOVE:                      // mouse moves and
            if(wParam & MK_LBUTTON)             // left button is down
                {
                ptNew = MAKEPOINT(lParam);      // get current point
                hDC = GetDC(hWnd);              // open DC
                // draw temporary lines using R2_NOT drawing mode
                SetROP2(hDC, R2_NOT);           // opposite of bkgnd
                MoveTo(hDC, ptBegin.x, ptBegin.y); // erase old line
                LineTo(hDC, ptOld.x,   ptOld.y);
                MoveTo(hDC, ptBegin.x, ptBegin.y); // draw new line
                LineTo(hDC, ptNew.x,   ptNew.y);

                ReleaseDC(hWnd, hDC);           // close DC
                ptOld = ptNew;                  // old becomes new
                }
            break;

        case WM_LBUTTONUP:
            hDC = GetDC(hWnd);                  // open DC
            // draw final line using default drawing mode
            MoveTo(hDC, ptBegin.x, ptBegin.y);
            LineTo(hDC, ptNew.x, ptNew.y);      // last ending point
```

```
        ReleaseDC(hWnd, hDC);                    // close DC
        break;

    case WM_DESTROY:
        PostQuitMessage(0);
        break;
    default:
        return( DefWindowProc(hWnd, msg, wParam, lParam) );
    }    // end switch(msg)
return 0L;
}   // end WndProc
```

The WM_LBUTTONUP Message

The WM_LBUTTONUP message is similar to WM_LBUTTONDOWN. However, we don't need to look at the mouse coordinates contained in its lParam value, because we already have them from the last WM_MOUSEMOVE message. When we receive this message we redraw the last line we drew in the WM_MOUSEMOVE section. Notice that, because we started over with a new device context when we received this message, we are no longer using the R2_NOT drawing mode, but the default R2_COPYPEN mode. Thus our drawing commands create a permanent black line in the usual way, drawing it exactly on top of the last temporary one. In doing so, it eliminates the blank spot where the lines intersect. Figure 30-5 shows how the intersection has been filled in.

DRAWING RECTANGLES WITH THE MOUSE

If we can draw straight lines with the mouse, can we draw other shapes as well? No problem. Our next example, MOUBOX, shows how to draw rectangles. To make them stand out better, we use a brush to fill each rectangle with a red, diagonal hatch pattern. Figure 30-6 shows the output when MOUBOX is used to create a series of rectangles.

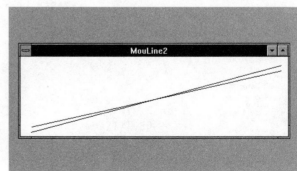

Figure 30-5
Output of
MOULINE2 Program

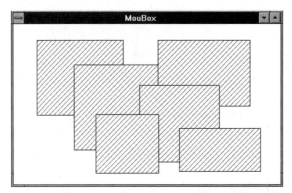

Figure 30-6

Output of MOUBOX Program

The user creates a rectangle by pressing the left mouse button where one corner of the rectangle will be, and moving the pointer to the opposite corner. While the mouse moves, the outline of the rectangle is displayed in temporary, rubber-banded form. When the user lifts the left mouse button, the rectangle is drawn permanently in the last position of the temporary version.

The code for this program is surprisingly similar to that for MOULINE2. Here's the listing for MOUBOX.C:

```
// moubox.c
// draws boxes, using outlines while dragging,
// filling final outline when button lifted

#define STRICT
#include <windows.h>
                                // prototype
LRESULT CALLBACK _export WndProc(HWND, UINT, WPARAM, LPARAM);

PSTR szProgName = "MouBox";    // application name
#include "stdmain.inc"         // standard WinMain()
/////////////////////////////////////////////////////////////////
// main window procedure -- receives messages                   //
/////////////////////////////////////////////////////////////////
LRESULT CALLBACK _export WndProc(HWND hWnd, UINT msg,
                                 WPARAM wParam, LPARAM lParam)
    {
    static POINT ptBegin, ptNew, ptOld;
    HDC hDC;
    HBRUSH hBrush;

    switch(msg)
        {
        case WM_LBUTTONDOWN:
            ptBegin = MAKEPOINT(lParam);        // get starting point
            ptOld = ptBegin;                    // it's first old point
            break;

        case WM_MOUSEMOVE:                      // mouse moves and
```

```
      if(wParam & MK_LBUTTON)                // left button is down
         {
         ptNew = MAKEPOINT(lParam);          // get current point
         hDC = GetDC(hWnd);                   // open DC

         SetROP2(hDC, R2_NOT);               // opposite of bkgnd
         hBrush = GetStockObject(NULL_BRUSH);  // don't fill
         SelectObject(hDC, hBrush);          // interior
         // draw rectangle outlines
         Rectangle(hDC, ptBegin.x, ptBegin.y,  // undo old
                        ptOld.x,   ptOld.y);
         Rectangle(hDC, ptBegin.x, ptBegin.y,  // draw new
                        ptNew.x,   ptNew.y);

         ReleaseDC(hWnd, hDC);                // close DC
         ptOld = ptNew;                       // old becomes new
         }
      break;

   case WM_LBUTTONUP:
      // red, diagonal-hatch brush
      hBrush = CreateHatchBrush( HS_BDIAGONAL, RGB(255,0,0) );
      hDC = GetDC(hWnd);                      // open DC
      SelectObject(hDC, hBrush);             // select brush
      // draw final rectangle, fill with current brush
      Rectangle(hDC, ptBegin.x, ptBegin.y,
                     ptNew.x,   ptNew.y);     // last ending point
      ReleaseDC(hWnd, hDC);                   // close DC
      DeleteObject(hBrush);                   // delete brush
      break;

   case WM_DESTROY:
      PostQuitMessage(0);
      break;
   default:
      return( DefWindowProc(hWnd, msg, wParam, lParam) );
   }    // end switch(msg)
return 0L;
}  // end WndProc
```

Instead of using MoveTo() and LineTo() to draw a line, we use Rectangle() to draw a
rectangle. Everything else works the same way as in MOULINE2, with one exception:
we must use a special kind of brush to make the temporary rectangles transparent.

The NULL Brush

When the user has pushed the mouse button, thereby anchoring one corner of the
rectangle, we draw temporary rectangles from there to the new mouse pointer
position. However, we don't want these temporary rubber-banded rectangles to
erase what's underneath, since the user may end up putting the final rectangle
someplace else. When we draw the rubber-banded rectangles, we want to draw a

"hollow" rectangle, one whose interior is transparent. We can do this with a stock object called the NULL_BRUSH. (Remember: do not delete a stock object.)

Later, we use the brush created with CreateHatchBrush(), which has the WH_BDIAGONAL style, to fill the permanent rectangle.

SUMMARY

You can go a long way programming the mouse with just three messages. They are: WM_MOUSEMOVE, which is sent whenever the mouse moves; WM_LBUTTONDOWN, sent whenever the left button is pressed, and WM_LBUTTONUP, sent whenever the left button is released. (WM_RBUTTONDOWN and WM_RBUTTONUP do the same thing for the right button.) Monitoring these messages allows you to handle the familiar clicking and dragging operations, as well as specialized actions like drawing with the mouse.

31

THE MINPAINT PROGRAM

*I*n this chapter we're going to put together what we learned about graphics to create a mini paint program. With this program you can use the mouse to draw freehand pixels, straight lines, rectangles, and ellipses. You can also create different pens, so your lines and shape outlines can have style, thickness, and color; and you can specify different brushes, so your figures can have color and patterns. Figure 31-1 shows some sample output from MINPAINT.

This application may not have all the bells and whistles of a real paint program, but it's surprisingly versatile. You can use it to draw just about anything, given enough time and patience.

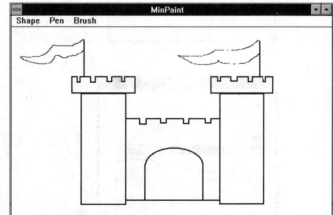

Figure 31-1

Output of

MINPAINT Program

DIALOG BOXES

Besides demonstrating graphics, this program also shows dialog boxes at work. These dialogs allow the user to change the characteristics of the pen and brush. They incorporate many of the controls we discussed in Part Four, *Dialog Boxes*. The Pen dialog box is shown in Figure 31-2, and the Brush dialog in Figure 31-3.

The Pen dialog allows the user to select the style of the line drawn by the pen: Solid, Dash, Dot, or Insideframe. (There are other styles; you're welcome to add them to the dialog if you want.) The user can also type in a line width (but remember that a width of 1 must be used with the Dot and Dash styles). Finally the user can select the color of the pen by clicking on the Color pushbutton, which brings up the Color common dialog.

The Brush dialog uses radio buttons to let the user choose between solid and hatched brushes. If the hatched brush is chosen, then the pattern can be selected from the list box. As with pens, a pushbutton calls up a Color common dialog so the user can select the brush color.

We've made the Cancel buttons into default pushbuttons in both dialogs. This means that if you press (ENTER), the dialog box will go away without changing any of its settings. This is a safety feature; it avoids changing the settings inadvertently. If

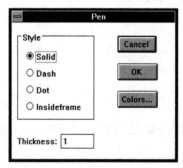

Figure 31-2
The Pen Dialog

Figure 31-3
The Brush Dialog

you don't like the way this works, you can make the Cancel buttons into ordinary pushbuttons, and make the OK buttons into default buttons.

PROGRAM FILES

There is only one pop-up menu in MINPAINT: Shape. This pop-up allows you to select from the menu items Pixel, Line, Rectangle, and Ellipse. Two other menu items, Pen and Brush, appear on the menu bar. Both call dialog boxes directly. Here's the listing for MINPAINT.RC:

```
// minpaint.rc
// resource file for minpaint

#include "minpaint.h"

MinPaint MENU
BEGIN
        POPUP "Shape"
        BEGIN
                MENUITEM "Pixel", IDM_PIXEL
                MENUITEM "Line", IDM_LINE
                MENUITEM "Rectangle", IDM_RECT
                MENUITEM "Ellipse", IDM_ELLIP
        END

        MENUITEM "Pen", IDM_PEN
        MENUITEM "Brush", IDM_BRUSH
END

PenDlg DIALOG 18, 18, 142, 114
STYLE DS_MODALFRAME | WS_POPUP | WS_CAPTION | WS_SYSMENU
CAPTION "Pen"
BEGIN
        CONTROL "Solid", IDP_SOLID, "BUTTON",
            BS_AUTORADIOBUTTON | WS_CHILD | WS_VISIBLE | WS_TABSTOP,
            13, 22, 28, 12
        CONTROL "Dash", IDP_DASH, "BUTTON",
            BS_AUTORADIOBUTTON | WS_CHILD | WS_VISIBLE | WS_TABSTOP,
            13, 36, 28, 12
        CONTROL "Dot", IDP_DOT, "BUTTON",
            BS_AUTORADIOBUTTON | WS_CHILD | WS_VISIBLE | WS_TABSTOP,
            13, 50, 28, 12
        CONTROL "Insideframe", IDP_INSIDE, "BUTTON",
            BS_AUTORADIOBUTTON | WS_CHILD | WS_VISIBLE | WS_TABSTOP,
            13, 64, 48, 12
        LTEXT "Thickness:", -1, 5, 95, 37, 8
        EDITTEXT IDP_EDIT, 43, 93, 29, 12,
            ES_LEFT | WS_CHILD | WS_VISIBLE | WS_BORDER | WS_TABSTOP
        CONTROL "Style", 106, "button",
            BS_GROUPBOX | WS_CHILD | WS_VISIBLE, 5, 7, 67, 74
```

```
        DEFPUSHBUTTON "Cancel", IDCANCEL, 92, 11, 34, 14,
            WS_CHILD | WS_VISIBLE | WS_TABSTOP
        PUSHBUTTON "OK", IDOK, 92, 34, 35, 14,
            WS_CHILD | WS_VISIBLE | WS_TABSTOP
        PUSHBUTTON "Colors...", IDP_COLORS, 92, 57, 35, 14,
            WS_CHILD | WS_VISIBLE | WS_TABSTOP
END

BrushDlg DIALOG 18, 18, 152, 122
STYLE DS_MODALFRAME | WS_POPUP | WS_CAPTION | WS_SYSMENU
CAPTION "Brush"
BEGIN
        CONTROL "Solid", IDB_SOLID, "BUTTON",
            BS_AUTORADIOBUTTON | WS_CHILD | WS_VISIBLE | WS_TABSTOP,
            12, 8, 28, 12
        CONTROL "Hatched", IDB_HATCH, "BUTTON",
            BS_AUTORADIOBUTTON | WS_CHILD | WS_VISIBLE | WS_TABSTOP,
            56, 8, 40, 12
        LISTBOX IDB_LIST, 11, 47, 79, 59,
            LBS_NOTIFY | WS_CHILD | WS_VISIBLE | WS_BORDER | WS_VSCROLL
        DEFPUSHBUTTON "Cancel", IDCANCEL, 103, 46, 35, 14,
            WS_CHILD | WS_VISIBLE | WS_TABSTOP
        PUSHBUTTON "OK", IDOK, 103, 67, 36, 14,
            WS_CHILD | WS_VISIBLE | WS_TABSTOP
        PUSHBUTTON "Colors...", IDB_COLORS, 103, 89, 37, 14,
            WS_CHILD | WS_VISIBLE | WS_TABSTOP
        LTEXT "Patterns", -1, 12, 36, 31, 8
END
```

The header file contains definitions for the menu and dialog control constants. Here's the listing for MINPAINT.H:

```
// minpaint.h
// header file for minpaint

#define IDM_PIXEL       101
#define IDM_LINE        102
#define IDM_RECT        103
#define IDM_ELLIP       104
#define IDM_PEN         200
#define IDM_BRUSH       300

#define IDP_SOLID       1001
#define IDP_DASH        1002
#define IDP_DOT         1003
#define IDP_INSIDE      1004
#define IDP_EDIT        1005
#define IDP_COLORS      1006

#define IDB_SOLID       2001
#define IDB_HATCH       2002
#define IDB_LIST        2003
#define IDB_COLORS      2004
```

This is a somewhat larger program than those we've seen before. It handles quite a few messages, and uses two dialog procedures in addition to the window procedure. However, almost everything in it should be familiar (with the exception of checking menu items, which we'll discuss later). Here's the listing for MINPAINT.C:

```c
// minpaint.c
// mini paint program

#define STRICT
#include <windows.h>
#include <commdlg.h>                // for ChooseColor() common dialog
#include "minpaint.h"
                                    // prototypes
LRESULT CALLBACK _export WndProc(HWND, UINT, WPARAM, LPARAM);
BOOL CALLBACK _export PenDlgProc(HWND, UINT, WPARAM, LPARAM);
BOOL CALLBACK _export BrushDlgProc(HWND, UINT, WPARAM, LPARAM);

int iPenStyle = PS_SOLID;          // initial pen style
int iPenWidth = 1;                 // initial pen width
COLORREF rgbPenColor = RGB(0,0,0);   // pen color (initially black)

int iHatchStyle = HS_HORIZONTAL; // hatch pattern constant
BOOL bHatchSet = FALSE;            // true if hatch brush, not solid
COLORREF rgbBrushColor = RGB(0,0,0); // brush color (initially black)

PSTR szProgName = "MinPaint";      // application name
#include "stdmain.inc"             // standard WinMain()
//////////////////////////////////////////////////////////////////////
// main window procedure -- receives messages                       //
//////////////////////////////////////////////////////////////////////
LRESULT CALLBACK _export WndProc(HWND hWnd, UINT msg,
                                 WPARAM wParam, LPARAM lParam)
   {
   HINSTANCE hInst;                    // instance handle
   DLGPROC lpDlgProc;                  // pointer to dialog procs
   static POINT ptBegin, ptNew, ptOld; // points
   HDC hDC;                            // device context
   HPEN hPen, hOldPen;                 // pen handles
   HBRUSH hBrush, hOldBrush;           // brush handles
   static int nSelect = IDM_PIXEL;     // ID of Shape menu item
   static HMENU hMenu;                 // menu handle
   int j, k;                           // loop variables


   switch(msg)
      {
      case WM_CREATE:
         hMenu = GetMenu(hWnd);         // get menu handle
         CheckMenuItem(hMenu, nSelect, MF_CHECKED); // check 1st item
         break;
```

```
case WM_LBUTTONDOWN:
   ptBegin = MAKEPOINT(lParam);            // get starting point
   ptOld = ptBegin;                        // it's first old point
   break;

case WM_MOUSEMOVE:                         // mouse moves and
   if(wParam & MK_LBUTTON)                 // left button is down
      {
      ptNew = MAKEPOINT(lParam);           // get current point

      hDC = GetDC(hWnd);                   // open DC
      SetROP2(hDC, R2_NOT);                // opposite of bkgnd
      hBrush = GetStockObject(NULL_BRUSH);    // don't fill
      hOldBrush = SelectObject(hDC, hBrush);  // interior
      switch(nSelect)                      // Shape menu selection
         {
         case IDM_PIXEL:
            SetROP2(hDC, R2_COPYPEN);   // use pen color
            // draw square of pixels, size of pen width
            for(j= -iPenWidth/2; j<=iPenWidth/2; j++)
               for(k= -iPenWidth/2; k<=iPenWidth/2; k++)
                  SetPixel(hDC, ptNew.x+j,
                                   ptNew.y+k, rgbPenColor);
            break;
         case IDM_LINE:
            // draw temporary line
            MoveTo(hDC, ptBegin.x, ptBegin.y);  // undo old
            LineTo(hDC, ptOld.x, ptOld.y);
            MoveTo(hDC, ptBegin.x, ptBegin.y);  // draw new
            LineTo(hDC, ptNew.x, ptNew.y);
            break;
         case IDM_RECT:
            // draw temporary unfilled rectangle
            Rectangle(hDC, ptBegin.x, ptBegin.y,  // undo old
                           ptOld.x,   ptOld.y);
            Rectangle(hDC, ptBegin.x, ptBegin.y,  // draw new
                           ptNew.x,   ptNew.y);
            break;
         case IDM_ELLIP:
            // draw temporary unfilled ellipse
            Ellipse(hDC, ptBegin.x, ptBegin.y,  // undo old
                         ptOld.x,   ptOld.y);
            Ellipse(hDC, ptBegin.x, ptBegin.y,  // draw new
                         ptNew.x,   ptNew.y);
            break;
         } // end switch nSelect
      SelectObject(hDC, hOldBrush);        // restore old brush
      ReleaseDC(hWnd, hDC);                // close DC
      ptOld = ptNew;                       // old becomes new
      }
   break;
```

```
case WM_LBUTTONUP:
    // create pen, based on pen dialog box settings
    hPen = CreatePen(iPenStyle, iPenWidth, rgbPenColor);
    // create hatch or solid brush, based on brush dialog box
    if(bHatchSet)
        hBrush = CreateHatchBrush(iHatchStyle, rgbBrushColor);
    else
        hBrush = CreateSolidBrush(rgbBrushColor);

    hDC = GetDC(hWnd);                           // open DC
    hOldBrush = SelectObject(hDC, hBrush);   // select brush
    hOldPen = SelectObject(hDC, hPen);       // select pen
    switch(nSelect)
        {
        case IDM_LINE:
            // draw permanent line with current pen
            MoveTo(hDC, ptBegin.x, ptBegin.y);
            LineTo(hDC, ptNew.x,   ptNew.y);
            break;
        case IDM_RECT:
            // draw permanent rectangle with current brush
            Rectangle(hDC, ptBegin.x, ptBegin.y, ptNew.x, ptNew.y);
            break;
        case IDM_ELLIP:
            // draw permanent ellipse with current brush
            Ellipse(hDC, ptBegin.x, ptBegin.y, ptNew.x, ptNew.y);
            break;
        }   // end switch nSelect
    SelectObject(hDC, hOldBrush);                // restore old brush
    SelectObject(hDC, hOldPen);                  // restore old pen
    DeleteObject(hBrush);                        // delete brush
    DeleteObject(hPen);                          // delete pen
    ReleaseDC(hWnd, hDC);                        // close DC
    break;

case WM_COMMAND:                   // user selected menu item
    switch(wParam)
        {
        case IDM_PEN:             // user selected Pen
            hInst = (HINSTANCE)GetWindowWord(hWnd, GWW_HINSTANCE);
            lpDlgProc = (DLGPROC)MakeProcInstance(
                                    (FARPROC)PenDlgProc, hInst );
            DialogBox(hInst, "PenDlg", hWnd, lpDlgProc);
            FreeProcInstance( (FARPROC)lpDlgProc );
            break;

        case IDM_BRUSH:               // user selected Brush
            hInst = (HINSTANCE)GetWindowWord(hWnd, GWW_HINSTANCE);
            lpDlgProc = (DLGPROC)MakeProcInstance(
                                    (FARPROC)BrushDlgProc, hInst );
            DialogBox(hInst, "BrushDlg", hWnd, lpDlgProc);
            FreeProcInstance( (FARPROC)lpDlgProc );
            break;
```

```
        case IDM_PIXEL:              // item on Shape menu
        case IDM_LINE:
        case IDM_RECT:
        case IDM_ELLIP:
                                     // uncheck old item
           CheckMenuItem(hMenu, nSelect, MF_UNCHECKED);
           nSelect = wParam;         // get ID of current item
                                     // check current item
           CheckMenuItem(hMenu, nSelect, MF_CHECKED);
           break;
        }   // end switch wParam
      break;  // end case WM_COMMAND

   case WM_DESTROY:
      PostQuitMessage(0);
      break;
   default:
      return( DefWindowProc(hWnd, msg, wParam, lParam) );
   }   // end switch(msg)
 return OL;
 }  // end WndProc

//////////////////////////////////////////////////////////////////////
// PenDlgProc() -- dialog window procedure                           //
//////////////////////////////////////////////////////////////////////
#pragma argsused

BOOL CALLBACK _export PenDlgProc(HWND hDlg, UINT msg,
                                    WPARAM wParam, LPARAM lParam)
   {
   static int nPen;                 // IDP_SOLID, etc.
   BOOL bError;                     // error from GetDlgItemInt()
   CHOOSECOLOR chc;                 // structure for color info
   DWORD rgbCustColors[16];         // for ChooseColor()

   switch(msg)
      {
      case WM_INITDIALOG:
         // set radio buttons to current pen style, check button
         if(iPenStyle==PS_SOLID)    nPen=IDP_SOLID;
         else if(iPenStyle==PS_DASH) nPen=IDP_DASH;
         else if(iPenStyle==PS_DOT) nPen=IDP_DOT;
         else                       nPen=IDP_INSIDE;
         CheckRadioButton(hDlg, IDP_SOLID, IDP_INSIDE, nPen);
         // set current width in edit field
         SetDlgItemInt(hDlg, IDP_EDIT, iPenWidth, TRUE);
         break;

      case WM_COMMAND:              // msg from control
         switch(wParam)
            {
            case IDP_COLORS:        // user pushed Colors button
```

```
                    // call Colors common dialog
                    chc.lStructSize = sizeof(CHOOSECOLOR);
                    chc.hwndOwner = hDlg;
                    chc.rgbResult = rgbPenColor;
                    chc.lpCustColors = rgbCustColors;
                    chc.Flags = CC_FULLOPEN | CC_RGBINIT;
                    if( ChooseColor(&chc) )
                        rgbPenColor = chc.rgbResult;  // got the color
                    break;

                case IDP_SOLID:             // user presses radio button
                case IDP_DASH:
                case IDP_DOT:
                case IDP_INSIDE:
                    nPen = wParam;          // save ID of button
                    break;

                case IDOK:                  // user pushes OK button
                    switch(nPen)
                        {
                        case IDP_SOLID:  iPenStyle = PS_SOLID; break;
                        case IDP_DASH:   iPenStyle = PS_DASH; break;
                        case IDP_DOT:    iPenStyle = PS_DOT; break;
                        case IDP_INSIDE: iPenStyle = PS_INSIDEFRAME; break;
                        }
                    iPenWidth =             // read width from edit field
                        (int)GetDlgItemInt(hDlg, IDP_EDIT, &bError, FALSE);
                    EndDialog(hDlg, NULL);  // terminate dialog box
                    break;  // end case IDOK

                case IDCANCEL:              // user pushes Cancel button
                    EndDialog(hDlg, NULL);  // terminate dialog box
                    break;
                }  // end switch wparam
            break;  // end case WM_COMMAND

        default:
            return FALSE;
        }  // end switch msg
    return TRUE;
    }  // end PenDlgProc


////////////////////////////////////////////////////////////////////////
// BrushDlgProc() -- dialog window procedure                            //
////////////////////////////////////////////////////////////////////////
#pragma argsused
#define NUMHATCH 6                  // number of hatch patterns
PSTR aList[NUMHATCH] =              // hatch patterns
        { "Horizontal", "Vertical", "Forward diagonal",
          "Backward diagonal", "Crosshatch",
          "Diagonal crosshatch" };
```

```
BOOL CALLBACK _export BrushDlgProc(HWND hDlg, UINT msg,
                                   WPARAM wParam, LPARAM lParam)
   {
   int j;
   static int nHatch;           // index of currently selected hatch
   CHOOSECOLOR chc;             // structure for color info
   COLORREF rgbCustColors[16];  // for ChooseColor()

   switch(msg)
      {
      case WM_INITDIALOG:
         // put hatch-pattern caption strings in list box
         for(j=0; j<NUMHATCH; j++)
            SendDlgItemMessage(hDlg, IDB_LIST, LB_ADDSTRING, 0,
                               (LPARAM)((LPCSTR)aList[j]));
         // select the current hatch pattern
         SendDlgItemMessage(hDlg, IDB_LIST, LB_SETCURSEL, nHatch, 0L);
         // set radio buttons to hatch or solid
         if(bHatchSet)
            CheckRadioButton(hDlg, IDB_SOLID, IDB_HATCH, IDB_HATCH);
         else
            CheckRadioButton(hDlg, IDB_SOLID, IDB_HATCH, IDB_SOLID);
         break;

      case WM_COMMAND:                   // msg from dlg box control
         switch(wParam)
            {
            case IDB_COLORS:             // user pushes Colors button
               // call Colors common dialog
               chc.lStructSize = sizeof(CHOOSECOLOR);
               chc.hwndOwner = hDlg;
               chc.rgbResult = rgbBrushColor;
               chc.lpCustColors = rgbCustColors;
               chc.Flags = CC_FULLOPEN | CC_RGBINIT;
               if( ChooseColor(&chc) )
                  rgbBrushColor = chc.rgbResult;
               break;

            case IDOK:                   // user pushes OK button
               // get index of currently-selected string
               nHatch = (int)SendDlgItemMessage(hDlg, IDB_LIST,
                                       LB_GETCURSEL, 0, 0L);
               switch(nHatch)  // set style according to index
                  {
                  case 0: iHatchStyle = HS_HORIZONTAL; break;
                  case 1: iHatchStyle = HS_VERTICAL; break;
                  case 2: iHatchStyle = HS_FDIAGONAL; break;
                  case 3: iHatchStyle = HS_BDIAGONAL; break;
                  case 4: iHatchStyle = HS_CROSS; break;
                  case 5: iHatchStyle = HS_DIAGCROSS; break;
                  }
               // find if hatch or solid radio button checked
               bHatchSet = (BOOL)SendDlgItemMessage(hDlg, IDB_HATCH,
```

```
                                              BM_GETSTATE, 0, OL);
          EndDialog(hDlg, NULL);   // terminate dialog box
          break;  // end case IDOK

       case IDCANCEL:              // user pushes Cancel button
          EndDialog(hDlg, NULL);   // terminate dialog box
          break;
       }  // end switch wparam
     break;  // end case WM_COMMAND
  default:
     return FALSE;
  }  // end switch msg
return TRUE;
}  // end BrushDlgProc
```

A key variable in the program is nSelect. The user selects an item from the Shape menu, either Pixel, Line, Rectangle, or Ellipse. This sets nSelect to the ID of that menu item. In the WM_MOUSEMOVE and WM_BUTTONUP sections, switch statements based on nSelect then execute the code to draw the specified shape.

Handling WM_MOUSEMOVE

When the mouse moves, indicated by WM_MOUSEMOVE, the shapes (except for pixels) are drawn in rubber-banded 1-pixel-wide black lines. This is the default pen, so no pen needs to be created. As we discussed in the last chapter, the R2_NOT drawing mode is used so each outline will erase the one it's drawn on top of.

Drawing Pixels

Pixels are handled differently than the other shapes. Pixels are drawn as soon as the mouse moves; there's no waiting for the button to be lifted. In this case the drawing mode is reset to R2_COPYPEN, the default, so the pixels will be drawn with the current pen.

We allow the user to vary the number of pixels drawn at each point. Nested **for** loops and the SetPixel() function draw a square block of pixels whenever the mouse moves. The dimensions of the block are derived from the pen width, using the iPenWidth variable. Thus if the user typed in a width of 5 in the Pens dialog, a 5-by-5 square of pixels will be drawn. The current pen color, rgbPenColor, is used in SetPixel(), so the pixels have the width and color of the current pen.

Handling WM_LBUTTONUP

When the WM_LBUTTONUP message is received, the final shapes are drawn. Here we create pens and brushes using the data supplied by the user in the dialog boxes. The pen is set to iPenStyle, iPenWidth, and rgbPenColor. The brush is created with either CreateHatchBrush() or CreateSolidBrush(), depending on whether the Solid or Hatched radio button is selected in the Brush dialog. The brush is given the style specified by the iHatchStyle variable.

We don't need to reset the drawing mode, since when we receive WM_LBUTTONUP we start over with a new device context, which resets the drawing mode, as well as the pen and brush, to their default values. Again we use a **switch** statement based on nSelect to decide which shapes to draw.

CHECKING MENU ITEMS

It's nice if, when the user clicks on the Shapes pop-up, there's an indication of which shape is currently selected. This way the user can verify which shape will be drawn, without actually making a selection.

This situation is typically handled by checking a menu item. A small check mark placed next to the item indicates the currently selected shape. If the user selects a different shape, the check moves to the new item. Only one item can be checked at a time. Figure 31-4 shows the Shapes pop-up with the Rectangle item checked.

Checking a menu item is easily carried out with the CheckMenuItem() function. This function takes three arguments: the menu handle, the ID of the menu item to be checked, and a flag that indicates whether the item is to be checked or unchecked. The possible values of this flag are MF_CHECKED and MF_UNCHECKED. The menu handle can be obtained using the GetMenu() function, which takes as its only argument the handle of the window whose menu you want to find. Here's how these functions look in the WM_CREATE section:

```
case WM_CREATE:
   hMenu = GetMenu(hWnd);
   CheckMenuItem(hMenu, nSelect, MF_CHECKED);
   break;
```

The nSelect variable holds the ID of the selected menu item. This variable is set whenever a WM_COMMAND message is received with a wParam equal to any of these menu item IDs.

```
case IDM_PIXEL:            // if any item on the Shapes menu is selected,
case IDM_LINE:
case IDM_RECT:
case IDM_ELLIP:
   CheckMenuItem(hMenu, nSelect, MF_UNCHECKED);  // uncheck old menu item
   nSelect = wParam;                             // get new item
   CheckMenuItem(hMenu, nSelect, MF_CHECKED);    // check new item
   break;
```

These sections of code handle checking and unchecking, and also keep nSelect set to the appropriate ID so the other sections of the program can figure out what shapes to draw when the mouse is moved.

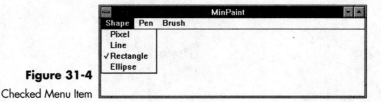

Figure 31-4

Checked Menu Item

SUMMARY

The mini-application in this chapter shows that you've learned enough to create fairly sophisticated graphics applications. You can improve and extend this program if you want. For example, it would be easy to add the capability to draw additional shapes, such as polygons. Just insert additional menu items and additional **case** statements to draw the new figures. You could also add an erase facility. (As it is now, if you want to erase something you can select a white pen or rectangle and draw over the offending area.)

Of course the graphics techniques we demonstrated apply in many more situations than paint programs. You can create scatter graphs with individual pixels, make bar graphs with rectangles, draw a graph's axes with lines, and in general create almost any image you like. The possibilities are limited only by your imagination.

PART SIX
GETTING FANCY WITH THE GUI

a major use of medieval art was the embellishment of existing objects. Manuscripts were illuminated with complex decorations in the margins. Religious scenes on altarpieces were bordered by vines or geometric patterns. Swords were engraved, shields were emblazoned, clothes were embroidered, bowls were enamelled. Angels, devils, knights, battles, dragons, griffons, unicorns, gargoyles, and abstract swirls ran rampant over every surface. It was as though people in King Arthur's day had a fear of blank space.

In the same way, Windows allows you to embellish the user interface. There is an amazing variety of ways to do this. In fact, if you can think of something you want to do, then you can probably find a way to do it (or often several ways). In Part Six we're going to introduce several useful user-interface features: inserting and deleting menu items while the program is running, adding menu accelerators, creating an icon to represent your program when it's minimized, and creating a main window that is really a dialog box (or is it the other way around?).

The topics we discuss here are not central to Windows programming; you can write many programs without using them. But they do demonstrate how flexible and rich the Windows user interface is, and they will help to give your programs a professional touch.

435

32

DYNAMIC
MENU ITEMS

So far we've created menu systems by specifying all their details in a menu
resource in an .RC file. The menu resource specifies the pop-ups and all
the menu items on each pop-up. Sometimes, however, you want to vary
the contents of menus *dynamically*—that is, while your program is running.
Examples of this are the Save, Close, and Print items that appear in a File menu
only when a file is open; font names that appear in a Font menu depending on
what fonts a program finds available in the system, Edit menu items like Cut,
Copy, and Paste that only appear if a document is open, and a Stop item that
appears when a process is running and is replaced by a Start item when it isn't.

A related approach is to *gray* menu items. A grayed item is still visible in a menu,
but it's drawn in gray instead of black, and it cannot be selected by the user. The
examples mentioned above (with the possible exception of the fonts list), could be
handled by graying menu items instead of by deleting and inserting them.

The example program in this chapter demonstrates both approaches: it inserts
and deletes menu items depending on the state of the program, and it grays and
ungrays other items.

THE CHNGMENU PROGRAM

The CHNGMENU program has two pop-ups: File and Edit, just like the
EZMENU program of Chapter 11, *Menus*. When you first start CHNGMENU
the File menu has only one item: Open, as shown in Figure 32-1. The Edit menu
has two items, Cut and Copy, but they can't be selected by the user and appear as
gray text, as shown in Figure 32-2.

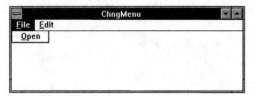

Figure 32-1

Initial File Menu

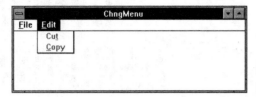

Figure 32-2

Initial Edit Menu

When the user selects Open from the File menu, both menus change. The Open item is deleted from the File menu and replaced by Save and Close; and the Cut and Copy items in the Edit menu are enabled and appear in black instead of gray. Figures 32-3 and 32-4 show the two menus in this state.

This example models an application that can open only one file at a time. If no file is open, it can't be saved or closed, so these items aren't shown on the menu. Also, there's no file to edit, so the items on the Edit menu are grayed. Once the file is opened, no other file can be opened until the first is closed, so the Open selection is removed, and Save and Close items are installed. An opened file can be edited, so the items on the Edit menu are enabled (ungrayed). When Close is selected, the menu items all revert back to their previous state.

Of course this program doesn't actually open or close files; making any menu selection simply results in a message box. The program's purpose is merely to show how to manipulate menu items. However, many real applications use similar schemes to dynamically rearrange File, Edit, and other menus.

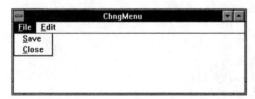

Figure 32-3

File Menu After Open Selected

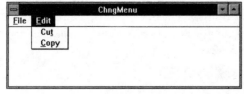

Figure 32-4

Edit Menu After Open Selected

Because this program uses menus, it requires the usual three files. In the resource script for the menu, you don't need to define any menu items that will appear dynamically later on, so the File menu has only the Open item. Also, we've added the GRAYED keyword to both items in the Edit menu:

```
MENUITEM "Cu&t", IDM_CUT, GRAYED
MENUITEM "&Copy", IDM_COPY, GRAYED
```

This keyword causes the items to start out grayed: when the user tries to select them, nothing happens. We can also gray items dynamically, as we'll see. Here's the listing for the CHNGMENU.RC file:

```
// chngmenu.rc
// resource script file for chngmenu

#include "chngmenu.h"

ChngMenu MENU
    BEGIN
        POPUP "&File"
            BEGIN
                MENUITEM "&Open", IDM_OPEN
            END
        POPUP "&Edit"
            BEGIN
                MENUITEM "Cu&t", IDM_CUT, GRAYED
                MENUITEM "&Copy", IDM_COPY, GRAYED
            END
    END
```

Even if a menu item will be added dynamically, it still needs an ID number, so the header file shows IDs for the Save and Close items, even though they don't appear in the .RC file. Here's the listing for CHNGMENU.H:

```
// chngmenu.h
// header file for chngmenu

#define IDM_OPEN    101
#define IDM_SAVE    102
#define IDM_CLOSE   103
#define IDM_CUT     201
#define IDM_COPY    202
```

A **switch** statement in the .C file handles the different menu selections: Open, Save, Close, Cut, and Copy. However, when the program first starts, the Save and Close cases are inoperative because the user can't select these items. Here's the listing for CHNGMENU.C:

```
// chngmenu.c
// changes menu items

#define STRICT
```

```
#include <windows.h>
#include "chngmenu.h"          // header file for IDM_OPEN, etc.

LRESULT CALLBACK _export WndProc(HWND, UINT, WPARAM, LPARAM);

PSTR szProgName = "ChngMenu";       // application name
#include "stdmain.inc"              // standard WinMain function
//////////////////////////////////////////////////////////////////
// main window procedure -- receives messages                    //
//////////////////////////////////////////////////////////////////
LRESULT CALLBACK _export WndProc(HWND hWnd, UINT msg,
                                 WPARAM wParam, LPARAM lParam)
   {
   HMENU hMenu;                         // main menu handle
   static HMENU hFileMenu, hEditMenu;   // pop-up handles

   switch(msg)
      {
      case WM_CREATE:
         hMenu = GetMenu(hWnd);              // get main menu handle
         hFileMenu = GetSubMenu(hMenu, 0);   // get File pop-up handle
         hEditMenu = GetSubMenu(hMenu, 1);   // get Edit pop-up handle
         break;

      case WM_COMMAND:
         switch(wParam)
            {
            case IDM_OPEN:
               MessageBox(hWnd,"You Chose Open", szProgName, MB_OK);

               // delete Open item using item ID
               DeleteMenu(hFileMenu, IDM_OPEN, MF_BYCOMMAND);

               // insert Save and Close items by position
               InsertMenu(hFileMenu, 0, MF_BYPOSITION,
                          IDM_SAVE, "&Save");
               InsertMenu(hFileMenu, 1, MF_BYPOSITION,
                          IDM_CLOSE, "&Close");

               // ungray Cut and Copy items
               EnableMenuItem(hEditMenu, IDM_CUT,
                              MF_BYCOMMAND | MF_ENABLED);
               EnableMenuItem(hEditMenu, IDM_COPY,
                              MF_BYCOMMAND | MF_ENABLED);
               break;

            case IDM_SAVE:
               MessageBox(hWnd,"You chose Save", szProgName, MB_OK);
               break;

            case IDM_CLOSE:
               MessageBox(hWnd,"You chose Close", szProgName, MB_OK);
```

```
                    // insert Open item just before Close
                    InsertMenu(hFileMenu, IDM_CLOSE, MF_BYCOMMAND,
                               IDM_OPEN, "&Open");

                    // delete Save and Close items by position
                    DeleteMenu(hFileMenu, 0, MF_BYPOSITION);
                    DeleteMenu(hFileMenu, 1, MF_BYPOSITION);

                    // gray Cut and Copy items
                    EnableMenuItem(hEditMenu, IDM_CUT,
                               MF_BYCOMMAND | MF_GRAYED);
                    EnableMenuItem(hEditMenu, IDM_COPY,
                               MF_BYCOMMAND | MF_GRAYED);
                    break;

                case IDM_CUT:            // user selects Cut
                    MessageBox(hWnd,"You chose Cut", szProgName, MB_OK);
                    break;

                case IDM_COPY:           // user selects Copy
                    MessageBox(hWnd,"You chose Copy", szProgName, MB_OK);
                    break;
            }    // end switch wParam
        break;   // end case WM_COMMAND

        case WM_DESTROY:
            PostQuitMessage(0);
            break;

        default:
            return( DefWindowProc(hWnd, msg, wParam, lParam) );
        }    // end switch(msg)

    return 0L;
}   // end WndProc
```

DELETING MENU ITEMS

When the user selects Open, we want to delete from the File menu that same Open item used to make the selection. To do this, we'll use the DeleteMenu() function. However, this function requires the handle of the menu from which the item will be deleted. We obtain the menu handles when the WM_CREATE message arrives. There are two steps. First we execute the GetMenu() function to get the handle for the entire menu system. Then we use the GetSubMenu() function to get the handles of the two pop-ups.

```
hMenu = GetMenu(hWnd);               // get main menu handle
hFileMenu = GetSubMenu(hMenu, 0);    // get File pop-up handle (position 0)
hEditMenu = GetSubMenu(hMenu, 1);    // get Edit pop-up handle (position 1)
```

Table 32-1 Arguments to DeleteMenu()

Argument Type	Symbolic Name	Type
HMENU	hSubMenu	Pop-up's handle
UINT	idItem	Item ID, if uFlags is BY_COMMAND
		Item position, if uFlags is BY_POSITION
UINT	uFlags	MF_BYCOMMAND or MF_BYPOSITION

The GetSubMenu() function takes two arguments: the menu system handle and the position of the pop-up menu, where 0 indicates the leftmost pop-up, 1 is the second from the left, and so on.

Once we have the pop-up handle we're ready for the WM_COMMAND message that arrives when the user selects Open. When that happens we use the DeleteMenu() function (which would be better named the DeleteMenuItem() function) to delete the Open item:

```
DeleteMenu(hFileMenu, IDM_OPEN, MF_BYCOMMAND);  // delete Open
```

This function takes three arguments. The first is the handle of the submenu in which the item to be deleted appears. The second argument, at least in this example, is the ID of the item to be deleted; but it can also specify the position of the item in the submenu. The third argument is a flag that determines which interpretation will be given to the second argument. Table 32-1 shows the situation.

We use the BY_COMMAND approach in the statement shown above to delete the Open item. It works when you know the ID number of the item.

The BY_POSITION method lets you delete items whose ID numbers you don't know, and may sometimes be more convenient even when you do know the IDs. We use this approach to delete the Save and Close items when the user selects Close:

```
DeleteMenu(hFileMenu, 0, MF_BYPOSITION);  // delete Save (first item)
DeleteMenu(hFileMenu, 1, MF_BYPOSITION);  // delete Close (second item)
```

INSERTING MENU ITEMS

Inserting menu items is slightly more complex than deleting them. We use the InsertMenu() function (which might be better named InsertMenuItem(), but hey, we can handle these minor inconsistencies). Here's how we insert the Save and Close items when the user selects Open:

```
InsertMenu(hFileMenu, 0, MF_POSITION, IDM_SAVE, "&Save");
InsertMenu(hFileMenu, 1, MF_POSITION, IDM_CLOSE, "&Close");
```

We also use this function to reinstall the Open item when the user selects Close:

```
InsertMenu(hFileMenu, IDM_CLOSE, MF_BYCOMMAND, IDM_OPEN, "&Open");
```

As you can see, there are two different ways to use this function, just as there were with DeleteMenu(). InsertMenu() takes five arguments, as shown in Table 32-2.

It's important to distinguish between the second and fourth arguments, both of which can be item IDs. The second argument tells *the position in the menu* where the new item will be installed; it is *not* the ID of the new item. The third argument is the flag that tells how the second argument will be interpreted. If the flag is MF_BYCOMMAND, the second argument is interpreted as an item ID and the new item is installed just above it in the pop-up. If the third argument is MF_BYPOSITION, the second argument is interpreted as a position in the pop-up (0 at the top), and the new item is installed at that position. The fourth argument is always the ID of the new item, and the fifth argument is the text that will be placed in the item.

Other flags can be ORed with the third argument to modify the new menu item. Table 32-3 shows the most common flag values.

Another function, AppendMenu(), is similar to InsertMenu(), but is less flexible in that it always installs an item at the bottom of an existing menu.

Table 32-2 Arguments to InsertMenu()

Argument Type	Symbolic Name	Purpose
HMENU	hSubMenu	Pop-up's handle
UINT	idItem	Item ID, if uFlags is BY_COMMAND
		Item position, if uFlags is BY_POSITION
UINT	uFlags	MF_BYCOMMAND, etc.
UINT	idNewItem	ID of new item
LPCSTR	lpNewItem	Text to be placed in new item

Table 32-3 Additional Flag Values for InsertMenu()

Flag Value	Effect
MF_CHECKED	Places check mark on menu item
MF_SEPARATOR	Makes item into separator (line)
MF_GRAYED	Grays the item

GRAYING MENU ITEMS

A grayed menu item appears as gray text instead of black. It indicates to the user that an item can't be selected at the moment, although it may be enabled under other circumstances.

As we've seen, you can gray an item by using the GRAYED keyword in the MENUITEM statement in the resource file. You can also gray an item when you create it dynamically with the InsertMenu() function, by using the MF_GRAYED flag. Can you gray an already-installed item? Yes, you use the EnableMenuItem() function. It takes only three arguments: the handle of the submenu that holds the item to be grayed, the ID of the item (or its position), and a flag. Table 32-4 shows the arguments to EnableMenuItem().

Table 32-4 Arguments to EnableMenuItem()

Argument Type	Symbolic Name	Purpose
HMENU	hSubMenu	Pop-up's handle
UINT	idItem	Item ID, if uFlags is BY_COMMAND
		Item position, if uFlags is BY_POSITION
UINT	uFlags	MF_BYCOMMAND, MF_BYPOSITION,
		MF_GRAYED, MF_CHECKED, etc.

Table 32-5 Additional Flag Values for EnableMenuItem()

Flag Value	Effect
MF_DISABLED	Disables item (it can't be selected, but is not grayed)
MF_ENABLED	Enables item (it's black and can be selected)
MF_GRAYED	Grays the item (it's gray and cannot be selected)

This function interprets the meaning of its second argument in the same way DeleteMenu() and InsertMenu() do, depending on the value of the third argument. This third argument may also OR together one of the constants shown in Table 32-5.

MF_DISABLED is similar to MF_GRAYED in that it disables the item; however, it does not gray it. The item stays black even though it can't be selected. This is a less user-friendly approach, since there's no visual indication that the item can't be selected, and the user may conclude that the item is "broken."

SUMMARY

In this chapter you've learned to install and delete menu items on existing pop-ups with the InstallMenu() and DeleteMenu() functions. You've also learned to enable and disable existing items with EnableMenuItem(). Not every program requires these actions, but in many cases you can improve and simplify the user interface by hiding or graying menu items that aren't relevant in a particular circumstance.

CHAPTER 33

MENU ACCELERATORS

*a*n accelerator is a key combination that has the same effect as selecting a pop-up menu item. Accelerators, as the name implies, are provided to speed up the selection of certain menu items; they are usually used for frequently used actions. Accelerators are also called *shortcut* keys. You can think of accelerators as being like the spurs that a medieval knight digs into the side of his horse: you can get the job done without them, but they make things go faster.

Usually the key combination for the accelerator is indicated next to the item on the pop-up menu. This makes it easy for the user to see which items have acclerators and to learn the key combinations. Figure 33-1 shows a File menu with some accelerator key combinations, and Figure 33-2 shows an Edit menu.

Accelerators can provide added speed or convenience: it's often faster (especially for the mouse-impaired) to press a few keys than it is to select an item from a menu. However, it's hard to remember a great many key combinations, so accelerators are usually used only for the most common operations.

Some accelerator key combinations are standardized for all applications. Table 33-1 shows Microsoft's recommendations, which were instituted in Windows version 3.1.

Note how easy it is to use the Cut, Copy, and Paste commands with the left hand alone.

An older set of accelerators was used for edit commands before Windows 3.1. They are still seen in some applications, and some users may prefer them. If you're creating

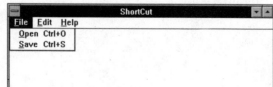

Figure 33-1

File Menu with Accelerators

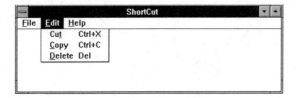

Figure 33-2

Edit Menu with Accelerators

an editor program you may want to build in the ability to handle these accelerators as well as the more modern ones. Table 33-2 shows these older accelerators.

Programmers can invent their own accelerators for other menu items. Microsoft offers the following guidelines (among others).

- Use (CTRL) plus a key, such as (CTRL)+(A), for most items. The letter should be chosen to make the accelerator easy to remember.
- Use function keys for frequently performed tasks (such as (F1) for help), but use them sparingly because they are hard to remember.
- Avoid (ALT) key combinations, since they are used for system functions such as accessing menus.

We might add that, while you can use letter keys such as 'A' alone (with no accompanying (CTRL) or other key) as accelerators, you probably don't want to because single characters are too easy to type by mistake and are used for ordinary text input.

Table 33-1 Recommended Accelerators

Key Combination	Corresponding Menu Item
(CTRL)+(X)	Cut
(CTRL)+(C)	Copy
(CTRL)+(V)	Paste
(DEL)	Delete
(CTRL)+(Z)	Undo (reverse last action)
(F1)	Help
(CTRL)+(N)	New
(CTRL)+(O)	Open
(CTRL)+(P)	Print
(CTRL)+(S)	Save

Table 33-2 Old-Style Accelerators

Key Combination	Corresponding Menu Item
SHIFT + DEL	Cut
CTRL + INS	Copy
SHIFT + INS	Paste
CTRL + DEL	Delete
ALT + BACKSPACE	Undo

Our example program shows how to implement various key combinations as accelerators. There are several steps involved. In the .RC file you must create an accelerator table resource, and modify the text of items in the menu resource to display the key combination. In the .C file you must load the accelerator resource, and—surprising—modify the message loop.

CREATING AN ACCELERATOR TABLE

Statements that specify all the accelerator key combinations are gathered together into something called an *accelerator table*. This accelerator table is a resource, just like a menu or a dialog script, and it appears in the .RC file. Let's look at the complete .RC file, which contains both a menu and an accelerator resource. Here's the listing for SHORTCUT.RC:

```
// shortcut.rc
// resource script file for shortcut

#include "shortcut.h"  // for IDM_ defines

ShortCut MENU
   BEGIN
      POPUP "&File"
         BEGIN
            MENUITEM "&Open\tCtrl+O", IDM_OPEN
            MENUITEM "&Save\tCtrl+S", IDM_SAVE
         END
      POPUP "&Edit"
         BEGIN
            MENUITEM "Cu&t\tCtrl+X", IDM_CUT
            MENUITEM "&Copy\tCtrl+C", IDM_COPY
            MENUITEM "&Delete\tDel", IDM_DELETE
         END
```

```
        MENUITEM "&Help", IDM_HELP  // (can't use tab)
    END

ShortCut ACCELERATORS
    BEGIN
        "^O",       IDM_OPEN                            // Ctrl+O
        "^S",       IDM_SAVE                            // Ctrl+S
        "^X",       IDM_CUT                             // Ctrl+X
        VK_DELETE,  IDM_CUT,     VIRTKEY, SHIFT         // Shift+Del
        "^C",       IDM_COPY                            // Ctrl+C
        VK_INSERT,  IDM_COPY,    VIRTKEY, CONTROL       // Ctrl+Ins
        VK_DELETE,  IDM_DELETE,  VIRTKEY                // Del
        VK_F1,      IDM_HELP,    VIRTKEY                // F1
    END
```

The menu resource is created in the usual way, either typing it in by hand or using the Resource Workshop approach. Like a menu, an accelerator table is easy to type in as a text file, but it can also be created with the Resource Workshop. Here we'll show how to type it in by hand; in the next section we'll see how to create it with the Resource Workshop.

In this example we've installed accelerators for the Cut and Copy items, using both the new and old systems. That is, the user can invoke Cut in three ways: by selecting it from the menu, by typing the new (CTRL)+(X) accelerator, or by typing the older (SHIFT)+(DEL) accelerator.

The header file contains the usual constants for the menu items. These same constants are used by the accelerator resource as well. Here's the listing for SHORTCUT.H:

```
// shortcut.h
// header file for shortcut

#define IDM_OPEN   101
#define IDM_SAVE   102
#define IDM_CUT    201
#define IDM_COPY   202
#define IDM_DELETE 203
#define IDM_HELP   300
```

Specifying the Accelerator Table

The accelerator table resource is specified with the same format as menus and dialog boxes: a name and a keyword, followed by BEGIN and END delimiters. Here's how that looks:

```
ShortCut ACCELERATORS
    BEGIN
    // individual accelerators
    END
```

The accelerator-table name (ShortCut in this example) can be, but doesn't have to be, the same as the menu name. Since they're different kinds of resources, Windows doesn't get confused.

There are two important formats for specifying individual accelerators. The first is for (CTRL) key combinations, and the second is for noncharacter keys such as the function keys, (DEL), (INS), the arrow keys, and so on.

Specifying Control-Key Combinations

The most common accelerator key combination is the Control key in combination with a single character key. We use four such accelerators in our resource:

```
"^O",      IDM_OPEN      // Ctrl+O
"^S",      IDM_SAVE      // Ctrl+S
"^X",      IDM_CUT       // Ctrl+X
"^C",      IDM_COPY      // Ctrl+C
```

The circumflex (^) indicates the (CTRL) key, so "^S" represents the (CTRL)+(S) key combination. The constant IDM_SAVE is the same constant used for the Save menu item in the menu resource. That's how Windows connects a particular accelerator with a particular menu item. When the user presses (CTRL)+(S), a WM_COMMAND message with a wParam value of IDM_SAVE will be sent to the program's window procedure, just as if the Save item had been selected from the File menu.

Specifying Virtual Key Combinations

We discussed virtual key codes in Chapter 21, *Text Input: The Hard Way*. They are constants with the VK_ prefix, like VK_ESCAPE, which represent each key on the keyboard. We can use virtual key codes, alone or in combination with (SHIFT) and (CTRL), to specify accelerators. Here are the four accelerators in SHORTCUT.RC that use this method:

```
VK_DELETE, IDM_CUT,    VIRTKEY, SHIFT      // Del+Shift
VK_INSERT, IDM_COPY,   VIRTKEY, CONTROL    // Ins+Ctrl
VK_DELETE, IDM_DELETE, VIRTKEY             // Del
VK_F1,     IDM_HELP,   VIRTKEY             // F1
```

The accelerators start with a virtual key code like VK_DELETE. Then comes the menu item identifier (IDM_CUT), and then the keyword VIRTKEY. You can add the SHIFT or CONTROL keywords to specify that the virtual key must be used in combination with the (SHIFT) or (CTRL) keys.

USING THE RESOURCE WORKSHOP

You can create accelerator tables using the Resource Workshop. This is probably worthwhile if you're already using the RW to create dialog box resources, but it doesn't really buy you much in the way of convenience otherwise, since you have to type in almost all the same information using RW that you do using a text editor. In any case, here's how to use the RW to create an accelerator table.

Creating an Accelerator Resource

We'll assume you've already opened an .RC window and created a menu resource, as described in Chapter 23, *The Resource Workshop*. To invoke the Accelerator editor, select New from the Resource menu, and when the dialog box appears, click on ACCELERATORS and click on OK. The Accelerators editor will appear, as shown in Figure 33-3.

You enter data into the panel on the left. The panel on the right then lists the accelerators you've entered so far.

First, type the numerical value of the accelerator's ID, like 101, into the Command field and press (ENTER). Then type over this value with the constant, like IDM_OPEN, and press (ENTER) again. At this point the constant should be in the Command field, and the number in the gray field to its right.

If you're going to enter (CTRL) key combinations, click on the ASCII button. If you're going to enter virtual key codes, click on the Virtual Key radio button.

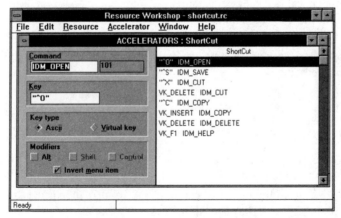

Figure 33-3

The Accelerators Editor

Specifying Control-Key Combinations

To specify a (CTRL) key combination, make sure the ASCII radio button is pressed. Then enter a string into the Key field, using the same format that we described above when doing it by hand. That is, for (CTRL)+(S), enter

```
"^S"
```

Include the quotes. When you're done, press (ENTER) and you'll see this specification recorded in the list on the right.

Specifying Virtual Key Combinations

To specify a vitual key, make sure the Virtual Key radio button is pressed. Then type in the vitual key constant. That is, for the (DEL) key, enter

```
VK_DELETE
```

Don't use quotes. If you want the virtual key to be used with the (SHIFT) or (CTRL) key, check the Shift or Control check box. Then press (ENTER). You'll see the specification recorded in the list to the right.

Notice that you don't need to create new identifiers for accelerators, since you use the same identifiers, such as IDM_OPEN, that you already created for the menu resource.

When you're done creating the accelerator resource, rename it the same way you do other resources, by clicking on it in the .RC window and selecting Rename from the Resource menu.

When you're done with the Accelerators editor, select Close from the document menu to return to the .RC window. Then select Save Project from the File menu to save the entire .RC file.

The result is an accelerators resource script that is very much the same, although perhaps not so nicely formatted, as one you would create by hand.

MODIFYING THE MENU RESOURCE

It's desirable for the user to have a quick way of finding out which accelerators work with which menu items. This is accomplished by adding a description of the keys to the menu item text string. Thus Open and Save items become

```
Open     Ctrl+O
Save     Ctrl+S
```

The C-language tab character '\t' is used to provide the separation between the item name and the accelerator. Here's how the menu resource looks for these two items:

```
MENUITEM "&Open\tCtrl+O", IDM_OPEN
MENUITEM "&Save\tCtrl+S", IDM_SAVE
```

You can modify these lines in the menu resource either manually or using the RW. Note that you shouldn't try to add this accelerator notation to pop-ups on the menu bar; it's only appropriate for menu items within the pop-ups. The user must learn in some other way that (F1) invokes the Help pop-up. (In fact, you can't use the tab character '\t' in pop-up names.)

MODIFYING THE SOURCE FILE

To handle accelerators, two additions to the source file are necessary. The accelerator resource must be loaded into memory, and the message loop must be modified to translate accelerator keystrokes. Our example program incorporates these changes. It responds to the resulting WM_COMMAND messages by putting a different message box on the screen for each item. These messages are generated when a menu item is selected, or when an accelerator key combination is pressed. Here's the listing for SHORTCUT.C:

```
// shortcut.c
// demonstrates menu accelerators

#define STRICT
#include <windows.h>
#include "shortcut.h"               // header file for menu IDs

LRESULT CALLBACK _export WndProc(HWND, UINT, WPARAM, LPARAM);

PSTR szProgName = "ShortCut";       // application name
///////////////////////////////////////////////////////////////////
// main window procedure -- program entry point                   //
///////////////////////////////////////////////////////////////////
#pragma argsused

int PASCAL WinMain(HINSTANCE hInstance, HINSTANCE hPrevInst,
                   LPSTR lpCmdLine, int nCmdShow)
    {
    HWND hWnd;
    MSG msg;
    WNDCLASS wndclass;
    HACCEL hAccel;                   // accelerator table handle

    if(!hPrevInst)
```

```
      {
      wndclass.style        = CS_VREDRAW/CS_HREDRAW;
      wndclass.lpfnWndProc  = (WNDPROC)WndProc;
      wndclass.cbClsExtra   = 0;
      wndclass.cbWndExtra   = 0;
      wndclass.hInstance    = hInstance;
      wndclass.hCursor      = LoadCursor (NULL, IDC_ARROW);
      wndclass.hIcon        = LoadIcon(NULL, IDI_APPLICATION);
      wndclass.lpszMenuName = szProgName;
      wndclass.hbrBackground = GetStockObject(WHITE_BRUSH);
      wndclass.lpszClassName = szProgName;
      RegisterClass(&wndclass);
      }  // end if

   hWnd = CreateWindow(szProgName, szProgName, WS_OVERLAPPEDWINDOW,
                     CW_USEDEFAULT, CW_USEDEFAULT, CW_USEDEFAULT,
                     CW_USEDEFAULT, NULL, NULL, hInstance, NULL);

   ShowWindow(hWnd, nCmdShow);

   // load accelerator table
   hAccel = LoadAccelerators(hInstance, "ShortCut");

   // message loop, modified to handle accelerators
   while( GetMessage(&msg,0,0,0) )  // get message from Windows
      {                             // translate keystrokes
      if( !TranslateAccelerator(hWnd, hAccel, &msg) )
         {
         TranslateMessage(&msg);    // convert keystrokes
         DispatchMessage(&msg);     // call window procedure
         }
      }
   return msg.wParam;
   }  // end WinMain

/////////////////////////////////////////////////////////////////////
// main window procedure -- receives messages                        //
/////////////////////////////////////////////////////////////////////
LRESULT CALLBACK _export WndProc(HWND hWnd, UINT msg,
                                 WPARAM wParam, LPARAM lParam)
   {
   switch(msg)
      {
      case WM_COMMAND:             // user selects a menu item
         switch(wParam)           // wParam holds item ID
            {
            case IDM_OPEN:          // user selects Open
               MessageBox(hWnd,"You chose Open", szProgName, MB_OK);
               break;

            case IDM_SAVE:          // user selects Save
               MessageBox(hWnd,"You chose Save", szProgName, MB_OK);
```

```
            break;

        case IDM_CUT:           // user selects Cut
            MessageBox(hWnd,"You chose Cut", szProgName, MB_OK);
            break;

        case IDM_COPY:          // user selects Copy
            MessageBox(hWnd,"You chose Copy", szProgName, MB_OK);
            break;

        case IDM_DELETE:            // user selects Delete
            MessageBox(hWnd,"You chose Delete", szProgName, MB_OK);
            break;

        case IDM_HELP:              // user selects Help
            MessageBox(hWnd,"You chose Help", szProgName, MB_OK);
            break;
        }   // end switch wParam
    break;  // end case WM_COMMAND

    case WM_DESTROY:
        PostQuitMessage(0);
        break;

    default:
        return( DefWindowProc(hWnd, msg, wParam, lParam) );
    }   // end switch(msg)

    return 0L;
}   // end WndProc
```

Loading an Accelerator Resource

A menu resource is loaded into memory automatically (if it's specified in the lpszMenuName member of the WNDCLASS structure). However, an accelerator resource must be loaded explicitly. To do this, we use the LoadAccelerators() function:

```
hAccel = LoadAccelerators(hInstance, "ShortCut");
```

Because we need to modify the message loop (which we'll discuss next), we can't use our usual STDMAIN.INC file. Instead, WinMain() must appear overtly at the beginning of the program. (You'd almost forgotten what it looked like, hadn't you?) Since WinMain() is handy, it serves as a convenient place to put the LoadAccelerators() function. In WinMain() we have easy access to the instance handle hInstance, which we would otherwise need to discover with GetWindowWord().

We could also execute LoadAccelerators() when we receive a WM_CREATE message.

The TranslateAccelerator() Function

Ordinarily there is no mechanism in Windows that translates key combinations into WM_COMMAND messages. If the user presses a key or key combination, we'll receive WM_CHAR or WM_KEYDOWN messages. We can, as we saw in Chapter 21, *Text Input: The Hard Way*, use these messages to figure out what key was pressed. However, pressing keys doesn't generate WM_COMMAND messages, which is what we want to happen for accelerators.

To cause key combinations to be translated into WM_COMMAND messages, we must use the TranslateAccelerator() function. This function must look at every queued message that arrives at our window procedure. If the message is WM_CHAR or WM_KEYDOWN, it checks to see if the key is one that's listed in the accelerator table. If it is, TranslateAccelerator() changes the message into the appropriate WM_COMMAND message. If it's some other message, or a WM_CHAR or WM_KEYDOWN message for a key that isn't in the table, it does no translation.

The only place that TranslateAccelerator() can access the queued messages is in the message loop. Here's what the loop looks like with this function installed:

```
while( GetMessage(&msg, 0, 0, 0) )
    {
    if( !TranslateAccelerator(hWnd, hAccel, &msg) )
        {
        TranslateMessage(&msg);
        DispatchMessage(&msg);
        }
    }
```

Whenever GetMessage() returns, signifying that we've received a queued message, we first examine the message with TranslateAccelerator(). If this function finds a key combination that really is an accelerator command, it tells Windows to send a WM_COMMAND message (which will be received after the current message) and returns a nonzero value. This causes the **if** statement to fail, and we go back to the top of the loop without further processing. For other messages, TranslateAccelerator() returns a zero value which causes the TranslateMessage() and DispatchMessage() functions to be executed in the usual way.

SUMMARY

Here are the steps necessary to install accelerators in your program:

1. Create an accelerator table resource in the .RC file. You can do this by hand with a text editor, or with Borland's Resource Workshop.

2. In the menu resource in the .RC file, add the accelerator key combinations to the menu item text in each MENUITEM statement. Use a tab character (\t) to separate the menu text from the key combination: "Save\tCtrl+S".

3. Install a LoadAccelerators() function to load the accelerator resource into memory. Usually you'll want to do this during initialization or when WM_CREATE is received.

4. Place a TranslateAccelerators() function in the message loop to intercept all queued messages and translate any that report accelerator keypresses.

34

ICONS AND CURSORS

$\mathcal{I}$ n King Arthur's time, every knight had a coat of arms emblazoned on his shield and, for those knights rich enough to have castles, carved into the stone above the main gate. The design of the coat of arms was amazingly complicated, involving the knight's ancestry, royal connections, valiant deeds, and so on, all expressed in symbolic form. Each color used on a coat of arms had a specific meaning, as did symbols like dragons, lions, and fluers de lis. The design and granting of coats of arms was called heraldry, and was one of the subjects studied by aspiring knights.

In Windows programming the *icon* serves a function similar to a coat of arms. An icon is the small rectangular design that appears when your program is minimized. It provides a symbolic representation of an application, and the form of the icon can reflect the purpose of the application.

The first part of this chapter shows how to add an icon (a shield with a tiny coat of arms) to your program. At the end of the chapter we'll also discuss how to change the cursor (the common name for the mouse pointer). Icons and cursors are similar in that they are small bitmapped graphics objects, although they are different in other ways, as we'll see.

ADDING AN ICON TO YOUR PROGRAM

The user can minimize any application by clicking on its minimize button (the down-pointing triangle in the upper right corner of its main window). This causes the application's window to shrink to an icon, which appears with any other icons in the lower left corner of the desktop. The icon indicates that the program is

Figure 34-1

Icons on the Desktop

running, but it takes up very little space. Figure 34-1 shows the desktop with some typical icons.

Windows provides a default icon for programs that don't have their own. In Figure 34-1, two icons are for the ShortCut and ChngMenu examples from the last chapters, each displayed as the default icon. The default icon, while functional, isn't too exciting. Creating your own custom icon adds a professional touch to your program.

To create an icon you must exercise your artistic skills. Fortunately Borland's Resource Workshop makes this easy. Our example program, BINICON, displays a custom icon when it's minimized. Since that's all the program does, it's rather simple. The trick is to create the icon.

The Resource Script File

An icon is a resource. However, unlike the resources we've seen so far (menus, dialogs, and accelerators), an icon is not usually stored as a text script within the resource file. Instead, since it consists of graphics information, an icon resource is placed in a separate binary file with the .ICO extension. This binary file is then referenced in the .RC file. Here's the listing for BINICON.RC:

```
// binicon.rc
// resource file for binicon

Shield ICON "binicon.ico"
```

Shield is the name of the icon. The ICON keyword indicates that we're defining an icon resource. Then "binicon.ico" specifies that the resource is a file called BINICON.ICO. This file describes the icon in binary format.

There are no identifiers in this program, as there are for menu items and dialog controls, so we don't need a header file.

Creating Icons with the Resource Workshop

Creating an icon is similar to creating other resources, as described in Chapter 23, *The Resource Workshop*. You create an .RC file by selecting New Project from the File menu. Then you save it under the appropriate name, BINICON.RC in this example, by selecting Save File As from the File menu.

To invoke the Paint editor, which you'll use to design icons, select New from the Resource menu, select ICON from the list, and click on OK.

Specifying the Icon File

At this point a dialog will ask if you want the resource to be created in source form, or as a binary file. The source form, which consists of many lines of numbers in hexadecimal format, is not usually necessary or useful, so click on the Binary button.

Another dialog, New File Resource, appears. Enter the file name of the resource in the File Name field. Usually you'll use the name of the application for this file. Icons always use the .ICO extension, so the resulting name in this example is BINICON.ICO. Make sure the correct .RC file name is displayed in the box (BINICON.RC), then click on OK. Answer Yes when asked if you want to create this file.

Drawing the Image

Yet another dialog appears, this one called New Icon Image. Radio buttons show different size boxes and different numbers of colors. Click on 32x32 and 16 colors, and press OK. You'll see the Paint editor window, as shown in Figure 34-2.

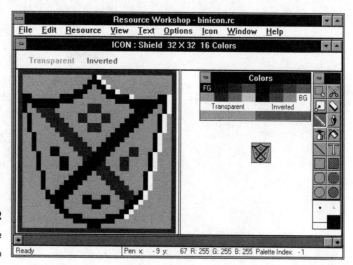

Figure 34-2

The Paint Editor in the Resource Workshop

The Paint editor works like a small paint program. It is surprisingly sophisticated, so we won't cover all its features here—just enough to get you started.

The pane on the left contains a box representing an enlarged version of an icon. You draw in this box to create the icon, using the cursor, which initially appears in the form of a pencil. Holding down the right mouse button while you move the pencil causes large square pixels to appear in the icon box.

The pane on the right contains a Colors palette and a Tools palette, in addition to a lifesize representation of the icon.

The left and right mouse buttons control separate colors. You'll probably want to use the left button for the foreground color and the right button for the background color, (which is useful for erasing mistakes). To change colors, move the pencil to one of the colors in the Colors palette. Click the left mouse button to set the foreground color, and the right button to set the background color.

The icon editor has other features as well. These are selected from the Tools palette, which is shown in Figure 34-3.

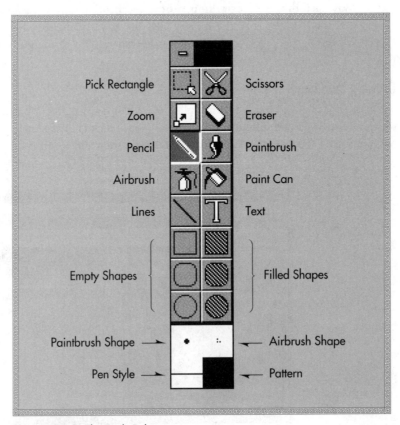

Figure 34-3 The Tools Palette

Here are some of the features on the Tools palette:

- 🔳 Lines. You can draw straight lines by clicking on the Lines icon in the Tools palette and then dragging the line in the Icon window.
- 🔳 Shapes. You can create rectangles, rounded rectangles, and circles by dragging the shape from the Tools palette and positioning it in the icon window.
- 🔳 Fill. You can fill areas with color by selecting the desired color from the Colors palette, clicking on the Paint Can icon, and then clicking with the cross hairs on the area you want filled.
- 🔳 Text. You can insert text into the icon by clicking on the Text icon to create an insertion point, moving the insertion point to the desired location, and typing in the characters.

Borland's *Resource Workshop User's Guide* describes the other icons on the Tools palette, as well as other features of the Paint editor.

Naming the Icon

When you've completed the icon, dismiss the Paint editor by selecting Close from its document menu. In the .RC window, you'll see that your icon is called ICON_1. Rename it to something more descriptive, in this case Shield, by selecting Rename from the Resource menu and filling in the name in the New Name field in the resulting dialog.

Saving the Icon Resource

Save the .RC file and the .ICO file by selecting Save Project from the File menu. If you examine the .RC file, you'll see the single line invoking the icon:

```
Shield ICON "binicon.ico"
```

There is also the binary file containing the icon, BINICON.ICO, but you can't examine this file directly. We'll need to run the program to see how the icon looks.

Modifying the Source File

You need to modify the .C source file to load the icon when the program runs. This is done in the definition of the hIcon member of the WNDCLASS structure for the main window. Since this takes place in WinMain(), we can't use our STDMAIN.INC approach to hiding WinMain(). Instead we must show WinMain() overtly at the start of the program. Here's the listing for BINICON.C:

```
// binicon.c
// adds icon to program using binary file

#define STRICT
```

```
#include <windows.h>
                                  // prototype
LRESULT CALLBACK _export WndProc(HWND, UINT, WPARAM, LPARAM);

PSTR szProgName = "BinIcon";    // application name
//////////////////////////////////////////////////////////////////
// WinMain() -- program entry point                              //
//////////////////////////////////////////////////////////////////
#pragma argsused

int PASCAL WinMain(HINSTANCE hInstance, HINSTANCE hPrevInst,
                   LPSTR lpCmdLine, int nCmdShow)
  {
  HWND hWnd;
  MSG msg;
  WNDCLASS wndclass;

  if(!hPrevInst)
     {
     wndclass.style         = CS_HREDRAW/CS_VREDRAW;
     wndclass.lpfnWndProc   = WndProc;
     wndclass.cbClsExtra    = 0;
     wndclass.cbWndExtra    = 0;
     wndclass.hInstance     = hInstance;
     wndclass.hCursor       = LoadCursor (NULL, IDC_ARROW);
     wndclass.hIcon         = LoadIcon(hInstance, "Shield"); // note
     wndclass.lpszMenuName  = NULL;
     wndclass.hbrBackground = GetStockObject(WHITE_BRUSH);
     wndclass.lpszClassName = szProgName;
     RegisterClass(&wndclass);
     }  // end if

  hWnd = CreateWindow(szProgName,
                      szProgName, WS_OVERLAPPEDWINDOW, CW_USEDEFAULT,
                      CW_USEDEFAULT, CW_USEDEFAULT, CW_USEDEFAULT,
                      NULL, NULL, hInstance, NULL);

  ShowWindow(hWnd, nCmdShow);

  // message loop
  while( GetMessage(&msg,0,0,0) )
     {
     TranslateMessage(&msg);
     DispatchMessage(&msg);
     }
  return msg.wParam;
  }  // end WinMain

//////////////////////////////////////////////////////////////////
// main window procedure -- receives messages                    //
//////////////////////////////////////////////////////////////////
LRESULT CALLBACK _export WndProc(HWND hWnd, UINT msg,
```

```
                        WPARAM wParam, LPARAM lParam)
{
switch(msg)
   {
   case WM_DESTROY:
      PostQuitMessage(0);
      break;
   default:
      return( DefWindowProc(hWnd, msg, wParam, lParam) );
   }    // end switch(msg)
return 0L;
}  // end WndProc
```

In previous programs we always used the stock application icon, invoked with the following line:

```
wndclass.hIcon = LoadIcon(NULL, IDI_APPLICATION);
```

This statement invokes the LoadIcon() function to load the stock icon, represented by IDI_APPLICATION. It also assigns the icon's handle to the hIcon member of WNDCLASS. This causes the stock application icon to be displayed when the main window is minimized.

In BINICON we modify this line to

```
wndclass.hIcon = LoadIcon(hInstance, "Shield");
```

This changes the icon to our newly created custom icon, which we named Shield in the .RC file. (Notice that the first argument is the instance handle, not NULL.) That's all you have to do. Figure 34-4 shows our custom icon on the desktop with other program icons.

A custom icon is a nice finishing touch for your application. It's an opportunity for promoting your product: an attractive icon creates a favorable impression when the user isn't actively interacting with the application.

Figure 34-4

Custom Icon on the Desktop

Table 34-1 Stock Cursors (Mouse Pointers)

Constant	Type of Cursor
IDC_ARROW	Standard up-left arrow
IDC_WAIT	Hourglass (indicates user must wait)
IDC_CROSS	Cross hairs (for fine detail)
IDC_IBEAM	I-beam (for text insertion)
IDC_UPARROW	Vertical arrow
IDC_SIZE	Square within a square
IDC_SIZENS	Double arrow, north-south
IDC_SIZEWE	Double arrow, west-east
IDC_SIZENWSE	Double arrow, northwest-southeast
IDC_SIZENESW	Double arrow, northeast-southwest
IDC_NULL	No cursor

USING STOCK CURSORS

The default cursor (mouse pointer) is an arrow that faces up and left. In many situations this cursor does just fine. Often, however, you'll encounter situations where the default cursor isn't appropriate. For instance, you may be writing a word processing program in which you want the cursor to have a vertical I-beam shape, to more accurately indicate the space between two characters. Or in a mapping program or adventure game you may want to precisely indicate points on a map, while hiding a minimum of the underlying detail. In these cases a small cross is easier to use than the arrow. Perhaps the most commonly used cursor, besides the normal arrow, is the hourglass, which is displayed when the user must wait for some lengthy process to complete, like a print job or disk access.

Windows makes available a number of stock cursors for these common situations. Table 34-1 shows the different stock cursors.

The various cursors with SIZE in their identifiers are used by Windows when the user is resizing a window by dragging the sizing border.

Permanent Cursor Replacement

Sometimes you want to change to a different stock cursor and keep this new cursor the entire time your program is running. You do this by calling the LoadCursor() function and assigning the resulting handle to the hCursor member of the wndclass structure in WinMain(), like this:

```
wndclass.hCursor = LoadCursor(NULL, IDC_IBEAM);
```

To do this you'll need to put WinMain() in your program overtly, as we've shown in several previous examples. We won't show an example of this, but it's easy to implement. The line shown above will cause the I-beam shape to appear whenever the cursor is in your window (or any window of the same class, for that matter).

Hourglass Cursor Indicates Lengthy Tasks

The hourglass cursor is used to indicate that a process is taking a long time to complete (from a fraction of a second to minutes). This typically happens when a file is being read or written to disk, or when a file is being printed. Here's how the cursor would be handled in the case of a program that uses a menu command to save a file to disk:

```
case IDM_SAVE:                            // user selects Save
   // open file and so on
   hCursor = LoadCursor(NULL, IDC_WAIT);  // load hourglass cursor
   hOldCursor = SetCursor(hCursor);       // display it
   _lread(...)                            // read the file (takes time)
   SetCursor(hOldCursor);                 // restore old cursor
   break;
```

We save the original cursor when we set the new one, and restore it when the reading process is complete. In many cases you don't need to restore the old cursor, since the default arrow cursor is reinstalled frequently by Windows. We'll see an example of this when we discuss printing in Part Seven, *Other Topics.*

Dynamic Cursor Replacement

If you want to change the cursor while the program is running, you'll need to monitor a new message: WM_SETCURSOR. This message arrives whenever the cursor should be reset. If you take the opportunity to reset the cursor to the desired shape whenever you get WM_SETCURSOR, the cursor will keep its new shape. If you don't reset the cursor when you get this message, the cursor will revert back to the default cursor.

Our example program shows how this works. It allows you to switch back and forth between two stock cursors. When you press the left mouse button, you'll get

the cross; and when you press the right mouse button, you'll get the up arrow.
Here's the listing for STOCUR.C:

```c
// stocur.c
// demonstrates stock cursors

#define STRICT
#include <windows.h>

                            // prototype
LRESULT CALLBACK _export WndProc(HWND, UINT, WPARAM, LPARAM);

PSTR szProgName = "StoCur";            // application name
#include "stdmain.inc"                 // standard WinMain() function
////////////////////////////////////////////////////////////////////
// main window procedure -- receives messages                      //
////////////////////////////////////////////////////////////////////
LRESULT CALLBACK _export WndProc(HWND hWnd, UINT msg,
                                 WPARAM wParam, LPARAM lParam)
    {
    static HCURSOR hCurrentCur, hUpCursor, hCrossCursor;

    switch(msg)
        {
        case WM_CREATE:
            hUpCursor =  LoadCursor(NULL, IDC_UPARROW);  // load stock
            hCrossCursor = LoadCursor(NULL, IDC_CROSS);  // cursors
            hCurrentCur = hCrossCursor;
            break;

        case WM_LBUTTONDOWN:
            hCurrentCur = hCrossCursor;     // it's the cross
            break;

        case WM_RBUTTONDOWN:
            hCurrentCur = hUpCursor;        // it's the up arrow
            break;

        case WM_SETCURSOR:
            SetCursor(hCurrentCur);         // set cursor
            break;

        case WM_DESTROY:
            PostQuitMessage(0);
            break;

        default:
            return( DefWindowProc(hWnd, msg, wParam, lParam) );
        }   // end switch(msg)

    return 0L;
    }  // end WndProc
```

When the WM_CREATE message is received, we use the LoadCursor() function to load the up arrow and the cross stock cursors. The variable hCurrentCur keeps track of which cursor is currently active. It starts out to be the cross cursor, but switches whenever a different mouse button is pushed. When the WM_SETCURSOR message arrives we reset the cursor to whatever the value of hCurrentCur is. If we don't do this, the cursor will revert to the default arrow whenever we get a WM_SETCURSOR message, which occurs whenever there's any mouse activity.

It's possible to create custom cursors, in much the same way we created custom icons earlier in this chapter. However, the stock cursors handle most situations.

SUMMARY

Here are the steps for adding an icon to your program:

1. Create an icon resource with the Resource Workshop. The icon will have a name, and will be stored in an .ICO file. There will be a statement invoking the icon in the .RC file.
2. Call the LoadIcon() function with arguments of hInstance and the name of your icon resource, and assign the result to the hIcon member of the WNDCLASS structure used to define the class of your main window.

There are several ways to change the cursor (mouse pointer) that's displayed in your program's main window. For a permanent change, you can change the value given to the hCursor member of the WNDCLASS structure used to define the class of your window.

You can use the LoadCursor() and SetCursor() functions together to change the cursor at any time. However, if you want to keep the cursor set after your window procedure returns (that is, after the current message has been processed), you'll need to monitor the WM_SETCURSOR message and use SetCursor() to keep the cursor reset to the proper value whenever this message is received.

35

STAND-ALONE DIALOGS

indows is amazingly flexible. For example, controls such as pushbuttons and edit fields are usually placed in dialog boxes, using statements in the resource script file. However, as we've already seen (in the EZEDIT program in Chapter 20, *Text Input: The Easy Way*), we can also use the CreateWindow() function to install an edit control directly in a main window.

In this chapter we're going to demonstrate another example of Windows' flexibility: using a dialog box as a main window. Why would we want to do that? Sometimes it's necessary to put many controls directly on a main window, and it's easier to install controls in a dialog box. Examples of programs that do this are desktop calculators (such as the CALCULATOR accessory in Windows) and games. In Part Eight, *Larger Programs,* we include another program that uses this approach: a calculator that converts between Roman and Arabic numerals.

THE 15-PUZZLE

The example program in this chapter models the classic "15-Puzzle" game. In this puzzle, 15 small blocks, numbered from 1 to 15, are confined in a square with 16 spaces. By repeatedly moving one of the adjacent blocks into the empty space, you can rearrange the pattern of the blocks. You can move blocks vertically or horizontally, but not diagonally. Figure 35-1 shows a 15-Puzzle in its initial position, before any of the blocks have been moved. In Figure 35-2 the blocks have been rearranged, forming a different pattern.

Figure 35-1
The 15-Puzzle
in Initial Position

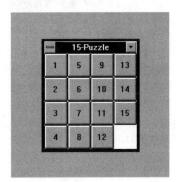

Figure 35-2
The 15-Puzzle
in New Position

Devotees of the 15-Puzzle try to arrange the numbers in different patterns, such as ordering them vertically, or in a spiral. It's interesting to note that not all the possible patterns can actually be achieved; only half of them are accessible. If you can't make a particular pattern no matter how hard you try, it may turn out to be one of the impossible ones.

MAIN WINDOW AS DIALOG

As you can see from the figures, the program's main window contains 15 pushbutton controls. (There are actually 16, but one is invisible.) We could place these controls in the window using a CreateWindow() function for each individual button, but figuring out the arguments for these functions to specify the button's positions would need to be done by hand, a tedious job. It's far easier to use the Resource Workshop to place the buttons in a dialog box, and then cause this dialog box to be the main window. Actually, dialog boxes and main windows are both just windows; there's really no essential difference between them. That's what makes this sort of interchangeability possible.

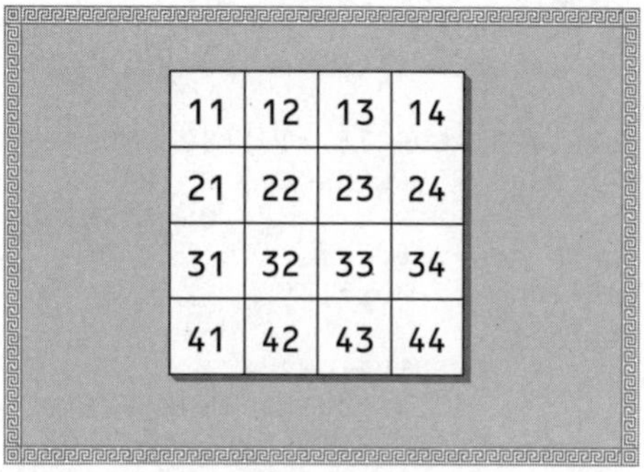

Figure 35-3 Pushbutton IDs

Creating the .RC File

You must first create a dialog box in the usual way with the Resource Workshop. Move 16 pushbuttons into it to form a 4-by-4 square. Size the dialog so it just holds the buttons. Give each button a caption that is a number from "1" to "15", as shown in Figure 35-1. The 16th button can be given any caption you like, such as "XX", since it will be made invisible later.

Each pushbutton must also be given a numerical ID value. These values depend on the position of the button. Figure 35-3 shows what values to assign. These values are critical because they'll be used to check the validity of the user's moves.

We don't use symbolic identifiers (like IDP_BUTTON15 or whatever) in this program because the numerical values are more informative than any such names would be. Thus there is no need for an .H header file.

You must specify a window class name for the dialog resource. We haven't done this before, but it's not hard. In the Dialog Editor, double-click on the dialog frame to bring up the Window Style dialog. Fill in the Class field with a class name, which can simply be the application name, "PuzzleClass" in this example. This produces the statement

```
CLASS "PuzzleClass"
```

in the description of the dialog in the PUZZLE.RC file.

Still in the Window Style dialog, fill in the Caption field with "15-Puzzle." We want to add a minimize button to the dialog, so click on the Minimize Box radio button. The System Menu and Modal Frame radio buttons should already be checked, the Window Type should be set to Pop-up, and the Frame Style to Caption.

Rename the dialog resource to Puzzle and save the project. Here's the listing for the resulting PUZZLE.RC file:

```
// puzzle.rc
// resource file for puzzle

Puzzle DIALOG 18, 18, 80, 80
STYLE DS_MODALFRAME | WS_POPUP | WS_CAPTION |
                    WS_SYSMENU | WS_MINIMIZEBOX
CLASS "PuzzleClass"
CAPTION "15-Puzzle"
BEGIN
        PUSHBUTTON "1", 11, 0, 0, 20, 20,
            WS_CHILD | WS_VISIBLE | WS_TABSTOP
        PUSHBUTTON "2", 12, 20, 0, 20, 20,
            WS_CHILD | WS_VISIBLE | WS_TABSTOP
        PUSHBUTTON "3", 13, 40, 0, 20, 20,
            WS_CHILD | WS_VISIBLE | WS_TABSTOP
        PUSHBUTTON "4", 14, 60, 0, 20, 20,
            WS_CHILD | WS_VISIBLE | WS_TABSTOP
        PUSHBUTTON "5", 21, 0, 20, 20, 20,
            WS_CHILD | WS_VISIBLE | WS_TABSTOP
        PUSHBUTTON "6", 22, 20, 20, 20, 20,
            WS_CHILD | WS_VISIBLE | WS_TABSTOP
        PUSHBUTTON "7", 23, 40, 20, 20, 20,
            WS_CHILD | WS_VISIBLE | WS_TABSTOP
        PUSHBUTTON "8", 24, 60, 20, 20, 20,
            WS_CHILD | WS_VISIBLE | WS_TABSTOP
        PUSHBUTTON "9", 31, 0, 40, 20, 20,
            WS_CHILD | WS_VISIBLE | WS_TABSTOP
        PUSHBUTTON "10", 32, 20, 40, 20, 20,
            WS_CHILD | WS_VISIBLE | WS_TABSTOP
        PUSHBUTTON "11", 33, 40, 40, 20, 20,
            WS_CHILD | WS_VISIBLE | WS_TABSTOP
        PUSHBUTTON "12", 34, 60, 40, 20, 20,
            WS_CHILD | WS_VISIBLE | WS_TABSTOP
        PUSHBUTTON "13", 41, 0, 60, 20, 20,
            WS_CHILD | WS_VISIBLE | WS_TABSTOP
        PUSHBUTTON "14", 42, 20, 60, 20, 20,
            WS_CHILD | WS_VISIBLE | WS_TABSTOP
        PUSHBUTTON "15", 43, 40, 60, 20, 20,
            WS_CHILD | WS_VISIBLE | WS_TABSTOP
        PUSHBUTTON "XX", 44, 60, 60, 20, 20,
            WS_CHILD | WS_VISIBLE | WS_TABSTOP
END
```

Creating the .C File

In the .C file, two changes are needed to treat a dialog box as a main window. Both involve changes in WinMain(), so we must include this function overtly in our listing rather than using our standard STDMAIN.INC file.

First, when we define the window class, we must set the cbWndExtra member to a constant:

```
wndclass.cbWndExtra = DLGWINDOWEXTRA;   // NOTE!!
```

This reserves a few dozen extra bytes in each instance of the program for the use of a part of the system called the dialog manager. If you don't reserve this space, the dialog manager will write into Never-Never Land, which is like falling into the clutches of the evil enchantress Morgan le Fey (who was King Arthur's sister, but that's another story).

The second change in WinMain() is using CreateDialog() instead of CreateWindow(). This function creates the dialog box/main window:

```
hWnd = CreateDialog(hInstance, szProgName, NULL, NULL);
```

The first argument is the instance handle, and the second is the name of the dialog resource, which is "Puzzle" in PUZZLE.RC. The next two arguments are the handle of the dialog's owner and the address of the dialog procedure. This dialog box is a main window, so its owner is NULL. It has no dialog procedure, since it uses WndProc(), which was specified in the class definition, so the fourth argument is also NULL. Here's the listing for PUZZLE.C:

```
// puzzle.c
// makes a "15-Puzzle"

#define STRICT
#include <windows.h>
                                    // prototype
LRESULT CALLBACK _export WndProc(HWND, UINT, WPARAM, LPARAM);

WORD wEmpty = 44;              // ID of button 16 (empty cell)
HWND hWndButton;              // button handle
char acBuffer[3];            // for button captions
//////////////////////////////////////////////////////////////////////
// WinMain() -- program entry point                                   //
//////////////////////////////////////////////////////////////////////
#pragma argsused

int PASCAL WinMain(HINSTANCE hInstance, HINSTANCE hPrevInst,
               LPSTR lpCmdLine, int nCmdShow)
   {
   HWND hWnd;
   MSG msg;
   WNDCLASS wndclass;

   if(!hPrevInst)
      {                                 // define the class
```

```
        wndclass.style          = NULL;
        wndclass.lpfnWndProc    = WndProc;
        wndclass.cbClsExtra     = 0;
        wndclass.cbWndExtra     = DLGWINDOWEXTRA;  // NOTE!!
        wndclass.hInstance      = hInstance;
        wndclass.hCursor        = LoadCursor (NULL, IDC_ARROW);
        wndclass.hIcon          = LoadIcon(NULL, IDI_APPLICATION);
        wndclass.lpszMenuName   = NULL;
        wndclass.hbrBackground = GetStockObject(WHITE_BRUSH);
        wndclass.lpszClassName = "PuzzleClass";  // must match class in
                                                 // dialog resource
        RegisterClass(&wndclass);        // register the window
        }  // end if
                                         // create a dialog window
    hWnd = CreateDialog(hInstance, "Puzzle", 0, NULL);

    ShowWindow(hWnd, nCmdShow);          // make window visible


    hWndButton = GetDlgItem(hWnd, wEmpty);  // get button 16 handle
    ShowWindow(hWndButton, SW_HIDE);        // make it invisible

    while( GetMessage(&msg,0,0,0) )
        {
        TranslateMessage(&msg);
        DispatchMessage(&msg);
        }
    return msg.wParam;
    }  // end WinMain


//////////////////////////////////////////////////////////////////
// main window procedure -- receives messages                    //
//////////////////////////////////////////////////////////////////
LRESULT CALLBACK _export WndProc(HWND hWnd, UINT msg,
                                 WPARAM wParam, LPARAM lParam)
    {
    switch(msg)
        {
        case WM_COMMAND:                          // button pressed
            if(wParam-wEmpty == 1 || wParam-wEmpty == 10 ||  // legal
               wEmpty-wParam == 1 || wEmpty-wParam == 10)    // move?
                {
                GetDlgItemText(hWnd, wParam, acBuffer, 3); // copy text
                SetDlgItemText(hWnd, wEmpty, acBuffer);
                hWndButton = GetDlgItem(hWnd, wParam); // active handle
                ShowWindow(hWndButton, SW_HIDE);       // make invis
                hWndButton = GetDlgItem(hWnd, wEmpty); // empty handle
                ShowWindow(hWndButton, SW_SHOW);       // make visible
                wEmpty = wParam;                       // save empty ID
                }
            else
                MessageBeep(0);                   // not a legal move
```

```
        SetFocus(hWnd);                       // no focus on button
        return 0;

    case WM_DESTROY:
        PostQuitMessage(0);
        return 0;
    }   // end switch(msg)
return( DefWindowProc(hWnd, msg, wParam, lParam) );
}   // end WndProc
```

PROGRAMMING TRICKS

We've used several tricks to simplify the code in PUZZLE.C. These include the scheme for numbering the button IDs, and copying one button's text to another. These tricks are specific to the Puzzle program; they're not applicable to all programs that use a dialog as a main window. However, you may find it interesting to see how they're applied.

They Don't Really Move

The central trick in Puzzle is that the buttons don't really move. They appear to move because a caption ("1" , "15" and so on) is copied from one button to another. Related to this is the fact that the empty space (the square where no button appears) is really just another button. The empty space moves from button to button. We'll call the button that is the temporary home of the empty space the *empty button*. The empty button is like the other buttons except that it's made invisible. Invisible controls don't generate messages and (of course) can't be seen by the user.

Let's call whatever button the user clicks on, the *active button*. We want the active button to appear to move into the empty space (assuming they are adjacent). To make it appear that a button is moving into the empty space we do three things:

▨ Copy the caption from the active button to the empty button.
▨ Make the active button invisible.
▨ Make the empty button visible.

In addition we save the ID number of the active button in a variable called wEmpty, so we can keep track of which button is the empty button. This all happens when we receive a WM_COMMAND message. The only controls are the 16 buttons, so we can assume that any WM_COMMAND message is the result of a button press. The ID of the button is in the wParam argument, so we treat this variable as the active button.

Remember that because the buttons don't move, the same button ID always applies to the button in a particular position, no matter what the caption on the button is, or whether the button is invisible (empty) or not.

Button Numbering

How can the program tell if a move is legal? For legal moves, the user must click on a button that is adjacent to the empty space: above it, below it, to the left, or to the right. If the move is legal we move the active button into the empty button; for illegal moves, we beep to alert the user.

The trick we use to determine the legality of a move is to give the button IDs numerical values that are related to their position. As you can see from Figure 35-3, if a button is below another button, its ID is 10 greater; if it's above, its ID is 10 less. If a button is to the right of another button, its ID is 1 greater, if it's to the left, its ID is 1 less.

For example, starting with the initial position in Figure 35-1, suppose we want to move the "12" button down into the empty space. The ID of the "12" button is 34, and the ID of the empty space is 44. These differ by 10, so the move is legal. The "11" button, on the other hand, has an ID of 33. It's illegal to move this button, since it differs from 44 by neither 1 nor 10.

We express these relationships in an **if** statement. Only if one of the four position possibilities is true do we move the button into the empty space.

SUMMARY

Here are the steps necessary to use a dialog box, created with the Resource Workshop, as a main window.

1. Create an .RC file and a dialog resource in the usual way with the RW, and place the controls in the dialog.
2. In the Window Style dialog for the dialog resource in the dialog editor, fill in the Class field with the same name you used for the lpszClassName member of the WNDCLASS structure.
3. In WinMain(), define a class in the usual way (as in our standard STDMAIN.INC file), but set the cbWndExtra member of WNDCLASS to the constant DLGWINDOWEXTRA.
4. Instead of using CreateWindow() to create the window, use CreateDialog(). The second argument to this function is the dialog's name (which appears in the dialog script in the .RC file).

5. Messages from the dialog controls will arrive in WndProc() as WM_COMMAND messages.

In Part Six we've looked at just a few of the many modifications you can make to the user interface to achieve interesting and useful effects. In Part Seven, *Other Topics,* we'll look at several different issues: memory management, printing, and debugging. In Part Eight, *Larger Programs,* we'll show several more complex example programs, some of which include techniques discussed in this chapter.

PART SEVEN
OTHER TOPICS

*I*n King Arthur's time there were rogue knights who didn't fit into the established categories. They weren't members of the Round Table, but they weren't part of the infamous Orkney faction (like Sir Gawain or King Lot) and they weren't foreigners like the French or Italians. The most well-known rogue knight, made famous by Robert Malgre Louis, was King Galavant the Unpredictable, who changed sides in the middle of the battle of Willbury Downs.

This section concerns programming activities that also don't fit into established categories, at least not the user-interface topics we've discussed so far. Nevertheless, these subjects—memory management, printing, and debugging—are important for writing serious Windows programs. Memory management is necessary when you need larger amounts of memory; printing creates a permanent record of text and graphics displays; and debugging is, alas, a necessary activity in any programming environment, and especially a complex one like Windows.

CHAPTER 36

MANAGING MEMORY

$\mathcal{K}$ing Arthur is thought to have been an actual person who lived in the 5th century and fought many successful battles. However, the evidence for this is tantalizingly slim. The problem is that no one (as far as we know) wrote down anything about Arthur's reign until many hundreds of years after it ended. In the meantime, the stories of his exploits survived only in the memories of individual Britons, who passed them down from generation to generation. Because we humans tend to embellish and romanticize our memories, it is difficult at this late date to separate fact from fiction; it is hard to know how much of the Arthurian legend is true.

Computers are less likely to romanticize the contents of their memories; usually we can count on them not to alter any of the data we entrust to them. Indeed, in the example programs we've seen so far in this book, we haven't paid much attention to memory at all. These programs used RAM (Random Access Memory) the way normal, small-scale C programs do, by defining automatic, static, and external variables. For such variables the compiler takes care of obtaining the proper memory from the system, and the programmer doesn't need to worry about the allocation process. However, there are situations where you cannot take such a cavalier attitude toward memory management. Instead, you may need to obtain memory directly from the system, as the program runs, rather than letting the compiler do it. This is called *dynamic memory allocation.*

Dynamic memory allocation may be necessary for several reasons. First, you may not be able to obtain enough memory any other way. If you're working with many variables, or even a few large ones (such as large arrays), they may not fit in the memory normally assigned to your program. Second, programs running in a multitasking environment like Windows should, like the knights of old, behave in a chivalrous manner. That means using the minimum amount of memory necessary, so that other applications will have room for their own data. This implies that an application should wait to allocate memory until it knows exactly how much to obtain, rather than allocating an enormous amount at the beginning and hoping everything will fit (as programs often do in single-tasking DOS systems). An example of this is a program waiting to allocate memory for a data buffer until it has examined the size of a disk file to be read into the buffer.

In this chapter we're going to examine how Windows applications allocate memory dynamically. We'll get to the nuts and bolts of memory allocation in the second part of the chapter. First, however, you need to know a few details about Windows memory management. The next few sections provide this background.

WINDOWS MEMORY MANAGEMENT

One of the keys to understanding Windows memory management is knowing that memory segments can be moved, discarded, and otherwise manipulated by the system while our program is using them. Let's review what segments are, and why they should be treated in this unchivalrous fashion.

Segments

In Windows 3.x, memory is allocated in *segments*. A segment is a quantity of memory that is convenient for the hardware to access as a unit. Because of the architecture of the Intel processors on which Windows runs, a segment cannot exceed 65,536 bytes, or 64K. (At least that is true of Windows 3.x. In Windows NT, which uses 32-bit memory addressing, this limitation disappears.) A segment may be smaller than 64K, but it can't be any larger.

A memory segment can be used for either code (program instructions) or data, but not (usually) both at once. The Windows programs that we've demonstrated in this book are all small-model programs, which use two segments: one for the program's code and one for its data. Another segment may be used for resources. This sets a limit on the amount of memory available to ordinary (non-dynamic) variables. However, as we show in this chapter, a program can dynamically allocate additional data segments as needed.

Memory Fragmentation

We said that Windows can move segments around in memory. Why would it want to do this? In Windows, memory is a shared resource. When several different programs are active, all of them, as well as Windows itself, are using memory at the same time. If a program takes up too much memory, or if there are too many

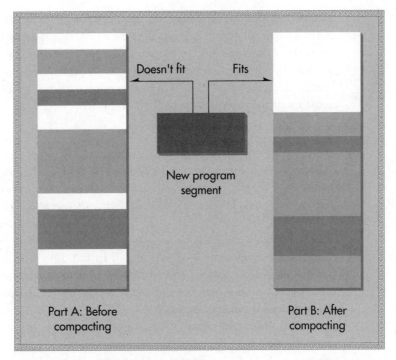

Figure 36-1 Memory Fragmentation

programs in memory at once, it's possible to run out of memory. Windows goes to considerable trouble to prevent this from happening. One way to conserve memory is to avoid *memory fragmentation*. Memory fragmentation occurs as a result of Windows allocating and deallocating different-sized memory segments for programs as they run. Eventually, "holes" develop between active segments, as shown in Figure 36-1, Part A.

If a new program requests memory, small segments can fit in the holes, but large ones may not find enough room. Windows tries to fix this by moving segments around in memory to create larger contiguous memory spaces, as shown in Figure 36-1, Part B. This is called *compacting* memory.

Moveable Memory

For Windows to compact memory, it must be able to move most memory segments. However, some segments should remain fixed. When you allocate memory you must specify whether it is to be moveable or fixed.

As a programmer, you may ask if it isn't dangerous to move parts of a program around in memory. Doesn't the program get confused? Don't pointers and addresses change, causing the program to access the wrong addresses? Not at all. Windows takes care of all the details, so that data will continue to be addressed by the program in the same way, no matter where it is in memory. In fact, most programs are not even aware that they have been moved. In simple programs you can pretty much ignore the whole issue, except that when dynamically allocating memory you must specify whether it is moveable or fixed, as we'll see.

Other Kinds of Memory

A memory segment can also be marked as *discardable*. That means that if Windows runs out of memory it can abandon the segment's contents and write over it with another segment. Later, if it's needed, Windows can reload the discarded segment from the disk. A discardable segment cannot be modified during program execution. If the information in it could be changed, then the changes would be lost when it was written over and reloaded from disk. Code and resources, which are not modifiable, can be treated this way, but not data. We won't worry about discardable memory here. It's not usually necessary for an application to mark the memory it allocates as discardable.

In 386-Enhanced mode, Windows can swap parts of programs to disk when memory becomes limited. This is called *virtual memory*. It allows programs to operate as if there were more RAM in the system than there really is. Virtual memory is a completely different mechanism than moving and discarding memory. It allows modifiable data segments to be swapped to the disk as well as code and resource segments. The use of virtual memory is completely invisible to the program, and can be ignored by applications programmers except in special circumstances. (From the user's viewpoint, however, applications will run more slowly when using virtual memory, since disk access is much slower than access to RAM.)

THE DEFAULT DATA SEGMENT

You can allocate two different kinds of memory in Windows: local and global. When should you use local, and when global? To answer this question, you need to understand the limitations of something called the *default data segment*, which holds local memory.

In Windows, every program—actually every *instance* of a program—includes exactly one default data segment. Figure 36-2 shows how this segment is arranged.

Let's look at a fragment of a program to see how different kinds of variables use memory, and how this relates to the default data segment.

```
// sample code

char acAlpha[100];    // external variable
int iBeta;            // external variable

func()
   {
   int iGamma;        // automatic variable
   char* pDelta;      // another automatic variable
   static int iZeta;  // static variable

   pGamma = (char*)malloc(100);   // don't do this in Windows
   }
```

This code shows memory being allocated in four different ways. There are external variables, static variables, automatic variables, and dynamic memory allocation with the C-language malloc() function, which should not be used in Windows but which may be familiar to you from C programs on other systems. All these kinds of data are stored in the default data segment.

Let's examine these different ways to store data with regard to their lifetime (how long the data remains in existence), visibility (what parts of the program can access them), and location (where they're stored in the default data segment).

Static Data

The part of the default data segment called *static data* contains your program's external and static variables.

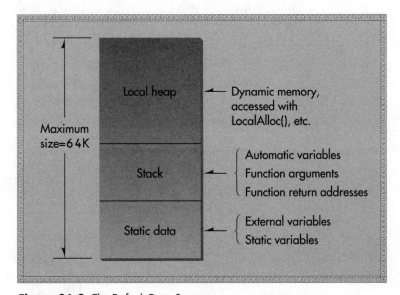

Figure 36-2 The Default Data Segment

External Variables

In the previous fragment, the variables acAlpha and iBeta are *external* variables. The memory they occupy is obtained when the program first starts to run, and remains available until the program terminates. If you put a value in an external variable, it will remain fixed for the life of the program (or until you change it). The lifetime of external variables is the same as that of the program itself.

External variables are accessible, or visible, from anywhere in the program (actually from the point at which they're declared to the end of the file).

Static Variables

The variable iZeta is declared static. This is a hybrid storage class. Like automatic variables, static variables can be accessed only from the function in which they're declared. However, like external variables, their lifetime is the same as that of the entire program.

The Stack

The second part of the default data segment is the *stack*. The stack is a data area that grows and shrinks dynamically while the program runs. It contains a program's automatic variables, function arguments, and function return addresses.

Automatic Variables

The variables iGamma and pDelta in the previous fragment are examples of automatic variables. Automatic variables are created (automatically; hence the name) when a function starts to execute, and are destroyed when the function returns. Their lifetime is thus the same as the function's. Also, they aren't accessible outside the function, so they have function visibility.

Remember that because the lifetime of automatic variables is the same as that of their function, such variables in window procedures like WndProc() won't retain their values between messages.

Arguments and Return Addresses

The stack also holds a function's arguments and its return address. When the function is called, its automatic variables, its arguments, and its return address are placed on the stack. When the function returns, this data is removed from the stack. Thus the stack's size at any moment depends on what functions are in operation.

Windows uses your stack whenever it calls any of your window procedures. This is why the linker automatically sets the stack size to a fairly large value, like 5K.

The Local Heap

The third major area of the default data segment is the *local heap*. You can allocate memory dynamically from the local heap. You may be familiar with malloc() and similar C functions, which allocate memory dynamically. You call them, and they return a pointer to an area of memory of the requested size. You then access this memory indirectly using pointers. In Windows you shouldn't use malloc(), but similar functions allow dynamic allocation of the local heap, as we'll see.

One Per Instance

Since each instance of a program has its own default data segment, each instance also has its own set of global and static variables, its own stack, and its own local heap. This makes it possible to run multiple instances of the same program without their data becoming catastrophically intermingled. Note, however, that if you declare two windows (and therefore two window procedures) of the same class, they must share all their local data. This can lead to problems if you use external or static variables. In this book we avoid the problem by never allocating more than one window of the same class; although there are times when you might want to do this.

GLOBAL MEMORY

We've seen that local memory is obtained from the local heap in the default data segment. However, you aren't limited to the local data segment for all your data storage. A Windows application can obtain global memory as well. This gives you the opportunity to allocate as much memory as you want, up to the amount available in the system, from the global heap. It is obtained in much the same way as local memory.

If there is so much global memory available, why would you want to use local memory? Let's compare the two kinds of allocation.

Advantages of Local Memory

The good news about local memory obtained from the default data segment is that it's fast. This is because its data is accessed with near pointers. Global memory is accessed with far pointers, which are twice as big as near pointers, and require considerably more overhead for each memory access. Also, the allocation process itself is more efficient for local memory, requiring less time and fewer bytes of memory.

Advantages of Global Memory

The problem with local memory is that the entire contents of the default data segment must not exceed 64K. This includes the stack and static data. Turbo (or Borland) C++ for Windows determines automatically how large the Stack will be (unless you use a .DEF file, which allows you to specify it yourself). This will be at least 5K. The Static Data area is sized to hold all your program's static data (external and static), however large that may be. There is also a small amount of overhead. The balance of the default data segment, perhaps 50K or less, is all that's available for local allocation.

Thus allocating from the local heap is appropriate for small amounts of memory. You'll need to keep track of how much memory you're using for your stack, static data, and local heap. If the total starts to approach 64K, you'll need to think about using global instead of local memory. But until this point is reached, local memory is superior, since it's faster and easier to access.

Now let's see how local and global memory are actually obtained from the system.

LOCAL ALLOCATION

When it first starts, our example program, LOCAL, allocates 5,000 variables of type UINT from the local heap. This is equivalent to 10,000 bytes. When the user presses the left mouse button, the program fills this memory with data, which is the sequence of numbers from 0 to 4,999, and checks to see if the data is correct. When the program terminates, it frees the memory. There are no .RC or .H files. Here's the listing for LOCAL.C:

```
// local.c
// allocates local memory

#define STRICT              // strict type checking
#include <windows.h>        // include file for all windows apps
                            // prototype
LRESULT CALLBACK _export WndProc(HWND, UINT, WPARAM, LPARAM);

UINT  uSegSize = 10000;     // number of bytes to be allocated
UINT  cVars =     5000;     // number of variables of type UINT

PSTR szProgName = "Local";  // application name
#include "stdmain.inc"       // standard WinMain() function
///////////////////////////////////////////////////////////////////
// main window procedure -- receives messages                    //
///////////////////////////////////////////////////////////////////
LRESULT CALLBACK _export WndProc(HWND hWnd, UINT msg,
                                 WPARAM wParam, LPARAM lParam)
   {
   static HLOCAL hLocal;    // handle to local memory
```

```
static UINT* pStart;          // pointer to memory block (note: near)
UINT j;                       // loop variable (note: unsigned int)

switch(msg)
    {
    case WM_CREATE:
        // allocate memory from local heap, get handle to memory
        hLocal = LocalAlloc(LMEM_FIXED | LMEM_ZEROINIT, uSegSize);
        if(!hLocal)
            { MessageBox(hWnd, "Can't allocate memory", szProgName,
                    MB_SYSTEMMODAL | MB_OK);   break; }

        pStart = (UINT*)LocalLock(hLocal);  // get pointer to memory
        break;   // end WM_CREATE

    case WM_LBUTTONDOWN:
        for(j=0; j<cVars; j++)                 // fill memory with data
            *(pStart+j) = j;

        for(j=0; j<cVars; j++)               // check data
            if(*(pStart+j) != j)
                { MessageBox(hWnd, "Memory error", szProgName,
                        MB_ICONHAND | MB_OK);   break; }

        MessageBox(hWnd, "Successful memory test", szProgName,
                MB_ICONINFORMATION | MB_OK);

        break;   // end WM_LBUTTONDOWN

    case WM_DESTROY:
        LocalUnlock(hLocal);                 // unlock memory
        LocalFree(hLocal);                   // free memory
        PostQuitMessage(0);
        break;

    default:
        return( DefWindowProc(hWnd, msg, wParam, lParam) );
    }   // end switch(msg)
return 0L;
}  // end WndProc
```

When you run this program and press the left mouse button, a message box appears (provided that all goes well) saying "Successful memory test." You can then select Close from the System menu, terminating the program. This is easy from the user's viewpoint, but there's considerable activity behind the scenes.

The LocalAlloc() Function

The function that allocates memory from the local heap is LocalAlloc(). You might expect that this function would return a pointer to the memory block, but things don't work that way in Windows. Instead what you get from LocalAlloc() is a handle to a memory *object*. An object in this context is a segment less than 64K long. As you recall from previous chapters, a handle is simply a numerical ID number that identifies an object and allows it to be accessed.

The first argument to LocalAlloc() can be one of the constants shown in Table 36-1.

You normally want to make local data segments fixed (as opposed to moveable). This installs the segment at the bottom of the local heap where it won't interfere with other memory activities. For this you want the LMEM_FIXED constant. Also, it's usually convenient if the allocated memory is initially set to all zeros. The LMEM_ZEROINIT constant accomplishes that. Multiple constants are ORed together. (You can also substitute the LPTR constant, which combines LMEM_FIXED and LMEM_ZEROINIT; we don't use it since it's less obvious what its purpose is.) The second argument to LocalAlloc() is the number of bytes to allocate.

Check the Return Value

The return value of LocalAlloc() is NULL (0) if the function is unsuccessful in obtaining memory. *It's vitally important to check this return value.* We have not emphasized the need to check the return values of API functions (although we'll have more to say about this in Chapter 38, *Debugging*). However, there is a fairly high probability that any given memory access attempt will fail. Why? Because Windows and other applications may be using all available memory at that particular instant.

Of course, if you take care not to run any other programs at the same time as your application, you may get away with not worrying about the return value of

Table 36-1 Allocation Attributes for LocalAlloc()

Constant	Allocated Memory
LMEM_MOVEABLE	Can be moved
LMEM_DISCARDABLE	Can be discarded (written over)
LMEM_FIXED	Can *not* be moved or discarded
LMEM_ZEROINIT	Is initialized to zeros
LMEM_NOCOMPACT	Does not cause local heap to be compacted
LMEM_NODISCARD	Does not cause local heap to be discarded

LocalAlloc(). But in the general situation where the user has started an unknown number of other programs, LocalAlloc() may not find the memory your program requests. In this case it's important to deal with the situation gracefully. In LOCAL we display a message box and skip the rest of the memory processing. In a serious program you might want to suggest that the user close other applications to free up some memory, and then try again.

System Modal Message Box

Notice that we use the MB_SYSTEMMODAL constant in the message box. This has the effect of shutting down all the other programs in the system until the user clicks on OK. Why take such a draconian step? Not being able to allocate memory is a problem with system-wide repercussions, and things may get weird at any moment. It's safest to bring everything to a halt until the user has been informed of the problem.

The LocalLock() Function

One question you may be asking is, if LocalAlloc() returns only a handle to memory, how do we get the actual memory address (that is, a pointer to it), so we can access the memory? The function LocalLock() solves this problem. It takes the memory handle as an argument, and returns a pointer to that memory. The pointer will be valid until the memory is unlocked with another function: LocalUnlock().

The need for separate functions for allocating and locking memory arose in the time of Real mode, in versions of Windows before 3.1. In Real mode, when a memory segment was moved, its pointer value changed. To guarantee a valid pointer value, the segment had to be locked to prevent it from moving while it was being accessed. However, now that Windows has abandoned Real mode, it can take advantage of the sophistication built into Intel's 80x86 processors, and locking data is no longer necessary. Thus a single function would probably suffice for both allocation and "locking" (obtaining a pointer). But the two-function approach lingers on for historical reasons. For the programmer, the result is that you must remember to allocate and lock together, in that order.

LocalUnlock() and LocalFree()

When you've finished with the memory you allocated, you should free it as soon as possible, so it will be available to Windows and other applications. In any case you should free it before exiting from the program. In LOCAL we free the memory when we get a WM_DESTROY message, indicating that the user has selected Close from the System menu.

Two functions, LocalUnlock() and LocalFree(), are necessary to unlock and free the memory. These functions require the memory *handle* (not the pointer) as an argument. You should always unlock and free together, in that order. The complete sequence is

```
hLocal = LocalAlloc(...        // allocate memory
pData = LocalLock(hLocal);     // get pointer to it
...
// access memory using pData
...
LocalUnlock(hLocal);           // release the pointer
LocalFree(hLocal);             // free the memory
```

GLOBAL ALLOCATION WITH FAR POINTERS

While local memory is stored in the default data segment, global memory consists of other data segments that are allocated by the system, as necessary. Thus the amount of global memory you can obtain is limited only by the amount of RAM and virtual memory in the system. For this reason, most of your memory allocation will probably be from global rather than local memory.

When the data object to be stored in global memory is less than 64K, it can be accessed with far pointers. Our next example shows how this is done. Later we'll see how to handle objects greater than 64K.

Our example program, GLOBAL, is similar to LOCAL. However, it allocates 10,000 variables of type DWORD, which is equivalent to 40,000 bytes, from global memory. You can use this memory as individual variables, but most commonly it will be used as an array. When you click the left mouse button, GLOBAL fills the memory with data and verifies that it is correct. When the WM_DESTROY message is received, it unlocks and frees the memory. Here's the listing for GLOBAL.C:

```
// global.c
// allocates global memory

#define STRICT               // strict type checking
#include <windows.h>         // include file for all windows apps
                             // prototype
LRESULT CALLBACK _export WndProc(HWND, UINT, WPARAM, LPARAM);

DWORD dwSegSize = 40000L;     // size of segment to be allocated
UINT  cVars =     10000;      // variables of type DWORD

PSTR szProgName = "Global";   // application name
#include "stdmain.inc"        // standard WinMain() function
////////////////////////////////////////////////////////////////
// main window procedure -- receives messages                  //
////////////////////////////////////////////////////////////////
LRESULT CALLBACK _export WndProc(HWND hWnd, UINT msg,
```

```
                            WPARAM wParam, LPARAM lParam)
{
static HGLOBAL hGlobal;      // handles to global memory
static DWORD FAR* lpStart;  // pointer to memory block (note: far)
UINT j;                      // loop variable

switch(msg)
   {
   case WM_CREATE:
      // allocate memory block, get handle to it
      hGlobal = GlobalAlloc(GMEM_MOVEABLE | GMEM_ZEROINIT,
                            dwSegSize);
      if(!hGlobal)
         { MessageBox(hWnd, "Can't allocate memory", szProgName,
                   MB_SYSTEMMODAL | MB_OK);   break; }

      // get pointer to memory block
      lpStart = (DWORD FAR*)GlobalLock(hGlobal);
      break;  // end WM_CREATE

   case WM_LBUTTONDOWN:
      for(j=0; j<cVars; j++)     // fill memory with data
         *(lpStart+j) = j;

      for(j=0; j<cVars; j++)     // check data
         if(*(lpStart+j) != j)
            { MessageBox(hWnd, "Memory error", szProgName,
                      MB_ICONHAND | MB_OK); break; }

      MessageBox(hWnd, "Successful memory test", szProgName,
               MB_ICONINFORMATION | MB_OK);
      break;  // end WM_LBUTTONDOWN

   case WM_DESTROY:
      GlobalUnlock(hGlobal);     // unlock memory
      GlobalFree(hGlobal);       // free memory
      PostQuitMessage(0);
      break;

   default:
      return( DefWindowProc(hWnd, msg, wParam, lParam) );
   }   // end switch(msg)
return 0L;
}  // end WndProc
```

Global Memory Functions

You manipulate global memory in much the same way as local memory. However, there are several important differences. Perhaps the most obvious is that we use the functions GlobalAlloc(), GlobalLock(), GlobalUnlock(), and GlobalFree() instead of their local counterparts.

The second argument to GlobalAlloc() is the segment size, dwSegSize. Note that this argument is the type DWORD, instead of UINT, as it is in LocalAlloc(). LocalAlloc() is restricted to memory that will fit within the 64K local data segment, but GlobalAlloc() has no such restriction, so it needs a larger data type to hold the size.

As with LocalAlloc(), it's important to check the return values of GlobalAlloc(). It's quite possible your application will be unable to obtain memory, and the more memory you ask for the truer this is.

Moveable Memory

In the LOCAL example we specified that local memory should be fixed, but in GLOBAL we specify that global memory should be *moveable*. This allows Windows to move our memory segment from place to place to aid in memory compacting and other activities. You aren't required to make your global memory moveable, but it's really nice if you do, because it helps Windows and all the other applications in the system operate efficiently.

In GlobalAlloc() we use the GMEM_MOVEABLE and GMEM_ZEROINIT constants to allocate a moveable segment initialized to all zeros. (You could also use the GHND constant, which combines GMEM_MOVEABLE and GMEM_ZEROINIT.)

Far Pointers

Because we're working with data in a segment other than the default data segment, we must use far rather than near pointers to access it. Thus the return value of GlobalLock() is type **void** FAR*, rather than type **void** NEAR*. These far pointers take 4 bytes rather than 2. The high-order 2 bytes are called the *selector*, and the low-order 2 bytes are called the *offset*. A near pointer has only an offset. We want to access data of type DWORD, so the pointer lpStart to the allocated segment is type DWORD FAR*.

GLOBAL ALLOCATION WITH HUGE POINTERS

If you use far pointers to access your data, you are restricted to memory objects smaller than the 64K maximum segment size. If your program requires a single memory object (usually an array) that excedes 64K, then huge pointers must be used. Our final example program, HUGE, is similar to GLOBAL, except that it demonstrates access to such huge objects. It allocates 50,000 variables of type DWORD. Since we deal with these variables as occupying contiguous memory addresses, they can be thought of as constituting a single array.

We allocate the necessary 200,000 bytes with GlobalAlloc(). Since segments have a maximum size of 65,536 bytes, this allocation requires four segments: three of 64K and one of 3,392 bytes. We treat the resulting memory as one huge object by filling it with data using a single **for** loop. Since we're using huge pointers, the compiler takes care of generating the code to correctly cross the segment boundaries. Here's the listing for HUGE.C:

```c
// huge.c
// allocates more than 64K of global memory

#define STRICT                  // strict type checking
#include <windows.h>            // include file for all windows apps
                                // prototype
LRESULT CALLBACK _export WndProc(HWND, UINT, WPARAM, LPARAM);

DWORD dwSegSize = 200000L;      // size of segment to be allocated
DWORD cVars =       50000L;     // variables of type DWORD

PSTR szProgName = "Huge";       // application name
#include "stdmain.inc"          // standard WinMain() function
/////////////////////////////////////////////////////////////////////
// main window procedure -- receives messages                      //
/////////////////////////////////////////////////////////////////////
LRESULT CALLBACK _export WndProc(HWND hWnd, UINT msg,
                                 WPARAM wParam, LPARAM lParam)
    {
    static HGLOBAL hGlobal;       // handle to global memory
    static DWORD huge* hpStart;   // pointer to memory (note: huge)
    DWORD j;                      // loop variable (note: DWORD)

    switch(msg)
        {
        case WM_CREATE:
            // allocate memory, get handle to it
            hGlobal = GlobalAlloc(GMEM_MOVEABLE | GMEM_ZEROINIT,
                                  dwSegSize);
            if(!hGlobal)
                { MessageBox(hWnd, "Can't allocate memory", szProgName,
                        MB_SYSTEMMODAL | MB_OK);   break; }

            // lock memory, get pointer to it
            hpStart = (DWORD huge*)GlobalLock(hGlobal);
            break;  // end WM_CREATE

        case WM_LBUTTONDOWN:
            for(j=0; j<cVars; j++)      // fill memory with data
                *(hpStart+j) = j;

            for(j=0; j<cVars; j++)      // check data
                if(*(hpStart+j) != j)
                    { MessageBox(hWnd, "Memory error", szProgName,
                            MB_ICONHAND | MB_OK); break; }

            MessageBox(hWnd, "Successful memory test", szProgName,
```

```
                          MB_ICONINFORMATION | MB_OK);
           break;  // end WM_LBUTTONDOWN

       case WM_DESTROY:
           GlobalUnlock(hGlobal);       // unlock memory
           GlobalFree(hGlobal);         // free memory
           PostQuitMessage(0);
           break;

       default:
           return( DefWindowProc(hWnd, msg, wParam, lParam) );
       }   // end switch(msg)
   return 0L;
}   // end WndProc
```

Here the pointer hpStart, used to access the data, is a huge pointer. Also, because the **for** loop must count so many elements, we use type DWORD for the loop variable j.

Don't Straddle Segment Boundaries

As we've seen, an array may straddle segment boundaries if you use huge pointers. However, you must be careful that an individual element in that array does not straddle a segment boundary. This isn't a problem with normal variables, which, with sizes of 1, 2, 4, or 8 bytes, divide evenly into 64K. However, if you have an array of structures, and each structure is, say, 37 bytes (or any other number that doesn't divide evenly into 65,536), you'll have trouble because one or more such structures will straddle a segment boundary, as shown in Figure 36-3. One solution to this problem is to size your structures so that an integral (even) number of them fit in 64K. Any power of 2, such as 64, 4,096, 16,384, and so on meet this criterion.

Memory Selector Limit

There is another limitation on global memory allocation. The memory handles obtained by GlobalAlloc() are one kind of *global selector*. Selectors are used for many other things besides memory handles. Each data segment, code segment, and resource segment requires a selector, as do many other items used by Windows. You don't need to know exactly what a selector is to allocate memory, but you should keep in mind that, due to the architecture of Intel chips and the way Windows interacts with it, there are only 8,192 global selectors available in the entire system. If your application uses too many selectors, it's possible to exhaust the supply, with disastrous results. Also, every allocation imposes a time and memory overhead, which it's nice to minimize.

The moral is to allocate global memory in a few larger segments; avoid allocating thousands of small ones.

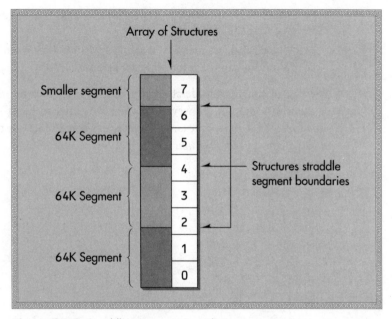

Figure 36-3 Straddling Segment Boundaries

SUMMARY

The sequence for obtaining memory, whether local or global is

1. Allocate memory with LocalAlloc() or GlobalAlloc().
2. Immediately lock the memory with LocalLock() or GlobalLock().
3. Use the memory for as long as you need it.
4. Unlock the memory with LocalUnlock() or GlobalUnlock().
5. Immediately free the memory with LocalFree() or GlobalFree().

Here are some quick-and-easy rules for memory allocation in simple Windows programs.

1. Make sure that your stack, static data, and local heap together are less than 64K.
2. Use the local heap for memory objects that need fast access.
3. Use the global heap for memory objects that don't fit in the local heap.
4. Make local memory fixed (LMEM_FIXED), and global memory moveable (GMEM_MOVEABLE).
5. If you're allocating more than 64K from global memory for a single memory object (like an array), access it with huge pointers.

6. Don't make too many separate allocations from the global heap. Use just a few large allocations instead.

7. Unlock and free memory as soon as possible after you're done with it, so Windows can use it for other applications.

There is, of course, considerably more to memory allocation than we have covered in this short chapter. However, we've shown how to handle the most common situations. We'll show an example that uses GlobalAlloc() in the database example in Part Eight, *Larger Programs.*

37

PRINTING

e've shown in numerous examples in this book how to display text or graphics on the screen. This is all very well, but many programs also need to provide a permanent record of their output. In this chapter we show how to send output to a printer. We'll first see how to write a single line of text to the printer. Then we'll explore writing multiple lines on multiple pages. We'll finish up with an example that displays graphics on the printer.

PREPARING TO PRINT

Drawing on the printer is, in theory, very much the same as drawing on the screen. You obtain a device context for the printer, execute functions like TextOut() and Rectangle() to draw text and graphics, and then delete the device context. Unfortunately, a printer requires considerably more preparation than the screen before these functions can be executed.

Before the program actually carries out the printing process, the user should be given a chance to select things like the number of copies, the print quality, the page range, the paper size, the page orientation, and even the particular printer, when several are installed in the system. This means that your application is responsible for finding out what printers are available and listing them, along with their characteristics, for the user's edification and decision-making.

Reading about the printing process in Windows is like listening to your grandfather tell how he had to walk miles to school through snow drifts higher than he was, and how kids nowadays have it easy. Before Windows 3.1, obtaining the necessary information about a printer was a truly baroque process. Information about the printers installed in the system is stored in the WIN.INI file. A special function,

GetProfileString(), was used to extract this information, which then had to be picked apart to find the printer description, driver name, and port name. And this was just the beginning. Various complex dialog boxes also had to be constructed.

Fortunately, Windows 3.1 introduced the Print common dialog, which makes setting up and using the printer far easier, as we'll see.

Another complication is that a printer's output is divided into pages. Special functions are necessary to manage the page-oriented aspect of printer output. Finally, we must be aware that more than one program may want to use the printer at the same time. In Windows the Print Manager resolves such disputes, but we need to help it out.

THE PRINT COMMON DIALOGS

The PrintDlg() API function is the key to printing in Windows. This function uses dialog boxes to discover the user's preferences. It then handles all the details of initializing the printer. From the programmer's standpoint, the result of executing PrintDlg() is the return of a device context handle. This handle is used to draw on the printer, just as the handle obtained from BeginPaint() is used to draw on the screen.

The PrintDlg() function can actually display several related dialog boxes: Print, Print Setup, and Options. Figure 37-1 shows the Print common dialog.

One printer in every Windows system is designated the default printer. (This can be changed with the Windows Control Panel utility.) It's this default printer that is described in the Print common dialog. In the figure, the default printer is listed as an HP LaserJet Series II.

In some situations, the user can choose the page range, or specify that only selected text is to be printed. In the figure these options are not available, so they are grayed. The print quality in dots per inch can be selected, along with the number of copies. The printer can also be instructed to collate the copies.

If the Setup button is pressed, the Print Setup common dialog appears, as shown in Figure 37-2.

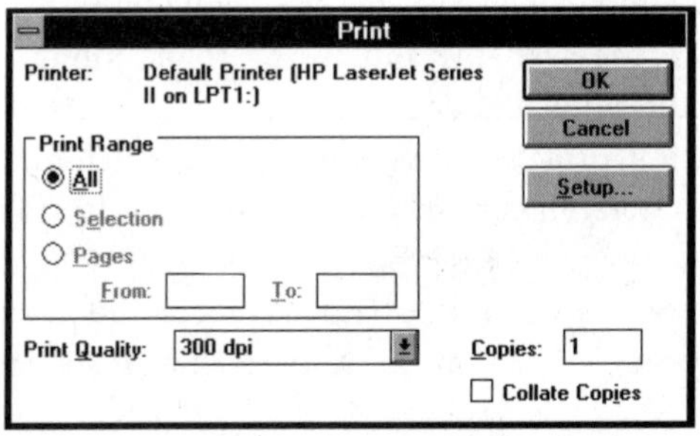

Figure 37-1
The Print Common Dialog

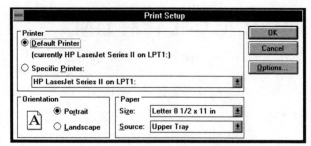

Figure 37-2

The Print Setup Common Dialog

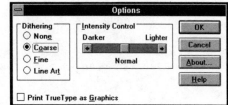

Figure 37-3

The Print Options Common Dialog

This dialog allows the user to specify a printer other than the default printer, to change the orientation of the page ("portrait" is vertical and "landscape" is horizontal), and to select different paper sizes. The type of printer determines some of the options that appear in the printer common dialogs, so they may look different on your system than they do in the figures.

If the user presses the Options button on the Print Setup dialog, a third dialog called Options appears, as shown in Figure 37-3. This dialog allows you to adjust the dithering (see Chapter 29, *Pens, Brushes, and Color*) and intensity of the printed output.

Once everything is set up appropriately, the user can click on the OK button in the Print dialog. This causes the actual printing process to begin. Figure 37-4 shows the resulting printer output for our first example program, EZPRINT.

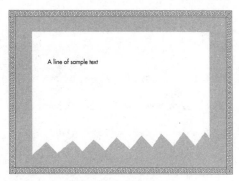

Figure 37-4 Output of EZPRINT

503

PRINTING ONE TEXT LINE

Let's see how to invoke the printer common dialogs from within the EZPRINT application. We use a menu selection to call up the common dialog, so there are .RC and .H files as well as the .C file. Here's the listing for EZPRINT.RC:

```
// ezprint.rc
// resource file for ezprint

#include "ezprint.h"

ezPrint MENU
BEGIN
    POPUP "&File"
        BEGIN
            MENUITEM "&Print...", IDM_PRINT
        END
END
```

There's not much to the menu system in this program: just one pop-up called File, with one menu item, Print. The .H file contains the ID for this one menu item. Here's the listing for EZPRINT.H:

```
// ezprint.h
// header file for ezprint

#define IDM_PRINT        101
```

As you can see from the .C file, the PrintDlg() function may have made things easier than in the old days, but there are still some details to worry about. Here's the listing for EZPRINT.C:

```
// ezprint.c
// uses print common dialog to print text

#define STRICT
#include <windows.h>
#include <commdlg.h>        // for common dialogs
#include <memory.h>         // for memset()
#include "ezprint.h"        // for menu #define

                            // prototype
LRESULT CALLBACK _export WndProc(HWND, UINT, WPARAM, LPARAM);

PSTR szDocName = "Test Document";    // document name (32 chars max)

PSTR szProgName = "ezPrint";         // application name
#include "stdmain.inc"               // standard WinMain() function
/////////////////////////////////////////////////////////////////////
// main window procedure -- receives messages                       //
/////////////////////////////////////////////////////////////////////
LRESULT CALLBACK _export WndProc(HWND hWnd, UINT msg,
```

```
                         WPARAM wParam, LPARAM lParam)
{
PRINTDLG pd;          // for PrintDlg()
DOCINFO di;           // for StartDoc()

switch(msg)
   {
   case WM_COMMAND:
      switch(wParam)
         {
         case IDM_PRINT:            // user selected Print

            // set up PRINTDLG structure for PrintDlg()
            memset( &pd, 0, sizeof(PRINTDLG) );  // clear it
            pd.lStructSize = sizeof(PRINTDLG);   // size
            pd.hwndOwner = hWnd;                 // our window
            pd.Flags = PD_RETURNDC |       // return dev context
                       PD_NOPAGENUMS |     // gray Pages button
                       PD_NOSELECTION |    // gray Selection button
                       PD_HIDEPRINTTOFILE; // hide Print-to-file

            // call Print common dialog
            if( !PrintDlg(&pd) )           // if null return,
               break;                      // then forget it

            // print the text
            di.cbSize = sizeof(DOCINFO);   // set up DOCINFO struct
            di.lpszDocName = szDocName;    // for StartDoc()
            di.lpszOutput = NULL;

            StartDoc(pd.hDC, &di);  // tell printer new document
            StartPage(pd.hDC);      // tell printer new page
            TextOut(pd.hDC, 100, 100, "A line of sample text", 21);
            EndPage(pd.hDC);        // tell printer end page
            EndDoc(pd.hDC);         // tell printer end document

            // clean up
            DeleteDC(pd.hDC);              // remove device context
            if(pd.hDevMode != NULL)        // free any memory
               GlobalFree(pd.hDevMode);    // allocated
            if(pd.hDevNames != NULL)       // by StartDoc()
               GlobalFree(pd.hDevNames);
            break;
         }   // end switch wParam
      break;  // end case WM_COMMAND

   case WM_DESTROY:
      PostQuitMessage(0);
      break;
   default:
      return( DefWindowProc(hWnd, msg, wParam, lParam) );
   }   // end switch(msg)
return 0L;
}  // end WndProc
```

The program sets up various structures and then executes PrintDlg() to get a device context handle. It tells the printer to start a new document and a new page, and then sends output to the printer. Finally it tells the printer that the page and the document are finished, and cleans up. Let's look at these steps in detail.

Setting Up the PRINTDLG Structure

The PrintDlg() function takes as its only argument the address of a structure of type PRINTDLG. An important purpose of this structure is to contain various flags that we use to tell PrintDlg() how to display the dialog boxes. Table 37-1 shows some of the possible values for these flags, which are ORed together and assigned to the Flags member of PRINTDLG.

You will usually want to use the PD_RETURNDC flag, which instructs PrintDlg() to return the device context handle for the printer. We'll use this handle for all our instructions to the printer, so this is an important flag. The PD_NOPAGENUMS flag and the PD_NOSELECTION flags disable (gray) the Pages and Selection radio buttons. The PD_HIDEPRINTTOFILE flag causes the Print To File check box to be hidden (not just disabled). You can call up the Print Setup common dialog directly by using the PD_PRINTSETUP flag.

There are other flag values we don't show here. In particular, consult your Windows API reference (see the Bibliography) for the PrintDlg() function if you want the Pages or Selection buttons to be active.

The PD_HIDEPRINTTOFILE flag has a value of 0x00100000, which is a value of type **long**. This generates a warning message from the compiler, "Constant is long," which you can ignore.

Table 37-1 Flag Values for the PRINTDLG Structure

Constant	Effect
PD_RETURNDC	Return device context (the most commonly used value)
PD_PRINTSETUP	Show Print Setup dialog instead of the Print dialog
PD_NOPAGENUMS	Disable the Pages radio button and the From and To edit fields
PD_NOSELECTION	Disable the Selection radio button
PD_HIDEPRINTTOFILE	Disable the Print To File check box

Executing PrintDlg()

Actually executing PrintDlg() is something of an anticlimax after all these preparatory details. However, it does the real work of displaying the dialogs, figuring out what the user wants to do, and returning a handle to the printer device context. This handle is placed in the hDC member of the PRINTDLG structure, where it can be accessed as pd.hDC.

Setting Up the DOCINFO Structure

Printing in Windows is complicated by the fact that several applications may want to use the printer at the same time. One way to avoid confusion is to give a name to each document, and refer to this name when starting a print job. This helps the Print Manager keep track of what's going on. We use the StartDoc() function to give our document a name and tell the printer that it should be printed. This function takes as its second argument the address of a structure of type DOCINFO. This structure's lpszDocName member contains the name of the document.

Also, the Print common dialog may contain a check box called Print To File, which the user can check to indicate that the output created for the printer should be stored in a disk file instead. If we want to use this option, we must store the name of the disk file in the DOCINFO structure. EZPRINT doesn't use this option, so we disable the Print To File box, and insert NULL in the lpszOutput member of DOCINFO.

Starting the Document and/or Page

The StartDoc() function tells the printer that we're ready to start printing a document. The first argument to this function is the device context handle pc.hDC. The second argument is the address of the DOCINFO structure whose members we already filled in. As we noted, the name of the document is passed to the Print Manager in this structure.

The StartPage() function causes the printer to begin at the top of a new page, and prepares the printer driver to accept data.

Output

There is only one output statement in EZPRINT. The TextOut() function causes a single line of text to be sent to the printer's device context. Here the line is "A line of sample text."

The second and third arguments to TextOut() are the coordinates on the page where the text will be displayed. Depending on the printer, these units may be much smaller than those used on the screen. Laser printers typically have resolutions of 300 or 600 dpi (dots per inch), while the screen is typically 70. Thus the values used for the coordinates may need to be made correspondingly larger.

Ending the Document and/or Page

The EndPage() function tells the printer that output to the page has been completed. Both EndPage() and StartPage() must be executed between pages, and EndPage() must be executed after the last page (which in this example is the only page).

The EndDoc() function ends the print job that was started with StartDoc(). It signals the Print Manager that it's free to begin another print job. You should send it as soon as you're done printing, so as not to slow down the rest of the system.

Cleaning Up

When printing is completed, after we have executed EndDoc(), the device context should be deleted. The DeleteDC() function is used for this.

Also, PrintDlg() may have caused memory to be allocated for two internal structures. We don't need to worry about these structures, but we do need to release the allocated memory, if any. To do this we examine the hDevMode and hDevNames members of PRINTDLG. If either of these memory handles is not NULL, we use the GlobalFree() function to free the allocated memory. This is a bit of a drag, especially since we didn't even use these structures; but it beats walking to school through snow drifts higher than your head.

PRINTING MULTIPLE TEXT LINES

Printing a single short line of text, as we did in EZPRINT, allowed us to avoid various details of drawing on the page. To print multiple lines we need to address these details. Specifically, we need to know how to find the dimensions of the lines of text to be displayed, and the dimensions of the page. With this information we can figure out how to space the lines appropriately and start a new page when the old one is full.

Our next example, PRINTEXT, prints 80 lines of text, enough for several pages. The text itself isn't very exciting; in the interest of saving space in the listing, we've avoided the temptation to print Hamlet's soliloquy. Instead we use wsprintf() to construct lines of the form "This is line number 33". Figure 37-5 shows what this looks like.

Again we use a Print menu item on a File menu, requiring an .RC file. Here's the listing for PRINTEXT.RC:

```
// printext.rc
// resource file for printext

#include "printext.h"

PrinText MENU
BEGIN
   POPUP "&File"
      BEGIN
         MENUITEM "&Print...", IDM_PRINT
      END
END
```

Here's the corresponding header file, PRINTEXT.H:

```
// printext.h
// header file for printext

#define IDM_PRINT        101
```

The source file is similar to that for EZPRINT, down to the point where the PrintDlg() function is executed. Once we have the device context handle for the

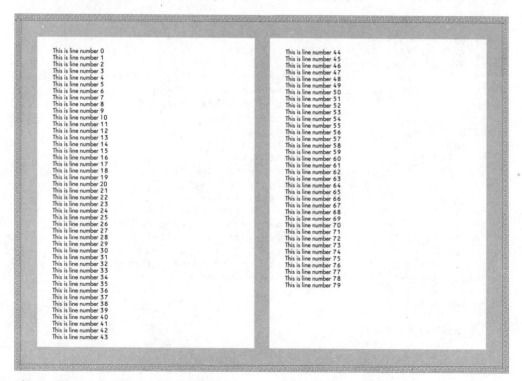

Figure 37-5 Printer Output from PRINTEXT

printer, however, we first get the text and page dimensions. Printing takes place in a **for** loop, where we position each line and execute page breaks. Here's the listing for PRINTEXT.C:

```c
// printext.c
// uses print common dialog to print text

#define STRICT
#include <windows.h>
#include <commdlg.h>          // for common dialogs
#include <memory.h>           // for memset()
#include "printext.h"         // for menu #define

                             // prototypes
LRESULT CALLBACK _export WndProc(HWND, UINT, WPARAM, LPARAM);

#define LINES       80          // lines of text to print
#define HORZMARGIN  1.0         // horizontal margin
#define VERTMARGIN  1.5         // vertical margin
#define BUFFSIZE    256         // buffer size
char szString[BUFFSIZE];        // space for general string
PSTR szDocName = "Test Document";   // document name

PSTR szProgName = "PrinText";       // application name
#include "stdmain.inc"              // standard WinMain() function
/////////////////////////////////////////////////////////////////
// main window procedure -- receives messages                   //
/////////////////////////////////////////////////////////////////
LRESULT CALLBACK _export WndProc(HWND hWnd, UINT msg,
                        WPARAM wParam, LPARAM lParam)
    {
    PRINTDLG pd;          // for PrintDlg()
    TEXTMETRIC tm;        // for GetTextMetrics()
    DOCINFO di;           // for StartDoc()
    HCURSOR hCursor, hOldCursor; // cursor handles
    int yChar;            // line height, in pixels
    int yPage;            // page height, in pixels
    int yPos;             // vertical position, in pixels
    int xPixels;          // pixels per inch in horizontal direction
    int yPixels;          // pixels per inch in vertical direction
    int xMargin;          // margin at left of page
    int yMargin;          // margin at top and bottom of page
    int iLine;            // current line number

    switch(msg)
        {
        case WM_COMMAND:
            switch(wParam)
                {
                case IDM_PRINT:            // user selected Print
                    // set up PRINTDLG structure for PrintDlg()
                    memset( &pd, 0, sizeof(PRINTDLG) );  // clear it
```

```
pd.lStructSize = sizeof(PRINTDLG);   // size
pd.hwndOwner = hWnd;                    // our window
pd.Flags = PD_RETURNDC |        // return dev context
           PD_NOPAGENUMS |      // gray Pages button
           PD_NOSELECTION |     // gray Selection button
           PD_HIDEPRINTTOFILE;  // hide Print-to-file

// call Print common dialog
if( !PrintDlg(&pd) )            // if null return,
   break;                       // then forget it

// change cursor to hourglass
hCursor = LoadCursor(NULL, IDC_WAIT);
hOldCursor = SetCursor(hCursor);

// get text and page dimensions
GetTextMetrics(pd.hDC, &tm);
yChar = tm.tmHeight + tm.tmExternalLeading;
yPage = GetDeviceCaps(pd.hDC, VERTRES);
xPixels = GetDeviceCaps(pd.hDC, LOGPIXELSX);
yPixels = GetDeviceCaps(pd.hDC, LOGPIXELSY);
xMargin = xPixels * HORZMARGIN;
yMargin = yPixels * VERTMARGIN;

// print the text
di.cbSize = sizeof(DOCINFO);  // set up DOCINFO struct
di.lpszDocName = szDocName;   // for StartDoc()
di.lpszOutput = NULL;
StartDoc(pd.hDC, &di);  // tell printer new document
StartPage(pd.hDC);      // tell printer new page
yPos = yMargin;         // start at vertical margin
for(iLine=0; iLine<LINES; iLine++)
   {
   yPos += yChar;       // move down one line
   if(yPos > yPage - yMargin - yChar)
      {                         // if past bottom margin,
      EndPage(pd.hDC);         // then go to new page
      StartPage(pd.hDC);
      yPos = yMargin;          // start at top again
      }
   wsprintf(szString, "This is line number %d", iLine);
   TextOut( pd.hDC, xMargin, yPos,
            szString, lstrlen(szString) );
   }
EndPage(pd.hDC);             // tell printer end page
EndDoc(pd.hDC);             // tell printer end document

// clean up
DeleteDC(pd.hDC);             // give up device context
if(pd.hDevMode != NULL) // free StartDoc() memory
   GlobalFree(pd.hDevMode);
if(pd.hDevNames != NULL)
```

```
                GlobalFree(pd.hDevNames);
                SetCursor(hOldCursor);  // restore original cursor
                break;
            }   // end switch wParam
        break;  // end case WM_COMMAND

    case WM_DESTROY:
        PostQuitMessage(0);
        break;
    default:
        return( DefWindowProc(hWnd, msg, wParam, lParam) );
    }   // end switch(msg)
return 0L;
}   // end WndProc
```

Text and Page Dimensions

We encountered the GetTextMetrics() function in Chapter 17, *Text Size*. Here we use it to find the line height, yChar. If we were concerned about the length of the lines, we could use the GetTextExtent() function, but in this example we assume the lines are short enough to fit on the page.

We use a new function to find the dimensions of the page: GetDeviceCaps(). This function returns a variety of information about a device (its name means Get Device Capabilities). Its first argument is the device context handle, in this case for the printer. The second argument is a flag that indicates what sort of information should be returned. There are a large number of possible values for this flag. Table 37-2 shows a few of the possibilities.

Table 37-2 Some Flag Values for GetDeviceCaps()

Constant	Return Value
HORZSIZE	Page width, in millimeters
VERTSIZE	Page height, in millimeters
HORZRES	Page width, in pixels
VERTRES	Page height, in pixels
LOGPIXELSX	Pixels per inch horizontally
LOGPIXELSY	Pixels per inch vertically

Other flags instruct GetDeviceCaps() to find out if a device has color capability, whether it can draw lines, curves, or polygons, has brushes or pens, and so on; we won't be concerned with these. Here we're interested in the height of the page, measured in pixels, and in the vertical and horizontal resolution, measured in pixels per inch.

```
yPage = GetDeviceCaps(pd.hDC, VERTRES);       // height of page, pixels
xPixels = GetDeviceCaps(pd.hDC, LOGPIXELSX);  // horiz resolution, ppi
yPixels = GetDeviceCaps(pd.hDC, LOGPIXELSY);  // vert resolution, ppi
```

The values for the horizontal and vertical page margins are the constants HORZMARGIN and VERTMARGIN, which we define as 1.0 inch and 1.5 inches. We convert these two dimensions to pixels by multiplying by xPixels and yPixels, respectively, to obtain xMargin and yMargin.

Displaying Lines

We print one text line with each iteration of a **for** loop. Each line has a horizontal coordinate of xMargin. The vertical position, yPos, starts at yMargin and increases by yChar pixels for each new line.

If yPos becomes greater than the page size (less one line), we execute EndPage() and StartPage() and reset yPos to yMargin, the top of the page.

When all the text lines have been sent to the printer, we execute EndPage() and EndDoc() and clean up as before.

The Hourglass Cursor

In Windows, printer data doesn't go directly to the printer. Instead it goes to the Print Manager (unless it's disabled), which takes care of orchestrating print jobs from different applications. The Print Manager can speed up the time your application spends in the printing process, since it can store the printer data prior to sending it on to the printer. Even so, during long print jobs there will usually be a period of time during which your program will not be able to respond to user input. To indicate this fact to the user, it's customary to change the cursor (mouse pointer) to an hourglass. As we discussed in Chapter 34, *Icons and Cursors*, this is handled with the LoadCursor() and SetCursor() functions. When printing is completed, the previous cursor is restored.

Different Fonts and Text Sizes

Although we don't show it in these examples, you can use the Font common dialog, described in Chapter 16, *Installable Fonts*, to select different fonts for the printer as

Figure 37-6 Printer Output of PRINTPIX

well as for the screen display. The techniques shown in PRINTEXT for finding the text size will work for different fonts and different text sizes.

PRINTING GRAPHICS

We can print graphics (pictures) almost as easily as text. Our example program, PRINTPIX, displays the same figure on the printer that various programs in Part Five, *Graphics,* displayed on the screen. Figure 37-6 shows the result.

PRINTPIX is modelled roughly on the ENGLISH program from Chapter 28, *Drawing Shapes.* It uses almost the same coordinates to specify the dimensions of the figure. (The discrepancy has to do with the origin.) This shows how easy it is to achieve WYSIWYG (What You See Is What You Get): the screen image and the printer image look just the same.

Again we use a File menu with a Print item that invokes the Print common dialog. Here's the listing for PRINTPIX.RC:

```
// printpix.rc
// resource file for printpix

#include "printpix.h"

PrintPix MENU
BEGIN
```

```
    POPUP "&File"
       BEGIN
          MENUITEM "&Print...", IDM_PRINT
       END
END
```

The header file is also the same as in previous examples in this chapter. Here's the listing for PRINTPIX.H:

```
// printpix.h
// header file for printpix

#define IDM_PRINT        101
```

The source file for PRINTPIX is similar to the previous ones in this chapter. The functions that actually draw the figure are the same as those in the ENGLISH program, except that they use a different device context. What's different is the way we calculate the size of the figure and where to draw it. Here's the listing for PRINTPIX.C:

```
// printpix.c
// uses print common dialog to print graphics

#define STRICT
#include <windows.h>
#include <commdlg.h>          // for common dialogs
#include <memory.h>           // for memset()
#include "printpix.h"         // for menu #define

                             // prototypes
LRESULT CALLBACK _export WndProc(HWND, UINT, WPARAM, LPARAM);

#define LINES       80               // lines of text to print
#define BUFFSIZE    256              // buffer size
char szString[BUFFSIZE];             // space for general string
PSTR szDocName = "Test Document";    // document name

PSTR szProgName = "PrintPix";        // application name
#include "stdmain.inc"               // standard WinMain() function
////////////////////////////////////////////////////////////////////
// main window procedure -- receives messages                     //
////////////////////////////////////////////////////////////////////
LRESULT CALLBACK _export WndProc(HWND hWnd, UINT msg,
                           WPARAM wParam, LPARAM lParam)
    {
    PRINTDLG pd;            // for PrintDlg()
    DOCINFO di;             // for StartDoc()
    HCURSOR hCursor, hOldCursor; // cursor handles
    int xPage, yPage;      // page dimensions, in pixels
    int xOrg, yOrg;        // coordinates of origin
    int xSize, ySize;      // dimensions of drawing, in pixels
    int xPixels, yPixels;  // pixels per inch on printing surface
```

```
      int xLeft=0, yTop=2000, xRight=3000, yBottom=0;
      POINT apt[] = { {0, 1000}, {1500, 2000},
                  {3000, 1000}, {1500, 0} };

      switch(msg)
         {
         case WM_COMMAND:
            switch(wParam)
               {
               case IDM_PRINT:              // user selected Print
                  // set up PRINTDLG structure for PrintDlg()
                  memset( &pd, 0, sizeof(PRINTDLG) );  // clear it
                  pd.lStructSize = sizeof(PRINTDLG);   // size
                  pd.hwndOwner = hWnd;                 // our window
                  pd.Flags = PD_RETURNDC |      // return dev context
                             PD_NOPAGENUMS |    // gray Pages button
                             PD_NOSELECTION |   // gray Selection button
                             PD_HIDEPRINTTOFILE; // hide Print-to-file

                  // call Print common dialog
                  if( !PrintDlg(&pd) )          // if null return,
                     break;                     // then forget it

                  // change cursor to hourglass
                  hCursor = LoadCursor(NULL, IDC_WAIT);
                  hOldCursor = SetCursor(hCursor);

                  // get printer output dimensions
                  xPage = GetDeviceCaps(pd.hDC, HORZRES);
                  yPage = GetDeviceCaps(pd.hDC, VERTRES);
                  xPixels = GetDeviceCaps(pd.hDC, LOGPIXELSX);
                  yPixels = GetDeviceCaps(pd.hDC, LOGPIXELSY);

                  // set map mode and origin
                  SetMapMode(pd.hDC, MM_HIENGLISH); // 1/1000th inch
                  xSize = ((float)(xRight-xLeft)*xPixels)/1000;
                  ySize = ((float)(yTop-yBottom)*yPixels)/1000;
                  xOrg = (xPage-xSize)/2;   // lower left of drawing,
                  yOrg = (yPage+ySize)/2;   // so drawing centered
                  SetViewportOrg(pd.hDC, xOrg, yOrg);

                  // get printer ready
                  di.cbSize = sizeof(DOCINFO);  // set up DOCINFO struct
                  di.lpszDocName = szDocName;   // for StartDoc()
                  di.lpszOutput = NULL;
                  StartDoc(pd.hDC, &di);  // tell printer new document
                  StartPage(pd.hDC);      // tell printer new page

                  // draw the usual design
                  Rectangle(pd.hDC, xLeft, yTop, xRight, yBottom);
```

```
                Ellipse(pd.hDC, xLeft, yTop, xRight, yBottom);
                MoveTo(pd.hDC, xLeft, yTop);
                LineTo(pd.hDC, xRight, yBottom);
                Polygon(pd.hDC, apt, 4);

                EndPage(pd.hDC);        // tell printer end page
                EndDoc(pd.hDC);         // tell printer end document
                SetCursor(hOldCursor);  // restore original cursor

                // clean up
                DeleteDC(pd.hDC);
                if(pd.hDevMode != NULL)
                   GlobalFree(pd.hDevMode);
                if(pd.hDevNames != NULL)
                   GlobalFree(pd.hDevNames);
                break;
            }   // end switch wParam
         break;  // end case WM_COMMAND

      case WM_DESTROY:
         PostQuitMessage(0);
         break;
      default:
         return( DefWindowProc(hWnd, msg, wParam, lParam) );
      }   // end switch(msg)
   return 0L;
}  // end WndProc
```

Drawing Size

One of the major issues when printing graphics is deciding how large the drawing should be. For example, if a line is 100 pixels long on the screen, how long should it be on the printer?

It's usually a mistake to make a drawing the same size in pixels on the printer as it is on the screen. A line that is 100 pixels long will be a bit more than an inch long on the screen, but on a printer with 300 dpi resolution it will only be 1/3 inch long. Generally we want a drawing to appear roughly the same size on the printer as it does on the display. To achieve this result we often use a mapping mode that allows us to specify dimensions in inches or millimeters. This permits the dimensions to be used both on the screen and on the printer.

The ENGLISH program in Chapter 28 used the HIENGLISH mapping mode. This mode uses coordinates measured in thousandths of an inch. We'll use this same mapping mode in PRINTPIX. Now if we specify a rectangle 2 inches high and 3 inches wide, it will appear to have approximately these dimensions on both the screen and the printer.

Drawing Location

Let's assume that we want to put the drawing in the center of the page. To do this, we'll need to know the page size and the drawing size. We already know how to find the page size, using GetDeviceCaps().

In our particular case the width of the drawing is xRight–xLeft, and the height is yTop–yBottom. (Remember that in the HIENGLISH mapping mode the Y-coordinate increases upward, not downward.) Although it's easier to work in inches when specifying the dimensions of the drawing, it's easier to work in pixels when specifying the location. To convert the drawing's dimensions from thousandths of an inch to pixels, we multiply by the resolution, xPixels or yPixels, and divide by 1,000. The result is stored in xSize and ySize. Now we have both the page and drawing sizes in pixels.

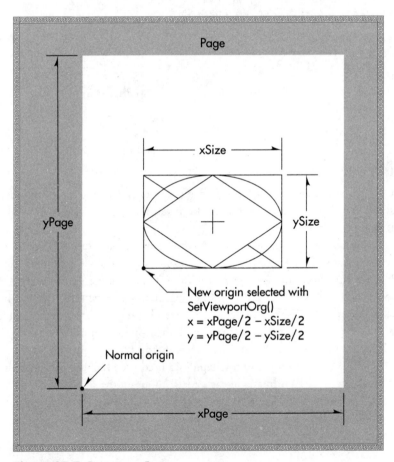

Figure 37-7 Centering a Figure

In the HIENGLISH mapping mode the normal origin is located at the bottom left of the figure. The coordinates of the new origin are found by going to the center of the page (which is at xPage/2 and yPage/2), and then moving back, toward the old origin, half the size of the drawing (which means subtracting xSize/2 and ySize/2). This is shown in Figure 37-7.

The SetViewportOrg() function places the origin at the new location. The arguments to the drawing functions Rectangle(), Ellipse(), and so forth are measured from this point, so the drawing appears in the center of the page.

You can use a similar approach to place drawings at other locations on the page.

SUMMARY

Printing involves calling up the Print common dialog, using the PrintDlg() function. This function allows the user to select the printer and other aspects of the printing process. It returns a handle to a device context, which is used as an argument to most graphics functions.

The same functions that write text to the screen, like TextOut(), work on the printer. The size of a text line can be found with GetTextExtent(). The size of a page, and the number of pixels per inch, can be found with GetDeviceCaps(). With these dimensions, a program can decide where to place lines of text on the screen.

Normal graphics functions like Rectangle() and Ellipse() work on the printer in the same way they do on the screen. For graphics, a mapping mode that uses inches or millimeters is easier to work with than the default MM_TEXT mode, which uses pixels. To locate a picture on the page, the programmer needs to take into account the picture size and the page size.

38
DEBUGGING

$\mathcal{H}$ere they come, charging toward you, dozens of them, in slimy black armor, mounted on mutant steeds. Their banner, waving in a toxic wind, reads "Insecti Vencit Omnia," which is Latin for "There are more where we came from." They are program bugs, and you must do battle with them every day, whether you want to or not.

A bug is a problem with a program. Bugs are usually caused by the programmer, but they can also be the result of errors in the system software (DOS and Windows), or the underlying hardware. In a multitasking system like Windows, they can even result from interactions with other applications.

Debugging is a difficult topic to discuss in concrete terms, because bugs can take such a variety of forms. Also, every programmer is prone to certain bugs that never seem to happen to other programmers. Nevertheless, there are a few things to be said about debugging. In this chapter we'll discuss how to avoid bugs, and ways to remove those that can't be avoided.

DEFENSIVE PROGRAMMING

Defensive programming is like a suit of armor: it keeps bugs from getting into your program. It's always easier to keep a bug out in the first place than it is to find it once it has embedded itself deep in the flesh and bone of your code. In this section we'll mention several programming techniques you can use to keep bugs at arm's length.

Incremental Development

Perhaps the most effective way to keep bugs under control is to develop your program incrementally—that is, one small step at a time. As we've seen, there is considerable code that is common to all Windows programs. Start with a program template that includes this code, such as the EZWIN program in Chapter 7, the EZMENU program of Chapter 11, or the EZDIAL program of Chapter 23. Rename the program, then compile it and run it to make sure it's error free.

Now—and this is the important point—add the smallest amount of code you can that will actually do something and result in a working program. Then compile and run the program again. If there's a problem, you know it's in the code you just added, and you can go back and fix it. Repeat the process, building up the program in small steps, checking each time that the added code operates as expected. You may want to keep backup files to make it easier to return to a previous bug-free version.

Let the Compiler Help You

Don't forget to define the STRICT variable in all your programs, and set the compiler so that it notifies you of all possible warnings. The compiler is very good at finding certain kinds of programming errors, and the more help you give it, the easier it will be for it to help you.

Common Pitfalls

Some programming errors are so easy to commit that probably every Windows programmer has fallen afoul of them at one time or another. Here are a few of the most common. We've already mentioned many of these, but it doesn't hurt to repeat them.

Retaining Values Between Messages

Whenever a variable in a window procedure (like WndProc) must retain its value between messages, it must be declared either static or external. Otherwise the value given the variable during the processing of one message will probably be gone when the next message arrives. The bugs that result from a failure to heed this precept are particularly difficult to track down. This is one of the first things to look for when your program behaves in mysterious ways.

Also, be careful if you create more than one window of the same class. All such windows share the same external and static variables, which essentially means you shouldn't use external or static variables in this situation.

Resource Identifiers

Make sure that the names given to resources agree in the source file and the resource file. Menu names must be the same in the .C and the .RC files. The same is true of dialog box names. If the menu bar or a dialog box doesn't appear, this is the first thing to look for.

If you haven't given values to the control identifiers (such as IDC_BUTTON1) in the .RC file, you'll get strange error messages from the resource compiler, like "Expected End." Make sure all such identifiers are defined in the .H file.

Predefined Class Names

When naming your window class, avoid names used by Windows for predefined window classes: STATIC, EDIT, BUTTON, SCROLLBAR, LISTBOX, and COMBOBOX. It's best to use names that are long and idiosyncratic, so they won't turn out to be the same as a name used elsewhere.

The wsprintf() Function

Typecast string arguments to the wsprintf() function to LPSTR, as in this program line:

```
wsprintf(szBuffer, "The string szString is %s", (LPSTR)szString);
```

If you don't do this, the string is not placed in szBuffer. Also, remember that wsprintf() does not handle floating-point numbers and lacks many other formatting niceties. For these you'll need to revert to the C-library function sprintf().

Don't Make Assumptions About Data Types

You can get into trouble by making assumptions about constants and data types that are defined in WINDOWS.H.

For example, you might look up the constant MB_OK (which is used to install an OK button in a message box), and find it has a value of of 0L. You might be tempted to use this value instead of MB_OK. Resist this temptation, since if Microsoft changes the definition in a future release of Windows, your program won't work.

Similarly, you might find that WPARAM is typedefed to be **unsigned int**. Don't make use of this fact either, since the definition may change, again rendering your program inoperative in different situations.

Use the sizeof() Operator

We have been rather lax in this book in that we have sometimes used the size of data types as explicit numbers. That is, we've assumed that a a variable of type **int** occupies 2 bytes. We've done this for clarity and to simplify the listings, but it's not really the best approach. On other machines, or in other versions of Windows, this size may be different: an **int** may be 4 bytes instead of 2, for example. So do as we say, not as we do. Use sizeof(int) or a similar construction whenever you need the size of a data type.

Mental Debugging

You probably know this already. When your program doesn't work, sit down, take a deep breath, relax, and look at the program listing from a different perspective. Focus on every statement that could be involved with the problem (and maybe some that couldn't possibly be). Often the solution will leap out at you. Old knights-errant might say that the answer appeared to them in a vision. Whatever you call it, it's often easier—and quicker—to find bugs with this approach than to plod through reams of code with more linear techniques. This is especially true in Windows programming.

Restart from Scratch

The compiler, or Windows itself, may behave oddly after you attempt to execute a buggy program. You will save yourself a lot of trouble if you always reboot your computer after any such weird behavior, or after any serious Windows error, such as a General Protection Fault. Don't keep plugging away, hoping things will get better. Your program has probably irreparably trashed the compiler, Windows, or DOS. The trouble with this is that you won't be sure from then on whether bugs in your program are caused by the program or by the system. Sometimes you can get away with restarting Windows without rebooting, but not always. When in doubt, reboot.

MESSAGE BOXES

One crude but effective debugging tool is the MessageBox() API function. If you have ever used printf() statements as debugging tools in a DOS program, you're familiar with the technique. Simply insert MessageBox() functions at critical points in your program code. When the program reaches the function, it stops and displays a message box. This reveals where the program is, and also gives you a chance to display the value of any variables you think might be relevant. For example, the following code fragment displays the values of two variables, iAlpha and szBeta:

```
wsprintf(szBuffer, "iAlpha=%d, szBeta=%s", iAlpha, (LPSTR)szBeta);
MessageBox(hWnd, szBuffer, "Debug Info", MB_OK);
```

A good first step is to put message boxes at the beginning of the code that handles each message (just after the **case** statement for WM_COMMAND and so on). If the program dies just after you see the WM_COMMAND message box, you'll know that the code for processing this message is probably faulty. You can then insert more message boxes in this code to isolate the problem further.

When the bug has been found, you can remove the message box code. Or you can surround it with the #ifdef and #endif directives, like this:

```
#ifdef DEBUG
wsprintf(szBuffer, "iAlpha=%d, szBeta=%s", iAlpha, (LPSTR)szBeta);
MessageBox(hWnd, szBuffer, "Debug Info", MB_OK);
#endif
```

This code will compile only if you insert the directive

```
#define DEBUG
```

at the beginning of the listing. This lets you activate or deactivate many sections of debugging code at once.

If there's no main window, such as when you get a WM_CREATE message, you can still use a message box, but the first parameter to MessageBox() should be NULL rather than the window handle.

You can use a message box in WM_PAINT code with Turbo (and Borland) C++ for Windows, but with some compilers you'll need to insert a ValidateRect() function following the message box:

```
MessageBox(hWnd, szBuffer, "Debug Info", MB_OK);
ValidateRect(hWnd, NULL);
```

This prevents an infinite loop that occurs when closing the message box generates another WM_PAINT message.

Message boxes have an advantage over debugger programs (such as Turbo Debugger for Windows, described next) in that they interfere only minimally with the normal functioning of the program and of Windows itself. They are a standard programming element, so in general they don't produce unexpected side effects. On the other hand, a good debugger can do many things that message boxes can't, and in many cases may prove to be essential.

CHECKING RETURN VALUES

In the example programs in this book, we have not (except in a few cases) made a point of checking the return values of API functions. Doing so would have made the program listings longer and less readable (and Windows programs need all the help they can get in the readability department). However, it is important for serious programs to check the return value of potentially troublesome functions. When the return value signals a problem, the program should alert the user. A message box may be used for this, with a short description of what caused the error. This will help the programmer during program development. Even after the program is in the hands of users, error messages can help pinpoint problems and aid in program maintenance.

The CHECKRET example program demonstrates how return values can be handled for some typical functions. This program draws a simple design on the screen, along with some text. Either of two pen colors can be used for the text. A dialog box, invoked when the user selects the Pen item on the menu bar, allows the user to select one of the pens.

The resource file defines the menu and the dialog, which has radio buttons labelled Blue and Red, and the usual OK and Cancel buttons. There's nothing unusual in this file. Here's the listing for CHECKRET.RC

```
// checkret.rc
// resource file for checkret

#include "checkret.h"

CheckMenu MENU
BEGIN
        MENUITEM "Pen", IDM_PEN
END

PenDlg DIALOG 18, 18, 142, 60
STYLE DS_MODALFRAME | WS_POPUP | WS_CAPTION | WS_SYSMENU
CAPTION "Pen"
BEGIN
        CONTROL "Blue", IDP_BLUE, "BUTTON",
           BS_AUTORADIOBUTTON | WS_CHILD | WS_VISIBLE | WS_TABSTOP,
           13, 22, 28, 12
        CONTROL "Red", IDP_RED, "BUTTON",
           BS_AUTORADIOBUTTON | WS_CHILD | WS_VISIBLE | WS_TABSTOP,
           13, 36, 28, 12
        DEFPUSHBUTTON "Cancel", IDCANCEL, 92, 11, 34, 14,
           WS_CHILD | WS_VISIBLE | WS_TABSTOP
        PUSHBUTTON "OK", IDOK, 92, 34, 35, 14,
           WS_CHILD | WS_VISIBLE | WS_TABSTOP
END
```

The header file has only three identifiers: one for the menu, and two for the Blue and Red radio buttons in the dialog. Here's the listing for CHECKRET.H:

```
// checkret.h
// header file for checkret

#define IDM_PEN         100

#define IDP_BLUE        1001
#define IDP_RED         1002
```

The source file is similar to those in programs we've seen before, such as EZDIAL and PENS. However, it contains checks for crucial return values, which makes it a bit longer than usual. Here's the listing for CHECKRET.C:

```
// checkret.c
// checks return values of API functions

#define STRICT
#include <windows.h>
#include "checkret.h"                    // for menu and dialog IDs
                                         // prototypes
LRESULT CALLBACK _export WndProc(HWND, UINT, WPARAM, LPARAM);
BOOL CALLBACK _export PenDlgProc(HWND, UINT, WPARAM, LPARAM);

HPEN hBluePen, hRedPen, hCurrentPen; // pen handles

PSTR szProgName = "CheckRet";         // application name
/////////////////////////////////////////////////////////////////////
// WinMain() -- program entry point                                 //
/////////////////////////////////////////////////////////////////////
#pragma argsused                       // ignore unused arguments

int PASCAL WinMain(HINSTANCE hInstance, HINSTANCE hPrevInst,
                LPSTR lpCmdLine, int nCmdShow)
    {
    HWND hWnd;                          // window handle from CreateWindow
    MSG msg;                            // message from GetMessage
    WNDCLASS wndclass;                  // window class structure

    if(!hPrevInst)                      // if this is first such window
        {
        wndclass.style          = CS_HREDRAW | CS_VREDRAW; // style
        wndclass.lpfnWndProc    = (WNDPROC)WndProc; // WndProc address
        wndclass.cbClsExtra     = 0;            // no extra class data
        wndclass.cbWndExtra     = 0;            // no extra window data
        wndclass.hInstance      = hInstance;    // which program?
                                                // stock arrow cursor
        wndclass.hCursor        = LoadCursor (NULL, IDC_ARROW);
                                                // stock blank icon
        wndclass.hIcon          = LoadIcon(NULL, IDI_APPLICATION);
        wndclass.lpszMenuName   = "CheckMenu";  // menu name
                                                // white background
        wndclass.hbrBackground = GetStockObject(WHITE_BRUSH);
        wndclass.lpszClassName = "CheckClass"; // window class name

        if( !RegisterClass(&wndclass) )         // CHECK RETURN VALUE
            {
            MessageBox(NULL, "Can't register class", "CheckRet", MB_OK);
            return FALSE;                       // exit program
            }
        } // end if (!hPrevInst)
```

```
        hWnd = CreateWindow("CheckClass", szProgName, WS_OVERLAPPEDWINDOW,
                        CW_USEDEFAULT, CW_USEDEFAULT, CW_USEDEFAULT,
                        CW_USEDEFAULT, NULL, NULL, hInstance, NULL);
        if(!hWnd)                       // CHECK RETURN VALUE
            {
            MessageBox(NULL, "Can't create window", "CheckRet", MB_OK);
            return FALSE;               // exit program
            }

        ShowWindow(hWnd, nCmdShow);         // make window visible

        // message loop
        while( GetMessage(&msg,0,0,0) ) // get message from Windows
            {
            TranslateMessage(&msg);         // convert keystrokes
            DispatchMessage(&msg);          // call windows procedure
            }
        return msg.wParam;                  // return to Windows
        }  // end WinMain

//////////////////////////////////////////////////////////////////////
// main window procedure -- receives messages                        //
//////////////////////////////////////////////////////////////////////
LRESULT CALLBACK _export WndProc(HWND hWnd, UINT msg,
                            WPARAM wParam, LPARAM lParam)
    {
    HDC hDC;
    PAINTSTRUCT ps;
    HPEN hOldPen;                   // old pen handle
    HFONT hOldFont, hFixedFont;     // font handles
    HINSTANCE hInst;                // instance handle
    DLGPROC lpDlgProc;              // pointer to dialog procs

    int xLeft=20, yTop=20, xRight=320, yBottom=220;
    int xText = 100, yText = 110;

    switch(msg)
        {
        case WM_CREATE:                 // create pens
            hBluePen = CreatePen(PS_SOLID, 5, RGB(0,0,255));   // blue
            hRedPen = CreatePen(PS_SOLID, 5, RGB(255,0,0));    // red
            if(!hBluePen || !hRedPen) // CHECK RETURN VALUES
                {
                MessageBox(hWnd, "Can't create pen", "CheckRet", MB_OK);
                break;
                }
            hCurrentPen = hBluePen;     // initial pen
            break;

        case WM_COMMAND:                    // user selected menu item
            switch(wParam)
                {
```

```
    case IDM_PEN:               // user selects Pen item
       hInst = (HINSTANCE)GetWindowWord(hWnd, GWW_HINSTANCE);
       lpDlgProc = (DLGPROC)MakeProcInstance(
                            (FARPROC)PenDlgProc, hInst);
       if(lpDlgProc)            // CHECK RETURN VALUE
          {                     // if OK, do dialog
          DialogBox(hInst, "PenDlg", hWnd, lpDlgProc);
          FreeProcInstance( (FARPROC)lpDlgProc );
          }
       else
          {
          MessageBox(hWnd, "Can't invoke dialog box",
                     "CheckRet", MB_OK);
          break;
          }
       InvalidateRect(hWnd, NULL, TRUE);
       break;

    default:                    // USE EXPLICIT DEFAULT
       break;
    }   // end switch wParam
 break; // end case WM_COMMAND

case WM_PAINT:
   hDC = BeginPaint(hWnd, &ps);
   if(!hDC)                     // CHECK RETURN VALUE
      {
      MessageBox(hWnd, "Can't get device context",
                 "CheckRet", MB_OK);
      break;
      }
   hOldPen = SelectObject(hDC, hCurrentPen);  // select pen
   if(!hOldPen)                 // CHECK RETURN VALUE
      {
      MessageBox(hWnd, "Can't select pen", "CheckRet", MB_OK);
      EndPaint(hWnd, &ps);
      break;
      }
   hFixedFont = GetStockObject(SYSTEM_FIXED_FONT);
   if(!hFixedFont)              // CHECK RETURN VALUE
      {
      MessageBox(hWnd, "Can't get font", "CheckRet", MB_OK);
      EndPaint(hWnd, &ps);
      break;
      }
   hOldFont = SelectObject(hDC, hFixedFont);   // select font
   if(!hOldFont)                // CHECK RETURN VALUE
      {
      MessageBox(hWnd, "Can't select font", "CheckRet", MB_OK);
      EndPaint(hWnd, &ps);
      break;
      }
```

```
            Rectangle(hDC, xLeft, yTop, xRight, yBottom);
            Ellipse(hDC, xLeft, yTop, xRight, yBottom);
            TextOut(hDC, xText, yText, "Check Return Values", 19);

            SelectObject(hDC, hOldPen);    // restore old pen
            SelectObject(hDC, hOldFont);   // restore old font
            EndPaint(hWnd, &ps);
            break;

        case WM_DESTROY:
            if(hBluePen)                   // if they exist,
                DeleteObject(hBluePen);    // delete new pens
            if(hRedPen)
                DeleteObject(hRedPen);
            PostQuitMessage(0);
            break;

        default:
            return( DefWindowProc(hWnd, msg, wParam, lParam) );
        }   // end switch(msg)
    return 0L;
    }   // end WndProc


//////////////////////////////////////////////////////////////////
// PenDlgProc() -- dialog window procedure                       //
//////////////////////////////////////////////////////////////////
#pragma argsused

BOOL CALLBACK _export PenDlgProc(HWND hDlg, UINT msg,
                                 WPARAM wParam, LPARAM lParam)
    {
    static HPEN hTempPen;

    switch(msg)
        {
        case WM_INITDIALOG:
            hTempPen = hCurrentPen;
            CheckRadioButton(hDlg, IDP_BLUE, IDP_RED,
                        (hTempPen==hBluePen) ? IDP_BLUE : IDP_RED);
            break;

        case WM_COMMAND:                   // msg from control
            switch(wParam)
                {
                case IDP_BLUE:             // user presses radio button
                    hTempPen = hBluePen;   // remember which one
                    break;
                case IDP_RED:
                    hTempPen = hRedPen;
                    break;
                case IDOK:                 // user pushes OK button
                    hCurrentPen = hTempPen; // record last choice
```

```
            EndDialog(hDlg, NULL);   // terminate dialog box
            break;
        case IDCANCEL:                // user pushes Cancel button
            EndDialog(hDlg, NULL);   // terminate dialog box
            break;
        } // end switch wparam
      break;  // end case WM_COMMAND

    default:
        return FALSE;
    } // end switch msg
return TRUE;
} // end PenDlgProc
```

Notice the functions whose return values are examined. The RegisterClass() function may produce a FALSE return value because another application has registered the same class. CreateWindow() may fail because there isn't enough memory to create the window. BeginPaint() may fail because there aren't any device contexts left. Any function that gets or creates something, such as CreatePen(), CreateBrush(), and GetStockObject(), may fail if there is a lack of memory or other system resources.

When creating a dialog box, check the return value of MakeProcInstance(). If it's FALSE, forget about invoking the dialog box, and display a message box instead.

We don't show it in this example, but GetDlgItem(), which returns the handle to a dialog control, may fail because there wasn't enough memory to create the control; so it's return value should be checked. Many other functions return error values when they're not successful. When in doubt, check the value.

TURBO DEBUGGER FOR WINDOWS

Turbo C++ for Windows and Borland C++ for Windows include a debugger called Turbo Debugger for Windows (TDW). We don't have room in this chapter for a detailed description of TDW. Borland's *Turbo Debugger User's Guide* does that. However, we will show you a few key points about TDW to get you started.

Using a debugger in Windows poses some special problems. For one thing, the event-driven architecture of Windows programs makes it more difficult to look at different parts of the program with the debugger. For another, when you mix a debugger and Windows, the whole system tends to become unstable. System crashes are common. It's prudent not to run any other applications while debugging, lest you lose their data. Be careful to save your source files before invoking the debugger.

The debugger doesn't work well for certain kinds of bugs. If it consistently crashes the system in certain situations, you may need to revert to the message-box debugging approach.

Starting TDW

There are two ways to start TDW: as a stand-alone program, or from within Turbo (or Borland) C++ for Windows.

TDW as a Stand-Alone Program

To use TDW as a stand-alone program, start by compiling and linking your program to generate an .EXE file. Make sure the .EXE file is in the same directory as the source file. Now exit from the compiler and start the debugger by double-clicking on the TDW icon in the Turbo C++ (or Borland C++) group. TDW runs in character mode, but it has menus and windows that work the same way as the Windows GUI.

When TDW loads, select Open from the File menu, switch to the proper directory, select the .EXE file you want to debug (the target program), and click on OK. You should see the beginning of your program's WinMain() function displayed, with a marker pointing to the first line.

TDW as a Compiler Accessory

To run TDW from Turbo (or Borland) C++ for Windows, first open the project if there is one, or the source file if there isn't. Compile and link the program, making sure the process doesn't generate any errors or warnings.

Now, select Debugger from the Run menu. After a few seconds the character-mode window will appear.

Trapped in an Endless Loop

If you're used to debugging DOS programs, you may be tempted to start single-stepping through WinMain(), whose listing is shown on the TDW screen. You can do this by pressing the (F8) key. The marker at the left edge of the screen will move from line to line. The screen will go blank briefly when Windows API functions such as LoadIcon() and GetStockObject() are called.

Unfortunately, when you get to the message loop at the end of WinMain(), you'll find that you're stuck. You can go round and round in the message loop, but you can't get to the window procedure where most of your program's code is.

The problem lies in Windows' event-driven architecture. While the debugger is going round and round the message loop, Windows is busy calling the program's window procedure with various messages. Unfortunately, TDW has no way of knowing this. However, we can tell TDW to break (stop executing the target program and return to the debugger screen) whenever certain messages are received. This is the key to Windows program debugging.

Breaking on Messages

The following steps set up TDW to break whenever a window procedure receives a message.

Select Windows Message from the View menu. A window appears, which is divided into three panes. Each pane has its own menu. The cursor should be in the top left pane, which is called Windows Messages. Press (ALT)+(F10) to bring up the menu for that pane. Select Add from this menu. A dialog window appears. Fill in the Window Identifier field in this new window with the name of your window procedure (which is WndProc in the examples in this book). Make sure the Window Proc radio button is selected, then click on OK. You'll be back in the three-pane window.

Click in the upper right pane, which may say something like Log All Messages. Bring up the menu for this pane by pressing (ALT)+(F10). Select Add from this menu. Now a dialog window appears that allows you to select what messages you want to break on. The options are All Messages, Single Message, or one of a number of message categories such as Mouse, Window, Input, and Initialization.

Break on All Messages

Choosing All Messages is educational in that you can learn how many messages Windows sends to your application. There are dozens, many of which we haven't mentioned in this book. The ones not handled by your program are handled by DefWindowProc(), so you don't need to worry about them, but it's still interesting to watch them go by.

To select this option, click on the All Messages radio button. Then click on the Break radio button in the Action box (don't forget this), and then on OK. The entry in the pane should now be "Break on all messages."

Break on a Specific Message

You can also focus on the action of a specific message. This is more efficient if you have some idea where the bug is. If you think there's a problem with WM_PAINT processing for example, click on the Single Message radio button, and then type WM_PAINT (use all caps) into the Single Message Name field. Similarly, if the problem is with menu commands, insert WM_COMMAND; and if the wrong thing happens when the left mouse button is pressed, insert WM_LBUTTONDOWN. Once the appropriate message name is inserted, click on the Break radio button (again, don't forget this), and then on OK.

Running the Program

Now that TDW knows what messages to break on, you can run the program. To do this, select Run from the Run menu, or press (F9). You'll see the listing for the window procedure WndProc() appear on the screen, with the pointer on the first line. The program has stopped here because you installed a breakpoint for one or more messages. If you installed a breakpoint for only a single message, you may find yourself in the target program rather than the debugger. Do whatever generates that message. To generate WM_PAINT, for example, make the main window larger. To generate WM_COMMAND, select something from the menu. This causes the break and you'll be back in the debugger.

Stepping and Tracing

From the debugger you can press (F8) to single-step through the program. Use (F7) instead if you want to trace into functions rather than stepping over them. Press (F9) to run the program full speed from the message breakpoint.

Every time you press (F9) or step all the way through WndProc(), you'll see a new message name appear on the lower pane of the Windows Messages window. If you elected to break on All Messages, then each new message is different. When interesting ones appear, you can trace through the code with (F8).

If you chose Single Message, then the same message name will appear over and over. (You may need to make the debugger window larger to see all the data on each message.) The listing for WndProc() will appear as before; but if you then step through the procedure, you'll find that you go directly to the **case** section that processes the particular message. This is usually a more efficient approach than breaking on all messages.

Switching Between TDW and the Target Program

You may find yourself stuck in the target program. Perhaps it's doing something that doesn't generate the message you chose to break on. You can get back to the debugger at any time by pressing the (CTRL)+(ALT)+(SYSRQ) key combination. (The (SYSRQ) key is the same as the (PRTSCN) key.) Once in TDW, you can set additional message breaks. To return to the target program from TDW, press (F9) to run it again.

Exiting from TDW

To exit from TDW, first shut down the target program in the usual way (by selecting Close from the system menu, for example). When you're back in TDW, select Quit from the File menu.

Be careful when you escape from the target program to TDW with the (CTRL)+(ALT)+(SYSRQ) key combination. Doing this leaves the target program in an unstable state. Don't do anything but set the necessary additional breakpoints. If you try to do something more radical, like exiting from TDW, you'll see a message box that says "Ctrl-Alt-SysRq interrupt, system crash possible, continue?" If you answer Yes, you may (in fact probably will) crash the system. Answer No, press (F9) to return to the program, and shut down the program normally. Now you can exit from TDW with no problem.

Normal Debugging

Once you get to specific message-handling sections of your program, you can use TDW as you would debuggers in DOS or other systems. There are many tools available in TDW, but the most useful are breakpoints and watch windows.

Setting Breakpoints

A breakpoint allows you to run the program up to a certain statement and stop at that point. From there you can single-step or examine variable values. Breakpoints let you zip through sections of code that would be too slow to single-step through, such as loops.

To set a breakpoint, position the cursor on the appropriate line in the program listing and select Toggle from the Breakpoints menu, or press (F2). To undo the breakpoint, repeat the process.

When a breakpoint is set you can run the program with (F9), and it will execute from the marked line up to the breakpoint.

Watch Windows

A watch window allows you to monitor the value of a variable. You can watch this value change as you single-step through the program, or you can examine it when the program stops at a breakpoint.

To set a variable in a watch window, select Add Watch from the Data menu. Type in the name of the variable in the resulting window, and click on OK. A window called Watches will appear on the bottom of the screen. It shows the variables you want to watch, and their values. (You may need to make this window larger to see the values.)

To delete a variable from the watch window, select it by clicking on it, and then press (DEL).

Other Features

We've only scratched the surface of TDW's features. Explore TDW's menus, use the Help menu, and read the documentation. You'll find it a powerful and perhaps even an indispensable ally in the battle against bugs.

SUMMARY

Try this sequence for debugging your program:

1. Make sure your program compiles and links without warning messages (unless you're very sure they're not causing the problem).
2. Try mental debugging. Check for common errors.
3. Insert a few message boxes to see if the program is going where you expect, and if variables have the correct values at strategic points.
4. Use Turbo Debugger for Windows.

PART EIGHT
LARGER PROGRAMS

The finishing touches for a knight's education were often provided by a *quest*. This was an expedition with a prescribed goal, such as aiding a damsel in distress or redressing an injustice. Ideally, a quest involved considerable hardship and danger, which were thought to build character. The most famous quest was the search for the holy grail, the cup used by Christ at the Last Supper.

Understanding a lengthy Windows program involves its share of hardship and danger (at least to one's sanity) and is thus a fitting subject for a quest. In this final section of the book, we present three example programs that are more challenging than those we've seen before. Previous examples have been, for the sake of clarity, as short as possible. These new programs are longer and more complex. They don't use any new features; they're constructed with the Windows building blocks we've discussed in previous chapters. Our intent is to show that it is possible to create interesting and useful Windows programs with the techniques described in this book.

There are three examples: a graphics program that uses fractal techniques to generate flowers and plants in an almost infinite variety of shapes; a calculator that converts between Roman and Arabic numerals; and a database program to organize your personal library (probably containing cheap novels and textbooks you'll never use again).

It is not our intention to explain every detail of these programs. We'll discuss in a general way how they work, and delve more deeply into any unusual features. Don't worry if you don't understand everything; the focus here is on how the building blocks you've learned about already relate to each other in larger programs. Remember that these programs are not intended to be full-scale commercial applications, but instead platforms that you can explore and modify. If you don't like the way something works, feel free to change it.

39

FRACTAL FLOWER GENERATOR

ractals may be defined as something that looks the same when you magnify it as it does when you don't. An example is the coastline of a country shown on a map. At a certain scale, the coastline looks all wiggly. But if you change the scale to show, say 10 times as much detail, then the coastline still looks all wiggly in the same sort of way. This turns out to be true no matter what scale you use. The characteristic of looking the same at different scales is called *self-similarity.*

Fractals have a wide variety of uses, but what we're concerned with in this chapter is their ability to create images that look like nature: landscapes, mountains, and plants. Our example program, FRACTAL, uses fractal techniques to draw a variety of plant-like images. The user, by changing parameters in the program, can define

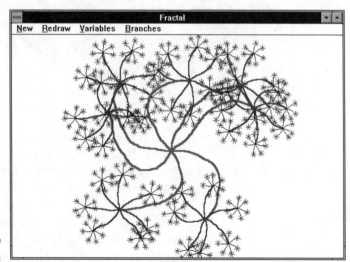

Figure 39-1
Queen Anne's Lace
(Default Plant)

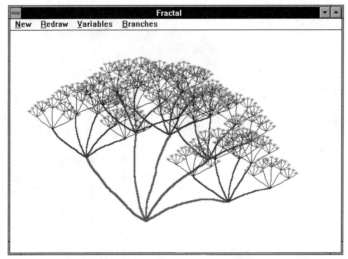

Figure 39-2

Jacaranda Tree

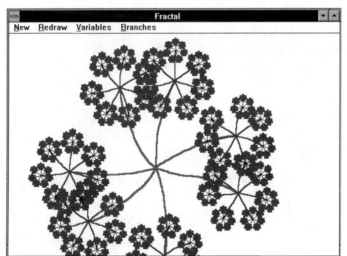

Figure 39-3

Geranium

the shape and color of these objects to make them resemble different varieties of trees, plants, and flowers. Figures 39-1, 39-2, and 39-3 show some of the possibilities. The colors of the various components of the plant can also be changed; unfortunately the figures can't reproduce these colors.

Conceptually, all the plant shapes are composed of only two elements: clusters and branches. A cluster is a point where several branches originate. They fan out in different directions from the cluster. A branch is a line that curves in an irregular way. It's composed of a number of straight-line segments.

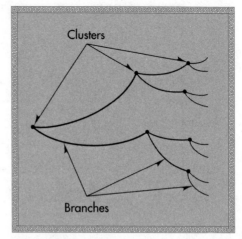

Figure 39-4 Clusters and Branches

Fractals enter the picture with the concept that at the end of every branch there is another cluster, smaller than the one from which the branch originated. This is shown in Figure 39-4.

A plant consists of a cluster with branches shooting out from it, clusters at the ends of these branches, smaller branches shooting out from these clusters, and so on.

An element of randomness is introduced to help create a natural look. This causes every branch to be a little different shape than the other branches. Thus every plant, which consists of many branches, is unique.

USING THE PROGRAM

When you first run the program you'll produce a variation of the plant shown in Figure 39-1. We'll call this the *default plant*. Every time you select New from the main menu, you'll see another drawing of this *type* of plant, but not this identical plant. Because FRACTAL involves random numbers, it can imitate nature's dictum that no two living objects are ever quite the same. If you select Redraw, on the other hand, the same exact plant will be drawn. You can also cause the same plant to be drawn by clicking anywhere on the screen. The plant will be redrawn starting at the cursor position. This allows you to reposition a plant to help you fit it in the window.

The Variables Dialog

To draw different types of plants, you need to change the values of certain variables in the program. If you select Variables from the main menu, you'll see the dialog box shown in Figure 39-5.

Variables	
Cluster fan-out angle (30-360):	360
Turn probability (0=right, 100=left):	30
Branches per cluster (2-12):	7
Segment length (1.0-20.0):	5
Segment-to-segment angle (0-90):	3
Segments per branch (10-200):	30
Branch-length reduction (2-20):	3
Recursion depth (2 to 5):	5

OK   Cancel

Figure 39-5

The Variables Dialog

There are eight variables in this dialog, each of which alters the shape of the plant in a different way. Understanding these variables is the key to understanding how the program works. Figure 39-6 shows some of these variables.

Cluster Fan-Out Angle

The branches can all shoot off from the cluster in more or less the same direction, or they can be evenly distributed around the circle. The angle in which all the branches lie is called the *cluster fan-out angle*. It can vary from 360 degrees, where the branches are distributed around a complete circle, to about 30 degrees, where they are too close together to distinguish.

Turn Probability

Each branch is composed of a number of straight-line segments. By connecting these segments at a small angle, we can make the branches appear to curve. If the angles all turn to the right, the branch appears to curve to the right.

It is in this segment-to-segment angle that the role of chance appears in the program. If the angles usually turn in one direction, but sometimes turn in the other, the branches appear to curve in a random and natural-looking way.

The turn probability specifies how often the angle will turn to the left and how often to the right. A value of 0 means they always go to the right; 50 means they turn either way with equal probability, and 100 means they always go to the left. A value of 30 produces life-like curves that tend to go right, while a value of 70 does the same for left-hand curves.

Branches per Cluster

There are 7 branches per cluster in the default plant. This value can be varied from 2 to 12 (or even higher). A value of 2 is appropriate for some kinds of trees; flowers generally require higher values.

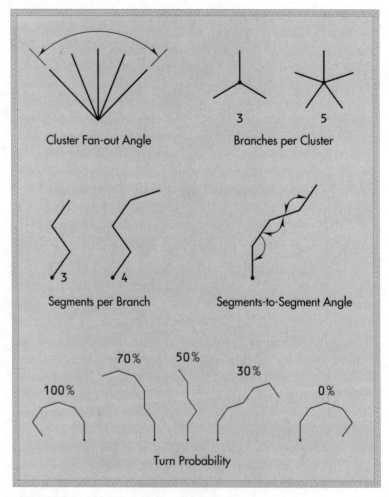

Figure 39-6 Some Variables in FRACTAL

This number has a major effect on the drawing time. If the recursion depth is 4 (we'll explain what that is in a moment), then the time required to draw 3 branches on every cluster is proportional to 3*3*3*3 or 81, while the time to draw 6 branches is 6*6*6*6 or 1,296, and the time to draw 12 branches is 12*12*12*12 or 20,736. The moral is, don't use large numbers for this variable without experimenting first with smaller ones; or you may find your computer taking many minutes to finish a drawing.

Segments per Branch

The number of segments per branch is one factor that influences the overall size of the drawing. The higher this number, the larger the drawing.

Segment Length

This is the second factor that influences the overall size of the drawing. If you make the segments twice as long, the whole drawing becomes twice as big; if they're half as long, the drawing is half the size.

The segments per branch and the segment length can be adjusted together to change the smoothness of the curves formed by the branches. If you double the number of segments per branch, and at the same time make each segment only half as long, the curves become smoother because they are composed of more segments, but the drawing remains the same size. On the other hand, drawing time is increased.

Segment-to-Segment Angle

Each segment in a branch is connected to the next segment at a fixed angle. The angle can bend either left or right, but it is always the same angle. Smaller angles create straighter branches; large angles create branches that are more curly. Unless the turn probability is close to 50, large angles create branches that curl up on themselves like springs.

If this angle is 0, all the branches are straight, and the resulting image takes on a geometrical look; more like a snowflake than a plant.

Branch-Length Reduction

In the default plant this value is set to 3, which means that the branches on each cluster are 1/3 the size of the branch that produced the cluster. If you change the number to 4, each set of branches will be 1/4 the length of the last set, and so forth.

Recursion Depth

The recursion depth is initially set to 4. That means there are four sizes of branches. The branch size is measured in the number of segments used to make the branch. The initial branches might be composed of 60 segments. Assuming a branch-length reduction of 3, the next-smallest branches will be 20 segments (60 divided by 3), still smaller branches will be 6 (20 divided by 3), and the smallest ones will be 2 segments. If the recursion depth is set to 3, there will be only 3 sizes of branches: 60, 20, and 6.

You can't have branches less than 1 segment long, so a recursion depth of 5 doesn't produce an additional branch size unless you start with a larger value of segments per branch. If you want to do this and keep the same scale, you can reduce the segment length. For instance, you can make the segment length 2, the segments per branch 120, and the recursion depth 5. This results in a more complicated image that's suitable for certain kinds of trees.

Branches

The Branches item on the main menu produces a drop-down menu with seven items: Branch #1, Branch #2, and so on up to Branch #7. Branch #1 represents the

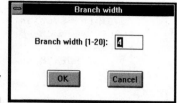

Figure 39-7
The Width Dialog

set of the largest branches: those that start from the first cluster. Branch #2 represents the next-smallest group of branches, which start from the clusters at the ends of the #1 branches, and so on for the other branch sizes. Usually branch numbers above 4 or 5 aren't used, and it's highly unlikely there will be more than 7 branch sizes, since they are too small to see at this depth.

Each of these Branch menu selections produces a submenu with two selections, Color and Width. With these selections you can change the color and the line width of any size branch. The Color selection brings up the Colors common dialog, so you can set the color of a particular size of branch. The Width item brings up the dialog shown in Figure 39-7, which allows you to type in a width.

In the default plant, produced when you first run the program, the last level of branch is #4. If you make this last-level branch thicker (say 3 to 5 pixels), the program generates a design that looks like flowers, as shown in Figure 39-3. We might call this branch size a "petal." Changing the color of the petals can produce spectacular results.

PROGRAM LISTING

The program listings are longer than those you've seen before, but all the elements should be familiar. In addition to the files listed here, there is an icon file, FRACTAL.ICO, that depicts a flower.

The Resource File

The resource file contains specifications for the menu system and for the Variables and Width dialog boxes. Here's the listing for FRACTAL.RC:

```
// fractal.rc
// resource script file for fractal

#include "fractal.h"    // constant #defines

FractalIcon ICON "fractal.ico"  // icon

Fractal MENU
    BEGIN
        MENUITEM "&New", IDM_NEWDRAW
```

```
            MENUITEM "&Redraw", IDM_REDRAW
            MENUITEM "&Variables", IDM_VARIAB
            POPUP "&Branches"
               BEGIN
                  POPUP "Branch #&1"
                     BEGIN
                        MENUITEM "&Color", IDM_COLOR1
                        MENUITEM "&Width", IDM_WIDTH1
                     END
                  POPUP "Branch #&2"
                     BEGIN
                        MENUITEM "&Color", IDM_COLOR2
                        MENUITEM "&Width", IDM_WIDTH2
                     END
                  POPUP "Branch #&3"
                     BEGIN
                        MENUITEM "&Color", IDM_COLOR3
                        MENUITEM "&Width", IDM_WIDTH3
                     END
                  POPUP "Branch #&4"
                     BEGIN
                        MENUITEM "&Color", IDM_COLOR4
                        MENUITEM "&Width", IDM_WIDTH4
                     END
                  POPUP "Branch #&5"
                     BEGIN
                        MENUITEM "&Color", IDM_COLOR5
                        MENUITEM "&Width", IDM_WIDTH5
                     END
                  POPUP "Branch #&6"
                     BEGIN
                        MENUITEM "&Color", IDM_COLOR6
                        MENUITEM "&Width", IDM_WIDTH6
                     END
                  POPUP "Branch #&7"
                     BEGIN
                        MENUITEM "&Color", IDM_COLOR7
                        MENUITEM "&Width", IDM_WIDTH7
                     END
               END
      END

// Variables dialog box
Variab DIALOG 24, 25, 176, 162
STYLE DS_MODALFRAME | WS_POPUP | WS_CAPTION | WS_SYSMENU
CAPTION "Variables"
BEGIN
   LTEXT "Cluster fan-out angle (30-360):", -1,
      12, 7, 98, 8
   LTEXT "Turn probability (0=right, 100=left):", -1,
      12, 23, 113, 8
```

```
    LTEXT "Branches per cluster (2-12):", -1,
        12, 39, 90, 8
    LTEXT "Segment length (1.0-20.0):", -1,
        12, 55, 101, 8
    LTEXT "Segment-to-segment angle (0-90):", -1,
        12, 71, 109, 8
    LTEXT "Segments per branch (10-200):", -1,
        12, 88, 111, 8
    LTEXT "Branch-length reduction (2-20):", -1,
        12, 104, 100, 8
    LTEXT "Recursion depth (2 to 5):", -1,
        12, 120, 111, 8
    EDITTEXT IDV_FANANGLE, 129, 5, 32, 12
    EDITTEXT IDV_PROBA,    129, 21, 32, 12
    EDITTEXT IDV_BRANCHES, 129, 37, 32, 12
    EDITTEXT IDV_LENGTH,   129, 53, 32, 12
    EDITTEXT IDV_TURN,     129, 69, 32, 12
    EDITTEXT IDV_SEGMENTS, 129, 85, 32, 12
    EDITTEXT IDV_REDUX,    129, 101, 32, 12
    EDITTEXT IDV_DEPTH,    129, 117, 32, 12
    CONTROL "OK", IDOK, "BUTTON",
        BS_PUSHBUTTON | WS_CHILD | WS_VISIBLE | WS_TABSTOP,
        50, 139, 30, 14
    CONTROL "Cancel", IDCANCEL, "BUTTON",
        BS_PUSHBUTTON | WS_CHILD | WS_VISIBLE | WS_TABSTOP,
        89, 139, 33, 14
END

// Widths dialog box
Widths DIALOG 25, 29, 142, 71
STYLE DS_MODALFRAME | WS_POPUP | WS_CAPTION | WS_SYSMENU
CAPTION "Branch width"
BEGIN
    CONTROL "Branch width (1-20):", -1, "STATIC",
        SS_LEFT | WS_CHILD | WS_VISIBLE | WS_GROUP,
        20, 18, 73, 8
    EDITTEXT IDD_EDIT,
        90, 16, 25, 12
    CONTROL "OK", IDOK, "BUTTON",
        BS_PUSHBUTTON | WS_CHILD | WS_VISIBLE | WS_TABSTOP,
        31, 46, 29, 14
    CONTROL "Cancel", IDCANCEL, "BUTTON",
        BS_PUSHBUTTON | WS_CHILD | WS_VISIBLE | WS_TABSTOP,
        84, 46, 31, 14
END
```

The Header File

The header file should hold no surprises, except for the number of constants it defines. Here's the listing for FRACTAL.H:

```
// fractal.h
// header file for fractal

#define IDM_NEWDRAW    100
#define IDM_REDRAW     200
#define IDM_VARIAB     300

#define IDM_COLOR1     401
#define IDM_WIDTH1     411
#define IDM_COLOR2     402
#define IDM_WIDTH2     412
#define IDM_COLOR3     403
#define IDM_WIDTH3     413
#define IDM_COLOR4     404
#define IDM_WIDTH4     414
#define IDM_COLOR5     405
#define IDM_WIDTH5     415
#define IDM_COLOR6     406
#define IDM_WIDTH6     416
#define IDM_COLOR7     407
#define IDM_WIDTH7     417

#define IDD_EDIT       1001

#define IDV_FANANGLE 2001   // cluster fan-out angle
#define IDV_PROBA    2002   // turn probability
#define IDV_BRANCHES 2003   // branches per cluster
#define IDV_LENGTH   2004   // segment length
#define IDV_TURN     2005   // segment-to-segment angle
#define IDV_SEGMENTS 2006   // segments per branch
#define IDV_REDUX    2007   // branch-length reduction
#define IDV_DEPTH    2008   // recursion depth
```

The Source File

The source file contains five functions. There is the usual WndProc() window procedure, which handles menu selections and creates the drawing. Two other procedures, VarDlgProc() and WidthDlgProc(), process messages sent to the Variables and Width dialog boxes, respectively. We'll see what the Cluster() and Branch() functions do next. Here's the listing for FRACTAL.C:

```
// fractal.c
// draws fractal plants

#define STRICT
#include <windows.h>
#include "fractal.h"        // for menu and dialog IDs
#include <commdlg.h>        // for ChooseColor common dialog
#include <stdlib.h>         // for srand(), rand()
#include <time.h>           // for time()
#include <math.h>           // for sin(), cos()
```

```
#define TWOPI 6.28318        // two times pi (same as 360 degrees)
#define DENOM    100         // denominator of probability
#define BUFFSIZE 256         // size of utility buffers

// set default values
float fan = TWOPI;           // angle of spread of branches (radians)
int prob = 30;               // numerator of probability (over 100)
int number = 7;              // number of branches per cluster
float seglen = 3.0;          // length of straight line segments
float turn = 0.1;            // change in segment angle (radians)
int segs = 60;               // max line segments per branch
float redux = 3.0;           // how much to divide # of segments
int maxdepth = 4;            // how many branch sizes

float x, y;                  // coordinates of line
int depth;                   // what size branch we're working on
time_t StartTime;            // random number seed
char szEditInput[BUFFSIZE];  // buffer for user input from dialog
char szEditOutput[BUFFSIZE]; // buffer for writing to dialog

HPEN hOldPen, hPen[7];       // pens
COLORREF clrref[7];          // pen colors
int nWidth[7];               // pen thicknesses

                             // prototypes
LRESULT CALLBACK _export WndProc(HWND, UINT, WPARAM, LPARAM);
BOOL CALLBACK _export VarDlgProc(HWND, UINT, WPARAM, LPARAM);
BOOL CALLBACK _export WidthDlgProc(HWND, UINT, WPARAM, LPARAM);
void Cluster(HDC hDC, int segs, float x, float y);
void Branch(HDC hDC, int segs, float theta, float x, float y);

//////////////////////////////////////////////////////////////////
// WinMain() -- program entry point                             //
//////////////////////////////////////////////////////////////////
#pragma argsused                        // ignore unused arguments

int PASCAL WinMain(HINSTANCE hInstance,  // which program are we?
                   HINSTANCE hPrevInst,  // is there another one?
                   LPSTR lpCmdLine,      // command line arguments
                   int nCmdShow)         // window size (icon, etc)
    {
    HWND hWnd;                   // window handle from CreateWindow()
    MSG msg;                     // message from GetMessage()
    WNDCLASS wndclass;           // window class structure

    if(!hPrevInst)               // if this is first such window
        {
        wndclass.style       = NULL;         // default style
        wndclass.lpfnWndProc = (WNDPROC)WndProc; // WndProc address
        wndclass.cbClsExtra  = 0;            // no extra class data
        wndclass.cbWndExtra  = 0;            // no extra window data
        wndclass.hInstance   = hInstance;    // which program?
```

```
                                              // stock arrow cursor
      wndclass.hCursor        = LoadCursor (NULL, IDC_ARROW);
                                              // custom icon
      wndclass.hIcon          = LoadIcon(hInstance, "FractalIcon");
      wndclass.lpszMenuName    = "FractalMenu";  // menu name
                                              // white background
      wndclass.hbrBackground = GetStockObject(WHITE_BRUSH);
      wndclass.lpszClassName = "FractalClass"; // window class name

      RegisterClass(&wndclass); // register the window
      }  // end if

   hWnd = CreateWindow("FractalClass",       // window class name
                       "Fractal",            // caption
                       WS_OVERLAPPEDWINDOW,  // style
                       CW_USEDEFAULT,        // default x position
                       CW_USEDEFAULT,        // default y position
                       CW_USEDEFAULT,        // default width
                       CW_USEDEFAULT,        // default height
                       NULL,                 // parent's handle
                       NULL,                 // menu handle
                       hInstance,            // which program?
                       NULL);                // no init data

   ShowWindow(hWnd, nCmdShow);      // make window visible

   // message loop
   while( GetMessage(&msg,0,0,0) )  // get message from Windows
      {
      TranslateMessage(&msg);       // convert keystrokes
      DispatchMessage(&msg);        // call window procedure
      }
   return msg.wParam;               // return to Windows
   }  // end WinMain

//////////////////////////////////////////////////////////////////////
// main window procedure -- receives messages                       //
//////////////////////////////////////////////////////////////////////
LRESULT CALLBACK _export WndProc(HWND hWnd, UINT msg,
                                 WPARAM wParam, LPARAM lParam)

   {
   static HINSTANCE hInst; // instance handle
   HDC hDC;                // device context handle
   PAINTSTRUCT ps;         // paint info
   DLGPROC lpDlgProc;      // pointer to dialog procedures
   int i;                  // loop variable
   CHOOSECOLOR chc;        // structure for color info
   DWORD dwCustColors[16]; // for ChooseColor()
   static DWORD dwColor;   // color chosen

   switch(msg)
      {
```

```
case WM_CREATE:
   // get instance handle
   hInst = (HINSTANCE)GetWindowWord(hWnd, GWW_HINSTANCE);

   // initialize colors for pens
   clrref[0] = RGB(127,127,0); // yellow
   clrref[1] = RGB(0,127,0);   // light green
   clrref[2] = RGB(0,0,0);     // black
   clrref[3] = RGB(255,0,0);   // red
   clrref[4] = RGB(0,255,0);   // green
   clrref[5] = RGB(0,255,255); // cyan
   clrref[6] = RGB(0,0,255);   // blue

   // initialize widths for pens
   nWidth[0] = 3;
   nWidth[1] = 2;
   nWidth[2] = 1;
   nWidth[3] = 1;
   nWidth[4] = 1;
   nWidth[5] = 1;
   nWidth[6] = 1;

   // create all the pens
   for(i=0; i<7; i++)
      hPen[i] = CreatePen(PS_SOLID, nWidth[i], clrref[i] );
   time(&StartTime);   // initial random seed in StartTime
   break;  // end WM_CREATE

case WM_SIZE:
   x = (float)LOWORD(lParam) / 2;  // start in center of window
   y = (float)HIWORD(lParam) / 2;
   InvalidateRect(hWnd, NULL, TRUE);
   break;

case WM_LBUTTONDOWN:                  // start at mouse click
   x = (float)LOWORD(lParam);
   y = (float)HIWORD(lParam);
   InvalidateRect(hWnd, NULL, TRUE);
   break;

case WM_COMMAND:             // user selects a menu item
   switch(wParam)            // wParam holds item ID
      {
      case IDM_REDRAW:           // old random seed
         InvalidateRect(hWnd, NULL, TRUE);
         break;

      case IDM_NEWDRAW:
         time(&StartTime);      // new random seed
         srand( (unsigned)StartTime );  // initialize random
         InvalidateRect(hWnd, NULL, TRUE);
         break;
```

```
        case IDM_VARIAB:
            lpDlgProc=(DLGPROC)MakeProcInstance(
                                (FARPROC)VarDlgProc, hInst );
            DialogBox(hInst, "Variab", hWnd, lpDlgProc);
            FreeProcInstance( (FARPROC)lpDlgProc );
            break;  // end case IDM_VARIAB

        case IDM_COLOR1:
        case IDM_COLOR2:
        case IDM_COLOR3:
        case IDM_COLOR4:
        case IDM_COLOR5:
        case IDM_COLOR6:
        case IDM_COLOR7:
            chc.lStructSize = sizeof(CHOOSECOLOR);
            chc.hwndOwner = hWnd;
            chc.rgbResult = clrref[wParam-IDM_COLOR1];
            chc.lpCustColors = dwCustColors;
            chc.Flags = CC_FULLOPEN | CC_RGBINIT;

            if( !ChooseColor(&chc) )
                break;
            dwColor = chc.rgbResult;
            clrref[wParam-IDM_COLOR1] = dwColor;
            DeleteObject( hPen[wParam-IDM_COLOR1] );
            hPen[wParam-IDM_COLOR1] =
                CreatePen(PS_SOLID, nWidth[wParam-IDM_COLOR1],
                            clrref[wParam-IDM_COLOR1]);
            break;  // end case multiple IDM_COLORs

        case IDM_WIDTH1:
        case IDM_WIDTH2:
        case IDM_WIDTH3:
        case IDM_WIDTH4:
        case IDM_WIDTH5:
        case IDM_WIDTH6:
        case IDM_WIDTH7:
            itoa(nWidth[wParam-IDM_WIDTH1], szEditOutput, 10);
            lpDlgProc=(DLGPROC)MakeProcInstance(
                                (FARPROC)WidthDlgProc, hInst );
            DialogBox(hInst, "Widths", hWnd, lpDlgProc);
            FreeProcInstance( (FARPROC)lpDlgProc );
            nWidth[wParam-IDM_WIDTH1] = atoi(szEditInput);
            DeleteObject( hPen[wParam-IDM_WIDTH1] );
            hPen[wParam-IDM_WIDTH1] =
                CreatePen(PS_SOLID, nWidth[wParam-IDM_WIDTH1],
                            clrref[wParam-IDM_WIDTH1] );
            break;  // end case multiple IDM_WIDTHs

        }   // end switch wParam
    break;  // end case WM_COMMAND
```

```
    case WM_PAINT:
        hDC = BeginPaint(hWnd, &ps);
        depth = 0;                          // start at the top
        srand( (unsigned)StartTime );  // initialize randoms
        Cluster(hDC, segs, x, y);      // display the cluster
        EndPaint(hWnd, &ps);
        break;

    case WM_DESTROY:
        for(i=0; i<7; i++)          // delete pens
            DeleteObject( hPen[i] );
        PostQuitMessage(0);
        break;

    default:
        return( DefWindowProc(hWnd, msg, wParam, lParam) );
    }   // end switch(msg)

    return 0L;
    }  // end WndProc


/////////////////////////////////////////////////////////////////
// Cluster() -- draws a cluster of tendrils                     //
/////////////////////////////////////////////////////////////////
void Cluster(HDC hDC, int segs, float x, float y)
    {
    int i;
    float theta;                            // angle of next segment

    // for each branch in this cluster
    for(i=0; i<number; i++)
        {
        if(fan >= TWOPI)                    // full circle
            theta = i*TWOPI/number;
        else                                // fan-shape
            theta = i*fan/(number-1) - fan/2;
        MoveTo(hDC, (int)x, (int)y);        // cluster center
        depth++;                            // down one level
        Branch(hDC, segs, theta, x, y);     // display branch
        depth--;                            // up one level
        }
    return;
    }


/////////////////////////////////////////////////////////////////
// Branch() -- draws a branch, with cluster at end             //
/////////////////////////////////////////////////////////////////
void Branch(HDC hDC, int segs, float theta, float x, float y)
    {
    int j;                                  // loop index
    int newsegs;                            // reduced # of segments
    int sign;                               // -1 or 1, left or right
```

```
    // select pen based on depth
    hOldPen = SelectObject( hDC, hPen[depth-1] );

    // draw all the segments that constitute one branch
    for(j=0; j<segs; j++)
        {                                    // turn left or right?
        sign = ( (rand() % DENOM) < prob ) ? -1 : 1;
        x = x + seglen*sin(theta);       // x and y of
        y = y - seglen*cos(theta);       // end of segment
        LineTo(hDC, (int)x, (int)y);     // draw segment
        theta = theta + sign*turn;       // new angle: bend the branch
        }
    SelectObject(hDC, hOldPen);          // restore old pen

    if(depth < maxdepth)                 // gone deep enough?
        {
        newsegs = segs / redux;          // make new cluster, but
        Cluster(hDC, newsegs, x, y);     // smaller than before
        }
    return;
    }


/////////////////////////////////////////////////////////////////////
// VarDlgProc() -- dialog window procedure -- gets variables       //
/////////////////////////////////////////////////////////////////////
#pragma argsused

BOOL CALLBACK _export VarDlgProc(HWND hDlg, UINT msg,
                                 WPARAM wParam, LPARAM lParam)
    {
    HWND hControl;                       // handle of control

    switch(msg)
        {
        case WM_INITDIALOG:
                                         // set text in edit controls
            // cluster fanout angle (radians to degrees)
            SetDlgItemInt(hDlg, IDV_FANANGLE,
                                (int)((fan*360)/TWOPI), TRUE);
            // probability of right or left turn
            SetDlgItemInt(hDlg, IDV_PROBA, prob, TRUE);
            // number of branches
            SetDlgItemInt(hDlg, IDV_BRANCHES, number, TRUE);
            // segment length
            gcvt( (double)seglen, 5, szEditOutput );
            SetDlgItemText(hDlg, IDV_LENGTH, szEditOutput);
            // turn angle from segment to segment (radians to degrees)
            SetDlgItemInt(hDlg, IDV_TURN, (int)((turn*360)/TWOPI), TRUE);
            // number of segments per branch
            SetDlgItemInt(hDlg, IDV_SEGMENTS, segs, TRUE);
            // amount to reduce branch size at each depth
            gcvt( (double)redux, 5, szEditOutput);
```

```
    SetDlgItemText(hDlg, IDV_REDUX, szEditOutput);
    // recursion depth (number of different branch sizes)
    SetDlgItemInt(hDlg, IDV_DEPTH, maxdepth, TRUE);

    hControl = GetDlgItem(hDlg, IDD_EDIT);  // get edit handle
    SetFocus(hControl);              // set focus to edit control
    break;

case WM_COMMAND:                     // msg from dlg box control
    switch(wParam)
        {
        case IDOK:                   // user pushes OK button
            // get cluster fanout angle (degrees to radians)
            GetDlgItemText(hDlg, IDV_FANANGLE, szEditInput, BUFFSIZE);
            fan = (float)((TWOPI*atoi(szEditInput))/360);
            // get probability (0=always left, 50=either way, etc.)
            GetDlgItemText(hDlg, IDV_PROBA, szEditInput, BUFFSIZE);
            prob = atoi(szEditInput);
            // get number of branches per cluster
            GetDlgItemText(hDlg, IDV_BRANCHES, szEditInput, BUFFSIZE);
            number = atoi(szEditInput);
            // get length of each segment
            GetDlgItemText(hDlg, IDV_LENGTH, szEditInput, BUFFSIZE);
            seglen = atof(szEditInput);
            // get angle between segments (degrees to radians)
            GetDlgItemText(hDlg, IDV_TURN, szEditInput, BUFFSIZE);
            turn = (float)((TWOPI*atoi(szEditInput))/360);
            // get segments per branch
            GetDlgItemText(hDlg, IDV_SEGMENTS, szEditInput, BUFFSIZE);
            segs = atoi(szEditInput);
            // get amount to reduce branch size at each recursion
            GetDlgItemText(hDlg, IDV_REDUX, szEditInput, BUFFSIZE);
            redux = atof(szEditInput);
            // get depth recursion depth
            GetDlgItemText(hDlg, IDV_DEPTH, szEditInput, BUFFSIZE);
            maxdepth = atof(szEditInput);

            EndDialog(hDlg, NULL);  // terminate dialog box
            break;

        case IDCANCEL:               // user pushes Cancel button
            EndDialog(hDlg, NULL);  // terminate dialog box
            break;
        } // end switch wParam
    break;  // end case WM_COMMAND
default:
    return FALSE;                    // if we don't handle msg
} // end switch msg
return TRUE;                          // if we handled message
} // end VarDlgProc
```

```
//////////////////////////////////////////////////////////////////
// WidthDlgProc() -- dialog window procedure -- gets pen widths   //
//////////////////////////////////////////////////////////////////
#pragma argsused

BOOL CALLBACK _export WidthDlgProc(HWND hDlg, UINT msg,
                                   WPARAM wParam, LPARAM lParam)
   {
   HWND hControl;                       // handle of control

   switch(msg)
      {
      case WM_INITDIALOG:
                                        // set text in edit control
         SetDlgItemText(hDlg, IDD_EDIT, szEditOutput);
         hControl = GetDlgItem(hDlg, IDD_EDIT);   // get edit handle
         SetFocus(hControl);            // set focus to edit control
         break;

      case WM_COMMAND:                  // msg from dlg box control
         switch(wParam)
            {
            case IDOK:                  // user pushes OK button
                                        // read text from edit field
               GetDlgItemText(hDlg, IDD_EDIT, szEditInput, BUFFSIZE);
               EndDialog(hDlg, NULL);   // terminate dialog box
               break;

            case IDCANCEL:              // user pushes Cancel button
               EndDialog(hDlg, NULL);   // terminate dialog box
               break;
            }  // end switch wParam
         break;  // end case WM_COMMAND

      default:
         return FALSE;                  // if we don't handle msg
      }  // end switch msg
   return TRUE;                         // if we handled message
   }  // end WidthDlgProc
```

HOW THE PROGRAM WORKS

The heart of the program lies in the functions Cluster() and Branch(). They figure out what to draw, and draw it.

The Cluster() Function

Cluster is initially called from WM_PAINT. It draws the entire design on the screen, but it has help from Branch() and also from itself, as we'll see. The arguments to Cluster() are the device context handle, the number of segments per branch, and the position of the cluster. These variables change with the branch size, while the other variables remain constant. The segments per branch is initially 60, but this can be changed from the Variables dialog. The cluster position is initially either the center of the screen or the location of a mouse click.

Cluster() cycles through a loop, calling the Branch() function as many times as there are branches in the cluster. Each time through the loop, Cluster() figures out the starting angle of the branch. It sends this, and the starting position for the branch (which is the same for all the branches in a cluster) to Branch().

The Branch() Function

The Branch() function draws the branch by cycling through a loop, drawing one segment for each iteration, until the branch is finished. When it's finished with a branch, Branch() then calls Cluster() to draw the cluster on the end of the branch. This is the tricky part of the program: it's recursive. Cluster() calls Branch(), and Branch() calls Cluster().

Branch() decides whether each new segment should bend to the left or right by finding a random number with the Borland C library function rand(). It calculates the ending position of the new line segment, selects the correct pen for the current depth so the segments are drawn in the appropriate width and color, and finally draws the segment with LineTo(). This LineTo() function is the only place in FRACTAL where pixels are actually placed on the screen. It draws the entire plant.

Every recursive function (or in this case pair of functions) must have some way to know how to exit; otherwise the program will cycle forever. Branch() checks to see if the depth is still less than maxdepth (the recursion depth). If it is, Branch() reduces the segment size and calls Cluster(). If not, it simply terminates, and the chain of Cluster() and Branch() functions that have called each other then return, working their way back up to the original call from WM_PAINT.

Other Details

The seed for random number generation is based on the current system time. The time is sampled only when the user selects New from the menu. This generates a new flower. If the user clicks the mouse, selects Redraw, or causes a WM_PAINT message by enlarging or uncovering the window, then the old value of the time is used for the random number seed, which causes the same plant to be redrawn.

In VarDlgProc() we use the itoa() and gcvt() functions to convert integer and floating-point numbers to strings to be placed in the edit controls with SetDlgItemText() when the dialog is first called. When the user presses OK, we use atoi() to convert the strings obtained from the controls with GetDlgItemText() back into numbers.

To simplify the programming, we use arrays to hold the 7 pen handles, colors, and thicknesses. The IDs of the colors and widths are chosen so the color or width can be found from the wParam value by subtracting a fixed value. The result is used as an index into the arrays holding the pen colors and widths.

SUMMARY

The user-interface part of this program is fairly simple, consisting of a few menu items and two dialog boxes. Yet the program can afford hours of amusement for would-be plant creators. Using a somewhat similar approach, you could create all sorts of applications, such as ray-tracing programs and draw, paint, and animation programs. Windows graphics functions make this easy.

If you're interested in fractals, you might want to try The Waite Group's book-disk *Fractals for Windows*, described in the Bibliography.

CHAPTER 40

ROMAN NUMERAL CONVERTER

$\mathcal{A}$rabic numerals were unknown in King Arthur's time. Instead, Roman numerals were used for all arithmetic calculations, from recording dates to tallying up the number of grain sacks in the castle storehouse. The inefficiency of Roman numerals was probably one of the factors that prevented progress in science and mathematics during medieval times. (Fortunately, Arabic numerals were invented during this period, and found their way to Europe in the later Middle Ages.)

Our example program in this chapter creates a calculator that allows you to convert between Roman and Arabic numerals. Although they are obsolete for most modern calculations (thank goodness), Roman numerals are still widely used for the dates of publications, movies, buildings, and gravestones. They're also used to number parts of books, verses of the Bible, and Super Bowls. They even turn up in formal outlines; at a sufficient depth of indentation, your word processor may automatically generate paragraphs numbered with Roman numerals.

But how many people can flawlessly convert between Roman numerals and ordinary Arabic numerals? Quick now, what's 1995 in Roman numerals? What does L stand for? What important event took place in MDCCLXXVI? Our program solves these kinds of problems. Figure 40-1 shows the calculator with an Arabic number, and Figure 40-2 shows it with the equivalent Roman numeral.

The program uses the dialog box as a main window, a technique we introduced in Chapter 35, *Stand-Alone Dialogs*. AROMAN's structure is similar to that of the PUZZLE program from that chapter, but the conversion routines and the number of buttons make it more complex.

Figure 40-1
Arabic Number

Figure 40-2
Roman Number

USING THE PROGRAM

Operating the calculator is easy. Use the mouse to click on the buttons. Enter either an Arabic number with the buttons on the left, or a Roman numeral with the buttons on the right. Then click on the Convert button. The number on the screen will be converted from one system to the other. For example, if you type MDCCLXXVI and press Convert, you'll see 1776. If you type 1776 and press Convert, you'll see MDCCLXXVI. If you click on Convert repeatedly, the number will flip back and forth between the two representations.

AROMAN can even understand nonstandard kinds of Roman numerals. The number 4, for example, is usually expressed as IV (5 less 1); but if you type in IIII (four Is), it will convert it to 4 (and back to IV if you press Convert again).

Press the Clear button to clear the existing number so you can enter another. You can also click on the number itself to make it go away.

Since there are no generally recognized Roman symbols for numbers greater than M (1000), it becomes inconvenient to express numbers greater than 3,999 or so. AROMAN hangs in there gamely until 5,999 and then tells you that the number is too big.

PROGRAM LISTING

As with the other programs in this chapter, AROMAN includes an icon file. It's called AROMAN.ICO. The resource file for AROMAN defines the pushbuttons and the edit field used to display the answer. Here's the listing for AROMAN.RC:

```
// aroman.rc
// dialog window for aroman

#include "aroman.h"

aromanICON ICON "aroman.ico"

aroman DIALOG 14, 21, 106, 114
CAPTION "Arabic <-> Roman"
STYLE WS_OVERLAPPED | WS_CAPTION | WS_SYSMENU | WS_MINIMIZEBOX
CLASS "aroman"
BEGIN
    PUSHBUTTON "I", 73, 66, 69, 16, 14
    PUSHBUTTON "V", 86, 82, 69, 16, 14
    PUSHBUTTON "X", 88, 66, 55, 16, 14
    PUSHBUTTON "L", 76, 82, 55, 16, 14
    PUSHBUTTON "C", 67, 66, 41, 16, 14
    PUSHBUTTON "D", 68, 82, 41, 16, 14
    PUSHBUTTON "M", 77, 66, 27, 16, 14
    PUSHBUTTON "0", 0, 6, 69, 16, 14
    PUSHBUTTON "1", 1, 6, 55, 16, 14
    PUSHBUTTON "2", 2, 22, 55, 16, 14
    PUSHBUTTON "3", 3, 38, 55, 16, 14
    PUSHBUTTON "4", 4, 6, 41, 16, 14
    PUSHBUTTON "5", 5, 22, 41, 16, 14
    PUSHBUTTON "6", 6, 38, 41, 16, 14
    PUSHBUTTON "7", 7, 6, 27, 16, 14
    PUSHBUTTON "8", 8, 22, 27, 16, 14
    PUSHBUTTON "9", 9, 38, 27, 16, 14
    PUSHBUTTON "Convert", ID_CONVERT, 17, 91, 33, 14
    PUSHBUTTON "Clear", ID_CLEAR, 59, 91, 26, 14
    CONTROL "", ID_EDIT, "EDIT", ES_RIGHT | ES_MULTILINE |
             WS_CHILD | WS_VISIBLE | WS_BORDER | WS_TABSTOP,
             18, 7, 69, 12
END
```

The header file has only three entries; the display edit control, the Convert pushbutton, and the Clear push button. We use numerical values for the pushbutton IDs, so they don't need identifiers. Here's the listing for AROMAN.H:

```
// aroman.h
// constants for aroman

#define ID_CONVERT   101
#define ID_CLEAR     102
#define ID_EDIT      103
```

Most of the work in the program takes place when the user presses the Convert key. There are two sections in **case** ID_CONVERT, one to translate from Arabic to Roman, and one to go the other way. Here's the listing for AROMAN.C:

```c
// aroman.c
// converts between Arabic and Roman numerals

#define STRICT
#include <windows.h>
#include "aroman.h"        // for control IDs
#include <string.h>        // for strstr()
#include <stdlib.h>        // for itoa(), etc.

#define SIZE 20
#define ARABIC 1
#define ROMAN 2
                           // prototypes
LRESULT CALLBACK _export WndProc(HWND, UINT, WPARAM, LPARAM);
void replstr(char*, char*, char*);

///////////////////////////////////////////////////////////////////
// WinMain() -- program entry point                              //
///////////////////////////////////////////////////////////////////
#pragma argsused

int PASCAL WinMain(HINSTANCE hInstance, HINSTANCE hPrevInst,
                LPSTR lpszCmdLine, int nCmdShow)
    {
    HWND hwnd;
    MSG msg;
    WNDCLASS wndclass;

    if(!hPrevInst)
        {
        wndclass.style        = NULL;
        wndclass.lpfnWndProc  = (WNDPROC)WndProc;
        wndclass.cbClsExtra   = 0;
        wndclass.cbWndExtra   = DLGWINDOWEXTRA;  // note: extra bytes
        wndclass.hInstance    = hInstance;
        wndclass.hCursor      = LoadCursor (NULL, IDC_ARROW);
        wndclass.hIcon        = LoadIcon(hInstance, "aromanICON");
        wndclass.lpszMenuName = NULL;
        wndclass.hbrBackground = GetStockObject(WHITE_BRUSH);
        wndclass.lpszClassName = "aromanClass";

        RegisterClass(&wndclass);
        }  // end if
                                      // create *dialog* window
    hwnd = CreateDialog(hInstance, "aromanDlg", 0, NULL);

    ShowWindow(hwnd, nCmdShow);
```

```
    while( GetMessage(&msg,0,0,0) )
       {
       TranslateMessage(&msg);
       DispatchMessage(&msg);
       }
    return msg.wParam;
    }  // end WinMain

//////////////////////////////////////////////////////////////////////
// main window procedure -- receives messages for dialog           //
//////////////////////////////////////////////////////////////////////
LRESULT CALLBACK _export WndProc(HWND hWnd, UINT msg,
                            WPARAM wParam, LPARAM lParam)
    {
    static char acAtoR[4][10][5] = {  // for values of Arabic numerals
       {"", "I", "II", "III", "IV", "V", "VI", "VII", "VIII", "IX" },
       {"", "X", "XX", "XXX", "XL", "L", "LX", "LXX", "LXXX", "XC" },
       {"", "C", "CC", "CCC", "CD", "D", "DC", "DCC", "DCCC", "CM" },
       {"", "M", "MM", "MMM", "MMMM", "MMMMM", "", "", "", "" }  };

    static unsigned int acRtoA[26];    // for values of Roman numerals

    static char szInput[SIZE];         // input string buffer
    static char szOutput[SIZE];        // output string buffer
    char szDigit[SIZE];                // digit buffer

    static int iMode = FALSE;          // neither Arabic nor Roman
    DWORD dwNum, dwNumTemp;
    int nPlace, nPlace2, nDigit, nLength, nValue1, nValue2;
    char ch;

    acRtoA[3]  =   100;    // C       // fill in values of Roman
    acRtoA[4]  =   500;    // D       // numerals in array ordered
    acRtoA[9]  =     1;    // I       // by letter values 1 to 26
    acRtoA[12] =    50;    // L
    acRtoA[13] =  1000;    // M
    acRtoA[22] =     5;    // V
    acRtoA[24] =    10;    // X

    switch(msg)
       {
       case WM_COMMAND:
          SetFocus(hWnd);             // no focus on controls
          switch(wParam)
             {
             case ID_EDIT:            // user clicks "output" window
             case ID_CLEAR:           // or "Clear" button
                szOutput[0] = '\0';   // clear buffers
                szInput[0] = '\0';    // clear display
                SetDlgItemText(hWnd, ID_EDIT, szOutput);
                iMode = FALSE;
                break;
```

```
case ID_CONVERT:
   nLength = lstrlen(szInput);   // get length of input

   if(iMode==ARABIC)              // convert to Roman
      {
      if(atol(szInput) > 5999L)
         {
         MessageBox(NULL, "Number too big", NULL, MB_OK);
         szOutput[0] = '\0';  // clear buffers
         szInput[0] = '\0';    // clear display
         SetDlgItemText(hWnd, ID_EDIT, szOutput);
         iMode = FALSE;
         break;
         }
      szOutput[0] = '\0';        // start with clean output
      for(nPlace=nLength-1; nPlace>=0; nPlace--)
         {                       // convert with acAtoR table
         nDigit = szInput[nLength-nPlace-1] - '0';
         lstrcat( szOutput, acAtoR[nPlace][nDigit] );
         }                       // check for special cases
      replstr(szOutput, "CMXCIX", "IM");  // 999
      replstr(szOutput, "XCIX", "IC");    //  99
      replstr(szOutput, "CMXC", "XM");    // 990
      }

   if(iMode==ROMAN)               // convert to Arabic
      {
      dwNum = 0;
      for(nPlace=0; nPlace<nLength; nPlace++)
         {
         ch = szInput[nPlace];                 // get char
         nValue1 = acRtoA[ch-'A'+1];           // convert it
         if(nPlace==nLength-1)                 // last char?
            {
            dwNum += nValue1;                  // add it to value
            break;                             // exit for loop
            }
         dwNumTemp = 0;                        // clear temp value
         // compare next character with nValue1
         for(nPlace2=nPlace+1; nPlace2<nLength; nPlace2++)
            {
            ch = szInput[nPlace2];             // get next char
            nValue2 = acRtoA[ch-'A'+1];        // convert it
            if(nPlace2-nPlace == 1)            // first compare?
               dwNumTemp = nValue1;
            if(nValue1==nValue2)               // II, XX, etc.
               {
               dwNumTemp += nValue2;
               if(nPlace2==nLength-1)          // last char?
                  {
                  dwNum += dwNumTemp;          // add temp value
                  nPlace = nLength;
```

```
            }
          }
        else                            // different chars
          {
          if(nValue1 > nValue2)     // MC, XI, etc.
            {
            dwNum += dwNumTemp;      // add temp value
            nPlace = nPlace2;
            }
          else                      // CM, IX, etc.
            {
            dwNum += nValue2 - dwNumTemp;
            nPlace = nPlace2 + 1;
            }
          ch = szInput[nPlace];     // get char
          nValue1 = acRtoA[ch-'A'+1]; // convert it
          if(nPlace==nLength-1)     // last char?
            {
            dwNum += nValue1;       // add it to value
            break;                  // exit for loop
            }
          dwNumTemp = 0;
          } // end else
        } // end for nPlace2
      } // end for nPlace
    ultoa(dwNum, szOutput, 10);        // convert to str
    } // end if iMode
  SetDlgItemText(hWnd, ID_EDIT, szOutput); // display
  lstrcpy(szInput, szOutput);        // switch modes
  iMode = (iMode==ARABIC) ? ROMAN : ARABIC;
  break;

default:
// assume command is a digit, add to input string
  if(wParam<10)                      // Arabic digit (0-9)
    {
    if(iMode==ROMAN)                 // wrong mode
      break;
    iMode = ARABIC;
    itoa(wParam, szDigit, 10);       // convert integer
    }                                //   to string
  else                               // Roman digit (I-M)
    {
    if(iMode==ARABIC)                // wrong mode
      break;
    iMode = ROMAN;
    szDigit[0] = (char)wParam;       // convert char
    szDigit[1] = '\0';               //   to string
    }
  lstrcat(szInput, szDigit);         // add new character
  SetDlgItemText(hWnd, ID_EDIT, szInput);  // display
  }
```

```
            break;

        case WM_DESTROY:
            PostQuitMessage(0);
            break;
        default:
            return( DefWindowProc(hWnd, msg, wParam, lParam) );
        }   // end switch(msg)
    return 0L;
    }   // end WndProc

///////////////////////////////////////////////////////////////////////
// replstr() -- finds oldtext in source, substitutes newtext          //
///////////////////////////////////////////////////////////////////////
void replstr(char* source, char* oldtext, char* newtext)
    {
    char* ptr;
    int nOld, nNew, nDiff, nRight, j;

    // note: assumes new text shorter than old text
    if( !(ptr=strstr(source, oldtext)) )  // find oldtext in src
        return;                           // return if no match
    nNew = lstrlen(newtext);
    nOld = lstrlen(oldtext);
    nDiff = nOld - nNew;            // assumed positive
    nRight = lstrlen(ptr) - nOld;  // chars to right of oldtext in src

    for(j=0; j<nNew; j++)          // copy newtext into source
        *ptr++ = *newtext++;
    for(j=0; j<=nRight; j++)       // shift remainder of source left
        {
        *ptr = *(ptr+nDiff);
        ptr++;
        }
    return;
    }
```

Arabic and Roman Digits

When the first digit is typed, the program decides whether the number being input is Arabic or Roman, and sets the iMode flag to either ARABIC or ROMAN. Subsequent characters of the wrong type are ignored. Characters of the correct type are converted to a string, szDigit, and concatenated with the string szInput, which holds the complete number, whether Arabic or Roman.

The Convert Button

When the user presses the Convert button, the appropriate conversion is applied. The conversion to use depends on the mode, which was set when the number was entered.

Arabic to Roman

If the mode is ARABIC, the number is converted to Roman. Each digit in szInput is examined. Its position in the string (the 1s position, the 10s position, and so on) and its value (0, 1, 2, and so on) are used to generate indexes into the two-dimensional array of strings acAtoR. The strings in this array represent the equivalent Roman numerals. For example, a 4 in the 1s position is equivalent to IV, while a 4 in the 10s position is equivalent to XL.

Several Roman numerals can be replaced with simplified versions, as shown in Table 40-1. When the program finds one of these long versions in the szOutput string, it replaces it with the corresponding short version. To do this we use the homemade string-handling routine replstr(), which replaces a substring (oldtext) within a longer string (source) with a different, shorter substring (newtext).

These conversions are controversial; some Roman-numeral experts prefer the long versions, which look more impressive but are not so readable. If you're of this persuasion, you can delete the calls to the replstr() function, the function itself, and its prototype. Or you could add radio buttons to the calculator so the user could choose between the long and short versions.

Roman to Arabic

If the number is Roman, it's converted to Arabic. This is more complex. A one-dimensional array of characters, acRtoA, holds the value of each Roman numeral at the position corresponding to the character's value. For example, C is the third letter of the alphabet, and is equivalent to 100, so acRtoA[3] holds 100. Each character position in szInput is examined in turn, and converted to an Arabic value using acRtoA. The results are accumulated in dwNum.

However, the value of a Roman numeral compared with adjacent numerals must be taken into account. For example, the X in XL means −10, while the X in LX means +10. There are three possibilities for two adjacent characters. They have the

Table 40-1 Shortened Versions of Roman Numerals

Long Version	Short Version	Arabic Equivalent
CMXCIX	IM	999
XCIX	IC	99
CMXC	XM	990

same value, the first is less than the second, or the second is less than the first. The program looks at these three situations in turn, and adds or subtracts the appropriate value from dwNum.

SUMMARY

It's easy to use the ideas in AROMAN to create different kinds of screen calculators. Special scientific calculators might handle geometrical formulas or complex numbers. Engineering calculators could be constructed for antenna design, stress analysis, or other specialized electrical or mechanical situations. You can even make really oddball calculators for such things as converting old-style British money in pounds, shillings, and pence into other currencies. Finally, as we demonstrated in the PUZZLE program in Chapter 35, *Stand-Alone Dialogs*, you can create games and puzzles that use the same approach.

CHAPTER 41

ORGANIZE
YOUR BOOKS

Have you ever wished you could find a particular book in your personal library? You think it's around the house somewhere, and you remember that it's about raising bees, but you can't remember where it is, who wrote it, or what it's called. Or perhaps you're curious how many books you have by John Updike, or you know you have a book called *Cider House Rules,* but you can't remember who wrote it.

Our final program, DATAB, helps you answer these questions. It's a database program that keeps track of your books. It presents forms you can fill in to describe each book. The resulting database is stored as a disk file. You can search for titles, authors, or the book's location; or for words used in a summary of the book.

The major features of this program are equally applicable to any kind of data; not just books. You could modify DATAB to handle stamp collections, phone lists, geology specimens, movie reviews, or what have you.

USING THE PROGRAM

When you start the program you'll see three items on the menu bar: File, Add, and Search. You can open an existing database file, or enter data for a new file. Here's what to do.

Opening an Existing File

If you have already created a database, you can open it by selecting Open from the File menu. This brings up the Open common dialog. Enter the name of the database file you want to open. The files for this program use the .BLS extension (for Book LiSt). When you've entered the file name, click on OK.

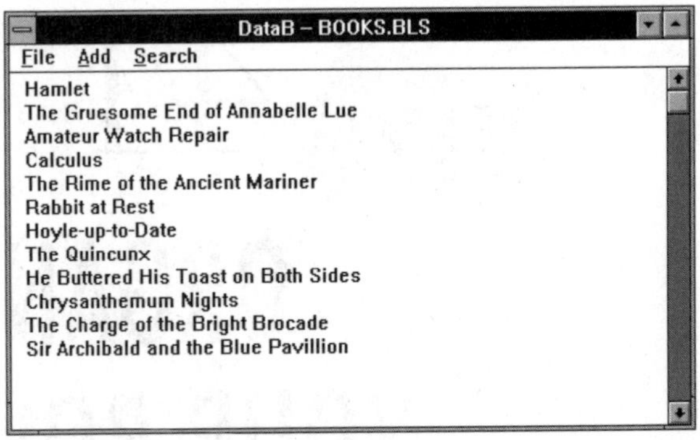

DataB – BOOKS.BLS

File   Add   Search

Hamlet
The Gruesome End of Annabelle Lue
Amateur Watch Repair
Calculus
The Rime of the Ancient Mariner
Rabbit at Rest
Hoyle-up-to-Date
The Quincunx
He Buttered His Toast on Both Sides
Chrysanthemum Nights
The Charge of the Bright Brocade
Sir Archibald and the Blue Pavillion

Figure 41-1

List of Book Titles
in Main Window

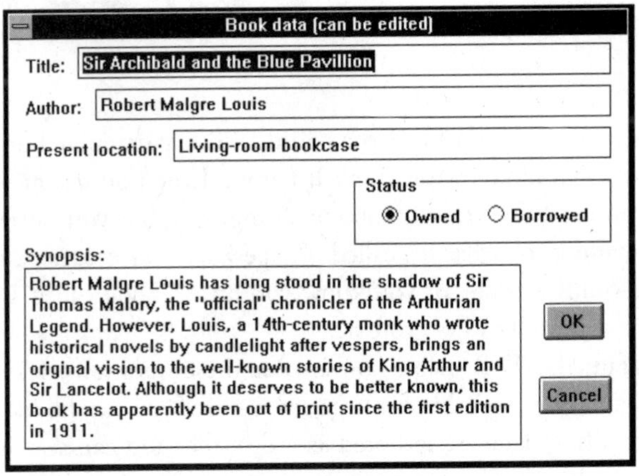

Book data [can be edited]

Title: Sir Archibald and the Blue Pavillion

Author: Robert Malgre Louis

Present location: Living-room bookcase

┌─ Status ──────────────────┐
│ ⦿ Owned   ○ Borrowed   │
└───────────────────────────┘

Synopsis:

Robert Malgre Louis has long stood in the shadow of Sir
Thomas Malory, the "official" chronicler of the Arthurian
Legend. However, Louis, a 14th-century monk who wrote
historical novels by candlelight after vespers, brings an
original vision to the well-known stories of King Arthur and
Sir Lancelot. Although it deserves to be better known, this
book has apparently been out of print since the first edition
in 1911.

OK

Cancel

Figure 41-2

The Book Data Dialog

When the file opens a list of book titles appears in the main window, as shown in Figure 41-1.

If you double-click on one of these titles, a dialog appears with the data about the book, as shown in Figure 41-2.

Adding New Data

You can add a book to the database by selecting the Add item on the menu bar. This brings up the Enter Data dialog, which is the same as the Book Data dialog except for the title. Type in the information about the book, including the title, author, location of the book (living room shelves, attic, garage, under the bed, or whatever), and a synopsis (a brief description). If you use words in the synopsis that accurately describe the book, it will be easier to search for them later.

Click on the appropriate radio button to indicate whether the book is owned or borrowed. When you're done, click on OK. The information for the new book will

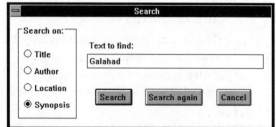

Figure 41-3

The Search Dialog

be added to the data in memory, and the new book's title will appear on the list in the main window.

If you have no existing database, start one by entering the data for some books. For each book, click on the Add menu item and fill in the data in the Enter Data dialog.

Saving a File

If you're saving a previously opened file, select Save from the File menu. If you just started your database, or want to save the information to a different file, select Save As. This brings up the Save As common dialog. Change to the appropriate directory and type in the name of the file, using the .BLS extension. Click on OK. The data is written to the file, but also remains in memory. You can continue to add to it, or you can exit from DATAB.

Searching

You can search for any word in any of the text fields. Selecting Search from the menu bar brings up the Search dialog, shown in Figure 41-3. Click the appropriate radio button for the field you want to search (Author, Title, and so on), and type in the text you want to search for. Click the Search button. If a match is found, the Book Data dialog will appear with the appropriate book. Click on Cancel to make the Book Data dialog go away. To find the next book that meets the search criteria, click on Search Again in the Search dialog. You can repeat this process until you've found all the matching books. Matching takes place without regard to case, so "shakespeare" works the same as "ShakeSpeare".

PROGRAM LISTINGS

The program uses the usual resource, header, and source files. They are all somewhat longer than usual, especially the source file. However, with a little study you shouldn't have too much trouble figuring out what they do.

The Resource File

The icon file for this program is DATAB.ICO. The resource file contains the menu resource and dialog resources for the Enter and Search dialog boxes. The Enter dialog resource plays two roles: both the DisplayDlgProc() and EnterDlgProc() procedures use it. Here's the listing for DATAB.RC:

```
// datab.rc
// resource file for datab

#include "datab.h"              // for defines

databICON ICON datab.ico       // icon

databMenu MENU
   BEGIN
      POPUP "&File"
         BEGIN
            MENUITEM "&New", IDM_NEW
            MENUITEM "&Open", IDM_OPEN
            MENUITEM "&Save", IDM_SAVE
            MENUITEM "Save &as...", IDM_SAVEAS
            MENUITEM SEPARATOR
            MENUITEM "E&xit", IDM_EXIT
         END
      MENUITEM "&Add" IDM_ADD
      MENUITEM "&Search", IDM_SEARCH
   END

// Enter dialog box
EnterDlg DIALOG 6, 18, 246, 162
STYLE DS_MODALFRAME | WS_POPUP | WS_CAPTION | WS_SYSMENU
CAPTION "Enter data"
BEGIN
   LTEXT "Title:", -1, 7, 6, 17, 8
   EDITTEXT 201, 28, 3, 211, 12
   LTEXT "Author:", -1, 7, 22, 30, 8
   EDITTEXT 202, 35, 19, 204, 12
   LTEXT "Present location:", -1, 7, 38, 58, 8
   EDITTEXT 203, 66, 35, 173, 12
   LTEXT "Synopsis:", -1, 6, 78, 32, 8
   CONTROL "", 204, "EDIT",
      ES_LEFT | ES_MULTILINE | WS_CHILD |
      WS_VISIBLE | WS_BORDER | WS_TABSTOP,
      6, 87, 197, 69
   RADIOBUTTON "Borrowed", 205, 190, 62, 42, 12
   RADIOBUTTON "Owned", 206, 148, 62, 34, 12
   CONTROL "Status", 207, "button",
      BS_GROUPBOX | WS_CHILD | WS_VISIBLE,
      137, 51, 102, 28
   PUSHBUTTON "OK", IDOK, 212, 102, 24, 14
   PUSHBUTTON "Cancel", IDCANCEL, 210, 130, 29, 14
END
```

```
// Search dialog box
SearchDlg DIALOG 7, 82, 226, 92
STYLE DS_MODALFRAME | WS_POPUP | WS_CAPTION | WS_SYSMENU
CAPTION "Search"
BEGIN
    EDITTEXT 301, 66, 31, 153, 12
    CONTROL "Search on:", 302, "BUTTON",
        BS_GROUPBOX | WS_CHILD | WS_VISIBLE | WS_GROUP | WS_TABSTOP,
        7, 6, 50, 79
    RADIOBUTTON "Title", 303, 12, 25, 28, 12
    RADIOBUTTON "Author", 304, 12, 39, 32, 12
    RADIOBUTTON "Location", 305, 12, 53, 36, 12
    RADIOBUTTON "Synopsis", 306, 12, 67, 40, 12
    LTEXT "Text to find:", -1, 68, 20, 114, 8
    CONTROL "Search", IDOK, "BUTTON",
        BS_PUSHBUTTON | WS_CHILD | WS_VISIBLE | WS_TABSTOP,
        73, 60, 32, 14
    PUSHBUTTON "Cancel", IDCANCEL, 178, 60, 30, 14
    CONTROL "Search again", 307, "BUTTON",
        BS_PUSHBUTTON | WS_CHILD | WS_VISIBLE | WS_TABSTOP,
        116, 60, 50, 14
END
```

The Header File

The header file contains constants for the menu items and the two sets of dialog controls. Here's the listing for DATAB.H:

```
// datab.h
// header file for datab

#define IDM_NEW       101
#define IDM_OPEN      102
#define IDM_SAVE      103
#define IDM_SAVEAS    104
#define IDM_EXIT      105
#define IDM_ADD       200
#define IDM_SEARCH    300

#define IDE_TITLE     201
#define IDE_AUTH      202
#define IDE_LOC       203
#define IDE_SYNOP     204
#define IDE_BOR       205
#define IDE_OWN       206

#define IDS_EDIT      301
#define IDS_TITLE     303
#define IDS_AUTH      304
#define IDS_LOC       305
#define IDS_SYNOP     306
#define IDS_AGAIN     307
```

The Source File

The source file consists of the usual WinMain() and WndProc() functions; the procedures EnterDlgProc(), DisplayDlgProc(), and SearchDlgProc() to handle dialog boxes; and Open(), SaveAs() and Save(), which handle menu selections related to file activities. Now, hang on to your hat; here's the listing for DATAB.C:

```c
// datab.c
// database program

#define STRICT
#include <windows.h>
#include <commdlg.h>          // for GetOpenFileName(), etc.
#include <string.h>           // for strstr()
#include <memory.h>           // for memset()
#include "datab.h"            // for menu and control #defines

#define TMARGIN     3         // top margin, in pixels
#define LMARGIN     10        // left margin, in pixels
#define SBSIZE      100       // buffer size: title, author, location
#define LBSIZE      722       // buffer size: synopsis

                             // prototypes
LRESULT CALLBACK _export WndProc(HWND, UINT, WPARAM, LPARAM);
BOOL CALLBACK _export EnterDlgProc(HWND, UINT, WPARAM, LPARAM);
BOOL CALLBACK _export SearchDlgProc(HWND, UINT, WPARAM, LPARAM);
BOOL CALLBACK _export DisplayDlgProc(HWND, UINT, WPARAM, LPARAM);
void SaveAs(HWND);
void Save(HWND);
void Open(HWND);

HINSTANCE hInst;             // global instance handle
HFILE hFile = NULL;          // file handle
char szFile[SBSIZE];         // file name
char szPath[SBSIZE];         // path+file name
char szString[SBSIZE];       // general string
                             // filters for Open and Save as
LPCSTR szFilter[] = { "Book lists (*.bls)", "*.bls",
                      "All files (*.*)",    "*.*",
                      "" };
struct Book
    {                        // structure for book data
    char szTitle[SBSIZE];    // book title
    char szAuthor[SBSIZE];   // author
    char szLocat[SBSIZE];    // location
    char szSynop[LBSIZE];    // synopsis
    int status;              // borrowed or owned
    } aBook;

HGLOBAL hGlobal;             // handles to global memory
HGLOBAL hTempGlobal;
char huge* pStart;           // pointer to start of memory block
```

```
char huge* pOffset;          // pointer into memory block
char* pBook = (char*)&aBook; // pointer into aBook structure
int cBooks = 0;              // number of books in memory
int iBookNumber;             // number of a particular book
BOOL bValidFile = FALSE;     // true if a valid file is open
BOOL bMemChange = FALSE;     // true if data in memory has changed
                             //    without being written to disk
//////////////////////////////////////////////////////////////////////
// WinMain() -- program entry point                                   //
//////////////////////////////////////////////////////////////////////
#pragma argsused

int PASCAL WinMain(HINSTANCE hInstance, HINSTANCE hPrevInst,
                   LPSTR lpCmdLine, int nCmdShow)
    {
    HWND hWnd;
    MSG msg;
    WNDCLASS wndclass;

    hInst = hInstance;       // save instance in global variable
    if(!hPrevInst)
        {
        wndclass.style         = CS_DBLCLKS;  // for double-clicking
        wndclass.lpfnWndProc   = (WNDPROC)WndProc;
        wndclass.cbClsExtra    = 0;
        wndclass.cbWndExtra    = 0;
        wndclass.hInstance     = hInstance;
        wndclass.hCursor       = LoadCursor(NULL, IDC_ARROW);
        wndclass.hIcon         = LoadIcon(hInstance, "databICON");
        wndclass.lpszMenuName  = "databMenu";
        wndclass.hbrBackground = GetStockObject(WHITE_BRUSH);
        wndclass.lpszClassName = "databClass";
        RegisterClass(&wndclass);
        }  // end if
    hWnd = CreateWindow("databClass", "DataB",
                        WS_OVERLAPPEDWINDOW, CW_USEDEFAULT,
                        CW_USEDEFAULT, CW_USEDEFAULT, CW_USEDEFAULT,
                        NULL, NULL, hInstance, NULL);
    ShowWindow(hWnd, nCmdShow);
    while( GetMessage(&msg,0,0,0) )
        {
        TranslateMessage(&msg);
        DispatchMessage(&msg);
        }
    return 0;
    }  // end WinMain


//////////////////////////////////////////////////////////////////////
// main window procedure -- receives messages                        //
//////////////////////////////////////////////////////////////////////
LRESULT CALLBACK _export WndProc(HWND hWnd, UINT msg,
                            WPARAM wParam, LPARAM lParam)
    {
```

```
DLGPROC lpDlgProc;            // pointer to dialog procs
HDC hDC;                      // handle for the device context
PAINTSTRUCT ps;              // holds PAINT information
TEXTMETRIC tm;               // holds text information
static int cyChar;           // character height
static int cyClient;         // client-area height
static int nVscrollPos;      // vertical scroll bar position
int index, j;                // loop indexes

switch(msg)
   {
   case WM_CREATE:
      // find height of characters
      hDC = GetDC(hWnd);          // get device context
      GetTextMetrics(hDC, &tm);   // get font info
      cyChar = tm.tmHeight;       // get character height
      ReleaseDC(hWnd, hDC);       · // release device context
                                  // set file name in window
      SetWindowText(hWnd, "DataB -- UNTITLED.BLS");
      break;      // end of WM_CREATE

   case WM_SIZE:   // find new height of client area
      cyClient = HIWORD(lParam);
      break;      // end of WM_SIZE

   case WM_VSCROLL:      // handle scroll bar messages
      switch(wParam)
         {                    // one line up or down
         case SB_LINEUP:   nVscrollPos--; break;
         case SB_LINEDOWN: nVscrollPos++; break;
                              // one screen up or down
         case SB_PAGEUP:   nVscrollPos -= cyClient/cyChar; break;
         case SB_PAGEDOWN: nVscrollPos += cyClient/cyChar; break;
         case SB_THUMBTRACK:      // whenever thumb moves
                     nVscrollPos = LOWORD(lParam); break;
         default: break;
         }                          // keep in range
      nVscrollPos = max( 0, min(nVscrollPos, cBooks-1) );
                                 // has thumb moved at all?
      if( nVscrollPos != GetScrollPos(hWnd, SB_VERT) )
         {                          // then reposition it
         SetScrollPos(hWnd, SB_VERT, nVscrollPos, TRUE);
         InvalidateRect(hWnd, NULL, TRUE);  // redraw window
         }
      break;      // end of WM_SCROLL

   case WM_PAINT:                      // repaint the screen
      memset(&ps, 0x00, sizeof(PAINTSTRUCT));  // zero the ps
      hDC = BeginPaint(hWnd, &ps);       // get device context
      if(cBooks==0)                     // if no books, don't paint
         { EndPaint(hWnd, &ps);  break; }
      // display those lines of output buffer that go on screen
      for(index = nVscrollPos;
```

```
         index < min(cBooks, nVscrollPos+cyClient/cyChar+1);
          index++ )
         {
         // copy from global memory into aBook
         for(j=0; j<SBSIZE; j++)
            *(pBook+j) = *((pStart+(long)index*sizeof(aBook))+j);
         // display the title of each book
         TextOut( hDC, LMARGIN,
                  TMARGIN + cyChar*(index - nVscrollPos),
                  aBook.szTitle, lstrlen(aBook.szTitle) );
         } // end for
      EndPaint(hWnd, &ps);        // tell Windows painting complete
      break;  // end of WM_PAINT

   case WM_LBUTTONDBLCLK:
      // translate vertical mouse coordinate into book number
      iBookNumber = nVscrollPos + HIWORD(lParam)/cyChar;
      if(cBooks==0 || iBookNumber >= cBooks)
         break;
      // transfer data from memory to aBook
      for(j=0; j<sizeof(aBook); j++)
         *(pBook+j) = *(pStart+(long)sizeof(aBook)*iBookNumber+j);
      // display dialog box with book's data in it
      lpDlgProc=(DLGPROC)MakeProcInstance
                           ( (FARPROC)DisplayDlgProc, hInst );
      DialogBox(hInst, "EnterDlg", hWnd, lpDlgProc);
      FreeProcInstance( (FARPROC)lpDlgProc );
      break;  // end of WM_LBUTTONDBLCLK

   case WM_COMMAND:                   // process menu selections
      switch(wParam)
         {
         case IDM_NEW:                // user selects New or Open
         case IDM_OPEN:
            if(bMemChange)            // if unsaved data in memory
               {
               if( MessageBox(hWnd,
                  "There is unsaved data. Save it?",
                  "DataB", MB_YESNO | MB_ICONQUESTION) == IDYES )
                  if(bValidFile)      // if file already open
                     Save(hWnd);      // save to file
                  else
                     SaveAs(hWnd);  // get user to save data
               }
            if(cBooks > 0)          // if memory in use
               {                    // it's for old data
               GlobalUnlock(hGlobal);          // unlock it
               hGlobal = GlobalFree( hGlobal ); // free it
               if( hGlobal != NULL ) {
                  MessageBox(hWnd, "Can't free memory", "DataB",
                     MB_OK | MB_ICONSTOP);  break; }
               cBooks = 0;
               }
```

```
                    InvalidateRect(hWnd, NULL, TRUE);  // clear screen
                    SetWindowText(hWnd, "DataB -- UNTITLED.BLS");
                    bMemChange = FALSE;  // fresh start
                    bValidFile = FALSE;
                    cBooks = 0;
                    if(wParam==IDM_OPEN) // if user selected Open
                       Open(hWnd);       // go open new file
                    break;  // end case IDM_NEW & IDM_OPEN

                 case IDM_SAVEAS:
                    SaveAs(hWnd);        // do "Save as..." dialog
                    break;  // end case IDM_SAVEAS

                 case IDM_SAVE:
                    if(bValidFile)       // if file already open
                       Save(hWnd);       // save it
                    else                 // otherwise
                       SaveAs(hWnd);     // get user to save data
                    break;  // end case IDM_SAVE

                 case IDM_SEARCH:
                    if(cBooks==0)        // if no books in memory
                       {                 // forget it
                       MessageBox(hWnd, "No data loaded", "DataB",
                                  MB_OK | MB_ICONINFORMATION);
                       break;
                       }                 // go do Search dialog
                    lpDlgProc=(DLGPROC)MakeProcInstance(
                                       (FARPROC)SearchDlgProc, hInst );
                    DialogBox(hInst, "SearchDlg", hWnd, lpDlgProc);
                    FreeProcInstance( (FARPROC)lpDlgProc );
                    break;  // end IDM_SEARCH

                 case IDM_ADD:          // do Enter data dialog
                    lpDlgProc=(DLGPROC)MakeProcInstance(
                                        (FARPROC)EnterDlgProc, hInst );
                    DialogBox(hInst, "EnterDlg", hWnd, lpDlgProc);
                    FreeProcInstance( (FARPROC)lpDlgProc );
                    break;  // end IDM_ADD

                 case IDM_EXIT:         // same as WM_CLOSE
                    SendMessage(hWnd, WM_CLOSE, 0, 0L);
                    break;
                 }   // end switch wParam

              // various commands affect cBooks and thus the scroll range
              SetScrollRange(hWnd, SB_VERT, 0,
                             cBooks + cyClient/cyChar, // maximum
                             FALSE);
              InvalidateRect(hWnd, NULL, TRUE);        // redraw window
              break;  // end case WM_COMMAND

           case WM_CLOSE:
```

```
            if(bMemChange)              // if unsaved data in memory
               {
               if( MessageBox(hWnd,
                   "There is unsaved data. Save it?",
                   "DataB", MB_YESNO | MB_ICONQUESTION) == IDYES )
                  if(bValidFile)        // if file already open
                     Save(hWnd);        // save the data
                  else
                     SaveAs(hWnd);      // get user to save data
               }
            DestroyWindow(hWnd);
            break;

         case WM_DESTROY:
            if(cBooks > 0)              // if memory in use
               {
               GlobalUnlock(hGlobal);            // unlock it
               hGlobal = GlobalFree(hGlobal);   // free it
               if( hGlobal != NULL )
                  MessageBox(hWnd, "Can't free memory", "DataB",
                           MB_OK | MB_ICONINFORMATION);
               }
            PostQuitMessage(0);
            break;

         default:
            return( DefWindowProc(hWnd, msg, wParam, lParam) );
         }   // end switch(msg)

      return 0L;
      }   // end WndProc

//////////////////////////////////////////////////////////////////
// SaveAs   -- "Save as..." dialog box                           //
//////////////////////////////////////////////////////////////////
void SaveAs(HWND hWnd)
   {
   OPENFILENAME ofn;                 // create structure
   LPSTR szDefExt = "BLS";           // default extension
   long cbWrite;                     // for _hwrite()

   if(cBooks==0)                     // if no data in memory
      { MessageBox(hWnd, "No data in memory", "DataB",
               MB_OK | MB_ICONINFORMATION); return; }
   lstrcpy(szPath, "UNTITLED.BLS");  // default file name
   // set up structure for GetSaveFileName()
   memset( &ofn, 0, sizeof(OPENFILENAME) );  // clear structure
   ofn.lStructSize = sizeof(OPENFILENAME);   // size of structure
   ofn.hwndOwner = hWnd;             // owner is main window
   ofn.lpstrFilter = szFilter[0]; // filter
   ofn.lpstrFile = szPath;          // path+name buffer
   ofn.nMaxFile = SBSIZE;           // size of above
   ofn.lpstrFileTitle = szFile;     // file name buffer
```

```
    ofn.nMaxFileTitle = SBSIZE;     // size of above
    ofn.Flags = OFN_PATHMUSTEXIST | OFN_HIDEREADONLY;
    ofn.lpstrDefExt = szDefExt;     // default extension

    if( !GetSaveFileName(&ofn) )    // get the path+name
        return;                     // user pressed Cancel
    hFile = _lcreat(szPath, 0);     // create new file
    if( hFile == HFILE_ERROR )
        { MessageBox(hWnd, "Can't create file", "DataB",
                MB_OK | MB_ICONSTOP);  return; }
                                    // write the data
    cbWrite = _hwrite(hFile, pStart, (long)sizeof(aBook)*cBooks);
    _lclose(hFile);                 // close the file
    if(cbWrite==HFILE_ERROR)
        { MessageBox(hWnd, "Can't write to file", "DataB",
                MB_OK | MB_ICONSTOP);  return; }
                                    // set file name in window title
    wsprintf(szString, "DataB -- %s", (LPSTR)szFile);
    SetWindowText(hWnd, szString);
    bMemChange = FALSE;             // memory is saved to disk
    bValidFile = TRUE;              // valid file opened
    return;                         // successful return
    }  // end SaveAs function

//////////////////////////////////////////////////////////////////
// Save function  -- saves memory to file                        //
//////////////////////////////////////////////////////////////////
void Save(HWND hWnd)
    {
    long cbWrite;                   // for _hwrite()

    if(cBooks==0)                   // if no data in memory
        { MessageBox(hWnd, "No data in memory", "DataB",
                MB_OK | MB_ICONINFORMATION);  return; }
    if( !bValidFile)                // if no valid file
        { MessageBox(hWnd, "File not open", "DataB",
                MB_OK | MB_ICONINFORMATION);  return; }
    hFile = _lopen(szPath, WRITE);  // open file
    if( !hFile )
        { MessageBox(hWnd, "Can't open file", "DataB",
                MB_OK | MB_ICONSTOP);  return; }
                                    // write data to file
    cbWrite = _hwrite(hFile, pStart, (long)sizeof(aBook)*cBooks);
    _lclose(hFile);                 // close file
    if(cbWrite==HFILE_ERROR)
        { MessageBox(hWnd, "Can't write to file", "DataB",
                MB_OK | MB_ICONSTOP);  return; }
    bMemChange = FALSE;             // memory saved to file
    return;                         // successful return
    }  // end Save function

//////////////////////////////////////////////////////////////////
// Open -- "Open" dialog box, opens a file                       //
//////////////////////////////////////////////////////////////////
```

```
void Open(HWND hWnd)
   {
   OPENFILENAME ofn;                   // create structure
   long cbFileSize;                    // size of file to read
   long cbRead;                        // return from _hread()

   szPath[0] = '\0';                   // empty name field
   memset( &ofn, 0, sizeof(OPENFILENAME) ); // clear structure
   ofn.lStructSize = sizeof(OPENFILENAME);  // size of structure
   ofn.hwndOwner = hWnd;               // owner is main window
   ofn.lpstrFilter = szFilter[0];      // filter
   ofn.lpstrFile = szPath;             // path+name buffer
   ofn.nMaxFile = SBSIZE;              // size of above
   ofn.lpstrFileTitle = szFile;        // file name buffer
   ofn.nMaxFileTitle = SBSIZE;         // size of above
   ofn.Flags = OFN_PATHMUSTEXIST       // require valid path and file
             | OFN_FILEMUSTEXIST;
   if( !GetOpenFileName(&ofn) )        // get the path+name
      return;                          // user pressed Cancel
   hFile = _lopen(szPath, READ_WRITE); // open new file
   if( !hFile )
      { MessageBox(hWnd, "Can't open file", "DataB",
                   MB_OK | MB_ICONSTOP); return; }
   cbFileSize = _llseek(hFile, 0L, 2); // seek to end of file
   if( cbFileSize == HFILE_ERROR )
      { MessageBox(hWnd, "Can't access file", "DataB",
                   MB_OK | MB_ICONSTOP); return; }
   hGlobal = GlobalAlloc( GMEM_MOVEABLE, cbFileSize );  // get memory
   if(!hGlobal)
      { MessageBox(hWnd, "Can't allocate memory",
                   "DataB", MB_ICONSTOP | MB_OK); return; }
   pStart = (char huge*)GlobalLock(hGlobal);  // lock memory
   _llseek(hFile, 0L, 0);              // seek to start of file
   cbRead = _hread(hFile, pStart, cbFileSize);  // read file
   _lclose(hFile);                     // close file
   if(cbRead == -1L)
      { MessageBox(hWnd, "Can't read file", "DataB",
                   MB_OK | MB_ICONSTOP); return; }
   cBooks = (int)( cbFileSize / sizeof(aBook) );  // books in memory
                                       // set file name in window title
   wsprintf(szString, "DataB -- %s", (LPSTR)szFile);
   SetWindowText(hWnd, szString);
   bMemChange = FALSE;                 // no memory changes yet
   bValidFile = TRUE;                  // valid file in memory
   return;                             // successful return
   }  // end Open()


//////////////////////////////////////////////////////////////////
// EmterDlgProc -- Gets data from "Enter Data" dialog box         //
//////////////////////////////////////////////////////////////////
#pragma argsused

BOOL CALLBACK _export EnterDlgProc(HWND hDlg, UINT msg,
                               WPARAM wParam, LPARAM lParam)
```

```
                    {
                    int j;                          // loop variable

                    switch(msg)
                        {
                        case WM_INITDIALOG:
                                                    // check "Owned" radio button
                            CheckRadioButton(hDlg, IDE_BOR, IDE_OWN, IDE_OWN);
                            aBook.status = IDE_OWN;
                            break;

                        case WM_COMMAND:            // msg from dlg box control
                            switch(wParam)
                                {
                                case IDOK:          // user pushes OK button
                                                    // read data from dialog
                                    GetDlgItemText(hDlg, IDE_TITLE,
                                                aBook.szTitle, SBSIZE);
                                    GetDlgItemText(hDlg, IDE_AUTH,
                                                aBook.szAuthor, SBSIZE);
                                    GetDlgItemText(hDlg, IDE_LOC,
                                                aBook.szLocat, SBSIZE);
                                    GetDlgItemText(hDlg, IDE_SYNOP,
                                                aBook.szSynop, LBSIZE);
                                    if(cBooks==0)    // if this is first book
                                        {            // allocate memory block
                                        cBooks = 1;  // one book in mem block
                                        hGlobal = GlobalAlloc(GMEM_MOVEABLE, sizeof(aBook));
                                        if(!hGlobal)
                                            { MessageBox(hDlg, "Could not allocate memory",
                                                    "DataB", MB_ICONHAND | MB_OK);  break; }
                                        pStart = (char huge*)GlobalLock(hGlobal); // lock it
                                        // transfer data from aBook to memory block
                                        for(j=0; j<sizeof(aBook); j++)
                                            *(pStart+j) = *(pBook+j);
                                        }
                                    else  // not first book, so expand memory block
                                        {
                                        cBooks++;                       // one more book
                                        // expand memory to hold one more book
                                        GlobalUnlock(hGlobal);          // forget old pointer
                                        hTempGlobal = GlobalReAlloc(hGlobal,   // reallocate
                                                    sizeof(aBook)*(cBooks+1),
                                                    GMEM_MOVEABLE);
                                        if(!hTempGlobal)                // check new handle
                                            { MessageBox(hDlg, "Could not reallocate memory",
                                                    "DataB", MB_ICONHAND | MB_OK);  break; }
                                        hGlobal = hTempGlobal;          // handle is OK
                                        pStart = (char huge*)GlobalLock(hGlobal); // lock it
                                        // copy data from aBook to end of memory block
                                        pOffset = pStart + (long)sizeof(aBook)*(cBooks-1);
                                        for(j=0; j<sizeof(aBook); j++)
                                            *(pOffset+j) = *(pBook+j);
```

```
                  }  // end else (not first book)
              bMemChange = TRUE;                  // memory changed
              EndDialog(hDlg, NULL);              // terminate dlg box
              break;  // end case IDOK

          case IDE_BOR:          // user pushes radio button
          case IDE_OWN:
              aBook.status = (BOOL)wParam;
              CheckRadioButton(hDlg, IDE_BOR, IDE_OWN, wParam);
              break;

          case IDCANCEL:         // user pushes Cancel button
              EndDialog(hDlg, NULL);  // terminate dialog box
              break;
          }  // end switch wParam

      break;  // end case WM_COMMAND
   default:
      return FALSE;                        // if we don't handle msg
   }  // end switch msg
   return TRUE;                            // if we handled message
   }  // end EnterDlgProc


/////////////////////////////////////////////////////////////////////
// SearchDlgProc -- finds field and text to search for              //
/////////////////////////////////////////////////////////////////////
#pragma argsused

BOOL CALLBACK _export SearchDlgProc(HWND hDlg, UINT msg,
                              WPARAM wParam, LPARAM lParam)
   {
   static int iSearchField;         // radio buttons IDS_TITLE, etc.
   char szSearch[SBSIZE];           // for search string
   int j, k;                        // loop variables
   char szTemp[LBSIZE];             // text to search
   static int iDisp;                // displacement into Book struct
   DLGPROC lpDlgProc;               // for Display dialog proc
   static int iBookStart;           // book number to start search

   switch(msg)
      {
      case WM_INITDIALOG:
                                 // check Title radio button
          CheckRadioButton(hDlg, IDS_TITLE, IDS_SYNOP, IDS_TITLE);
          iSearchField = IDS_TITLE;
          iBookNumber = -1;          // if user starts with Again
          break;

      case WM_COMMAND:             // msg from dlg box control
          switch(wParam)
             {
             case IDS_TITLE:         // user pushes radio button
             case IDS_AUTH:
```

```
case IDS_LOC:
case IDS_SYNOP:
  iSearchField = wParam;
  CheckRadioButton(hDlg, IDS_TITLE, IDS_SYNOP, wParam);
  break;

case IDOK:               // user pushes Search button
case IDS_AGAIN:          // user pushes Search-Again
  if(wParam==IDOK)
     iBookStart = 0;    // if Search, start with book 0
  else                   // if Search-Again, start with
     iBookStart = iBookNumber + 1; // last book found + 1
switch(iSearchField) // set displacement into aBook
   {
   case IDS_TITLE:
      iDisp = 0;                          break;
   case IDS_AUTH:
      iDisp = (int)&(aBook.szAuthor) -
              (int)&(aBook.szTitle);  break;
   case IDS_LOC:
      iDisp = (int)&(aBook.szLocat) -
              (int)&(aBook.szTitle);  break;
   case IDS_SYNOP:
      iDisp = (int)&(aBook.szSynop) -
              (int)&(aBook.szTitle);  break;
   }
                        // read text from edit field
GetDlgItemText(hDlg, IDS_EDIT, szSearch, SBSIZE);
                        // look at each book in turn
for(j=iBookStart; j<cBooks; j++)
   {
   // copy field from global memory to szTemp
   for(k=0;
      *(pStart+((long)sizeof(aBook))*j+iDisp+k); k++)
      *(szTemp+k) =
             *(pStart+(long)(sizeof(aBook))*j+iDisp+k);
   szTemp[k] = '\0';        // terminate string
   AnsiLower(szSearch);     // convert both strings
   AnsiLower(szTemp);       // to lower case
   // search for search-string in field
   if( strstr(szTemp, szSearch) != NULL )
      {                     // found
      iBookNumber = j;      // save for display dialog
      // display dialog box with book's data in it
      lpDlgProc=(DLGPROC)MakeProcInstance
               ( (FARPROC)DisplayDlgProc, hInst );
      DialogBox(hInst, "EnterDlg", hDlg, lpDlgProc);
      FreeProcInstance( (FARPROC)lpDlgProc );
      SetFocus(hDlg);   // give focus back to "Search"
      goto search_ended;    // escape from loop
      }  // end if match
   }  // end for j
```

```
                MessageBox(hDlg, "No match", "DataB",    // not found
                         MB_OK | MB_ICONINFORMATION);
search_ended:  break;

            case IDCANCEL:                  // user pushes Cancel button
                EndDialog(hDlg, NULL);  // terminate dialog box
                break;
            }  // end switch wParam
        break;  // end case WM_COMMAND

    default:
        return FALSE;                       // if we don't handle msg
    }  // end switch msg
  return TRUE;                              // if we handled message
  }  // end SearchDlgProc


///////////////////////////////////////////////////////////////////////
// DisplayDlgProc -- Displays data using "Enter Data" dialog box     //
///////////////////////////////////////////////////////////////////////
#pragma argsused

BOOL CALLBACK _export DisplayDlgProc(HWND hDlg, UINT msg,
                             WPARAM wParam, LPARAM lParam)
  {
  int j;                                // loop variable

  switch(msg)
    {
    case WM_INITDIALOG:
        SetWindowText(hDlg, "Book data (can be edited)");
                                        // transfer data from
        for(j=0; j<sizeof(aBook); j++) // memory block to aBook
          *(pBook+j) = *(pStart+(long)iBookNumber*sizeof(aBook)+j);
        // transfer text from aBook to dialog fields
        SetDlgItemText(hDlg, IDE_TITLE, aBook.szTitle);
        SetDlgItemText(hDlg, IDE_AUTH, aBook.szAuthor);
        SetDlgItemText(hDlg, IDE_LOC, aBook.szLocat);
        SetDlgItemText(hDlg, IDE_SYNOP, aBook.szSynop);
        if(aBook.status == IDE_OWN)     // set radio button
            CheckRadioButton(hDlg, IDE_BOR, IDE_OWN, IDE_OWN);
        else
            CheckRadioButton(hDlg, IDE_BOR, IDE_OWN, IDE_BOR);
        break;  // end WM_INITDIALOG

    case WM_COMMAND:                        // msg from dlg box control
        switch(wParam)
            {
            case IDE_BOR:                   // user pushes radio button
            case IDE_OWN:
                aBook.status = (BOOL)wParam;
                CheckRadioButton(hDlg, IDE_BOR, IDE_OWN, wParam);
                break;
```

```
        case IDOK:                     // user pushes OK button
          // copy data from dialog into aBook
          GetDlgItemText(hDlg, IDE_TITLE,
                        aBook.szTitle, SBSIZE);
          GetDlgItemText(hDlg, IDE_AUTH,
                        aBook.szAuthor, SBSIZE);
          GetDlgItemText(hDlg, IDE_LOC,
                        aBook.szLocat, SBSIZE);
          GetDlgItemText(hDlg, IDE_SYNOP,
                        aBook.szSynop, LBSIZE);
          // transfer data from aBook to memory block
          for(j=0; j<sizeof(aBook); j++)
            *(pStart+(long)iBookNumber*sizeof(aBook)+j)
                                        = *(pBook+j);
          EndDialog(hDlg, NULL);    // terminate dialog box
          bMemChange = TRUE;        // user may have changed entry
          break;  // end case IDOK

        case IDCANCEL:               // user pushes Cancel button
          EndDialog(hDlg, NULL);    // terminate dialog box
          break;
        } // end switch wParam
      break;  // end case WM_COMMAND
    default:
      return FALSE;                  // if we don't handle msg
    } // end switch msg
  return TRUE;                       // if we handled message
} // end DisplayDlgProc
```

HOW THE PROGRAM WORKS

We can't describe every detail of DATAB's operation, but a brief explanation of some of its major elements should make it easier to figure out how it works. You need to know about the structure used to store the data for each book, how many such structures are stored in a buffer in memory, how this data buffer is saved to disk, and how the program reacts to file-oriented menu selections.

The Book Structure

The information for each book is stored in a structure of type Book. All but one of the members of this structure are strings. The szTitle, szAuthor, and szLocat (location) members are each 100 bytes long. The szSynop (synopsis) member is 722 bytes long. The status member is an integer, which is 2 bytes; it can have the values IDE_OWN or IDE_BOR (for owned or borrowed). Thus the total size of the Book structure is 1,024 bytes. This fits evenly into the 65,536-byte buffer, so we can use a multisegment data buffer, as described in Chapter 36, *Managing Memory*.

A fixed-length structure is the simplest approach to storing data. Another approach, storing strings in just enough memory to hold them, would use memory more efficiently in many circumstances but would, in this case, complicate the programming.

Buffers

All the data for a given database is stored in memory as an array of structures of type Book. The data from this array is written to disk as one file. When a file is read back in, it all goes into a single memory buffer. The memory to hold this array is obtained with the GlobalAlloc() function, locked with GlobalLock(), and pointed to by the variable pStart.

With this approach we're gambling here that the user won't have more books than will fit in memory at once. Two megabytes of memory (which is available on most Windows systems) can hold the data for 2,000 books, so this approach is probably adequate for most home libraries. If you have more books than this, or less memory, you may want to modify the program to read in only a portion of a file at a time. For simplicity we've avoided this nicety.

Display

There can be many more book titles in a file than will fit in the main window. We use scroll bars in the usual way to scroll through the list. When we receive a WM_PAINT message, we don't want to execute TextOut() for hundreds of titles that won't actually be displayed, so we calculate how many titles will actually fit in the window, and display only those.

Files

A program designer must decide how to deal with two file-related issues: how long to keep a file open, and how to handle the various file-oriented menu commands. Let's see how these are handled in DATAB.

Does "Open" Really Mean Open?

As we discussed in Chapter 12, *Disk Files,* there are two philosophies about how long files should be left open. The first approach maintains that a file should be open only long enough to read data into memory. That is, the file should be closed before WndProc() returns. The second school of thought allows you to keep the file open as long as you want (except for floppies).

We use the first approach in DATAB: we open the file, read or write to it, and close it while processing a single message. This means that what the user may think of as a file being "open" doesn't correspond to a file really being open. When the user selects Open, the information is read from the file into memory, but the file is closed again. "Open" in this sense means that the program is working with data from a particular file and is aware what file it is. If the user selects Save, the program will open this same file, write the data back to it, and close it again.

Files and Menu Commands

The file-oriented menu commands in DATAB are New, Open, Save, Save As, and to some extent, Exit. These commands must work together in a coherent way. Two flags are important in coordinating these commands. The bMemChange flag is set to TRUE if new data has been added to memory since the file was last saved. The bValidFile flag is set to TRUE if a file is "open," that is, if the program is currently working with data from a specific file (but remember, this doesn't mean the file is really open).

Table 41-1 shows in outline form the effect of these menu commands for different combinations of these flags.

The notations in the table are somewhat cryptic. "Open" in quotation marks in the column heads means that bValidFile is true. The column heading New Data corresponds to the bMemChange flag being true, while No New Data means that it's false.

"Read new file" means that the program opens the file, reads the data into memory, and closes the file. "Write file" means that the program opens or creates the file, writes data to it, and closes it. The string "Save changes?" represents a message box that asks this question. This box appears if newly entered data would be lost as the result of the user selecting a menu item. If the user answers Yes to the message box, the actions shown indented following the string are executed; otherwise they aren't.

Memory

Global memory is used to hold the entire database. It is allocated when a file is opened. The file size is ascertained with _llseek(), and this amount of memory is allocated. The variable cBooks keeps track of how many books this memory represents. It is calculated by dividing the file size by the size of one Book structure, sizeof(aBook).

Global memory is also allocated when the user enters the data for a book. If it's the first book, GlobalAlloc() is used; but if there are already other books in memory, then the GlobalReAlloc() function is used to expand the memory to hold the additional book. This function leaves the contents of a memory object undisturbed, but changes the size of the object. GlobalReAlloc() takes three arguments: the handle of the memory object to be reallocated, the new size of the object, and a flag indicating how the memory should be reallocated (GMEM_MOVEABLE and so on).

Table 41-1 Actions of Menu-Oriented File Commands

	File Not "Open" No New Data	File Not "Open" New Data	File "Open" No New Data	File "Open" New Data
New		If "Save changes" Save As dialog Write old data		If "Save changes?" Write old data
Open	Open dialog Read new file	If "Save changes?" Save As dialog Save old data Open dialog Read new file	Open dialog Read new file	If "Save changes? Write old data Open dialog Read new file
Save	Save As dialog Write file	Save As dialog Write file	Write file	Write file
Save As	Save As dialog Write data	Save As dialog Write data	Save As dialog Write data	Save As dialog Write data
Exit		If "Save changes?" Save As dialog Write data		If "Save changes?" Write data

Any global memory still in use when the program exits is freed during WM_DESTROY. Also, global memory used for an old file is freed before a new file is opened or when New is selected.

Since each Book structure in memory is the same size, it's easy to walk a pointer through memory, looking at each book in turn. Because all the data is kept in memory, searches are fast. If the program had to read data from the disk, the search would be much slower.

Huge pointers are used to access global memory, since the array of Book structures may well be larger than a single segment, which is limited to only 64 books (65,536 bytes).

Other Details

The user can double-click on items in the list in the main window, thereby bringing up the Display dialog for a particular book. To make this possible, the style member of the main window's WNDCLASS structure must be given the CS_DBLCLKS style constant:

```
wndclass.style = CS_DBLCLKS;
```

The WM_LBUTTONDBLCLK message responds to double-clicks. In the code for processing this message, the vertical mouse coordinate is used to calculate which book the user is indicating with the double-click, and the display dialog is called for that book.

The C-library string-handling functions don't work with huge memory, so we copy the data for each book "by hand," using a **for** loop, into a local structure, aBook, where we can access it more conveniently.

ARISE, SIR KNIGHT

So, at last, we've reached the end of our story. You have learned all we can teach you about the dreaded dragons of Windows programming. You can wield the mighty Excalibur to create common dialog boxes, gallop full speed with your lance levelled at Events, and don a full suit of armor to ward off sharp and deadly bugs. You have suffered through lengthy lessons on knightly lore such as messages, controls, and device contexts. We've even dropped a few hints about chivalry, in the form of coexisting gracefully with other applications.

Therefore, kneel, while we tap your shoulder with the flat side of a dialog procedure. By the powers vested in us (don't ask by whom), we hereby dub thee a Knight of the Windows Pain. Arise, Sir Knight, and ride out into the wide world of GUI programming. We have every confidence that with your newfound skills you can overcome the dragons we have met in this book, and that you can likewise learn the wily ways of the other Windows dragons, wicked knights, and strange monsters that you will encounter on your own quests.

DERIVED DATA TYPES

Here are some of the more common derived data types used in Windows programming. The definitions of all these types, and many more, can be found in the WINDOWS.H file. A few common macros and structures are also listed.

DERIVED TYPES

Table A-1

Notation	Meaning
FALSE	0
TRUE	1
BOOL	int (0 or nonzero)
BYTE	unsigned char
WORD	unsigned short
UINT	unsigned int
DWORD	unsigned long
FAR	_far
NEAR	_near
LONG	long
VOID	void

Table A-1

Notation	Meaning	
PASCAL	_pascal	
NULL	0 (or 0L, depending on memory model)	
WPARAM	UINT	
LPARAM	LONG	
LRESULT	LONG	
FARPROC	int (FAR PASCAL *)() far pointer to function	
DLGPROC	FARPROC	
WINAPI	_far _pascal	
CALLBACK	_far _pascal	
HANDLE	const void NEAR* (if STRICT defined, otherwise UINT)	
HWND	HANDLE (window handle)	
HINSTANCE	HANDLE (instance handle)	
HDC	HANDLE (device context handle)	
HMENU	HANDLE (menu handle)	
HLOCAL	HANDLE (local memory handle)	
HGLOBAL	HANDLE (global memory handle)	
(and other Hxxx handles too numerous to mention)		
PSTR	char _near *	Pointer to a string
LPSTR	char _far *	Far pointer to a string
LPCSTR	const char _far *	Far pointer to read-only string
Pxxx	xxx _near *	Pointer (PWORD is WORD NEAR *)
LPxxx	xxx _far *	Far pointer (LPWORD is WORD FAR *)

MACROS

Table A-2	
Name	Purpose
LOWORD(dw)	Extracts low WORD of a DWORD
HIWORD(dw)	Extracts high WORD of a DWORD
LOBYTE(w)	Extracts low BYTE of a WORD
HIBYTE(w)	Extracts high BYTE of a WORD
MAKELONG(w,w)	Makes DWORD out of two WORDS
max(a,b)	Extracts maximum of a or b
min(a,b)	Extracts minimum of a or b
MAKEPOINT(dw)	Makes structure of type POINT out of a DWORD

STRUCTURES

```
// Input message data
typedef struct tagMSG
    {
    HWND        hwnd;
    UINT        message;
    WPARAM      wParam;
    LPARAM      lParam;
    DWORD       time;
    POINT       pt;
    } MSG;

// Window class data
typedef struct tagWNDCLASS
    {
    UINT        style;
    WNDPROC     lpfnWndProc;
    int         cbClsExtra;
    int         cbWndExtra;
    HINSTANCE   hInstance;
    HICON       hIcon;
    HCURSOR     hCursor;
    HBRUSH      hbrBackground;
```

```
    LPCSTR      lpszMenuName;
    LPCSTR      lpszClassName;
    } WNDCLASS;

// Data for drawing within a window
typedef struct tagPAINTSTRUCT
    {
    HDC         hdc;
    BOOL        fErase;
    RECT        rcPaint;
    BOOL        fRestore;
    BOOL        fIncUpdate;
    BYTE        rgbReserved[16];
    } PAINTSTRUCT;

// Rectangle
typedef struct tagRECT
    {
    int left;
    int top;
    int right;
    int bottom;
    } RECT;

// Point
typedef struct tagPOINT
{
    int x;
    int y;
} POINT;
```

HUNGARIAN NOTATION

Hungarian notation is a mnemonic device to help the programmer ensure that variables have the correct data type and are used appropriately. Each variable name is preceded by a lowercase letter or letters that indicate the basic data type or the purpose of the variable. The following list shows some common examples of Hungarian notation as used in Windows programming.

Table B-1 Hungarian Notation

Hungarian	Meaning	Examples
ch	character	chKeyboard
w	unsigned int (WORD)	wParam, wSeg, wFlags
dw	unsigned long (DWORD)	dwAlloc, dwCount
n	number (int)	nCount, nSize, nIDComboBox
i	integer (int)	iValue, iReturn
l	long integer	lParam
a	array	aBuffer[]
ach	array of characters	achBuffer[]
b	bytes (int)	bItems
b	boolean (BOOL)	bEnable, bFlag

Table B-1

Hungarian	Meaning	Examples
p	pointer	pString
np	near pointer	npBuffer
lp	long (far) pointer	lpCmdLine, lpPoints, lpString
lpfn	long pointer to function	lpfnDlgProc
i	index (into array)	ichNames (to char array)
h	handle	hWnd, hInstance, hDC, hIcon
c	count	cItems
cb	count of bytes	cbItems
sz	null-terminated string	szFileName, szStreet
x	x-coordinate	xTarget
y	y-coordinate	yTarget

BIBLIOGRAPHY

For any sort of serious Windows programming you'll need a reference that describes the API functions, structures, messages, macros, and so on. The standard is the *Microsoft Windows 3.1Programmer's Reference* (Microsoft Press, Redmond, WA 1992). This is a multivolume set, and is rather expensive, but it is the definitive reference.

A more approachable, and considerably cheaper, Windows reference is *The Waite Group's Windows API Bible*, by James L. Conger (Waite Group Press, Corte Madera, California, 1992). This book has the information you need for all but the most complex programming situations, and includes clear mini-tutorials on many topics. It is organized for quick reference.

If you are lucky enough to own the Borland C++ & Application Frameworks product, you'll find that it includes a three-volume Windows reference, the *Windows API Reference Guide*.

To brush up on your C programming, we can't help but recommend *The Waite Group's C Programming Using Turbo C++* by Robert Lafore (Sams Publishing, Carmel, Indiana, 1990). It covers all aspects of C programming in the PC environment in an easy-to-follow style, using Borland products.

If you're intrigued by the FRACTAL program in Chapter 39, you might want to try *Fractals for Windows* (Waite Group Press, 1992). This book explains many types of fractals, and contains a disk with a sophisticated fractal generator. Also try *Computers, Pattern, Chaos and Beauty* by Clifford A. Pickover (St. Martin's Press, New York, 1990), which has many ideas for programming fractals.

E

H